P9-CDV-603

mr. mike

AD Biography
O'Donoghue Mic 1998

Perrin, Dennis. Mr. Mike : the life and work of
Michael O'Donoghue   9000819381

Mich

8/98

9000819381

DISCARDED BY
MEAD PUBLIC LIBRARY

mr. mike: the life and work of
michael o'donoghue

dennis perrin

AVON BOOKS  NEW YORK

Pages 431–32 are an extension of this copyright page.

AVON BOOKS, INC.
1350 Avenue of the Americas
New York, New York 10019

Copyright © 1998 by Dennis Perrin
Interior design by Rhea Braunstein
Visit our website at **http://www.AvonBooks.com**
ISBN: 0-380-97330-8

All rights reserved, which includes the right to reproduce this book or portions thereof in any form whatsoever except as provided by the U.S. Copyright Law. For information address Avon Books, Inc.

Library of Congress Cataloging in Publication Data:

Perrin, Dennis.
   Mr. Mike : the life and work of Michael O'Donoghue / by Dennis Perrin.—
1st ed.
      p.   cm.
   Includes index.
   1. O'Donoghue, Michael, 1940–1994.   2. Television comedy writers—United
States—Biography.   3. Actors—United States—Biography.   I. Title.
PN1992.4.036P47   1998   98-10955
812'.54—dc21   CIP

First Avon Books Printing: July 1998

AVON TRADEMARK REG. U.S. PAT. OFF. AND IN OTHER COUNTRIES, MARCA REGIS-
TRADA, HECHO EN U.S.A.

Printed in the U.S.A.

FIRST EDITION

QPM   10   9   8   7   6   5   4   3   2   1

819381

To Nancy Bauer, my inspiration and third eye

185381

acknowledgments

First, my deepest gratitude and thanks to Cheryl Hardwick, without whom there would be no book. Cheryl provided me with everything I needed to adequately research Michael O'Donoghue's life and work, including complete access to his files. She never wavered in her support of this project. For that I'm indebted to her.

I also wish to thank my agent Mary Evans, Lou Aronica of Avon Books, my editor Tom Dupree, Jane Donohue, Angie Brown, Frank Springer, Paul Krassner, Matty Simmons and Tony Hendra for allowing me to quote heavily from their respective books, Lorne Michaels, Mike Bosze at Broadway Video, Lee Hill, Mark Mitchell, Eric Boehlert, Stephanie Parker, Peter Becker, Tim Smith, Kim Otis, Steve Gilbert, A. M. Buria, Donna Kobe, David Thomas, Maura Driscoll-Thomas, Christine Walker, Adrian Buckmaster, John and Ramona Corey, Chic and Patti Perrin, Don Perrin, Clare and Conn Bauer, Virginia Basham, Tami Napier, and my children Katrina Bauer and Henry Perrin.

mr. mike

introduction

Death is the flip side of life.

His brain exploded. Once the source of sinister concepts, premises that cut deep and touched bone, routines so precise and intense that the punch lines were hideous screams, his brain ran short of fuse and detonated. As deaths go, his was dramatic. It mirrored somewhat the anatomy of his jokes: a swift buildup to a violent finish, "The End." He had given millions of television viewers a glimpse of his demise whenever he pretended to plunge steel needles into his eyes, whereupon he'd grab his face, writhe in anguish, and emit sharp, piercing cries. It is rare that the artist's physical passing resembles his work in form and tone, but here it became the final fact.

When Michael O'Donoghue died of a massive brain hemorrhage on November 8, 1994, the era of comic innovation he helped to define pitched onto the carpet with him. This was understood immediately by his friends and colleagues when they learned of his death; even those O'Donoghue had dismissed from his life knew the meaning of his passing. Although many of his peers had long abandoned the slashing humor of the early *National Lampoon* and *Saturday Night Live,* O'Donoghue kept his blade within arm's reach. He didn't always wield it, and at times forgot that it was there. But unlike those whom he inspired, O'Donoghue never lost sight of the blade's power to wound.

He believed that things could be funny and not funny at the same time, that comedy and tragedy were indivisible. He saw it as his, if not every humorist's, duty to inflict a "second smile"—the slit that appears when a throat has been cut. Laughter alone was one-dimensional; deeper emotions were to be exposed, then assaulted. But few found desirable this approach to comedy in 1994. To most, O'Donoghue's sensibility belonged on the garbage heap of pantomime, slapstick, and Catskill one-

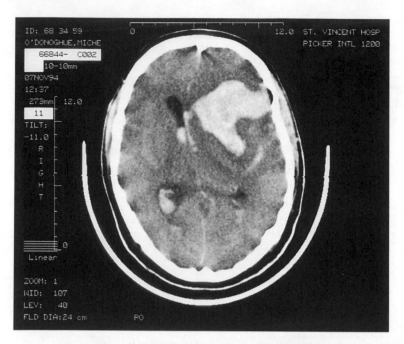

X ray of Michael O'Donoghue's brain, November 8, 1994

liners. His day had passed, his blade left to rust. Yet when news of O'Donoghue's demise spread, those familiar with his work sought exposure to its force one last time.

On the night of November 12, the Saturday following his death, a wake was held in O'Donoghue's Manhattan residence. White candles lined the outdoor steps and led mourners to the front door. Inside, past the flock of coats hanging in the hallway, stood the actress Margot Kidder, a former girlfriend of O'Donoghue's and a bit player in his not-ready-for-late-night special, *Mondo Video*. Kidder looked shaken, distraught. A cigarette dangled from her lips as she handed mourners their choice of black sashes. Behind her sat baskets filled with sashes and mass cards. Above the baskets were two small signs: the first read JEWS; the second, OTHERS.

As the signs indicated, the wake was to evoke O'Donoghue's comic spirit; the cobra might have died, but his fangs retained venom. Yet for most of the evening this and other attempts to revive O'Donoghue's stalk-and-slash style (at times fitting, at other times like CPR performed with a mallet) would knock against the raw, genuine feelings of loss. One would look at up the JEWS sign, nod to its dig at segregation, then look down to a mass card and absorb the peaceful Irish verse:

But since it fell into my lot
That I should rise
and you should not
I gently rise and softly call
Good night
And joy be to you all

Beneath the verse was a photo of O'Donoghue dressed in black and standing before the Virgin Mary, Baby Jesus, and rows of prayer candles. The photo captured both the sinister and the soft sides of the man, the comedy assassin who believed in order, subverted tradition, and insisted on respect. Here on a flat, two-dimensional surface, the twin halves of O'Donoghue were joined, fusion the wake itself didn't achieve. But the effort was made and should have been made; unfortunately, the ingredient essential to success existed only in memory.

When alive, O'Donoghue was known for his theme parties, extensions of his theatrical and generous (to his friends) nature. He put as much effort into the creation of the proper party atmosphere as he put into his work; weeks, sometimes months, were spent polishing every last detail. And each party would have a specific guest list to match its specific theme. "The grand gatherings at his turn-of-the-century Village town house," wrote Dan Aykroyd in a *Rolling Stone* eulogy, "always attracted a great mix, and you dressed in church clothes . . . Writers, wits, humorists and artists would attend, the fare being an elixir of continuous irreverence." The wake marked the first time that O'Donoghue did not attend his own party. Its theme was the

Mr. Mike attends his own wake; a photo that greeted the guests

shock of sudden death, its guest list nonspecific. Everyone dies, so all fit the theme.

The apartment was framed in ribbons of black tulle, and within this frame milled celebrities of various stripes, from Penny Marshall to James Taylor to Paul Shaffer to Bret Easton Ellis (whose novel *American Psycho* O'Donoghue thought hilarious); former *Lampoon* and *SNL* staffers; ex-lovers and old acquaintances of O'Donoghue's, as well as his closest friends. Alcohol was served to those who honored the drunken tradition of Irish wakes, Poland Spring water to those of the New Age. Tobacco smoke mixed with marijuana. Light music played over the din of O'Donoghue anecdotes.

The television in O'Donoghue's bedroom was tuned to the "new" *SNL* (1994 model), hosted that night by Sarah Jessica Parker. The sound was muted but the visuals appeared as dull as the comedy was bound to be. Since that week's show was still being written the day O'Donoghue died, one had hoped that the writers would toss the crap they were assembling and put forward some twisted, dark, fucked-in-the-head concepts to honor the man who helped build the house they lived in. Of course, nothing of the sort happened: Amish would sooner steal cars before these writers attempted such a leap. But as a lame-looking *Wizard of Oz* sketch emerged on-screen, someone walked by the set and said, "They're doing something for Michael at the end of the show."

Just before *SNL* went to a commercial, members of the show's house band were shown. On the right side of the home base stage was an untended piano wreathed in darkness, quiet as a coffin. The piano belonged to Cheryl Hardwick, *SNL*'s co-musical director and Michael O'Donoghue's wife of nine years. But she was not on the stage; she stood near the front door of the apartment, shrouded in widow's black and receiving the condolences of arriving guests. Small, pretty, her features partially hidden behind a veil of black tulle (fashioned from the same ribbon decorating the apartment), Hardwick held it together as best she could. She was devastated, sure, but her size and manner belied an inner core of strength that O'Donoghue himself had come to rely on in his later years.

It was nearing one A.M., and the guests (now officially a throng) were told to enter the bedroom for the *SNL* tribute to O'Donoghue. As the final person crammed into the last available space, the image of Bill Murray filled the TV's screen. He referred to O'Donoghue's passing as a "death in the family," the *Saturday Night* "family" headed by Lorne Michaels—"a family," O'Donoghue once sneered, "I did not choose." Murray joked that O'Donoghue was roasting in Hell, awaiting the arrival of blaxploitation legend Pam Grier. Murray then introduced a clip of O'Donoghue at work in his prime.

It was a sketch from 1977, *SNL*'s third season and O'Donoghue's final year with the show's original cast. The piece is set in a waterfront dive called the Coral Waters Bar & Grill (though inside a colorful neon sign proclaims the place to be Mr. Mike's Coral Waters Cafe—under new management?). The joint is ratty and in shambles; a lone sailor looks on the verge of passing out as Laraine Newman, clad in a shoddy cocktail dress, enters. Inebriated, she stumbles past the piano player on her way to the bar. The tune being played is "Have Yourself a Merry Little Christmas." The person playing it is a young Cheryl Hardwick.

Behind the bar stands O'Donoghue as Mr. Mike. While technically a recurring character in the *SNL* mold, Mr. Mike is but a slight exaggeration of O'Donoghue's persona, and at this point in the show's run he appears on camera *solely* as Mr. Mike. He wears a dark blue suit and a tropical print shirt with the collar open. His eyes are masked by the dark lenses of his glasses; a thin brown More cigarette burns perfectly in his mouth. Mr. Mike is the essence of cold precision in a world of disease and decay.

Laraine Newman hits the bar and is in very bad shape. She needs a "Least-Loved Bedtime Tale" the way a junkie needs smack. Only Mr. Mike, black market dealer of sad, violent stories, can provide one. "Sure thing, Laraine," he says in answer to her request. "But I'm afraid you're gonna have to sing for it." Laraine is thrown: *Sing?* In the shape she's in? But Mr. Mike is unbending. Laraine must sing the aria from *Madame Butterfly* if she's to receive her fix. Left with no option, Laraine grudgingly complies as "Fingers" Hardwick provides the music from the opera.

As Laraine sings the aria, Mr. Mike mixes her one of his specialties, a drink called the Soiled Kimono—two-thirds "costly French champagne" and one-third Japanese plum wine, topped with a paper butterfly. The Soiled Kimono was created by a Japanese aviator who was angry with an unfaithful geisha. In a fit of passion, he flung two-thirds "costly French champagne," one-third Japanese plum wine, and a paper butterfly into the geisha's face. She loved the taste and kissed the aviator before hitting him in the lungs with a gardening tool.

But Laraine is unaware of this. She's struggled through the aria while we read of the drink's history in a narrative crawl on-screen. She finishes and is given her Soiled Kimono. Laraine peers over the paper butterfly, her pupils in dilation: Can she have her story *now*? she pleads.

"I'm afraid not, doll face," says Mr. Mike.

"But *why*?"

"Because you sang lousy, that's why. Because you don't deserve a 'Least-Loved Bedtime Tale.'"

"Oh, Mr. Mike, Mr. Mike, you're so cruel!"

"Well, sometimes you have to be cruel, Laraine."

"In order to be kind, Mr. Mike?"

"No, in order to be even crueler. Now scram. Put an egg in your shoe and beat it. It's closing time."

And with that Laraine is left to ponder whether she should eat the paper butterfly.

The old sketch faded to a live picture of Bill Murray, who held a Soiled Kimono. The studio audience applauded. Whether they liked what they saw on the monitors is unknown, but in terms of comic energy and intelligence, the sketch was the best thing presented that evening. When compared to the current troupe's clumsy execution of one-joke material, the O'Donoghue tape must have seemed to them otherworldy.

Murray, on the other hand, understood the grammar of the piece. After all, he had been a member of the cast that had benefited from O'Donoghue's work. He raised his Soiled Kimono and said, "It takes a great man to make a great wake." He saluted Hardwick, who sat directly in front of the television on the bed she'd shared with O'Donoghue. Mitch Glazer, O'Donoghue's screenwriting partner and closest friend, held Hardwick's hand throughout.

After the on-air tribute, mourners spilled from the bedroom and into the rest of the apartment. Still more arrived. Space became limited and people sought a spot where they could stand without getting jostled. Hal Willner, a close friend of O'Donoghue's and a longtime music coordinator for *SNL*, found space near the fireplace. There on the mantel before him was a small model house. Tiny naked Barbies lounged on its roof. Intrigued, Willner looked through one of the windows and saw a vial filled with gray ash. It was, as he suspected, O'Donoghue's cremated remains. While other mourners tried to conjure Mr. Mike's aura, Willner viewed the man himself, now so much dust in the house of Barbie.

The real meat of the evening arrived with a reading of O'Donoghue's poetry. It was a form O'Donoghue practiced since childhood; and though he was not known primarily as a poet, his work, especially his print pieces, possessed poetic rhythms. The crowd of mourners fell silent as Mitch Glazer, Laila Nabulsi (friend to the *SNL* crowd and former flame of Hunter S. Thompson), and others took turns reciting some of O'Donoghue's more obscure and peculiar verse. There was a dirty limerick:

> *A gay Irish priest in New Delhi*
> *Tattooed the Lord's Prayer on his belly.*
> *By the time that a Brahman*
> *Read down to the "amen,"*
> *He'd blown both salvation and Kelly.*

A poem from his later years:

> *The pediment is broken*
> *And the bayonets are fixed.*
> *The F—word's never spoken*
> *When the company is mixed.*
> *The teardrops fall like teardrops*
> *And the raindrops fall like rain.*
> *I'm sure this can't be pleasure*
> *'Cause it feels so much like pain.*
> *Take me home, Dr. Jesus.*
> *Take me home, Dr. Jesus.*
> *Take me home, Dr. Jesus.*
> *Take me home.*

And one titled "Panda Puffs":

> *Chinamen in the icebox.*
> *Chinamen on the stairs.*
> *With hatchet, sword,*
> *And silken cord,*
> *Chinamen stalk the bears.*
>
> *Tickety-tock they whisper.*
> *Clickety-clack their shoes.*
> *In old Cathay*
> *They used to say,*
> *"Chinamen never lose."*
>
> *Pitterpat down the bellrope.*
> *Pitterpat up the sinks.*
> *With button eyes*
> *And big bow ties,*
> *Panda bears stalk the Chinks.*
>
> *Blackety-white their whiskers.*
> *Blackety-white their skin.*
> *The winds that sway*
> *The bamboo say,*
> *"Chinamen never win."*

Upon hearing "Panda Puffs," a portly man, not unpandalike himself, said rather stiffly, "My Chinese friends wouldn't find that funny." He spoke to no one in particular, but it was clear that his righteous button had been pushed. Yet it seemed curious that someone who knew enough about O'Donoghue to attend his wake would find offensive so absurd, though tender, a poem. After all, O'Donoghue never pandered to tribal emotion and identification: He saw these as barriers worthy of destruction, more so if it would yield a great image or a humorous line. A true mourner would understand this. The Panda Man was there for a party (as were many others at that hour), and Mr. Mike kicked him in the nuts.

From poetry came reminiscence. Those with anecdotes stood on a chair so to better address the mourners and, still filtering in, partygoers. Penny Marshall spoke of O'Donoghue as a guest in her Hollywood home. Marilyn Suzanne Miller, a former *SNL* scribe, talked about O'Donoghue the collaborator and close friend. Tom Davis, ex-half of the *SNL* comedy team of Franken and Davis, delivered a brief, passionate speech praising O'Donoghue's "fuck-you" attitude, which he unleashed on those who didn't get his jokes.

Bill Murray, fresh from his television appearance, was hard-core and emphatic. He recalled that O'Donoghue had berated him when he was new to *SNL* in 1977, and that he didn't win O'Donoghue's respect until he threatened to seriously hurt the guy. Murray stressed that, above all else, O'Donoghue taught "you how to hate. He hated the horrible things in life, and the horrible people in life—and he hated them so good." The tension underlying this hatred surfaced and flared as Chevy Chase stepped up on the speaker's chair.

Chase and O'Donoghue had once been very close. They had known one another since the early 1970s, and their friendship had tightened during the first year of *Saturday Night.* But down the line O'Donoghue felt betrayed by Chase, and from that time on theirs was a fragile, love/hate relationship. Still, Chase adored O'Donoghue and appreciated his brilliance. He looked stunned by O'Donoghue's death, and when the opportunity arrived for him to speak, he seized it.

Chase rose slowly on the chair, his forehead covered in sweat. He looked directly down to his feet as if to avoid the hostility of those who felt he had no place at the wake. His voice was soft and a touch serene, a far cry from the cocksure delivery of his Weekend Update days. He recalled the time when he and O'Donoghue, then collaborators on the *National Lampoon Radio Hour,* shared a cab in Manhattan. O'Donoghue had joked about Chase's acting ability, or lack thereof, and had predicted that Chase would someday be a mediocre movie star, a personality on permanent *Vacation.* Chase smiled as he said this, acknowledging the accuracy of the prediction.

He then spoke of O'Donoghue's needles-in-the-eyes routine, first performed on the *Radio Hour* and then later a staple on *SNL.* In the routine's embryonic form, O'Donoghue merely tortured a celebrity he disdained by ramming long, sharp needles into the celebrity's eye sockets. Chase identified the first celebrity victim as talk show host Merv Griffin, but was soon corrected. "It was Mike Douglas, *Chevy!*" yelled an angry Tom Davis from the middle of the room. A few people laughed at Chase's expense as he muttered, "Oh, yeah, Mike Douglas . . ." He finished by saying, "I loved Michael, and I'm crushed that he's dead. I said it like an actor, that's how I said it."

Chase stepped down, and as he moved from the center of attention some in the crowd pushed a reluctant Lorne Michaels into it. Michaels, the creator of *SNL* who gave O'Donoghue access to millions of viewers, appeared slightly nervous as he followed Chase. After all, O'Donoghue was renowned for his public and often vicious attacks on Michaels, comparing him to everything from a petty thief for whom nothing was too small to steal to a show-biz pimp who paid lip service to art as he peddled the lowest form of rubbish. The history of attacks, in addition to Michaels's low reputation among O'Donoghue loyalists and the cool reception Chase had received, certainly contributed to Michaels's reticence to speak.

Michaels was soft-spoken and brief. He recognized O'Donoghue as a major influence on the early *SNL* and on him. "He was an incredibly important person in my life," said Michaels. He ended by confessing: "I loved him deeply. And it would embarrass him as it embarrasses me to say so." Michaels wasn't heckled, but neither was he applauded. In fact, both he and Chase unwittingly set themselves up for what was perhaps the punch line of the evening.

Michaels was followed by Buck Henry who, as a first-rate humorist, saw an opening and pounced to seal it with barbed wire. An early *SNL* fixture, Henry became a regular part of the show's recurring bits: He acted as straightman to John Belushi's Samurai; he was Jane Curtin's comic foil in countless talk show parodies; and he played the emcee who introduced O'Donoghue's needles-in-the-eyes act. Henry and O'Donoghue respected one another artistically, and the two got on quite well; but Henry had avoided any close relationship with O'Donoghue so as not to invoke his famous temper and be placed on O'Donoghue's "shit list," where one could find, presumably underlined, the names Chevy Chase and Lorne Michaels.

Aware of O'Donoghue's mixed feelings for the two, Henry stood on the chair, smiled as he looked down at Chase and Michaels, and said, "Thank you, Lorne; thank you, Chevy. I think we all know how much Michael loved *you.*" On paper the line looks tame, no stronger than a remark tossed off at a Dean Martin roast. But the room held a certain tension, and the laughter the line inspired was not good-natured in spirit:

It was a release of anger on O'Donoghue's behalf, the first and only truly cathartic display of the evening.

Many felt that Henry captured and expressed perfectly O'Donoghue's sentiments, and in a sense this was so. (Think of Henry's dry manner and cold stare that fluster Dustin Hoffman in the hotel scene in *The Graduate.*) Had he been able to see Chase and Michaels speak so sincerely of him—in his *apartment,* no less—chances are good that O'Donoghue would have stared at them unblinking for an extended beat, drag on his More cigarette, exhale the smoke in their faces, and whisper through its cloud, "Blow me."

Still, the sincerity expressed by Chase and Michaels appeared genuine, and it took some courage for them to enter a hostile room and open themselves to almost certain ridicule. This was especially true for Michaels, who, although powerful, had always been controlled and publicly discreet, his comments carefully arranged. After Henry's verbal jab and the laughter that followed, several people moved away from Michaels as if to escape the line of fire. Susan Forristal, Michaels's ex-wife and a veteran of the *SNL* scene, saw this and made her way to him. Forristal recognized the producer's discomfort with the situation and she tried to lend support. But Michaels soon departed, leaving behind the anti-Lorne revelers who stayed to eat the food, drink the booze, and avail themselves of other party favors that had been financed largely by Michaels himself.

The wake was described the following week in *New York* magazine as "the hippest party in New York," and O'Donoghue was said to be "the coolest one there. That's because he was dead." The *New Yorker* took a less collegiate view of events in its "Talk of the Town" section, though writer Anthony Haden-Guest did incur the wrath of Chevy Chase with his depiction of the comedian's behavior at the wake. Haden-Guest accurately reported the reception Chase received, but he seemed to take delight in the spectacle. Chase invited the writer to discuss the piece face-to-face, an offer Haden-Guest thought best to decline.

Both magazines missed the cultural significance represented by the wake, their correspondents content to survey the scene as just another celebrity gathering. But those close to O'Donoghue felt strongly about the wake. To them it was not a mere "cool party": It not only highlighted the effect O'Donoghue had on his peers but brought home the point that O'Donoghue had been a singular and inimitable talent.

To Tom Davis, it was "the best wake I've ever been to. I've never seen a better wake. I was especially distraught, I suppose in part because I sort of see myself in Michael, and I feel frustrated about not being able to do what I want to do, and he died before he got to do what he wanted to do. So it really hit me." Regarding the crowd, Davis observed that "there were people there whom Michael hated, and I thought had real balls showing up—but they did. The zeitgeist of the evening was interesting." No doubt Davis meant Chase and Michaels (who would have shown worse form had they not attended), but also his former partner, Al Franken, who decided to make an appearance. O'Donoghue thought little of Franken, whom he considered be be at best a minor club comic. As Davis put it, "Mr. Mike went to his grave not speaking to people he did not speak to. Unto death."

Two of O'Donoghue's significant collaborators took stock of the wake as well. George W. S. Trow, a *New Yorker* writer and former *Lampoon* contributor who with O'Donoghue co-authored the Merchant/Ivory film *Savages*, saw the wake as "studded with true mourners. Everyone felt deep sorrow for Cheryl [Hardwick] because Michael really found an important life with Cheryl, and he loved it and she loved it. Everyone was aware that she was losing this, so the first concern was for her.

"Other than that, I would say [the wake] was like a party for the death of the founder of Bloomingdale's, attended by a lot of people who were still showing at Bloomingdale's or hoping to show at Bloomingdale's, and in a certain way didn't give a shit. They accommodated themselves, as I think people should not, to the idea that 'Oh well, creative people check out early.' "

Trow noted the importance parties played in O'Donoghue's life, that they "were serious avant garde parties done meticulously from his point of view. The wake was not a serious avant garde party. There was no control, and Michael always insisted on control of what he did. My idea of what he would have wanted would have been a small party of people who really loved him, or a barely tongue-in-cheek high mass, or if everyone was really feeling desperate and angry, a party in the East Village with a woman with a dildo. Michael would have gotten all that. Michael did not like disrespect to Michael, in any form at any time."

Nelson Lyon, with whom O'Donoghue worked on several screenplays and on *SNL* in 1981, and who along with Trow helped to influence O'Donoghue's artistic persona, was "alarmed" by the wake's "party atmosphere." "Being half-Mick," he said, "I guess I should have had some experience with wakes. But . . . I didn't think it was very funny. There were pockets of people I knew or could relate to and [I understood] they were grieving at the sudden loss of Mike. But there were a lot of people having a party and giggling. I just found that aspect to it disgusting."

But what specifically irked Lyon was that prominently taped to a glass case were the CAT scans that showed in graphic detail the hemorrhage in O'Donoghue's brain. "That's people trying to be daring and honest and carrying on the irreverent black humor spirit, which to me was just wrong and out of place. People were trying to be clever: 'Oh, Mr. Mike would really have *loved* that.' Well, why not have his blood in a plastic bucket? That was truly bad taste, and I speak as a person who thinks bad taste is the only good taste. But that was really tacky.

"Once again, it's people not having a connection and pretending they have a connection and pretending they're moved. I had the feeling about the wake that it was jam-packed and full of those people. We always hear, 'Well, Mike's life touched everybody,' and it just didn't. Mike's life stabbed a lot of people, it didn't just touch a lot of people. He was precious, he was unique, and the death affected me profoundly. He was somebody I could talk to in the most nonverbal, psychic way."

A lot of my humor is like Christ coming down from the cross—it has no meaning until much later on.

Michael O'Donoghue is, or was, what media types call a well-known unknown; that is, someone known to those in entertainment and publishing circles—the pop cultural elite, the ones who *matter*—but an absolute nobody to the majority of people who consume with gusto the endless images and deceit poured into their homes via television and glossy magazines. Although O'Donoghue was a personal god to me for as long as I can remember, I sensed that many of my friends and acquaintances, as well as the strangers I spoke to, were clueless as to what this guy did.

This sense was confirmed when I finalized my deal with Avon Books—"You're writing about *who*?" I was asked over again. It was then that I realized that my task, which initially brought me joy, would be a treacherous one. How do I, a not-very-well-known unknown, illuminate the life and work of a humorist who on the current American popularity scale ranks somewhere in the vicinity of John Bunny, Frank Tashlin, and Raymond Griffith? Forget that these three were at one time prominent in American humor; when were they last mentioned on E!? And how does one dredge them up and analyze them in the present day without resorting to academic tools? Such was the dilemma I faced with O'Donoghue once the contract was signed and the first advance check had been cashed.

It should be said here that *Mr. Mike* is not a standard biography, at least not in the Leon Edel/Henry James, Richard Ellmann/Oscar Wilde sense of the word. Nor does it reflect the values of the late Albert Goldman, a necro-porn artist whose corpse-rape of Lenny Bruce, Elvis, and John Lennon was loud and messy enough to wake the celebrity dead. ("Seal the casket! Here comes Goldman!") *Mr. Mike* is what the English call a biographical sketch, an attempt, albeit an extensive one, to convey the importance of O'Donoghue's contributions to American humor without bogging down in minutiae and excessive detail—the "kitchen sink" school of biography. As you will see in the *Lampoon* and *SNL* sections, I veer dangerously close to the porcelain edge.

In O'Donoghue's files alone there is enough material, personal and comedic, to easily fill a thousand-plus-page book. Add to this the interviews I conducted with his friends, family, and colleagues, and the needle starts pointing to a two-volume set, much too much for a man whose best work spanned just over a decade. Thus I've had to excise a large amount of material and shape what I believe is essentially a primer to the world of Michael O'Donoghue. To those whose names do not appear or who are briefly noted, my sincere thanks for your help and my genuine apologies for not getting you in. To quote the Stoics (or was it Kitty Kelley?), the bio biz is one *nasty* motherfucker.

Some of the areas covered in this book have been dealt with elsewhere. The legacy of the *National Lampoon* was addressed in *Going Too Far* by Tony Hendra, and in *If You Don't Buy This Book, We'll Shoot This Dog* by Matty Simmons. The books paint conflicting pictures of the *Lampoon,* which is only to be expected as Hendra and Simmons are vets of the magazine and so have scores to settle and private points to make. As for *SNL*, there are two compilations of scripts and a volume of *Rolling Stone* profiles; but as far as a narrative history of the show is concerned, there is one book, *Saturday Night: A Backstage History of Saturday Night Live* by Doug Hill and Jeff Weingrad. All mention O'Donoghue, and I will acknowledge each contribution to this effort as is warranted.

The story of seventies humor, which altered the culture in ways that remain evident and unprecedented, cannot be told without Michael O'Donoghue. He was as vital to modern comedy as was Buster Keaton to silent film and Ernie Kovacs to early television. O'Donoghue said he was in a satirical line that ran from Mark Twain to Nathaniel West to Terry Southern to himself. Impressive company, and not altogether untrue. At his best O'Donoghue parodied and satirized the darker elements of American life like no one else around him, and thus stood alone as he watched his influence spread.

But while in debt to the above writers, Southern especially, he also owed plenty to Lenny Bruce, who made the small openings that O'Donoghue later ripped wide. Bruce allowed comedy to flourish, and sometimes flounder, in areas that were anathema to the previous generation of gagmeisters: disease, war, drugs, hypocrisy, racism, and death. Because of this, Bruce faced steady harassment from cops, prosecutors, and judges who didn't get the joke—and didn't want to. O'Donoghue himself wasn't particularly sentimental when it came to Bruce's criminal violations of American obscenity laws. After all, he later mused, if Lenny Bruce were any good he would've gotten the chair.

O'Donoghue often referred to himself as America's greatest living

humorist, and although this boast was delivered with a smile, O'Donoghue did believe in his own importance. He saw the effect his humor
had on his peers and in the culture. Perhaps anticipating a study of his
life and work (he discussed the possibility with Darius James, a writer
and novelist whom he befriended), O'Donoghue decried the practice of
praising the dead and issued a challenge to writers tempted to appraise a
subject "objectively":

> If you attack people even as an act of faith—just assume they're scum
> because I'm scum, you're scum, we're all scum—just attack on the assump-
> tion that something's there somewhere, we'll get to it. History will bear you
> out. The guy will die, they'll find a door that's never been opened and all
> those dead cheerleaders are inside. . . . And I haven't been wrong yet. We're
> human beings, that is to say, assholes.

Within a week of saying this, O'Donoghue died. Whether he would
have wanted the above criteria applied to him no one can say. While I
knew O'Donoghue in the last four years of his life, our relationship was
roughly that of Zen master and acolyte. He was friendly and generous
but aloof, and I confess that I always felt intimidated by his presence.
But O'Donoghue, "scum" though he could be, did teach me much in
the way of humor and of delivering a joke—or, as was often the case
with him, the *anti*-joke. What follows is not so much an attack as it is
an attempt to explain his work, how it intersected with his life, and the
ways in which it defined a high-powered era of humor.

A kangaroo walks into a bar and says to the bartender, "Blood is the lipstick
of wounds." The bartender does not know how he said it or why.

one

Life is not for everybody.

In the midst of mediocrity, the climate in which American culture thrives, it is sometimes necessary to commit terrorist acts. But due to the relative dearth of crazed, determined artists in the mainstream, the promise of creative bloodshed (ever needed for renewal) remains distant. Also, the financial rewards offered to those who ply their skills "constructively" are significant: Money fattens the trigger finger. The best one can hope for is that lone talent who puts it *all* on the line, who kicks, slashes, and destroys as much as he can before either he is subdued or his story is bought by Disney and is made into a summer film starring Tim Allen.

Michael James and Barbara Donohue with their infant son

Interior demolition would become the forte of Michael Henry Donohue, born January 5, 1940, at St. Elizabeth Hospital in Utica, New York. He was taken to the house where his mother was raised in nearby Sauquoit, though over the course of the year the family moved to Albany, then to nearby Cassville. Michael was third-generation Irish-American; his ancestors, the O'Donoghues, hailed from Killarney, and the family name was "Americanized" by his great-grandfather, James O'Donoghue, upon his arrival in the States.

Michael's parents, Michael James Donohue, born September 16, 1917, and Barbara Ann Zimmerman, born August 18, 1919, were natives of Sauquoit who met while studying advanced biology at Sauquoit Valley Central High School. Both were well-read and displayed a flair for public speaking. Michael James twice won the American Legion Annual High School Oratorical Contest, choosing as his topics the seditious figures of Benedict Arnold and Spartacus. Barbara was equally loquacious, having won a similar contest before her high school graduation.

Young Michael soon displayed his own gift of gab. Before he turned two, "he could talk in long sentences," according to Barbara. It is not known what he said or had to say: Michael merely responded to the output of words produced by his parents; the language organ in his brain played all the right notes. At the suggestion of her cousin, Barbara began referring to the talkative Michael as "Pete" in order to avoid confusion with Michael Senior.

Politically, the Donohues were Republicans in the Republican town of Cassville. Michael James was less ideological than was Barbara (who turned up her nose at anything resembling a liberal—or, worse, a Democrat), and this might have led their son to state in later interviews that his father was the more liberal of the two. Barbara agreed that her husband was indeed warm and open to ideas, but this in no way meant that he was liberal in the conventional political sense. "We were Republicans," she insisted. "Everybody [in town] was." When America entered World War II, Michael James worked for the illiberal-sounding but appropriately named Savage Arms munitions plant. Barbara remained at home with Pete.

As for religion, the Donohues were mildly Presbyterian, and Barbara, who performed the straitlaced role in her son's eyes, made sure that Pete attended church on Easter and on occasion went to Sunday school. "One of my earliest memories is reciting the Twenty-third Psalm in church when I was three," he later said. "That line, 'He leadeth me beside the still waters,' terrified me," he later recalled. "I thought it was about Martian canals." To Pete, the Bible was less the literal Word of God than it was a fascinating work of fiction, the ultimate narrative of Good versus Evil. What child would find dull a tale in which characters are created from dust and ribs? a flood covers the globe and a sea is parted on command? sinners are turned to pillars of salt? a Messiah is conceived inside a virgin girl? the world ends in a pyro-Technicolor climax? The

**Pete Donohue, in 1944, before
the rheumatic fever**

Lord's talent for mass slaughter is particularly eye-grabbing and renders pathetic the efforts of Pol Pot—or even Henry Kissinger. These and other Good Book images, bursting with magic, violence, and passion, stimulated young Pete Donohue's imagination.

His father remembered that Pete often wondered, "If Christ came back, where would He fit in?" Far from viewing the Son of Man in a devotional light, Pete saw Christ lost in contemporary life: the Savior as yesterday's news, His gesture on the cross either forgotten or misunderstood by the philistine mass. Pete identified with this rendering of Jesus and continued to do so throughout much of his life. Yet he also held the Devil in awe, telling his father that Lucifer was his favorite biblical character because "that guy had guts. He stood up to God even though he knew he was going to get it." The force and allure of Lucifer's defiance were not lost on Pete, and he thought the Devil interesting enough that he christened the family cat "Satan."

Life is one big minefield and the only place that isn't a minefield is the place they make the mines.

Taught the value of reading, Pete once broke out crying in a movie theater after a newsreel showed German Nazis shoveling books onto a bonfire. At home his reading skills developed as his attention span lengthened into concentration. Access to the family's library, combined with the endless free hours of childhood, allowed him the time to reflect as he learned, and this proved invaluable when he was hit by rheumatic fever after his fifth birthday.

His mother had suffered from the same disease at the same age, so Pete's affliction was at least a familiar one. Indeed, rheumatic fever—an infectious disease that occurs in children between the ages of five and fifteen and that is characterized by fever and inflammation of the joints and can result in permanent damage to the heart—reached epidemic levels in the United States during the 1940s and 1950s. In many cases the disease was quite deadly. The discovery of penicillin during World War II and the wide use of antimicrobial therapy in the decade following the war helped to diminish the rate of rheumatic outbreak.

However, penicillin was not widely used in 1945. In Pete's case, the treatment was that of "wait and see"; he was ordered by the family's doctor to stay inside the house and avoid physical exertion. "It was a real negative turning point," he said, looking back, adding that the disease was "the main influence in my life." The doctor essentially sent Pete to his room for a year, and to a child of his intellect, the closing of doors and the pulling of shades was especially depressing.

Prior to Pete's contracting rheumatic fever, Barbara had given birth to her second child, Jane, on January 21, 1945. Under the best circumstances an infant and a boy of five present a challenge to their parents. But in the Donohue home the demands of newborn Jane were amplified by Pete's woeful condition.

Predictably, Barbara and Michael James were tested by stress on a daily basis. Both children required constant attention; and with Michael James working full-time, Barbara was left to balance the needs of the two. At times the pressure must have been profound, but if so it was never admitted to by either parent. In those predysfunctional days, bitching about one's family burden was considered bad form.

Pete certainly felt tremendous pressure, though for him there was no chance to unwind at the end of the day. Ill and isolated, he withdrew into his room and began to create an alternate world; but unlike the fantasy worlds that children usually conceive and later abandon, Pete's was beset by the intense heat of sickness and burned accordingly. As the fever enveloped Pete it smothered his young senses and forced him to resist as best he could. Part of his resistance was physical as he strained to find breathing space beyond the heat. Much of his resistance, though, was mental, and here his attachment to books served to alleviate some of the discomfort.

Pete enjoyed Laura Lee Hope's Bobbsey Twins, a popular series of stories that featured twin sets of . . . twins. He also showed interest in some of the more advanced literature in the house: Longfellow's poetry; the stories of Nathaniel Hawthorne and Robert Louis Stevenson. Later, he delved into Shakespeare's sonnets. Is it possible that his reading skills were exaggerated by himself and his parents once he achieved notoriety in the late 1970s? Of course. But the children of the pre-video/home computer era enjoyed a literary advantage over today's cyber-youth (and the pre–post/post-post-cyber-youth of tomorrow); to them the written word was real, familiar, and accessible. So it was for Pete. He scanned the pages of the antique volumes available to him, picked up a word here, a phrase there. Barbara guided him across the inevitable rough patches. Being sick, Pete received plenty of attention, but his precocity cut through the fever to generate its own heat. His parents observed in wonder—pleased, but a bit amazed.

In particular, the work of two English authors helped to steer his attention away from his suffocating condition. Kenneth Grahame's *The Wind in the Willows*, the classic children's tale that featured the diligent Mole, the practical Rat, the pompous Toad, and the wise Badger, enchanted Pete. He walked along River Bank and through Wild Wood, where animals wrote poetry, sang songs, dined well, lounged in parlors in front of cozy fires, wore tweed overcoats, and smoked tobacco. There is action amid wit; conversation and reflection precede broad comedy.

Here Pete found specific items relevant to his own world. He loved the titles "Mr. Mole" and "Mr. Badger," a style he would employ in many of his later print and television pieces. Also, the animals' observance of social customs such as afternoon tea, picnics, and banquets appealed to him. And being a child, Pete was drawn to the cute depictions of Grahame's characters. His affection for the "cute" remained for life; it defined part of his softer side as an adult and served as a setup to savage punch lines in his humor.

Primarily, though, it was the picture of "home" in *Willows* that connected with the fever-stricken child. Himself housebound, he warmed to the book's images of animals padding about their underground lairs in dressing gowns and slippers, sipping warm ale. Nature in the guise of disease forced Pete indoors; nature in the form of winter kept Badger, Rat, and Mole confined (though Mr. Mole took an ill-advised hike through the snow as Ratty emerged to catch him), and they made the most of their situation. As Mole told Badger:

> Once well underground you know exactly where you are. Nothing can happen to you, and nothing can get at you. You're entirely your own master, and you don't have to consult anybody or mind what they say. Things go on all the same overhead, and you let 'em, and don't bother about 'em. When you want to go up, up you go, and there the things are, waiting for you.

Pete couldn't "go up" when he wished, and "the things" overhead would have to wait. But his will to master his private lair grew strong as his young body weakened, a monstrous task for a five-year-old boy to face, regardless of his intelligence.

Then there was Sir Arthur Conan Doyle's master creation, Sherlock Holmes. Impersonal, precise, brilliant beyond the fancies of dull humans (save for his brother, Mycroft), Holmes embodied individual tenacity. He filtered reality as it moved slowly, awkwardly around him. His perception allowed him to pick apart criminal motives and solve the cases that stumped Scotland Yard; but it also removed him from common emotion. Although he maintained cordial relations with his friend and chronicler, Dr. James Watson, Holmes was a touch misanthropic and took a decidedly dim view of the general public. His superior tools of deduction and reasoning were used less for the betterment of society than they were to help relieve him of life's monotony, the ultimate terror in Holmes's eyes.

When the loner-genius of 221B Baker Street entered Pete's mind, he never left. As had generations of boys before him, Pete enjoyed Holmes the clever translator of clues, the eccentric, the amateur chemist, the sloppy keeper of files. But what primarily caught Pete's attention was Holmes the singular presence from which all else stemmed. Holmes was the master of intense deliberation, one who plumbed the "deep waters" of any given case or intrigue. He would spend days in his study pacing and meditating, stretched out along the floor or staring, knees held to his chest, into the grain of a fire. All the while his brain moved at tremendous speed and slowed only to retrieve stray bits of evidence: "The facts, gentlemen! *The facts!*"

> While I'm laughing on the outside, there is a little man inside me who is crying. And inside him is an even smaller man who is throwing up. And inside him is a tiny man who is farting. And then there comes this itsy-bitsy man who is pissing and shitting and draining his boils and God-knows-what. And inside him is a baby field mouse who is bleeding profusely from the ears.

Months passed. Pete's condition remained unchanged. He continued to read, think, pretend. He collected stamps and baseball cards—the Brooklyn Dodgers was his favorite team. He began to assemble scrapbooks that consisted of photos and drawings culled from magazines and newspapers. At times the images he clipped and pasted related to a specific story he was reading; at other times he'd pick something that simply pleased his eye—diamonds, for instance. In silence, Pete arranged each item until it fit the theme of a particular page. He played with the position of an image as he would a puzzle's piece, his eye trained on a spot to be filled, his mind sharpened by the emergence of precision.

Pete found some escape in radio, particularly in serials such as *Jack Armstrong: The All-American Boy* (best listened to while eating Wheaties), *The Shadow* (best listened to in the dark), and of course *Sherlock Holmes*. In every appreciation of the radio era we are reminded that it was the absence of visuals that stimulated the listener's imagination. Radio compelled one to picture acts of heroism and valor privately, thus ensuring that the mind received some exercise, and Pete gave his mind a decent daily workout. He applied the same intensity to radio listening that he did to reading; dialogue and plots filled his head and served to offset the fever's weight. It was a habit that continued after the fever passed. When not memorizing radio bits, Pete would clip the radio listings from the newspaper and add them to his scrapbooks.

Despite Pete's efforts to pierce his feverish haze and lessen the pain of isolation, he was unable to shield himself from the sadness that normally accompanies a long illness. His sanctuary glistened with what he would later call "Irish black mist." Anger, too, held sway, and would become a prominent part of his emotional and creative makeup. Gradually, though, he channeled these negative emotions into the same area where his creative instincts were taking shape.

"I became kind of misanthropic," he later said, echoing Sartre's belief that Hell is other people. "I developed a concept of 'others.'" The "others" were, plainly enough, everyone else "other" than Pete. They did not feel as he felt, did not see the world as he saw it, did not think the same thoughts he did. "I have a difficult time understanding others, their wants, their desires. It gave me a certain distance from which to observe things."

The concept of "others" was at first abstract. After all, having no contact with anyone *other* than his parents, it was impossible for Pete to apply the concept directly—to measure the emotional and intellectual growth of a peer and find him inferior. But the "others" were out there running, jumping, and playing, and he knew in time he'd encounter them (a moment when the "others" would certainly know of *him*). Until that time, Pete gazed out the window in serious thought; his imagination added color to the dull rural landscape beyond the glass, but the colors would fade to eventual boredom.

It is doubtful that Pete saw his parents as "others." They nurtured him, read to him, did what they could to make his solitary hell tolerable. But their close attention and constant presence had an additional effect on Pete, for he was more than an ill boy who needed his mother and dad; he was an exceptional child forced to mature at an accelerated rate. His intellect outpaced his emotions, a disparity that would remain with him as an adult; consequently, his perspective was modified at speeds unnatural for someone his age. On the periphery of this private storm stood Barbara and Michael James.

Pete's mother stirred within him a mix of emotions. Later, in interviews, he spoke fondly of Barbara and often credited her with influencing his comedy. "I got my mean sense of humor from my mother," he told *People* in 1979. "I've watched her my whole life trying to suppress herself. But it would come out—little dessert forks in the back." That same year he described her to *Rolling Stone* as "a mean woman" who inspired most of his "search-and-destroy humor." For her part, Barbara downplayed the image advanced by her son; she said that if anything her humor was "weird," not mean. In private, to friends, he maintained that Barbara was a strong influence. But in these accounts fondness gave way to resentment. At times he felt that his success was achieved in spite of his mother, that his drive and ambition were in some way a reaction to her authority. At other times he thought that she was responsible for his becoming the artist he became, that he was and would always be in her debt. Neither assessment sat well with him, and he could grow furious if he brooded for too long.

Barbara was The German, the family's center of power, its force. Though physically slight, she nevertheless commanded his respect. She was literate, controlled, unshakable. She embodied the strength that Pete came to admire. He would kid and tease Barbara (that is, when he didn't resent her), but on occasion he would romanticize her as well.

A fine example of this can be found in the second installment of the *National Lampoon Radio Hour* from 1973. Several *Lampoon* editors trade stories about a bygone Golden Age in New York City. Someone remembers that during this fantasy era, butter was made available in taxicabs. Then came World War II and with it shortages and rationing, which put an end to the courtesy butter. This prompts Michael to share one of his childhood "memories":

When I first came to New York City—my mother brought me to New York City in 1944, so I was four years old, and she was pretty excited about coming to New York City because she's a small-town girl and she didn't get here very often, maybe her third or fourth trip. There were a lot of things she wanted to do: Radio City, eat at the, what's that place in Grand Central Station? . . . the Oyster Bar. Pretty excited. She had no idea—you know, living in a small town—she had no idea that there had been no butter in a taxicab for four years because of the war. So we get down here . . . she hails a cab, gets in, looks for the butter, there's *no* butter of course, she asks the taxi driver and he kind of sneers. . . . And she's *so* disappointed 'cause she's looking forward to this. Well, and this is my mother all over, here's what she does: She asks the cab to pull over to the side by a grocery store, she walks in, buys her *own* pound of butter, brings it out, puts it in the cab and . . . well, we left the unused portion in the cab, so I can only assume that that is the *last* butter in a taxicab in New York City, and it was my mom that put the butter there.

Pete's feelings for his father were equally varied. In interviews he painted Michael James as a "softhearted" Irishman who loved to laugh (his was a high, sweet laugh, not unlike Pete's) and tell jokes and funny stories. He told *High Times* magazine, "My father did a minstrel show when I was about four . . . amateur theatrical PTA or something . . . that obviously was one of the turning points in my life. I got quite enraptured by his minstrel jokes. Why do mice have small balls? Because very few mice know how to dance. I find those very amusing jokes."

Michael James could be sarcastic as well as jovial. When answering a call from an encyclopedia salesman, he cut off the fellow in mid-pitch by stating that as the Donohues didn't believe in education a set of encyclopedias would be of no use to the family. When a salesman for princess phones asked what color phone would suit him should he choose to place an order, Michael James answered "Black," adding that the Donohues' house was painted entirely in black, appliances included.

If his father's humor made an impression on Pete, he never admitted to it. All credit for instilling in him a cutthroat sensibility went to Barbara. Pete felt that her personality and temperament overwhelmed her husband, that she possessed the drive, ambition, and style that his father sorely lacked. Pete later illustrated the differences between his mother and his father by saying that the Germans love to kill and the Irish love to die. The soft-focus picture of the amiable minstrel was effaced in this harsh light. Pete found his father crude as well as passive; as an adult he would do his version of "Michael James" for friends. Affecting a small-town accent, he would grab his crotch and walk hunched over in a simian fashion: Dad as the ultimate yahoo, farting and belching and drinking beer. Pete's sister, Jane, took issue with this and said that their father was anything *but* a loud, drunken lout. There was a close relative who drank, she said, but Michael James hardly touched the stuff. Why her brother lapsed into this caricature she couldn't say; yet he did, and he would do so to prove how evolved he was from the commoners back home.

Pete turned six, and soon after the illness began to wane. Still, he remained frail, sickly. Barbara sought to strengthen him by taking him outside for brief periods of time. He breathed in the rural air, coughing now and then; he walked in the yard so as to recapture his outdoor footing. These excursions lasted several minutes and then Pete was taken back into the house. As his stamina increased, so too would his time outside. But Pete's natural habitat was now inside his head. There he moved swiftly and without hesitation, his footing sure, his vitality never in question. It was his environment, one he controlled with a firm, pale fist.

Was young Pete Donohue's affliction tinged with romanticism? To a certain degree, yes, and this can be traced primarily to statements made by him as an adult. The lore of the ill artist boasts deep cultural roots, and Pete was in this sense classically romantic. But since his bout with rheumatic fever did much to mold his character, which in turn affected his craft, one cannot downplay its significance. Like Marcel Proust, who hacked and wheezed while arranging his sentences, or Martin Scorsese, who suffered from asthma in childhood and stared out his tenement window while composing scenes in his head, Pete Donohue's muse first sparked during his sickness. His take on that experience was simply a nod to tradition.

While sick, Pete was forbidden to show excitement or be animated. This, of course, led him to suppress the emotion and anger his isolation helped to generate. So as the fever receded it left behind ragged feelings as an outgoing tide leaves broken shells in sand. It also left Pete extremely sensitive: His already keen antennae now vibrated at shadows. A peculiar awareness soon emerged, one that Pete would fight to control and keep focused—a rough job considering the elements involved. But, again, he had little choice in the matter. Rheumatic fever had erased the possibility of a return to "normal" childhood.

Pete spent much of his recuperative time reading and fantasizing as before. Radio commanded more of his attention. "Radio is fine," he once said when looking back to this period. "Sound is very comforting." Comfort was found in Pete's favorite serials, where action, intrigue, and suspense kept him near the dial; but there was comedy, too. In fact, American radio in the 1940s was essentially defined by Jack Benny, Fred Allen, Abbott and Costello, Bob Hope, Ed Wynn, and Burns and Allen, the first true wave of mass media comedians. Each show revolved around a comic who played himself and who in turn was supported by a "gang" of regular characters. Some shows, such as Fred Allen's, sported a variety format; other shows, such as Jack Benny's, established more of a domestic tone. All took their single acts and stretched them to commercial length: *Seinfeld* minus the masturbation references, *Ellen* without the cute lesbian gags.

It is not known whether Pete preferred any one comic or program, but his exposure to these performers taught him the basic structure of jokes and one-liners (a structure he would later smash when it suited him), and it was here that the idea of creating humor was tapped.

Again, look to the *National Lampoon Radio Hour*. One of the *Hour*'s recurring segments was "Laughs from the Past," in which routines and songs performed by comedians of previous generations were presented in their original form. Many of the bits used were taken from radio shows of the 1940s, the time when young O'Donoghue had been absorbed by the medium. As producer and director of the *Hour,* he saw to it that the comedians he had listened to as a boy were brought to a 1973 audience, one made up of males aged eighteen to twenty-four who presumably understood the "head" humor of Cheech and Chong or Firesign Theatre far better than they did a George Jessel joke.

Of the many "Laughs" heard on the *Hour,* there was one bit that mirrored Pete's later contempt for corporate authority. Henry Morgan was one of the sharper and wittier radio comedians of the 1940s, and as such was doomed to oblivion in a country where wit is seldom understood—when it is recognized at all. (The same fate befell the great Fred Allen, whose brilliant comic wordplay is now so much ether.) Morgan had little patience for fools, which naturally led him to look down on commercial sponsors, especially those sponsors fool enough to advertise on his show. One sponsor, Schick, had Morgan write and perform its ads himself. This led to a then–celebrated series of ads/routines that the company felt undermined its revolutionary new product, the injector razor. Schick soon abandoned Morgan, but not before he skewered the image of the company as millions of patriotic razor users listened in.

One of Morgan's Schick ads aired on the *Hour* (he teaches a dumb jock the difference between an injector razor and cornflakes). Though mild when set next to *Lampoon* takes on sex and death, it fit the show's format in a way the other "Laughs from the Past" did not. Morgan was ahead of his time in the attitude he conveyed toward commercials and the companies that financed them. After all, his minor rebellion took place in a nonrebellious era. But Morgan *did* anticipate the approach to humor that the *Lampoon* would later adopt, and the spirit he displayed might have had some impact on Pete. Not only did he use Morgan's bit, but he himself would attempt a similar, yet bloodier, assault on corporate sponsors and, in one instance, a television network.

When not engrossed in radio or books, Pete listened to music, primarily classical. The works of the great composers had always been played in the Donohue home, and Pete was exposed to various symphonies and sonatas from infancy. As he aged, Pete discovered that music could establish a mood—or, more common in his case, *reflect* a mood already established.

Gabriel-Urban Fauré's *Pavane: Opus 50* became a particular favorite; Pete found fascinating its melancholy tone and chorus, at once distant and passionate. He identified with the mournful progression of the piece, and when one listens to the music closely the reason appears evident: A year of illness and detachment must have seemed a funeral march for a boy of five, especially since time passes slowly for children. *Pavane* expresses sorrow in a deliberate manner, sorrow that is rich and timed to rise and fall. It's impossible to say whether Pete's own sadness matched what he heard in Fauré's composition. But *Pavane* makes clear that darkness always looms and that art can capture its essence. An important lesson, one that Pete knew instinctively but had yet to fully comprehend.

Head packed with words, words tied to images, images extending to emotion: Was there any question that Michael Henry Donohue would write, if only to burst this mental dam? Barbara and Michael James were part of a family oral tradition that, according to Barbara, went back a few generations. Yet to anyone's knowledge, none of the talk-happy O'Donoghues or Zimmermans on either side of the family's fence ever published any thoughts or stories. The Sauquoit Donohues kept the tradition alive and off-the-record—that is, until Pete began marking up pieces of scrap paper with sentence fragments and bits of dialogue copied from books.

If it's true that writers write what they know or pretend to understand, then beginning writers copy what they read. Pete's own reading tended toward Victorian fiction and English children's stories, and his appreciation of Sherlock Holmes deepened as he matured. He always enjoyed the detective's casebooks as exciting tales, but now he looked beyond the action to learn how the action was sustained. He studied Conan Doyle's prose, its rhythm, its pace; he examined each story's content and saw how meticulous Conan Doyle could be in establishing plot. Much of the information was necessary to the story and its conclusion, but minor details suggested different, far-off episodes, never to be grasped or explained. Pete picked up on Conan Doyle's interest in obscure items listed in the Holmes mysteries. Not only did these offhanded references appeal to Pete's growing interest in matters strange and inexplicable, they inspired the need for minute detail in his own writing.

Stop and compare: In *The Musgrave Ritual,* Holmes brings before Watson the records of his early cases. "They are not all successes, Watson," says Holmes, "but there are some pretty little problems among them." Holmes then surveys the bundles of paper that contain the relevant information. "Here's the record of the Tarleton murders, and the case of Vamberry, the wine merchant, and the adventure of the old Russian woman, and the singular affair of the aluminum crutch, as well as a full account of Ricoletti of the clubfoot and his abominable wife . . ." Holmes moves on to the case of Reginald Musgrave and leaves one to wonder what intrigue is tied to that aluminum crutch.

In much of his adult work, Pete employed the same technique. He arranged a series of images for no purpose other than to suggest an odd story or a joke that never arrived; "the penguin, the soap dish, and the invisible cowgirl" was a favorite combination. He did this in longer pieces as well. In "What Marks on the Neck?" from the November 1971 *National Lampoon,* a collection of old photographs is adorned by captions that positively burst with Conan Doyle's influence. The caption under a photo of a tall, thin woman in 1920s garb reads, "More interesting was the case of René Jacquet, the Le Havre vampire, who, affecting the shape of a lungfish, would steal onto fishing vessels and feed upon the sailors. A yachting party off Saint-Jean-de-Luz finally stabbed him in the heart with a dessert fork . . ."

Another photo shows a stern man, Ned Shale, holding a folded newspaper; he rants, "Just look at these headlines—'Colossal Centipede Flattens Flatiron Building,' 'Cabinet Minister Loses Hands,' 'Search Continues for Missing Governess,' 'Chinese Illusionist Nabbed in Spore Theft,' 'Army Seizes Tungsten Deposits'! I tell you, Aubrey, something strange is going on, and I intend to get to the bottom of it!"

Shale never does and neither do we. But then that's the point. Here and in numerous other bits and pieces the young Pete Donohue is present, the boy who discovered early a formula that he could later remix as desire dictated.

Pete's desire to write and understand writing intensified. He flirted with poetry and strove to construct simple rhymes. He wrote and rewrote sentences until frustration gave way to anger. Unlike the child who plays "grown-up" and pretends to be who he wants to be, Pete wasn't playing or pretending; he was engaged in serious exploration. Writing became a primary part of his young life and was not a game. His sweating over sentence structure and his anger when stuck on a word marked the beginning of his creative style. Ideas would expand, concepts would bloom, tone would sharpen, but the sheer hell of translating all to paper would never really change.

However, Pete was no slave to the grindstone. There were enthusiasms and some happiness. The mind that would later pull humor from madness and violence was presently consumed with family life nestled in the slowness of Cassville. Soon Pete would play Little League baseball; he would pitch and play first base, but would find it difficult to run the bases due to his lingering asthma. He later tried out for the school track team but couldn't sustain a decent sprint. Still, he was very competitive, no matter the sport or game; his sister described his attitude as "ruthless" and "win at all costs" and said that as an opponent he "was not friendly."

When I was fairly young, they had migrant camps in upstate New York. My mother would always shudder as she went by the migrant camps. And they weren't in my books about the policeman stopping traffic so the little baby ducks could cross the street; I knew that. And no one was explaining that if they paid those people a decent wage, you'd have to pay a dollar and a half for a can of beans. So everyone looked the other way, and that's when I began to see that those books about our society were lying to me. Once you know that, you find confirmation everywhere.

Still weak but nearly well, seven-year-old Pete Donohue was sent to a one-room countryside school in Cassville, itself a part of the Sauquoit Valley public school system. It was his first real exposure to other children, and he lacked the social skills necessary to interact with them. But Pete wasn't there to chat. Behind in his studies (that is, studies required by the state), he was to make up both first and second grade in one year, which he neatly did. The following year, at the age of eight, he covered the third and fourth grades. His teachers were impressed with the knowledge he already possessed (Pete's reading skills were beyond those of the other students) and with his hunger for and ability to digest new information.

After a brief move to nearby Clayville in 1949, where Pete started and finished the fifth grade, the Donohues returned to Sauquoit, and there they would stay. Michael James found work as an industrial engineer and sold real estate on the side, at times assisted by Barbara. She also helped make ends meet by selling cosmetics in a Utica clothing store. Pete maintained his scholastic pace at Sauquoit Valley Central School. In seventh and eighth grades he collected numerous awards for math, science, and English; he expanded his studies to include algebra and Latin. In eighth grade he began to play the clarinet. His grades were consistently among the highest of his class, and on the surface Pete seemed the model student.

To his classmates he was the model geek. They either shunned him socially or, in the case of a few farm boys, hammered him physically. Pete's appearance, that of a tall, skinny boy who wore thick, unflattering glasses, made him a conspicuous

Pete with sister Jane, late 1940s

and inviting target of attack. He fit the physical stereotype of the brainiac dork. But Pete was no pacifist. The anger that welled within could be used to strike back at his redneck aggressors. If confronted, he would remove his glasses and crouch in a coiled fighting stance. If assaulted, he would try to match punch for punch: "I learned that the secret to fighting is surprise, so I'd hit them in the back with a two-by-four, which gives you most of the edge for the first three or four minutes. I'd take advantage of their momentary surprise to hit them again with the two-by-four."

Still, Pete's intellect was faster and more punishing than his use of fists or weapons. "I got pretty good at fighting," he later bragged, "but I figured out a much better way to get back at people. Tell them their nose looks like a ruptured bicycle horn. Then you've hit them not once, you've hit them many times. They'll wake up at six in the morning with tears on their pillow. Physical deformity was—still is—the greatest thing to go for. Never challenge people's ideas. What a silly waste of time. Give them a remark to stick in their memory book: 'You look like an asshole.' "

I was a wiseass. Not surprising, really; you could almost have guessed that. In fact, it's always thrilled me that I have actually made my money out of essentially being a wiseass. All the time I was mouthing off, wising off about God knows what sobersided subject, I was actually preparing for my future. A professional wiseass; that's just a lovely thing to be.

Pete's teachers, though pleased with his grades, took a dim view of his attitude and his style of study. A ninth grade instructor wrote on his report card that Pete "should become more orderly in his approach" to school, that he took "too long to settle down to work." His eleventh grade English teacher, Mrs. Owens, noted next to his A that "Michael's English work is satisfactory, but his attention in class is poor—sometimes to the point of discourtesy. I should like to see him improve in this respect."

That didn't seem in the cards. Barbara recalled that Pete "spent more time in the principal's office than the principal did," and that he could be, and often was, "holy hell" in school. He did do his best to keep his teachers off balance. In grade school, when given a test to identify various colors, Pete refused to label a green panel as "green." Miffed, his teacher sent Pete home with a note for his parents. When Barbara asked him why he had failed to correctly identify the panel as "green," Pete replied, "It wasn't *green;* it was *chartreuse.*"

"I found that humor could cut 'em up pretty good," he stated later, "like going back to the third grade when you take the doggy-doo and put it on the teacher's chair. Or when the substitute teacher would come in and you'd write the name 'Mike Hunt' and she would ask, 'Mike Hunt? Has anybody seen Mike Hunt?' Which, really, in the third or fourth grade, can really put you in the aisles, a good joke like that. That's a grand joke. Still a good joke, still a great, witty joke."

In Pete's sophomore year of high school a fellow student ran afoul of a substitute teacher. The teacher started to send the boy to see the principal, then announced that any other student who thought what the boy had done was funny could join him. Pete rose from his desk and went to the door. "Where are you going?" the teacher asked. "I thought it was funny," answered Pete. Furious, the teacher sat the other boy down and sent Pete in his place. After the vice principal condemned his behavior, Pete was asked, "Now, do you still think it's funny?" He delivered a deadpan look, then replied, "No, I think it's *hilarious*." His father was summoned, and after reviewing the evidence Michael James sided with his son.

School was where Pete's "others" concept took firm root. Walking the hallways, watching the various cliques in action, he witnessed a social order that both disgusted and frightened him. Yes, they were by and large "dumb farmers." But dumb or not, they were in the mainstream of the school and shared a sense of place. To a teen left outside of this arrangement that represented power to be used against him, either in the form of banishment or by way of a big rube's fist. Yet Pete wouldn't allow this state of affairs to ruin his life. After all, the "others" might have clung together, but when left alone they were lost. "To this day," he said at age forty-three, "I love rainy weather because I have a scrap-book and the other kids are fucked."

There is a popular portrait of the comedian-as-adolescent-wiseguy, the unpopular kid who made the larger kids laugh lest they choose instead to pound the shit out of him. Mel Brooks and Richard Pryor painted themselves thus, and it informed their later work (especially Pryor, who had a routine about his being a funny coward as a kid). Pete Donohue, on the other hand, sought not to amuse the louts. Humor was his defense, but not in the sense of deflecting or disarming any aggressive intent held by the big boys; humor was to be a weapon, a source of power, a leveler in a war of wills. Pete wanted, as he said, to hurt those who looked to hurt him and to leave them sobbing in their pillows. What did not destroy him made him funnier.

During his time at Sauquoit Valley Central School, Pete met and became friends with a boy named Philip Ray. Like Pete, Phil was smart and theatrical; he too felt out of place in Sauquoit but was not quite as isolated as was Pete. However, he warmed to Pete's intelligence and his nasty sense of humor. He saw in Pete a kindred soul, and together the pair would amuse one another while rattling those around them.

Crank calls were a favorite activity (and a much safer one in the days before caller ID). Pete and Phil would set a small phonograph and a stack of records next to a phone. They'd pull names at random from the Sauquoit directory, call those chosen, and inform them that they were to win a prize if they could correctly identify a piece of music. A few seconds of a record were played; if the piece was correctly identified, Pete or Phil would answer "No, that's wrong!" and would then repeat the prank until the person either hung up or they broke out laughing. Hours were spent on the Donohue phone for just this purpose.

The two boys shared a fondness for makeup and costumes. As a child, Pete would dress—in coats, hats, sheets—as various characters from his imagination. He'd roam the house as though it were a stage, affecting postures and accents. With Phil he decided to take the production out-doors. They went to a nearby cemetery that was located next to railroad tracks. Each day passenger trains ran past the columns of headstones, behind which sat Pete and Phil in vampire costume: black capes on their backs, macaroni on their incisors. As the trains whizzed by the boys leaped toward the passengers' windows, waving their arms and baring their semolina fangs. They would then return to the headstones to await the next audience.

Pete liked the stillness of the graveyard; there his imagination kicked up human dust. He also enjoyed exploring hidden, abandoned spaces. Once he entered a Victorian house that was owned by an older woman who had recently died. However, her furniture and belongings remained, and Pete soon found himself in the deceased woman's bedroom. He went through her closet and tried on scarves and silk sleeping wear. He later said it was there that he first felt arousal when wearing women's clothing, especially lingerie. Though not a transvestite per se, he discov-ered early the pleasure of fine silky things, and this he carried with him for the rest of his life.

Pete and Phil were inseparable and largely kept to themselves. An-other boy, Barton Cobain, was on the pair's wavelength and came to know the two for a brief while. Pete acknowledged that Barton was "pretty bright" and that he would have "been tough competition" for him, but tragedy intervened. During the freshman picnic, Barton went for a swim in a lake and drowned. As the entire class watched the police drag the lake for his body, Pete had his eye on the food. "[W]e hadn't eaten yet and I was hungry. I grabbed a sandwich and the gym teacher started yelling at me, 'You monster, you *monster!*' Hell, I thought you could grieve and eat at the same time."

The picnic drowning anecdote was told to *Rolling Stone* in 1979, and it certainly fit the notorious O'Donoghue profile of that period. Yet the incident described above had been dramatized in the 1956 film *The Bad Seed*, which starred young Patty McCormack as Rhoda Penmark, the murderous little miss from whose *Seed* evil sprouts. Rhoda attends a school picnic near a lake. While the other children play games it is discovered that Claude Dagel, Rhoda's scholastic rival, has drowned. Word of his death quickly spreads. When Rhoda returns home from the picnic, her mother is struck by Rhoda's nonchalance and immediate request for a peanut butter sandwich. While the rest of the small town grieves, Rhoda eats her lunch.

Barton Cobain did indeed drown at his freshman picnic; and it's certainly conceivable that Pete reached for a sandwich after the fact (though his sister said he was devastated by Cobain's death). But the similarity found in both real and reel incidents is noteworthy in that Pete Donohue plucked elements from various sources and merged them into the persona he created for himself. Like Rhoda, Pete was a smart kid who detested the majority of his peers—though he possessed no homicidal intent toward Barton as Rhoda did toward Claude. But although he never killed anyone, Pete fantasized about the ultimate crime and would later wish death upon those who crossed him.

> *One morning you wake up dead*
> *Teddy bear by your bed*
> *They want to give you head—*
> *Stones, the baby ghouls.*

> *Bloodstains on the party dress*
> *Little white gloves a mess!*
> *Look out for the pre-pu-bes*
> *Of the baby ghouls.*

His writing developed; his approach remained intense. He stared off into space for extended periods of time, consumed with himself as ideas evolved. Whatever attention disorder he might have shown at school, Pete did not lack focus when alone. In fact, his focus was total and at times would result in rage. He broke pencils; he threw tantrums. Physically he was weak, but his temper knew strength. Before long pencil halves and scraps of paper littered his bedroom. Matchbook covers bearing concepts piled up. Barbara tolerated the mess until it reached critical mass; she would then clean the room, taking care not to throw away the matchbook covers. *That* could lead to more anger, a larger mess.

Barbara believed that Pete's tantrums stemmed from impatience caused by his "sickly" condition. If something didn't go right, if he failed to realize any objective, no matter how minor, he would snap; he'd scream, stomp his feet, kick the walls. He'd work himself to full lather until one of his parents stepped in. The principal punishment was grounding (though keeping Pete in his room might not seem a stern approach), and on one occasion Pete's outburst was so explosive that Barbara doused him with a pan of ice water. But once he got going he could sustain a tantrum for days, albeit at varying levels of passion.

Pete's tantrums were disruptive but directed mainly at himself; anger was the lubricant that kept the engine humming. Concentration, precision, and execution were the creative ends to his sometimes turbulent means. By his early teens Pete was writing regularly, in class and by himself. In his eighth grade English class Pete experimented with half sentences. Although he could easily produce an essay or book report or any standard assignment on request, Pete preferred to tinker with epigrams and other brief arrangements. His teacher, Mr. Taylor, who recognized Pete's talent, insisted he learn the basics: "When you're published you can use all the half sentences you want," he intoned.

As it so happened, Pete had written an essay that traced the life of Sir Arthur Conan Doyle and his struggles as a writer. Meticulously detailed and researched, the essay revealed how much Conan Doyle had received for his first Sherlock Holmes story (twenty-three pounds) and that he'd modeled the physical features of Holmes after those of "Joseph Bell, his old teacher." Pete mailed the essay to the *Baker Street Journal*, the publication of the Baker Street Irregulars, a Sherlock Holmes fan club based in London. To Pete's surprise the *Journal* published the piece, his first—the family's first—appearance in print. He then presented Mr. Taylor with the issue of the *Journal* bearing his piece. Mr. Taylor was impressed and from then on allowed Pete to write in the style he desired.

At home, Pete amused himself in varied ways. He'd place toy soldiers atop his electric train set, then pick off each one with a pellet gun as the cars moved along the tracks. Also, he enjoyed tormenting his kid sister, Jane. If she fell down a flight of stairs, Pete laughed; he did this, too, when she broke her arm—the children, she later said, were taught to laugh off injury or pain. When Jane was six or seven years old, Pete devised a game for her. He took a broom handle and rapped out a piece by, say, Beethoven against a wall. He then asked Jane, who knew only "Jingle Bells," "What song was that?" If she didn't know, and she often didn't, Pete nudged or playfully hit her legs with the broom handle. Jane was happy to receive the attention, as her brother often ignored her while he pursued his private interests.

Pete also dabbled in art. He sketched in pen the family's cats, Truman and Satan, as well as other items in the house. But his favorite medium was watercolor. He considered several themes before settling on dead trees. Amid the leafless branches and faded bark Pete saw beauty; he brought to canvas spare tree lines and set them against gray skies. He toiled in the attic and turned out a number of dead tree originals, each evoking the barren climate of a small town sliding from fall to winter.

Recognizing their son's talent for painting, Pete's parents sent him to Utica to attend summer art school when he was fifteen. There Pete learned about form and perspective, and he studied the history of art movements and the artists that defined them. He became somewhat en-amored of the British artist Aubrey Beardsley, friend of Oscar Wilde and illustrator of the playwright's *Salomé*. Beardsley was of a crowd described as the Decadents, a collection of writers and artists who either ignored or flouted Victorian sensibilities during the mid- to late-1890s. Beardsley worked with pen and ink and always in black and white. His drawings convey a fine dark grace; as Fraser Harrison, editor of an anthology of Beardsley's work, put it:

> The world inhabited by [Beardsley's] figures is essentially artificial; the clothes they wear are elaborate, preposterous, and, above all, suggestive; their rooms and gardens are sheer masquerade; men and women alike wear masks, cosmetics, beauty spots and absurdly elaborate coiffures; their bodies are often unnaturally elongated, and their feet reduced to miniatures; they keep company with satyrs, pierrots, embryos and grotesques. His scenes are lit by candles, foot-lights, gas-lights, or an unearthly twilight, but, whatever the source, shadows are never cast.

Beardsley's world, light-years from Sauquoit, was clearly seen by the teenager; the smooth, peculiar lines found in Beardsley's drawings soon appeared in Pete's pen-and-ink sketches. But it was Beardsley's tilt to the eccentric that attracted Pete; those rooms and gardens where human and beast mingled in costume opened his eyes and laid the mental groundwork for comic settings, theme parties. Even the titles of Beard-sley's drawings—"The Repentance of Mrs. ★★★★," "The Comedy-Ballet of Marionettes, as performed by the troupe of the Theatre Impossible, II"—nudged Pete in a certain artistic direction. (Flip back to the page where Ned Shale rants about bizarre headlines; and the name of the person to whom he is speaking . . . ?)

Pete's time at art school produced little in the way of output: Barbara recalled a "weird" sculpture of plaster of paris and glass he once brought home. But Utica, which the family visited every weekend, offered Pete no real alternative, and he began to think more and more about leaving the area entirely. He found the town as dead as his trees; that is, if one chooses to view his paintings as watercolor Rorschachs.

Back at Sauquoit Valley Central High, Pete threw himself into his

Senior year, 1957, Sauquoit Valley Central High School

studies and extracurricular activities. His grades were still among the highest of his class, and although he was still unpopular with girls he did manage a few dates with one named Kelly. He learned to play chess and joined the Chess Club, then gave up the game because it consumed too much of his time. He continued to play the clarinet and teamed with Phil Ray, who played piano, as a member of the school band. Their collaboration proved so successful that they were asked to perform at special school functions, including as warm-up for a PTA meeting in 1956. And as a nod to family tradition, Pete won the American Legion Annual High School Oratorical Contest in his senior year.

Pete also assumed the presidency of the Dramatics Club. His duties kept him busy both onstage and off; he participated in every aspect of a play's production, from acting to helping with set and costume design. The school's drama teacher, Mrs. Pritchard, wanted plays with myriad parts: less *Charley's Aunt,* more *Chuck's Numerous Relatives.* She wanted to get as many kids as she could in a production. Pete was thus consigned to small roles, although once cast he made the most of his time onstage. In one production he was directed to fall over a couch. Not content to merely drop, he spent hours at home honing the perfect fall. He plunged, collapsed, and tumbled from a variety of angles until he found the right combination. He stood just next to the couch's arm and, body fully erect, fell in a straight line, hit the cushions, bounced slightly, then struck the floor. Minor character though he was, Pete choreographed his brief bit of action so he would steal the scene and secure the audience's complete attention.

Pete finished his high school years in pretty much the same fashion: He wasn't terribly popular but he was recognized. "I was so damned bright that the other kids really couldn't keep me out of their lives," he said in retrospect. A glance at his senior yearbook supports this; several pages are filled with friendly, even enthusiastic, salutations—the "nork," as he was called, had left his mark. But the most genuine entry came from Phil Ray whose casual tone signified his closeness to Pete. "See you in Rochester," Phil wrote at the end, referring to Pete's decision to attend the University of Rochester in the fall of 1957. Rochester was not a world capital, but compared to Sauquoit it was Paris. Rochester pointed the way out of an existence that Pete likened to "being walled up alive."

two

It's very interesting to teach children what you hoped your society would be like. But you should teach them as truth that it did, indeed, turn out this way.

As Sauquoit disappeared in the distance and Rochester rose into view, Pete Donohue felt for the first time a sense of true freedom. Sauquoit had been an extension of his bedroom, a place to practice his craft, to fantasize and play artiste while the "others" scratched their heads, their mouths agape. Pete saw college as an opportunity to develop and hone the temperament that had surfaced within the walls of Sauquoit. He also believed that his imagination and talent would be appreciated once his professors were exposed to his work.

The University of Rochester was, like many of the nation's centers of "higher learning" in 1957, a pillar of social and political conformity. The university's primary focus was business education, its students raw material to be cut and formed to meet the needs of corporate managers. This was a golden era for American business, a time of high profits and extended corporate control of the national economy. Consequently, corporate ladder climbing was reflected in the culture, usually in light fare such as *Will Success Spoil Rock Hunter?* Although the alienating aspects of big business were explored as well (the film *The Man in the Gray Flannel Suit* starring Gregory Peck, the book *The New Industrial State* by John Kenneth Galbraith), most Americans viewed the corporate state as natural and corporations as providers of the good life. Those who did not were godless and Marxist, and no doubt homosexual.

Business held little appeal for Pete, the corporate treadmill less so. But Rochester was close to Sauquoit and affordable. Its curriculum included English and philosophy, subjects he chose to major and minor in respectively. Also, he sought to invent himself: "I wisely pretended to be another type of person—suave, confident, popular," and the first thing this new person did was lose "Pete" as a nickname. ("It sounds like a butcher," he complained to his mother.) He introduced himself to his fellow freshmen as simply Mike Donohue.

The Rochester climate was typical of the time. Fraternities and sorores governed the social scene; crew cuts and neckties were favored by boys, sweaters, cinch belts, and crinolines by girls; ROTC cadets and football players ranked among the most popular students on campus; Dwight Eisenhower was admired, if not revered. Wholesome, nativist *Happy Days*, a climate in which Mike Donohue revealed his "suave, confident" side to those he hoped to impress, to show that despite his small-town roots he was more cosmopolitan than rube.

Naturally, Mike was not one to chase the Pat Boone crowd. His theatrical demeanor and literary knowledge precluded his consorting with jocks and business school squares. Besides, he was thin and wiry, not the strapping alpha male type then celebrated as All-American. Definite boundaries were in place. (To make himself seem less the academic stiff, he chose not to wear his glasses in public.) Still, he looked to branch out, make connections, put into action ideas he had conceived since his time at Sauquoit High.

Another Rochester freshman held a few ideas of his own. Dan Rattiner hailed from Milburn, New Jersey, where as a high school student he had fancied himself avant-garde. Rattiner's primary interest was humor, Lenny Bruce being one of his favorites. He also appreciated the work of Eugene Ionesco and Samuel Beckett. He was not prime business school stock, but Rattiner attended Rochester anyway because his high school faculty adviser "said I should go there."

After settling in the Hoeing Hall dorm, Rattiner strove to establish a lounge for students bored with or put off by the campus status quo. Though new to the Rochester scene, Rattiner felt that there had to be some level of dissidence in the midst of such conformity and that this would be worth tapping into. He combed the campus in search of a space, and eventually reserved a room in the Student Center. He then arranged to have audiotapes of Jean Shepherd's radio show sent to Rochester by a friend in Brooklyn, New York, and the tapes became the centerpiece of Rattiner's alternative gatherings.

At the time Jean Shepherd was considered the "leading satirist of the underground." He was best known for his short stories, droll little digs at human absurdity. He was deceptively "folksy" in his approach to humor; an "aw shucks" delivery helped mask his acid tongue. (This is a feature commonly found in other Hoosier-bred wits such as Kurt Vonnegut, David Letterman, and the no longer read George Ade, whose work Shepherd anthologized.) Though he practiced a dying art form— the bones of which were later bleached by Dave Barry and Lewis Grizzard—Shepherd enlivened his pieces with fine comic vigor and timing.

The rhythms of his titles evoked S. J. Perelman: "Miss Bryfogel and the Frightening Case of the Speckle-Throated Cuckold"; "The Day Shift Drops By for a Belt"; "Leopold Doppler and the Great Orpheum Gravy Boat Riot." Above all, Shepherd was a quality stylist, a rarity in American humor writing.

Shepherd's radio show (which emanated from WOR-AM in Manhattan) was hyped energetically by Rattiner. He pasted posters across campus and played up Shepherd's "underground" cachet. Students who arrived at the center to hear the show were charged fifty cents admission. Once inside they were guided to a dark room illuminated by colored lights. They sat on leather sofas or Indian rugs and listened as Shepherd's voice rose from a reel-to-reel tape player. The turnouts were modest; as Rattiner remembers it, there was a "small number of people who considered [themselves] outcast from the main part of the community." Among this number was, of course, Mike Donohue.

It is unclear whether Donohue and Rattiner met at one of the Jean Shepherd events, but it certainly seems likely. After all, Donohue absorbed what he could in matters of culture, and his desire to learn intensified when he entered college. He was also drawn to the offbeat, for it was there that new ideas dwelled. And though Shepherd, celebrated by the Associated Press and *Newsweek*, didn't quite fit into this category, his reputation cut against the Rochester grain, and this was bound to attract Donohue. In any event, Rattiner did meet Donohue around this time. Soon, each would see the other as ally and collaborator.

Although Rattiner was influenced by the likes of Shepherd and Lenny Bruce, he was nevertheless thrown by the seventeen-year-old Donohue. He would refer to his new friend's humor as, for lack of a surgical description, "wacko." Donohue's perspective, though evolving, was striking even to one fond of the experimental in art and comedy. Rattiner wasn't aware of Donohue's medical history, the childhood isolation that fed his often punishing introspection; to him, Donohue was an odd but bright freshman from small-town America. But he understood Donohue and recognized the potential of a creative relationship. To Donohue, Rattiner was the only person other than Phil Ray who appreciated his ideas. And since Phil did not attend Rochester (he would occasionally visit), Donohue grew closer to Rattiner.

The two Young Turks cast their cold eyes on the surrounding environment. They consciously set themselves apart from the other freshmen and stood polar-opposite to all that Rochester represented. They spent hours in the Student Union's rathskeller and watched various Rock Hudsons (robust and straight) chase numerous Doris Days and the occasional Sandra Dee. "We were on the outs," said Rattiner. "Neither of us were particulary ladies' men." Rather than join in a fruitless pursuit, Rattiner and Donohue sat at a corner table and applied lit matches to plastic spoons and forks, melting them into unusual shapes. They cracked wise in the wake of those who passed by; they played Dave Brubeck's "Take Five" again and again on the jukebox; they behaved like bad boy bohemians who threw paint on a colorless world. They then decided to take their act to a larger audience.

Early in 1958, Rattiner asked for and received a weekly slot on the campus radio station, WRUR. He and Donohue threw together a show that had no title, no format, no clear purpose other than to provide an outlet for the pair's nervous energy. The only recurring element heard on the show was its theme song, "The Poet and Peasant Overture" as horribly rendered by an amateur polka group called the Guggenheim Sauerkraut Orchestra. (The sound was roughly that of a car crashing into rented instruments.) The hosts sat close to the microphone and whispered, "You're hearing this program from deep in the underground. The authorities don't want you to listen to this . . ." They played cuts from Lenny Bruce albums, recited poetry, read from newspapers, satirized current events.

The experience enriched Mike Donohue. Unlike the high school stage, where he had to compete to be seen, radio placed him directly in the minds of the audience. His mellifluous voice ran counter to the aggressive pitch favored by mainstream announcers and their imitators, and this, too, attracted attention. Unfortunately for Donohue and Rattiner, not everyone at Rochester found their act amusing. Complaints were heard that the boys were dabbling in obscenity and sedition, and after four months the show's plug was quietly pulled.

Those fucking prick professors just wanted their ideas parroted back to them. I went berserk when I figured that out. The ultimate lie: freedom in academia.

Despite his bohemian display, Mike Donohue took seriously his education: He truly felt that college was a center of intellectual refinement. He knew that if he was to advance in his thinking and perfect his methods of research and study he had to submit to academic discipline. But Rochester soon dampened this awareness before it could become enthusiasm. The social conformity, the emphasis on business, the leaden pace of university life shut young Mike down (more accurately, he allowed it to shut him down). Distracted and bored, he went through the motions of being a "good student" while focusd on other realities. Despite his outer "new" self, Donohue remained nestled in the world he had created while in Sauquoit.

He wasn't helped by the fact that many academics (then as now) live in a shadow world, speak and write in a strange, dense language, and view imagination as an impediment to tenure. This was especially true in the 1950s, when a student's duty was to parrot the observations made by his all-knowing professor. There were, of course, a fair number of creative minds in academe at the time. One wonders how Donohue would have fared at, say, Columbia University, its faculty staffed by the the likes of Lionel Trilling, Mark Van Doren, and F. W. Dupee. Would he have been more engaged? more willing to struggle? (Or, to turn the question around, Would *they* have been tolerant of him?) Impossible to say, though the possibilities are enticing. Rochester offered no comparable academic lineup, and this left Donohue to test his talents under what he considered to be adverse conditions.

At times Donohue provided his professors an easy target. In his freshman drama class he was to summarize the plots of several plays, among them *Volpone, All for Love, The Jew of Malta.* The result is a mishmash of interpretations, misspellings, and haphazard analysis. (In response to one question, Donohue answers with "no idea!" then adds that he thinks his professor "invented" the basis for the question "to make it hard.") Donohue was given a D-plus, but not before his professor commented, "You strive manfully, but the hard truth is too clearly manifest for us decently to ignore. You simply haven't read a lot of the plays and despite ingenious improvising you continually betray your lack of preparation." There is some recognition of talent; a few of Donohue's insights, though "isolated," are "ones of good quality." But he was caught inventing a dance in mid-step, and the music was killed and the curtain brought down.

Though he would wait until the last minute to tackle an assignment, Donohue could, and did, attempt an original approach. In a paper from his sophomore year, he was to analyze the mythological tragedy of Troilus and Cressida, a pair of Trojan lovers whose saga was adapted by Geoffrey Chaucer and later by William Shakespeare. Donohue chose to compare the two interpretations through the character of Pandarus, who appears first as Cressida's wise, matchmaking uncle in Chaucer's poem, and then as a more scheming relation in Shakespeare's play. (The action in each version is set against the Trojan War.) The title of his paper "The Characters of Both Shakespeare's and Chaucer's Pandarus, With the Result of Occurrence When That of Chaucer's Is Substituted Into That of Shakespeare's Play, *Troilus and Cressida*," is as overwrought as the contents are revealing.

Donohue's initial mistake was to fill the paper with British spellings. The result of this Anglo influence shines on every page, but his professor marks as wrong each use of "ou" in words such as *humour* and makes clear that a simple American "o" will suffice. She is confused, then put off, by Donohue's insistence that the "nucleus of Shakespeare's play is lust"; that Troilus and Cressida do not possess the "sacred emotions" of love and that this results in their "separation" and "general disillusionment." Here, Uncle Pandarus "appears as a vile cynic, a nasty old man" who, in dealing his niece to Troilus, is little more than "a pimp"—that is, when he doesn't have incestual designs on the girl himself. It is only when Donohue replaces the bad Pandarus with the good that "the lust becomes love" and all are redeemed.

Apart from his desire to write as an Englishman (predictable, given his influences), Donohue's paper reveals an emerging set of values that would remain pretty much intact through his adult years. He sees love as nobility itself, made of crystal and easily damaged when handled by brutes. Lust is the language of the savage, the drool that hangs from animal teeth. There is honor in tenderness, degradation in cynicism. Those who feel with their hearts transcend those who think with their crotches. It is a black-and-white world tinged with rose, one that revolves around the young romantic.

Donohue's prose is suitably analytical but nonacademic; this is not a guy gunning for the ivory tower. He writes of literature in a literary way; and although rough patches exist (as do numerous misspellings, the consequence of eleventh-hour effort), his handling of the subject matter is rather inspired. His characterization of Shakespeare's Pandarus as a pimp with incest on his mind is a daring move. After all, *pimp* was not commonly used in 1958, especially by college sophomores attending conservative universities. Had he desired to shock his professor, some coarseness would have shown. But here Donohue is straightforward; he looks down on vulgarity and describes his distaste without blinking.

His professor felt it to be "a thoughtful paper, showing interest in and understanding of both pieces." However, she wasn't fully taken with Donohue's Pandarus switch and saw the maneuver as half-baked. Then the boom is lowered: "Obvious errors mar the presentation of your ideas in this paper in fact as well as mechanics. What you have to say about the complex relation of Troilus and Cressida does *not* follow the text." Troilus, at least "in the opinion of Ulysses," is "an outstanding young man who has idealized Cressida." And finally, Shakespeare's Pandarus is not a pimp, so, presumably, there was no need to replace him with Chaucer's kinder model.

For coloring outside of the lines, Donohue received a fine fat D. There is the possibility that his professor recognized his talent but disapproved of his brashness, thus the low grade. If this is true, her notes to Donohue offer scant evidence. The line about Troilus's being "an outstanding young man" is at best meaningless; it sounds as if he brought Cressida home before curfew and was content with a kiss on the cheek. Contrary evaluations are unwelcome. Whatever the professor's reasoning,

Mike Donohue, near the end of his first stint at Rochester University, 1959–60

Donohue felt that his writing would never be taken seriously in class; that is, when he chose to seriously write.

Most of Mike Donohue's serious compositions were labored over outside of class. He set aside time to write poetry and short humorous stories. Writing had always provided solace, and as he completed his sophomore year he was determined to develop a personal style regardless of faculty opinion. His friendship with Dan Rattiner remained strong, for Rattiner, too, felt restricted by the regimented thinking that dominated campus life. As individuals and as a team they tried to set fire to the twigs that passed for Rochester ivy but never fully succeeded. In the fall of 1959, Rattiner moved to take hold of a campus fixture with the hope that he and Donohue might turn the thing . . . if not on its head, then flat on its back.

The college humor magazine was once an integral part of many American universities, the most famous being Harvard's *Lampoon*. Rochester had *Ugh*; and though the name suggested something "sick" in *Mad*'s jugular vein, *Ugh* was a quaint little mag devoted to good-natured mischief. Rattiner had been a contributor during his sophomore year, and when he returned as a junior he was offered the position of editor-in-chief. Unlike the august *Lampoon*, where editorial succession resembled secret tribal rites, *Ugh* was handed to whomever happened to be around—in this case, Rattiner. Turned off by the magazine's tongue-in-cheek approach, Rattiner wanted *Ugh* to be volatile. He hated the mag's name but was in no position to change it. This was just as well. Before long Rochester's paragons of taste and virtue would utter the word *Ugh*, not in appreciation, but as though they had been hit in the gut.

If a young, enterprising satirist wishes to make waves, he naturally drops poison in the fount of superstition: religion. Rattiner had pellets in hand but recognized the risk involved. After all, it was—is—generally assumed that God personally created the United States in His image, and there was—is—little doubt that Heaven's throne sports a red, white, and blue finish. So any swipe taken at the Lord was seen as unpatriotic; and in 1959 patriotism itself was a state religion, while the IRS burned incense and the Pentagon passed the collection plates.

Inspired by Lenny Bruce and a new satirical magazine—*The Realist*, founded by Bruce's friend Paul Krassner—Rattiner floated a few ideas to friends. He was playing with various depictions of the Crucifixion in cartoon form. One showed an overstressed Jesus trying to carry a twenty-five-foot cross on his shoulder. Another portrayed the Son of Man as a reluctant Savior; He is seen kicking and screaming on his way to the cross, and as the nails are produced He attempts to escape. This latter concept horrified Rattiner's friends and acquaintances. Their reaction was so negative that he chose not to publish the cartoon. But disbelief dies hard, and eventually Rattiner did print a parody of the Last Supper, "Table for Eight: A Soap Opera in Half an Act" by Fredric Kaplan. It was milder than the "Run Jesus Run!" idea (the Supper guests included Nietzsche, Chaucer, and the Marquis de Sade), but it nevertheless angered students and faculty alike.

Mike Donohue was not among the offended. He knew in his heart that Rochester was provincial, that those who set the academic and social standards were contemptible and worthy of insult. He delighted in Rattiner's dissent and saw *Ugh* as a place where his private musings could be publicly expressed. But Donohue was not on a satirical mission. He was too guarded for so grand a gesture. His interest in *Ugh* was plain: He wanted to write what he wanted to write without interference or correction. Rattiner provided him the opportunity to do so, and Donohue accepted.

Normally, *Ugh* was published once each semester. Under Rattiner it appeared three times in the 1959–1960 school year, and in every issue there was material by Mike Donohue (though his byline was spelled "Donahue"). While other contributors sent up various campus customs and symbols, Donohue kept to his own world. He wasn't interested in razzing university officials, despite his distaste for the administration. And even when he took on a seemingly "satirical" assignment he wrote it on his terms, used his references, and gave the piece his personal stamp.

In the spring 1960 *Ugh*, Donohue penned a "President's Address" to the graduating senior class. "As you receive your diploma and turn to face the radioactive world of reality," he begins, "you might best remember and be guided by this little parable which I now relate." He then tells the story of an Eskimo medical student named Nangooknic whose goal in life was to be "the only Eskimo stomach expert" so that he could "aid his fellow man" and "make gobs of money" in the bargain. For months Nangooknic searched America for a stomach he could study.

Finally, "down to his last haddock," the poor Eskimo encountered a professor who just happened to own a stomach that he kept in a jar of formaldehyde. The professor agreed to exchange the stomach for the Eskimo's fish; but the jar was accidentally dropped, though "the stomach contained within was unharmed. However, Nangooknic refused to trade, left the [professor's] house and returned to Eskimoland, there to become a Renault dealer." The parable's moral? "Why trade a haddock for an upset stomach?"

Apart from the passing reference to radioactivity, there is nothing remotely "satirical" in this absurd little tale—unless one finds relevant bumbling professors or the odd Renault dealership. There are, however, early signs of what would become Donohue's tendency to mix unusual images with puns. In "The Green Fox," published in the fall 1959 *Ugh*, Donohue produces some truly awful plays on the word *fox*: A fox's fixation is a "foxation"; when Green Fox stands guard against an evil hunter, he is the "twentieth sentry fox," and so on. But what is striking about this piece is that it contains a root idea that Donohue would convert to formula on *Saturday Night Live*.

Green Fox was at odds with his color-specific cousins (Red Fox, Yellow Fox, et al.). Though they shared a common enemy, the ruthless Bad Jake, whose hobby it was to trap Easter rabbits and sell their pelts, Green Fox decided to turn against his kin. Once the other foxes were asleep and unguarded, Green Fox ran through the woods to Bad Jake's cabin to tell the hunter where his sleeping cousins could be found, but "Bad Jake, seeing Green Fox running toward him, took out his twenty gauge and shot him through the head. Green Fox lay, looking like a busted tube of chlorophyll toothpaste . . . The End."

Mr. Mike in utero.

Subverting fairy tales and children's stories provided Donohue with plenty of material; and although he broke no new ground, he was in serious training. *Ugh* was essential to his development as a humorist, and his experience with the magazine yielded far better results than did any of his classes—hardly surprising since he put everything he had into his private work. Yet despite his dismissal of this "jerkwater college," Rochester was open enough for Donohue to find the work of Beckett, Ionesco, and Jean Cocteau. Also, he became aware of surrealism and Dada. To this point Donohue had been an enthusiastic student of the classics. Well-grounded, he could now ignite his imagination and watch as twisted images shot off in all directions. The powder keg met the right spark.

Rattiner had steered *Ugh* away from the bland and toward the provocative, and he took pride in his accomplishment. But when Donohue submitted a poem titled "That That Is, Is" for the Winter 1960 issue,

Rattiner was conscious enough of the prevailing campus atmosphere to stick a disclaimer on the piece: "The opinions expressed in this article represent only those of the author and do not in any way resemble the opinion of the staff or the editors or anyone else who has seen this thing so far." Perhaps Rattiner intended this as a joke, as if to say "You think *we're* bad? Get a load of this!" But joke or no, Rattiner knew he couldn't run the poem unless he covered the magazine and himself.

A large human eye stares at the reader. The mood is one of detachment, forcefully expressed. Then

> *The taffata coloured marble sinks slowly into the bubbling pavement*
> *Picyune splatterings to incarnate a glowing purple rapture*
> *Futile all is*
> > *(If you melt a flower pot*
> > *Is it a melting pot?)*
> *Madness explodes in flaming blackboards and nauseous goldfish*
> *Steaming axle grease foams down upon the dacron city*
> *Futile all is*
>
> *Let the insipid alligators be*
> *Touch not the sand that lies in constant wait to rise again*
> *Look not for the good 5¢ martini*
>
> *Futile all is*
>
> *Armidillos*
> > *make crummy soup*
> *and even if they made good soup*
> *the whole idea sounds so ridiculous*
> *that no one would eat it*
> > *the same goes for Ant-Eater steak*
> *thus life is limited*
> > *by people who*
> > *don't really like good soup*
> *NOW*
> *THERE IS ONLY ONE VERMILLION STARFISH*
> > *IN THE WORLD*
> *THERE USED TO BE MANY*
> > *(alas)*
> *WHEN ANCIENT GREECE'S TEMPLES SHOWN*
> > *STILL*
> *ONE COULD GAZE UNTO THE SEA*
> *AND WATCH THEM*

CARTWHEELING GIDDILY O'ER THE WAVES
REVELING IN THE UNSOPHISTICATED JOY
    OF LIFE ITSELF
    (alas)
NOW THERE IS ONLY ONE VERMILLION STAR-
    FISH IN THE WORLD
    and today it died. . . . .

Pebbles are very nice for
    beaches and
    goldfish bowls and
    chicken grit
But They Are Not Absolutely Essential
To Life!
    because they can be replaced
    by imitation pebbles.

is your road of life under con-
struction?

At the poem's close is a photo of Donohue dressed as Hitler, tightly wound with fist in hand. The Führer as struggling poet? or simply vexed by degenerate art?

"That That Is, Is" is a touch overdone but striking nonetheless. (How often did Donohue visualize "flaming blackboards" while sitting bored in class?) As with his other *Ugh* material, "That" contains ideas that would infuse much of his mature work: No matter how exotic or special the species, extinction is inevitable; life is so cheap that imitations are equal to the genuine article. Futile all is, indeed.

It was around this time that Donohue discovered three new and lasting influences. First was Antonin Artaud, the insane French poet and playwright who founded the Theatre of Cruelty and whose creative intensity Donohue sought to match; Franz Kafka, the brilliant composer of bureaucratic

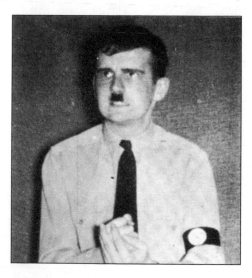

As Hitler, from *Ugh*

nightmares who suggested that people should read only the books that wound and stab them; and Terry Southern, whose novel *Flash and Filigree* leveled Mike Donohue. "I wanted to be a writer," he later said. "I was good at writing and I was good with words. I thought it was just an amusing hobby because there wasn't anyone like me around." But then he encountered *Flash* and thought, "Shit, this is writing also! I can do this!" The plot of *Flash*—a Beverly Hills dermatologist is pulled by one of his patients into a series of strange adventures—captivated Donohue; and the methodical way in which Southern built his story (start slow, pick up incredible speed, swerve into the ending) lay before Donohue as a luminous blueprint of comic invention. From that moment on he felt that Southern "gave me permission to be a writer."

In some ways Southern resembled his young admirer. He was the product of a small town (in Texas), spent much of his time from age eleven teaching himself to write. He was heavily influenced by Edgar Allan Poe and would, as exercise, rewrite some of Poe's stories as well as those by Nathaniel Hawthorne. Eventually he moved to original material. "I used to write a lot, then show it to my friends—one or two of them anyway—with the idea more or less of astonishing or confounding them with the contents of the pages. I knew they had never seen anything like this before . . . but finally I went too far, and alienated one of the readers—my best friend . . . and this slowed me down for a while—no daring. But finally I learned not to care too much, and would write wholly for an imaginary reader whose tastes were similar to my own. And this is, of course, the only way to work well."

When Donohue discovered his work, Southern's star was beginning to rise. In pieces for the *Paris Review* and *Harper's Bazaar*, and also in *Flash and Filigree*, Southern looked to "astonish" his readers. In Mike Donohue, Southern touched a profound nerve.

As he immersed himself in various new stimuli, Donohue kept one foot in the university's door. In 1959, the middle of his sophomore year, he was accepted as a "neophyte" by the Kappa Nu fraternity. Why Donohue chose to join a frat is not known; perhaps it was a way to mitigate his bad grades, to show that he could be a solid student. If that is true, the facade weathered quickly; within weeks he was thrown out for initiating a cocoa fight that stained the frat's newly painted walls. Also that year he ran for the office of social chairman. He typed up and distributed flyers announcing his candidacy:

Sophomores
I'm going to vote for Mike Donohue because:
(check one)
1) He promised to give me his Samoan fertility idol.

2) He'll do a bang-up job, really top-drawer.
3) I'm secretly married to him.
4) He plays a dandy game of "Monopoly."
5) . . . Why not?

*Actually, your reasons are not of importance. Whatever the motives,
please vote Mike Donohue as social chairman of the class of '61.*

Though he lacked the voter base necessary to win office, Donohue's talent as a writer proved alluring to his fellow students. In fact, some offered him money to anonymously author their assignments. This he did, at least a few times; and his mercenary impulse led him to see, up close, disparity in grading. The papers he ghosted received As and Bs, his own received Cs and Ds. Either his professors were conscious of the deception and wished to teach Donohue a lesson or they were as thick as he believed them to be and graded according to their natural prejudice. Regardless of their motive, he felt frustrated, angry, and above all betrayed.

He had thought about teaching, but that notion withered. As his junior year wore on he began to cut loose. He gave sarcastic answers to his professors in class. When invited to a costume party he arrived in full Hitler getup with the intention to shock. He stole a campus policeman's scooter and rode it through a nearby park until he was nabbed.

The Angel of death —

An example of Donohue's art, c. 1958–59

(So said his mother. Donohue himself said he'd stolen a police *car*, which conveys real felonious derring-do. What student outlaw worth the name would bother snatching a *scooter*?) He felt the odds were against him and decided to go on autodestruct, a pattern that would deepen as time went on.

As he pondered his future he continued to write. He played with humorous verse, attempted haiku. In one of his many unpublished poems from this period, "The Slowest Gun Alive," Donohue created the legend of a mediocre gunfighter obsessed with survival at any cost.

> *I'm the slowest gun alive, my boys, the slowest gun alive.*
> *Yet notches in my colt I have, one less than 35.*
> *Oh many men shot sure and fast, but one thing did they lack . . .*
> *A coward's heart like I had, and I shot them in the back.*
> *Yippeeiioooo, Yippeeiiaaaa, I shot them in the back.*
>
> *I remember one-eyed Jake, my boys, remember one-eyed Jake.*
> *He could shoot the pearly fangs off of a movin' rattlesnake.*
> *But I snuck me up behind him with my trusty twenty gauge,*
> *And now Jake's fertilizer, for the tumbleweed and sage.*
> *Yip . . . . . . Yip . . . . . . , Tumbleweed and sage.*
>
> *And then there's old Jack Daw, my boys, and then there's old Jack Daw.*
> *They say that he could almost beat his shadow to the draw.*
> *But he never knew who shot him in the middle of the spine,*
> *And I really doubt he'll find out, in a small box made of pine.*
> *Yip . . . Yip . . . . , small box made of pine.*
>
> *And so I shot them all, my boys, and so I shot them all.*
> *I'd always fire from behind and then I'd watch them fall.*
> *For it doesn't really matter if you're faster than the rest,*
> *The man that goes on living, must really be the best,*
> *Yip . . . Yip . . . . , Must really be the best.*

Television was choked with western programs and commercial tie-ins, and parodies of the gunfighter myth were common—from Ernie Kovacs to *Mad*. But Donohue laced seemingly "funny" pieces with ideas he believed to be significant: He attacked the cowardly and corrupt with an aggressive tone and upheld the concept of honor. His enthusiasm for college a memory, Donohue took refuge in what he considered valorous. His poem may mock *Gunsmoke*, but he felt he had been ambushed by those he once idealized. In the final stanza one can see Donohue holding a warm pistol, standing atop his academic prey.

In one of his last papers submitted for a grade, Donohue seemed to dare his professor to judge him harshly. Titled "A Renaissance Drama," it is a convoluted story of love, violence, madness, and, yes, betrayal within the Scottish monarchy. There is careful attention to detail—right down to the correct spelling of ancient Scottish names. And since old Scottish castles were in need of constant light, thousands of candles surround the action and serve as metaphors. King Rossguire laments, "Each night a thousand candles pass to nothing, a futile effort to sustain the day." Lady Rossguire observes, "A candle doth become the burning sun," to which the king later replies that one "gains no warmth from a burn." Two servants enter the scene as Renaissance vaudevillians:

ROSS: Would that I'd been born a candle maker. I might find wealth upon this house alone.
GUNN: Still remember, sire, that candle business tends to wax and wane. Better for a trade you slaughter hogs, for then the palm is always greased.

The servants return later in the story to provide mirth amid the shedding of blood (human, not porcine). Lady Rossguire goes mad, the king kills himself, then the lady recovers to tell the surviving royal relatives to "live and forget." The curtain drops on candlelit despair.

In his summation, Donohue refers to the "difficulties I encountered in writing this paper," primarily those of "fitting thought into the iambic pentameter form." He then states bluntly, "Of all the profits gained from the writing of this play, the over-shadowing benefit was an appreciation of the importance of rythm [*sic*]; something not received in two and one half years of English concentration." In a lengthy response, Donohue's professor says, "Yes, I agree, we do badly with *rhythm* [student's nose rubbed in the misspelling]—although part of what we've been studying is the *rhythm of action*." After citing difficulties encountered in following the dense plot, the professor concedes that Donohue's paper "is a very interesting experiment . . . You have a mind of fine ad hoc virtues. You say a number of valid and perceptive things . . . You need to respect your own gifts enough to learn to stand behind them and deliver yourself through them (how 'moral' can I get?)." Before he could answer, Donohue was rewarded with a rare B. But by this time he was already looking beyond academic redemption.

Turning away from university life to embrace its alternative, Donohue became what was known as a "beatnik." The word itself was by 1960 a commercial tag, thanks to the PR efforts of Allen Ginsberg (primarily on behalf of Jack Kerouac) and the mass media hunger for a marketable stereotype. The Beats did boast original talent—Ginsberg,

Kerouac, William S. Burroughs—whose disparate styles, though lumped under a single definition, sliced through the complacency of American literature. But it was the Beat lifestyle that interested the caption writers of newspapers and magazines, and they heeded the call of the bongo drum. Those interested in the *work* of specific authors or poets looked to a number of small literary journals, the most prominent of which was the *Evergreen Review*.

Evergreen grew out of Grove Press, which was responsible for publishing such verboten fare as D. H. Lawrence's *Lady Chatterley's Lover* and Henry Miller's *Tropic of Cancer* (both books were banned by the U.S. Postmaster-General for reasons of "obscenity," a ruling later overturned by the Supreme Court), as well as *Waiting for Godot* by Samuel Beckett, *Naked Lunch* by William Burroughs, and *Last Exit to Brooklyn* by Hubert Selby Jr. *Evergreen* first appeared in 1957 and came out quarterly. Its second issue, "San Francisco Scene," highlighted work by Lawrence Ferlinghetti, Kenneth Rexroth, Kerouac, and Ginsberg, whose seminal poem, *Howl*, was published in full. This lent the Bay Area bohemian luster and made San Francisco seem a refuge for those trapped in the philistine mass.

When Mike Donohue first read *Evergreen*, he saw his future flash before his eyes. "Oh god, it was like pornography, it was so hot!" he later said. "They had articles by Kerouac and [the poet] Gary Snyder. Very cool stuff about driving across the Golden Gate Bridge as the dawn is coming up with a six-pack on the seat, a Lucky in your mouth, Coltrane on the radio, and you're with a . . . Negro—and I thought, 'This is cool! I gotta be a part of this!' " *Evergreen* was to the new literature as manifestos were to the Surrealists. Donohue appreciated and was influenced by the European avant garde of the 1910s and 1920s, but that world had died and existed only in fossil form. The Beats, however (Generation B?), were alive and in motion, and this electrified him.

Donohue's early Beat days were spent in Rochester. He and Rattiner frequented a downtown coffee house where they played chess, drank cappuccino, and listened to folk musicians tell of the black man's misery. Donohue dressed in dark clothes and wore his thick black glasses. Later, on *Saturday Night Live*, he would parody his younger self in a sketch set in a 1950s coffeehouse. As an ultrahip patron, he would trade trite observations with Jane Curtin as bad poetry and music swirled around them. It would be an affectionate send-up tempered by hindsight. But his younger self, too, saw the absurdity in the coffee-and-guitar scene, and this he expressed in an unpublished poem:

> They wave a pennant, for Dyer-Bennet; They'll give their lives,
>   for Burl Ives; From intellectual to homosexual, they're
>   singing folksongs.

*They'll walk for Miles, to J. J. Niles; They'll stay all night,
    to hear Josh White; the latest fad, for mom and dad;
    is singing folksongs.*

Donohue appreciated nonconformity and dissidence but often stopped short of direct participation. When Rattiner joined a demonstration outside a local Woolworth's to protest lunch counter segregation, Donohue happened by and saw his friend picketing. Rattiner held a placard that read SEGREGATION IS WRONG. Donohue glanced at the statement, looked to Rattiner, and replied, "No, *prejudice* is wrong. What's wrong with segregation?"

Donohue's interest in dissident literature and obscure art led to other discoveries: "I'd been studying philosophy. I got up to Immanuel Kant and threw the book across the room. It had taken me four hours on a pleasant summer day to read and understand one page. I slid off into Oriental religions. Zen was the only thing I studied in college that did me any good. In terms of humor, it's the real mechanism." His connection to the creative elements of Zen came in handy when, at the end of 1959, he helped establish a new campus theater group, Experiment 60.

In the *Campus Times*, Rochester's official student newspaper, Donohue made public the group's agenda: "While the Stagers [Rochester's official theater company] handle their own type of drama admirably, they do not venture into the experimental field, and there is a definite need for a group which would present this type of drama." Donohue himself had acted in Stager productions: He appeared as the third slave in George Bernard Shaw's *Androcles and the Lion* in his freshman year. But Experiment 60 hoped to knock the cobwebs from Shaw's white beard. In the group's constitution it was decreed that the "organization" was to "inspire creative drama, to promote achievement in theatrical artistry, and to bestow the rich rewards of stage experience upon our members." Assisted by Rattiner and another student, Debbie Downs, Donohue found the ideal material for the group's first production, which was to be staged in a small room in the Student Union.

In accordance with his enthusiasm for Zen, Donohue chose three short Japanese Noh plays, which were portrayed as "delicate in nature and a combination between acting and dancing." In a flyer, Donohue described a few of the major roles to be cast, and one can see clearly what attracted him to the plays. "Yama: The King of Hell. A pompous overbearing tyrant. Princess: Sophisticated woman driven insane by her own cruelty. Gardener: Old man destroyed by the rages of young love." And then there is Rosei, whose character description paralleled the self-image of his American interpreter: "A deep sensitive young philosopher. A wanderer."

Experiment 60 was not confined to the Japanese muse; the group was committed to everything from "the extentionist drama to whatever pops up." This, of course, included two mainstays of the dramatic avant-garde, Samuel Beckett and Eugene Ionesco. (An evening of their work was produced by the group in April 1960.) For Donohue the experience confirmed that his choice to be an artist was the correct one. The thought of attending more classes, of earning a bachelor's degree in English, seemed pointless. He wanted to participate in and contribute to the new directions being charted in drama and literature. Like Sauquoit, Rochester became so much dead skin to be brushed away.

In the spring of 1960, Mike Donohue decided to quit college—or perhaps he was expelled. In later interviews he leaned toward the expulsion story, perhaps because it bolstered his reputation as student agitator-turned-cutting-edge-artist. Considering his adult work, this story makes the most sense (and for exciting copy). However, in a résumé from 1968 he debates whether he "flunked or was thrown out" of Rochester (his grades were indeed on the lower end of the curve); in a 1993 interview with a Canadian journalist he says that he "left school." But it is in a long, hurried letter to his father, typed in lower case and at times a mess grammatically, that Donohue fully explains his reasons for not finishing school.

> dear dad
> i don't know how to preface this letter. i'm quite good with the glib phrase and clever remark but this has no place here. the thing is i don't plan to return this fall to school. i'll try and explain why . . . college can not do me much good. it has done me alot of good both socially and intellectually. socially i can talk to people, meet them and handle them in some degree. before school i was pretty well out of it in this angle. i had a tremendous inferior attitude from high school. hell, i could hardly look a girl in the eye. maybe it was good for me in some manner as it forced me to amuse myself, to turn toward sherlock holmes, reading, writing, and pursuits of more introspective nature. anyway college helped me out of this . . .

Donohue contends that although college opened "new worlds of knowledge," there were definite limits that he could not or would not abide.

> i grew bored with classes, interested in other things. the things that professors had given me a glimpse of, the curiosity that they had seeked to evoke was successful, but it was too early, too soon. i neglected classes, put time into my interests and flunked . . . i forgot

that i was in school, that i even went there to study. the whole thing had no more meaning for me, it was as if it did not exist. i still thought i could pull through like always, with a smile and lots of study the night before . . . yet i still snuck thru with the minimum of effort, still wrapped my self up in my own pursuits.

Son then informs father what it is he wants to do.

 i want to make a stab at writing plays. this may sound pretty silly and very unrealistic, which perhaps it is. but someone, every-writer from shakespeare down to steinbeck has had to make this decision . . . now i don't know that i'm any shakespeare or steinbeck. i do know that i feel that i'm good, very good . . . i know i still have alot to learn, alot that i'm unsatisfied with . . . do not judge my works from that silly poem i sent home. this is like a hobby with me, writing poetry—mostly bad poetry, but i know this. however my plays are something else, i think i can do great things with them. i have tremendous faith in myself. i believe that i will do things that i will be proud of and satisfied with. perhaps i am wrong. but i want to prove that i am wrong. if i do not i will never have confidence in myself.

Donohue fears that Michael James will react angrily to his decision, but feels no alternative exists. He asks his father to "explain to mother for me. we have always disagreed on just about everything and she will think i am some kind of a nut . . . but tell her that i really do love her however much i disagree with her and that i do not want to hurt her by this." He closes the letter as "pete."

Donohue's letter was written well over a year after he left Rochester. In that time he traveled west, twice attempted academic redemption (and fell short, thus the explanation to his father), began to explore and test his talent as a writer. He embarked on this journey confident but uncertain. For him there was no other choice; the move had to be made.

Actually, I am just as proud as hell that I do not have the old sheepskin or anything to fall back to. If I fall I am going right into the gutter.

The British critic Kenneth Tynan visited San Francisco in 1960 and discovered "a new America" in mid-creation. "Eccentricity is cradled here; more extremes of thought and feeling are cherished than anywhere else in the country." There was nothing strange in this. After all, as Tynan noted, the city was at one time or another home to such writers as Mark Twain, Bret Harte, Ambrose Bierce, Sinclair Lewis, and Robert

Louis Stevenson. They, along with less-famous talents, provided balance to the provincial America of their day. By 1960, the provincial was eveloped by the atomic. Television evolved and expanded, advertising slickened, pop culture erupted, space travel commenced. If San Francisco was fostering "a new America," it would be hard-pressed to touch, much less balance, the larger nation.

Mike Donohue arrived in San Francisco the same year as Tynan's visit. Unlike the future author of *Oh! Calcutta*, Donohue viewed the Bay Area with a less-clinical eye. If indeed the city was awash in alternative lifestyles and ways of making art, he was intent to join that current. Donohue was tinkering with his own creation: himself. What began in his bedroom in Sauquoit had grown to inexorable proportions. By the time he left Rochester he either had to shape this mass of ideas and influences or kill the thing outright and return to chasing grades. His move to San Francisco revealed his need to engage what was consuming him; but lingering doubts—and where his parents were concerned, guilt—kept him from rejecting academia completely.

It is not known whether Michael James and Barbara were angry with their son's decision to quit school. As shown in his letter to his father, Donohue expected a negative reaction and did what he could to soften the blow. But the fact that he had been indulged by his parents since the time of his sickness suggests that their reaction would be one of disappointment, not anger. Donohue's parents were quite conscious of their son's intelligence and talent. They didn't fully comprehend some of his college pieces and found strange his artistic temperament. But they recognized his intensity and commitment to his work. Even if they disapproved of his actions there is no evidence that they failed to assist him when he was in need. In fact, it was they who financed his move to San Francisco in the fall of 1960.

After a brief stay at a residence on Waller Street, Donohue settled into the Conard House at the beginning of October. Located in the city's Pacific Heights neighborhood, the Conard House was a Victorian-era mansion that had been converted into a home for "mentally ill" youth: "Fourteen of the residents are post-hospitalized psychiatric patients, six are mentally retarded young people who are employable or trainable," read a pamphlet for the house. Rooms were rented to "non-patients" as well; Donohue took advantage of an opening and became the roommate of a young man visiting from London.

Over the next few months Donohue took courses at San Francisco State University and the University of California at Berkeley. His antipathy toward the academy was tempered by the realization that he could use additional formal training, specifically in creative writing and dramatic technique. Also, he couldn't ignore that his parents were footing the bill and that they wanted him to complete school. Though he came to the Bay Area with bohemian intentions, he had to consider the Republicans who held the purse strings.

In a letter to his mother, Donohue plays up the positive aspects of his West Coast move. He describes Conard House as a cozy hostel, a magnet for globe-trotting youth: "It [is] a huge Victorian place, filled with fireplaces and winding staircases. Out back it has a Japanese garden with a fishpond, wicker chairs, and cypress trees. Very nice place to write and no one disturbs you." Of course, Donohue omits mention of mentally ill boarders or anything to do with psychiatry; Barbara the German would not approve (remember her disdain of the migrant workers). She is given a static-free tour of the house and is assured that her investment is a wise one. "The people living here are really all right and make for a good group," her son says convincingly, then adds: "Have received all the money you sent me so feel free to send as much as you like."

Donohue stresses to Barbara the importance of his writing—*the* reason for his move, after all. He speaks of a play that he struggles to finish so it may be read to the rest of his playwriting class. For creative writing he was to submit two haiku; out of eighty submissions, his were judged to be the best.

> *The moon is gold now;*
> *In the ripening buckwheat,*
> *Fireflies, asleep.*

> *His horse runs so fast*
> *That he does not even see*
> *The fallen pinecones.*

To show Mother that after schoolwork there is time for personal creation, he includes a poem titled "House of the Disenchanted" (*Conard House?*) and is convinced of her reaction in advance: "You won't like it but I send it anyway."

> *Hear within a family grieve,*
> *Reason they to mourn,*
> *O're the sobs a shriller cry—*
> *Baby has been born!*

> *Pity that he'll hear the bird,*
> *Seizing bow and arrow,*
> *Send a shaft into its breast—*
> *Down falls pretty sparrow!*

When the baby has grown old,
And come home to die,
Family gives a partytime—
Bon Voyage! Goodbye!

As he did in his letter to his father (and would do in all family correspondence), Mike signed off as "pete." His parents knew he hated the nickname; yet there was a certain tenderness in his use of it, a suggestion that despite rapid change he would always be the smart, difficult son whom they adored and held in awe. "Pete" was the piece he gave them in the midst of his private makeover. "Donohue" was next to go.

To the serious writer, or to the writer who takes himself seriously, everything flows from the byline. Perspective can change, style can be polished or abandoned; marquee value enhanced, market value diminished. But the name remains at the center of all effort. "Mike" was hamfisted, better suited to a maker of pulp; "Michael" projected intelligence and distinction. "Donohue" was too common, too American to work; "O'Donoghue" looked and felt as literary as Ireland itself. His greatgrandfather might have tossed the O' overboard as he neared the shoreline of the States, but Michael O'Donoghue found it intact and serviceable a continent away.

Apollinaire's head explodes starlike into fragments.
Men scamble for pieces to carry in their pockets.
A belief exists in many countries that a poet's head
Brings good luck.
Even pieces of a poet's head bring good luck.

O'Donoghue's experience with Experiment 60 in Rochester and his exposure to the Theatres of Absurdity and Cruelty led him to believe that playwriting was perhaps his best artistic option. Here was a form that demanded dialogue, and O'Donoghue discovered that he possessed a knack for creating . . . if not *natural* discussions, then speeches and exchanges subordinate to ideas. The influences had yet to settle. Meantime, he revised his various plays in the quiet areas of Conard House, usually at night—if possible, in front of a fire. As he searched for the right word, the transitional phrase, he realized startling images that, were he to reveal them in conversation, might betray him as another mentally "challenged" resident. Art, on the other hand, provided his thoughts refuge—for the moment, at least.

The playwright emerges, San Francisco, 1960

The one advantage to his living in Conard House (other than the affordable rent) was the opportunity to be somone else. At Rochester, O'Donoghue had had moderate success with this tactic, but the university's climate allowed for little growth. Among the recovering mentally ill and those passing through to other cities, however, there was less pressure to conform to a central ideal: You were who you said you were. Also, this was San Francisco, not upstate New York; one wasn't compelled to perpetually rebel in order to generate breathing space.

O'Donoghue attended his classes and, when back at Conard, read, wrote, ruminated. He showed his plays to other boarders and at times took part in group activities, particularly when it came to making meals. But there was one person who made an immediate impression: a young Puerto Rican woman, Gabrielle Benat. Gabrielle, or Gaby, was around five feet eight inches tall, with short black hair. Michael told Barbara that Benat's mother was the landlady of Conard House, but no such position existed. Perhaps Benat's mother was connected to Conard's administration; then again, perhaps not. What is certain is that Michael refused to tell Barbara the specific purpose of Conard House, and whether Benat was there as a supportive daughter or simply as a boarder is unclear. Yet she stood out, and O'Donoghue was smitten.

Unlike the button-nose debs of Rochester, Gaby Benat was dark, attractive, and displayed some edge. Politically she was radical, but politics and commitment to causes mattered little to O'Donoghue. He grasped the passion without entering the fray. Yet Benat engaged him and exposed his romantic urge; for her he peeled back layers of intensity and offered the softness within. This wrinkle in his persona would remain. Regardless of how aloof or self-contained he was, love or the prospect of love served as a skeleton key. Benat was to be his first real romance; she opened the lock when it was bright silver and new.

She referred to O'Donoghue as "m." (which he would use as an

alternate byline) and "cherie." It's doubtful that she was aware of his
childhood sickness and relatively unhappy adolescence, as he usually kept
this to himself; but then, the soft Michael might have made these facts
known. In any case, Benat was enamored of the current model. She
found him to be intelligent, talented, and charming. In turn, O'Donoghue lavished Benat with his complete devotion, emotionally and physically. To O'Donoghue the art of getting laid had till then been largely
a conceptual one. Women, at least those who stirred his desire, rarely
gave him the time of day, if anything at all. With Benat there was much-
needed fusion of mind *and* body. As in his writing O'Donoghue sought
through experimentation the essence of carnal relations—or, How many
ways could one get off?

*If the grass is always greener on the other side of the fence, what color is
the fence?*

O'Donoghue's reading habits took a mystical turn. He consumed the
works of Aleister Crowley, and for a time carried with him Crowley's
Magick in Theory and Practice. He was also absorbed by the legend of
Atlantis, particularly as interpreted by the nineteenth-century Russian
occultist Madame Helena Petrovna Blavatsky. In her book, *The Secret
Doctrine*, Madame maintained that she received her information from the
Brotherhood of the Mahatmas, ethereal beings who lived in Tibet and
communicated through astral visitation. In addition to Atlantis—destroyed by black magic—Madame was obsessed with the other lost continent, known as Lemuria. The Lemurians were described as large, apelike
creatures, some of whom had four arms, an eye in the back of the head,
and advanced telepathic capabilities. According to Blavatsky and other
occultists, modern civilization can be traced to the twin ancient lands,
modern humans to the inhabitants. Such tales fired O'Donoghue's imagination; his interest in the occult revealed a measure of superstition that
would later extend to psychic phenomena and the symbolic power of
dreams.

It's a safe bet that O'Donoghue's Republican parents would have
disapproved of his flirtation with the occult, Barbara especially. Yet his
dabbling in matters Black and Mysterious was a part of his overall fascination with religion: The cathedral spire was equal to the pentagram. Thus
he read and listened; he came to appreciate Anglican ritual, enjoyed the
deep timbre of Gregorian chants as well as the music of choirs.

Nuns intrigued him. He saw them in a variety of lights, from domi-
natrix to lesbian to nightclub stripper. He also envisioned the ultimate
violation: the rape of a nun, an assault on flesh and faith. In a letter to
O'Donoghue, Benat suggests that he realize this fantasy in a staged set-

ting: "I do think you should get it out of your system, perhaps have some willing chick dress up as one and have her kneel in a church, the most grand one you can find . . . then sneak up, be high as hell of course so you won't keep thinking she's just faking it, and then whomp on her . . ." Apparently, Benat never offered herself in an enticing habit.

After several months in San Francisco, O'Donoghue grew restless artistically and poorer financially. He survived on money from home but knew that the pipeline wouldn't, shouldn't, remain active; he fine-tuned his plays and poems but had no place to publish them. At the beginning of 1961, while in the Conard House office, O'Donoghue met John Bryan, who was then a general assignment reporter and jazz editor for the *San Francisco Examiner*. Bryan was dating a woman involved in Conard's administration and, like Dan Rattiner before him, was intrigued by O'Donoghue at first sight. The young writer struck Bryan as sardonic, skinny, and morose—"quite Gallic" in appearance, resembling "a Faustian scholar." Bryan was aware of Conard's mentally ill clientele, so he naturally assumed that O'Donoghue was there to banish his demons.

Like O'Donoghue, John Bryan moved to the Bay Area in 1960. Originally from Cleveland, Bryan had worked in Houston, Texas, as a mainstream newspaper reporter. In the spring of 1959 he assembled what was to be Houston's first alternative publication, *Gusher*. This brought him in touch with a variety of artists and writers, including the poet Charles Bukowski, who sent Bryan some forty to fifty manuscripts for his use. Though *Gusher* lasted only one issue, it proved that even in culturally narrow cities such as Houston creative options could exist. Also, *Gusher* was an antisegregation, interracial paper, an achievement not only unique for late-1950s Houston but potentially dangerous for Bryan as well.

Bryan followed Phil Ray and Dan Rattiner as someone with whom O'Donoghue could share ideas and enthusiasms. The two discussed books, art; Lenny Bruce's importance was, of course, noted and agreed upon. Bryan thought O'Donoghue to be a "brilliant and loquacious" person who "knew that he was witty" in an obscure sort of way. O'Donoghue also was given to long periods of silence, his stare the sole sign that his mind was engaged.

Bryan began to socialize with O'Donoghue and Benat. The trio frequented the Coffee Gallery, a venue that allowed patrons to express themselves if the urge proved too strong. Another hangout was Vesuvio's Bar, once the watering hole of Jack Kerouac. O'Donoghue was a social drinker who sipped red wine. Bryan preferred heavier spirits in larger doses. (He later thought that his drinking habits disgusted O'Donoghue, which, considering the latter's contempt for drunkenness, was probably true.) While he enjoyed O'Donoghue's company, Bryan found his friend to be "a bit of a snob." This was and would always be the measure of Barbara's influence, something her son would never shake. It was a trait that contrasted with the Beat sensibility—which had initially lured him to the West Coast.

O'Donoghue's haughtiness did not extend to his wardrobe. He dressed in work shirts and jeans, allowed his hair to grow to a suitable bohemian length. The black-framed glasses were replaced by wire rims. He took up smoking, a habit his parents fancied but one he had resisted until then. Though he worked to remain detached from the common world, O'Donoghue did engage in public spectacle. A favorite routine involved a forty-five-foot-high plastic lumberjack—a Paul Bunyon like-ness—that stood in front of a local store. O'Donoghue would dance at the lumberjack's feet and sing of the French-Canadian woodsman who gave his own sister syphilis, a routine he performed several times with occasional alteration of lyrics.

Singing and dancing did nothing to alleviate O'Donoghue's eco-nomic problem: He was broke. He also had tired of asking his parents for money. "when one does not work for what he eats," he said in the letter to his father, "he does not appreciate it, he does not appreciate the bed in which he sleeps or the clothes he wears. he has no stake in them, he cannot recognize the value . . . being supported robs me of your respect, of my pride and of my virility itself. it saps the drive for life. i feel guilty and you feel you're supporting a worthless parasite."

In the spring of 1961, thanks to Bryan, O'Donoghue got a job as a copy boy/reporter trainee for the *Examiner*. He cut his hair, donned a cheap green suit, and entered the press world of Hearst. O'Donoghue did not find the bright lights and bustle of the paper's city room terribly inspiring. But as far as day jobs were concerned, the *Examiner* position beat any number of menial or service-oriented tasks. At least O'Dono-ghue was able to work with, if not *writers*, then people familiar with current events who typed. Things went smoothly for a couple of months; O'Donoghue adjusted to the bustle. During his lunch hours he joined Bryan on trips to a bookstore nearby called, appropriately, Holmes. They browsed and bought the occasional volume. But soon O'Donoghue pulled back and slacked off. He arrived late to the office several days in succession and was fired. Bryan helped him win back his job. Then, not long into his second chance, O'Donoghue became involved in an alterca-tion: "I got into a fight in the city room. I grabbed a man's tie and pulled him across a desk. I was gonna hit him with a lead type bar, which can really leave some kinda *Tom and Jerry*–type indentation in the skull, but someone stopped me."

No one remembers what instigated the fight. O'Donoghue's ongoing frustration with his life combined with his volatile temper most certainly contributed to the blowup. A final pink slip was issued and all appeals were denied.

In the face of unemployment, O'Donoghue and Benat strengthened their ties. They lived together at Conard House but desired privacy. Low on funds, they managed to afford an apartment located on the second floor of a house at the intersection of Hayes and Laguna Streets. Their initial happiness soon gave way to fear. Bryan found their place to be "a strange old flat" that the couple felt was "definitely haunted." During a visit Bryan noticed that the pair had moved their bed from bedroom to living room. The reason, they said, was that each suffered the identical nightmare in which a woman was murdered by her husband. The image of butchery was so graphic and intense that both O'Donoghue and Benat woke up screaming. Intrigued, Bryan asked to sleep in the bedroom for a night, and he, too, experienced the murder and awoke with a scream. Later, Bryan checked into the history of the house and discovered that in 1910 a woman was indeed slain by her husband in the room that all now avoided.

Conard House had been too confining. The new place fomented blood-splattered dreams (which no doubt deepened O'Donoghue's interest in the mystical). O'Donoghue and Benat looked for new and hopefully sedate living quarters; Bryan again provided aid. He resided in a large two-story Victorian house located in Potrero Hill, near the Mission District. It was owned by a married couple who subscribed to Maoism. (The place was painted red and had been dubbed "The House of Treason" by one of Bryan's co-workers at the *Examiner*.) The rooms had been turned into rental units, and Bryan's room was the smallest in the house. Still, he invited O'Donoghue and Benat to move in with him. The arrangement was to be temporary and part of a project then being considered.

In the midst of their many discussions, Bryan and O'Donoghue were stuck on the idea of starting their own literary magazine. Both had liked *Big Table*, a dissident publication at the University of Chicago created for the expressed purpose of printing sections of William Burroughs's *Naked Lunch*. (The official university journal, *Chicago Review*, published excerpts of *Lunch* in the spring and autumn 1958 issues. This led to cries of "filth" from local columnists and puritans on campus, which in turn led to the suppression of the *Review*'s spring 1959 issue, which excerpted more of Burroughs's book.) And, of course, they appreciated *Evergreen Review*. Each had ideas he wanted to pursue, and as manifestos and journals filled the San Francisco scene, they felt it was the perfect time to add their voices to the mix. Living together lent immediacy to their collaboration.

Whatever the literary intentions of their living arrangement, Bryan's room was simply too small to accommodate three people. Naturally, some embarrassing, if not compromising, situations arose. There was the matter of sex: O'Donoghue and Benat engaged in rather vocal lovemaking, which Bryan could not avoid hearing. Oftentimes Bryan would find their mattress and the floor around it covered in olive oil. He once joked to O'Donoghue that if he or Benat were ever short of oil for salad dressing they could always wring out their mattress. O'Donoghue stared at him unsmiling. He found Bryan's remark less than amusing and made his feelings known. Moments like this one led Bryan to observe that O'Donoghue "had a blind spot to his own absurdity," even though he was adept at detecting absurdity in others.

Throughout the late spring of 1961, Bryan and O'Donoghue pushed forward with their project. Thanks to his experience with *Gusher* in Houston, Bryan had manuscripts from and connections to a number of writers, Charles Bukowski included. As Bryan pursued those he thought perfect for the new magazine, now called *renaissance*, O'Donoghue went to bars and coffeehouses and tacked to the walls cards that called for contributors:

> *depression and war*
> *sapped the vitality*
> *of the american*
> *"little"*
> *magazine*
>
> *a post war pall*
> *of conformity*
> *obscured its slow*
> *rebirth*
> *and a wave*
> *of nihilistic*
> *but necessary*
> *rebellion*
> *distorted its aims*
> *RENAISSANCE*
> *now affirms*
> *that maturity*
> *must backstop genius*
>
> *criteria:*
> >   *is it good?*
> >   *is it vital?*

Many who read the "prospectus" thought so and sent examples of their work. O'Donoghue, said Bryan, "brought in some interesting talent": poet David Meltzer; artist Mel Fowler, a specialist in woodcuts; another artist, Clara Lopez, who, according to Bryan, ate human flesh on occasion (holidays? weekends?). The project quickly took shape, and now Bryan and O'Donoghue needed a place to typeset the magazine. After several dead ends, Bryan approached James A. Pike, bishop of the Episcopal church in San Francisco. Bryan first met Bishop Pike when he covered the controversial religious figure for the *Examiner*. The bishop was renowned for his opposition to the Episcopal hierarchy (which eventually brought him up on heresy charges in 1966), his radical politics, and his interest in the psychic world. (Pike would later disappear in the Israeli desert; his body was never found.)

The bishop liked Bryan; he gave the young editor the keys to his office in the Episcopal Diocese, located on Nob Hill. There Bryan discovered two IBM Executive electric typewriters, which at the time were top of the line. This was a bit of a boon; Bryan had expected *renaissance* to have the pica look associated with manual typewriters. By using the IBM Executives, he could make the magazine appear a tad slicker than the standard bohemian sheet. As O'Donoghue helped sort the manuscripts, Bryan typed out the first issue in a matter of days. They worked alone, and although they liked and respected Bishop Pike (O'Donoghue once knelt before Pike and kissed his ring, which made the bishop laugh), they feared he would read and disapprove of the material. This never happened; and given the bishop's stand on social issues, their fear of censure was probably misplaced.

With *renaissance* set in type, Bryan approached several printers. But unlike the amoral Xerox hustlers of today, print shop workers in 1961 had high standards and strong beliefs. When they came across the word *fuck*, which appeared once in the first issue, they balked and returned the pages to Bryan. Determined to persevere, Bryan asked a friend who worked in a print shop if he could make copies after hours under cover of the dark of night. Being a communist (thus godless and unprincipled), the guy agreed to help. Bryan and O'Donoghue solicited additional labor by turning the work into collating parties. Inspired by a sense of mission and many glasses of white wine (red, if spilled, would stain a page), the friends of *renaissance* delivered a first printing of one thousand copies.

By the time the July issue of *renaissance* was completed and printed, the novelty of small literary magazines had passed, especially in the Bay Area. Poet and bookstore owner Lawrence Ferlinghetti certainly thought so: his venue, City Lights, was more tourist site than source of outlaw literature. When told about *renaissance*, Ferlinghetti opined that the last thing San Francisco needed was yet *another* magazine. But he saw merit in its pages and displayed several copies in the window of his store. Priced at seventy-five cents, *renaissance* sold nearly three hundred issues; the remaining copies were later given away.

renaissance was O'Donoghue's first exposure as a "professional" writer—professional in that the magazine was commercially available; he wasn't about to earn a living wage through his work. Still, just a year out of Rochester, an example of his writing could be found among the work of the contemporary talents he admired—Ginsberg, Kerouac, Burroughs, and Gary Snyder, as well as Beckett, Artaud, and Cocteau. *renaissance* lacked the name recognition of *Evergreen Review*, but it did resemble the journal in spirit and tone: heavy on poetry and art, self-conscious in its rejection of dominant literary values. Those who read the first issue could sample the mood on the opening page:

the poets rebelled and wrote it with a small "g". but no one heard. and so the poets again rebelled and wrote it with no "g" at all. in the beginning od created the heavens and the earth. now the people heard. and they wrote it with a large "O".

john bryan
michael o'donoghue

This is akin to the observation that *god* spelled backward is *dog*, but it's still a nice slap to the superstitious mind. There was plenty of phonetic sacrilege being practiced at the time, and Bryan and O'Donoghue (whom despite the dual byline, Bryan credits with sole authorship) were not above applying blue pencil to the Bible.

A few pages later the mood darkens. An ink sketch by Michael Fender shows a malformed teenage boy sitting on a sofa. His right arm stops just above the elbow, the result, we soon learn, of amputation; the right half of his face is scarred to distortion. Above him is the title "to dwell in zo'ar," O'Donoghue's dramatic ode to isolation, cruelty, coercion, and despair.

"zo'ar" is set in the cellar of an old house. Trunks, boxes, and bundles of paper litter the stage. Darkness prevails, "save for a dull and feeble backlight permitted by the [cellar] windows." The colors that dominate both costume and set are black, gray, and brown. The unnamed boy sits alone in silence; footsteps are heard on the stairs leading to the cellar. The door is opened and a man appears. He is "slightly obese" and dressed in a black suit; his hair is gray and he wears steel-rimmed glasses. "His features are broad and very ugly." He enters, turns on the cellar light, addresses the boy.

MAN: Quiet again, I see . . . Eyes still red. Don't cover them.
Or can't you bear the shame, the betrayal of your precious
masculinity. It's so feminine to cry. . . . Isn't it? Won't talk?
Can't talk. Hoarse from all that screaming. Pity. One can't
carry on as you did and not expect to strain one's voice. . . .

The immediate impression is one of abuse: What has this sick, fat
bastard done to the frightened, disfigured teen? The boy begs to be
released, but the man, though on the opposite end of the cellar, insists
upon toying with his prey.

BOY: What do you want?
MAN: To hurt you. Rather fascinates you, doesn't it? How I can
hurt you and still be this far away.
BOY: If you touch me—
MAN: I want . . . I want to strip you of your childhood . . . to
castrate your youth. I want . . . to impregnate the anxieties
of adolescence . . . and watch the virgin blood . . . clot into
fear . . .

The boy chastises the man, now revealed as his botany teacher, for
attempting to "make love" to him. The man scoffs at the boy's "naiveté," admits he attempted to seduce him, insists it was a minor gesture.

MAN: And then, after I, who have always gone out of my way to
help you, after I asked you to become better friends and
merely stroked your hair or something like that, then you
launch into this hideous tantrum, yell all sorts of beastly things
and race all about the house. . . . I think you frightened my
poor Mynah bird partly to death. He'll probably keep
squawking all week: "Please get your hands off me, please sir.
Don't touch me. Don't touch me you dirty old man." Poor
bird. Oh . . . I don't know what we're going to do with you.
Dirty old man indeed . . . indeed . . . Did you enjoy my
phrase about childhood, castrating youth etc. Objectively. I
mean not directed at you but for their own sake, just as
phrases.
BOY: Yes sir . . . I suppose I did.
MAN: You really did?
BOY: Yes sir. I didn't quite understand them.
MAN: But you liked them.
BOY: Yes.

The boy has ceased to be a victim and appears, in a curious way, intrigued by the man and his motives. While the man fluctuates between flattery and abuse (he makes light of the fire that damaged his student), the boy gains strength; he remains a bit frightened but uses fear to his advantage. In the middle of another tirade the boy begins to laugh.

MAN: Stop. Stop it this instant. You can't laugh . . . You're not . . . supposed to laugh.
BOY: Why?
MAN: Because you're not laughing at the right things.
BOY: The right things . . . If I'm everything you say, stupid and ugly, no one likes me, if I'm all this, what else have I to do but laugh.
MAN: One doesn't laugh at himself . . . One laughs at what made him this way.
BOY: I know why.
MAN: Indeed.
BOY: Why you can't laugh. You're ugly inside.
MAN: A grotesque liver perhaps.
BOY: You called me ugly but you're uglier than I am. Old and uglier. I'm only on the outside but you're ugly all over. You're old and it's all inside you and you can't get it out. You can't get it out ever.
MAN: And you think you'll be any different at my age?
BOY: I won't be like you.

The odd flirtation continues. They speak of the lies of poetry, the nastiness of sex, the corruption of beauty. The boy is a romantic, the man a realist—or, to be more precise, a broken romantic. Each sees in the other features that he detests but cannot avoid. After more chat the boy is released so as not to alarm his parents.

Like some of O'Donoghue's earlier efforts ("That That Is, Is," for instance), "to dwell in zo'ar" strains for effect yet delivers a few arresting images. The characters alone catch the eye, and once their "relationship" is established the dialogue becomes secondary. What led them to this place? Is this part of an ongoing game or a fumbled attempt at seduction? (Does the man go on to found NAMBLA?) O'Donoghue's contempt for teachers shines through as he loads the man down with nonsense. The man is a bore with buggery on his mind. And what does the boy, abbreviated, disfigured, yearning for love, represent? Best leave that to the specialist in tweed.

O'Donoghue's play demonstrated his growth as a writer. He understood despair and learned to weave it into his work. His sense of humor tapped his darker impulses, so much so that at times a joke was missed or an aside obscured by surrounding shadows. This would need adjusting. As O'Donoghue developed stranger, better material, Marsh Maslin, a *San Francisco Call-Bulletin* columnist, who reviewed *renaissance*, said that "zo'ar" was "a sad tough play that might even be produced someday. It has power." Naturally, the blurb pleased O'Donoghue; his work was taken seriously, singled out from the work of over a dozen other contributors (Maslin found "appealing" Bryan's essay on blues guitarist Lightin' Hopkins). His future as a Bay Area writer/editor seemed promising, but the sparkle would soon fall to ash.

The living situation at Bryan's apartment became tense. What was to be a short-term arrangement dragged on for months. Had Bryan lived with O'Donoghue alone there might have been room to negotiate. After all, the two produced a magazine that impressed Lawrence Ferlinghetti while it grabbed some favorable notices. A second issue and the probability of further success might have diverted their minds from their cramped quarters. But Benat lived there, too, and this—as any single person who's shared space with a couple can attest—placed additional stress on Bryan, especially since he felt that he and Benat were rivals for O'Donoghue's attention. Bryan was forced to listen to her and O'Donoghue's theatrical fucking; he had to deal with O'Donoghue as a friend *and* as a collaborator *and* as a roommate, which, given O'Donoghue's moods, proved burdensome. For their part, O'Donoghue and Benat grew tired of the arrangement. No one was happy. So Bryan informed his friends that it was time for them to leave.

This did not sit well with O'Donoghue. Although he recognized the reality of the situation, he nevertheless felt betrayed by Bryan. His pride, which equaled in intensity his art, had been tarnished: Asked to *leave*? Who the fuck asks *him* to *leave*? As O'Donoghue and Benat sought temporary accommodations, O'Donoghue, angry and put out, needed to make a decision. He could remain in San Francisco, settle down with Benat, and pursue a writing career, or he could return to Rochester, regroup, and try to enter the writing game from a different angle.

The San Francisco option had little to recommend it. Once he broke with Bryan, O'Donoghue lacked a serious connection to anyone who knew of his work and could assist him in getting published. *renaissance* was his ticket, and this he tore in half. (He and Bryan had discussed the possibility of publishing O'Donoghue's poetry in the second issue, but nothing came of it.) Also, months earlier, O'Donoghue had ceased attending his classes, and since he'd asked his parents to stop sending him money there was no realistic chance of his returning to school. All San Francisco held for him was his relationship with Benat and the very real prospect of a dull day job to help pay the rent.

In his letter to his father, written just before *renaissance* went to press, O'Donoghue spoke favorably of his life in San Francisco and of his unwillingness to return home and to the university:

> it would be very easy for me to go back to rochester. i would have all my old friends and slip into the old groove again . . . i could give my plays in the local theater group—the one i started 2 years ago [Experiment 60] and i would have all sorts of little things to tell about san francisco . . . i could play my guitar [which he had recently taken up] at the fraternity and be assured of feminine company . . . please do not think that i am being egotistical. i know very well the school, what my position was in the school and how they would react to me now. but this would be the lazy way out.

As 1961 drew to a close, O'Donoghue was forced to dine on these words. Seeing no immediate future for himself in San Francisco, he asked his mother to finance his trip back east. Barbara was happy to do so; she would have her son home where he belonged. But O'Donoghue had seen too much during his time on the West Coast to be hemmed in at home. His work had been published in the literary capital of the country and had been well received; he was completing and revising a variety of new plays. Yes, he had to return to upstate New York, but this, he felt, would be a temporary retreat.

three

Today is the first day of the rest of your life . . . and already you've fucked it up.

f it's true that failure spurs genius—or at least slaps it awake—then the twenty-one-year-old Michael O'Donoghue was in a prime position to realize his goals. After some sixteen months in San Francisco, where he flirted with the beatnik life, chose not to finish school or hold a steady job, engaged in his first adult relationship, published a play no respectable publication would touch, and severed all ties to the one person who could help him professionally, O'Donoghue found himself back in his bedroom in Sauquoit. Despite evidence of growth, his persona had failed to take root near the bay. He hoped that the warmth of familiar ground would push him to full maturation.

First, O'Donoghue had to see if Benat could make the transition with him. Since he refused to stay with her in San Francisco, perhaps she might adapt to small-town life. With Barbara's help, O'Donoghue paid for Benat's plane ride east. It is not known whether she blanched at the sight of farms and dirt roads, or if O'Donoghue couldn't appreciate her in a rural setting (perhaps each had lost interest in the other during this time), but soon after she stepped off the plane, O'Donoghue put Benat on a bus and sent to her back to the land of poetry, jazz, and overpriced coffee.

Next, O'Donoghue enrolled in the University of Rochester, this time to pursue a teaching degree in English. Why he returned to school—especially the school he despised and had once fled—is a mystery. The one explanation that fits the existing picture is that O'Donoghue felt he owed it to his parents to have something to "fall back on." After all, they had financed his first two forays into college, as well as his move west and his retreat to Sauquoit; they again put up the cash for a third stab at a degree. It is clear that academia held little interest for him, but he again hit the books to placate Michael James and Barbara.

Michael James had an apartment in a Rochester suburb called Medina, and here he stayed when conducting business in the area. O'Donoghue moved in with his father, enrolled in the university, and soon found himself strolling the campus he'd thought was in his past. In a sense this was still true: His class, the class of 1961—including Dan Rattiner, who was now in graduate school at Harvard—had graduated the previous spring. Although he wasn't much older than the current senior crop he was, like a soldier or a sailor on the G.I. Bill, years beyond them in life experience. And most important, he was no longer Mike Donohue, the headstrong student who had sought to rattle and razz his professors; he was the elegant *m.*—poet, playwright, artiste. The former had crammed bits of experimental prose into the academic papers he'd bothered to finish on time. The latter knew the difference between Art and the Academy, and would in his assignments keep these conflicting worlds separate.

Indeed, in his papers from this period, one is struck by the serious, dry finesse employed by O'Donoghue. Gone are the crowbar dents and scratches that marked his earlier assignments. The conflicting tones are absent because O'Donoghue the writer was no longer conflicted. He had discovered his voice—patchy and wavering though it could still be—and did not need to raise it in improper surroundings. Besides, all the fury and intensity was being poured into the plays that he continued to polish in his lone hours. When asked to write an academic paper, that is what he delivered. Once he was rid of the need to impress and show off, O'Donoghue proved that he was a capable analyst and critic of literature, theater, and art.

He liked to highlight the theme of a subject that he himself understood and shared. In his paper on the German artist Kaethe Kollwitz, O'Donoghue notes that despite her lack of innovation Kollwitz "remained steadfast to a cold, uncompromising image . . . it is an image indicative of no ideology, no time, no place; an unvarnished vision of the lost, the defeated. . . . She never relented this image." O'Donoghue discusses some of her "death" works—"Mother with a Dead Child," "Death Reaches for a Child," "Death as a Friend," "Death with a Girl in Lap"—with real appreciation; he praises Kollwitz for capturing in her art stark tragedy, and adds that she freed her dramatic agony through a superior use of imagination.

O'Donoghue's professor did not grade the Kollwitz paper but did confess to liking it. Here O'Donoghue is sure of foot and balanced throughout every argument. Kollwitz's fascination with death and despair fascinates *him*. He has learned that The End is a recurring theme in art, but it takes someone who creates a "cold, uncompromising image" to give this theme the power necessary to disturb and disrupt those complacent with life. O'Donoghue came to this realization well before he wrote of Kollwitz; it steadied his aim as he prepared to pick off a few targets of his own.

In another paper, a study of the French playwright Molière, O'Donoghue evaluates the role of comedy in theater. He notes Molière's captivity to commercialism, that he "like Shakespeare, could not risk financial destruction by writing on what his audience did not wish to hear, or what they could not understand." Still, Molière penned scathing characterizations of the rogues of his day; his speeches fit together perfectly and were "firmly held by an encompassing comic spirit, piled to the height of pleasure"; his plays gained speed until "stopped by a curtain." O'Donoghue then states that "the future of modern theater must lie in Molière's single rule: the giving of pleasure." Yet one wonders: Pleasure for whom? The audience conditioned to applaud commercial tripe? Or the playwright caught between muse and savings account? Perhaps O'Donoghue means "pleasure" in producing experimental plays, for this is what he would soon commit himself to doing.

Analysis of comedy was new to O'Donoghue. Whatever his thoughts were of humor, they had until now remained private. In fact, O'Donoghue didn't consider himself as strictly a humorist. True, he had contributed to *Ugh* and played Lenny Bruce records on college radio, but this was in part defiance; O'Donoghue was stirred by *art*, serious, at times savage, depictions of existence. If he was funny it was in the way that Artaud and Beckett were funny: Jokes were scattered among the dying and the dead, laughter coughed up with blood and bile. This was how he defined the bulk of his work from *renaissance* on.

In man's long climb up the evolutionary ladder, when did he first learn to drown?

Six months into his third attempt to finish school, Michael O'Donoghue called an end to the charade. He was not, nor would he ever be, faculty material. Although he had performed well academically, his principal focus was on his plays and assorted poems. His desire to write for the stage remained strong throughout this final academic phase and thus diminished any passion he held for earning a degree. By now O'Donoghue's parents knew that he would never "settle down" in the conventional manner. Their daughter, Jane, was about to enter college, so at least one of their children would earn the all-important sheepskin. Mi-

Back in Rochester, c. 1961–62

chael (forever Pete to them) inhabited a different place where degrees and traditional honors are but small dead leaves in the dirt down the road.

Unlike the last time he left the University of Rochester, O'Donoghue decided to stay put. He hadn't come to like the Rochester area, but he recognized that he was in no position to depart for distant climes—not yet, anyway. Besides, he was getting reacquainted with the local scene, albeit in his own theatrical fashion. He liked to pretend he was blind and did so with great attention to detail: white cane; dark shades; halting, tentative gait. As the Blind Man, O'Donoghue walked into traffic and heard the skidding sound of sudden braking; he walked into stores so he could "browse," and proceeded to trip and fall and knock over merchandise. Naturally, the proprietors never showed anger. They helped him up and out of their stores lest the poor fellow stumble into something else.*

Religious symbols captivated him, and so during the Christmas season of 1961 O'Donoghue cased a nativity scene in a Rochester park. When darkness fell, he grabbed the Baby Jesus and smuggled Him back to the apartment in Medina. He placed the plastic Savior in a variety of positions as he sought the perfect display. Finally, O'Donoghue hung Him by the

---

*Playing blind was something of a hobby for O'Donoghue. In 1987 he managed to get himself into a public service announcement with Mary Tyler Moore. Ms. Moore, a diabetic, listed the many ill effects caused by diabetes. When she mentioned blindness, the camera cut to a shot of O'Donoghue wearing his trademark dark glasses.

neck from the ceiling (in preparation for a life of suffering?), and there Jesus remained until the arrival of Christmas 1962. O'Donoghue then returned to the park and set Him next to the new Baby Jesus, thereby creating a (brief) countermyth that Mary had Immaculately Conceived twins.

Clearly, O'Donoghue pined for the stage—if not proscenium, then the street would suffice. His theatrical nature began to break seams. The leaving of school allowed him time to seek a dramatic outlet, though Rochester was not known as a theater town; but were it Stratford-on-Avon, who in the "legitimate" theater would hire an intense, unpredictable type like O'Donoghue? Happily for him, Rochester's small but energetic underground had grown since his first exposure to it in 1957. By early 1962, Rochester's "bohemia" had garnered some attention from the local mainstream press, so there existed an opening for nontraditional expression, just enough room for O'Donoghue's needs.

Somewhere in his search for an outlet, O'Donoghue happened upon two people who shared his interest in alternative theater. One was Thomas David, "a young man long practiced in the art of stage design," as O'Donoghue later described him to a local newspaper. The other was a young woman, Arloha McVinnie. If David and McVinnie were unaware of O'Donoghue's previous involvement with Experiment 60, he certainly informed them of the fact. After all, Experiment 60 looked to widen the minor cleft in the university's theater department; wasn't this what David and McVinnie had in mind for Rochester as a whole?

David's and McVinnie's impressions of O'Donoghue are not recorded. Obviously they took to him and involved him with the project at hand: the formation of a new theater group that would perform experimental plays written by the known (Ionesco, Beckett) and unknown (members of the company) alike. By May a stage was secured in the basement of a coffeehouse called Galerie 65, located at 250 Court Street. A name for the group was then considered, a task not lightly taken. Indeed, the designation was of equal importance to the type of plays that the company would perform. Identity and image had to be established, marketed. (One thinks of Group, Mercury, Living . . .) Soon they settled on Panem et Circenses, then thought better of the Latin tag. The English translation worked just as well: Bread and Circuses.

The purpose of the new group, as stated in a densely worded set of bylaws, was to "encourage the development of the dramatic arts in all their forms, and particularly the development and expansion of the modern experimental theatre . . . to encourage and promote the composition of new dramatic works, the discovery or rediscovery of forgotten or neglected dramatic works . . . [t]o write, design, produce, sponsor, disseminate, and present to the public, theatrical works of all varieties and in all forms . . ." And so on. So detailed are the pages of this document that one might mistake Bread and Circuses for a law firm. The group's founders were quite serious about their intentions, expressed in blocks of humorless text.

The Bread and Circuses document was written with members in mind. The first public announcement of the group's formation and theatrical mission came on May 29, 1962, in the *Rochester Times-Union*. Hamilton B. Allen, in his column, "Two on the Aisle," spoke of a visit he had received from a "young man, stranger in these parts," who wished to publicize Bread and Circuses. The young man was O'Donoghue playing the role of West Coast Writer to the fullest. Allen appeared unaware of O'Donoghue's local connections, and this suited the "stranger" fine. It helped give the group a cosmopolitan air, said that this was more than another collection of Rochester amateurs who wanted to put on a show. "This is what the Roman emperors ordered for the people," O'Donoghue told Allen in reference to the name Bread and Circuses. "More loosely it translates, 'Give 'em what they want; keep 'em happy.' " Molière's edict of "giving pleasure" was now to be applied to upstate New York.

O'Donoghue outlined the group's initial production, which was to be staged a month later. As did Experiment 60, Bread and Circuses would bow with a trio of Japanese Noh plays. The plays he described sound almost identical to the ones he and Dan Rattiner produced several years before. The comedy deals with the king of Hell; the first tragedy shows a girl gone insane over unrequited love; the final tragedy depicts "an old woman, a courtesan, [who] is driven mad after killing her suitor." Since no titles exist from either production (just a brief summary of each play), an accurate comparison cannot be made. It's highly probable that O'Donoghue pushed the idea of Noh plays to his fellow thespians; if he did not, then it is certain he supported the decision to do the same.

The Noh plays ran for two consecutive weekends in July. According to the *Times-Union*, the group "packed the basement of 'Galerie 65' . . . for six performances." (There is no record of whether O'Donoghue performed in any of the plays.) An unnamed spokesman for Bread and Circuses added that the "production closed with a profit" and that the group would use "the proceeds to continue our efforts in the experimental vein." By September, Bread and Circuses took over the management of Galerie 65, renamed the place Le Galerie, and established its headquarters there. Buoyed by the success of their opening production and by the growth of the company to over fifty members, the group announced ambitious plans: a Punch-and-Judy show with live actors; dramatizations of Rudyard Kipling's "Just So Stories"; projects that incorporated ballet, opera, and filmmaking.

"We're not in competition with anyone," the spokesman said, "but hope to bring together creative forces of Rochester for the production of stimulating entertainment." In its quest for stimulation, the group decided to stage a one-act comedy by a local mathematician who worked for General Dynamics, Richard W. Bonker. His play, *The Pedestal*, was set to run for three weekends in November with Bonker as director. The cast consisted of two Rochester-bred actors and O'Donoghue, who was to play two roles. The three main characters were described by Bonker as being "the irrational, the human nostalgia and the absurd that is born of their encounter." *The Pedestal* was pitched as a "contemporary passion play" about the inner struggle of man.

That's one way of viewing it. *The Pedestal* opens with a prologue by a troubador named Arlecchino, who is seen tuning a lute as the lights come up. He turns to the audience, welcomes them, introduces himself, then dives into exposition. Lest anyone miss the point of the play, Arlecchino refers to its "experimental nature" engulfed by "the author's ecclesiastical rhetoric" and set in "an artificial situation." He asks, "How, then, can you, as spectators, believe that what you see is more sham and delusion? The answer is; drama is a ritual, ambiguous as the surf, which while appearing to carry you to shore, pulls you out from it until your feet can no longer feel the bottom, and your cries, like the sea tern's, are heard only by the open sky."

Since O'Donoghue played Arlecchino, the comparison of drama to drowning in the ocean is fitting. One can hear his young voice, touched by sarcasm, giving the image a finer edge—which is important because this is the strongest passage in the prologue. After additional exposition Arlecchino exits, but not before advising that the audience discount everything he has said, for "I am not a musician—and the strings of this lute are missing." Apparently, the cries of the audience would be heard after all.

The remainder of *The Pedestal* is a pseudo-existential conversation between the archbishop of Toledo, Tomás de Torquemada, and Henry Plantagenet, the king, who are, in "reality," a bread baker and a pork butcher, respectively. The roles they've adopted help them come to grips with a world out of control. Before long they pull poor Papolis, a machinist they cast as court jester, onto the stage. Papolis has trouble adapting to the game, partly because he's a conscript, chiefly because the two other characters bury him in bad Beckett-speak. Papolis threatens to quit the game, but Torquemada and Plantagenet make him a prince and they his humble servants. Papolis accepts; his servants call for a war against an imagined enemy. Papolis refuses to fight; his servants call for his crucifixion. The play ends as Papolis is dragged to the cross by his tormentors.

Bonker's debt to Pirandello is a rather heavy one; *The Pedestal* could easily have been called *Three Characters in Search of a Mathematician*. But the character Papolis seems tailored specifically for the young O'Donoghue. He calls for sanity where none exists; he's wise to the game being played but is helpess to resist its pull. There's an earnestness here that O'Donoghue understood and to a certain degree shared. And, Papolis being a jester, there's a brush with cornball humor, something O'Donoghue would use for his own ends. When his tormentors briefly leave the stage, Papolis turns to the audience (the fourth wall in this play was presumably the fire exit) and delivers a couple of bad jokes about politicians—including the use of the word *election* to mean "erection" when uttered by the Japanese. The jokes were Bonker's, but in the margin of the script O'Donoghue jotted down his own joke about the "French politician who got elected by kissing all the babies . . . before they were born." The line is subtler than those penned by Bonker, and the anti-French tone anticipates O'Donoghue's later skewering of Germany's favorite doormat.

O'Donoghue's copy of *The Pedestal* script is filled with notes to himself. His character's lines are circled and underlined in thick pen marks, which suggests an intensity he surely brought to this small part. There is an emphasis on his being emphatic, to make Papolis his *own* creation. By the time Torquemada tells Plantagenet to "Get the nails" for the crucifixion, Papolis is so frantic and desperate that he smears his makeup so as to reveal his "true" self. But the nails are produced and his cap and bells soon become the clown's crown of thorns.

The Pedestal received kind notices and plenty of publicity. Far from being viewed as a band of theater outlaws, Bread and Circuses intrigued and at times delighted local mainstream observers. The audience that filled Le Galerie's basement for the Noh plays trickled in for *The Pedestal*. Opening night drew only eight people, the next evening twenty-eight. (The basement could seat forty.) Business picked up as the play closed its run, and Bread and Circuses, now a fixture of sorts, planned for its winter series of productions. Among them: Eugene Ionesco's *Jack*; the original *Barber of Seville* by Beaumarchais, upon which the famous opera was later based; and a nineteenth-century melodrama by George Baker, *Among the Breakers*.

In order to create interest in *Among the Breakers*, O'Donoghue wrote a "commercial" for the play that was to be performed onstage during the run of *The Pedestal*. (This leads one to ask: How "experimental" is theater when it borrows from television?) It's unclear whether the *Breakers* ad indeed ran, but O'Donoghue's script survives, and for so short a piece it is rich in detail. The set is made up of a chaise lounge, an end table with books on top, bookends, a candle, and a gilded picture hanging above the lounge. A man (O'Donoghue?) "foppishly dressed" and "flagrantly homosexual" enters.

> Assuming an exaggerated attitude of trés fatigué, he mops his fevered brow and flings himself upon the chaise lounge, totally devastated. With an aura of elaborate relief at being safe within his aesthetic sanctuary, he plucks a slim mauve volume of Ronald Firbank's works from between the massive bookends and is about to peruse it when he takes notice of the audience:
> "Well, Hi there. You know, after a hard day of interior decorating, I find I need a real cigarette. And VOGUE (producing package) gives it to me. Not only in the taste that I require, but the pretty colours match my underwear. (Lights up on imposing candle.) Honestly now, these cigarettes are really elegant. Do what millions of others are doing . . . smoke VOGUE. Why not just bounce right down to your local tobacconist and nab a few cartons. And you tell him . . . Helen sent you."

The connection to George Baker's melodrama is at best tenuous, but O'Donoghue's grip on specifics is firm. The images in his head are by now distinct, down to the color and size of Firbank's book. His handling of homosexualist "manners" is clumsy, and he would learn to better exploit stereotypes to achieve full comic effect. Yet O'Donoghue shows that no piece is too small to accommodate his overflowing ideas.

Success with Bread and Circuses gave O'Donoghue a lift but no living wage. As in San Francisco, he was a semiprofessional writer (and actor) whose work brought him little more than critical praise. Thus he was compelled to take the dreaded day job. Through the early months of 1963 he performed a variety of tasks, from hawking costume jewelry door-to-door to selling *Life* magazine subscriptions by telephone. He also became a credit manager for the Sherwin-Williams paint company in Medina. Though ostensibly committed to covering the Earth with his company's fine product, O'Donoghue concentrated on furthering his education. He typed up extensive notes that dealt with kinetic sculpture, abstract art, the Futurists, and individual artists such as Marcel Duchamp and Jean Tinguely. When not conducting business from his office, he developed ideas for Bread and Circuses and took some interest in film.

O'Donoghue's first film treatment, *The Action Painter*, was written during this period. It is not known if he had a contact who was involved in making films or if he wrote the treatment as a mere exercise. But *The Action Painter* reflects O'Donoghue's creative passion and his need to capture it intact. The "story" centers on an artist who drives to the country so he may execute his "action" art: paint blown at a canvas by way of dynamite. That, in essence, is the film. O'Donoghue commits the majority of page space to camera angles, art direction, scene changes, and so on. In his zeal to convey what he has in mind, O'Donoghue reveals his inexperience: Attempting to describe a "LONG SHOT, HIGH ANGLE," he suggests that it be done "like in the westerns." Another time he advises the "cameraman" to avoid being "reflected in the hubcap" when shooting a scene involving a Volkswagen.

The treatment for *The Action Painter* is so overthought that O'Donoghue devotes nearly half a page to the opening credit sequence: "The colours of the titles should not be so arresting as to negate or diminish from the natural outdoor colours; nor so brash as to anticipate the shock of the actual painting itself. Have the colours spring-colours to harmonize with the subject . . ." Though reminiscent of the instructions Myrna Loy gives to the painter in *Mr. Blandings Builds His Dream House*, O'Donoghue's "colour" scheme may be traced to his long days at Sherwin-Williams.

What is of interest in *The Action Painter* is the name O'Donoghue gives to his film "company": Mirbeau Productions. Here one finds another influence—rarely acknowledged by O'Donoghue but important nonetheless. A drama critic, author, and playwright who warred with the cultural and political conventions of late-nineteenth-century France, Octave Mirbeau sought confrontation. So sharp were his attacks on public figures that he was obliged to fight (and win) at least four duels. In 1882, Mirbeau founded an acidic weekly, *Les Grimaces*, which lasted some six months. But it was in 1899 that Mirbeau's sensibility bore petal and thorn when his novel, *Le Jardin des Supplices*, otherwise known as *The Torture Garden*, was published.

Vivid, brutal, and beautifully written, *The Torture Garden* was once denounced as "the most sickening work of art of the nineteenth century." The novel tells of a bourgeois Frenchman whose obsession with an Englishwoman of independent mind and spirit leads to a garden in China where torture is art, atrocity erotic. By composing so graphic a work, Mirbeau meant to assail hypocrisy and the corruption of French "morality"; but the point of his novel was missed by its critics, who, overwhelmed by the violence, confused the writer for his art and so considered Mirbeau depraved. Such critical thinking would one day interpret O'Donoghue's work, yet the parallels to Mirbeau do not end there. *The Torture Garden* teems with razor-fine thoughts and observations:

Murder is born of love, and love attains the greatest intensity in murder.

There is something more mysteriously attractive than beauty: it is corruption.

In all the black countries the whites are the only cannibals.

Desire can attain the darkest human terror and give an actual idea of hell and its horror.

Murder is the very bed-rock of our social institutions, and consequently the most imperious necessity of civilized life.

Did you know that pearls had souls?

Like Mirbeau, O'Donoghue saw the poetry in mayhem and would put it to satiric use. And like Mirbeau, O'Donoghue would strive to draw blood with his pen. He would also become fond of the aphorism and bon mot. Indeed, *The Torture Garden*, with its blend of elegance and barbarity (peacocks strut among corpses, flowers are nourished by blood), its wit and rough sexual tension, anticipated much of O'Donoghue's later work and reads like the novel he neglected to write.

Sometime in mid-1963, O'Donoghue worked as a classical music disc jockey for WBBF-FM in Rochester. While not the free-form radio he knew in college, WBBF allowed him the opportunity to perform within limits. After all, he was not broadcasting from "the underground" but from the Midtown Tower Building. No taped record of his radio stint exists, but O'Donoghue later told *Rolling Stone* that one of his responsibilities was to read the hourly newscast. He would find on the wire a disaster of some magnitude, whether natural or man-made, and expand on the more horrific aspects until the story was distorted beyond reason. When not reading the news, O'Donoghue made use of the station's electric typewriters and worked out ideas on WBBF stationery.

Among these ideas was another film treatment, *The Big Movie*, in which $50 million is wasted through the random destruction of priceless antiques, artifacts, and works of art. Two film executives machine-gun a half dozen Old Masters, including Botticelli's *Venus* and Gainsborough's *Blue Boy*; piss on the Dead Sea Scrolls; shred to bits Shakespeare's folios. A bonfire is lit and every expensive item imaginable is tossed onto the flames, the camera included. Obviously, O'Donoghue meant for *The Big Movie* to be a joke, perhaps something he showed to other staffers. But film treatments and radio mischief were bubbles rising slowly to the surface. The true creative force was about to emerge.

Life is just another snuff movie.

By the fall of 1963, O'Donoghue had worked as both actor and set designer in a number of Bread and Circuses productions (his set design

Teaching an acting class, c. 1962–63

for Ionesco's *Jack* reflected Andy Warhol's pop art aesthetic). During this time he put the final polish on five short plays, some of which he had conceived in San Francisco, and was eager to have them staged. But O'Donoghue was not content to present his plays as just another Bread and Circuses offering; he'd grown too self-aware as an artist to allow so common a production. What he desired was nothing less than *An Evening with Michael O'Donoghue*. Bread and Circuses would, of course, provide the stage for this event, but the company itself would be relegated to backdrop. Instead, O'Donoghue devised a more suitable frame for his work: *le théâtre de malaise*, or, as the local press would call it, "sick theater."

In his studies of theater history and of the French language, O'Donoghue clearly encountered the Grand Guignol. Founded in 1897 by Parisian playwright Oscar Méténier, Grand Guignol came out of the Théâtre Libre, where plays tended to naturalism, turning the stage into another facet of everyday life. Secondhand furniture doubled as scenery. Sides of beef and live chickens served as props. The audience was more or less ignored; at times the actors would speak their lines with their backs to the house. The plays were usually set in a squalid environment and focused on the lower elements of Parisian life. Also, Théâtre Libre plays were brief, so an evening could consist of five or six dramas, a format O'Donoghue looked to borrow.

The Grand Guignol pushed the immediacy of Théâtre Libre toward the extreme. Although the plays that dramatized the gutter remained, plays based on police blotters and sensational newspaper stories added a topical edge. Yet Méténier, feeling he could add little more to Libre/Guignol, vanished. His place was taken by Max Maurey, the Malcolm Maclaren of the French theater scene. He possessed no real love for the avant-garde but recognized the commercial appeal of horror and savagery. Thus his Grand Guignol was the ultimate in "bad taste" that incorporated graphic depictions of rape, torture, and murder. Blood dripped and spurted from chests and heads; animal eyeballs popped from gouged sockets and bounced off the stage; wounds and severed limbs were as common as soliloquies in Shakespeare's work. Maurey guessed right, and the Grand Guignol was a success. Years later Maurey was joined by a prolific, death-obsessed playwright, Andre de Lorde. Known as the Prince of Terror, de Lorde created a style of drama called "slices of death," and he hoped to write a play so horrifying that the audience would flee within minutes of exposure.

O'Donoghue's work would anger its share of souls. But for all that *le théâtre de malaise* owed to Théâtre Libre and Grand Guignol (as well as to Artaud's Theatre of Cruelty), it was not intended to horrify or to frighten as much as to disorient, and here O'Donoghue leaned more to Cocteau and absurdity. On a slip of paper given to those attending his plays, he announced the creation of the " 'O'Donoghue-Cocteau Award—1963,' to be presented to the person who best completes the following statement in 100 words or less: 'I believe that Michael O'Donoghue sincerely deserves the title—*The Jean Cocteau of the Americas* because . . .'" The Rochester man who won the award wrote that O'Donoghue was not only "the very embodiment of Jean Cocteau," he was "the true reincarnation of Jesus Christ, Esq., our Lord and Savior and Grand Inquisitor of all times . . ."

When speaking to local journalists, O'Donoghue assumed a slightly lower profile. On the day his plays premiered, November 15, the *Rochester Democrat and Chronicle* referred to O'Donoghue as "a West Coast writer now living in Rochester," and mentioned his involvement with *renaissance* and the *San Francisco Examiner*, where he had worked "as a reporter." An old hand at shaping a persona, O'Donoghue now grasped the importance of self-promotion. His time in San Francisco, marked by poverty, unemployment, and *one* brief success, became in the Rochester press a period of sustained professional achievement. No journalist thought to ask *why* a "reporter," editor, and writer who had done so well in the Bay Area would suddenly move to Rochester and take up with an experimental theater group. It seemed enough that O'Donoghue was bringing some "Off-Broadway flavor" to the local scene, and that his plays would "be given their world premiere" in the basement of a coffeehouse.

O'Donoghue's use of the Rochester press helped to generate interest in *le théâtre de malaise*, and on opening night the small space under Le Galerie was filled with patrons curious to see just how "sick" this production could be. The cast included O'Donoghue; Bobbie Neely and Janice Bickel, who were billed as the "Insatiable Tripp Sisters"; and Ephram Robbins. O'Donoghue decided that he and three actors could effectively translate his words to the stage—a sizable gamble given the complications written into the work. There were to be several character and costume changes throughout the many blackouts and shifts in narrative. Several dozen props were to be used. Also, the actors had to contend with the various sound cues and voice-overs O'Donoghue threw in their, and his, path. What appeared tight and precise on the page was certain to unravel once set in motion, and did. Nevertheless, O'Donoghue and company survived the lighting and sound failures that occurred on opening night. They made their way through patches of affected writing and brought to life some truly brilliant material.

Lights up on O'Donoghue's set design. In the center of the tiny stage sits a large white block sporting "m." on its sides. This remains fixed through the evening. To its left hangs a bone-white, one-armed female mannequin wearing a long black wig and with her legs missing below the knees. Suddenly, a woman is chased onstage by a man.

Her clothes are torn. She is frantic. Brusquely, he corners her, presses her against the wall and brutally kisses her resisting lips. Weakened, she struggles against his advances (pounding his back, squirming, etc.) until he finally releases her. Without hesitation, she whips from her handbag a revolver and fires three shots into the groin of the attacker. Bang. Bang. Bang. Flashing a toothy grin, he retorts: "You have spirit. I like that." Then drops dead.

O'Donoghue is then introduced to the audience as "Western New York State's newest and most exciting playwright," and he delivers a brief synopsis of his "life." "I was born the son of Greek peasants in 1941," he begins. "I have no memory of my early childhood." His parents were slain in the Greek Civil War, he says, and then he tells how the Red Cross found him and nursed him back to health. He was later adopted by an RAF officer and his wife, a "pretty, tight-faced woman of Norman descent. I recall that she could make tiny ballerinas out of the hollyhocks." His adoptive parents split up and placed him in a Canadian private school. He saw neither of them again. His mother then died of a brain tumor, and his father began work on a secret atomic project in Livermore, California. "I have taken no steps to contact him."

No mention of Sauquoit or rhuematic fever; instead, we have entered one of his darker scrapbooks and are sent through its pages at a rapid clip.

Much of the action is described or set to pantomime as it is impossible to stage. Yet the effects, however uneven and marred by mistakes, pile up and take form. The first play, *Michael Hip and the Pale Dry Death-Machine*, consists of several episodes that merge "to make the bitter tapestry, a persistent day-dream" that lurks in O'Donoghue's unconscious. Here "among cobwebs and dull roots" flash poems, dreams, and television commercials. T. S. Eliot and Aldous Huxley stroll arm in arm until suddenly "this monstrous, huge, ugly, painfully complex, disturbingly eclectic and TERRIFYING machine *springs* into the street and begins to 'bear down'" on the pair and "runs right over them CRUNCH leaving them all dead, mushed into the cobblestones, a disheartening mass of tread marks." James Baldwin is forced by a civil rights group to use a white men's room while Carl Sandburg is transformed into a grain elevator. A flannel-clad O'Donoghue steps forward to pitch "Cajones," the "MAN'S cigarette" that has wild animals "ground right into the tobacco." He strips to a white shirt and becomes a tortured artist in *Icarus*. Here he is quizzed on the type of pictures he paints.

(2): I paint . . . pictures of birds.
(1): Oh, birds. Sparrows? Cardinals? Robins? Ravens? Orioles? Crows? Finches? Blue-Jays? Scarlet Tanagers? Owls? Meadow Larks?—
(2): Hummingbirds. I paint pictures of hummingbirds.
(1): Oh, hum—
(2): Black hummingbirds. Actually, I paint pictures of Big Black Hummingbirds THAT HATE THEIR *MOTHER*!!!

O'Donoghue cringes as he spits out the last line. Are the humming-birds by chance Irish-German?

Good Grief, More Genesis? travels less distance to demolish its target. We are in the Great Courtroom of God on Judgment Day. An old bearded man wanders into court. He produces a scroll, reads down its length, mumbles to himself, then, eyes wide, fingers tense, he throws the scroll into the air and yells out: "THE GREAT MAN! THE GREAT MAN DEAD AT LAST! THE GREAT MAN DEAD!" An angel hears the news and the two discuss what possible fate awaits the deceased. The judge, "the Right Honourable Girolamo Savonarola," enters and court is in session. The old man makes the judge aware of the "special significance" of the first case, and the deceased is ushered in to a blast of trumpets. He is the humanitarian Albert Schweitzer. The gallery of onlookers are in awe as "Al humbly mounts the witness box and stands trembling in senility . . ."

Judge Savonarola is as impressed as the onlookers. He asks Schweitzer as "a formality" the customary question: "State the good you have performed in your corporeal existence." Schweitzer says he has done his best to serve his fellow man. Formality complete, judge and jury accept Schweitzer into the Kingdom of Heaven. The gallery shakes with applause and cheers. But the judge forgot to consult "Him-From-Whom-All-Blessings-Flow" and asks for His Final Mercy. *"REJECTED,"* comes His reply from behind black curtains. The courtroom erupts in gasps. Schweitzer recounts his many selfless acts, including his spurning of modern convenience so he could assist the starving in Africa. *"REJECTED."* Angry, Schweitzer goes on about Africa as he is forcibly removed from the courtroom: "Listen you. It was hot. It was very hot in Africa. . . . It was just awful. I went out of my way to help those filthy black bastaaaaaaaaaarrrrrrrrrrddddsssssss . . ." The good doctor kicks and screams and is tossed into Hell by a pair of demons.

The judge, bewildered by this decision, asks for an explanation. The black curtains part and out steps Jesus Christ.

GOOD. I'M GLAD YOU ASKED THAT. NOW I COULD HAND YOU A LOT OF GARBAGE FROM THE BIG BOOK, BUT THIS TIME I'M TELLING YOU RIGHT FROM THE SHOULDER. COME ON NOW. WHO THE HELL HOLES UP FIFTY YEARS IN A CRUMMY JUNGLE POPPIN' PENICILLIN TO SOME GRUBBY NATIVES? WHO? SOME KIND OF NUT, THAT'S WHO. OR, A REAL OPERATOR: A GUY WHO THINKS AHEAD. THIS IS WHAT IT ALL BOILS DOWN TO: SCHWEITZER WAS SHOOTING FOR THE RIGHT-HAND THRONE. AND I'M TELLING YOU NOW SO EVERYBODY GETS IT STRAIGHT. NO OBSEQUIOUS GOODY-GOODY IS GONNA JERK ME AROUND!!!

Praise be to God.

In *The Twilight Maelstrom of Cookie Lavagetto,* a flurry of notes compete to be heard. Like experimental jazz, *Twilight* is a hit-or-miss affair. But themes are introduced here that O'Donoghue would develop over time. We begin in prewar Germany, circa 1927. The Scheidewasser Imperial Players are about to stage their production of *Der Fang-Fruh.* Der Herr Professor, wearing a clownish hat with a bent flower (shades of Emil Jannings in *The Blue Angel*), introduces "The Rat-Flog Song." Der Fang enters the scene, "an infant firmly affixed to his bayonet," and sings in German, the English translation coming from loudspeakers:

> *Life always kicks you hard in the stomach;*
> *Especially if you are with child.*
> *All honest effort dead-ends in despair.*
> *Your bicycle is stolen.*
> *And you are apprehended attempting to steal another.*
> *The gods are weak.*
> *Man is weaker.*
> *Ho! Ho!*
> *Rat-Flog.*

Der Herr Professor, flanked by the Düsseldorf honky-tonk angels, adds, "Fallen to the final crib in a Chicago Bordello, the Dirty Sisters warn—'True Love Can Not Survive The Change Of Life.' " This he repeats until the stage darkens. The sound of howitzers exploding and machine guns firing rips through the dark. War has arrived, and O'Donoghue sticks our noses in a blood-lined trench. Amid the killing and mutilation a soldier finds his friend Ricky "half-buried in the mud. Already the sparrows and finches had eaten away much of his face. But I knew it was Ricky, all right. There was no mistaking that winsome grin."

Most of Europe is in flames. In Salerno, Italy, on August 24, 1943, a crack American combat unit known as Fart d'Art destroys "axis art treasures, thus crushing the enemy's aesthetic backbone." The Nazis might have allowed Paris to remain intact, but this team of Yanks plays a different game. Spotty, Ace, and "Touchhole" Johnson machine-gun a Botticelli (an image taken from *The Big Movie*) and talk of punching fags. In the background a radio crackles and "America's Doll-Face," Neruda HeartShaped, is heard singing "You'll Be Marching Home to Mother, in the Victory Parade."

But O'Donoghue plays no favorites. He allows Spotty and another army buddy, Jim, to be captured by the Nazis and sent to Stalag 23. They are interrogated by the Commandant (O'Donoghue). He orders the Americans to sign papers that denounce the very way of life the boys are sworn to defend. Spotty tears them in two and gives the kraut a quick lesson in democracy: "Attending the church of your choice. Rooting for the Yankees. Scarfin' a hot-dog. The right to 'have your say' . . ." The Commandant is unimpressed.

> What you say is all very interesting but, alas, pitifully naive. The people *desire* to be dominated, to be "trod upon." They are too weak and stupid to rule themselves. They need a strong Master. They ask to be beaten, to be awakened in the middle of the night, to be unmercifully tortured, to be raped. It is their inalienable right as human beings . . .

The Commandant sends orders by phone that forty more lesbians will be needed to work at the various camps. They are to wear leather slacks, a halter, an armband, a riding crop, and jackboots. They must be made ready, for soon the photographers from the men's magazines will arrive. What type of pictures does he want? "The usual things. Bulldozer shots, twins, trenches, ovens, spectacles, teeth, etc." The Commandant

The Nazi Commandant breaks down in *Cookie Lavagetto*

boasts of his "nice 8' x 10' glossy of 'The Duchess of Dachau pouring lye into the ears of trussed and screaming rabbis' "; he then casually pulls his revolver and shoots Jim in the groin. Jim dies, his final move an attempt to show a snapshot of his loved ones. The German breaks down: "OH MY GOD. IT IS THIS TERRIBLE WAR. IT HAS MADE ANIMALS OF US." Spotty pats him on the shoulder and assures him that all will be fine.

When mining the Holocaust for humor, one forever risks a cave-in. The mere mention of Nazi ovens provokes either anger or tears; laughter is rarely linked to a pile of gassed bodies. Like "dead baby" jokes or remarks that mock disaster, most gas chamber jokes are brutally free of nuance. One particular joke in this line compares Jews to pizza, the difference being that pizza doesn't scream when put in an oven. This is tin-plated shock, artless and lacking in wit; some may say anti-Semitic, but as true anti-Semites dismiss the Holocaust as fiction or believe it to be exaggerated, acknowledgment of ovens and gas chambers would contradict their claims. Those who make the jokes concede the horror and use it to bolster their punch lines.

Although O'Donoghue could and did toss off crude one-liners, he groped for deeper meaning. That the Holocaust could happen, that for all the piety expressed after the fact, millions of humans, German and American among them, allowed mass murder to flourish—this he found compelling and worthy of satire. There was also the dark energy of the swastika, perhaps *the* most potent symbol of the late twentieth century. This, too, intrigued O'Donoghue; the swastika possessed unspeakable power, and he would spend the better part of his career trying to artisically harness its symbolic force. Here O'Donoghue was pretty much on his own and his efforts would confuse—if not infuriate—those looking.

Few people found death camps amusing in 1963. When the Commandant went on about lesbians in jackboots posing with teeth and the torture of rabbis, the satire was missed (or unappreciated) by a number of patrons who promptly walked out of the performance. It should be remembered that at the time *no* one—not even Lenny Bruce—portrayed Nazis in such a fashion. In *Hogan's Heroes*, the Gestapo resembled the Keystone Kops; in *The Producers*, "Springtime for Hitler" parodied the Broadway musical and its audience, not anti-Semitism. Even so, these treatments were still years away. When O'Donoghue staged *Twilight,* the primary artistic comment on the Holocaust and the men who had engineered it was *Judgment at Nuremberg,* a film rather short on comic tension.

After Spotty commiserates with the Commandant, the war ends and German "guilt" is displayed:

Genosite

The Minister of Defense (also Vice-President in charge of Overseas Operations for a leading motor car company) is about to unveil a grim monument at Buchenwald—a stern reminder of man's-inhumanity-to-man.

THIS MUST NOT HAPPEN AGAIN

© VOLKSWAGEN OF AMERICA, INC.

Minister of Defense: We have gathered here to pay homage to these stones; stones that once ran yellow with Jewish blood.

We are then taken to the Slovik Memorial Veterans Hospital in Schenectady, New York, named after the one American soldier shot for desertion during the war. It is Christmas Day, 1953. Here a quadruple amputee hopes to win an old nurse's love by making thousands of poppies for her with his teeth. However, she plans to retire after forty years of service to "the sick, the suffering, the maimed, the crippled, the undone and irrepairable, the deformed, defiled, stigmatic, misshapen, blotchy, warped, fecculent, odious, repellent, abhorrent, offensive, disgusting, sickening, noxious, abominable, despicable, loathsome, nauseating, vile, foul, nasty . . . Echhhhhhhh . . ." She exits, vomiting. If Albert Schweitzer and Jesus Christ can express distaste for those they supposedly champion, why not a nurse who's had her fill of compassion?

The amputee is left to deal with the sadistic attendant Heine, played by O'Donoghue. As he flops about the stage in an effort to impress his new caretaker, the amputee endures verbal abuse and threats of physical harm. Left alone, he yells out: "OH DEAR GOD! OH CHRIST SAVE ME HELP ME PLEASE OH GOD . . ." His slab of a body succumbs to muscular spasms that send him twitching across the floor. The sound of Connie Francis singing "God Bless America" surrounds him, and a strange presence is felt. "Who are you?" the amputee asks.

I am the Spirit of American Bravery. I walked side by side the buckskinned pioneers as they spread small-pox to the Indians. I was a sentry at Andersonville and rode with Sherman when he gutted the Appomattox . . . I fought with MacArthur against the Bonus Marchers. I rode the cockpit as a plucky

Berating the amputee

little plane struck back against a "still tough" yellow peril at Hiroshima and Nagasaki. I heard your desperate cries and came to comfort you.

The amputee begs to be made whole, a request the spirit denies. "How would it be if every hero who ever lost an arm or a leg, just grew it back again?" he says to the truncated vet. "Then being a hero wouldn't mean very much, would it? Mutilation is the better part of glory." Instead the spirit turns the amputee into a form better suited to his needs: a gigantic red poppy. As the lights faded on this scene, more patrons left the theater. The sight of O'Donoghue haranguing an armless and legless man (an effect achieved by placing Ephram Robbins in a sack) was a bit much for some audience members. But O'Donoghue was pleased; and when others walked out of subsequent performances, he intensified his screams and threats to a degree that it appeared he was haranguing *them*. He found audience defections to be "so much more satisfying than applause."

Perhaps. But he breaks the vow, made nearly two years earlier, to give the audience "what they want" and to "keep 'em happy." What caused O'Donoghue to shift his position? At the birth of Bread and Circuses his enthusiasm for the group was genuine and in public statements bordered on the collegiate. This might have stemmed from his failure in San Francisco and his need to begin anew. By the time of the *malaise* plays, however, O'Donoghue had detached himself somewhat from his surroundings. Also, the reaction to his work was at best mixed, and he felt he deserved better. O'Donoghue might have intended to keep his audience happy, but when they walked out on *Twilight* he labelled them rubes and claimed to be content with their rejection.

Audience rejection alone did not account for O'Donoghue's change of heart. Because he was smitten with Cocteau and had immersed himself in the French artist's work, it is likely that he came across Cocteau's comments on the "tragic gag." "I did not invent the tragic gag," Cocteau said to a critic in 1932, "but I used it as much as possible. The gag is a great find. Here is an example. Charlie Chaplin swallows a whistle and all the dogs follow him. The audience bursts into laughter. With the tragic gag I don't expect the audience to laugh (if they do, I have failed) but I expect a black silence from them that is almost as violent as laughter." In *le théâtre de malaise*, O'Donoghue created his own version of the tragic gag; drama and comedy were one. Patrons sickened by Nazis and the mistreatment of amputees might indeed have given O'Donoghue what he wanted. Their outrage was laughter, their exit an ovation.

Those who left during *Twilight* were spared *Take 3 Big Giant Steps, Honey, Toward the Key to My Heart*. A man and woman discuss sex, contraception, and the consecutive number of times a samurai must ejaculate "without taking it out" in order to earn his title (the answer: six). Few props are used; movement is minimal. Since it is the weakest of the evening's plays and could never stand on its own, *Take 3 Giant Steps* provides cast and crew a breather after *Twilight* and before the final, demanding, play, *the automation of caprice*.

Like *Twilight*, *caprice* is episodic. "The Big Ocean" (or "death to the lifeboats") finds Captain Contrabando, skipper of the *Swarthy Clipper*, carving the ship's log into the chest of the Indian cook, Mahatma. As his penknife cuts through brown bleeding flesh, the captain, played by O'Donoghue, misspells a word and begins to erase with a pair of scissors. Mahatma screams; a sailor enters to report the shooting of the White Albatross. The captain signs his name to the log (which sends poor Mahatma to new depths of agony) and goes to the deck to have a look. Once there he is peeved.

> o.k. enough is enough. first you shot the white dolphin, then you shot the white elephant, then it was a white locomobile, then a white dove, then the white buffalo, then norman mailer, and now this. now really, all kidding aside, you guys are just askin' for it.

O'Donoghue as Captan Contrabando in *caprice*

The crew fears retribution—"the sky grows dark, the wind is screaming, god is angry, he will punish us for our misdeeds"—and the captain gives the order to submerge. "But this isn't a submarine," says a sailor. Contrabando remains firm. "That, matey, is my concern, not yours."

Next, we are taken to "A Lestoil Community Sing." O'Donoghue is a folksinger who performs a tune called "Them Seeds" that he picked up while in prison. It tells of a girl named Barbara who slips into jail cells at night to "pleasure" the convicts before they are executed. ("Jus' before you s'pose to die/Barbara opens up your fly.") The folksinger then mentions Muffo' Hopkins, "the great grand-daddy of United States folk-singin'." When Muffo' died, he had taped to his leg pounds of illegal white powder and thousands of pills. Every year junkies look for Muffo's unmarked grave and the "treasure" therein. To honor Muffo's memory the folksinger strums "The Octoroon Blues," in which a man of mixed parentage beats his mother from evening to morn: "The gopher-eyed bitch/that a-made me born."

We are brought to the play's final piece, "The Automation of Caprice," a "contemporary anti-play . . . employing small caps and pornography." As in *Twilight*, some of the difficult action is described or pantomimed. Images blend as hallucinations: an old Ecuadoran woman sinks a dagger into a young man's chest and calls it love eternal, then hands him a plastic lollipop and calls it love tangible; Henry Miller and F. Scott Fitzgerald arrive and exit as they melt like Salvador Dali's clocks; the old woman and young man follow suit. The scene is in the mind of an Indian on peyote. The Indian is a hunchback with webbed feet and countless boils. He rapes a fourteen-year-old quadruple amputee just as a chain gang approaches. The prisoners are black, their attire from Neiman-Marcus. The "Boss Spade" begins to sing but is beaten by the overseer, who wields a bicycle chain. Fade to a radio announcer's voice: "when we last left ramona, you will remember that she had succeeded in eluding the myopic leader of the icelandic underground . . ."

But ramona wedgewood's escape leads to an auto mishap, and she lies bleeding and battered beneath her mauve Daimler-Benz. A Saint Bernard comes to ramona's aid. She calls to him—"go boy, go to the village & fetch help." The dog opts instead to lick ramona's exposed genitalia. Three days pass; the dog stops licking and chases a ground squirrel; ramona sinks into a deep coma.

A car drives past the crash site, stops, backs up. A man holding a black bag gets out. He is a doctor, and he rushes to ramona's side and administers first aid. He rises, stands motionless over ramona's broken form, considers the situation in silence. Then, after extended deliberation, the doctor kneels, lifts ramona's skirt, and begins to lick her exposed genitalia. Organ music swells.

> tune in tomorrow for the next garish chapter in the misanthropic life of ramona wedgewood . . . be with us when: renegade gypsies, under the erroneous belief that golden pubic hair, taken externally, can cure pellagra; pluck clean poor ramona's delicate fertile areas.

Static consumes the announcer; the radio goes dead. O'Donoghue damages ramona but he cannot dispose of her, for within months she will take another name and become one of his greatest creations.

From here *caprice* quickly winds down. James M. Barrie, author of *Peter Pan*, sprinkles himself with magic dust and alights. The peyote-addled Indian is revealed to be O'Donoghue. He is slain by a Boy Scout leader who mistakes him for a "deviate redskin." Before he surrenders to death, O'Donoghue, "svelte, undaunted, places his burning kiss upon the old man's cold and bloodless lips, and exits. silently."

The evening is complete, though an "optional" ending is sometimes staged. A mock white horse is led in. The announcer produces a shotgun and blows away the horse's head. The cast run on stage, strip to their underwear, and smear warm equine blood on their bodies. While they race about the theater shouting obscenities, the announcer steps into a lone, blue spotlight. "Well, folks. I guess that just about wraps it up. I hope you enjoyed yourselves as much as we enjoyed having you with us." Kisses are blown as the spotlight dims.

Those who stayed to the end of the show must have wondered what the hell hit them. *Le théâtre de malaise* was unlike anything ever offered in a Rochester theater. The following day, fellow WBBF-FM staffer

Dick Moses reviewed the production in a station segment called "Critics Corps." Moses favored the shorter plays and felt O'Donoghue to be "a careful and clever writer" in parts. Yet the weight of the evening pressed him to caution:

> This is far out theater, no question about it, but I wonder if Mr. O'Donoghue isn't overreaching a bit—for his own good and that of the things he wants to put before us. Certainly both he and the audience seemed to feel more comfortable when things were a bit closer and tighter. Go ahead and see it—it won't hurt a bit, but I warn you: Michael O'Donoghue makes no bones about attacking everything: your religion, your politics, your morality, your composure, even at times your patience. But he gives you a chance to get back at him in the intermission—in writing no less [the O'Donoghue-Cocteau Award]. What can you lose except a buck and a half—and certainly the cause of experimental theater is worth that.

The notion that O'Donoghue's work served the "cause of experimental theater" is a dubious one. Though a member of a company, O'Donoghue's main concern was getting *his* vision right: first on paper, then on stage. He made certain that people knew who was responsible for the material. In the promotional posters for *malaise*, his name is dwarfed only by the production's title; in the local press he was mentioned as much if not more than Bread and Circuses. If this was "experimental," then Hollywood celebrities are eternally in the avant-garde.

Behind the publicity lay a central fact: As a writer, O'Donoghue was superior to his fellow company members. This he knew, and he recognized the American reality that talent will go unnoticed unless it is relentlessly advertised. The single cause to which O'Donoghue was committed was himself. If experimental theater benefited from his efforts, it came through fallout and not by design.

Despite audience defections, *le théâtre de malaise* did reasonably well and sustained Le Galerie's notorious reputation, which was enhanced when two cast members suffered physical injury on opening night. Ephram Robbins fractured his ankle and Bobbie Neely cracked three ribs while scuffling onstage. It is unclear when the injuries occurred; in both the opening scene and in *Take 3 Steps* a man and woman fight, so it is likely that Robbins and Neely hurt each other during one of these exchanges. After receiving medical attention, Robbins and Neely literally limped through that weekend's remaining two shows. The following Friday, November 22, O'Donoghue announced in the *Rochester Times-Union* that, though still injured, Robbins and Neely were ready to perform that night.

But events in Dallas that afternoon insured that no one would take the stage: President Kennedy was gunned down and died. For the next three days the nation witnessed on television one of the more gripping and engaging state productions ever mounted. From Walter Cronkite choking back tears to the murder of Lee Harvey Oswald to John-John's farewell to his father, Americans were presented live and largely un-scripted imperial tragedy that the ancient Greeks and Romans would have appreciated and been hard-pressed to match.* Bread and Circuses chose not to compete, and the weekend's performances of *le théâtre de malaise* were cancelled. Many Americans stayed home to mourn their fallen "father-leader" (Oliver Stone's rather accurate description of JFK, given the national hymnals). O'Donoghue didn't mourn but studied the drama to its conclusion. He took note of the major themes and sketched out ideas for another production.

The Friday following the assassination, November 29, the cast were set to perform when, minutes before the opening scene, Bobbie Neely became ill and was hospitalized. There was no understudy, so the audi-ence's money was refunded and another weekend was lost. On December 2, O'Donoghue sent a press release to local media outlets that explained the company's predicament. "Two weeks of inactivity . . . have sapped public interest," he stated, then asked that the new performance schedule be advertised. The company planned to resume *malaise* on December 14 and had added another weekend of shows beginning December 21. The weekend of December 6, however, was kept free for another, smaller, theatrical event: Michael O'Donoghue's wedding.

After leaving San Francisco and Gaby Benat behind, O'Donoghue kept free of serious romantic entanglement. He was perpetually broke and could not (or would not) hold a steady job, though he did on occasion conduct acting classes at Le Galerie. His moods swayed from bright to sullen, and unless directly stimulated he became bored and removed. He was devoted to the advancement of his work and career, and it was here, while involved with Bread and Circuses, that O'Dono-ghue met Janice Bickel. Little is known about Bickel, and in later years O'Donoghue consigned their relationship to a footnote. What *is* known is that Bickel was a divorced mother of three children, Suzanne, Jeff, and Christopher. She was a native of Rochester who worked as a recep-tionist for a life insurance company. Having some theatrical ambition, Bickel, along with her sister, Bobbie Neely, joined Bread and Circuses soon after its inception. She was four years older than O'Donoghue, blond, and considered amiable by those who met her. O'Donoghue shared this sentiment, and the two became romantically involved.

---

*Coverage of JFK's death and funeral was eventually outdone in 1997 with the media-led orgy on behalf of Diana Spencer, "England's Rose."

They married in Rochester on Saturday, December 7, 1963. O'Donoghue wore a conservative black suit, his bride a dress made of black velvet and satin. The ceremony was a small and quiet one. For Bickel marriage meant a father for her three kids; for O'Donoghue it was an attempt to bring stability to his chaotic life. Not since his brush with a fraternity in college had he opted to join the "others" in the conventional world. Whether he was pressured from without or felt desperation within is unclear; there was nothing in his makeup that suggested a wife and children were desired. Still, his mother, Barbara, endorsed his decision. She liked Bickel and as always preferred her son to be more "responsible" and less "bohemian." But to O'Donoghue, Mother's approval was the least of his worries. Barely able to support himself, he now was responsible for a family of five. A month shy of his twenty-fourth birthday, O'Donoghue dove face-first into waters where depth and strength of current had not been properly measured.

O'Donoghue was less than adequately equipped to handle the responsibilities of fatherhood. He continued to hold mixed and at times violently negative emotions for his parents and sister—which was notable, as they constituted the only family structure he had known. Also, he suffered bouts of depression and kept a thin lid on a cauldron of anger. He hated upstate New York, despised the provincialism of Rochester, and loathed the thought of settling into a "straight" job. Yet by marrying Janice Bickel he all but guaranteed that he would remain chained to that which he reviled for many years to come.

Before his marriage O'Donoghue had moved from Medina and into Rochester proper. He lived in an apartment at 29 Thayer Street, and Janice and the children soon joined him there. A veteran of cramped quarters, O'Donoghue was used to sharing space. But now he had kids to contend with, and the pressure to be a good parent exacted a gradual toll. Apparently he got on well with the two older children, Jeff and Suzanne, both of whom were under age ten. There was a side to O'Donoghue that appreciated the world of children, where games, projects, and rainy-day activities are commonplace. He remembered his own childhood and the need to entertain himself, so to a degree he indentified with Jeff and Suzanne and their need to connect with him. Infants, however, were a lower species. "You can't talk to babies," he would complain, and Janice's six-month-old son, Christopher, gave O'Donoghue no end of problems. The baby's incessant crying drove his new dad nuts. So Dad opted for a different form of communication.

O'Donoghue loved costumes and props and kept in his possession many of the items used in his plays. Among the props was a gun that shot blanks, the very weapon his Nazi Commandant had fired into the groin of an American soldier. One night when Christopher began to wail, O'Donoghue tried to calm him. But "hush little baby" was not his strong suit and O'Donoghue resorted to other means. He saw the gun, grabbed it, and returned to the side of the crib. He stared down at Christopher, whose face was now tear-streaked and red. In the casual manner of his stage Nazi, O'Donoghue raised the gun to the ceiling and fired twice. The loud pops startled the baby into stunned silence, and he remained quiet for the better part of the evening.

When he acquired some fame, O'Donoghue loved to tell this story. It sharpened an already stiletto reputation, and he was so taken with the story's effect on journalists that he embellished it to make it appear that he had fired *live* rounds into the ceiling above the crib. This thrilled those who profiled him, and no one ever considered (at least in print) the reality of firing a loaded handgun above a baby's head. Nor did they ask why O'Donoghue had never faced arrest or rebuke; after all, a guy who pumps bullets into the ceiling of his apartment would at the very least attract his neighbors' or landlord's attention. (O'Donoghue later said that Bickel knew nothing of his cribside manner until she read of it in *Rolling Stone*. If this is true, then Bickel was far too trusting a mother and O'Donoghue a duplicitous husband.) Perhaps journalists didn't fully buy O'Donoghue's tale but saw its value as great copy—something along the lines of William S. Burroughs's shooting his wife, Joan, in the head, which *did* result in death and arrest. In any case, the story of the baby and the gun defined O'Donoghue's disastrous first marriage.

His home life tense, his prospects for steady work slim (Bickel kept her day job and Barbara would help in a financial pinch), O'Donoghue sank into his writing. The *malaise* plays ended their run on December 23, and O'Donoghue rushed to finish his newest project, based on the Kennedy assassination. Titled simply *The Death of JFK*, the play treats the president's death as the serious television spectacle it became. Thus *JFK* is less a play and more a television satire for the stage. The one true "character" is Felix Ravenwood, an NBC News correspondent who guides us through the postassassination landscape as only an objective journalist can. He reviews the actions of a dozen CIA agents who, when shots rang out in Dealy Plaza, ran for their lives and trampled and killed an eighty-two-year-old widow. But the widow's family will not sue for damages because that would be "decidedly unpatriotic" at "this dark hour."

Reports filter in from a nation in shock. In Los Angeles, a suicide attempt by Kennedy impressionist Vaughn Meader is thwarted and the popular entertainer is sedated. In Indiana, a nine-year-old boy phones his school and threatens to kill President Johnson. Though the call was a prank, a mob of two thousand proud Hoosiers hangs the boy from the flagpole of the local courthouse, cuts him down, and burns the body.

Ravenwood stops for a special bulletin . . . In Dallas, accused assassin Lee Harvey Oswald is about to be transferred to another jail. We are taken live to police headquarters.

Reporters look on as sheriffs escort Oswald to an armored truck. Suddenly, Jack Ruby steps forward and drills Oswald in the gut; Oswald then groans and slumps to the ground. The officers wrestle with Ruby until someone from CBS shouts out that he forgot to switch on his camera. His request that the principals run through the action again is granted. Oswald gets up, retraces his steps, and the shooting is repeated. Now the people from *The March of Time* want to get Oswald's death from a different angle. The sequence is restaged, and this time Oswald eats lead and collapses in slow motion.

Back at the White House, members of Congress file past the body of the slain chief executive, at rest in the Blue Room. Ravenwood is impressed by Jackie's fine taste in funeral decor. He surveys the art and furniture that augment the presidential casket and notes that the rug, which bears the Colonial-era slogan "Don't Tread On Me!" was a gift to Ida Saxton McKinley, whose husband, President William McKinley, "also fell prey to an assassin's bullets." The casket itself, purchased by President Warren Harding, was found collecting dust in the White House cellar. Now put to use, the casket holds not the late Mr. Kennedy, Ravenwood tells us, but the remains of Abraham Lincoln. This, added to McKinley's rug, unites the three whose terms ended with the pulling of triggers—a shell-pocked Hall of Presidents.

We are switched to Arlington National Cemetery for President Kennedy's (or is it Lincoln's?) burial. The First Lady lights the temporary eternal flame as Cardinal Cushing prepares to say a few words. But the cardinal is confused; he knows that a president is being buried yet is unsure of the country represented. His assistant whispers, "United Sta—" which Cushing picks up and finishes with a flourish. But what is the president's name?

ASSISTANT: John.
CUSHING: Yes . . . Yes . . . John . . . uh . . . uh
ASSISTANT: Fitzgerald.
CUSHING: Fitzgerald . . . FITZGERALD . . . . . .
ASSISTANT: Kennedy . . . you ass.
CUSHING: KENNEDY YOU ASS. Holy . . . Holy . . . Holy . . .
ASSISTANT: Mary.
CUSHING: Mother of . . . of . . .
ASSISTANT: God.
CUSHING: Huh?
ASSISTANT: GOD!

Cushing becomes agitated but no less confused. As the service ends he prays somewhat appropriately, "Blessed . . . is the fruit of thy . . . Wound?" and is corrected once again. While the cardinal stumbles over Jesus, Ravenwood turns to tell us that Kennedy foe Richard Nixon has expressed his regrets to the grieving family. The ex–vice president then contributed $5,000 to a fund to benefit Oswald's widow, Marina, established the night of the assassination by Kennedy cabinet member and former political foe Adlai Stevenson. And finally, the CIA will take no action against agent Lester Forsythe, who, upon hearing the first shot in Dealy Plaza, threw down his gun and shouted, "I surrender. Long live Lenin!" before passing out. In fact, CIA Director John McCone considers Forsythe "a hero" since he was the sole remaining agent at the scene of the killing. Ravenwood concludes his report, normal broadcasting activities are resumed. We are returned to *Ozzie and Harriet* and, one trusts, a happier climate.

The Death of JFK was performed at Le Galerie in the first weeks of 1964 as part of a Bread and Circuses "satirical revue." The stage was barely cleared of swastikas, abused amputees, and horse blood before O'Donoghue dragged Kennedy's corpse into view. The country remained in official mourning at the beginning of the new year, and to satirize what is regarded by many as *the* profound moment in American affairs required a willful neglect of "good taste"—and perhaps common sense, given the intensity of public emotion. But O'Donoghue was equally intense and on somewhat of a roll following the *malaise* plays. If not the leader of Bread and Circuses, he was certainly the troupe's keenest shot, and what better way to prove this than to fix aim on the taboo of the hour.

He smelled blood in Dallas, but it was media and political reaction to the killing that sent him into a frenzy, and here O'Donoghue stood virtually alone. (Ephram Robbins wrote the Cardinal Cushing bit, its tone influenced by O'Donoghue.) Few comics risked routines based on the assassination for fear of offending the public and the Holy Family itself. *The Realist*'s editor, Paul Krassner, referred to Oswald and the "lone nut" theory in a performance the day after Kennedy's (and the day before Oswald's) death; Lenny Bruce followed his friend's lead a week later at the Village Theater in New York.

Bruce's take on the assassination was perhaps the most anticipated of any humorist's in the country. When he took the stage audience tension was acute. Bruce removed the microphone from its stand, allowed the applause to subside, and said, "*Whew!* Vaughn Meader is *screwed*. . . ." Bruce chided Jackie for not being a good wife at the moment of truth, and noted that the First Widow was "hauling ass" when the fatal shot burst her husband's skull. Police detectives in the audience were appalled by Bruce's ribbing of Mrs. Kennedy and would use it as evidence in later obscenity charges against the comedian.

O'Donoghue was not as high-profile as Lenny Bruce and did not risk arrest, so he was free to plow straight into the issue sans care or caution. Performed in the postassassination atmosphere, *The Death of JFK* appeared intentionally tasteless, and to a degree this was true and quite necessary. If a satirist is unwilling to be soiled by sacred ground—or in this case, splattered by sacred blood—he then is unworthy of the title and should instead tell jokes about airline food. *JFK* rates definitely as satire, yet O'Donoghue did not view himself strictly as a satirist: he was a playwright, and satire was but one of his weapons. Still, his strikes against official mendacity and cowardice, mob thinking, hero worship, media manipulation of death and tragedy were accurate and forceful. *JFK* lacked the layers of absurdity he so carefully (and in parts pretentiously) designed for *le théâtre de malaise*. In what was a swiftly penned one-act play, O'Donoghue had time only for direct hits; images and gags he would otherwise expand upon, edit, or discard were brought promptly to the page and performed.★

As he would with much of his work, O'Donoghue reworked parts of *JFK* for potential use in other pieces. William Manchester's book on the assassination provided his mill fresh grist. Published by Harper and Row in 1967, *The Death of a President* was Manchester's hymnal to Camelot and its king. But prior to publication, Manchester received pressure from the Kennedy camp, primarily from Jackie and RFK speechwriter Richard Goodwin, to alter his already partisan manuscript to accommodate their every minor qualm; and his critical portrayal of Lyndon Johnson was softened so as not to anger the president and damage the party (and thus Bobby's and Teddy's presidential chances). The book's expurgated bits inspired considerable commentary: Just what did Manchester leave out? O'Donoghue imagined what Manchester was forced to exclude.

Page 43. "After the shots, I looked down at the scarlet blood that covered my pink wool dress and noted, with mounting horror, that it . . . it *clashed!*"

Page 226. "You know, he still looks better than Dick Nixon!"

★However, the play was not conceived and performed as quickly as O'Donoghue later claimed. Like the baby and the gun, O'Donoghue scrambled the facts for dramatic effect and said that he staged *JFK three* days after the assassination. His press release of December 2 made no mention of the play as he was still consumed by *le théâtre de malaise*, and the impossibility of such a sharp turnaround, especially with ailing actors, would have prevented his producing *JFK* in the time frame he later set.

Page 257. "Ah'm callin' it 'The Great Society'! Yawl kin take that 'New Frontier' shit an' shove it up yer ass! An' git them gawddam P-T boats outta muh office!!''

Page 292. "I guess my biggest disappointment came three days after the burial when Jack didn't arise from the dead."

Some of these Manchester book "excerpts" turned up in a July 1970 *National Lampoon* piece, "Diana Barrymore's Drinking Songs" (which also included John-John saluting from atop the Chappaquiddick bridge). But O'Donoghue's parody of Manchester paled when set against Paul Krassner's "The Parts Left Out of the Kennedy Book," which appeared in *The Realist*. In Krassner's version, Jackie walks to the back of Air Force One, where the body of JFK rests. There she spies Lyndon Johnson "crouching over the corpse . . . breathing hard and moving his body rhythmically. At first I thought he must be performing some mysterious symbolic rite he'd learned from Mexicans or Indians as a boy. And then I realized—there is only one way to say this—he was literally fucking my husband in the throat. In the bullet wound in the front of his throat. He reached a climax and dismounted. I froze. The next thing I remember, he was being sworn in as the new President."

Before his Manchester parody appeared on those newsstands that would display it (a good many did not), Krassner told Terry Southern of his idea and Southern in turn used the image in a short story, "The Blood of a Wig." In contrast to Krassner's clinical approach, Southern gave the hideous concept his own special touch: Jackie sees LBJ, "gasps, and is literally slammed back against the door by the sheer impact of the outrageous horror confronting her: i.e., the hulking Texan, silhouette at the casket, its lid half raised, and he hunching bestially, his coarse animal member thrusting into the casket, and indeed into the neck-wound itself. '*Great God,*' she cries, 'how heinous! It must be a case of . . . of . . . NECK-ROPHILIA!' "

In his *JFK* play, O'Donoghue caught perfectly the mood of national mourning and dealt with it viciously. On the Manchester front, however, O'Donoghue was surpassed by two master satirists. Jackie's obsession with style in the face of death is fine, and LBJ's coarse manner rings true; but Krassner and Southern take the rancor that existed between the Kennedys and Johnson to its extreme and fitting conclusion. (Surely the massacre of peasants wasn't LBJ's *only* deviate practice.) It was one of the few times O'Donoghue would find himself beaten to the knockout blow.

O'Donoghue's mother adored *The Death of JFK*; her hatred of liberals led her to love the play's defiant tone. But *JFK* and the revue it was part of enjoyed a short run and did not, as did *malaise*, stir up local theatergoers to a significant extent. This was of small importance to O'Donoghue as he looked past Bread and Circuses and toward other venues. Shortly after *JFK* closed, he struck a deal with a tiny publishing "house" (more likely a tent) called Plastique Press in nearby Pittsford, New York. Plastique agreed to print a "limited edition paperback" of all the *malaise* plays in March and granted readers an early glimpse of this "new and fresh playwright" by running *Michael Hip and the Pale Dry Hip-Machine* in its mimeographed organ, *Plastique*.

It's easy to see why *Plastique*'s editors were taken with O'Donoghue. Their publication reflected a self-conscious, bohemian "degeneracy." Misspellings and typos frequently appear, and the layout is inferior to that of an average high school newspaper. Clearly money was lacking, as was editorial competence. But when they read O'Donoghue's plays they knew—or someone knew—that his was quality work. Also, his reputation as an artistic risk-taker was well-known throughout alternative Rochester, so he would, in theory, help lift *Plastique* to a provocative level.

O'Donoghue himself had grown bored with Rochester, and his willingness to allow *Plastique* to publish *Michael Hip*, apart from the minor publicity he would receive from this and the subsequent collection, showed he was prepared for a transition. But *Plastique* laid out *Michael Hip* so poorly that it resembles a shopping mall flyer. The play's humor is smothered by the mess, typos included, and one cannot believe that O'Donoghue would tolerate such an amateurish display. If *Plastique*'s ineptitude stoked his anger (a plausible scenario, given his attachment to his work), a letter he received at the time of publication certainly doused it.

After *le théâtre de malaise* closed, O'Donoghue mailed a copy of *the automation of caprice* to the *Evergreen Review* in the hope that he might join the likes of Beckett, Burroughs, Southern, and Artaud. O'Donoghue had continued to read *Evergreen* since leaving San Francisco, and he recognized that this was the ultimate proving ground: If he was ever to be taken seriously as a playwright he needed to mix with the heavy hitters in their environment. And *Evergreen* represented the best in new/dissident literature and art. Though confident in his talent as a writer, O'Donoghue must have felt that *caprice* stood a slim chance of slipping through *Evergreen*'s gate. In form as well as tone, *caprice* resembled little else in the magazine, and it's likely that O'Donoghue sent it off and considered the matter closed. Why else would he then hand his best work to date to an outfit such as Plastique Press?

But O'Donoghue did hear from *Evergreen*:

GROVE PRESS, INC.
64 UNIVERSITY PLACE
NEW YORK 3, NEW YORK
OREGON 4-7200

February 13, 1964

Mr. O'Donohue:

Many thanks for letting us see THE AUTOMATION
OF CAPRICE which we have decided to use in
EVERGREEN REVIEW. When the manuscript is set
in type we will send proofs for your approval.

Would you be so kind as to send us a few lines
of biographical information?

Sincerely,

Martin Brynien

and its acceptance of his play set in motion his final departure from
"the sticks."

There exist no copies of the proposed Plastique book of the *malaise*
plays; O'Donoghue must have terminated the project. Now that he was
to be published in *Evergreen Review* and his work was to be the property
of Grove Press, there was no reason for him to honor the Plastique
agreement. More important than this was the effect the news had on his
marriage. By March it became clear to O'Donoghue that his decision to
marry a woman with three young children had been a huge mistake. By

all accounts he was enamored of his new family (save for the baby's crying—BANG!), but the pressure of raising and providing for them was too much for him. He longed to be a successful writer whose life matched the feeling of his words.

The strain had taken its toll on Bickel and the kids, too, and they often left O'Donoghue to himself. They traveled to Niagara Falls and sent postcards with love to "Daddy." They spent time with Barbara and Michael James in Sauquoit, and there were periods when the kids lived in the Donohue home. Back in Thayer Street, O'Donoghue wrote poetry and began work on a novel. He would show the *Evergreen* editors the other *malaise* plays, of course; but he had to develop new material to fully exploit the opportunity, and this required of O'Donoghue a shift in priorities. The days spent alone buried in work convinced him, if any doubt remained, of the need to return to single life.

The drift to divorce had been steady; by June the marriage sank from view after six months of negligible effort, at least on O'Donoghue's part. It is unclear if the ending was harsh, but it was certainly less than amicable. O'Donoghue had more to gain from a break than did Bickel (he later described the marriage as "traumatic"), but evidence suggests that both acknowledged the futility of the situation and simply called it quits. Apart from a few postdivorce phone calls, O'Donoghue and Bickel never again spoke to one another. She followed his career, and when O'Donoghue died, Bickel (her surname now Cronin) sent her condolences and called to comfort O'Donoghue's widow.

Released from the father trap, O'Donoghue concentrated on leaving Rochester. He had little money, although he could turn to Barbara for ready cash. He had few contacts in Manhattan but felt he could build on his exposure in *Evergreen*. To his parents, it seemed he had been there before: ready to bolt for the larger city, no job secured, no clear plan mapped out. But this time was different. When he had left college for San Francisco O'Donoghue had had only his *Ugh* experience to drive him. Experimentation lay ahead, his voice to deepen gradually. Four years later he began to hit his creative stride, and the next step, New York, could no longer be put off.

His Thayer Street neighbors were probably glad to see him go. O'Donoghue was not, as witnesses say at a murder scene, a quiet type who kept to himself. He drove a broken-down Datsun that he despised. When it rained the car's wires got wet and the thing failed to start. O'Donoghue would circle the Datsun in a rage, trusty blank revolver in hand, and fire shot after shot at the car while the neighbors peered out their windows. Other times he received complaints from the tenants who lived below his apartment. They felt that excessive noise issued daily from their ceiling. So O'Donoghue added to their torment by rolling a bowling ball back and forth on his hallway's long wooden floor.

After several complaints the police were summoned. O'Donoghue, who was either tipped off to their arrival or simply anticipated a response, was prepared. When he opened his door to the cops, he explained that the noise came from his cat's swatting a small plastic ball. The cops looked down and saw the cat sitting next to the ball; O'Donoghue casually smoked a cigarette and asked why such a fuss was being made. The police left, and O'Donoghue resumed the bowling ball routine.

O'Donoghue's feeling for landlords was equally charitable. Before he moved out of one apartment, he painted the apartment's interior completely black—including the phone, the windows, and the floor. To heighten the dramatic effect, he poured cement mix down the toilet. When he prepared to leave Thayer Street, O'Donoghue focused on *that* apartment's toilet since it routinely overflowed and his landlady had failed to have it repaired. During the week leading to his departure, O'Donoghue ceased to flush the toilet after each use and allowed the waste to stagnate. On his final day there he covered the waste with cleanser to kill the stench, then set the seat cover down to hide the mess. He knew that the next person to flush would encounter the remnants of a week's worth of meals. This served as O'Donoghue's exit line from the Rochester stage, delivered in absentia.

> *We are the holy*
> *men*
> *Am serving tea*
> *and singing*
> *Ra's feat over*
> *Broken mass.*
> *Between the*
> *reader*
> *And the poem*
> *Between the*
> *symbol*
> *And the meaning*
> *Falls the footnote*
> *OOO that*
> *Huxleyian raga—*
> *It's so mystic*
> *So polylinguistic*
> *Mistah Berlitz*
> *—he dead.*

It was late January 1964. Barney Rosset and Fred Jordan, editor and managing editor for *Evergreen Review*, respectively, riffled through a stack of unsolicited manuscripts. The two men were ensconced in Rosset's house in East Hampton, Long Island, searching for something of interest. Though *Evergreen* relied on a stable of famous noncommercial talent, the magazine made its name by publishing unknown writers and artists whose work was detested by most other editors. In order to find those few who could make the cut, Rosset and Jordan spent hours knee-deep in slush piles; on this particular January afternoon, their eyes strained by numerous bad submissions, Jordan spied an ususual-looking manuscript titled *the automation of caprice* by Michael O'Donoghue.

Jordan looked over the play. Sex, torture, random violence, beastiality, and drug-induced hallucinations rubbed the redness from his eyes. He showed *caprice* to Rosset, who read it and seconded Jordan's positive reaction. "It was a weird vision," Jordan remembered. O'Donoghue, he felt, "was obviously knowledgeable about literature." The editors were also impressed with the manuscript's appearance. O'Donoghue's placement of words and odd use of punctuation gave the play the look of a manifesto with stage directions. It was a wise move by O'Donoghue. Unknown and unsolicited, he needed to grab the editors' attention and guide them to the play's action in one swift motion, and he succeeded. His knack for precision ingrained, he now framed his professional work with the same care as he once designed his scrapbooks.

Eager to begin life as a New York writer, O'Donoghue traveled by bus to Manhattan in the early fall of 1964. The day he arrived he had no place to stay, but this was a secondary concern: O'Donoghue wanted his presence felt immediately. He went straight to the Caffe Cino, a coffeehouse/performance space in Greenwich Village, and asked for someone to read and evaluate his work while he waited. An actress there to rehearse a play titled *Happening* stared at O'Donoghue and said nothing; but the play's director, Larry Loonin, showed interest and was handed a black binder that contained the *malaise* plays.

Loonin scanned the scripts. From time to time he'd look up at O'Donoghue, who quietly smoked but bore an intense expression. The assault of the images in the plays combined with the severe presence of the author struck Loonin hard: O'Donoghue did not fail in his effort to impress. The two went out to eat and talk, and a bond was quickly formed. O'Donoghue sensed this and knew that he needed a bed for the night. So he abruptly asked if he could sleep at Loonin's place. Loonin hesitated. *Who* was this guy? he wondered. Was he dangerous? Crazy? Hoping to ease Loonin's anxiety, O'Donoghue offered his mother as a reference. "Call her," he said as he scribbled Barbara's phone number. Loonin replied that a call was unnecessary. O'Donoghue then produced his driver's license, and Loonin noticed that he and the young writer shared the same birthday. He went with his gut and relented.

For the next several days O'Donoghue stayed at Loonin's apartment at 126 MacDougal Street. He made a number of phone calls during this time, the majority long-distance to Rochester. Loonin overheard some of these calls, and it appeared that O'Donoghue used every contact he had, every friend of a friend, to secure an apartment uptown. Soon he arranged to share a tiny, fifth-floor walkup at 314 East Ninety-first Street with a social worker called Teddy. Though he preferred to live in the Village (on occasion he'd stay with Loonin), O'Donoghue had to settle for a railroad flat in the rather nonartistic neighborhood of Yorktown. Ultimately his address was unimportant. O'Donoghue was in New York as the city entered a vibrant artistic period. The opportunity to establish his name and work finally lay before him.

four

False dreams are the only dreams worth having.

The *Evergreen Review*'s circulation, higher than that of most other small arts magazines, continued to grow through the early 1960s. In the summer of 1964 *Evergreen* went from quarto, or roughly coat pocket size, to a glossy eight-by-eleven inches, the standard size for commercial magazines. The change led to a boom in circulation, from 100,000 to 250,000 per issue, and with it some national attention. A Republican congressman from Michigan, Gerald Ford, waved a copy of *Evergreen* while on the House floor and denounced it as pornographic. Ford objected to a photo of his future employer, Richard Nixon, set against the image of a nude woman who bore no resemblance to Nixon's wife, Pat.

Another issue of *Evergreen,* April–May 1964, was seized in a raid by the Hicksville, Long Island, vice squad. A woman who worked in the plant where *Evergreen* was printed found obscene the portfolio of photographer Emil J. Cadoo, whose work appeared in the issue. Her husband, a police detective with the local force, studied the nude portraits and agreed. The vice squad then confiscated 21,000 unbound copies and took them to the police station for, presumably, further study. The copies remained impounded until *Evergreen*'s lawyers entered the fray and three federal judges ordered the copies released.

On the tail of this and other skirmishes came Michael O'Donoghue's *Evergreen* debut. *The automation of caprice* was featured in the August–September 1964 issue, and to O'Donoghue's delight it was published exactly as he intended. So as not to confuse any reader taken with his work, O'Donoghue's name appears five times in the piece, and a sixth mention is made in the author's bio at the bottom of the page. He refers to *renaissance* and *le théâtre de malaise,* but the bio's final sentence promises something more: "He is presently writing a novel 'promoting mass suicide.' " The novel, conceived in Rochester, was at this point a mass of notes that formed a crude but lengthy outline titled *a death book*.

Set in the "surprisingly near future," *death book* focuses on a protagonist named Madison Avenue Man (who, for some reason, O'Donoghue dubs "MMA"). He is summoned to Freedom City, "the Capital of the World," by the Captain, a Greek national who runs a nameless, global empire. The Captain tells MMA that due to ceaseless breeding Earth's population will soon exceed man's technological ability to provide food, manage waste, and prevent the conflicts that will inevitably follow. MMA's mission is vital: to undermine optimism and project a future dystopia so bleak that people will choose suicide over life. "You will sell death," the Captain tells MMA. "It will be history's greatest advertising campaign. Life must become Brand X." Of course, MMA will be given unlimited funds and resources to achieve this goal.

The propaganda blitz begins, and consumers obediently drop like insects. A pleasant tasting suicide pill called Enditol is posthumously endorsed by dead celebrities and sales reach into the millions. Bodies pile up; funerals are performed on conveyor belts. The campaign is so successful that "civilized" methods of body disposal no longer work. Corpses rot in the street before they can be collected and buried. So Nazi gas ovens are dusted off and updated, and crematoriums operate around the clock to meet the demand.

Mass suicide escalates, and soon the world is a voluntary death camp. The Captain goes mad in the face of his "success" and disappears. Cut loose, MMA roams the grim landscape until he spots people dancing on a distant hill. Encouraged, he approaches them; but they are the Castration Society, a dissident population-control group turned to vigilantism. They grab MMA and pull down his pants as a beautiful woman in a ceremonial robe steps forward holding a small silver knife. She raises it, and the sun reflects on the edge of the blade . . .

O'Donoghue never expanded his notes into a novel. The plot, at least in outline form, is one-dimensional. A few minor characters pop up, but all lack the muscle necessary to support the two major figures. Still *a death book* contains some stunning imagery that leans more to cinema than to print.

The Captain's office is a space of majestic proportions fallen to disrepair. Paper and broken glass litter the polished floor; crystal ashtrays overflow with cigarette butts; a priceless Persian rug sports a large hole from a fire. Despite a thousand open windows, the air remains stale. A bird flies wildly across the office and the Captain attempts to shoot it down while he talks to MMA. He misses continually as bullets rip through plaster and chip marble. After several spent clips the bird is hit and falls; its broken wings flap as it dies, and the sound echoes around the two men, who continue their discussion.

O'Donoghue's notes for the next-to-last chapter suggest a Kafka/ Burroughs influence, and a certain Spanish master is cited, too:

> The ovens are cold. Bodies lie piled in decay, almost fused into each other as the carrion has rotted and given way. The ensuing scenes are tableauxs of horror, robbing reason from MMA. Stench and decay. Animals run wild in the streets, dogs eating people, Siamese cats gnawing neck of old lady. This is a Goya etching. Clean, vivid, surrealistic, so real that it is unreal. Outré and grotesque. The horror is overwhelming. . . .

O'Donoghue forges an interesting if makeshift link between advertising and human eradication; had he fleshed out this "etching" he might have realized in words the level of terror Goya captured on canvas. Indeed, *a death book* could have been, in its modest way, a satirical addition to the critiques of mass culture written by Vance Packard and C. Wright Mills.

But O'Donoghue abandoned the project. He had extensively researched the psychology of suicide, death symbols, castration anxiety, and mob mentality; but his notes came to nothing and were placed in his growing stack of files. At some point, he thought, the notes could be used for another project. Presently *Evergreen* wanted more material, and O'Donoghue typed up a list of new ideas. However, his abject poverty made enthusiasm difficult. When Fred Jordan first met O'Donoghue he thought the young writer was "deeply depressed. He had this take on the world which was very harsh and I felt very close to him. He wasn't terribly funny in conversation, but he had that sharp satirical vision which I liked so much."

Evergreen could pay only $100 per submission. And since the magazine was a monthly, O'Donoghue was left with a large gap in what passed for an income. His mother made sure that he would be able to buy food, but O'Donoghue was forced yet again to find other work. He wandered Manhattan in search of a job he could stand to perform, something that wouldn't darken his already bleak mood. Then, in midtown, he discovered Brentano's, a venerable New York bookstore located on Fifth Avenue. He applied for and received a job as a clerk. The position paid little, but O'Donoghue found ways to extend his measly salary—his primary tactic was to pocket small amounts of money from the store's till, just enough to avoid suspicion. After all, he was not a clerk but a writer published by one of America's more notorious magazines. Why should he starve on a clerk's wages? And what better place for a writer to rob than a bookstore?

At Brentano's, O'Donoghue was often asked by customers to recommend books. Doubtless he pushed his favorite authors, Kafka, Conan Doyle, Hawthorne; writers with cachet left to the discriminating few. There were new favorites as well, Nathaniel West and Vladimir Nabokov, whose novel *Lolita* O'Donoghue admired. Then there was another writer whose newest effort had been released in the States a few months before. *This* was a book that O'Donoghue relished in promoting. "Older women would come in and say, 'I'd like a book for my niece/daughter,' " he later recalled. "And I'd say, 'How old is she?' 'About sixteen or seventeen.' So I'd say 'Oh, I have just the book. It's a book about a girl her age who has all sorts of adventures and stuff and she'll just love it.' And then I'd sell them *Candy* by Terry Southern. One woman came back livid with rage. But I know that book changed some of those girls' lives. Forever."

Written by Southern and Mason Hoffenberg (the collaboration weighed heaviest at Southern's end), *Candy* was seen by many as a satire of pornography. Though the sex is in portions intimately described then turned to comic effect, *Candy* gently knocks a number of topics, from medicine to religion to academia. Still, sex drives the story. Like Nabokov's nymphet, Candy Christian is a girl who inspires lewd thoughts. Lolita is smarter than Candy—savvier, too. Where Lolita manipulates her mother and two older men, Candy simply accepts the sexual advances made by practically anyone, a pathetic hunchback included. She is the ultimate altruist. Through her the dregs of society have their way, and she is left tingling but she never feels complete. Thus her ongoing adventures.

There are grand moments in *Candy,* and the book contains some of Southern's best writing. But this was overlooked by French authorities in 1957, when *Candy* first appeared in Paris. (The authors originally shared the pseudonym Maxwell Kenton.) The government of Charles de Gaulle banned the book on grounds of indecency. Olympia Press, the underground house that delivered both *Lolita* and *Candy,* changed the novel's title to *Lollipop;* it re-emerged, original text intact, and was left alone to attract a sizable following. Seven years and countless pirate editions later, *Candy* came to America by way of Putnam and helped broaden the national debate over "obscenity" and artistic freedom.

O'Donoghue followed the debate as it related to *Candy.* He clipped reviews of the book from *Newsweek, Time,* the *New York Review,* and the *New York Herald Tribune* and placed them alongside Southern's magazine essays in a file devoted to the writer. Most critics liked *Candy* in parts, but many felt it light and uneven. Those critics beholden to Puritan ethics were, of course, put off by the book's depictions of premarital sex, a white girl violated by the darker breeds, etc. But instead of lashing out in the name of Morality, they took a different and rather inspired position. Alfred Chester, who reviewed *Candy* in *Book Week,* described it perfectly:

> What the reader should be on guard against is that posture now being assumed in some dubious American circles (*Time* magazine is a case in point) which pretends very noisily and very frequently to be already bored with sex in literature. This pretense at boredom is, in fact, a concealment of outrage, for a sexually free people, free to accept or reject the act or the art, are automatically disencumbered of numerous guilts and thus harder to control, to manipulate, to indoctrinate, to own.

Indeed, the *Time* hack who dismissed *Candy* feigned several yawns before concluding that the book was "outrageous in detail" and "dirty as hell." That perception, even by *Candy*'s defenders, helped keep the book high on best-seller lists during the summer of 1964. What had been considered daring in the late 1940s and through the 1950s was becoming commonplace—at least to the extent that not every new author was threatened with legal action, though a few were selectively targeted. The once rigid culture loosened and could no longer restrict the explicit in sexual and political art.

As he did with *Flash and Filigree* and Southern's novella *The Magic Christian,* O'Donoghue pored over *Candy* and studied its humorous rhythm. When it came to creative influence, O'Donoghue looked to an eclectic set of writers; but Terry Southern remained for him the ultimate source. He marveled at the way Southern caught the sound of everyday speech and set it perfectly in place. He envied Southern's knack for italizing the *right* word at key comic moments. O'Donoghue's self-confidence as a writer was so strong as to border on arrogance, but when faced with Southern's work he ceded ground, if not the game.

Candy did more than amuse and inspire O'Donoghue; the story touched off an idea that O'Donoghue had mulled over for the better part of a year. In *the automation of caprice,* the character Ramona Wedgewood, a wealthy, beautiful young woman, met with misfortune and abuse. The segment was brief, the character raw, but Ramona stuck in O'Donoghue's mind. As he developed her he dropped the name Ramona in favor of Holly and thought of ways to expand the original segment to either play or novel length. In *Candy* the heroine is not rich or sophisticated, yet her looks and disposition lead her steadily into trouble. O'Donoghue's Holly lived worlds away from Candy Christian, but the concept of her also suffering endless despair seemed to him the ideal approach.

Surely there are better gifts God could have given us than life.

Toward the end of 1964, Fred Jordan contacted Dell Comics. He wanted to modify *Evergreen*'s appearance a bit by bringing in an artist who could draw in the style of *Superman*. Jordan was referred to a free-lance cartoonist, Frank Springer, whose work for Dell included comic book adaptations of recent Hollywood fare. (At the time Jordan reached him, Springer had just finished an adaptation of *The Raven,* which starred Boris Karloff and a young Jack Nicholson.) The *Evergreen* editor asked Springer if he was interested in collaborating with one of the magazine's newer writers. Since Jordan's offer represented another paycheck, all-important to any freelance artist, Springer accepted, but said he wasn't familiar with Michael O'Donoghue.

A native of Queens, New York, and a graduate of Syracuse University, where he studied art from 1948 to 1952, Frank Springer was atypical for an *Evergreen* contributor. He did not smoke marijuana and work on the railroad like Jack Kerouac. Unlike William S. Burroughs, he'd never dabbled in heroin and handguns. He was neither bohemian nor revolutionary, and his work inspired no morality campaigns. Springer's road to *Evergreen* ran from the U.S. Army at Fort Dix (he drew sports cartoons in the base newspaper, the *Post*) and through his five-year apprenticeship on the popular comic strip *Terry and the Pirates*. He embodied the American suburban archetype: He lived with his wife and children in Greenlawn, Long Island, and was conservative in dress and demeanor. Springer's one similarity to the *Evergreen* crowd was perhaps his love of jazz.

Despite his "straight" persona, Springer recognized talent. He had his aesthetic biases but could see beyond them when shown, as is said, "the genuine article." Still, nothing in his professional background could have prepared him for Michael O'Donoghue; yet when the two were paired by Fred Jordan, Springer warmed to the arrangement with little fuss. O'Donoghue, too, appreciated what Jordan had in mind and rose instantly to the demands of the comic book format.

O'Donoghue and Springer first met over the phone. They were assigned to create an in-house ad for *Evergreen*; O'Donoghue tossed a few ideas Springer's way, Springer told O'Donoghue what could or could not be done, and soon they settled on a concept. There was no friction to speak of, no initial "feeling out" process; their seemingly disparate styles fell gracefully into line. If Jordan at all anticipated the brilliant collaboration that was to come, then his editorial instincts rivaled the calculations of any master chemist.

The standard *Evergreen* house ad was self-consciously "hip" and played off themes both intellectual and bohemian. The magazine emphasized its sexually charged and artistically seditious reputation to lure new subscribers, and here the combination proved successful. But Jordan wanted to vary *Evergreen*'s approach to the ads and was anxious to see his new creative team in action. So O'Donoghue repaired to his type-writer, lit the first of many cigarettes, and pounded out a script for Springer to illustrate.

Firm in his knowledge of dissident literature, O'Donoghue could have conformed to the *Evergreen* ad style. But he chose instead to parody what at the time was perhaps the nation's most recognizable print adver-tisement: the cartoon in which a weakling becomes a man after reading a book "by" Charles Atlas. O'Donoghue knew that Springer could dupli-cate the cartoon's look, and O'Donoghue himself easily captured its nar-rative. Indeed, the ad didn't satirize Atlas so much as it mocked the pretensions of the *Evergreen* faithful, a rather fresh approach to securing new readers.

"Buddy Can You Spare a Fin?" (next page) was completed and given to Jordan in early December of 1964. As Springer stepped on the elevator that would take him to Grove, he noticed a younger man there whose dress conveyed a "studied sloppiness." It was, of course, O'Donoghue; and though the collaborators had never met personally, they instinctively greeted one another and shook hands for the first time. Springer studied his new partner's appearance. O'Donoghue had longish hair and a wispy mustache that he would soon shave away. He wore "the uniform of the time"—that is, army jacket, jeans, crumpled shirt. This ran counter to Springer's suit and tie, which served as his uniform whenever he con-ducted business in Manhattan. They entered the Grove offices together, a mismatch in fashion but a force in combined talent.

> *Death is a virgin*
> *And snow is her veil.*
> *It covers a bride*
> *And it covers a trail.*

In early 1965, O'Donoghue quit his job at Brentano's and stayed at home writing and reading. He received money from his parents so he could eat, and he forged ahead with the "Holly" project. He scanned his *death book* notes for items that would fit his new novel and came across a reminder to "find out the meaning of 'Zeitgeist.' " O'Donoghue liked the sound of the word and thought it looked great when placed after Holly. Her first name lilted and was light on the tongue; her second name rushed forward and stopped on a dime. Satisfied, O'Donoghue conceived a gauntlet of exotic dangers through which Holly Zeit-Geist would pass. She would, he hoped, be true to her name and act as the guiding spirit of her time.

The Twilight Maelstrom of Cookie Lavagetto appeared in the March

J.P. SARTRE, NOTED AUTHOR, ASKS:

BUDDY CAN YOU SPARE A FIN?

ONLY **15 MINUTES** A DAY MOLDS A **VITAL** AND MORE **INTERESTING** YOU !!!

CHUCK, HANDSOME, YOUNG IBM EXECUTIVE, VISITS A COFFEE HOUSE...

75¢ FOR A **CUP OF COFFEE !!!** ARE YOU KIDDING?

AT A NEARBY TABLE, A GROUP OF BOHEMIANS DISCUSS CONTEMPORARY ARTS.

ORNETTE COLEMAN, SUMMERHILL, DJUNA BARNES!

LARRY RIVERS, DR. SAX!

EDDIE ALBEE, HAND-HELD CAMERA, ARRABAL!

CHUCK JOINS IN...

BOY, THAT **EDNA FERBER** IS ONE **HELL** OF A WRITER !!!

BAM!

EDNA FERBER !?!

J'ACCUSE!

BACK HOME...

WHAT'S **WRONG** WITH ME? WELL BUILT! NAIL DOWN 15 THOU A YEAR!

GLEN MILLER RECORDS

WALTER KEENE PRINT OF "NATALIE WOOD AS A CHILD"

DRAT IT ALL, ANYWAY !!!

BLAM!

COMPLETE COLLECTION OF NATIONAL GEOGRAPHIC SINCE 1938

BRIGHT IDEA!

HELLO! WHAT'S THIS? SUBSCRIBE TO THE **EVERGREEN REVIEW** — SIX ISSUES FOR FIVE DOLLARS — CLIP OUT COUPON... HMMM... IT'S WORTH A TRY!

ONE YEAR LATER...

CHUCK RETURNS...

LOOK! HERE COMES THAT *CREEP* AGAIN!

LET'S PUT HIM DOWN!

JAZZ TONIGHT

READ ANY *GOOD BOOKS* LATELY? HA, HA HA !!!

MARCEL DUCHAMP, MORNING GLORY SEEDS, TERRY SOUTHERN, MONK, SOREN KIERKEGAARD, NOVA EXPRESS, JOHN CAGE, PABLO NERUDA, BIG SUR, NORMAN MAILER'S "EXISTENTIALIST HERO", ROGER CORMAN, BEVERLY KENNY, GELBER...

...MALAPARTE, SATIE, MIRACULOUS MANDARIN, KIF, GENET, JOHN CHAMBERLAIN, MERCE CUNNINGHAM, KIKI, **-AND-** THE CABINET OF DOCTOR CALIGARI!

WOW!

GASP!

WE'RE WIPED OUT !!!

CHUCK BABY — LET'S FALL BY MY PAD AND DIG SOME HORACE SILVER!

I'M HIP!

EVERGREEN REVIEW

THE END

MAIL $$ SAVING COUPON TODAY !!!

EVERGREEN REVIEW   R114
80 UNIVERSITY PL., N.Y. 3, N.Y.

Yes, I am over 18 years of age. Please rush one year's subscription (6 issues) to Evergreen Review. One Fin ($5.00) enclosed.

Name ....
Street ....
City .... Zone ...... State ......
(please print)
I understand no salesman will call upon me.

SNIP ALONG DOTTED LINE

WRITTEN BY MICHAEL O'DONOGHUE, DRAWN BY FRANK SPRINGER

1965 *Evergreen Review.* Like *caprice,* the play was published precisely as O'Donoghue had designed it, no editorial "improvements" made. O'Donoghue received another hundred-dollar check, and starvation and homelessness were averted once again. One afternoon shortly after *Cookie* appeared, O'Donoghue and his roommate, Teddy, were on the floor of their apartment eating cherries. A fellow social worker named Kate came to visit and brought with her a friend, Paula Levy. Introductions were made; O'Donoghue and Levy immediately clicked. They talked for hours, though O'Donoghue dominated the conversation. That night he took her to *Citizen Kane,* a film Levy had never seen. They then drove around the city in Levy's car until sunrise.

Like O'Donoghue, Paula Levy was recently divorced. She lived in her hometown of West Orange, New Jersey, and had dropped out of Rugters University law school as her marriage broke up. She was five feet tall with medium-length black hair, was smart, and possessed a strong romantic streak. Levy wasn't looking for someone new, but she positively fell for O'Donoghue, who reciprocated Levy's affection. After their night together, O'Donoghue and Levy became nearly inseparable. Levy spent much of her time at the Ninety-first Street apartment until she moved to Manahattan several weeks later. She found a studio on Twenty-second Street off Gramercy Park; within days O'Donoghue joined her there. Teddy left Ninety-first Street for parts unknown, and O'Donoghue turned the apartment into his personal storage space. He brought his essential items to the studio downtown, and he and Levy set up house.

The move to Gramercy Park made sense. The studio was located in a better neighborhood, was within walking distance of Grove Press, was brighter and sunnier than the apartment uptown. It represented a fresh start for both, especially after an incident that occurred at Ninety-first Street just after the two met. Levy loved O'Donoghue but was less fond of his black cat, Octave. Named for the author of *The Torture Garden,* Octave liked lounging on the windowsill for hours on end. One day the window was open. Octave rolled back and off the sill and fell five flights to his death. O'Donoghue was devastated. When Levy arrived hours later he told her of the tragedy. He said that Octave had committed suicide because Levy hurt the cat's feelings. O'Donoghue expressed his grief with dramatic flair as Levy watched, intrigued.

The couple soon established a routine. Levy returned to Rutgers and law school, her days spent in class and in transit. O'Donoghue slept through much of the day and devoted the night to writing. Once Levy was in bed O'Donoghue began to type, occasionally jotting notes and asides on his pages with a black felt-tip pen. He preferred to write with the television on; the battle noise of war movies or the guttural dialogue of samurai films provided the right mix of sound. O'Donoghue drew energy from explosions and sword fights, and he hit the typewriter keys with a certain intensity. Cigarette smoke hung over the table as he pushed himself to complete or revise a piece by morning. Levy found comforting the sound of his typing, but the loud, all-night movies were sometimes an irritant. Yet the routine continued and pages of new material accumulated.

O'Donoghue worked on a number of items, but Holly Zeit-Geist took precedence over the rest. He made her a jet set socialite with long blond hair and an aquiline body. The idea was to send Holly from her world of rich friends into a cycle of torture and ceaseless hell. But O'Donoghue insisted that every reference be correct, no matter how minor the fact. And since Holly would suffer on several continents, he disappeared into the New York Public Library to research the customs and lore of obscure nations. When free of school, Levy assisted him. Fortunately for O'Donoghue, Levy's father gave her a living allowance, so he didn't need a day job. He was still poor but ends were met. Plus, he was with a woman who allowed him to concentrate on writing. Levy's indulgence made possible O'Donoghue's growth during this period, and he took full creative advantage of the opportunity.

Fred Jordan was pleased with the two *malaise* plays that appeared in *Evergreen*. Each served as an introduction to the twenty-five-year-old writer, brought a wider audience in touch with work seen only in Rochester. In the June 1965 issue, Jordan published a third *malaise* play, an altered version of *Michael Hip and the Pale-Dry Death Machine*. To assuage Jordan's request for new material, O'Donoghue changed the play's title to *M. A Column That Promotes Broken Watches for High School Dropouts*. He resurrects Captain Contrabando from *caprice,* makes him a baron, and sends him to die in the Spanish Civil War—but not before Ernest Hemingway, in a cameo appearance, enters a coma when the baron mentions castration. Also, Lenny Bruce shows up on *To Tell the Truth,* and mainlines "With an Enormous Hyperdermic Needle."

But Jordan wanted something written specifically for the magazine. He asked O'Donoghue for material and was given a few of the Holly Zeit-Geist pages. O'Donoghue said Holly was a novel-in-progress, but he would fashion the parts he had finished into an *Evergreen* piece. Jordan liked what he read; he forwarded the pages to Barney Rosset, who then suggested a change. The imagery was so dense, the references so exact, that Rosset felt Holly might work better as a comic strip. This stirred O'Donoghue. A comic, an *adult* comic, would strengthen the narrative and enhance its effect. Imagining Holly in danger was one thing, but to *see* her maltreated in a series of panels was preferable to O'Donoghue, and he brought the idea to Frank Springer's attention in late summer 1965.

Springer saw much in those early pages. He tapped into O'Dono-

ghue's extensive research and meticulous plot and began to visualize
Holly and her adventures. Springer traveled from Long Island to Manhattan for story conferences with O'Donoghue, who prepared for the meetings by studying a variety of comic books. As a child, O'Donoghue was
kept from reading comics by Barbara, who found them an insult to her
son's intelligence. Her snobbery had a lasting effect on him (and would
reflect on other areas of his life), and until he met Springer he never
thought to pick up *Detective Comics* or *Real Fantasy*. But once taken with
a project, O'Donoghue tended to full immersion.

He concentrated on superheroes and was drawn to the work of
Steve Ditko. A writer and artist for Marvel Comics, Ditko helped create
Spiderman, Dr. Strange, and the Incredible Hulk; but it was with Spiderman that Ditko made his name. The swift, smooth motion of the
character was combined with the smart-aleck wit of writer and Marvel
Comics founder Stan Lee. It was a combination O'Donoghue desired
for Holly—except the wisecracks in his strip were to carry real menace.
O'Donoghue asked Springer to approximate Ditko's style; he also sent
along a few pages of *The Flash* so Springer could study the comic's rapid
pace. O'Donoghue told his partner that they had to mix "a pop art and
pop literary concept" to bring Holly sufficiently to life. Springer was
impressed by O'Donoghue's groundwork and enthusiasm, but the young
writer needed to learn some of the rules of cartooning.

O'Donoghue had written far too much dialogue for each panel.
Springer explained to him that the comic book form, at least what they
were attempting, needed few words. "If you write a novel inside a
balloon," he said, "no one's going to read it." The same held true for
captions and narration. Springer urged O'Donoghue to think more in
visual terms and advised him to cut the bulk of his text. O'Donoghue
adjusted quickly. By their next meeting the text had been stripped down
to reasonable size, but O'Donoghue hoped to keep some of the lengthier
portions. He asked Springer to leave enough space in certain panels so
he could squeeze in the desired words. Springer accommodated where
he could, and this give-and-take continued throughout the strip's run.

The O'Donoghue-Springer collaboration lacked dramatic tension.
They did not argue or trade threats; O'Donoghue refrained from screaming, kicked no walls, destroyed no property. That behavior would later
arise from more volatile settings. Instead, the two polished characters and
action over many lunches. They met once at Ninety-first Street, and
then ever after at the Gramercy studio to discuss the story's development.
It was in every sense a business-only arrangement, save for O'Donoghue's
performances when explanations would not suffice. "Michael would act
out the stories and was very theatrical, almost like a stand-up comic,"
Springer recalled. "He was a little like Al Capp in this way. Capp was

Phoebe's creators: Frank Springer (l.) and O'Donoghue

extremely enthusiastic about his strip [*Li'l Abner*], and when he would describe a story he would collapse, laughing at his own stuff."

When the laughter ceased, O'Donoghue penned rough sketches of the action for Springer to follow. He clipped photos of models from glossy magazines. The women were sleek and wore chiffon dresses. All had black hair piled stylishly high; O'Donoghue preferred this to his original blond design. He also changed the name of the character from Holly to Phoebe. Holly was nice, but Phoebe, like Zeit-Geist, rhymed, and this made memorable the heroine's name. Where Holly seemed kittenish, Phoebe sounded plain, like Gertrude; her name stood in elegant contrast to the Bridget Bardot type Springer was drawing. O'Donoghue encouraged this angle, but he wanted balance. "She is very beautiful," he said in a note to Springer, "with features that can be a domineering icy handsomeness and yet can also be sweetly innocent."

Springer finished the first installment of *The Adventures of Phoebe Zeit-Geist* by early autumn. He incorporated most of O'Donoghue's changes, which at times were as wordy as his original text. But the revisions worked, the script was tight and funny, and Springer captured the balance his partner requested: Phoebe was as beautiful as O'Donoghue had pictured her. Fred Jordan loved the strip and approved it for publication in the November 1965 issue. There Phoebe would share space with an imported comic book heroine, Barbarella.

Created by Jean-Claude Forest, *Barbarella* became something of a cult comic in France in 1965. The action takes place in a fantasy world where the strip's heroine fucks a robot, battles an evil one-eyed queen, avoids venom spit out by a faceless monster, soars with a blindfolded angel named Pygar. Like Phoebe, Barbarella is beautiful and sex-driven; but she is clearheaded, strong, and able to sidestep danger and death. This, alas, was not to be with Phoebe.

Before *Phoebe*'s debut, O'Donoghue published a new piece, "Paris in the Twenties," in *Evergreen*'s September issue. It represented—apart from *Phoebe*—some of the best writing O'Donoghue would exhibit in the magazine. Narrated by an expatriate American named Jake, "Paris" deals with the "wild" behavior of the "Lost Generation" that gave the City of Lights its "madcap" reputation during that decade. The piece is episodic and opens at full speed (see left).

I recall I was fucking Josephine Boulanger (she was younger, of course). Yes, I was jazzing her—"Josephine" (as I called her). Jazzing her ON THE FLOOR, if I remember correctly. And all the while she sang "Trois Ballades de Mallarmé"—*beautifully*. After, we smoked long Russian cigarettes and chatted of Hitler's watercolors. The sun was warm and bright breezes moved the curtains. Paul Eluard came to visit later (we were still nude) and told us of Huneker's death. There was no more love-making that afternoon, I assure you.

Jake reminisces. A Hispano-Suiza, "a touring car the size of a locomotive," crashes into a crowd of people, killing twenty, their twisted bodies urinated on by a naked Chaim Soutine, who yells, "I PISS ON YOUR MIDDLE-CLASS MORALITIES!!!" This leads to laughter and rioting and bomb detonations. Later, Jake ravishes Madame Curie on a cobblestone street as a Negro saxophonist wails and couples tango on zinc tables. After dispensing with Madame, Jake joins the dancer Nijinsky for a bit of sniper fun. They rent a cheap Italian rifle and shoot at passersby while a heavy rain hinders their aim. A pumpkin vendor is hit, but no one is killed.

The week following sees Paris buried in Fauvist manifestos. Their "massive planes" strafe the city's streets with thousands of leaflets. Unfortunately for Jake's friend, Eugéne Brieux, a Fauvist pilot "carelessly left a bundle of manifestoes still crated and had tossed it from the plane, hitting Brieux." Since the leaflets are by now at shoulder level, it is an hour and forty minutes before Jake and Mata Hari reach their comrade who lies only yards away. Brieux dies, and Mata observes, "mustering a wan smile": "The ship is sinking." Thus the era ends. "Once their hearts belonged to DADA. Now their art belongs to MOMA."

As in parts of the *malaise* plays, O'Donoghue puts the notorious names of art and literature in strange and deadly situations. But in, say, *caprice,* Henry Miller and Scott Fitzgerald are pushed onstage for the sake of making an appearance, hallucination or not. However in "Paris," names are dropped casually, naturally; the thought of Nijinsky-as-sniper is ridiculous, yet it fits the tempo of the piece. One can visualize the dancer squeezing off rounds as bullets slice through a downpour. That O'Donoghue fills his piece with obscure figures of the period does help its flow; one avoids tripping over famous writers as they fuck, vomit blood, or lie in comas. In fact, O'Donoghue seems to test the *Evergreen* reader: You think yourself avant-garde? Well, who's *this* . . . ?

-2 Poems-*

The Untimely Demise of Madame X
(or)
"Shot in Her Box at the Opera"
... to Benjamin Peret, 1928.

My airplane is burning.
My formal gardens cross their legs.
Negroes have eaten up my sister.

My mother has been revoked.
Gypsies stole my father,
Repainted him,
And sold him across the border.

My wife is a sailor.

My wolves are housebroken.
My cat is a dog.
The goldfish drowned.

Emery dust in my monorail.

My arsenal is doves.
My caprice is annotated.
The bathtub tried to bite me
And did.

Hunchbacks gave me money.

My screams are dead snowflakes
Falling on dead people
Making them feel all warm and loved.

The Dynamite Museum

... after it happened, all these things we found
   in the ruins.

a stuffed indian with dead feathers.
a snare drum mouche for the inside thigh.
an enormous owl.
a mirror composed of white flesh.
3 zinc centipedes.
a blind fish.
another blind fish.
another zinc centipede.
a hand-painted virgin.
a broken grasshopper and a mallet to keep
   it that way.
a mezzotint made from a photograph of a
   zinc centipede.
a sign that read "DEFENSE DE FUMER".

.... after it happened, all these things we found
   in the ruins.

a glass monkey who sang Debussy.
a piano that told one's fortune.
a watch that guessed one's sex.

*author's note: I originally wrote these poems in French and
translated them into English. They lose quite a bit in translation.

Here O'Donoghue hit his stride, but "Paris," while great, passed with little notice. (It is featured in the *Evergreen* anthology.) For the next three years O'Donoghue would be known only as the master of *Phoebe Zeit-Geist.*

Phoebe, too, gets off to a fast start. The first installment, "Tarpit Terror," begins with our heroine already in trouble. We are told of her background in a densely worded précis:

24-year-old Phoebe Zeit-Geist, daughter of a Serbian aristocrat, raised in Northern Tibet where she mastered the mysteries of Oriental combat arts, studied ballet in Montevideo (*Uruguay*) with one whom many still refer to as "Sergei Diaghilev's most brilliant protégée" (*and who must at this time remain nameless*) danced briefly with the "Grand Ballet Du Marquîs Cuevas" and then, upon the insistence of her father (*her mother having perished of tuberculosis in 1947*), completed her education at an exclusive Swiss finishing school. Our story opens as Phoebe, while attending a garden party in Antwerp, has been slipped a drugged pousse-café and now comes to, scant hours later, at an oasis in Death Valley, California, the prisoner of a sinister stranger.

Our eyes move right to Phoebe and her tormentor, a nameless ex–Nazi clad in Luftwaffe garb. He stands over her, his riding crop raised

and ready to deliver punishment. He demands that she strip, but decides that he'll rip her dress off instead. Soon Phoebe stands naked in mud, and she'll remain unclothed for the better part of her adventures. But thoughts of future events are meaningless now as the ex-Nazi informs her of her fate.

Then, intent on her complete debasement, the mad German begins striking Phoebe's soft flesh with his riding crop.

She is tied to the helicopter and jerked by her wrists to the sky. "Does depravity triumph?" asks O'Donoghue at strip's end. Yes, it does. And will, again and again. This initial episode, brief as it is, makes it plain to all that Phoebe has merely stubbed her toe in comparison to the abuse she'll soon encounter.

O'Donoghue and Springer were well into the next installment by the time "Tarpit" was at newsstands. As they developed episode two, O'Donoghue wrote several more adventures during his night-long sessions at home. One leg bounced as he typed out the plots and filled in the specific action. He smoked continuously, would punch his thigh when blocked or stalled creatively, as though the next image or word was lodged in his leg. The television blared and flashed near his face as Paula Levy tried to sleep. In the night's darkest hours he let Phoebe (and

Paula) rest; with pen he honed his verse, assorted haikus. One poem, "The White Moth," echoes Phoebe:

She dreamt of drowning;
That, for many years, her unclothed body bobbed
In the Pacific.
Her eyes turned the color of iodine.
Her flesh was white.
In the afternoons, boys would swim out and play on her.
Sometimes, they would remove their trunks and
Rub against her.
When they pressed her breasts,
Bubbles emerged from her mouth and rose,
Slowly,
To the surface . . .

but the sound, distant, tapers off. Still, O'Donoghue could not shake Phoebe from his thoughts. Nor did he desire to. He became fully consumed with her saga and his plotlines grew ever more complex. When he acted out scenes for Springer, O'Donoghue assumed a number of personalities and postures; his voice fluctuated from dominant tones to submissive whines; even minor characters received stage time. One can imagine his appearance as he performed the ex-Nazi bit from the first installment: "In time, I would make you beg to obey me, no matter how . . . distasteful the command! *SEIG HEIL!!*" Springer watched and absorbed it all. The performances were instructive and amusing. But overseas, in the land of the former Reich, the ex-Nazi's riding crop struck a nationalist nerve.

I am reminded of an old German proverb: Kill the Jews.

Defeated in war, drawn and quartered at Nuremberg, the Germans were cleansed of impure thoughts and sent to separate corners: markets in the West; Marxism in the East. To the dismay of those citizens unable to book flights to Paraguay, symbols of the Nazi era, including the swastika, were outlawed. References to the past were restricted to lessons learned, and certain appetites and impulses were deemed inappropriate. By the mid-1960s Adolf Eichmann had been tried and executed in Israel, West German intellectuals searched for extended meaning in the previous generation's madness, and East German officials continued their fight against fascism by combating, among many things, jazz music. To put it in corporate terms, Nazism had lost significant market share. Into this scene fell Phoebe Zeit-Geist.

Evergreen's West German distributor, Internationale Presse, forwarded the November 1965 issue to the Bundesprüfstelle, or the Federal Censorship Office, for review. There an official named Robert Schilling examined the front of the book, expecting nothing in the way of interest. "But then I came upon the 'comic' story 'Phoebe Zeit-Geist' on pp. 58," he fumed in a letter to Internationale. "It goes beyond anything of this kind so far placed before me. In our view, the depiction in this form of the wildest kind of sadism, unleashed on a girl who must, in stages, undress herself completely before an observer and who is being whipped—this no doubt goes beyond all limits."

Indecency was the least of it; national honor was at stake, too, and here Herr Schilling's alarm rang loudest. He notes that the Nazi depicted in the strip was not connected to the SS, to war crimes, to concentration camps, but existed in the "postwar period in *California!*" In other words, the man is an impostor and definitely not German because Germany is free of the Nazi contagion . . . or something along these literal lines. This, Schilling protests, is a slur upon the new German character and could "endanger the understanding between the NATO nations, and is likely to do this both here as well as over there."

He believes that the strip "incites against the 'German officer' type and here it might make it appear as if, to this very day, and all diplomatic statements to the contrary, an anti-German campaign of significant proportions continues to be waged in the U.S." After sounding an obligatory "danger to youth" warning, Schilling closes with a line that is at once cautionary and poetic: "Only the dumbest of calves select their own butchers." Or, He who forgets the past is free to play victim.

While Schilling scanned *Phoebe Zeit-Geist* for further anti-German bias, *Evergreen* capitalized on his decision to ban the issue from circulation. A press release alerted media outlets to the controversy; ads were taken out in the *New York Times,* the *Village Voice,* and the *New York Review of Books.* "Will *Evergreen* split NATO?" the ad copy asked. "Will it tarnish the German officer type? Will you still be able to get this historic issue?" Of course, Grove Press had plenty in stock, and for the price of a year's subscription one could savor Phoebe's punishment sans German interference. As do all good censors, Schilling fanned the very flame he tried clumsily to extinguish. The number of German readers exposed to the first *Phoebe Zeit-Geist* is not known, but in the States the publicity brought the strip to an audience beyond *Evergreen*'s subscription base.

Naturally, *Phoebe* inspired its share of letters. Readers were divided from the first installment on. Many saw the strip as graffiti sprayed across serious literature and felt it sullied the look and purpose of the magazine.

Others were put off by what they believed to be degrading and pornographic scenarios; Puritans have always dwelled in Bohemia. *Phoebe*'s defenders took equally high roads. They analyzed O'Donoghue's satirical
narrative and Springer's comic art (one reader compared Springer to the
great Will Eisner of *Spirit* fame) and insisted that the team did indeed
belong in *Evergreen*.

Then there were those who enjoyed the strip at ground level. A
young woman from Massachusetts wrote in to say that she found *Phoebe
Zeit-Geist* to be "a captivating feature. I read it over many times to make
sure I hadn't missed any subtle meanings. . . . I found the ex-Nazi to
be amazingly fascinating; villains always are. It's a shame that more men
[don't] share some of his domineering qualities instead of being Momma's
boys. May *Evergreen Review* and the ex-Nazi prosper and may Phoebe
Zeit-Geist suffer forever." Instead, Phoebe would suffer for just over
three years, but her sacrifice helped make possible *Evergreen*'s subsequent
(and relative) prosperity.

O'Donoghue and Springer scarcely acknowledged the attention paid
to their creation. Indeed, Springer was unaware that the strip had attained
notoriety. He and O'Donoghue remained busy, focused. They were settling into a cycle of story conferences, writing and drawing jags, meetings
at Grove, and revisions. Springer had his hands full with the new scripts
O'Donoghue gave him. Minor details covered paragraphs; each bit of
action was painfully—at times, tediously—described. But O'Donoghue
made sure that Springer could move among panels without being stalled
by directions. When cutting was necessary, O'Donoghue obliged. Movement was vital to the strip, for without it Phoebe stays in Antwerp and
sips her pousse-café.

The helicopter that tugs Phoebe to her fate continued its flight in
the next *Evergreen* installment. As she ponders "What does it all mean?"
Phoebe is whacked against billboards, traffic lights, and neon signs. Then
"an arrow whistles past, splitting the rope that binds her hands," and she
dives into the river below. From here, acceleration.

• Caught in the river's current, Phoebe's life flashes before her eyes.
Wolves tear at her clothes; a dyke dance instructor begs to kiss her shoes;
caged Gila monsters strain to eat dead beetles off her breasts and mound;
her co-pilot dying, she trains a machine gun on a squadron of enemy
zeppelins; a giant jungle spider sets upon her; she is crucified by a mad
rabbi. The current takes Phoebe to the edge of a falls, but she is pulled
to shore by a blind Zen archer. His was the arrow that cut her bonds;
now he wants to kill her, point blank.

We are left with the words of a Kyoto poet: "The yellow butterflies count moments, not months, and have time enough." Phoebe's still eyes begin to glaze.

• Sunlight illuminates the dead heroine. A pair of Scarlet Tanagers build a nest beneath her chin. Come twilight, hooded members of the Moon Squad appear, toss her body in the trunk of their car, and speed off to the Terre Haute Federal Bank & Trust building. There Phoebe is carried into the bank's vault, which doubles as the entrance to the Temple of Necrophilia. She is to marry Thanatos, God of Death, in a private ceremony; and as the wedding begins, a voice cries "Stop!" from the back of room. The guests are startled. Will they get to cut the wedding cake, which bears the edible inscription, "Little white flowers will never awaken you"?

• The High Priests of the Temple are outraged by this

interruption. But the nameless intruder holds a hand grenade and keeps everyone frozen in place. He grabs Phoebe and races from the bank.

The Moon Squad, hot on his heels, arrives minutes later. But Phoebe is gone. Weeks later, her body arrives in Ceylon, where a deranged fungologist plans to use her as a garden on which he will grow an "avant-garde fungus" called Felicia. Within days spores multiply on Phoebe. However, the fungologist forgot to feed his dog, Bruno; he pounces on the spore-laden body and prepares to feast. Meanwhile, back in Terre Haute, the Moon Squad tracks down the intruder and incinerates him with a flamethrower.

• As Bruno lunges for Phoebe's throat, he is hit with a harpoon. An Eskimo, the dog's original owner, is responsible. Years before, his dog was stolen by a Yukon dog-napping ring; his search brings him to Ceylon and near-reunion when he notices that Phoebe resembles the Ice Princess of ancient lore. With her sacrifice, the Eskimo Nation will rise and drive the white man from its sacred tundra. So the Eskimo impales the dog and drags Phoebe back to Alaska. There he consults Nono Shanook, the Tribal Angakut, or "medicine man." Both agree that in order to be sacrificed, the Ice Princess must first be resurrected. Nono brews a potion in a cauldron, chants, then slips Phoebe in the mix. Minutes later . . .

She is taken to a remote ice floe, tied to a pair of ceremonial posts, and covered with fish. A ravenous polar bear approaches; like Bruno, it views Phoebe as its next meal.

• And like Bruno, the polar bear is killed before it dines. Fortunately for Phoebe, the *Black Narcissus,* an elegant submarine that boasts a ballroom, antique furniture, a fireplace, and chandeliers, surfaced and saved her from a painful, messy death. Unfortunately, the sub is manned by Puff and Flit, two gay white slave traders who look to sell their newest catch. But second thoughts prevail; Puff decides instead to defile poor Phoebe. Before the punishment can begin, however, a giant manta ray attacks the sub. Flit refuses to allow Puff to fire his prized, antique torpedoes (on each are hand-painted scenes of famous naval battles).

Phoebe is shot through the deep and toward the ray. An explosion rips wide the predator . . . and Phoebe?

• Amazing though it seems, Phoebe survives, intact. She washes up on a beach in Rio de Janeiro, stumbles about, falls into a deep pit, and is knocked senseless. Upon awakening, Phoebe finds herself at the mercy of a Brazilian foot fetishist and his Afro-Asiatic, single-legged assistant, Viola. They force her to wear a variety of shoes that are one size too small; the boxes as well. But this does not sate their twisted appetites.

The binding begins.

• Viola grabs the foot of a protesting Phoebe when, suddenly, she spots what foot fetishists most despise: a bunion. Sickened, they toss Phoebe in a trash can, where she attracts the attention of a Marxist garbage man. He is sickened, too, for here lies fallow a potential worker who can, *must,* contribute to international communism. He packs her in the can and ships it along "The Red Grapevine" to a bauxite mine in northern Albania. The mine is run by Peiping Tom, a ruthless Maoist functionary. He uses Phoebe as a human wheelbarrow and has bauxite loaded on her back.

The Komodo dragon nears the chained heroine. It hisses into her face and raises its right claw . . .

• Night in Macao. The back alleys teem with vermin and decay. Murder and pestilence lurk in shadows. A sailor drops a bag on the bar of a waterfront dive. He utters a single Serbo-Croatian word, then vanishes. The bag is taken by courier to a pagoda on the outskirts of town. A small, crazed-looking man accepts the delivery and empties the bag. Out spills Phoebe Zeit-Geist.

But conventional art is not his forté; humans are his canvas, the tattoo drill his brush. He leads Phoebe into a room where "earlier pieces"—tattooed corpses—hang from the ceiling. These are mere sketches. But with Phoebe he now has the perfect body on which to draw his masterpiece.

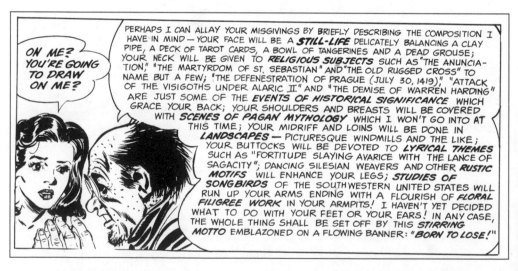

The lights go out. The tattooer neglected his electric bill, and before he can recover, the landlord, who resembles Norman Mailer, arrives to evict him for nonpayment of rent. The landlord impounds all of the tattooer's possessions, Phoebe included. He then boots the deadbeat out the door and turns to Phoebe, who thanks him for his deed. But the landlord has less than noble ideas for her.

He smuggles Phoebe to Tokyo and lashes her to the Haneda Monorail. The train bears down on her spread-eagled form; Phoebe yells, but the person nearest her is an elderly blind beggar who shuffles along the street below. What can he do?

• Plenty, for the beggar is in reality the blind Zen archer who killed Phoebe. He fires an arrow into a Yang bird that flies above the tracks. The bird falls face-first toward Phoebe; its razor-sharp beak slices through the ropes, and she plummets to the pavement that will kill her. But she drops instead through the vinyl top of a Toyota Land Cruiser, is cold-cocked by the driver, and taken from the city. Meanwhile, in France, a counterspy named Dirk Savage is assigned to find and rescue Phoebe. Savage is a fearless, effective agent, one of the best in the world of espionage. He leaves his briefing and approaches his car when, suddenly, a flower vendor pulls a revolver and shoots him in the head. Savage dies; Phoebe remains in danger.

• Phoebe comes to in a cage on the coast of New Zealand. Before her stands a hideously obese woman called the Blob Princess, who is flanked by a group of women known as the Incredible Lesbians. Phoebe begins to ask a question and the Blob flies into a rage. She beats Phoebe with fists and feet; a bullwhip is produced and Phoebe is mercilessly flogged.

THE HEFTY SAPPHIST PREPARES TO FLAIL THE COMELY CAPTIVE RELENTLESSLY, WHEN...

But two of the Lesbians scrap and this diverts the Blob. Phoebe bolts and runs for her life, over mountains, across ravines, through deserts and jungles until she she is overcome with exhaustion and collapses. She hears a noise and raises her head to find *all* her tormentors.

The villains descend upon her (opposite), and while Phoebe fights valiantly, the odds prove too great and she is stomped to a pulp. *Finis.*

The Adventures of Phoebe Zeit-Geist put O'Donoghue on the edge of New York's artistic map. His skill at satirical narrative was evident to those who followed the strip, but since *Phoebe* was a comic and so a "lighter" form, he would be tagged a "pop" curiosity—"The Twisted Mind Behind *Phoebe Zeit-Geist*" instead of "The Poet and Playwright, M. O'Donoghue." But this didn't faze him. Whatever his earlier pretensions of artistic splendor, of muses pure and grand, O'Donoghue now saw possibility in less-elevated areas of creative life. Until *Phoebe,* he'd

given comic books little, if any, thought. That changed, and with it came a shift in his approach to work.

The confidence he possessed as a playwright flowed into different forms, and once committed to a piece he pressed until either it broke apart or it assumed the shape he demanded. There was to be no middle way. O'Donoghue required that everything he did bear *his* stamp, extend *his* vision, and this was first fully realized in *Phoebe Zeit-Geist*. The story line is broad and sweeping and brilliantly paced, but O'Donoghue's distinctive touch is felt in the details.

When the Moon Squad steal Phoebe's corpse, they don't merely toss her in the back of a car; they stow her in the trunk of a silver 1934 Weyman Torpedo-Phaeton Duesenberg, Model SJ. When the crazed tattoo artist shows Phoebe his earlier "work," the bodies that hang before them bear images and slogans that are minutely rendered but clearly defined. So, too, are the naval battles drawn on the torpedoes of the submarine *Black Narcissus*. In nearly every panel can be found little items, from the lettering on a wrinkled Little League T-shirt to a portion of a bank sign that touts a "low" interest rate (19.9 percent in 1966) on loans. And so on. Details like these lent the strip texture, and most carried no comedic message or joke.

Still, O'Donoghue did see the humor in density; in various expositions and narrative turns he'd close a long passage with a line that was either silly or absurd, that tripped just slightly the rhythm of a speech. Each episode had this, but in the Eskimo segment the technique is pronounced. First, we are introduced to the Eskimo Angakut:

He then receives his guest and makes a discovery:

At times the turns O'Donoghue made were sharper, tighter, direct. In the introduction of episode four, he puts to rest any thoughts that Phoebe survived the Zen arrow.

> Our last episode ended on what might be considered a despondent note when Phoebe Zeit-Geist, wealthy 24-year-old sophisticate, was slain by a blind Zen archer who, for inscrutable reasons, sent a shaft into her breast, piercing her vital parts. Many readers of this strip might believe that Phoebe isn't *really* dead; that at the last moment we're going to pull some shoddy trick like an emergency operation and that Phoebe is only *severely wounded. Wrong!!!* Phoebe Zeit-Geist is *dead! Defunct! Morte! Kaput!* Sorry, but that's the way things turned out.

Above all, there is a casual acceptance of Phoebe's fate that pervades the strip. None of the characters appear ruffled when encountering her in a compromised state or sordid condition. They respond as if nothing is amiss. When the *Black Narcissus* surfaces near the ice floe where Phoebe is to be sacrificed, Flit looks into the periscope and says, "Now *there's* something you don't see every day—a naked woman covered with fish about to be eaten by a polar bear!" The same holds true when characters encounter each other. As the hooded and armed Moon Squad enters the post office to reclaim Phoebe's corpse, a squad member asks the clerk, "Did a guy about so tall just come in here and mail a dead woman?" The clerk takes a second to reflect and replies, "Can't rightly say! Too late to check 'cause the mail's on the hook waitin' to be picked up. . . ." Dead woman? Hooded men toting rifles? The clerk doesn't notice—or care.

From April 1966 to October 1967, *Phoebe Zeit-Geist* appeared in almost every other issue of *Evergreen*. The division among readers deepened, and as O'Donoghue and Springer polished Phoebe off they put her future to a vote: Should she die or undergo a fresh round of torture? Readers were told that only a resounding vote in favor of more installments would "stay the executioner's hand." Roughly three of every five ballots mailed in to *Evergreen* carried a "Phoebe Must Live!" vote. Of the over seven thousand readers who responded, 59 percent wanted the strip to continue, while 41 percent demanded termination. Comments accompanied each ballot.

Pheobe is the only reason I get your crummy paper. Keep your nipples high, Phoebe!

I think this is the only TERRIBLE part of the magazine. Very childish, immature, sick and perverted. The finest avant-garde literary review in the U.S. has no room for trash such as this.

Actually does it matter whether she lives or dies? After all, she's been dead once already. . . . I don't think the "Yes" answer is very meaningful. Just keep Mr. O'Donoghue's masterpiece going . . .

The insistence of your editors to publish this comic strip idiocy, this intellectual affront and, in fact, to feature it on the cover of the latest issue is one thing that will cause me to consider *not* to renew my subscription. . . .

By all means, let her live. But how about spanking her instead of all those bizarre tortures?

Yet it seemed that not even a "resounding" show of support for Phoebe could save her. O'Donoghue and Springer needed a break from their creation—Springer especially. Though he enjoyed his collaboration with O'Donoghue, Springer held a low opinion of *Evergreen*'s other material. He felt the magazine had become "raunchy" and that its editors were preoccupied with nudity for nudity's sake, and to a degree Springer was correct. *Evergreen* did feature more "tits and ass" as the 1960s went on; and since some of the nude photos lacked literary or satirical meaning, their display appeared gratuitous. But sexual freedom had always been a part of *Evergreen*'s agenda: Nudity was but an element of life and thus worthy of artistic attention, however absurd. A woman's breast painted green with the nipple kept pink might be meaningless to all save the woman and the person who painted her.

Springer saw matters differently: he feared that his association with the magazine would hurt his career, and early in *Phoebe Zeit-Geist*'s run he quit working on the strip. Looking back, Springer said that his decision stemmed in part from a flu he suffered at the time. His illness allowed him to act on his fear, and for a brief period *Phoebe* had no illustrator. Springer discussed his decision extensively with O'Donoghue and Fred Jordan, both of whom obviously urged him to resume work. The flu passed, and Springer was eventually convinced that further dealings with *Evergreen* would not sink his reputation in the mainstream of comic art. He returned to the strip and focused solely on its content, none of which he ever viewed as "pornographic."

O'Donoghue, however, had no problem with nudity, obscenity, or profanity. Though he jokingly referred to himself as "the Angel of Purity," he felt that sex and violence were necessary elements of his work. When *Phoebe* took off and O'Donoghue began to receive some press attention (mostly from small, downtown publications), he made no apologies for the strip, and he adapted quickly to the reputation that formed around him. "I'll defend to the death my right to be unstable and especially my right to never be cured," he said in 1967. "My morality is very elusive." Asked by a reporter if his work carried any message, O'Donoghue replied, "Just death and despair. No hope. It's not necessary." But he did find necessary a public image, a mask that complemented his volatile artistic temperament.

When it came to women and relationships, O'Donoghue publically said, "Cut any woman open and you find a cottage with a white picket fence. Women like to pretend I'm not what I write. They say, 'You're really a very sweet wonderful person.' Which I'd like to be but I'm not." The private reality was more a mixed affair. Paula Levy saw O'Donoghue's tender side, a "shadow area" that he carefully exposed. She noticed that when watching Japanese samurai films he became emotionally involved with the stories, sometimes to the point of tears. O'Donoghue also read to her, his voice soft and sentimental, his manner delicate. On occasion the couple would dine with Barbara's sister, Margaret, who lived in Queens. O'Donoghue treated his aunt with respect and lavished her with affection.

But there was the unsweetened side, in evidence since childhood, which Levy discovered soon after he moved into her apartment. O'Donoghue, she said, could get "disproportionately upset" over the smallest problem or obstacle. His voice rose dramatically; he punched the wall, his thigh, a table top; he was passionate but controlled, his violence more theatrical than threatening. While painting a section of the apartment yellow, Levy and O'Donoghue argued over the color, which he came to despise. Words led to action: O'Donoghue and Levy threw paint at one another, covering themselves, the furniture, and the walls in yellow streaks. Later, in a limerick, O'Donoghue explained to Levy his behavior:

A painter named Mike was neurotic
Chose a color he thought was exotic
He painted along,
But the color was wrong,
And Mike is a raving psychotic!

At Christmas, one of the cats knocked over the tree and O'Donoghue became hysterical. He ranted about how his Christmas was ruined
and he left the tree on its side until calm returned. Also, O'Donoghue
began to get migraine headaches. The pain was infrequent, but severe.

*Any asshole can take a piece of marble and sculpt something. It takes genius
to take a hammer and smash a face.*

Although much of his creative time had been occupied with *Phoebe
Zeit-Geist,* O'Donoghue never lost his love for the stage. In his story
conference bits for Springer and in his increasingly colorful tantrums at
home, O'Donoghue demonstrated a need to perform. This was reflected
in even the smallest of gestures. When smoking, he held his cigarette
between his middle fingers and affected a fey, George Sanders manner.
When talking, he removed his glasses and used them as a prop, accenting
his words with the movement of his frames. Though extremely self-
conscious in this regard, O'Donoghue delivered seamless performances;
affectation and personality merged. But a true outlet was needed, and his
friendship with Larry Loonin served to provide one.

A self-described "guilt-ridden Jew of Coney Island," Loonin was a
fixture in the Off-Off-Broadway scene. With short hair and sports jacket,
he did not fit the stereotype of the bohemian artist. By day he taught
English at Walden High School in Manhattan; after dark he staged odd
plays and performance pieces of varied quality. His work received notice
in the *New York Times* and the *Village Voice,* and the reviews, like his
work, were mixed. His direction of a Keith Cameron play, *The Hundred
and First,* which appeared at the Judson Poet's Theatre in 1964, was
panned by the *Voice* as "a one-joke revue sketch stretched out almost
beyond endurance. Larry Loonin's production is messy and lacking in
style, amateurish in the most plodding way." But criticism did not daunt
him. Loonin continued to write and direct, and he saw O'Donoghue as
the perfect vehicle for his work.

By moving to New York when he did, O'Donoghue was present
for the mid-1960s expansion of alternative theaters and performance
spaces—or Off-Off Broadway, as it came to be called. Plays, monologues,
various styles of "performance art" were staged in coffeehouses, base-
ments, lofts, abandoned garages, and studio apartments. Some spaces op-

erated under no fixed name, but most did: the Hardware Poet's Playhouse, the Village South Theater, the Open Stage, Cafe Engage, Cafe La Mama, as well as the Judson Poet's Theatre and Caffe Cino.

On small stages or an area of floor cleared of chairs, actors wrestled with the themes found in plays such as *Who Put That Blood on My Long-Stemmed Rose?*, *Shopping and Waiting*, *Lullaby for a Dying Man*, *It's Always the Same But Sometimes It's Different*, and *Unpacking the Black Trunk*. A few playwrights—Edward Albee, Lanford Wilson, Terrence McNally—were noticed and promoted to larger venues; established works by Tennessee Williams and Jean Genet were revived and reinterpreted. The daily newspapers and Sunday magazines all ran the requisite piece on this theatrical "movement," emphasis placed on "exotic." But most of Off-Off Broadway operated far from the bright lights and under bare bulbs instead.

In early 1965, Loonin altered one of his plays with O'Donoghue in mind. Titled *Our First Gobi Fossils,* it was billed as an "exposé on existence. A primitive rite. Or nothing at all. It is up to you." The play bowed in late February in the coffeehouse of the Spenser Memorial Church. O'Donoghue is the tyrant who quizzes, abuses, and ultimately kills the other characters. The play's action is "abrupt and non-literal," and the characters' motives are reduced to multiple choice by way of improvisation. The script provides a number of lines from which the actors may deviate. Thus, *Gobi* is formless and at times overwrought. The variety of routes a character can take ensures that the play is as "abrupt" as much of the dialogue is graceless.

"One may talk about death and not be there," says the tyrant. "One is less there than the deceased. One may talk and be dead. Talking is a way of not being there." Much of *Gobi* sounds this way, and the bulk of stiff lines were given to O'Donoghue. Yet it was his behavior, not his speeches, that electrified and startled the audience. Loonin conceived the tyrant as a puritan prone to violence. But O'Donoghue drove his character past such quaintness. He Nazified the tyrant; like the abusive caretaker in *The Twilight Maelstrom of Cookie Lavagetto,* his onstage screams appeared as threats against cast *and* audience. People squirmed as he shrieked in their faces. He dominated not only the stage but the room itself. O'Donoghue so worked himself into a dramatic rage that after many performances he visibly shook and kept to himself.

An actor in everyday life, O'Donoghue suffered from stage fright. Before each performance Loonin handed him a lollipop, which O'Donoghue sucked on while repeating to himself, "Well, here goes nothing. It will be interesting to see how it turns out." Loonin believed this to be O'Donoghue's mantra. As he sat backstage in the tyrant's costume, the fury he would soon display was summoned. After the show the cast stayed clear of their trembling co-star. Loonin spoke softly to O'Donoghue in an effort to relax him. Once he unleashed his anger pacification was difficult, but not impossible; and after many cigarettes the trembling ceased. In discussions with Loonin, O'Donoghue stressed his desire to push his work beyond "good and evil" to a place where conventional "morality" perished. In this he echoed Friedrich Nietzsche, and he and Loonin debated the merits of this philosophy well into the night.

Stage acting, however, was not of primary interest to O'Donoghue. Other actors employed various techniques to keep their performances fresh, but O'Donoghue built slowly to that *one* performance that crystallized whatever role he was playing. Once this peak was reached he lost interest in the part, and he would, in Loonin's words, "phone in" his performance. The one exception seemed to be *Gobi*'s tyrant, whose screams never lost their frightening pitch.

Loonin continued to cast O'Donoghue in plays he either wrote or chose to adapt. One such adaptation was *If You Please* by André Breton and Philippe Soupault, staged at the Martinique Theater. O'Donoghue played Létoile, an upstanding member of the Legion of Honor who speaks at length of the human condition. He is seen by some as a moral hero. "Everyone knows that Létoile is in possession of the same powers as God," admits a man to God himself. "[H]e sees all, hears all—and no one suspects it." Those who approach him for help or advice are suspected of wrongdoing and are turned over to the police. It is a tactic that catches up with him, and when Létoile is arrested he shows no interest in the crime of which he is accused. "What does that matter to me?" he tells the inspector.

Again, O'Donoghue was cast as a tyrant, though Létoile resembled George Sanders and was not given to tantrums. Still, his performance rippled the audience. Intensity was lowered but no less evident; a stare or a pause heightened the necessary tension, and O'Donoghue perfected this to the point where his quiet could equal his screams. O'Donoghue also saw the play differently than did its co-author, Breton. He and Loonin debated an observation made by Breton that an artist must stand away from the wall if he is to hear an echo. Loonin agreed; O'Donoghue dissented. He felt that not only should an artist be near the wall, he should slam against it and press his ear to it as tightly as possible.

Many coffeehouses and small theaters constituted Off-Off Broadway, but these spaces were also home to what were called "happenings"—a mid-1960s variation on "performance art" or "spontaneous theater." A "happening" could consist of just about anything, so abstract was its definition. Action was usually minimal, artist and audience interchangeable. The material and performances tended to blandness and passivity, as was proper for an ethereal form. O'Donoghue was drawn to this, but the ethereal left him cold. He favored short, quick pieces that punched and stabbed those watching. (Much of *malaise* reflected this thinking.) Thus the "happenings" he conceived were not abstract or dull. He committed himself to specific action where confrontation was inevitable.

In mid-1965, Loonin hosted a series of happening pieces at the Martinique Theater. Each piece was preceded and followed by Loonin delivering a dry monologue. This smoothed the way between acts, though in O'Donoghue's case no emcee could stave off what became the standard audience reaction. Every performer had been given a letter in the alphabet from which he or she was to construct a piece. O'Donoghue's letter was R. He came onstage, unfolded an American flag, and spread it out. He produced several green, plastic rhinoceroses and placed each one on either a red or a white stripe. He knelt on the flag and emitted what seemed a rumbling noise: "rrrrrrrrrrrrRRRonaldReaganRoutsRuthlessRevolutionaries . . ." As he continued in the R vein, O'Donoghue moved the plastic rhinos along the flag's stripes as if he were racing them. He took his time, the pace determined by audience response.

O'Donoghue's routine almost always elicited gasps. Although not a particularly violent abuse of the flag, his actions did not seem right to some. Even in the few demonstrations then being held against the Vietnam war, the flag was kept aloft and was used as one of the symbols of dissent. (As the war intensified, gasoline and matches were added.) Politics aside, flag worship was the norm. But here was some "beatnik" crawling on Old Glory and using it as he might a common playroom mat. One night three Marines witnessed O'Donoghue's act and were enraged by his conduct. The trio confronted O'Donoghue as he came off stage. Words were exhanged, then punches flew, the majority of which smashed against O'Donoghue's face. The assault was broken up and the Marines were thrown out; O'Donoghue was rushed to St. Vincent's Hospital. Though he bled quite a bit, no stitches were required. O'Donoghue was cleaned up and sent home with Paula Levy. In subsequent performances, the Martinique stationed a security guard between O'Donoghue and the audience.

Incidents like this horrified Levy, and her contempt for Loonin deepened. From the moment she met him, Levy detested Loonin. She thought he was mean, pretentious, devoid of talent, and she was mystified by O'Donoghue's fascination with him. She blamed Loonin for the Marine assault and felt that he pushed O'Donoghue to extreme behavior, including the backstage trembling that followed *Gobi Fossils*. O'Donoghue, Loonin contended, didn't need to be pushed, nor would he allow it: O'Donoghue acted independently and never sought another person's approval. It was this quality that attracted Loonin. In O'Donoghue he saw a fearless artistic spirit that he himself lacked. O'Donoghue was the Id and Loonin wanted a piece.

Levy's hostility toward Loonin was open, and this made for tense moments whenever they were together. She thought Loonin was a parasite; he felt that Levy was jealous of his friendship with O'Donoghue. The trio, then, was less than merry. Once, according to Levy, when driving Loonin to his new apartment in Brooklyn Heights, she and O'Donoghue witnessed a purse-snatching on a nearby corner. Loonin urged his friend to leave the car and race after the crook. O'Donoghue complied. But Loonin remained in his seat and refused to assist in the chase, which O'Donoghue soon abandoned. As O'Donoghue jogged back to the car, Levy steamed. She was furious with Loonin and feared that O'Donoghue could have been killed. Loonin remembers none of this and doubts that it ever happened. True or not, the story brings to light the bad blood that existed between the two.

Aware of the hostilities, O'Donoghue nevertheless went about his business. He assembled notes for two novels he wanted to write, one about passenger pigeons, the other about European lesbians. The latter pile of notes, titled *Le Coeur de Toile*—or, *The Cloth Heart*—was perhaps the more ambitious project. The idea was that the book had been written by an unknown French author, then lost. Years later it was unearthed and "translated" by O'Donoghue. When studying the scenes and scanning the outline, however, one sees that the French author held many of the same passions as his translator:

- "Novice" lesbians, held captive by older women, are punished for the slightest transgression.
- A foul-mouthed nun forces young girls to lick her clitoris—"Here is your God."
- Blood is drawn from sensuous lips; tears are collected in champagne bottles.
- Books bound in rare animal skins are read by nude women stretched out on fur chaise lounges. Houseflies mate on the art nouveau objects that surround them.

The "novices" endure much in the way of humiliation. A woman is forced to clean the boots of her captors with a brush made from her shorn hair. Another is sewn into the skin of her dead male lover and must wear "him" for a month. Through it all the unknown French author is made even more anonymous by the creator of Phoebe Zeit-Geist. O'Donoghue was to write *The Cloth Heart* "in character," but the mask kept hitting the floor. Had he developed the novel he might have found a better fit. He fiddled with the premise, changed the title to

Ghostflowers, and announced in *Evergreen* that it was due to be finished. Instead, the pages were put in an envelope and filed away.

The passenger pigeon notes, called *The Glass Vertebrae,* consist of extreme and varied images. Where *The Cloth Heart* stays focused on S&M, *Vertebrae* jumps all over the room. The "story" is of the demise of the last passenger pigeon in 1914 at the Cincinnati Zoo. But as O'Donoghue states in his notes, "Nobody is going to pay to read about some dumb passenger pigeon and the like." Indeed, there is very little about birds of any kind. The assassination of an African leader (called "Burning Spear" O'Donoghue) leads to a ribbon-cutting ceremony at Dachau, where Nazis tattoo their first Jewish prisoner, which is followed by a death ray, an underwater laboratory, a multiple-choice test, Arab curses, a dedication to Franz Kafka, and dirty limericks. The episodes lack connecting tissue; in no way does one sense a novel in progress. Yet again in *Evergreen,* O'Donoghue publicized *The Glass Vertebrae* as if it were nearly finished. But soon it, too, was consigned to the files.

One project that O'Donoghue pretty much completed might have worked as a novelty paperback. Written in the midst of 1960s liberalism, *The Liberal Book* captures accurately the passions and biases then held by the American mainstream left. For pages, every possible character trait is listed:

LIBERALS know all the verses to "We Shall Overcome."
LIBERALS drive Volkswagens, particulary if they are Jewish.
LIBERALS argue over what actually happened at the Yalta Conference.
LIBERALS are always careful to say "Afro-American."
LIBERALS approve of pre-marital intercourse. In fact, they call it that.

The Kennedys, wine-and-cheese parties, *Pogo,* boycotts, and literary quarterlies are cherished; Roy Cohn, TV dinners, *Little Black Sambo,* Barbie dolls, and book burnings are not. As satire, *The Liberal Book* is tame, the biases of liberals gently tweaked. Given the violent imagery in his other projects—and the fact that he wrote for a leftist magazine and lived in a liberal environment—one might expect a harsher response. But O'Donoghue began to vary his tones. He saw the advantage in stealth and appreciated the balance it lent his aggression. Why use an ice pick when a pillow can smother your prey?

But *The Liberal Book* died on the vine. Into the files it went, another project buried and forgotten. Phoebe remained popular, however, and like Conan Doyle, O'Donoghue considered reviving his star creation. If Sherlock Holmes could rise from the Reichenbach Falls, the more resilient Phoebe could again spring naked into harm's way.

In order to hide, he almost became a tree.
It was 4:30.
Father would be coming home soon.
The apricots at the bottom of the bowl had gone bad.
The inside of the clock was to be painted black.
Snails were mating in the piano.
"I'll join them," he thought.
"They'll never find me here."

In late 1966, O'Donoghue went apartment hunting. To be more precise, he asked around for the cheapest possible deal. He and Levy were still attached, but O'Donoghue wanted a place of his own, an objective unrealized since he'd moved to New York. The studio he shared with Levy was cozy but cramped; room was needed to accommodate his evolving style. Soon, word got back to him that a loft was available on Spring Street, in a downtown neighborhood called SoHo.

Before it became a shopping mall that catered to Euro-swill, SoHo was for the most part deserted. The downtown "scene" of art, music, and theater resided primarily in the West and East Village. This would spill southward, take root, and expand to monstrous dimensions. But when O'Donoghue surveyed the area it consisted of warehouses and factory lofts. Indeed, at the time SoHo was better known as the Factory District or the Cast-Iron District. Art gallery banners had yet to unfurl. O'Donoghue himself preferred the factory label to the trendier tag:

> I dislike the name SoHo, and I dislike the person who thought up the name, though I don't know him. He must have been very pleased with himself when he thought the name up. The Factory District is *south* of *Houston* Street. Get it? *South Houston*. I bet he wrote a letter to the *Village Voice* when he thought it up.

He disliked the name but not the location. It was quiet, removed. The space he inspected was an abandoned factory loft at 148 Spring Street—and much larger than he would ever need. The stairs that led to the loft were wide and steep; the loft itself took up the entire second floor of the building. The ceiling was high and lighting fixtures few. What light filtered in came through three large windows facing Spring; but as the loft was deep, light touched but a portion of the space. The remaining area was thus dark and gloomy. Its location and condition made it affordable to even the penniless O'Donoghue. He discovered, though, that the loft was an illegal rental and was not to be used as a living space. But whoever held the lease (unknown to this day) chose to overlook this problem, and with Levy's help O'Donoghue moved in.

Foul and dingy though it was, the loft suited O'Donoghue. Its darkness paralleled his somber side, its distance from crowds and "scenes" equaled his own. In a way the loft resembled his bedroom in Sauquoit; here he would design a private world, a sanctuary in which to think, write, and be depressed. Slowly he filled the loft with what broken-down furniture he could find. A mattress, shoved into a space beneath the stairwell, served as his bed. At the back of the loft was his kitchen. A table set near an old gas stove became his desk, atop which sat his Smith-Corona typewriter and a small gray metal box that held "idea" cards. Also, he procured a file cabinet that once belonged to a dentist; no longer would his folders and notes lie in piles. This was just as well, as the loft's floor had rotted in places, and O'Donoghue nailed old license plates over the holes.

Decoration, too, was important. In his Thayer Street apartment in Rochester, O'Donoghue had casually exhibited some props from his plays, but theme and narrative were missing. In Spring Street the arrangement of assorted items would be conscious, planned. As he strained to find the right word or image in a written piece, so too did he fuss over the location of a plaster female head, a twisted doll, his plastic rhinos. He'd set a curio in a specific spot, step back, smoke a cigarette, cock his head, study the placement, and gauge its effect. When items were added arrangements changed and O'Donoghue would toil as before. To visitors the loft seemed a strange and forbiding museum. They were haunted by the mood created. For the first but not last time, O'Donoghue projected fully his anxiety and obsessions. To visit the loft was to fall deep in his shadow.

Throughout 1966, O'Donoghue continued to collaborate with Loonin. During the summer Loonin organized a theater festival in Franconia, New Hampshire. He had been teaching at the local college there, and on occasion O'Donoghue drove up and addressed Loonin's students. For the festival O'Donoghue was to perform some of his short pieces and speak of his time spent in experimental theater. Levy joined him on the trip north. Despite Loonin's presence, she was at peace with the local environment and found beautiful the landscape, as did O'Donoghue. He also found attractive a Nazi war helmet that was worn by a sculptor named Robert Morris. O'Donoghue coveted the helmet; Morris let him wear it for several days, though on O'Donoghue it failed to evoke Panzer toughness. When not playing Stalag games, O'Donoghue fleshed out new performance ideas, including one in which he stabbed himself in the eye with a large needle.

Back in New York, O'Donoghue embarked on several stage projects. He had a small role in the Spencer Stage Company production of *The Revolution of the Lovers,* written by Ronald Merle and staged in Brooklyn

Heights. He again became the Tyrant in *Our First Gobi Fossils,* which was reprised in a number of Off-Off-Broadway haunts. He performed short pieces at the Café au Go Go and the Martinique Theater. With Loonin's help he convinced Joe Cino, owner of the Caffe Cino, to let him read from *The Twilight Maelstrom of Cookie Lavagetto.*

Cino allowed all manner of expression on his stage, but he was made nervous by O'Donoghue's script. Reluctant, Cino gave in to the request. As O'Donoghue read he worked himself into his familiar dramatic frenzy. As it did in Rochester, the Nazi Commandant's speech about ovens and lesbians startled and disgusted many in the audience; but it was the abuse of the quadruple amputee that led one person to snap. As O'Donoghue later told it:

> [A]n alleged faggot art director . . . pulled the light switch and started crying out in the darkness, "This man is sick, this man is horrible!" He was going to hit me when the lights came on but he decided instead I should be put away. And I should have been. I was convulsed on the floor with laughter.

If so, then laughter quickly gave way to righteous anger. According to Loonin, O'Donoghue tracked him down and screamed about the incident. He felt he'd been betrayed, that no one had a right to interrupt his performance. Loonin listened to the tirade and agreed; but he knew that O'Donoghue's material was much too cutting for New York's avant-garde crowd—especially if performed by O'Donoghue himself.

Loonin remained mesmerized by his friend's talent and linked himself to O'Donoghue whenever possible. He conceived the beginnings of stories, then asked O'Donoghue to fill in the rest. One premise: A band of Spanish actors approach "the unreachable hacienda" in order to perform a comic play. But the hacienda remains beyond reach. Danger looms. . . . From here O'Donoghue took control. The result is amusing, the ending wonderful. Exposed to a green chemical powder, the Spanish actors retch and rip away their outer skin to reveal their inner selves—enormous insects. The insects perform the play as planned, but instead of speaking they make "a grinding, chewing noise" through five long acts. Their performance fails to provoke laughter.

By 1967 O'Donoghue had grown wary of performing in cafés. His experience at Caffe Cino alerted him to the fact that "anything goes" had its limits. He then decided to stage performances at his Spring Street loft. There he could act as he desired, and the loft's sullen atmosphere would lend his work the proper frame. Also, there was enough space to accommodate an audience. With Loonin he put the word out. On Wednesday and Thursday, café dwellers were told of the happening, and by Saturday night anywhere from twenty to forty people would arrive

During the "happening" period, June 1967

at O'Donoghue's door. Loonin secured what chairs he could find, and on some nights a third of the audience would stand.

Once he had an audience, a *private* audience, O'Donoghue sought to demolish their notions of "art." He felt the downtown "avant-garde" to be conformist and meek. He believed that their "blind acceptance" of dull forms invited aggression, and he was only too pleased to comply. For a time he considered forming the Yellow Capezio School of Art, "something so repulsive that no one would accept it." The school's goal would be to so nauseate and upset patrons that they would vomit on their shoes, "which is where the name Yellow Capezios comes from," he'd add. One idea for a piece was to import dead children from Mexico or India, glue their bodies to a canvas, then shellac them to prevent their rotting. If dead children were unavailable, dead kittens were an acceptable replacement. Obviously, O'Donoghue never acted on this idea; its definition was enough to sicken those who heard it explained. This, he claimed, made him happy.

Kittens intrigued him. However, their being dead was too bland, the artistic possibilites limited. But devouring them . . . *that* was an image he could use. Under the title *Eating Kittens,* O'Donoghue united a series of recurring pieces that highlighted sorrow, pain, and death, and this he performed in his loft in the spring of 1967. Some of the material recalls *malaise:* Rochester lingered in his mind. But like *malaise, Kittens* contains some volatile imagery that cannot be categorized as "satire" or even "comedy."

Goldfish are boiled alive in their bowls; a crippled girl, erotically clothed, has her crutch kicked from under her and is stomped by a laughing O'Donoghue; thirty dolls, stabbed with bread knives, are thrown onstage to the refrain of "Pavane for a Dead Princess." Plus:

pink blood: Michael enters dressed as a nun. A girl kneels before him and hands him a bow. He tests it. Then snaps his fingers. The girl returns with an arrow in her mouth (much like a dog fetching a newspaper or stick). Michael fits the arrow, draws, aims, and sends a shaft straight into a large copy of Sandro Botticelli's "Birth of Venus." When hit, the painting trickles pink blood. Michael shoots 4 or 5 more arrows in a similar fashion.

the gypsy priest: Roll of drums. Shaky spotlight finds a mannequin ("My God! It's Tinkerbell!") poised high in the rafters. A girl sings: "When you wish upon a star . . ." The rope is cut and "Tink" swoops down smack into a concrete wall & smashes to bits. Nun uncorks and pours a bottle of blood over the pieces, quipping (in a shoddy imitation of Dylan Thomas): "DEATH SHALL HAVE NO DOMINION."

death mitigated: Huge banner flops down proclaiming: "MADAME CURIE IS DEAD." Straightaway, a girl dressed in only an aviator's helmet bursts through the banner, protesting: "Non! Non! This is not true, Monseiur. She's still alive!" Clutches her heart. And falls. Dead.

valentine's day: Nun returns to fire automatic rifle into perhaps 100 "Do Not Puncture" aerosol shaving cream cans mounted on a framed rectangle. When hit, the cans spout and billow white, creamy glop that falls on a girl writhing on the floor dressed in an American flag. This is augmented by a tape of a woman achieving orgasm at least 12 times in five minutes.

Light fades; the nun speaks: "IT WAS THIS WAY ONCE . . . IT WILL NEVER BE THIS WAY AGAIN." In darkness glow the hot plates that boiled alive the goldfish. Their bodies float in silhouette.

Not all of *Eating Kittens* was performed as written. No goldfish were boiled, no automatic rifle was fired (though apparently shaving cream was dispensed), no arrows were flung. The Botticelli was another artist's work. The impossible-to-stage parts were read by O'Donoghue, as agitated and dramatic as ever. Other segments, such as *the gypsy priest* and *death mitigated,* were sufficiently realized. The knifed dolls were tossed on cue. But perhaps most unsettling to those watching was O'Donoghue's abuse of the "crippled" girl. The segment, *you can't crawl away from life forever,* reached a level of sadism merely hinted at in O'Donoghue's earlier work.

It is one thing for a Nazi or a drill sergeant to torture a victim; no matter how brutal, their behavior can be explained. But for a man to stomp a helpless woman simply because it amuses him is something else entirely. Was it a "satire" of misogyny? An illustration of passion gone awry? A plea for better treatment of the sexually-charged handicapped? Whatever the point, it was just an act. But as O'Donoghue kicked away while emitting "unrestrained, joyous laughter," some in the audience felt that his performance was too realistic. Maybe the guy *was* fucking crazy.

Loonin began to think along these lines. He found unsettling O'Donoghue's temperament, even though it was this that had initially attracted him. In *Gobi Fossils* he saw a man handle emotion as if it were a grenade. He now had trouble discerning the "real" O'Donoghue from his "theatrical" persona, and he could no longer tell if his friend was serious or not when making cruel observations. The problem, if one can call it that, predated Loonin. When he met O'Donoghue, the "real" and "theatrical" sides were for the most part one. In essence, Loonin never really knew the "real" O'Donoghue; that body had been dumped upstate. What Loonin saw as a coarsening was yet another shift in character. The decoration of the loft should have served as a clue.

Loonin became convinced of O'Donoghue's severity during a rehearsal of a piece in the loft. The piece, titled *The Monkey Fuckers,* came from a story in *The Realist* about the curious mating habits of the baboon. An actor, Tom Bissinger, read the story aloud. The other players, cast as monkeys and kept in cages made from egg cartons, performed the story as Bissinger read. In one cage crouched Loonin and an actress, Ellen Gurin. They pantomimed the act of monkey love, but O'Donoghue, who slipped written bits of dialogue into the cage, wanted more. Caught up in the story line, O'Donoghue berated the two for their lack of "realism." From his rising voice came orders that they truly mate in rough simian fashion.

As he screamed—"like a Nazi," according to Loonin, Gurin became unglued. Like everyone else there, Gurin had smoked a fair amount of marijuana. Addled by the rush of THC and confronted by a ranting O'Donoghue, she began to cry and asked that the rehearsal be stopped. But the atmosphere was too charged to be changed so quickly, and on the piece went. Eventually things wound down and people began to leave, including Gurin, who remained shaken by the experience. One week later, at Andy Warhol's studio, the Factory, Gurin committed suicide by jumping out a window.

After they read of her death in the local papers, Loonin and O'Donoghue discussed the matter. Loonin believed that his friend had overstepped his bounds and was of no assistance to someone in need. O'Donoghue countered that Gurin knew what she was getting into and was emotionally rattled to begin with, so the fault rested with her. After all, no one else present that day had leaped from a window. To Loonin,

Posing with the heads in the loft. In the rear row, Maude Boltz, a rope sculptress, O'Donoghue's girlfriend at the time

O'Donoghue seemed untouched by Gurin's death, and when O'Dono- ghue named one of the plaster female heads in his loft "Ellen," Loonin thought O'Donoghue had rounded the bend.

It is difficult to judge O'Donoghue's mind-set at the time. Although his words and deeds suggest he was indifferent to Gurin's fate, O'Dono- ghue was in reality hypersensitive to the very concept of death and the fact that it is inescapable. This informed much of his work, and it's possible that he feigned indifference for the sake of artistic appearances. After all, how could a "sick and twisted" individual such as O'Donoghue be bothered with the suicide of one person? Had he felt responsible for Gurin's death, it's hard to believe he could have hidden it so well: O'Donoghue, at center, was soft, nonviolent. The thought that he'd had a hand in pushing her out the window would be too much for him to endure. Gurin's suicide, he felt, was inevitable, and this allowed him to crack wise about her passing as he would about the death of a com- plete stranger.

Still, O'Donoghue was possessed of extreme ideas, and he took de- light in the stunned reactions of others. Loonin joined the ranks of the stunned; O'Donoghue now functioned on a level that Loonin could not—or chose not—to approach. The gap between them widened, and the final break came, fittingly enough, over a play written by O'Donoghue.

Titled *Someday What You Really Are Is Going to Catch Up With You, I Just Hope It Isn't Too Late, Or, Don't Be a Fool! Once a Romance Is Dead . . . It Can Never Come to Life Again*, the play is one of O'Donoghue's weaker efforts of this period. The three characters, Leslie Howard, Clark Gable, and Vivien Leigh, form a love triangle in which passions and identities are randomly exchanged. But the dialogue is bland, soap opera mush, and no connection to *Gone With the Wind* is made. Indeed, the dialogue seems to be taken from lesser, cheesier fare. Romance clichés are stacked high, and one assumes that the "joke" is in these regal characters spouting nonsense. Quickly written, scarcely revised, *Someday* was staged in early 1967 at the Martinique Theater with Loonin as director.

O'Donoghue played Gable as George Sanders, whose mask he all but wore himself: fey demeanor, droll elocution, cigarette held lightly between middle fingers. The play ran for two weeks before O'Donoghue left, bored with the production. Loonin, however, wanted to keep *Someday* going. He recast the Gable role and staged a few additional performances. Then he received a letter from O'Donoghue's lawyer. Loonin was told that if he continued with the production he would be sued for $1,500. Loonin was taken aback; he phoned his friend and asked what this meant. O'Donoghue answered simply that if he wasn't in the play, the play would not go on. If he had to use legal muscle to enforce his decision, so be it. Angered but unwilling to fight, Loonin ceased production.

To this point Loonin and O'Donoghue's collaboration had involved some give-and-take. Thus Loonin felt he could freely use O'Donoghue's material, but here a crucial error was made. Unless O'Donoghue was personally involved, he allowed *no one* to touch his material. His work so intertwined with his name that separation was unthinkable, and attempts at separation were, to him, criminal. It was plagiarism by another name. This O'Donoghue did not tolerate, as Loonin quickly discovered.

The scuffle over the play effectively ended their relationship. Months later, Loonin saw O'Donoghue at a party on the Upper West Side and attempted reconciliation. But O'Donoghue complained of a headache and turned away. They met again in the mid-1970s when O'Donoghue was working on *Saturday Night Live*. The old acquaintances chatted amiably until Loonin raised the issue of their dispute. Another fight ensued, and Loonin and O'Donoghue never again spoke.

Loonin's case was unusual: He crossed O'Donoghue and was, albeit years later, granted a second chance. O'Donoghue was not so generous to others—or "others." He would, in the style of John Barrymore in the film *Twentieth Century,* close the iron door on those he felt had betrayed him. Over the next few years this iron door slammed with the frequency of a screen door on a back porch.

five

If you can't fuck it, blow it up.

eaten to death in her final adventure, Phoebe Zeit-Geist lay in her grave under the tombstone inscription "Golden lads and girls all must, as chimney sweepers come to dust." But unlike the average corpse, Phoebe kept her figure and stayed the hand of decay. Resurrection was inevitable, but in what form? And to what end? (What would it all mean?) In darkness she awaited her wake-up/curtain call.

At *Evergreen,* the desire for more *Phoebe Zeit-Geist* was strong. In its two-year run the strip made the magazine notorious, which in turn helped boost circulation. Conceptually, the editors preferred that attention be paid to the fiction of Kenzaburo Oë and Hubert Selby Jr., the criticism of Susan Sontag and Martin Williams, the plays of Brendan Behan and Arrabal. Here the *Evergreen* faithful complied, for the talent on display could not be found in most other magazines. Yet a score of readers overlooked the latest trends in literature, art, and poetry and focused instead on *Phoebe.* They studied the narrative for hidden meanings, concocted theories to explain her appeal. They bought *Evergreen* because it ran the strip; had *Phoebe* appeared in *Ceilings & Walls,* the monthly devoted to empty rooms would have seen a rise in sales.

With *Phoebe,* O'Donoghue and Springer had altered the *Evergreen* formula. Once tightly wound, the magazine loosened; a piece on student unrest or police brutality shared space with a study of lingerie. Barney Rosset and Fred Jordan did tilt in this direction before *Phoebe* emerged—*Barbarella* is one example. But it was *Phoebe*'s tone that shook up the magazine, text and all. O'Donoghue rendered sex, violence, and death with such creative grace that a change in format was the only way *Evergreen* could contain (or channel) the energy he unleashed. Jordan encouraged O'Donoghue to exploit similar themes in other pieces, and in a specific case he provided the writer with sexual material that he wanted O'Donoghue to adapt.

Jordan possessed a mass of photos that showed women, mostly nude, lounging seductively in various locations. The photos were taken by a freelancer named Roy Coleman, known professionally as "Chaz." He submitted the photos for publication, but Jordan found them simple and unerotic. The only way to use the photos, Jordan thought, was in a satirical sense, and who better to mesh nudity and satire than O'Donoghue?

But naked women alone did not inspire satirical thoughts. Instead, O'Donoghue filled their blank stares with odd story lines and captions. A topless woman on a lunch counter becomes "Cleo," a motorcycle gang nympho seeking thrills; cheerleaders strip, then shower together, so they may ease the pain of their team's defeat; a dress designer, "Marigold Flagg," reflects on owls, chess, and other topics (see next page).

He conceived similar bits for other photographers (nude women living in abandoned cars, a topless scuba diver), but to O'Donoghue the extra work meant more paychecks, little else. Money was scarce, and gone was the security that Paula Levy once provided him. Two years earlier he had been made a contributing editor to *Evergreen,* but this was an honorary editorship for which he received no salary. Jordan now began paying him fifty dollars a week to check the magazine's circulation numbers—among other vague, subscription-oriented duties. O'Donoghue pocketed the money, made up the numbers, and outlined a new set of *Phoebe* adventures.

Her termination in *Evergreen*'s October 1967 issue could not stem the strip's growing popularity. Like Barbarella, Phoebe became something of a cultural symbol. Middlebrows in the press sensed a trend in progress, and essays devoted to the scantily clad woman and her place in the comic world soon appeared. Most employed the tone demonstrated by a critic in *New York* magazine: "[E]ye-popping, if not brilliant, parodies of our preoccupation with perversity . . . they are self-conscious put-downs." Since *Barbarella* and *Phoebe Zeit-Geist* had, as protagonists, beautiful women with large breasts, the strips were often linked, and one was rarely mentioned independently of the other.

This suited Rosset and Jordan fine. They planned to publish the complete *Barbarella* to capitalize on the release of Roger Vadim's film. Why not a collection of the *Phoebe* strips? they thought. This certainly made more sense than a continuation of her adventures in *Evergreen.* A book would naturally appeal to the *Phoebe* crowd while it attracted new members to the fold (and to the magazine itself). It could be assembled quickly with minimum effort and cost, and could, potentially, lead to something larger—like a film version of the heroine's travails.

"Dr. Caligari," a pet owl, wings its way across the room and perches on her shoulder. Whooooooo. Whooooooo. When asked whether she thinks it strange for a young, attractive girl to choose an owl as a pet, Marigold replies: "Not nearly so strange as, let us say, a tapir. Not nearly so strange. Care for a game of chess?" The board is set up. After playing 5 minutes, she announces: "I mate in 19 moves." 19 moves later. Checkmate. "Chess originated in ancient Persia," she points out, flashing an engaging smile. "The word 'checkmate' is derived from the Persian *'shah mat'* meaning 'the king is dead'. Excuse me while I limber up." She leaps to the parallel bars and gives an awesome demonstration of dexterity and muscle control. It's over as suddenly as it began. Springing from the bars, she executes a mid-air double somersault and lands on both feet. Upright. Her body is glistening. Firelight plays on her thighs. "Wow! Half an hour on one of these things and I guarantee you'll feel fabulous." Then comes the near magical transformation from Marigold, the skilled gymnast, to Marigold, the gracious hostess. "Care for another drink?" But Marigold has many ever-changing faces, many fluctuating moods. Within seconds she is toying with a 1927 Sikorsky Amphibian S-38 propeller, discussing philosophy: "Frankly, I'm an existentialist. *Sartre et moi, nous sommes exactement comme ci. Il est gentil.*" The fire has burned low. The shadows lengthen. A great white owl flutters across the room. Whooooooo. Whooooooo. Whooooooo.

O'Donoghue liked the idea of a *Phoebe* book. It would give his creation the permanence that yellowing back issues of *Evergreen* could not; plus, there was the promise of money and additional *Phoebe*-related projects. All that was needed was an illustrated précis to better explain Phoebe's background and an ending where she is pulled from death and sent home. As he had in Levy's apartment, O'Donoghue, fueled by coffee and Silva Thins, wrote through many nights. The sound of his Smith-Corona pierced the silence of his loft, where in darkness roamed his cats, Pamela and Black Cat. Within a week he had produced a script that was ready for Springer's attention. They met, spoke briefly, and Springer returned to Long Island to complete his end of the assignment.

In the précis we are shown Phoebe's wealth: mansion, butler, polo pony, limousine, and chauffeur. Her childhood and adolescence sweep by, and at age twenty-four she finds herself at "one of those elegant garden parties in Antwerp." The guest of honor, Phoebe mingles with the upper crust, a jet set of aristocrats and heiresses that includes the pre–Sirhan Robert Kennedy and, in the corners of the room, O'Donoghue and Springer themselves. All goes swimmingly until Phoebe is slipped the drugged pousse-café that knocks her cold, and she is placed in a wicker portmanteau. While "suspended in the twilight world of heavy sedation," Phoebe remembers her eleventh birthday, spent alone at the Tavistock Goose Fair.

The Gypsy's reaction scars her for life—or what remains of it, for
destiny beckons Phoebe as she awakens in Death Valley under the glare
of the ex-Nazi . . .

In the closing chapter, "Abjection Overruled," Phoebe is rescued
from the mob of would-be assassins by an unseen "big weird machine"
that drops her "at *another* Antwerp garden party" (where again O'Donoghue and Springer appear). Here a mob of a different sort converge
on Phoebe:

Battered but alive, Phoebe rests; justice and truth are reaffirmed. But
does further trouble await our heroine? The old Gypsy knows—or rather

knew, as she had earlier succumbed to a brain tumor and died horribly. Only time, and the sale of thousands of *Phoebe* books, would tell.

Jordan approved the new chapters and plans to release the hardcover edition of *The Adventures of Phoebe Zeit-Geist* were made for the spring of 1968. In meetings with Jordan and Rosset, O'Donoghue pitched his idea for the book's cover illustration: a facsimile of a B-grade movie poster where none of the action portrayed appears in the film itself. Something, as O'Donoghue would become fond of saying, that got "the rubes in the tent." He saw Phoebe held by a giant robot that scorched everything in its path with a death ray: a city aflame, army tanks melted, soldiers killed. Rosset objected to the concept on the grounds that Phoebe never encountered a giant robot. O'Donoghue replied that this was precisely what he desired, and once he made clear his idea, Rosset gave in.

The Adventures of Phoebe Zeit-Geist was released in March 1968. A book party was held early that month in a small West Village bookstore at midnight. Author and artist were, of course, present to sign copies, chat with fans. O'Donoghue was in George Sanders mode, suave but subversive (this was, after all, a Grove Press signing), smoking cigarettes in his typically elegant manner. Turnout was modest; sales of the book slim: four copies were paid for and signed. The book did better with the general public. *Phoebe* sold relatively well but was not a blockbuster by any means. Critics were positive; some, like *Playboy*'s, enthusiastic. Even the right-wing *National Review* took time from cheering the slaughter of Asian peasants to "rejoice" in the book's arrival. This, however, would be the crest of *Phoebe*'s popularity.

Talk of a *Phoebe* film ended with *Barbarella*'s release. Roger Vadim's depiction of the French comic proved embarrassing to all involved, from the film's star Jane Fonda, to its screenwriter, Terry Southern. Though *Barbarella* attained "camp classic" status, this was not enough to encourage investors or studios to back another film about a sexy woman's strange adventures. But as bad as *Barbarella* was, its story line offered fewer obstacles to interpretation than did *Phoebe*'s. Any attempt to realize in live action the scope, density, and movement of the strip would doubtlessly have failed, especially in 1968. (Today, it would be directed by Joel Shumacher and would star Uma Thurman.) *Phoebe* animated could incorporate much of the original strip's action, but production costs would have been prohibitive. Still, a few voices rose in favor of a *Phoebe* project: Ultra Violet, a veteran of Andy Warhol's films, told the press that she was available to play Miss Zeit-Geist. Her call, as it were, was not returned.

Phoebe helped to make a notorious or "hip" reputation for O'Donoghue, but, as always, he received little money for his creation. During the latter part of *Phoebe*'s run, O'Donoghue took a job at an East Village discotheque called the Electric Circus. Located on St. Mark's Place, the Circus was billed as the "ultimate entertainment experience." The house bands were Sly and the Family Stone and the Chambers Brothers; jugglers and clowns moved through the crowd; an actor in a gorilla suit and an actress in a Bo Peep costume distributed hash brownies and acid in sugar cubes. It was a cavernous place that could accommodate over seven hundred people. Foam rubber, black-lit rooms lay adjacent to the big room, and there customers could go to either sort out or enjoy the state of their minds.

O'Donoghue was brought in by Denis Wright, who produced many of the stage shows at the Circus, and introduced to the venue's manager, Barry Secunda, who hired him as an "idea man." O'Donoghue was to help produce and act in various happenings and short theatrical scenes between the music acts. He also became part of the Circus's Saturday morning children's theater, called the Electric Ear, where, in one play, he was cast as a duck. O'Donoghue was given creative carte blanche and used this freedom to indulge his taste for spectacle. One such event occurred on Halloween night, 1967. Dressed as a monk, O'Donoghue walked onstage carrying a large crucifix as other actors chanted behind him. He had ordered that coconut oil be poured into the fog machine so that a coconut essence would envelop the crowd as he entered. But the oil burned and the machine emitted acrid smoke. Overcome by fumes, the crowd rushed the fire exits and the performance came to an abrupt end.

O'Donoghue spent over half a year at the Circus. His final night came when, after working as emcee, he inadvertently walked into a fight where "a guy was getting stabbed. And the brother of the guy who was getting stabbed was a security guard at the club and a black belt in karate. He was freaked out on something and got confused and thought I was the one who stabbed his brother, so he tried to kill me. It took five people to drive him off me, and since they couldn't hold him they said, 'You better leave, Mike.'" O'Donoghue showed up at Secunda's office in a hysterical state, his shirt ripped, wire glasses bent, and voice high-pitched: "*Barry!* That's it! Fuck it! I'm gone!" Secunda asked what happened.

"What happened?" O'Donoghue screamed. "I can't stay here any-more! They're animals! I just had the shit kicked out of me!"

"Sit down. Calm down. Let me get Security."

"No, no, no," said O'Donoghue. "*That's* who did it!"

O'Donoghue quit the Electric Circus. "I realized that probably this wasn't such a good job and maybe I should do other things to make a living," he said. But O'Donoghue and Secunda forged a bond, and within a year Secunda would become his manager.

Back at Grove, O'Donoghue met up with a cartoonist named Phil Wende. A product of Tennessee, Wende had moved to New York and sold a few illustrations to *Evergreen,* including "The Adventures of the Smith Brothers," a pair of idiot Klansmen. O'Donoghue and Wende discussed art and exchanged ideas. O'Donoghue had several he thought might sell, including one about the daily life of a single rock. He wrote the story for Wende to illustrate, then took the pages to Random House and pitched them to a young editor there, Christopher Cerf.

Cerf, son of the famous Bennett, hailed from Harvard and was a veteran of the *Harvard Lampoon.* He was of the generation that helped set the *Lampoon* on a more commercial course that ultimately led to its *National Lampoon* incarnation. Upon graduation in 1963, Cerf and fellow *Lampoon* alum Michael Frith went to work at Random House's Beginner Books division, where Dr. Seuss held sway. After a brief noncombat stint in the military, Cerf returned to Random House full-time as a senior editor for both adult and juvenile books. It was here in 1968 that O'Don-oghue approached him with the rock book idea, among others. Up to this point O'Donoghue had had no contact with the *Harvard Lampoon* crowd; yet, said Cerf, "He knew who I was and he knew I was there, and he knew I was doing crazy books, among other things." Cerf, who knew of O'Donoghue through *Phoebe,* looked over the illustrations and story and bought the idea immediately. He loved the concept but couldn't pay much for it. Indeed, his father gave him $150 to promote what was now *The Incredible, Thrilling Adventures of the Rock.*

Although not one of O'Donoghue's better ideas, *Rock* has its charm, especially for a book he knocked off in order to raise money. There is no plot. The same rock sits in the same spot in the same forest for thousands of years. Nothing much happens. Then, while two boys roam the wood in search of a Christmas tree, one sees the rock and is inspired (see pages 164 and 165).

"I don't recall it flying off the shelves," said Cerf of the book; but neither did he see it as a complete disaster. The experience led to a close friendship with O'Donoghue. "He wasn't as unbelievably weird at first as he became later," Cerf observed, "and I say that with great affection. I think he was definitely unusual, intense and crazy, but extremely funny and really very, very nice. That's the part that surprises people. I loved him right away. He was always paranoid, but he was paranoid in an extremely outgoing and funny way earlier, compared to what I think he was like later."

In 1969, Cerf brought O'Donoghue into a quickie project that sati-rized the then-famous "conspiracy" trial in Chicago. Following the police riots during the Democratic Convention the previous summer, a number of New Left activists—among them Abbie Hoffman, Jerry Rubin, Bobby Seale, and David Dellinger—were brought to court to face charges that

Then the smaller boy got an idea. "Hey! I got an idea! See that rock there? Why don't we take him home and paint him red and green and cover him with tinsel and glue a picture of Santa to him and put a candle on top and he could be a CHRISTMAS ROCK?"

they had driven Chicago's finest to behave like fascist thugs. Hoffman asked Cerf if he would produce a program that could be hawked on the courthouse steps. The trial was to be treated as a sports event, "The Chicago Conspiracy vs. the Washington Kangaroos," and Cerf, Michael Frith, and O'Donoghue contributed to the program. O'Donoghue wrote an ad for the "Action Army," where new recruits sent to Vietnam may enjoy Charlie's "light show" after "blowing some Saigon Red." Also, there was a "report" from "Bull" Penn of the "Conspiracy" sports desk, written by a younger friend of Cerf's, George W.S. Trow.

Trow had come to Harvard through Exeter. He joined the *Lampoon*

His older brother paused for a moment. Then he slowly turned, his face brightening, and replied, "A CHRISTMAS ROCK? HAH! HAH! THAT'S THE DUMBEST THING I EVER HEARD OF! YOU MUST BE OUT OF YOUR HEAD! A CHRISTMAS ROCK??? HAH! HAH! HAH! HAH! HAH! HAH! HAH!"

"at a time when the *Lampoon* was very interesting"—that is, when Cerf and Frith were pushing the magazine away from its staid, buttoned-down tradition. It was "a serious moment at Harvard" both culturally and politically, and over in Hearst's Castle, home of the *Lampoon,* a number of prep school boys "found a chance to run wild, largely around the talent of Cerf and Frith." And, of course, one of these boys was Trow. Fair-haired, stylish, eloquent, Trow had by his own admission a rather conventional aspect to his life. His prime artistic influence was H. H. Monroe, otherwise known as the short story master Saki; and like Monroe, Trow wasted few words in his written work. He was precise if prim, though once behind the *Lampoon* castle's walls he, along with Cerf, would cut loose, get drunk and play Ray Charles songs on the piano. "To like the Supremes or R&B was not done," said Trow, "and it was done by us."

Trow became president of the *Lampoon* in his senior year, 1965. After graduation and a brief time in the Coast Guard, Trow, as had many *Lampoon* vets before him, moved on to the *New Yorker* to serve an apprenticeship under the aegis of the magazine's editor, William Shawn. There Trow hoped to develop as a serious writer. But he never lost track of his *Lampoon* colleagues, and when Cerf asked him to contribute to the "Conspiracy" program, Trow composed his sports desk piece. During this period he attended a gathering for Abbie Hoffman that was held in O'Donoghue's Spring Street loft. When Trow walked into the space, "I saw Michael and he saw me and we understood that something was likely to happen that we had to check out a little bit." Each scoped out the other: O'Donoghue scanned Trow for hints of snobbishness or disrespect; Trow, taking in the flavor of the loft, wondered if his host was too strange to handle. Finally, O'Donoghue handed Trow a copy of the *Phoebe* book. As he read the opening panels set at the fateful garden party in Antwerp, Trow laughed. "What are you laughing at?" inquired O'Donoghue. They talked, connected. "There was no looking back," said Trow. "Once I got a taste of his loft and the way he was living, it was hard to stay away."

After this first meeting, Trow and O'Donoghue saw quite a bit of each other. They talked every day and got together at least four times a week. But for all of O'Donoghue's openness, Trow noticed a distinct behavorial pattern in his new friend. "In the sixties and early seventies, Michael had a rigid countercultural presence which kept everything at a distance," said Trow. "He did not like any conventional interaction with society. It was only when he began to discover that there could be a kind of high camp attitude toward life that would work for a certain aspect of conventional society that he did that, and he did it very quickly. He moved from one way of dealing with the world to quite another. But in fact they were the same way of dealing with the world." But O'Donoghue had yet to reach high camp. For now the cool distance remained, and his loft, noticed Trow, was a key element in this early posture.

Although their material appeared in the "Conspiracy" program, this did not constitute collaboration. That would soon come. Trow was friendly with a film producer, Ismail Merchant, through whom he'd met Merchant's associate, the director James Ivory. Sometime in 1968 or early 1969, Trow and Ivory discussed possible film projects. Both liked Luis

With George Trow, in the Soho loft, c. 1969–70

Buñuel's *Exterminating Angel,* in which a civilized dinner party goes to seed, trapping the guests as matters deteriorate. Ivory suggested making Buñuel's film in reverse, and Trow agreed. A band of primitive people enter a grand house, become civilized, and hold a lavish dinner party before they revert back to their crude origins. Ivory, to his amazement, received immediate financial backing for this rather obscure project. Trow brought O'Donoghue in to co-write the screenplay because, as he put it, "I could not imagine doing anything without Michael."

Trow and O'Donoghue worked quickly but separately. Trow devised the framework of a weekend house party within which many of O'Donoghue's scenes were played out. Their screenplay, *Savages,* though simple in plotline, contains subtle, richly textured passages and bits. A tribe of Mud People are about to sacrifce one of their own when, suddenly, a croquet ball bounces in their midst. The tribal priestess studies the ball, holding it aloft. It possesses a certain power that leads the priestess and her followers to its place of origin, a large, abandoned country house located near the deep forest where the Mud People live. Cautiously, they approach the house, enter it, look around. Before them lie the remains of civilized prosperity. They touch the picture frames, fondle objets d' art, try on once expensive clothes. No longer afraid, the Mud People immerse themselves in this strange environment, and a swift metamorphosis takes place. Their tribal masks drop, the mud peels away, and they soon become a stylish group of revelers, clean and impeccably dressed, there to enjoy a weekend party in the country.

Savages brings to life a theme O'Donoghue toyed with over the years: elegance that is slightly weathered and tattered; style that is a shadow of its former self. As *Savages* unfolds the now "civilized" Mud People slowly but steadily drift back to their primal state. It is here, in this inevitable return to the mud, that some of O'Donoghue's better images surface.

- An older woman, Carlotta, entertains a circle of guests by performing Bletology, a form of fortune telling done through the fondling of peaches. As Carlotta holds a slightly bruised peach, she enters a trance and sees duplicity, bale, remorse . . . a soiled kimono, explosions at the mill, laughter behind one's back . . . signals through the flames, webbed fingers, weevils in the tea . . . a punctured thumb, cheap emotions, faded carpets . . .
- Two women flirt and kiss in the backseat of a Pierce-Arrow. One, Iliona, instructs the other on the finer points of eliminating facial hair as she removes the young thing's clothes and embraces her naked form. Iliona turns on the car's headlights and sees in the near distance a woman, noose around her neck, hanging from a tree. Her body slowly turns in the dim light.
- A song, "Steppin' on the Spaniel," is played on the Victrola. Dancing begins as one of the guests mimes the words.

> We don't need no blackbirds to bye-bye!
> Or hooty owls to ask us "Who?" or "Why?"
> Wallabies and sheep need not apply!
> All we want are sleeping dogs that lie . . .
> We're . . .
> Steppin' on the Spaniel
> Fallin' off a log.
> Syncopate it and y'all
> Be puttin' on the dog!
> No difference if it's a pedigreed or a mutt, I know
> It doesn't matter when you're doin' that strut, hi ho!

But no amount of dancing can stave off the inevitable descent. Finally, during croquet on the lawn, the party guests begin swinging the mallets as clubs, whacking balls into the wood that awaits their return. . . .

Savages was shot in the fall of 1970. The filming was done on location in Scarborough, New York, at a neo-Georgian mansion called Beechwood. During production Trow and O'Donoghue worked line by line with each other on the film's trailer: "They lived as though every day were their last, and every night as though it were the first. Between the apes and the angels came . . . *Savages*." But the film would not be released for another two years. The duo began work on another screen project called *The War Room,* but this, Trow admitted, had no real plot or energy. O'Donoghue and Trow concentrated instead on a new magazine that both had recently helped bring to life.

A gun in the mouth is the new lampshade on the head.

Few magazines leave permanent dents in American culture, a culture now and forever steeped in the audiovisual. The early *New Yorker* made for electric reading before it slowed to a soft, comfortable hum. Then Tina Brown arrived with designer jumper cables and a crew of hack mechanics. In the 1960s, *Esquire* dealt beautifully, at times brilliantly, with American politics, literature, and pop culture. But eventually celebrity gossip drowned out the better voices; the best the magazine could hit was a minor, often flat, note. *Playboy*'s blend of airbrushed models and consumer items for men made its founder rich and legitimized the use of sex as a selling point. The formula staled, but not before countless other magazines copied Hef's example. And, of course, there was *National Lampoon.*

Most people familiar with the name *National Lampoon* connect it to *Animal House* and a string of Chevy Chase road films. Though its effect on American humor continues to reverberate, the magazine itself is now forgotten. This might in part stem from the fact that the *Lampoon* was never widely read. It was very popular among youth, primarily high school boys and college-age men—a coveted ad demographic. But it did not find a place on the American coffee table. Those in the mainstream whom the *Lampoon* touched were usually repulsed or confused by its humor. This was especially true of the mainstream press. Although reporters and editors admired the magazine's healthy circulation figures, they struggled to explain the jokes and references that hit them at odd angles. Thus their use of the labels "irreverent" (above the belt) and "tasteless" (below).

The beginnings of the *National Lampoon* were relatively modest. In the mid-1960s Henry Beard and Doug Kenney were editors of the *Harvard Lampoon.* Beard was clean-cut, smoked a pipe, wore wrinkled Brooks Brothers suits; Kenney played the prep school lad who would later become a hippie. Beard's humor was dry and shaped by his intellect; Kenney's humor was instinctive, free-flowing, but no less intelligent than Beard's. Beard hailed from a distinguished East Coast family; Kenney was a kid from Chagrin Falls, Ohio. In 1968 they put together a parody of *Life* magazine that was to be distributed nationally. Near the end of this project Beard and Kenney, along with their business confidant, Rob Hoffman, met with Harold Chamberlain, owner of one of the largest magazine distributorships in the nation. The trio intrigued Chamberlain, and he suggested that his friend Matty Simmons have a word with them.

Matty Simmons had worked in journalism and public relations; as executive vice president of the Diners Club he helped found the credit card business. In 1967 he and his partner, Len Mogel, left the Diners Club to enter the magazine world. Their company, Twenty First Century Communications, first published *Cheetah,* a failed attempt to cash in on the commercialized elements of the counterculture. Their second effort, *Weight Watchers Magazine,* met with success; but Simmons and Mogel were open to other ventures, and it was at this point that they met with Beard, Kenney, and Hoffman. "The meeting wasn't one of particular importance to Len and me," Simmons later wrote. "Any relationship agreed to would be for a one-shot publication [the *Life* parody]. No one in the room that day envisioned the possibility of a monthly magazine."

But the Harvard trio had plans beyond *Life.* Their college days were over, and the traditional route for ex-*Lampoon* editors—Wall Street, advertising, law—appealed to neither Beard nor Kenney. They wanted to play the parody game at a professional level. Their version of *Life* was, in content, a step toward this goal. But the parody sold poorly, and the production costs ensured that no profit would be realized. Yet Simmons saw possibility in the wreckage. After all, he and Mogel came late into the *Life* project and were unable to alter its tragic course. Were they to be in on the beginning of a new project, their knowledge of magazine production and distribution could make a sizable difference.

In late 1968, Simmons and Mogel brokered a deal with the *Harvard Lampoon* to publish a parody of *Time.* This was the second *Lampoon* take on the venerable American weekly (the first published in 1965). But the first *Time* parody was distributed locally in Cambridge; the new one was aimed at a national audience. The question posed on the parody's cover, "Does Sex Sell Magazines?" was answered in mid-1969 when the *Lampoon's Time* earned $250,000 in newsstand sales. As did *Life, Time* reflected Beard's and Kenney's humor; but thanks to Simmons and Mogel, the Harvard boys amused more than a handful of *Lampoon* enthusiasts. The shared success of *Time* made it plain to all that a national humor monthly was indeed a viable proposition.

In June 1969, the first meetings were held to discuss this idea. After much haggling between Hoffman, who represented Beard and Kenney, and Simmons, a final deal was agreed upon: Twenty First Century would own 80 percent of the new company's stock, and at the end of five years Simmons and Mogel would buy out the Harvard trio as though they owned 50 percent of the stock instead of the 20 percent they held.★

★Though Hoffman negotiated the *Lampoon* deal, he did not remain with the magazine. He returned to his native Texas to work for his father's Coca-Cola franchise.

The deal cleared the way for the magazine and created what would later be a crisis moment for the enterprise. (Those interested in the minutiae of the deal and the bargaining process that led to it are advised to read Matty Simmons's memoir, *If You Don't Buy This Book, We'll Shoot This Dog,* and Tony Hendra's *Going Too Far.*)

Where *Mad* merely thumbed a nose and made obnoxious noises, the *National Lampoon* employed the bullet and club. No one was innocent; all were considered targets. But this sensibility did not spring organically from the magazine's Harvard roots. The boys who penned the college *Lampoon* and its parody issues were unaccustomed to bloodletting; they lived in Hearst's Castle, not a slaughterhouse. Their wit didn't clash with their pants. Although rock 'n' roll inspired them to take new steps, their humor retained much of the Harvard tradition. The new magazine needed an outside agitator. In late summer 1969, Beard and Kenney put out the word; Christopher Cerf and George Trow responded by bringing them Michael O'Donoghue.

The moment was perfect for O'Donoghue. His connection to *Evergreen* remained, but his best days there were past. By 1969 all the magazine received from him were scraps of his lesser verse. He looked to publish elsewhere. However, outlets for the expression of his new ideas were few. The alternative press of *Screw* and the *East Village Other* offered plenty of uncensored space, and O'Donoghue knew well the editors of these publications. Although he did allow *Other Scenes,* a spin-off sheet from the *EVO,* to print the dirty limericks from *The Glass Vertebrae,* O'Donoghue saw no future in such venues. Had *The Rock* sold better, he might have turned out novelty paperbacks. But O'Donoghue was too restless to conform to single-premise books. Ambitious, he wanted the next step he took to leave a lasting print.

When they first encountered O'Donoghue, Beard and Kenney—especially Kenney—were struck by his authenticity. Like tourists in the bad part of town, the Harvard boys saw in their new collaborator dangerous and exotic qualities. In ratty clothes and a torn army jacket, with long, stringy hair and a wispy mustache, O'Donoghue did not fit the profile of the Hearst Castle occupant. Imagine him as a Harvard student who submits to the *Lampoon* surrealist poems and death camp jokes. Think of him in a Hasty Pudding show where his screams and taunts frighten all present. No amount of George Sanders would convince the boys to allow such a creature into their club. But on O'Donoghue's turf they opened their arms and announced the pleasure of his company.

To O'Donoghue this welcome confirmed his arrival. He was not in awe of the Harvard tradition, felt no uncertainty when advancing his ideas. He was older, was more experienced than the boys, and saw himself above their Ivy League wit. Cerf and Trow understood and accepted

O'Donoghue's stance; Beard and Kenney followed their lead. His talent was too evident to ignore. Kenney appreciated O'Donoghue's mastery of whatever topic he chose to engage. "When I was growing up in Ohio," Kenney said, "I wrote stories about beatniks. I'd have them getting off the IRT at Sixty-eighth and Bleecker and going into a coffeehouse. O'Donoghue had that stuff with authority."

In the early *Lampoon* meetings O'Donoghue was the lone non-Harvard voice. Surrounded by Beard, Kenney, Trow, Cerf, and Michael Frith (who soon fell away), O'Donoghue listened to their banter and studied their exchanges. They were bright and clever, he thought, but each lacked a taste for the jugular. He viewed them as "a bunch of Harvard snot faggots who thought it was wrong to shed blood. It was I that taught them that the true essence of comedy is a baby seal hunt, that rather than using the epee, try the bludgeon." Though it was presumptive to assume he could alter their humor—given that they were as different from one another as they were from O'Donoghue—he would, over time, push them to consider, if not adopt, his tactics. O'Donoghue believed that for the magazine to be good, inhibitions such as "taste" and "morality" had to be, well, snuffed.

The first meetings were held in an apartment shared by Beard and Kenney on East Eighty-third Street. By fall 1969 Matty Simmons had secured them office space at 1790 Broadway, but everyone preferred to meet in public, and soon planning dinners were held once a week at an old German restaurant called the Blue Ribbon. There, under faded photos of opera stars past, the group discussed format and content, what had worked in the parody issues and what could work in a monthly. As ideas flew about, Beard recorded everything said on a notepad. Trow described these meetings as "playful, mean dinners" where lulls were uncommon. As for O'Donoghue, Trow considered him "dominant from moment one. Artistically it was quite clear that this man was ready to go. He knew what he wanted to do; it was a matter of getting it in the magazine."

O'Donoghue knew what he wanted because he had a surplus of ideas. While the others engaged in rapid wordplay and sought to top a previous remark, O'Donoghue sat back, smoked, awaited an opening. His contributions to Beard's notepad came not off-the-cuff, but were already written, weighed for effect, and filed in his metal box at home. He was not improvisational; epigrams and concepts were memorized exactly as he had composed them. This gave him a leg up on his younger colleagues, who were brilliant in conversation but remained rookies in the big humor game. It was a gap, however, that would quickly close.

Matty Simmons was pleased with his roster. Since the *Time* parody, he'd wanted badly to publish a humor monthly, and as 1969 ended everything was set for the *Lampoon*'s debut in the spring. (The magazine's operations moved from Broadway to 635 Madison Avenue.) Simmons was especially impressed with O'Donoghue, whom he described affectionately as "alienated." Like Kenney and Beard, Simmons saw O'Donoghue as essential to the magazine. But neither he nor anyone else could convince O'Donoghue to accept a staff position.

O'Donoghue preferred his freelance status for a practical reason: As a *Lampoon* staffer his material would become the property of Twenty First Century Communications. This meant that the *Lampoon*'s parent company could reprint his work without giving him a dime—or worse, the proper credit. Whether there was a danger of this happening mattered not to O'Donoghue. He simply took no chances. He would sell his pieces to the magazine as an independent contractor. He reserved the rights to his work, which could not be touched without his approval. This also kept him clear of the daily struggle of assembling a new magazine. He valued the access but disdained the mechanics.

American humor is really angry rube humor. Very mean and aggressive. I've always liked American jokes.

The *National Lampoon*'s inaugural issue hit newsstands in March 1970. Its cover, a woman in a skimpy leather outfit leered at by a cartoon duck, the magazine's supposed "mascot," proved a drab combination. It was the first of many awful visual ideas executed by Cloud Studios, which had been hired to bring its version of art direction to the *Lampoon*. Cloud consisted of Bill Skurski, Michael Sullivan, and Peter Bramley, who, as described by Matty Simmons, "dressed in eighteenth-century knickers and stockings, a beaded jacket, and a scarf."

Bramley's drawings reflected this flamboyance; he favored the over-the-top approach then fashionable in "comix": bulging eyeballs, elastic features, sound effects like "Thud!" and "Splat!" written into the panel, and so on. He had illustrated some of O'Donoghue's poetry in *Evergreen Review,* and was well-known and liked throughout the downtown print world. Bramley's work dominated the early *Lampoon,* and this tipped the magazine more to a "countercultural" look that would, again and again, compromise its satiric thrust.

O'Donoghue had two major pieces in the first *Lampoon.* "Pornocopia," excerpts from erotic novels, could easily have appeared in *Evergreen.* O'Donoghue captured accurately the writing styles of the Marquis de Sade, Jacqueline Susann, the "Lost Generation" of the 1920s, and the ever handy Anonymous:

Upon seeing Prissy, a tall gaunt man, wearing but a pair of soiled galoshes, threw himself at her feet and commenced wildly kissing her feather duster.

"Allow me to introduce Professor Schadenfreude," interposed Lord Stoker as the bewildered miss blushed crimson under the Austrian's singular attentions. "His studies in aberrant sexual behavior have taken man's sexual urges out of the Dark Ages."

"And back to the Stone Age," added Lady Wick-Burner, crawling across the carpet to gnaw on the heel of Prissy's left shoe. . . .

The other piece, "Mondo Perverto," a mock subtabloid magazine, was written with George Trow. Here the Cloud style works, for "Mondo Perverto" is properly cheesy and ragged. Photos and text are slapped randomly together, and one gets a grimy feeling just touching the pages. Between the "top" stories—a nymphomaniac wills her heart to Eleanor Roosevelt, a case is made for killing the aged, vampire cows haunt a Wyoming town—are tiny ads for cheap porno paperbacks, elevator cowboy boots, a home sex change kit, and Spanish Fly bubble gum ("Your sweetheart will blow more than bubbles when she takes a chomp on this!"). Every detail, down to the addresses on the coupons, is rendered exact. "Perverto" was uneven, but it cleared the way for sharper parodies of the magazine format.

For all O'Donoghue's talk of spilling blood, his contributions to the first several issues were, for him, rather mild. After touching on the profane and bizarre in *Evergreen,* it was as if he had to show he could write straight satirical copy for the *Lampoon.* He initially focused on the absurdities of the New Left and the contradictions found in the "progressive lifestyle." If the *Lampoon* was to be read by the counterculture, or by those sympathetic with the Good Fight, then O'Donoghue made certain that his early pieces were shoved into each righteous face.

One such piece was "Crossing the Rubicam." The antiwar movement has been co-opted by Madison Avenue, and new ad campaigns are unveiled: a Dewar's profile of an armed feminist revolutionary; a pitch for Up-Against-The-Wall-To-Wall-Carpeting; a television spot in which a black militant prefers Super Shell gasoline in his Molotov cocktail. "Needless to say," he writes, "the same committed youths who were lobbing bricks through their windows are now skimping on their drug money so they can buy an I-Ching rug. Once more, Yankee know-how has triumphed over bubbleheaded idealism." O'Donoghue doesn't wait for the protesters to fatten into yuppie consumers; he knows where they'll end up before their first croissant is eaten.

In the September "Show Biz" issue is "Waiting in the Left Wings." We follow a "new breed" starlet named Nana Bijou through her busy day. She pontificates on ecology, sexism, the Vietnam War; but ultimately her favorite subject is herself. The downtrodden are props in her ongoing photo op. "When asked why Indians are denied membership in REABSORB (Radical Entertainers and Businessmen [to] Save Our Red Brothers), an organization Nana 'spearheads' from the den of her 47-room Pacific Palisades chateau, our attractive activist confides, 'Quite frankly, I think letting them in would tend to debase our image!' " Nana's lip service to causes allows her to wallow in luxury without guilt, though it is doubtful that she encountered so profound an emotion.

In this early *Lampoon* period, O'Donoghue seemed fascinated with the power of consumer culture. Not only did he assume that it would wear down and engulf dissenters (those pretending to dissent, like Nana, had already been digested), he felt that consumerism was the religion of Middle America—not an original thought, not even for O'Donoghue, whose disdain for consumerism and advertising can be seen in his *death book* notes. But in the above pieces and others, such as "Keeping Up With the Joneses," a television show in which a family of four celebrate the blind acquisition of goods, O'Donoghue advanced the notion that despite its material abundance, the America of 1970 was hollow and morally bankrupt. This approach is as literal as he would ever allow; before long he would slip into the shadows where human corruption is a given fact and the sane response is a hammer to the skull.

In the July "Bad Taste" issue of the *Lampoon,* O'Donoghue revealed a glimpse of what was to come. His piece, "Diana Barrymore's Drinking Songs," is a hodgepodge of various bits and one-liners, some of which appeared previously in *Evergreen* and on Le Galerie's basement stage. Among the newer material is "Deadland," a netherworld overseen by the jovial corpse of Walt Disney. Still faithful to children even after death, Uncle Walt tells the kids how they can join in on the postlife fun.

> The quickest way to reach Deadland is to fly here! Simply make two paper airplanes (don't forget to attach paper clips to the noses!), hold one in each hand, and jump from the highest window in your house!
>
> One of the best ways to reach Deadland is by the Magic Tunnel that lies just behind the Enchanted Door! And where is the Enchanted Door? Why, it's on the front of any old refrigerator! And once you're inside, don't forget to shut the Enchanted Door tight so Mommy can't follow you!
>
> See you soon! And be sure to tune in next week, when I tell you about the free toys that grow underneath trains and on the tops of high-power lines and in the bottom of deserted mining shafts!

In Deadland, Mouseketeers never age; their zombie smiles remain fixed as they march through eternal roll call.

Due to its seemingly "tasteless" and "offensive" nature, "Diana Barrymore's Drinking Songs" was printed backwards, so that one needed a mirror to read it. This gimmick was, of course, part of the joke; but the piece taken whole was less "offensive" than any number of items that O'Donoghue had penned for *Evergreen.* "Deadland" was the sharpest bit, but it pricked rather than cut. The image of Walt Disney luring children to their deaths might be taboo if handled by a lesser satirist. For O'Donoghue this was a barrel shoot. He needed something that inspired fear and disgust in the average reader, something that could not be laughed away as simply a "sick" joke.

In the August "Paranoia" issue of the *Lampoon,* O'Donoghue found that something: cancer. In earlier work he mentioned but did not highlight disease. Physical infirmity, torture, death—these were the themes he exploited and would continue to exploit. But terminal illness is tough to generalize; once "cancer" is mentioned the mind thinks immediately of tumors, trauma, chemotherapy, a host of specific horrors. Death, too, crops up, its presence made explicit through the pain caused by disease. Years later, O'Donoghue explained what led him in this direction:

> The things people are shocked by are no longer sexual. It's cancer that threatens people now, not blow jobs. So you can be shocking and dangerous and there is a perimeter that people get very nervous as you move close to. I used to smoke Marlboros and the guy [selling them] would say, "Soft pack or hard?" I'd say, "Listen, I don't really care as long as it gives me cancer." They'd just go "Hunnnnh?"

If cancer is blunt, then O'Donoghue's first treatment of the topic is equally so. In "21 Danger Signs of Cancer," he lists those "symptoms" that indicate the disease: bleeding gums, chapped lips, an itchy neck, headaches at the base of the brain, morning urination, nose hair growth, inability to salivate, being startled by loud noises, afternoon naps. "If you have one or two of the above symptoms," the reader is advised, "act swiftly and there is a *slim, remote possibility* that you can be saved. If you have three or more symptoms, don't bother consulting a physician because it's *too late.* You've reached what we of the medical profession call 'the point of no return.' In the few weeks left to you (*sometimes as much as four months!*), put your affairs in order, say a last goodbye to your loved ones, and prepare for the Eternal Darkness that lies ahead. . . . Brought to you as a public service by The Cancer Institute."

Beneath the "symptoms" is a black-and-white photo of a tomb. On the marble steps leading up to it read the inscriptions "Name of Deceased: You and Your Family. Date of Death: Sooner Than You Think. Cause of Death: Terminal Cancer." The punch line of the piece seems to be, If You Have Cancer You Will Die Horribly and There's Nothing

You Can Do to Stop It. Here one sees the first flecks of blood darkening Harvard crimson.

> *I have a subscription to your magazine,* National Lampoon. *Although I found it to be in poor taste occasionally, I realized it was a satirical magazine so I enjoyed it. However, while reading your August issue which I otherwise found amusing, I hit an advertisement on Cancer for which you should pray to G-d he forgives you for.*
>
> *I have worked as a hospital volunteer for the past 2½ years. During this time I have had to work with* too *many terminal patients, mostly those stricken and doomed with Cancer. Have you ever gone into a ward and have had to explain to 7 year-old child why G-d made him get Cancer and why he must die? Or go to your Land of Eternal Darkness??? Millions of lives are taken by terminal Cancer which you made into a disgusting, morbid, repulsive joke.*
>
> —*Letter from a Brooklyn high school student, 1970*

Although O'Donoghue was slow to follow his recipe for the magazine—sex, violence, and bad taste—his influence surfaced elsewhere, primarily from Kenney's work. Beard's dry style was firm and impervious to radical change. Trow, who often collaborated with O'Donoghue in that first year, retained his pointed elegance; if anything, O'Donoghue moved closer to Trow in their co-authored pieces than the reverse. But Kenney was open to experimentation. He respected O'Donoghue and looked up to him. The older writer could find art within chaos and ferocity. Such was not seen at Harvard, where however spontaneous or wild one's talent, certain boundaries were acknowledged.

The only boundaries O'Donoghue acknowledged were his own, though he never really defined them—"I have one of those minds that can't hold cohesive logic," he once (jokingly?) admitted. But he did make cohesive the ideas that sprang from the dark regions of his mind, and this stirred Kenney to trust fully his own comic instincts. As Thelonious Monk inspired the young John Coltrane to better utilize his natural gifts, so O'Donoghue showed Kenney the value of intuitive composition.

Different yet similar, these two sensibilities merged brilliantly in the November "Nostalgia" issue. In O'Donoghue's card box was an idea for a parody of high school yearbooks. When the theme of the November issue was discussed, he brought the idea to Kenney, who embraced it. Kenney had planned to satirize nostalgia of the 1950s, specifically teen nostalgia, and a high school yearbook fit neatly into the mix. "Nostalgia" for other periods of American history was also slated for the issue (including an 1896 Sears Roebuck "Sex Catalogue" conceived and written by Kenney), but the 1950s section would predominate. The decade was closer to the lives of the *Lampoon* editors, especially Kenney, who more than anyone else on the magazine found poetic and horrid the language and images of that time.

It was in the "Nostalgia" issue that Kenney's comic instincts bore exceptional fruit. Kenney was a child in the 1950s; his high school and college years were spent in the 1960s. Whatever his private view of the 1950s, it was not rooted in the peer wars of Eisenhower-era high schools. Kenney's 1950s would have been seen from an adolescent's perspective, colored by the mainstream culture of Davy Crockett, Dick Clark, soda shops, and white buck shoes. For him to capture the emotions of teens caught in this bland, repressive environment required that he make use of the pain he had experienced in school.

"He had a rough childhood," said Kathryn Walker, who was romantically involved with Kenney at the end of his life. "He had been an unusually talented and not especially popular student in school. It was hard for him to find his crowd there; he was such a rare talent, and such a sensitive person. There was a lot of damage inflicted, and loneliness endured." Though he graduated from high school in 1964, and from Harvard in 1968, Kenney placed his teen isolation in a mid-1950s setting. After all, if alienation is more or less the same for each generation, then Kenney's instincts here proved true. He covered his pain in 1950s slang and created a style of humor that would be copied endlessly by lesser talents.

O'Donoghue, on the other hand, *did* attend high school in the 1950s. Like Kenney, he was bright, unpopular and in need of a confident facade. Although O'Donoghue opted to become an aloof intellectual burning with savage concepts, Kenney played the preppie who delivered side-splitting jokes. Of the two personas, Kenney's was better suited to interpret the 1950s as "Nostalgia," and O'Donoghue recognized this when he gave Kenney the yearbook idea. The result, "Cat-Calls: Ezra Taft Benson High School Year Book 1956," showed that O'Donoghue was keen to the talents of his colleague; his artistic ego was large but it did not prevent him from making sound creative judgments.

"Cat-Calls" looks and reads like a small-town high school yearbook on a limited editorial budget. Photos of students and faculty are faded and stark as if snapped in a colorless void. Drawings of American flags and bobcats (the school's mascot) that appear in the margins are appropriately amateurish. The yearbook in front of us belongs to Mary-Elizabeth Flounce, or "Winkie," whose extracurricular activities include Honor Bowling, Honor Volleyball, and Honor Softball, as well as membership in Bobkittens and Whiskerettes. Winkie is described as a "pert 'n' perky" girl who is "nice to everyone." She stands in contrast to other departing seniors such as Wallace "Gus-Gus" Hooper, class clown and "spitball champ," and Marcia "Sarge" Perkula, the closet dyke who rides a "flame-red Harley Davidson." The descriptions of the senior class provide a partial but distinct narrative of life at Ezra Taft. Science nerd, brainless jock, female tramp, and ladies' man stare lifelessly from their portraits. They are trapped in roles dictated by society, roles that will probably define them as adults.

"Cat-Calls" reaches beyond satire. There is sadness here, a poignancy born of a world where hope is routinely demolished. The optimism expressed in school slogans and student inscriptions is forced and paper-thin. Awareness that life after high school promises drudgery and tedium emerges in spots, specifically in the "happy" news that "Moose," the jock and fag-basher, "has accepted a position as an automobile body repairman and Gus-Gus starts next month as a credit manager trainee for a whole chain of dry cleaning stores." Kenney grasped brilliantly the despair of young adulthood. Most of the characters depicted are pathetic and seemingly worthy of their fate, but a shred of sympathy remains. One reads "Cat-Calls" and thinks, "You poor bastards."

Though O'Donoghue shares the byline for "Cat-Calls," the piece is, by all accounts, Kenney's. Yet O'Donoghue's fingerprints, however light, do appear. The reference to Gus-Gus's becoming a "credit manager trainee" is certainly linked to O'Donoghue's time at Sherwin-Williams. The news that a "few of the guys are even going on to college to become engineers" reflects Michael James Donohue's career choice and his belief in the importance of a college degree. And in the dedication to Rupert Peen, a Senior Civics instructor who died during the school year, an apology is offered: "We are truly sorry, too, for the unkind jokes we made about your cough and those nicknames like 'Hacker' and 'Old Croupy.' We had no idea at the time you had cancer of the trachea." Kenney might have written this, but it was O'Donoghue who inspired such a joke.

With the "Nostalgia" issue, the *Lampoon* changed its appearance. The magazine showed a profit after its sixth month in existence, a remarkable feat given the high mortality rate among new periodicals, and Matty Simmons, who loathed the "underground" graphics of Cloud Studios, wanted a slicker look. In his search for a new art director he was contacted by a young artist named Michael Gross. A product of Brooklyn's Pratt Institute of Art and a seasoned professional in the magazine world (he had worked at *Cosmopolitan*), Gross approached the *Lampoon,* amazed there was an opening. His instincts were commercial—too commercial, he thought, to interest the *Lampoon*. Kenney shared this thought and opposed the hiring of Gross. But Beard and Simmons saw the value of Gross's talent and experience, and in the fall of 1970 he was hired to replace Cloud.

In his book *Going Too Far,* Tony Hendra explains what distinguished Gross from counterculture artists: "Gross was less interested in the cross-currents of political or intellectual commitment than he was in precision of form, and the satisfaction of getting it right . . ." Then Gross himself adds,

> Maybe because of that schizophrenia in me between liberal and conservative, I wanted to be successful and commercial. I couldn't see painting in a loft because I didn't know what I wanted to say as an artist. I liked working commercially because I thought I could translate people's ideas . . . It didn't matter to me a whole lot what I was saying or what I was doing, as long as I was translating it well.

In Gross, Simmons found someone who shared his commercial view. But Gross brought more than mainstream savvy to the *Lampoon*; as translator, he became the silent conduit between concept and finished piece. Unlike Peter Bramley, he added no cartoon sound effects, nor did he exaggerate the ideas of contributors. He ensured that the magazine's graphics complemented, not overwhelmed, a piece. If, say, a movie gossip magazine was parodied, then it should resemble the original in detail and not be "joked up." The parody issues of the *Harvard Lampoon* pretty much followed this rule, but the early *National Lampoon* rejected it; by opting for a "hip" and "underground" look, the magazine had weakened its potential lethal touch. Gross rid the *Lampoon* of its brash appearance so it might strike quietly, effectively.

In order to transform the *Lampoon* Gross had to adjust to the sensibility of each writer. At times he was handed material so

Self portrait, c. 1971–72

raw that he struggled to find the right visual angle. "I would often be doing things and I had no fucking idea what [the joke was] about," he later said. Some of the writers simply lacked a visual sense; they could not, for example, write a comic or think in comic book terms. Thus guidance was usually necessary. Beard preferred text to pictures, density to color. But he admitted his visual impairment and rolled with Gross's suggestions. Kenney had a better idea of what a piece required graphically, yet he could stray or drift off before explaining what he wanted. Trow utterly mystified Gross, who felt him too obscure. But O'Donoghue knew how his work should look down to the final period. He was, in Gross's estimation, "the most visually sensitive writer of the entire magazine."

But precision bred problems. O'Donoghue expected that every detail be perfectly realized, and this guaranteed the opposite. Some of the artists assigned to his pieces had trouble grasping the complete image. The sheer number of details swamped them. O'Donoghue's mania for "getting it right" added pressure. Certain items were left out or mishandled; punch lines were confused for setups, and vice versa. Gross did what he could to rectify mistakes. Indeed, looking back on O'Donoghue's *Lampoon* work one is impressed with the manipulation of specifics. But O'Donoghue recognized anything amiss; what was microscopic to others appeared glaring and obvious to him, and tantrums were thrown: "This *isn't* the way it should be!" he would scream, his voice rattling the office. "It's *got* to be the way I said!" O'Donoghue complained to Gross, who counseled the offending artist or made the corrections himself.

As the *Lampoon* found its footing, kindred spirits arrived in New York. From the beginning there were contributors other than the senior group, primarily John Weidman and Terry Catchpole, both of whom were Harvard vets. At first year's end, two prolific writers were added: John Boni, a member (along with Weidman) of the Doug Kenney school of humor; and Chris Miller, a specialist in sexually charged short stories. Then there was Michel Choquette, a French-Canadian comic from Montreal whose contributions were ultimately surpassed by the talent he introduced to Beard and Kenney. Indeed, Choquette brought to the *Lampoon* three writers who burned their names into the masthead.

Tony Hendra came from England teamed with Nick Ullett. The two met while at Cambridge, where Hendra performed with the future members of Monty Python, John Cleese and Graham Chapman. Hendra and Ullett bowed in the States in 1964 as the opening act for Lenny Bruce at the Café au Go Go. They became regulars on *The Merv Griffin Show* and made several appearances on *The Ed Sullivan Show*. By the late 1960s the team had settled in Los Angeles to write and perform for television, including *Playboy After Dark* and ABC's *Music Scene*, which

Hendra described as "a very, very early version of *Saturday Night Live*." There was also the rumor that the team had nearly been chosen to host what became *Rowan and Martin's Laugh-In*. Though moderately successful, Hendra and Ullett languished amid laugh tracks, dull premises, canned applause, predictable story lines. The team broke up; Hendra looked for something different. He then encountered Choquette, who told him about the new humor monthly in New York.

Sean Kelly was Choquette's neighbor in a Montreal apartment. Kelly had worked as a copywriter for an ad agency, McConnell Eastman, and taught English at Montreal's Loyola College. He also taught the history of "parody, satire, Dada, against the grain humorous writing" and was proficient as a lyricist and poet. Choquette suggested that he and Kelly work as *Lampoon* collaborators, and in mid-1970 their pieces began to appear in the magazine. Choquette would bring the finished work to New York while Kelly remained in Canada; for a time Beard thought Choquette had invented his partner, since Kelly was never seen in the office. But Kelly's phantom lurked there, its presence tangible, distinct.

Anne Beatts, a Buffalo native, attended McGill University in Montreal before joining the same ad firm as Kelly. Though she made a name for herself at McGill's campus newspaper, Beatts didn't see herself as Writer. She took up the pen solely to pay the rent, and she cut her professional teeth by writing gasoline, cigarette, and ice cream commercials. Kelly introduced Beatts to Choquette, and she began to work with him as a "weird cross between girlfriend and assistant." When Choquette attended the *Lampoon* dinners in New York, he brought Beatts along. She felt unwelcome at the all-male gatherings, but "they couldn't tell me to go home." Beatts found the verbal exchanges furious: "It was very competitive. The atmosphere was full of testosterone. And I would be the only girl there; sort of Wendy and the Island of Lost Boys." She tossed ideas into the fray and "if they liked the idea they'd sort of be stuck because they had to use me."

The three contributed to the *Lampoon* from various points: Hendra from Los Angeles; Kelly from Montreal; and Beatts when in New York with Choquette. At the end of 1970 Hendra and Choquette were made contributing editors, while Kelly and Beatts freelanced well into the second year. But a major editorial upheaval brought all to a single plane.

As editor and one of the key writers of the *Lampoon,* Doug Kenney lived daily with tremendous pressure. Unlike Beard, who faced his job with a workman's grit, or O'Donoghue, whose files were crammed with ideas (and who remained mercifully free of the office grind), Kenney, in Beard's words, "bore the burden. The *National Lampoon* was his design—all the departments . . . everything." Kenney supervised the creative end of the magazine, a backbreaking task in itself; plus, he was viewed as the leader, the boy genius who held aloft his generation's banner. On top of all else Kenney had to contribute *his* material to the mix, and this obligation could cause delays and missed deadlines. As Hendra saw it: "Kenney had to wait until 'it came,' which was usually late; he was one of those writers who need to build up a head of agitated guilt before the words will start to flow. This is bad enough on a one-time basis, but when the rhythm of monthly publication makes it necessary to build up a head of guilt every thirty days, it can be a killer."

Even so, Kenney found a way to get it done. His girlfriend at Harvard, Judith Bruce, noted that despite strain and chaos, "Doug could still produce; he'd sit down at the typewriter at 3 A.M. He did many of the celebrated *National Lampoon* pieces out of whole cloth—one draft. There was music in his head." But it seemed that the music grew distant as the pressure increased. Not only was Kenney responsible for the magazine, he had at home a wife, Alex Garcia-Marta, whom he rarely saw. "He was at work twenty hours a day," she said, "and I was left out altogether." Many of Kenney's friends felt that Garcia-Marta did not understand him, and the hours he spent at the office probably ensured a marital breach. Before long Kenney began an affair with the *Lampoon*'s managing editor, Mary Martello. Dicey enough when one is married; but here Kenney stepped on a mine that he hadn't anticipated.

O'Donoghue had an intense crush on Martello. Whether or not he and Martello coupled remains a matter of dispute among *Lampoon* vets, but O'Donoghue considered Martello his in some deep romantic sense. When he learned of her affair with Kenney, "Michael regarded this as a betrayal of his love," said Hendra. "He had a huge falling out with Kenney. . . . No amount of emotional maneuvering on Kenney's part could persuade O'Donoghue to reopen lines of communication. Anything Kenney tried—cajoling, explaining, apologizing, making light of it—was met with a wall of icy, white-lipped fury."

O'Donoghue's rage fed on Kenney's "betrayal" and this caused him considerable turmoil. "He was vulnerable," said Sean Kelly. "He was inconsolably weeping and smoking cigarettes. He couldn't speak he was so brokenhearted." O'Donoghue lay alone in Spring Street, doubtless obsessing on the affair and exaggerating its importance. Despite his outward confidence, O'Donoghue was indeed vulnerable when it came to relationships with women. To this point he had but a handful of romantic unions—his botched marriage included; and it was he who had ended every one. Kenney and Martello were beyond his control and he could do nothing to alter this reality. So O'Donoghue removed himself from Kenney's world, which was itself beginning to implode.

In July 1971, Kenney disappeared. Those close to him heard nothing for ten days. When Kenney did surface he was in Los Angeles visiting his college friends, Peter Ivers and Lucy Fisher. There he would stay for two months, leaving Beard to run the *Lampoon* and his wife financially and emotionally stranded. "That was pretty much the end," she said. "I was devastated and had no idea if he was coming back. He left me without a penny." Kenney mailed postcards to friends in New York to inform them of his whereabouts. On the postcard to Matty Simmons, Kenney advised, "Next time, try a Yalie."

Before Kenney's departure, Beard detected in his colleague signs of real stress: "I could see it but there was nothing I could do about it. Doug was becoming unglued." Lucy Fisher more or less concurred: "Doug couldn't take it anymore. He didn't like his job or his life." But at the *Lampoon* the business of publishing humor remained, and the pressure now dropped on Beard and Michael Gross. Beard quietly assumed leadership of the magazine. Gross, on the other hand, was visibly angry with Kenney. A consummate professional who took seriously his craft, Gross felt abandoned and left in the lurch. He thought Kenney was irresponsible and selfish and he dismissed the excuses offered to explain Kenney's defection. The *Lampoon* was a job, the enterprise itself a success. One simply did not abandon those committed to the task.

Back at the magazine, people rallied around Beard, whose challenge was to plug the hole left by Kenney. He still had O'Donoghue and Trow, major assets at any time, crisis or no. Also, there were Weidman, Boni, and Miller; but although Beard himself produced acres of words, fresh talent was needed to maintain the *Lampoon*'s ascension. This is where Hendra, Kelly, and Beatts came in, holding the coattails of Choquette.

Hendra had packed up his family and moved to a country house in New Jersey. Choquette had an apartment in Manhattan's East Village, and Beatts and Kelly stayed there when in town. The *Lampoon*'s second phase, which began with the hiring of Gross, was about to seriously bloom. Although Beard held everything together, the prime force behind the magazine now was Michael O'Donoghue.

"Foto Funnies" session in the *Lampoon* lobby, 1971

O'Donoghue's influence over the *Lampoon* came gradually. He was a major voice from the first issue on, but, in his view, "It took me a while to get into the groove." Before he joined the magazine he proved in his work that he could touch, indeed trounce, the untouchable. Once he returned to this area, where the base and vile aspects of life are eclipsed only by death, O'Donoghue's reign truly began. But not every piece drew blood or showed black. Banality and absurdity balanced the darkness, and in early 1971 O'Donoghue delivered a pair of *Lampoon* classics that established his primacy.

"How to Write Good" appeared in the March "Culture" issue. It is, on the surface, a parody of home study courses that give false hope to the untalented. The "student" is shown the "tricks" of the writing trade such as exposition, the development of raw material, and finding the proper ending to a story.

All too often, the budding author finds that his tale has run its course and yet he sees no way to satisfactorily end it, or, in literary parlance, "wrap it up." Observe how easily I resolve this problem:

Suddenly, everyone was run over by a truck.
—the end—

You'll be surprised at how many different settings and situations this ending applies to. For instance, if you were writing a story about ants, it would end "Suddenly, everyone was run over by a centipede." In fact, this is the only ending you ever need use.*

*Warning—If you are writing a story about trucks, do *not* have the trucks run over by a truck. Have the trucks run over by a *mammoth* truck.

But as the lesson progresses the focus shifts from the student's needs to the mania of the instructor, O'Donoghue himself. No longer does he wish to make the student a better writer; he looks to rouse in the student's potential readers fear and inadequacy so they will be ensnared. One method is to drop casually into a story "the punch line of an ancedote in a little-spoken foreign language." This, O'Donoghue insists, "is precisely why this device is best used in memoirs, whose sole purpose is to make the reader feel that you have lived life to the fullest, while his existence, in comparison, has been meaningless and shabby. . . ."

Another method is to disguise bad prose by conning the reader. If the student has written horribly a chapter and lacks the energy to rewrite it, he must "provide some strong ulterior motive" for the reader to complete the chapter and move on. O'Donoghue first suggests lust: "Artfully concealed within the next chapter is the astounding secret of an ancient Bhutanese love cult that will increase your sexual satisfaction by at least 60% and possibly more. . . ." If lust fails, threats may suffice.

DEAR READER,
THIS MESSAGE IS PRINTED ON *CHINESE POISON PAPER* WHICH IS MADE FROM DEADLY HERBS THAT ARE INSTANTLY ABSORBED BY THE FINGER-TIPS SO IT WON'T DO ANY GOOD TO WASH YOUR HANDS BECAUSE YOU WILL DIE A HORRIBLE AND LINGERING DEATH IN ABOUT AN HOUR UNLESS YOU TAKE THE SPECIAL ANTIDOTE WHICH IS REVEALED IN *CHAPTER SIX* AND YOU'LL BE SAVED.

If the student finds the above note tame, or fears that the reader will ignore it, he can up the ante in another note: "PRINTED ON *BAVARIAN POISON PAPER* WHICH IS ABOUT A HUNDRED THOUSAND TIMES MORE POWERFUL AND EVEN IF YOU'RE WEARING GLOVES YOU'RE DEAD FOR SURE UNLESS . . ." Appeals to vanity, greed, and sloth might also give the reader incentive to finish even the worst book ever written. These tips are among the many O'Donoghue has to offer, but before he can continue he is suddenly run over by a truck.

As with *le théâtre de malaise,* "How to Write Good" promotes above everything Michael O'Donoghue. Over five pages of copy his name is mentioned, in bold letters larger than the text, thirteen times. Part of this is self-parody: O'Donoghue as Writer Extraordinaire dispensing valuable "insights." But the pose is not a complete joke. O'Donoghue believed he was creatively without peer at the *Lampoon* (the exception being Kenney), a view he had little trouble expressing.

When it came to his physical appearance, however, O'Donoghue was less confident. Since his arrival in New York, O'Donoghue had struggled with weight gain; he lacked the muscle tone necessary to absorb or counter-act the fat. When he joined the *Lampoon* he tended to be overweight, particularly in the stomach. This worried him and inspired several diets. But the extra pounds remained and were exaggerated in the caricatures of O'Donoghue that illustrate "How to Write Good." Drawn by the artist Joe Orlando, the caricatures are unflattering, and in subsequent "Best Of" collections they were omitted at O'Donoghue's request.

In the April "Adventure" issue, O'Donoghue returned to the comic book format with "Tarzan of the Cows." For this piece O'Donoghue went outside the *Lampoon* stable of artists and brought in someone he knew would deliver the right look, Frank Springer. After *Phoebe Zeit-Geist,* Springer drew *Batman* for DC Comics, then moved on to Stan Lee's Marvel. These were lucrative jobs in the comic book world, and many mainstream artists would decline work from an "obscene" publication such as the *Lampoon.* But Springer respected and trusted O'Donoghue. Their previous collaboration had proved successful for both, their creative interplay unique to one another. Besides, Springer's reputation rested partly on *Evergreen;* how much more "profane" could the *Lampoon* be?

In "Tarzan of the Cows" O'Donoghue twists slightly the Edgar Rice Burroughs tale: A human baby is lost in the wild and is adopted and raised by beasts. But here the "wild" is southern Wisconsin, not Africa; the beasts that parent Tarzan are cows, not apes. Other than this, Tarzan looks and speaks the same as in the original story (with more than a slight nod to the films). His loyal chicken, Simba, at his side, Tarzan is sworn to uphold "The Law of the Pasture" and to keep meadow and field free of crime.

In this adventure, a group of rural crooks possess a map that will lead them to the Lost Gravel Pit of Waupaca County. But before they can steal the sacred gravel they must scare off the elderly farm couple who own the land where the Lost Pit is located. The solution? The crooks come across some groundhog costumes and

Simba learns of the crime through the poultry grapevine and runs to tell Tarzan.

Swinging on telephone lines that double for jungle vines, Tarzan confronts the crooks as they shovel gravel into a truck. They raise their "firesticks" and shoot at Tarzan, but the "mighty midwesterner" dodges the bullets and lands on a haystack, crying out (see opposite).

Thanks to Tarzan, the pasture is again at peace.

"Tarzan of the Cows" is O'Donoghue at his absurdist best. Gravel has the value of lost Egyptian treasure; men in ridiculous groundhog costumes confuse and frighten the locals; a veil of sinister mystery hangs over barns and old gas stations. As in *Phoebe Zeit-Geist,* the action is played straight, the panels drawn in a commercial, mainstream style. In *Phoebe* a dead naked woman travels the globe without inspiring second looks; in "Tarzan" a man in a loincloth who talks to chickens and cows swings through rural Wisconsin free of scrutiny. The preposterous is as natural as the wind that spins a weather vane.

There is more here than the story of Tarzan. The entire piece resembles a real comic book, complete with cover ("Kenosha Komics, 15¢"), an ad for war toys ("Special Forces Assault Outfit!"), a preview of the next "Tarzan" issue (in which the "Wurlitzer Graveyard" and the "Forbidden Jewel of Heafford Junction" are encountered), and informative tie-ins to the strip such as "Farmer Phil's Meadow Lore" (that you can "cut out and save") and "Cows Around the World." This latter bit is a factual description of a breed of cow and nothing more. But set against "Tarzan" it becomes humorous, as though readers of the strip will want to learn all they can about bovines.

Also, at the end of the strip, another Kenosha Komic character is promoted:

With "Tarzan of the Cows" O'Donoghue and Springer picked up where *Phoebe* died off. They collaborated on several other *Lampoon* pieces (Springer became a regular contributor), but as good as some of those later strips were, none ever matched the concentrated brilliance of "Tarzan."

All my life people have been saying it's so hard to build things up and so easy to tear things down. It's very difficult to tear things down!

The *Lampoon*'s new arrivals took immediate notice of O'Donoghue. Tony Hendra thought O'Donoghue was "spec-tacular. He was so different. I think one of the reasons why I gravitated towards him was that he was so different from the short sentence, brain-dead people" Hendra had dealt with in Los Angeles. At a time when it was easy to satirize Nixon or the "establishment" in general, O'Donoghue's "irreverence was about his own generation. I'd never met anyone who was funny about Warhol and Mick Jagger. That was very refreshing. . . . One of his favorite expressions was 'rock and roll pigs,' by which he meant any of our emerging 'leaders' who sought to manipulate, control, divide, and diminish others. . . . Most of all, though, O'Donoghue was simply good to be around, constantly funny, with a new kind of wit, a new kind of irreverence; someone for whom nothing had to be explained, modified, censored."

Sean Kelly's initial but not lasting impressions of the *Lampoon* staff were that Beard was "remote"; Kenney, when present, "seemed to me an insecure bully"; Trow "I found impossible the first few times I met him. George seemed like everybody who had been riding his horse through my ancestors' potato fields for generations." But with O'Donoghue, Kelly felt no real class difference. "At the time I thought these Harvard guys were very clannish; they had all their little in-jokes together, they were very WASPish, whereas Michael—I thought I knew who this guy was. He just seemed like an agreeable guy. He seemed like someone who was vulnerable and angry." Kelly knew of O'Donoghue from reading *Evergreen Review*. Above his desk at Loyola hung a frame from *Phoebe Zeit-Geist*.

Anne Beatts would come to know O'Donoghue intimately; but when she began to attend the *Lampoon* dinners and contribute to the magazine it was in concert with Choquette, who, although he collaborated primarily with Kelly, was taken with Beatts's ideas and knew he could not take sole credit. Beatts first met O'Donoghue when a contingent of *Lampoon*ers visited the Spring Street loft. To her the place was "very grimy" and O'Donoghue's personality matched: "I thought he was kind of mean, a mean cruel person" who lorded over headless mannequins, obese cats, odd plastic curios. Her initial impression never truly faded but did for a time subside. Their paths had crossed, and through O'Donoghue, Beatts would find her comic voice.

It was Hendra who initially was most smitten with O'Donoghue. By the fall of 1971 he and O'Donoghue were close friends, and Hendra spent more and more of his time on Spring Street. Hendra lived two hours away in western New Jersey. Since the "movable feast" of the *Lampoon* remained centered in Manhattan and Hendra worked there full-time, he was loath to commute late at night to his "remote if beautiful old house." So O'Donoghue allowed Hendra to sleep on "a hideously uncomfortable couch" in the loft whenever the need arose. "It was a very spooky place," Hendra recalled, its eeriness heightened by the mannequins "and dolls. I've always found dolls very scary. There were all these strange faces and things looking at you, and if you'd wake up in the night and had had too many chemicals, it could be quite scary."

While Hendra experienced O'Donoghue's inner sanctum, O'Donoghue elicited from his friend advice on matters of style and taste. Hendra felt O'Donoghue was drawn to his "British" (though in fact Irish) persona, that with it came a certain sophistication. He suspected O'Donoghue "had a real social inferiority complex. One of the ways this manifested itself was that he asked me to teach him about wine, as I was a big wine buff. He wanted to know more about wine. He was almost childlike in wanting to learn about wine but he didn't really like wine at that point. But he did find that he liked port a good deal, so I taught him what I knew."

O'Donoghue and Hendra drank port, smoked dope, held late-night discussions in the loft. A number of topics were broached, humor predominant among them. At one stage the two talked of camp, whether "being camp about camp became camp itself" and if camp could be connected to things shocking, how far could this be taken, and so on. The discussions were deep and lasted hours. "Then," said Hendra, "we came full circle. We decided that the most shocking thing you could do was to really, really start liking Mantovani," who was to classical music what Kenny G. is to jazz. Several Mantovani albums were listened to, evaluated. As the port warmed their palettes one said to the other, "That is the most beautiful rendering of 'Ave Maria' I've ever heard." Traces of irony were present, but Hendra insisted that "on some strange level" the sentiments expressed were genuine. After two or three ports, who knows?

Meanwhile, at the *Lampoon,* O'Donoghue produced a vivid succession of pieces that ran to the end of 1971. In the August "Bummer" issue, he wrote with Trow "Defeat Comics" (illustrated by "Crag W. Granite," whose style owed everything to Frank Springer), the story of four fascist brothers who can't wait to butcher dinks in 'Nam. Once there, however, corruption and malaise set in and the brothers become jaded and withdrawn. But before the comic is an ad for a wartime charity (opposite).

The reference is, of course, to My Lai—or "Pinkville," as it was called. On March 16, 1968, the members of Charlie Company, under the command of Lieutenant William Calley, spent the better part of the day there executing nearly six hundred Vietnamese men, women, and children while Calley's superiors watched from helicopters that hovered above the scene. Though later denounced by the military and press as an "isolated" incident, and though Calley was blamed solely for the deed, My Lai was but one of countless massacres of civilians committed by U.S. personnel during the war. In "Kill the Children" O'Donoghue caught perfectly the casual acceptance of such ongoing atrocities (including the endorsements of celebrities), and exposed the shady features of most "charities" for starving foreign children. Also, one cannot overlook Michael Gross, who gave the ad its realistic and ultimately chilling appearance.★

In the September "Kids" issue, O'Donoghue parodied "Eloise at the

★Calley's presence is felt throughout the "Bummer" issue. On the cover of the magazine, Calley is portrayed as Alfred E. Neuman (drawn by Kelly Freas), complete with the legend "What, My Lai?" In a piece written by Henry Beard and illustrated by Rick Meyerowitz, Calley is pitted against Charles Manson in a computer bout that Calley wins on a disputed TKO.

Lt. Calley's KILL THE CHILDREN FEDERATION

Dear Concerned Citizen,

This is Xena Puento. Xena is nine years old. She has never seen a glass of milk. Xena and her mother live in an abandoned packing crate on the outskirts of Manila, just one of thousands of deprived and impoverished families trapped by illiteracy, educational deficiency, unemployment, and disease. For just $15, I can shoot Xena in the head and toss her into a mass grave. But I need your help. Guns, bullets, and bulldozers cost money. While the need is great, the available funds are small.

There used to be no hope for Xena and those like her. They were doomed to a life of misery without chance of escape. But now your donation can provide that chance. Only $15 enables you to select your child from a score of countries overseas and areas at home. Soon you will receive a photograph of your child's resting place and an actual death certificate filled out by authorized U.S. personnel. An additional contribution of $5 will provide a small marker; $10 buys a wreath; $25 pays for a handsome urn; and $180 covers the cost of perpetual care.

Don't you think little Xena has suffered enough? Then act today and complete the sponsorship application below.

Thanks so much!

Sincerely,

Lt. William Calley, Ret.

Partial list of national sponsors and foster soldiers
Joey Heatherton
Brig. Gen. John W. Donaldson
Sen. Mendel Rivers
Morey Amsterdam
Walter Brennan
Capt. Ernest Medina
Mr. & Mrs. Samuel Yorty
George Jessel
Sen. James O. Eastland
Kate Smith

Available countries and areas
Taiwan
Peru
Korea
Iran
The Philippines
Bolivia
Ecuador
Brazil
S. Vietnam
Kurdistan
Mexico
Lebanon
Hong Kong
Paraguay
Syria
Africa
USA—
  Appalachia
  Watts
  Bedford Stuyvesant
  American Indian reservation
    and migrant camps

A division of the
Foster Soldiers' Plan, Inc.

We're not trying to destroy the world. Just a little piece of it.

NL-7-71

Lt. Calley's Kill the Children Federation
A division of the Foster Soldiers' Plan, Inc.
Box 711
Fort Benning, Georgia 23409

Name_____

Address_____

City_____State_____Zip_____

If for a group, please specify _____
                              (church, class, club,

_____
  school, business, etc.)

Registered (VFA-0880) with the U.S. GOVERNMENT'S ADVISORY COMMITTEE ON VOLUNTARY FOREIGN AID. Contributions are tax-deductible.

I wish to sponsor the death of a

☐ boy   ☐ girl in _____ _____.
                    (name of country)

I am enclosing $15 to cover cost of expungement & burial.

☐ Choose a child from an area of greatest need.

☐ I am enclosing an additional $_____ to pay for

_____
  (marker, wreath, urn, p. care)

☐ I cannot sponsor the death of a child, but want to give
$_____.

☐ Please send me more information.

Hotel Plaza" by taking the precocious little girl from her upscale setting and dropping her into the fleabag Dixee Hotel. Here Eloise romps among junkies and winos, hookers and child abusers. Despite the change in scenery, Eloise maintains a sunny disposition and finds fun where she can: "Every Tuesday I go see Yvonne. Yvonne is a meth freak and a transvestite. He lets me count his needle marks. Sometimes I hide his works." She also adapts quickly to her new environment: "Before I go to bed I put on my Felix the Cat mask so paint chips won't fall in my mouth. Oooooooooooooooo I absolutely love my Felix the Cat mask." On her bed lies a one-legged, armless doll; a gift from Uncle Mike?

Drawn by Donna Moody, "Eloise at the Hotel Dixee" is an effective if rather simple parody: the reversal of fortune, the horror faced by poor children, and so on. O'Donoghue's fascination with the underside of American life plays well here, but another, more ominous, theme continued to absorb him.

"Children's Letters to the Gestapo" immediately precedes "Eloise" in the same issue, and the title alone renders antiseptic the Dixee's squalor. In eight short notes sent to Himmler of the SS, the power of Nazi propaganda is uniquely dramatized. It's clear that these German children have learned their lessons well; anti-Semitism blends easily with childhood concerns, beliefs, senses of humor. Nazi kids *do* say the darnedest things.

Dear Heinrich Himmler,
How do you get all those peeple into your oven? We can hardly get a pork roast into ours.
Respectfully,
Uta Grotewohl

Aryan indoctrination is one thing; the real trick is to turn the despised gently against themselves:

Dear Mr. Himmler,
Thank you very much
for the gold star
to wear on my
jacket. Now I can
pretend I am
a cowboy sheriff.
     Best wishes,
     Naomi Feinberg

Is there doubt that young, doomed Naomi expected water from those showerheads?

"Children's Letters to the Gestapo" is focused in a way that O'Donoghue's early Nazi material is not, and thus is more effective as satire. Swastikas and death camps have become familiar if repellent images of collective insanity and this, as does all repetition, blunts the effect. But when jackboots and ovens reflect in the eyes of children, insanity is recast. Children can be made to accept just about anything, and this alone is horrifying enough. Stick swastikas on their arms and teach them to march and soon Our Gang finds mischief at Buchenwald instead of in vacant lots.

In the October "Back to School" issue, O'Donoghue took on the Beatles with "Magical Misery Tour" (which was given the *Yellow Submarine* look by artist Randall Enos). We join the post-Fab Four in their search for the magic Apple that will poison their relationship and cause intralegal wrangling. Along the way they fuck groupies, bestow upon the Mahareshi their worldy goods, and record "Helter Skelter," which gives Charles Manson and crew "the sign" to "Chop up a starlet! And a coffee heiress! And a Polish playboy! And a hairdresser! And a grocer! And a grocer's wife!" John marries Yoko; Paul marries Linda; George and Ringo go solo. Litigation begins. The Apple has rotted. "The Dream Is Over . . ."

In previous parodies of the counterculture, O'Donoghue had settled for general targets: do-good starlets, self-centered activists, the corruption of altruism. In "Misery" he sticks his knife directly through the name tag, especially John Lennon's. By 1971 Lennon-Ono were *the* megamedia couple. From television pulpits provided them by Mike Douglas and Dick Cavett, and in Jann Wenner's *Rolling Stone,* John and Yoko Inc. delivered sermons about art, politics, war, and above all themselves. They displayed a smugness born of fame and wealth, and this O'Donoghue assails. We see Lennon in overalls, his hair shorn to symbolize his and Ono's "Year Zero" conceit. With raised fist he lets free a primal scream:

I've had it with you grotty fucking guys! Everybody treated Yoko like fucking garbage! Yoko is a supreme intellectual! George said she gave off bad fucking vibes! I'm a fucking genius! Me fucking Auntie threw away all me fucking poems! Paul's music is fucking rubbish! And what about Mick wiggling his fucking arse! Where the fuck does he come off with all that fucking fag dancing! The fucking Stones always fucking imitated us!

Holding a portfolio of "Neurotic Lithographs," Yoko takes her husband by the ear and leads him down a path where Mark David Chapman and Albert Goldman lie in wait. The "Dream" is now another mutilated corpse.

In the fall of 1971 O'Donoghue was invited to "guest" edit the November issue of the magazine. O'Donoghue maintained his freelance status, and Matty Simmons sorely wanted his star contributor on staff. While an acknowledgment of the newer talent and their creative input to the *Lampoon,* the "guest editor" slot was in part designed to corral O'Donoghue. After all, his was not a new voice but a defining one, and it was high time that the formality of editorship be extended to him.

His theme of choice was "Horror," and it proved a decent but not an especially inspired issue. O'Donoghue's two offerings, "What Marks on the Neck?" the Conan Doyle-ish caption piece, and "The Incredible Shrinking Magazine" in which *Esquire* slowly disappears from sight, lacked the inventive aggression of his recent work. However, the "Horror" issue brought to the *Lampoon* the artist Edward Gorey, whose Victorian-style illustrations possessed a strange, subtle gentility that naturally appealed to O'Donoghue. (According to Michael Gross, O'Donoghue was the only editor who could communicate with Gorey: "They would go off and talk," he recalled.) Also, Paul Krassner was given a column, "The Unforgiving Minute," to, as he put it, "plug my *own* jams and jellies here in the lobby," namely, *The Realist* and his book, *How a Satirical Editor Became a Yippie Conspirator in Ten Easy Years.*

However, *this* satirical editor immediately felt the pressure advertising puts on a magazine's content. Unlike *The Realist,* which survived without ads, the *Lampoon* was dependent on the hawking of stereos, rock albums, jeans, and cigarettes. It was this latter commodity that caught Krassner's eye; as a militant foe of the tobacco companies he expressed his opinion regarding cigarettes in his first column:

Of course, it's easy to become self-righteous about such 1984-ish sounding plans, but didn't we approve of the anti-cigarette commercials on television to counteract the vicious, inhumane, exploitative pro-cigarette commercials? Yet, here is *Natlamp,* a somewhat anti-establishment magazine, coming to you partially by the grace of a couple of full-page cigarette ads.

Krassner then rationalizes his presence in a tobacco-funded magazine by noting his freedom to promote his wares, and adds, "anybody who buys cigarettes because they're advertised here deserves to die of cancer." On the surface this rather barbed reference to the Big C fit perfectly in an issue edited by O'Donoghue: Who better to appreciate the sentiment? But satire rarely holds sway over commerce; O'Donoghue occupied the editor's chair, but the real power in the magazine (Krassner suspected Beard) saw nothing funny in the remark. When the issue hit the street, "die of cancer" had been cut and the sentence read, "anybody who buys cigarettes because they're advertised here deserves to." The point was lost, R. J. Reynolds and its customers were spared, and Krassner was left holding the ashtray.★

In 1972 the *Lampoon,* and O'Donoghue, flourished. If uncertainty regarding the enterprise lingered, the growth shown in 1971 put it to rest. For instance, the *Lampoon* did just fine without Doug Kenney (though had he left in, say, late 1970, his absence might have crippled the magazine), and this encouraged those who stayed on or joined up after his exit. When Kenney returned from his California retreat in the autumn of 1971, the *Lampoon* was no longer "his." Beard was the creative boss and the contributors provided him, more often than not, with stellar material. Plenty of great music remained in Kenney's head—only now he was a featured soloist, not the conductor. In a sense this dimished role served him and his humor well.

What Kenney saw upon his return was a magazine in mid-evolution. Whatever its original "underground" or "countercultural" pretensions, the *Lampoon* became sleeker, sharper, more potent with each passing month. Circulation continued to rise. Matty Simmons and Henry Beard kept the magazine intact and turned a possible disaster (Kenney's departure) into a creative windfall. It helped, of course, to have O'Donoghue, whose execution of concepts showed the other writers what was possible. Had the *Lampoon* never published O'Donoghue, success may still have come; after all, the talent on hand was considerable, especially for an American magazine. But a *Lampoon* minus O'Donoghue would have

★To be fair, the *Lampoon* did lose several large accounts due to the magazine's content. But rattling Catholics or nationalists or Disney (which threatened to sue the *Lampoon* for showing Minnie Mouse with pasties) was one thing, even a good thing; pissing into the deep pockets of the tobacco companies certainly raised different questions.

At the _Lampoon_, c. 1972

been like a herbivore gnawing on dried beef: an amusing but bloodless effort to rouse the carnivore within. The scent of fresh kill was necessary to accomplish this, and it was O'Donoghue who knew best the lethal touch.

As bodies fell, other _Lampoon_ writers joined the fray. In the August 1971 issue, John Boni penned "As the Monk Burns," a Vietnamese soap opera in which the characters "steel themselves against the ravages of battle and concentrate on the all-important task (_organ music_) of living their lives day to day." Death makes living difficult, but the plucky Asian peasants make do: children give piggyback rides to their dead cousin who was strafed by an army helicopter; two lovers spat while napalm, bullets, and bombs remove limbs from each. A battle rages, scores of villagers are mowed down or crushed by tanks. Yet one peasant woman remains steadfast. Determined to begin life anew, she goes to live with her sister in another village—My Lai.

In the September issue, John Weidman skewered the _Peanuts_ gang with "Death Is," a series of quaint observations in the style of "Love Is." Here the Great Pumpkin finally arrives, dressed in Grim Reaper black: "Death is your first BB gun" shows Schroeder slumped on his piano after he is shot by Charlie Brown; "Death is playing Superman in a tree" shows Linus strangled by his cape; "Death is a Swiss Army knife for Christmas" shows Pigpen sliced to pieces. Lucy drinks poison from a medicine cabinet; Snoopy swims after a large meal and drowns. The _Peanuts_ characters are drawn to perfection by artist Herb Trimpe, and this is what gives the piece its delightful kick. In fact, so accurate are the likenesses that _Peanuts_ creator Charles Schulz threatened the _Lampoon_ with legal action. He was given an apology and a promise that never again would his sacred characters be so blasphemed.

Not known for death humor, Boni and Weidman explored their darker sides and came up with two fine pieces. O'Donoghue's influence is evident in each, especially in "Death Is." But there was more to O'Donoghue's influence than jokes about death and suffering. The point he stressed was that the best humorists do not flinch when committed to attack; once engaged they go all the way and use whatever it takes to bring down a target. O'Donoghue preferred the truncheon, then "kick them in the face with spiked shoes and hit them with the furniture." As other contributors followed his lead, O'Donoghue pushed himself into darker, stranger territory where the outline of humor is faint and laughter is the cry of the lunatic.

Though not as rabid as O'Donoghue, Kelly, Choquette, and Beatts sought to match his excellence. The three collaborated on several pieces throughout 1971, including a "Canadian Supplement" in the August issue in which the "Retarded Giant" of the north is celebrated and explained in appropriately bland terms. Kelly and Beatts teamed separately with Choquette, and then at times with each other. In the midst of this jumping about, a wide range of topics was satirized: *Sesame Street* was set in Harlem; *A Christmas Carol* staged in Nixon's White House. There was an eighteenth-century *Rolling Stone* devoted to the death of Mozart, and a twenty-sixth-century comic book written by and for Earth's dominant species, the cockroach. Kelly and Beatts also produced work individually. Beatts leaned more to the essay while Kelly spun out poetry and song lyrics, the most notable of this period being "I Dreamed I Was There in O.D. Heaven," where the "new Holy Trinity" consists of Brian Jones, Jimi Hendrix, and Janis Joplin.

Tony Hendra, too, lacked the taste for blood that so excited O'Donoghue. But like Kelly and Beatts, he could on occasion wound if not maim his prey. Hendra was adept at political satire. He understood the mechanics of the American military state and the political mythology that protected it.* But it was religion that inspired Hendra's better, early *Lampoon* work. In "Lamentations II," a "lost book" of the Old Testament is found, its author complaining to God about everything from bowel movements to the PR hustle of ancient tribes. In "The Story of Jessica Christ," the ditzy, gorgeous Daughter of God tours the Holy Land drawing lewd but worshipful attention. "You shall not enter the kingdom

---

*This can be seen in an eerily prescient piece of his called "(Classified)." A newsletter published by the CIA, FBI, and NSA, "(Classified)" deals with the "need" for better surveillance of the American public through wiretapping and other methods of domestic spying. Though written in the era of Nixon and J. Edgar Hoover, "(Classified)" could easily pertain to Bill Clinton and Janet Reno, as well as to their successors.

of heaven unless you enter through Me," she says, and a line quickly forms. But Judas is excluded; he turns Jessica over to Pontius Pilate, who is also rebuffed, and so the Saviorette is crucified. Nailed to the cross, Jessica's final word to the world is "Men!"

Hendra was chosen to oversee the first issue of 1972. Its theme, "Is Nothing Sacred?" was a rhetorical question as far as the *Lampoon* went, but Hendra's goal was to attack all that the counterculture held dear. For this effort he relied heavily on O'Donoghue, who had already clubbed to the ground his share of hippies, radicals, and feminists. Another round of thrashing seemed to him fine. He gathered from his files material that he and Hendra sifted through and worked up for the issue.

As far as sheer "tastelessness" goes, "Is Nothing Sacred?" could have been rougher or meaner. Its sharp edges are serrated, its dull patches few. One piece, "Where Do YOU Draw the Line?" throws rather illiberal images at the reader and asks "How depraved are you?" Baby bunnies are eaten by their mother; the ad line "when acid indigestion strikes . . ." appears next to a photo of a starving Third World peasant; a bull's-eye is placed on the head of Martin Luther King Jr. The piece ends with the ultimate in bad taste, the re-election of Richard Nixon. Elsewhere, a calendar for 1972 is decorated by a drawing of a kitten hanging dead from a yarn noose. Here the O'Donoghue touch is anonymous but plain.

The issue includes Henry Beard's parody of Buckminster Fuller, complete with geodesic penis and vagina. The parody is brilliant and exact, but offensive to whom? Science geeks? Kelly and Choquette paired to create "Son-O-God Comics," in which Jesus Christ is portrayed as Captain Marvel. Beatts assisted with the comic, but in her solo piece, "The American Indian: Noble Savage or Renaissance Man?" she spears liberal guilt and righteousness concerning the Natives, who are seen as pure, peaceful, and in all ways superior to the white man. Doug Kenney returned to the fold with "Che Guevara's Bolivian Diaries." The revolutionary's fall is recounted in absurd diary entries. Che's concern for his image exceeds his devotion to armed struggle; as he plots his escape from Bolivia he dreams up titles for Hollywood's film of his life. The razzing of Che is compounded on the issue's cover, where his famous visage is splattered with custard pie.

However, the issue belongs to Hendra and above all to O'Donoghue. Their friendship now extended to the pages of the *Lampoon*. They collaborated on two pieces, each a requisite blast against the hippie–New Left "lifestyle." In a parody of *The Whole Earth Catalog* (to which Beard and Kelly also contributed), a number of Aquarian-age sins are revealed, including liberal racism. Joan Baez is singled out here: Her tribute to the Black Panthers is a song titled "Pull the Triggers, Niggers." The constipated, humorless Weather Underground get theirs as well in a "public statement" written by Hendra: "The time has come for all of us to face up to the facts and take the right remedy. We are all of us, black and white, brothers and sisters, pigs; and if we have any sense of cosmic rightness left in our bodies, we owe it to humanity to off ourselves." Hanging is recommended, hemp rope preferred to nylon.

O'Donoghue's *Catalog* piece, "Kitty Glitter," attacks R. Crumb and his creation Fritz the Cat, renamed "Fritz the Star" due to his appearance in the popular Ralph Bakshi film. The strip, drawn by Randall Enos, approximates the Crumb style. We are shown how stardom has changed Fritz from a feline anarchist to a money-grubbing celebrity for whom no gig is too commercial. Apparently, Fritz is to Crumb as Mickey Mouse was to Disney, and this naturally leads to an amusement park called "Crumbland" where all the Zap Comix characters toil as mascots. Crumb himself appears wearing a monogrammed shirt and country club necktie; shamelessly he hawks a line of Fritz-related merchandise while maintaining "I haven't sold out!" The dean of underground comics is now the whore of Madison Avenue.

The problem with "Kitty Glitter" is that O'Donoghue shoots at a phantom target. In reality, Crumb resisted the commercialization of Fritz the Cat and had nothing to do with the Bakshi film. In fact, the result so incensed Crumb that he killed off Fritz in a subsequent strip by ramming an ice pick into the cat's head. Had Crumb wanted to sell out he certainly would have been quite wealthy; there was no end to the offers he received.* But Crumb remained true to his art, a mind-boggling concept to most Americans.

O'Donoghue, however, acted on his notion that everyone, no matter how gifted or noble, is at some level an asshole and thus deserving of abuse. This is what prompted his attack on John Lennon, whom he admired. But O'Donoghue couldn't effectively satirize Crumb since the cartoonist always admitted to—indeed, dramatized—his personal and artistic shortcomings. To call a self-described jerk a "jerk" is ultimately meaningless. Years later, O'Donoghue admitted as much: "It's impossible to do a parody of Robert Crumb. The man is almost impossible to hit; it's like attacking a Zen master. So I would just do it as an exercise."

O'Donoghue does better in "The Vietnamese Baby Book." Like his "Kill the Children" ad, the "Baby Book" shows children in war zones as disposable items: broken dolls scattered amid rubble. The starkness of "Kill the Children" is softened here in baby colors of pink and blue. The illustrations of maimed Vietnamese children, done by Newton Myers, evoke a cuteness and innocence that a new life embodies, even though arms and legs are missing. The baby whose book it is, Ngnoc

*All this and more can be seen in Terry Zwigoff's excellent documentary film, *Crumb*.

Tran Binh, was born to a teenage Vietnamese girl who was beaten and raped by an American soldier. Chemical defoliants inhaled during Mother's pregnancy leave Ngnoc born with three fingers and a thumb; and although his birth weight is normal, he shrivels to nothing in the space of a year.

Malnutrition is the least of Ngnoc's worries: He is wounded in a crossfire and is patched up by the "Cross of Red" people. He whimpers, cringes, has nightmares. At fourteen and a half months he utters his first word, "Medic." But there's not much to say in a world where napalm falls like rain, villages burn, the dead and dying litter roads and rice paddies. Soon the U.S. Air Force relieves Ngnoc of his misery by dropping a few bombs his way. Mother survives and fills the final page of her late baby's book (opposite).

"The Vietnamese Baby Book" is perhaps the best work of O'Donoghue's *Lampoon* years. Assisted by Michael Gross, who, it seemed, could do anything asked of him, O'Donoghue showed that to the Vietnamese the horrors of war were commonplace; if indeed a baby book was produced in such an environment, it would provide space for "Baby's First Wound" and give advice on how to stop a child from sucking her stump or bleeding in bed. If the Vietnamese were beyond or just numb to shock, they at least had a pretty good excuse. But for those Americans either indifferent to or unconcerned by the destruction unleashed in their name, O'Donoghue felt nothing but contempt:

I wrote [the "Baby Book"] at a time when you'd watch footage in Vietnam of people's heads being blown apart and salivate because it was dinnertime. You knew it was dinnertime because it would come on the six o'clock news . . . that book was cruel beyond fuckin' belief, because at that time people were so jaded that to wake them up, you couldn't just slap them across the face; you had to hit them with a fucking club ten times to get their fucking attention.

But attacking an unpopular war, either with club, gun, or cattle prod, required little courage. After all, Wall Street itself wanted a complete withdrawal from the Asian jungles by this late date, and only the more fascist elements of the American scene were clamoring for gook blood. Of course, "The Vietnamese Baby Book" was brilliant, and one imagines its satiric power had it appeared in the mid-1960s. But in 1972, O'Donoghue was piling on, however distinctive his leap. There simply was "Nothing Sacred" about the Vietnam War. But World War II was considered not only sacred but holy, and beneath its halo existed tragedy so profound that the very idea of a satirist's sniffing around for jokes seemed

Snapshots

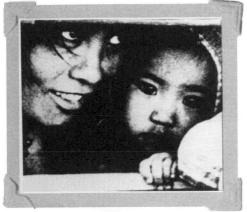

Ngoc and me

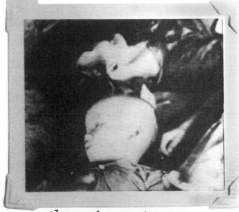

After the raid

Nursery Rhymes

Willy Calley, pudding and pie,
Shot the boys and made them die.
When the girls came to surrender,
Willy just ignored their gender.

Baa, baa, black market,
Have you any scag?
Yes sir, yes sir,
Would you like a bag?
Some for the master-sergeant,
Some for the pain,
Some for the hooker
Who goes down in the lane.

Monday's child is born dead.
Tuesday's child is underfed.
Wednesday's child is full of junk.
Thursday's child's a burning monk.
Friday's child is lame and blinded.
Saturday's child is feeble-minded.
But the children born on Sunday
Will be tossed in mass graves one day.

Baby's First Funeral

Date: *January 5, 1972*
Type of Service: *Buddhist*
Comments: *U.S. Air Force gave me
condolence payment of 80 piastres, enough
almost to buy another Baby Book.*

Paste Photo of Baby's Grave Here

at best repugnant. It was in war-torn Europe, not Southeast Asia, where
O'Donoghue showed real artistic courage.

Since his time with *le théâtre de malaise,* O'Donoghue had sought to
crack the sacredness of the Big One. A conflict that had ripped up one
continent and part of another, that had exhibited the depths of human
conduct, and in which millions of bodies lay in great heaps certainly
deserved, he felt, some comic scrutiny. And at the heart of this madness
stood the Third Reich, its theatrical devotion to mass murder an endless
source of fascination to O'Donoghue. For the "Is Nothing Sacred?"
issue, he brought Hendra aboard his private cattle car and there they
collaborated on a little-known but interesting piece.

Titled "Summer of '44," it begins by announcing the latest vogue:

Those fabulous forties are back in fashion news! You thought it was so far
and no Führer? Wrong! In the wake of high camp and low camp comes
death camp with trend- and jet-setters alike jumping on the bundwagon,
taking a trip back to that dear, dead decade when the best Polish joke was
the Munich Pact and it was Deutschland über Alles in Wunderland in gay
hun-loving Berlin.

So what does the 1972 woman desire most? The Total Death Camp
Experience, naturally. "It follows as Kristal Nacht the day that the fashion
Welt turns to the *last word* in abasement and nothin'-says-lovin'-like-
somethin'-from-the-oven suffering—the Middle European Jew. Make
way for the RAVENSBRUECK LOOK!" The look is created by Nancy
Weiss of *Harper's Bazaar,* who, while in the company of the Allied forces
that liberated the Ravensbrück women's death camp in 1945, "fell in
love" with the place. "And all those divine girls—skeletons with sunken
cheeks, lifeless eyes. Utterly perfect! I felt I'd died and gone to fashion
model heaven." Weiss convinced the army to turn the camp over to
Harper's. "We run it pretty much the same as the Germans," she says,
"except, of course, that the prettier girls get a chance to pose for the
magazine."

The Total Death Camp beauty regimen is laid out and advice is
given on the selection of the perfect makeup (dirt from Treblinka), fur
(gold star on each lapel), ornament (phone numbers tattooed on the
forearm), diet (a watery cabbage-and-turnip soup, with a mouse added
for flavor). It is the lifestyle that women die for. "Recreate the innocence
of '44. You know who you are, you know where you're going. Hide
in closets. Behind bookshelves. Betray friends. Ride trains. Crowd into
small rooms. Fight for trifles. Above all, follow orders. Resistance is
useless. . . ."

The equation of fashion with fascism requires no logical jump. Top designers and the magazines that promote them are forever beholden to power and celebrity. Amorality is the essence of couture, regardless of ribbons worn. If it turned out that the poor who stitch clothes in sweat-shops made for better material themselves, a human leather line of jackets and pants would be launched. After all, the claims of a non-English-speaking peasant are no greater than a mink's.★ When *Harper's* Nancy Weiss goes gaga over death camp chic, it seems plausible that mass suffering could be made to serve fashion, especially if no one of consequence objects. When a young model starves herself to maintain a rail-thin figure, is she not both commandant and prisoner?

Where "Children's Letters to the Gestapo" leaves deep puncture wounds, "Summer of '44" manages a few surface cuts. The bold language used somehow stays on the page, and no amount of oven references can contribute to its rising. Though minor, "Summer" is very much in line with O'Donoghue's thoughts of humor and the Holocaust (the models in the camp can be traced to *The Twilight Maelstrom of Cookie Lavagetto*). He does not flinch from the subject, nor does he hesitate when approaching it: Directness is vital in the demolition of taboos. But the symbol of genocide in the twentieth century transcended mere taboo and easily withstood the best shots O'Donoghue delivered. Here he would always be outmatched. What's a satirist to do when tourists can stroll through a sanitized Auschwitz?

It's not enough to tickle the ribs. Now you must drive an ice pick into the brain pan. Did I say "an ice pick?" I meant "nine hundred ice picks," of course.

Doug Kenney was back, the *Lampoon* continued its ascent, and through early 1972 the magazine added to its arsenal. Brian McConnachie had approached Beard and Kenney in 1970 with some poorly drawn but conceptually strange cartoons. Kenney was pleasant, Beard liked the ideas, but neither rushed McConnachie into print. During this period McConnachie was being phased out of his job at the Benton and Bowles ad agency; he continued to petition Beard until finally he appeared in the March 1972 "Escape" issue with a parody of *Papillon*.

Tall, bespectacled, a conventional dresser, McConnachie stood opposite the verbal sparring at the *Lampoon*. He was quiet, reflective; to him

★In "Manskin Is . . . As Manskin Does," which appeared in the May 1972 *Lampoon*, Tony Hendra imagines what human skin fashion might look like. The piece is a sequel of sorts to "Summer of '44," complete with the mock *Vogue* narration that O'Donoghue had down pat. Hendra said he was not directly influenced by O'Donoghue but that his friend "sharpened" him up. Still, the styles in "Manskin" suggest more than an indirect O'Donoghue influence.

the *Lampoon* was "very clever and bitchy, a real clever boys' club" where no one seemed to work in the office, though deadlines were met and pages filled with material appeared on Beard's desk. In childhood his mother read to him James Thurber, and Thurber's genteel oddness (primarily that of his drawings) resided in McConnachie's unconscious. His humor possessed a silent Zen quality in which sudden movement seemed static, the ethereal down-to-earth.

Even when writing "straight" parody, McConnachie's peculiar vision was clear: Tom Wolfe's run-on sentences burst with unexpected sound effects (a peg leg walking, a steamer trunk falling); Jack Anderson's Washington gossip column is filled with random, paranoid instructions to the reader ("PRETEND YOU'RE JUST READING THIS. DON'T LOOK AROUND . . . THEY'RE RIGHT OUTSIDE. KEEP READING") that by column's end would build to full rant. His was a style that no one could duplicate, and he created for himself a unique place in the *Lampoon.*

Bruce McCall, a self-described "renegade Canuck" from southwestern Ontario, also came to the *Lampoon* via advertising. He too loved Thurber, as well as Robert Benchley, Charles Dickens, the original *New Yorker,* and British comic Tony Hancock, whose radio show *Half Hour* made ridiculous the mundane. Though McCall could write, he was primarily an artist fascinated by technology, specifically the early days of automation. Much of his material was "by and large parodies of 1938 magazines" such as *Popular Mechanics,* "a curious form of beating up on the helpless past, but I always liked doing it. It allowed me to exorcize all the stuff that I'd read and found so moving." In McCall's world military tanks replaced horses in polo, sportsmen shot zeppelins over rolling plains. Each detail was drawn with the near-precision of photography; operator manual art worthy of a gallery.

Like O'Donoghue, McCall was older than the rest of the *Lampoon* crowd. He was pleasant and easygoing but was in no way connected to the counterculture. His attraction to the *Lampoon* was based solely on the excellence he found when reading it; so he approached the magazine in late 1971 with portfolio in hand. Again it was Beard who took interest in the newcomer, and McCall debuted in the April 1972 "25th Anniversary" issue with " '58 Bulgemobiles!" Cars the size of small houses are introduced to a public bored with the standard models. Space-age design has expanded to include Turbo-Glare Dual Headlights, Ultra-KlimaTron Interior Weather Control Units, and Pan-O-Wrap Full-Vu Windshields. McCall's ad experience shows in the slogans that promote the Bulgemobile line: "Mister, you just found a whole new way of going—not to mention a whole new way of saying you've arrived!" So advanced are these cars that "They Make Tomorrow Seem Like Yesterday!"

McConnachie and McCall came to the *Lampoon* with their comic sensibilities pretty much set. P. J. O'Rourke, however, was younger, adaptable, aggressive. He lived in the East Village and had contributed to several underground papers. A native of Toledo, Ohio, and a graduate of a creative writing program at Johns Hopkins University, O'Rourke, according to a friend, "knew his Byron from his Shelley" despite his tattered, dissident appearance. He arrived at the *Lampoon* "with the blessing of [George] Trow, which was a heavy credential," said Hendra. (Sean Kelly credits Dean Latimer, another contributor, with the discovery.) His energy and enthusiasm were noted, appreciated; Matty Simmons took an instant liking to him, which, for O'Rourke, would later prove profitable. He studied the work of the senior writers but drew inspiration chiefly from Kenney and O'Donoghue—not surprising, as they were *the* eminent *Lampoon* voices. Within two years of his arrival, O'Rourke would collaborate with both on major projects.

O'Rourke's early work shows a young writer determined to make the *Lampoon* grade. Various styles are tried on for size; most are abandoned, a few kept and modified. His ambition reveals itself in the energy that pushes many of his pieces along. A prime example of this is "The Iliad and the Ecstasy," in which white suburbanites shoot heroin for kicks and as a form of therapy. O'Rourke borrows freely from Kenney here but does not hit the same notes. "Iliad" moves at such a speed that the jokes become road kill before they are fully developed. One does not laugh so much as try to keep pace. In time O'Rourke would slow a bit and allow his humor a chance to breathe—that is, once he absorbed all he could from Kenney and O'Donoghue and at long last became, in O'Donoghue's words, "P.J. the humorist."

Among the newer talent was a writer who perhaps more than anyone at the *Lampoon* approached the level of darkness established by O'Donoghue. Ed Bluestone was a stand-up comedian who hailed from New Jersey. Many at the *Lampoon* found him disagreeable. "There was nothing pleasant about him," said McConnachie, who opposed the addition of Bluestone. "He was just fucking angry." Another writer thought Bluestone resembled a thalidomide baby with a deformed personality to match. But Beard liked his material, as did O'Donoghue and Simmons. In his work Bluestone could be brutal, but it was brutality from afar. He preferred detonation to hand-to-hand combat: A button was pressed; body parts rained in the near distance.

Like O'Donoghue, Bluestone located the absurdity in death. In "Telling a Kid His Parents Are Dead," tips are given to those who must inform a child that he is now an orphan. A boy holds his stomach and looks up at a man:

KID: I'm so hungry that my stomach hurts. We've been walking all day and haven't eaten a thing.

ADULT: I know, but I had a reason for not buying you food. *Right now* you've got *ten seconds* to choose between all the ice cream you can eat or seeing your parents alive again.

The same boy sits on the lap of a department store Santa:

SANTA CLAUS: . . . And your parents hadn't paid my bills in three years. So we paid them a visit last night; a couple of the elves got drunk and tore your mother's dress. Then for some reason your father got mad. It was a lot like *A Clockwork Orange*.

Religion, too, received Bluestone's attention. Indeed, some of the more blasphemous material ever to appear in the *Lampoon* came from a collaboration between Bluestone and O'Donoghue's old partner Frank Springer. Their series of strips called "Sermonette" inspired many of the *Lampoon*'s critics to complain of, among other sins, anti-Catholicism. Presented as a public service by the Archdiocese of Greater New York, "Sermonette" is hosted by Father Thomas Carlson. In the first installment the Father introduces his special guest, Jesus Christ. However, *this* Christ is at best twelve inches tall and is nailed securely to a miniature cross.

Father Carlson has a miracle in mind: To prove that the tiny Jesus is the real Son of God, "and not some little squirt we pulled in off the street," he proposes that Jesus eat a full-size communion wafer. Jesus asks that the wafer be halved as a whole one is too much to swallow. The Father agrees. "Listen," he says to the audience, "even if He only eats half a wafer, it's still a remarkable feat! Look how small His head is!" The half wafer is crammed down Jesus's throat; His stomach rumbles as Father Carlson orders Him to "keep it down, dammit!" But Jesus vomits and sprays wafer bits across the Father's desk. Carlson barks to the technicians: "Wrap up that wafer, boys, it's a priceless relic!" They do as a woozy Jesus looks on.

Bluestone's affinity for black humor made him seem to some at the magazine to be an O'Donoghue clone. The two shared a taste for the strange and bleak, but Bluestone's voice was distinctive, organic. He never imitated O'Donoghue the way others at the *Lampoon* sometimes did.* When Bluestone dealt with death he did so casually; there is an

---

*John Boni's "Death Is" and Tony Hendra's "Manskin" have been noted. But perhaps the most obvious imitation was Brian McConnachie's "Suicide Letters to Santa." The piece is funny but a warmed-over "Children's Letters to the Gestapo."

ease in his jokes about oblivion that almost negates the seriousness of the subject, yet somehow never does. This odd balance is best seen in the famous *Lampoon* cover for the January 1973 "Death" issue. A hand gun is held to the head of a dog. The gun's hammer is cocked, the dog stares nervously at the gunman. A threat is spelled out: "If You Don't Buy This Magazine, We'll Kill This Dog." A potentially cruel image is instead absurd. The vulnerable mutt inspires not pity but laughter, even though the reality of blowing a dog's head off would sicken most observers. The premise is simple, its effect enduring. If there is such a thing as an Ed Bluestone legacy, it can be seen in the eyes of that unfortunate dog.★

I don't want to do humor that helps people—the way Bob Hope tells Spiro Agnew jokes that build Spiro up. I want to demolish the people who need demolishing. The list is endless.

In early 1972, O'Donoghue remained a *Lampoon* freelancer. Tony Hendra, himself recently brought on staff by Beard and Simmons, was charged with convincing his friend to join him. O'Donoghue was reluctant but he recognized the power he had over the enterprise. If he was to take a staff position, certain conditions had to be met. First, he wanted the start-up capital for a film magazine he called *Rushes*. Editorially, *Rushes* was to cover film as *Rolling Stone* covered rock music. More important, it would complement and not compete with *Lampoon*. O'Donoghue even sketched out some *Rushes* ideas:

Salvador Dali once did a film for Disney which has never been heard of again. Do a piece on that film.

Guide to Cock Size: Big—Charlie Chaplin, Milton Berle; Small—Joel Grey . . .

Do reviews of the critics—one each month. Review them as a movie. [A concept later seen in *Spy* magazine—"Review of Reviewers."]

[Charles] Manson as America's top film critic. Pauline Kael just writes about how bad [a movie is], Manson goes out and does something about it. The sword mightier than the pen.

★Bluestone's premise of holding an animal hostage for laughs has been copied and adapted in countless arenas. The title of Matty Simmons's book is one example (and Simmons does credit Bluestone). Another, briefly celebrated, variation came in 1982 when *Saturday Night Live* threatened to boil "Larry the Lobster" unless viewers phoned in to stop it. Larry was spared and later retired to Florida, where he died of pincer cancer in 1990.

But *Rushes* went nowhere. O'Donoghue also asked that an issue of the *Lampoon* be done as a comedy album, a project that would take the magazine in a show business direction. Here Beard resisted: "We're literary people," he complained to Simmons, "and we should stay with that until we [get] it right." Beard's resistance eventually was beaten down by O'Donoghue's tenacity. In the spring of 1972 he approached the *Lampoon*'s advertsing director, Gerry Taylor, with the idea; Taylor discussed it with Simmons, who approved of the project. If nothing else, Simmons reasoned, a comedy album would "market the *Lampoon* name" and bring additional attention—and ad revenue—to the magazine. O'Donoghue teamed with Hendra, and the pair took time off from the magazine to produce what O'Donoghue called *Radio Dinner*.

In the early 1970s, the number of counterculture comedians recording albums was relatively small. One of the more popular releases was George Carlin's *AM-FM,* which showcased Carlin's transition from mainstream stand-up to dissident humorist. Groups such as Firesign Theatre and PDQ Bach had their followings. Also, the drug-damaged act of Cheech and Chong, with their rambling bits about pot and narcs, issued from the stereos of suburban white teenagers. In this environment the *Lampoon*'s brand of humor burned like phosphorous on skin. The challenge faced by O'Donoghue and Hendra was to transfer their humor from print to vinyl without losing the heat it generated. Sound production was vital, especially since five of the pieces planned were musical. As the two producers cast their album they found the right person for the job.

Of the talent hired for *Radio Dinner,* Christopher Guest was certainly the most important. His ability as an impressionist and his skill as a musician made him invaluable to O'Donoghue and Hendra, who saw that Guest could cover the ground they tilled for the album. But Guest contributed something more—his friend Bob Tischler. At the time Tischler worked as a sound engineer for Wendell Craig, where he helped produce radio spots and film trailers for television. He had the technical prowess and commercial instincts necessary to an ambitious project like *Radio Dinner,* and he too was hired.

When Tischler met with the album's producers, he recognized O'Donoghue from his time at Franconia College. Tischler was a student there in the summer of 1966 during Larry Loonin's theatre festival, and he remembered that O'Donoghue left in awe the audiences that gathered to watch him perform. As Tischler would discover, the O'Donoghue of 1972 was no less intense than the actor who had worked himself into crazed states of mind six years earlier. Only now the audiences were private, the performances for keeps.

Thanks to the deal made by Gerry Taylor, *Radio Dinner* was to be released by RCA and recorded in the company's "huge, antiquated Manhattan studios," as Hendra put it. As did his friend, O'Donoghue approached the project with the utmost seriousness; this was a prime opportunity to extend his creative reach and establish himself in a medium "hotter" than print. But he lacked the experience necessary to effectively produce an album, and here Hendra's involvement proved crucial. Hendra had recorded two comedy albums with his partner Nick Ullett; he knew his way around a studio and understood what was required to complete such a project. Thus a technical disparity existed between the two. This displeased O'Donoghue, who above all loathed secondary status.

"I had to pursue the position of producer," Hendra said. "[Michael] didn't know enough to produce it. There was a certain amount of friction." Hendra worked closely with Tischler to ensure that his and O'Donoghue's "elaborate aural plans" were realized. In so doing Hendra dominated the project, and in many instances he played director to O'Donoghue the actor whenever the latter recorded a piece. Not surprisingly, O'Donoghue was given to fits of temper. At one point during the recording, Hendra told O'Donoghue that "he had to re-do something." This ignited "one of his moderated explosions," voice raised, thigh repeatedly punched. "He just went ape shit because I was telling him what to do."

Although he recognized Hendra's authority as producer and was committed to the project, O'Donoghue felt he was a superior artist to his partner and was not in need of creative supervision. Hendra remembered that "Michael had definite ambitions; this album was his. I think he always resented, perhaps, that I had had that experience. There was no question that once the album came out, the things I had done on it were going to get more attention than the things he'd done." Despite this, both he and O'Donoghue were "very proud of the album and it was basically a great experience."

For all their creative tussling, Hendra and O'Donoghue turned out an album worthy of the *Lampoon* name. Targets are blasted, then brushed aside. Bob Tischler's sound production enhances the culmination of barbs, no matter how fleeting the joke. In "Concert in Bangladesh," the "tragedy team" of Hendra and Guest performs a routine of disease and starvation one-liners. Each punch line receives a sitar and triangle rim shot as an audience mumbles and moans in the background. The use of sound here is subtle, light, and the mind's eye sees the pair struggle in front of the dead and dying. This level of execution can be heard throughout *Radio Dinner;* Tischler's audio skills are equal to Michael Gross's visual sense, and so fine material is strengthened.

Hendra's claim that his material got "more attention" than O'Dono-

With Tony Hendra at the time of _Radio Dinner_

ghue's is difficult to verify. Two of his longer pieces are indeed prominent: a spoof of the then popular "Desiderata" poster in which human
existence is described as a fluke, the listener is told to "give up"; and
"Profiles in Chrome," a take-off on the 1972 election in which an
avacado-green Pontiac GTO runs against Nixon. This forces the president to forge yet another "new" persona, one with bumpers and headlights. ("Profiles" was later disowned by Hendra, who saw it as
"interminable and incomprehensible.") Yet despite Hendra's considerable
input, one cannot listen to _Radio Dinner_ and be unaware of O'Donoghue's presence. His voice is heard in various cuts, from a "Phono Phun-
nies" bit in which he pisses on a record executive's briefcase, to his plea
as "Barbra Streisand" for the killing of police, to a series of blackouts
called "Pigeons":

> "Once I had this whole box full of dead pigeons. Whole box full, say 12 to
> 14 pigeons. And I used to take them, you know, and play around with them,
> try to make them do things. Stuff like . . . well, I'd take them up to the roof
> and throw them off, to see if they'd fly or somethin' . . . or glide. And all
> they'd ever do is just fall into the street. That's all they'd ever do. That was
> about it."

"I used to get a kick out of hangin' around the park, 'cause there are a lot of trees and grass and drinking fountains and everything. And I used to go down and sit on one of the benches, you know? Every mornin' I'd go down to the park and then I'd feed the pigeons."

"What'd you feed 'em? Popcorn?"

"No. Every mornin' I'd go down to this park and I'd feed the pigeons to my cat."

"I can do these bird calls, you know? And all these birds would just fly over and see me when I did the bird calls. I can do the way I used to call the pigeons, if you care to hear it. Yeah? Well, it goes like this. HEY, YOU WITH THE FEATHERS. YOU WANNA STEP OVER HERE A SECOND?"

When not physically at the mike, O'Donoghue's writing comes through in "Catch It and You Keep It," a game show that drops heavy merchandise on contestants from a height of one hundred feet; the show ends lethally in a consumerist avalanche. An aphorism, "Nagasaki: The Art of Japanese Body Arrangement," also bears his initials. But it is in "Magical Misery Tour" that O'Donoghue's club swings beautifully and effectively. Adapted from his earlier *Lampoon* piece of the same name, "Misery" is a John Lennon song in which the ex-Beatle reveals the torment of being John Lennon. O'Donoghue took Lennon's own words from a *Rolling Stone* interview and arranged them as verse. But as Hendra recalled, there was no music and thus no real way to properly skewer Lennon.

The original concept was simply to shout the verses out, primal-scream style, but that was too blunt, given that they were Lennon's own words; and besides there would be no parody involved, no recognizability. After all, no one had ever heard Lennon scream. Beyond that, his voice was extraordinarily distinctive—perhaps the best-known male voice in rock.

After much thought, Hendra offered to do Lennon's voice himself. Though not an impressionist by nature, Hendra could approximate the Liverpool tone before "Tischler flattened and thinned my voice electronically," which then made it sound "at least promising." With voice and verses down, a music track was needed, and here producers and talent were stumped. Guest tried but failed to find the right style. Finally, the answer came from without. During a visit to the studio, Christopher Cerf, said Hendra, "asked if he could have a crack at setting the song to music and was instantly accepted.

"His solution was perfect—a simple, driving 'Imagine'-style piano [more like the ponderous riffs heard on *Plastic Ono Band*] that allowed the words to be chanted or perhaps ranted over it. He edited O'Donoghue's verses somewhat so that they roughly fit the beat, and added odd little Beatle-ish tags at the end of each. It worked perfectly."

"Magical Misery Tour" is just that: "Lennon" berates all around him save Yoko; his voice escalates with every complaint (a style of abuse familiar to O'Donoghue) until words cease to cut and he is left screaming into space. Hendra, with Tischler's technical help, pretty much grasps Lennon's voice. He begins slowly but acidly, telling his fans, Mick Jagger, and George Harrison to fuck off, get fucked: "Fuck this! Fuck that!/I don't owe you fuckers anything and all I've got to say is fuck you!/The sky is blue." Warmed up, "Lennon" kicks into self-righteous overdrive. Piano notes fly by in an attempt to avoid his wrath:

> Look you bastards I'm a genius like Shakespeare and Beethoven and van Gogh! Don't you dare criticize my work! "Don't Worry Kyoko" was one of the fucking *best* rock and roll records ever made! I'm a fucking artist! I'm sensitive as shit! I throw up before I go on stage! I can make a guitar speak! If I could be a fisherman I would but I can't because *I'm a fucking genius*! I was the Walrus! Paul wasn't the Walrus! I was just saying that to be nice but I was actually the Walrus! Even that rubbish he's been singing! *Eastman was an animal!! A fucking stupid middle-class pig!! I won't let fucking animals like that near me!!* Yoko is a supreme intellectual! I'll tell you why nobody likes her music! Because she's a woman and she's Oriental, that's why! Where are you Mother?! *They're trying to crucify me!!*

"Lennon" finally concedes that "genius is pain"; and as his genius is profound so too is his agony. He shrieks until he crumbles sobbing and moaning. Yoko pops in to again remind us, "The dream is over."

Hendra admitted to unprecedented nervousness when it came to his doing Lennon. "I had deep misgivings that I could pull it off," he said. But on the night he recorded the song, Hendra was possessed by his inner Lennon; a voice, "one I barely recognized," took hold and the words rushed forth "in a ferocious tumble of hate and disappointment"— "My Master's Voice," he called it, anticipating the West Coast channeling trend by nearly a decade. Whatever voice surfaced that evening, the result is easily the best cut on the album, and "Misery" remains funny to this day. Since Hendra sings/rants, he naturally receives the attention. But the song is O'Donoghue's and reflects his energy and aggression.

Radio Dinner was completed and delivered to RCA in April 1972. After listening to the recording the label's executives demanded that all references to Nixon be removed, including a minor bit of O'Donoghue's in which David and Julie Eisenhower struggle with their sex life. RCA had signed a lucrative military contract with the Nixon administration and sensibly wished to avoid conflict. But the demand did not go down well with O'Donoghue, who, according to Matty Simmons, "was apoplectic" and refused to comply. Hendra hated his Nixon piece and could see axing it on creative grounds, but RCA wasn't interested in maximizing the album's comic punch, so Hendra, too, refused. Simmons added his vote: "Fuck 'em. It stays or we go!" RCA returned *Radio Dinner* to the *Lampoon,* and through another deal secured by Gerry Taylor the album was released on Blue Thumb Records, a small label distributed by Epic.

Radio Dinner was modestly promoted and some mainstream media outlets showed interest. After all, the *Lampoon* was still a curiosity, and few journalists "got" the magazine's humor. Perhaps the best piece that highlighted the album and O'Donoghue appeared in the October 17, 1972, *Washington Post.* Portrayed by columnist Tom Donnelly as "a man for all decades," O'Donoghue speaks confidently of *Radio Dinner* and expands on some of his favorite bits. He explains the premise of "Magical Misery Tour" and adds, "It's always such a delight when you can hang someone with his own words." Of Joan Baez he observes, "There's one soul everybody wanted to crucify for years." He takes special pride in Hendra's "Tragedy Team" routine, which for him contains the album's satirical essence: "You just have to [do] a parody on the George Harrison–Bob Dylan mentality that thinks you can solve the problems of Bangladesh by having people buy rock concert tickets. . . . If you can sell guilt, you're in." Accompanying the piece is a photo of O'Donoghue, flop cap at a tilt, cigarette held by the middle fingers, eyes fixed coldly on the Beltway reader. No reassuring Mark Russell expression here.

With *Radio Dinner* completed and in stores (where it sold well over the next few years), O'Donoghue and Hendra returned to the magazine. Their friendship survived the stress of producing the album, and now, as Simmons observed, "the two had become inseparable. . . . They were colleagues. They were friends. They were two of the wittiest and most outspoken members of the group that regularly gathered for the staff dinners," which by this this time had widened into savage social events. "The dialogue was just incessant," said Hendra. "The level of verbal sparring was such that if you didn't hold up you were discarded."

The discussions, he added,

> were extreme. They would certainly shock—and *did* shock—anyone who was drawn into there. I don't think people said stuff like this at this point. Sometimes it was about dead babies. Sometimes it was about Nixon, and sometimes it was about being funny about Nixon. As with any collective—or

coalescence, if you like—of humorists, it's always very cannibalistic. They chew one another up, and they chew their own with great relish. Humorists are not nice people. There was a sort of piranha tank feeling to it.

Of the *Lampoon* piranhas, O'Donoghue could be—and was—the most vicious. His in-office outbursts grew in proportion to the magazine's circulation. Anger was occasionally vented in support of a piece he wanted done right; but many times O'Donoghue directed his fury at things independent of the magazine. The telephone could be a weapon. If he felt his phone bill was incorrect, for example, he would come to the office, call the phone company, and aggressively berate the luckless representative who took his complaint. His voice rose as epithets such as "cunt," "pig," and "scum" shot into the receiver. O'Donoghue often penned his insults in advance and built to an abusive climax that steamrolled the person on the other end. He wasted no words; no put-down was arbitrary.

Before long his phone calls became set pieces to be performed. A member of the Columbia Record Club, O'Donoghue once was sent and billed for albums he did not order. He arrived at his office and dialed the club. "This is Michael O'Donoghue," he began, then informed the operator of the crime committed. "Listen," he continued, "I'm going to pack up forty fucking tons of bricks and I'm going to send them to you C.O.D., YOU MOTHERFUCKER UNLESS YOU STRAIGHTEN THIS UP!!" The scripted pitch was reached, the receiver slammed down. By this time a number of the *Lampoon*'s office staff gathered near his door and listened in. O'Donoghue emerged looking solemn. He saw the small crowd and broke into laughter, clearly pleased with his performance.

If when dialing his prey the office phone malfunctioned, then *it* received the anger that O'Donoghue had built up. Phones were either ripped from their outlets and thrown against the wall or were smashed to bits by a heavy walking stick. When not destroying phones, O'Donoghue kicked the office walls and knocked over file cabinets. Onlookers were amazed that a man who lacked muscle tone could summon such strength. But O'Donoghue's temper, when flexed, more than made up for his physical shortcomings.

O'Donoghue's outbursts affected the magazine's editors and contributors in varied ways. Henry Beard tolerated O'Donoghue because he was vital to the *Lampoon,* but many felt that behind his quiet facade Beard resented the chaos O'Donoghue could wreak. Bruce McCall noted, too, O'Donoghue's sometime "berserk" nature and ability to "intimidate the shit out of anybody who crossed him in any way, particularly over creative matters." Yet McCall appreciated O'Donoghue's directness: "He was one of the few people I know who had the guts to insult someone to their face, and he would do it. In a curious way people loved it. I think they knew it was coming from somebody who *cared* so much, even though part of it was his need to impress himself on you."

George Trow believed O'Donoghue's temper was connected to psychological and physical torment. "Michael was depressed, and I knew that," he said. "He probably always had a permanent clinical depression." Also, the migraine headaches had increased in frequency, the pain so blinding at times "that to be in the same room with it was to suffer with him." But above it all was O'Donoghue's feeling of self-importance. "Michael had an enormous sense of his own dignity," said Trow, and thus was intolerant of any slight, whether real or imagined. This is why O'Donoghue despised large institutions such as the phone company or banks—because he was not accorded the respect due him. His aversion to banks was so extreme that Trow had to accompany O'Donoghue when a deposit or withdrawal was made "because if some asshole failed to give him the proper respect, he was very likely to want to kill if not kill."

This tension, seen in much of his *Lampoon* work, helped distinguish O'Donoghue from his fellow contributors. A following of sorts developed as readers keyed into the O'Donoghue style. Of course, some readers were more inspired than others, and one professed O'Donoghue fan decided to show his appreciation in a very dramatic way. In April 1972, O'Donoghue received a box containing nine sticks of dynamite. The note accompanying the package read: "Mike: Here, have some fun. A Friend. PS. Tell your boys in the mailroom to send out back issues soon or they won't have a mailroom any more. Ha. Ha. PPS. Cops will come soon."

According to Matty Simmons, O'Donoghue turned "white, green, and orange" when he saw the dynamite. According to the *New York Times,* "Mr. O'Donoghue said he had carried the dynamite around the offices of the magazine showing it to friends. He said that rather than call the police he telephoned a friend whom he described as a demolition expert [the writer George Plimpton]. 'He told me you can do anything with dynamite—toss it around, stick a fork in it—as long as it isn't sweating or discolored,' Mr. O'Donoghue said."

Eventually the police were called, and the bomb squad soon arrived. Six blocks along Madison Avenue were closed and hundreds of people were evacuated from the third, fourth, and fifth floors of the *Lampoon* building. After the package was removed, the *Lampoon* staff filtered back into the office, now crowded with police and reporters. A couple of cops questioned Simmons, who told them not to mistake the shabbily dressed O'Donoghue for the bomber. But O'Donoghue must have raised official eyebrows anyway, for he was livid that the dynamite had been taken. According to Tony Hendra, "in the middle of the furor, crouched in his attack mode, glasses held away from his face, being restrained by everyone, was my pal O'D: 'It's my dynamite, you pigs!' he was yelling. 'I want it! Give it back! It's mine!'" P. J. O'Rourke reported that O'Donoghue complained that the police "won't give me my bomb threat note back. Honest to God, *nine sticks of dynamite* never beat me up in the back of a squad car." The following day the punch line was delivered in the form of eight lengths of fuse and blasting caps.

Women—put a bag over their hearts and they're all the same.

In the spring of 1972, O'Donoghue fell deeply in love once again. While attending a literary party in Manhattan he met Amy Ephron, the younger sister of Nora, then a columnist for *Esquire*. Ephron was several years O'Donoghue's junior and an aspiring writer herself. She had been hired by Christopher Cerf to work for *The Electric Company,* a kind of preteen *Sesame Street*. She was, according to those who knew her at the time, smart, sweet, and demure, qualities that easily pierced O'Donoghue's tough hide and lodged in his soft center.

Hendra, who continued to frequent the Spring Street loft, saw his friend the night of the party. "He came back [to the loft] and said, 'I'm in love.'" O'Donoghue spoke of Ephron with a dandyish flair and was, to Hendra's eye, quite sincere. Before this the two spent their evenings sharpening each other's claws, and for one of them to "come home and say 'I'm in love' was an invitation to get ripped apart." But the dynamic changed, and Hendra realized that O'Donoghue "had gone over some kind of line, that this was not to be made fun of. . . . He was really just beside himself. He thought this was the love of his life, and he was really strange about it."

At the time he met Ephron, O'Donoghue was "very worried about his weight, very worried," said Hendra. The desire to be thin, always present, became urgent now that he was involved in a serious relationship. But mastering his body image proved hardest to O'Donoghue. Averse to exercise, he dieted, starved himself, smoked packs of Silva Thins to kill his appetite. Slowly the pounds fell away; before long O'Donoghue's clothes appeared baggy on his frame. Instead of buying a new pair of pants he cinched what he had at the waist with a long belt. Shirts and jackets hung loose over a once paunchy gut. Though his weight would always fluctuate, O'Donoghue never again surrendered to obesity. His new body image was to fit the artistic niche he carved out at the *Lampoon*.

As his involvement with Ephron deepened, O'Donoghue brought

her along to *Lampoon* functions. Because she dated the Presence, as O'Donoghue was now being called, Ephron was formally if not warmly embraced by the rank-and-file. Sean Kelly and his wife occasionally brunched with the couple, and Kelly stiffened in the face of their romantic small talk. "I remember being appalled that Ephron's name for O'Donoghue was 'Goo,'" he said. "Amy was effectively childish: 'Oh, Goo!' And I thought, 'Jesus Christ, Michael! What are you doing with someone who calls you Goo?'" Since O'Donoghue kept secret his past, colleagues such as Kelly were at a loss to explain his attraction to pet names and other "childish" features of new romance.

Hendra, too, was thrown. Not only did he find "strange" O'Donoghue's affection for Ephron, he dubbed it "corny." "I don't think I ever called him on it because I really knew that this was something you could not joke about," recalled Hendra, "but he was so corny. They were doing things like holding hands and sitting by fountains. He would come back and tell me stuff like this. And I would go, 'O'Donoghue, is this you?' [and he would respond] 'I won't hear a thing against her.'" Like Kelly, Hendra knew O'Donoghue in present time and so on O'Donoghue's terms. The small-town boy shunned by girls grew creatively but emotionally remained raw—especially when lost in romance. To him true love was honorable no matter how "corny" the arrangement. Parts of this were seen by Hendra, but the complete picture was obscured and missed. Thus he and Kelly scratched their heads as O'Donoghue reveled in "Goo"-speak.

Still, Hendra picked up on O'Donoghue's hunger for sexual prowess. "Michael said this wonderful thing in one of his rages: 'Why don't we start a humor magazine. I'll bring the women!' It was very telling. He thought he was the purveyor of sexuality in the magazine. But it was clearly Doug [Kenney]. Doug was the sexy guy in the magazine; Doug was the guy who did the sexual humor. But Michael really wanted to see himself as the sexual magnet." This was a key element to O'Donoghue's makeover, a weak spot he covered with bravado and confidence. If he envied Kenney in any way it surely was on sexual grounds, for Kenney seemed at ease with his classic looks and boyish charm—traits O'Donoghue coveted but did not have. His distress when told of Kenney's affair with Mary Martello was partially tied to his concept of "betrayal"; but it appears more likely that O'Donoghue was simply jealous of Kenney. The handsome guy got the girl that the weirdo "nork" had a crush on.

With Ephron, O'Donoghue allowed his infatuation to flow. Not since Paula Levy had he so fallen for a woman, but this was a different level and a different crowd. O'Donoghue was prominent among an emerging set of talents, his avant-garde obscurity now a mention on his résumé. The mainstream press showed interest in the *Lampoon* as reporters from the *New York Times* and *Newsweek* visited the magazine's offices and mixed with the editors. Always keen to publicity, O'Donoghue made himself available for interviews and kept at hand comments he penned in advance, but uttered casually as though off-the-cuff.* His lust for notoriety was integral to the making of his art. He believed in his own importance as a humorist and was not shy about sharing this fact with reporters. As the *Lampoon* expanded so did his confidence, the crest of which was his relationship with Amy Ephron.

Fresh confidence aside, O'Donoghue remained a prisoner to dark moods and migraines. In an office environment this provided onlookers with amusement, assuming they weren't in O'Donoghue's line of fire. But in a relationship outbursts and tantrums usually prove detrimental, as O'Donoghue knew from his "raving psychotic" episodes with Paula Levy. Apparently the same held true with Ephron, and those in *Lampoon* circles saw a pattern of quarreling develop between the two. In addition, O'Donoghue began to have an on-and-off affair with a woman named Mary Mitchell, who lived down the street from his loft. As the person then closest to O'Donoghue, Hendra witnessed the increase in the "sexual traffic" and was himself caught in it, for he too had a "brief, happy, and not very serious affair" with Mitchell that was encouraged by O'Donoghue. It was, in Hendra's words, part of "the hip happening, Going Too Far, nothing-is-sacred, dish-it-out world of the 1972 *Lampoon*." But for Hendra, an important part of this world was soon to collapse.

O'Donoghue and Ephron argued, made up, argued, made up. O'Donoghue kept Hendra apprised of everything, whether he complained to his friend about Ephron's shortcomings or kicked him out of the loft so he could be alone with her. After several more turns of the wheel, O'Donoghue claimed that he was forever through with Ephron. "No question about it," insisted Hendra, "Michael said, 'I never want to *see* that bitch again!'" Not long after this announcement, Ephron attended a *Lampoon* dinner where among those seated was O'Donoghue and Hendra. O'Donoghue reportedly left early and went home alone, but Hendra and Ephron remained. After several drinks, Ephron invited Hendra back to her apartment to smoke a joint. He did; the two got stoned and fell into bed.

*In a *New York Times Magazine* story on the *Lampoon* (December 10, 1972), author Mopsy Strange Kennedy was taken with O'Donoghue's act: "He sits on the windowsill and stares off into space, looking as if he's trying to remember somebody's last name, and then comic-strip light bulbs seem to come on in his mind, and he tries out some new joke or idea. 'How about soap ballets?' 'Love of Life' danced? Yes?'" In the days of Johnny Carson this was known as "panel," the bits used during an interview that a comedian thought too weak for his set—or in O'Donoghue's case, the *Lampoon*.

"It really was a one-night stand of the worst kind," said Hendra. "We smoked a lot of dope. I really was not attracted to Amy, but we ended up doing the deed and that was that." Not so far as O'Donoghue was concerned. Stories vary about how O'Donoghue learned of "the deed," but by the time Hendra arrived at the *Lampoon* the next day O'Donoghue was aware of the fact—and livid. A message was sent to Hendra that informed him he was no longer welcome at Spring Street. Caught off guard, he phoned Ephron, who told him of O'Donoghue's grief upon hearing the news, and Hendra, aware of his friend's operatic temper, readied himself for anything. In his book, Hendra describes his postdeed encounter with O'Donoghue:

> He came in late in the afternoon, lips the width of piano wire, talking in some odd Englishese: "You owe me an explanation, I feel . . ." "What was the purpose of this, might I ask . . . ?" It was ridiculous. I felt like I was on the set of *Savages*. But he was obviously in the eye of some powerful emotional storm, and though it didn't look quite like hurt, I didn't want him to stay that way. If there was any wrong here, I was in it. I told him what had happened and how I thought it had happened, but that to whatever degree he was hurt, I was sorry and regretted it.
>
> Nothing. My friend was looking at me as if he'd never seen me before. He was capable of staggering anger, which I had expected to have to survive, but while there was plenty of anger here, it was not the dominant emotion. Nor was rebuke. But it was intense and absolute. He sat there glaring through me, lips tight, breathing slightly too quickly through his nose. He seemed to be trying to will me to admit a wrong, a terrible wrong, an immeasurably terrible wrong, and then die.

However badly Hendra felt about the Ephron affair—though it seemed it meant relatively nothing to him—he was much more concerned with O'Donoghue. He honestly believed that fucking his friend's ex-lover constituted at best a misdemeanor, thus his feeling that O'Donoghue was "ridiculous" for being upset. But surely, at some level, Hendra must have anticipated such a reaction. After all, he spent hours and hours alone with O'Donoghue and doubtless glimpsed the man's vulnerable side, which had erupted in pain when Kenney slept with Martello. He saw O'Donoghue's response to what was essentially a minor affair; what did he think would happen when O'Donoghue learned of his night with Ephron, a woman for whom his friend expended deep emotion, "bitch" or not? O'Donoghue's ties to Ephron remained tangled, a mess further complicated by Hendra's involvement.

O'Donoghue's anger immediately affected the *Lampoon*. The office atmosphere, Hendra noted, "was as though the air had been sprayed with cyanide. The force of O'Donoghue's emotion rolled down the hallways, into other offices, other departments. People spoke in hushed tones. . . . It felt as though someone had been assassinated." The personal rift became professional as the magazine was pulled into the fray. Hendra went to Henry Beard and explained his side of the story. Beard listened, nodded, counseled Hendra to temporarily keep a low profile. As editor, his first concern was the health of the *Lampoon*. O'Donoghue went to Matty Simmons and demanded that Hendra be fired. If Simmons refused, O'Donoghue said he would quit. "Now, we had a problem," recalled Simmons. "O'Donoghue was 'A-Team.' Hendra was good but not nearly as valuable. The easiest way out for me would have been to fire Tony. He was replaceable. O'Donoghue was not and never would be. I had honestly believed what I told Michael. This wasn't my business."

But O'Donoghue ensured that it became just that. He kept calling for Hendra's dismissal. He then demanded that his office be moved away from Hendra's; in order to calm him, Simmons had Hendra's office moved instead, "a matter of eight feet," said Hendra, but this did nothing to soothe O'Donoghue. After several days, Hendra decided to confront head-on his now former friend.

I grabbed O'Donoghue one day and pulled him into my office. I think he thought I was going to beat him up. He had a way of taking off his glasses when attacking or being attacked—perhaps from bitter experience in the schoolyard. He took them off now and stood there looking defiant, daring me to deck him. Nothing could have been further from my mind. I begged him to cut the bullshit, and at least see if we couldn't salvage something from almost a year of friendship. And I repeated that if anyone was wrong I was, and that was our business. But now it was becoming everyone's business, and we should spare them that. As soon as I stopped standing between him and the door, he left. I never really spoke to him again.

Not that Hendra didn't try. He sent O'Donoghue a note on *Lampoon* stationery proclaiming "once and for all" that he never "at any time, for any reason" intended to hurt O'Donoghue. "I'm not enjoying all this one iota. It's sad, poisonous and terribly unfunny," he added. "So please, let's stop. I miss you." O'Donoghue never responded, and Hendra, who had seen O'Donoghue and Kenney reconcile after the Martello affair, was at a loss to explain why his former friend wouldn't forgive him as well: Hadn't O'Donoghue been as distraught then as now? Although it's true that O'Donoghue had felt "betrayed" by Kenney, he also knew that Martello was seeing more than one person, and this softened the blow. Also, he considered Kenney (as well as himself) a superior talent to Hendra, so if he was betrayed, he was betrayed by an equal. Ephron, on the other hand, was exclusively "his." That his best friend dared cross him O'Donoghue found unpardonable. That he had been crossed by a lesser talent galled him even more.

Beard and Simmons tried to stay clear of the feud, but other contributors could not avoid its impact. Still, many sympathized with O'Donoghue. "I could never buy Michael getting that upset about anybody copulating no matter who was involved," said Brian McConnachie. "I *could* buy him getting that way if it was personal, that he was betrayed by Tony. Then he saw Tony for who he is. It was the realization that Tony could be a user." Bob Tischler observed, "Michael put his trust in you, and if he felt you violated that trust it's a big fucking thing." George Trow confessed, "I don't know what happened between Tony and Michael, it was just as simple as *that*. [Tony] was scum, you didn't talk to him again, and it was over." Hendra believed that O'Donoghue "cowed" people into supporting him and thus divided the magazine into camps. But Trow disagreed:

It wasn't a matter of dividing people into camps. There was no camp in Michael's camp. People were terrified. It was a serious thing to walk around with this genius hating you. It was not a pleasant experience. Michael was dangerous. Michael was serious. Michael was not joking about what he was doing. I mean, this was an angry genius. This was not something to fuck with.

Perhaps the one contributor most affected by the feud was Sean Kelly. During his early *Lampoon* period, Kelly divided his time between Montreal and Manhattan. When in New York, he, along with Anne Beatts, spent many recreational hours in O'Donoghue's loft. Once, their host produced some blotter acid that the three ingested before going to see samurai films. When they returned to the loft they spent the entire night on the building's roof. "Suddenly it was dawn," said Kelly, "and there we are wrecked out of our minds, at which point Michael decided that I was, in fact, a fox and not a human being." Kelly thought this amusing, and soaked in the peculiar observations of a hallucinating O'Donoghue.

Kelly never felt that he and O'Donoghue were "asshole buddies," but O'Donoghue was generous and Kelly appreciated his vulnerable side. After suffering what Kelly termed a "domestic catastrophe," he received a call from O'Donoghue, who offered assistance. "He was there for me. It was an experience almost unique in my life. It was very moving. There was nothing he *could* do, but it was the gesture; there was no bullshit to it." The downside to the relationship was that Kelly was married with kids. O'Donoghue was single and enjoyed his freedom. When O'Donoghue and Beatts visited Kelly in Montreal, they implored him to join them for a night on the town. Kelly said that he couldn't afford to go, to which O'Donoghue asked, "Baby needs a new pair of shoes?" Kelly replied, "Precisely." He did, indeed, have a baby—several, in fact—all in need of shoes. Nothing kills one's social life faster than parenthood.

Hendra was closer to Kelly in life experience. Both had a wife and children; both were fallen Catholics; both were part of the *Lampoon*'s vital second wave. Their commitment to the magazine led to a strong friendship. The arrangement appealed to Kelly, as he enjoyed Hendra's company; but he also held O'Donoghue in high esteem. At the moment of the split, Kelly was faced with a decision he did not want to make. So he straddled the fence for as long as he could in the hope that conditions would change.

Simmons, too, wanted the atmosphere cleared, and he thought it best that Hendra be given a project outside of the office. Gerry Taylor and Blue Thumb Records had asked Simmons for another *Lampoon* album. Taylor was especially keen on the idea because *Radio Dinner* had helped boost ad sales and successfully marketed the *Lampoon* name. Since Hendra had put in more production work on *Dinner* than O'Donoghue, the new album was his to create. And since the new album was to be a collection of music parodies recorded live, Hendra turned to Kelly for assistance. "Kelly was a natural person to work with," said Hendra. "[H]is facility in lyric writing was staggering, and his knowledge of, and sensitivity to, rock was light-years ahead of mine. . . . Kelly's knowledge was encyclopedic from Elvis to Alice Cooper. He listened to lyrics, felt them, got their resonances. Like O'Donoghue, his first instinct was poetic, but his ear was far more complex, his wordplay Byzantine."

The live album concept soon gave way to a live stage show. Titled *Lemmings,* it was to be a collection of sketches buoyed by musical numbers. By going this route the *Lampoon* would have a play *and* a sound track album, a prospect that pleased both Taylor and Simmons. One of the *Lemmings* bits parodied Woodstock, and the sketch grew to become the second half of the show. As in the "Is Nothing Sacred?" issue and in *Radio Dinner,* the self-destructive and idiotic aspects of the counterculture were again targeted. Hendra was especially proficient on this front, having tossed his share of dirt on the 1960s grave. Part of the *Lemmings* Woodstock premise, that of rock festival as mass suicide, can be found in his Weather Underground "statement"—"We owe it to humanity to off ourselves"—from "Is Nothing Sacred?"

But the idea of a death-oriented Woodstock had been twice explored by O'Donoghue. In "The Daily Roach Holder" is a report from "The Montana Festival," the symbol of which is a vulture perched on the arm of a guitar. Here O'Donoghue parodies both Woodstock and its grimy cousin, Altamont, where the Hell's Angels, hired as "security," assaulted performers and spectators alike, the cresendo reached with the stabbing death of a black man. O'Donoghue portrays the Angels as "Hitler's Heroes," who "savagely attacked anyone within 150 feet of the bandshell with chains, tire irons and zip guns." The "Heroes" slew nine, but there was plenty of death to go around: "26 who OD'd on bad smack, six suicides, three who were run over in their sleeping bags, 11 who perished from amateur abortions, and at least one teen-age girl who was kicked to death in a ritual murder." Compared to this, bad brown acid is bland brown rice.

In "Woodstockade," O'Donoghue ushers the remaining crowd to a death camp, condemning the "rock and roll pigs" he so despised to a festival of torture and pain. Here hippies are Gypsies and Jews: they are given "Groovy Skin Decorations" such as identification numbers tattooed on the forearm, and "*Free* Crystal Acid!—Specifically Zyklon B, the crystallized prussic acid that blew the minds of thousands at Auschwitz"; they mix with the "cream of Rockdom," including Bob Dylan, Joan Baez, and Joni Mitchell, all of whom perfom under the watchful eyes of "vicious, sadistic guards"; they wear "freaky striped pajamas," are recycled as soap, and are urged to "get back" to the soil via "a mass grave." Unlike the festivals that preceded it, Woodstockade has enough space to "accommodate up to six million" blissed-out oven heads. It is a place for tribes to gather, then be gassed.

The true foundation of *Lemmings* lies in the pieces above. There are differences—*Lemmings* reflects voluntary self-annihilation, whereas "Woodstockade" is a state-run cultural cleansing—but the similarities outweigh them. Yet O'Donoghue never received the credit due him on this count—not from Hendra, Kelly, or Simmons. In fact, he is the only major contributor not named in connection with the project. Everyone else, from Kenney to Beard to O'Rourke to Beatts, had a hand in the writing of *Lemmings* and are so noted. But before the show was conceived there was O'Donoghue, painting killing fields of crimson and clover; a mass murdering van Gogh at Arles. There might have been a *Lemmings* minus his influence, but it would have lacked a similar edge.

As it stood, O'Donoghue wanted nothing of Hendra save the spectacle of his downfall and dismissal—which, of course, did not come. But neither did O'Donoghue's resignation, though one might suspect that Hendra's getting *Lemmings* would provide him the perfect cover to leave the magazine. For all his bluster about quitting, O'Donoghue knew he had no comparable place to go. As the *Lampoon* rolled through 1972, O'Donoghue was becoming one of the magazine's highest-paid contributors, second only to Beard. Once he was brought on staff his annual wage rose, and by year's end his salary reached $45,000—$10,000 more than Matty Simmons himself made. A decent chunk of this money came from special "Best Of" editions of the *Lampoon* in which O'Donoghue's pieces usually outnumbered those of the other writers. What other outlet would give him the same salary and the latitude found here?

There was during this period a brief dalliance with the *New Yorker*. Once home to humorists such as Thurber, Benchley, Perelman, and Dorothy Parker, the *New Yorker* of 1972 was not known for its comic range. Its formula dried and bore dust by the time O'Donoghue came around, and the thought that his aggressive humor would fit in such a stale environment was a fanciful one. But Trow was a contributor (though his better work appeared in the *Lampoon*), and this helped his friend receive consideration. Indeed, Trow had written about O'Donoghue twice in the "Talk of the Town" section of the magazine, including an examination of the Spring Street loft and SoHo itself. William Shawn, the *New Yorker* editor, was open to a submission from O'Donoghue, and in autumn 1972 he received "Mr. Lewis, Meet Mr. Clark," a study of "time's untarnished twosomes," individuals who joined forces in bids to "become rich, powerful, famous or, more often than not, infamous." The list includes:

Murphy and O'Flaherty, charismatic running mates whose White House dreams were dashed when opponents exposed their plan to put the Pope on the one dollar bill.

Hoofbeat and Tarbox, talented vaudevillians who became "America's best-loved Negroes" with the never-to-be-forgotten phrase "Ah hain't gwine to de ribber whne de ribber flan ham gwum gwub!"

Woolheim and Wesikopf, beloved herpetologists whose definitive monograph, "If a Hooded Adder Were to Fight an Orb-Weaving Spider, Who Would Win?" was greeted with hoots and jeers by the scientific community.

Doctor and Mrs. Nine, stylish chemists who unlocked the secret of the blue tulip to create the weird and troubling scent, "Never Touch Me There."

Skating Navajos, midget tap dancers, Siamese twin prizefighters—all obscure figures on the margins of history, and all a bit too exotic for the *New Yorker*. Shawn wanted to use the piece but in a toned-down form. He eliminated the broad ethnic jokes that gave the piece its sting—no Hoofbeat and Tarbox, no swipes against Irish papists—and made bland the odd material so it would not ruffle the magazine's gray feathers. He also changed the format of the piece from a survey of strange twosomes to a "miniquiz" in which the reader must match teams to feats.

Shawn presented this new version to O'Donoghue for his approval; O'Donoghue saw nothing of himself in the edited piece and rejected it. Soon after, he complained to Bruce McCall over lunch. "The *New Yorker* had the temerity to suggest changes to a piece he wanted to sell them," McCall remembered. " 'Fuck them!' he said. He refused Mr. William Shawn's 'pansy little changes' that were supposed to make it suitable to the *New Yorker*. And typical of Michael, he could've made a quick two grand and been in the *New Yorker*." But conditioned to the freedom at the *Lampoon* and secure in his identity as a humorist, O'Donoghue passed on what most writers would consider a golden opportunity.

Film was possibly another alternative, or at least it seemed so in the summer of 1972. After several years on the Merchant/Ivory shelf, *Savages* was finally released—first at Cannes, then in the States.* The British critics who saw the film at Cannes raved: "Director James Ivory achieves a kind of sophisticated apocalypse that is both witty and terrifying," wrote Richard Roud in the *Manchester Guardian;* "A triumph . . . The whole central section, a smart dinner party set sometime in the 1920s, is classic, the writing and playing match each other beautifully and a lot of what is said is very funny indeed," added John Russell Taylor in the *Times* of London. The *auteur*-mad French were no less reverent. Marcel Martin, writing in *Les Lettres Francaises,* stated, "The American representation in the Director's Fortnight is abundant and gripping. . . . The film is of an originality and intensity that are very rare. . . ." All credit goes to Ivory, whose title "director" becomes a proper, sacred, noun.

American critics were a bit more divided, though two major outlets passed favorable judgments. Penelope Gilliatt of the *New Yorker,* shadow partner to the magazine's big gun, Pauline Kael, found *Savages* a "glittering film . . . full of withering social commentary and a peculiar, erratic stateliness of style. . . ." Though taken with much of the film, Gilliatt concluded that *Savages* is less funny than it is "portentous." In the *New York Times,* Roger Greenspun was impressed with the film's escalating wit, yet: "Almost every moment in 'Savages' seems like part of a superb movie that has not been quite put together. . . . But whatever is missing from 'Savages,' we are left with a good deal—from the almost lyrical direction, to the always intelligent screenwriting [the *auteur's* true nemesis], to the lush and delicate photography . . ." Combined, these above reviews helped drown out negative appraisals by John Simon in *New York* magazine ("*Savages* pounds away at the obvious with half-baked and witless comments on matters so banal they barely merit comment") and Stuart Byron in *Rolling Stone* ("a most interesting failure").

*It is unclear whether O'Donoghue and Trow attended the film's premiere at Cannes. A couple of *Lampoon* vets thought the two went to France, but Matty Simmons believes they stayed at home.

On the editorial page of the *Lampoon*'s November issue, O'Donoghue "plugged" the film in mock ad-speak:

IF RAW SEX, TWIN-FISTED ACTION, and HIGH-VOLTAGE THRILLS are your cup of TNT, you won't want to miss *Savages,* A POWERHOUSE OF A MOVIE that BRISTLES WITH TENSION . . . Actually, *Savages* is about as exciting as a six-pack of Carnation Instant Breakfast, but we thought maybe they could pull a few of these phrases for reviews. In fact, here are a few more: FAIRLY EXPLODES ONTO THE SCREEN, RIPS THE LID OFF HOLLYWOOD, MAKES *THE GODFATHER* LOOK LIKE *BAMBI,* MAKES *THE STEWARDESSES* LOOK LIKE *I REMEMBER MAMA,* AT LAST—A BLACK JAMES BOND, and I CAN'T REMEMBER WHEN I'VE ENJOYED A FILM MORE.

In the end, *Savages* received more critical attention than paying customers, and after a limited run the film quietly faded from theaters. But the *Savages* experience brought into O'Donoghue's life two lasting influences: George Trow, of course, whose elegant manner and urbane sensibility deeply impressed him; and Nelson Lyon, whom O'Donoghue met prior to the film's New York premiere.

A native of Troy Hills, New Jersey, Lyon immersed himself early in the darker waters of American popular culture, primarily horror and mystery films but also EC comics, which Lyon considered some of the greatest literature the United States had to offer. Boasting titles like *Tales From the Crypt* and *Weird Science,* EC plumbed the depths of horror and fantasy and laid the groundwork for *The Twilight Zone* and *The Outer Limits,* as well as *Nightmare on Elm Street* and kindred cinematic fare. This naturally alarmed (alarms) official tastemakers. EC's founders, Al Feldstein and William Gaines, who would later create *Mad,* came under congressional attack in the early 1950s for their supposed corruption of American youth. EC was used to enact the Comics Code, under which "subversive" images and ideas were softened or eliminated so as to not divert impressionable minds from wholesome activities such as public school prayer and "duck and cover."

Lyon was not among those pulled from EC's grip. Although he became conversant in Dickens, Thackeray, and Shakespeare, and went on to attend Columbia University, where he studied under Lionel Trilling and F. W. Dupee, Lyon never lost his appreciation for the "lesser" art forms. Along with EC, he was fond of 1930s pulp fiction and the theater of Grand Guignol. A large, imposing figure, Lyon was serious, intellectually intense, and drawn to humor—partly as a defense mechanism, primarily because he recognized that humor was the one route that allowed for honest appraisal of the madness of the world. He believed that "the best comedy deals with the abyss of horror," and wished to make films that embodied this belief.

When he met O'Donoghue, Lyon had worked in advertising and conceived numerous campaigns promoting MGM films. He also won a Grammy award for his art direction of the *Dr. Zhivago* sound track album. In 1971 Lyon was asked to fix, then film, a screenplay that was sitting on his boss's desk. He quit his ad job, attended film school at New York University and the City College of New York, rewrote the screenplay, and called it *The Telephone Book,* the title based on an old joke that if you find the right actor, the right director, and the right producer, you can make a profitable movie of the telephone book.

However, Lyon's *Telephone Book* was an *Alice in Wonderland*/porno satire about a sexually depraved nymphet who is burned out and bored at age sixteen. She is ultrarich and blasé about life. She receives an obscene phone call that cuts through the boredom and reignites her passion. When she tracks down the caller he turns out to be an ex-astronaut who went insane in a weightless chamber. (He wears a pig mask while making the calls, an unconscious nod to Terry Southern's character Guy Grand in *The Magic Christian*.) In the end, the man cannot physically consummate his relationship with the girl; he pours his energy into an all-night phone call that leaves her collapsed and presumably dead.

The Telephone Book, which featured unknowns Jill Clayburgh and William Hickey, was influenced by the Warhol aesthetic: a simple, "primitive" style of filmmaking where the camera focuses solely on the "personality" in front of it. But the film didn't quite work, and Lyon added interview footage of real obscene callers in an effort to salvage what he said was like "looking at death." Yet Avco Embassy bought and released the film in 1971. *Telephone Book* flopped in New York; critic Judith Crist trashed it, while the *New Yorker*'s Pauline Kael chose not to review the film and dismissed it as "exploitative." But *Telephone Book* played well in Los Angeles, where Kevin Thomas of the *Times* gave it a positive review. Still, Lyon was displeased with the final cut and sought to learn from and build on this flawed first effort.

At the time of *Telephone Book*'s New York release, Lyon was dating an actress named Asha Puthli, who had a small role in *Savages*. Puthli spoke enthusiastically of O'Donoghue and this inspired Lyon to meet him. Lyon was familiar with *Phoebe Zeit-Geist* and recalled his thoughts when he first read the strip: "Who the fuck is this weird Mick with the 'O' apostrophe?" He asked Puthli to invite O'Donoghue to dine with them at the Russian Tea Room before attending the screening of *Telephone Book*. "We really just hit it off, right off the bat," Lyon remembered. "Mike liked EC comics. He immediately picked up on everything

I was tallking about. I took him to the screening and he didn't like the movie much, but he loved the spirit." Months later, in the summer of 1972, Lyon attended the New York premiere of *Savages*. So began a creative, sometimes turbulent, relationship.

O'Donoghue took immense delight in the way Lyon affected some of the *Lampoon* regulars—Brian McConnachie saw Lyon as "Michael's pit bull," though O'Donoghue preferred to call him the "Swamp Monster," the "Swamp Beast," or the "Dark One." Lyon acted the way O'Donoghue wished to act, talked the way O'Donoghue wished to talk, had the presence O'Donoghue wished to possess. Lyon did fancy himself a "verbal gunslinger," especially when drinking, but he never had to express this in a direct physical manner as his size and energy were intimidation enough. At times Lyon was seen by people as overbearing, at other times he was soft-spoken and courteous. But above all Lyon was erudite and he conveyed a humorous, literary air.

Similar in temperament and outlook, and each with a film to his credit, Lyon and O'Donoghue collaborated on a film treatment called *Georgia Bobo, or The Dose From Outer Space*. The idea was originally Lyon's: An alien intelligence comes to Earth in the guise of a venereal disease. It strikes an average guy, ruins his life, destroys his marriage. The alien virus slowly tranforms him into a hideous monster of the EC variety. O'Donoghue thought the virus should be a shapeless blob with decomposing flesh that was wheeled about by devoted slaves. He and Lyon debated and incorporated various ideas, finished the treatment, and pitched it to one of Lyon's Hollywood contacts. At the time the film industry was experiencing creative rebirth; producers backed new projects such as *The Last Picture Show* and *The Godfather,* but the concept of an all-consuming, incurable alien virus did not appeal to them. Once the treatment was rejected, Lyon eked out a living producing film trailers while O'Donoghue brought his full attention back to the *Lampoon*.

What you really want in life you get stuck with.

If he was stuck with the *Lampoon,* then he wanted something more, especially since Hendra had been handed such a show biz plum. O'Donoghue was not pleased with the *Lemmings* situation, to put it mildly. He went to Simmons and railed against what he considered an extended betrayal. "This is great!" Simmons recalled his saying. "Hendra doublecrosses me, and he's punished by being given a show to create." Simmons tried to assure him that this wasn't so, but O'Donoghue demanded satisfaction, namely his own project. After all, wasn't he the *other* person responsible for *Radio Dinner*? Where was his reward? Simmons agreed, and the two "discussed Michael doing a special issue of the magazine over which he would have total control. He'd been talking for some time about an 'Encyclopedia of Humor.' This would be an A-to-Z book in which topics of every nature would be satirized. Special editions of the magazine with reprints had been quite profitable, but this would be the first original special edition."

The *Encyclopedia* would also consume O'Donoghue and stretch him to his creative limits. Sensing this, Simmons assigned P. J. O'Rourke to assist O'Donoghue. O'Rourke had yet to distinguish himself in the magazine, and many contributors viewed him contemptuously as too eager to please or felt him unfunny and imitative. Oftentimes editors spoke softly lest O'Rourke overhear and know which pub they planned to hit after work. Despite this cool reception, O'Rourke was ambitious and put in extensive hours at the *Lampoon*. This endeared him to Simmons, who admired the young writer's loyalty to the magazine and his determination to succeed. It was the very reason O'Rourke was chosen to work with O'Donoghue: Simmons knew he would devote himself fully to the project, no questions asked. And to the aspiring O'Rourke, working alongside O'Donoghue certainly was motivation enough.

Anne Beatts was ambitious as well, determined to leave her mark. Beatts asserted herself within the male bastion of the *Lampoon,* but as the magazine's sole female contributor she often fought uphill against an unspoken but prevalent mind-set that "girls aren't funny." She learned to roll with the *Lampoon* punches and deliver a few of her own. Beatts's assertion was expressed in a "Foto Funnies" strip in the May 1972 "Men!" issue—of which she was "guest editor."★ In yet another parody of the Charles Atlas ad, Beatts has sand kicked in her face, is berated by her boyfriend for being "a weakling," then learns to toughen up through "NatLampCo." She returns to the scene of her humiliation, defeats the bully, and becomes the "Hero of the Beach"—"You're a real woman, after all," says her boyfriend, squeezing her flexed muscle. In the image of a fighting-trim Beatts one cannot miss the obvious symbolism: In order to hold her own with the male editors, Beatts had to stay in creative shape. The only way she would be respected was if she "kicked ass" like the boys—but even this was no guarantee.

Though she had been brought to the *Lampoon* by Michel Choquette, with whom she collaborated on page and off, Beatts looked to stand alone. Her excellent "American Indian" piece in the "Is Nothing Sacred?" issue promised much, as did her work in subsequent issues. But she remained a humorist-in-development whose comic voice, while strong, had yet to fully mature. She worked all sides of the magazine,

★This issue includes a piece by Amy Ephron titled, amusingly enough, "How to Make It With Men." It was paired with Doug Kenney's "How to Score With Chicks." The piece represents Ephron's only appearance in the *Lampoon*.

and this included many dinners with Henry Beard. Beatts liked and respected Beard, who proved a droll dining companion, but soon she told herself, "I can't take another dinner with Henry." She phoned O'Donoghue and asked him to take Beard's seat. He accepted, and thus began for both a relationship of intensity and high drama.

Before they moved to the dinner stage, O'Donoghue and Beatts had socialized in the company of others, most often with Sean Kelly. Beatts continued to view O'Donoghue as "mean and evil," but she was attracted to his sense of humor, the germ of which existed in her. As the dinners became more than dates to eat food, Beatts's aversion to O'Donoghue steadily faded. He allowed her to see past his iron exterior. "Michael had a very cuddly, very sweet and vulnerable side" to him, she noted. "It was a double-edged sword because as you got close you saw that [side], and the more you saw that, the more resentful and suspicious he became because he allowed you to see it."

Through 1972 Beatts commuted between Montreal and New York, where she stayed with Choquette in his East Village apartment. Once she became a *Lampoon* fixture, Beatts took a place of her own, a sublet on Charles Street. She saw more and more of O'Donoghue, their time together made easier by Choquette's being in Europe. His relationship with Ephron effectively over, O'Donoghue seductively advanced on Beatts, movement she did not discourage. They shared ideas for the magazine and spoke of collaboration. This enticed Beatts: O'Donoghue was clearly superior to Choquette as a humorist, and collaboration with the Presence could only sharpen her perspective and hone the edge that partially appeared in her work. Professionally, it made sense. Privately, they grew closer.

In their early work together, it seemed that O'Donoghue and Beatts found humorous—or at least worthy of parody—board games. In "OD: The Game of Drug Abuse," the object of the game is "to remain on the board after all the other players have OD'd." There follows a list of rules, then a board and drug cards are provided. The piece is constructed so that the reader can cut out the cards and actually play the game. As the list of rules is mildy amusing, this must have been the intended joke. In "Checkmeat: Fish and Poultry," chess pieces are replaced with fried chicken (knight), meatloaf (rook), cheeseburger (pawn), poached mackerel (bishop). King and queen are rib roast and tongue, respectively. Again, game pieces are there for the cutting, this time on "specially-selected-extra-rugged paper"; and although the list of rules and the possible moves are slightly funnier than those in "OD," the joke is again in the premise, which here is inadequately "fleshed" out.

In the byline to "Checkmeat," Beatts's name appears before O'Donoghue's, a move Beatts felt was part of her collaborator's seduction, even

though the piece was her idea. No matter: Beatts was falling for O'Donoghue creatively and romantically. "He was very much a mentor to me.
Definitely," she conceded. "He really had created this role for himself
where he was very much the Supreme Dictator of humor. I felt somewhat annointed by his recognition of me as funny, and I would pay a
lot of attention to what he had to say and I learned a lot of things from
him. I think he was very glad to share it and he was very good in that
role." However, Beatts remained attached to Choquette. When he returned from Europe, Beatts was torn but thought it proper to resume
their relationship. But too much passion and creative interplay had occurred with O'Donoghue, and for Beatts there was no going back. Her
reunion with Choquette was brief, and she took up permanently with
O'Donoghue.

After putting to bed the November 1972 "Decadence" issue,
which he edited, O'Donoghue dove completely into the *Encyclopedia
of Humor* project.

The premise seemed
simple enough, and
O'Donoghue had
had time to thor-
oughly mull it over.
But when he began
work he soon rec-
ognized the com-
plexity of the task
before him. Fortu-
nately for him there
was O'Rourke, who,
as the project wore
on, became indis-
pensable, and Beatts,
who was now part of
O'Donoghue's life.
Both helped bring
the *Encyclopedia* to
term and without
them one wonders
what O'Donoghue
would have done.
He might have
posed as humor's
Supreme Dictator,
but when it came

In the Soho loft with curios, 1972

to handling the nuts and bolts of a major project O'Donoghue was less sure of his position. Delegation of authority did not come naturally to him; he lacked the spontaneity and quick judgment that a good director needs when harnessing talent.

Slowly, slowly, the *Encyclopedia* was put together. As Sean Kelly observed, the book "was never going to come out. It was taking for-fucking-ever. They missed a couple of press dates, and P.J. got involved and made it happen. He wrote stuff that wasn't that good, but it filled spaces. He bugged people," *Lampoon* regulars, for material. In his dust jacket introduction to the *Encyclopedia,* O'Donoghue mocks his own shortcomings as the book's editor, because "while Michael may be a prolific writer of humor, a prolific doer of work he isn't." On the other hand,

> P.J. O'Rourke, he's not too *funny* but he does get the job done. Not that he thought very much of this project but it was better than what he was doing at the time which was sorting the mail. Besides, P.J.'s so easy to work with and he doesn't mind O'Donoghue's name being smeared all over the front cover of this book. I mean, as far as he's concerned, if that little piece of human garbage who calls himself an editor wants to splash his unmemorable name across the jacket of this em—

The introduction supposedly jumps to the back flap, but there instead is a meditation on rug mats, set to a *Savages* beat: "The curious tan rug mats of Central Asia . . . The haunting russet rug mats mentioned by Thomas Hardy . . ." Somehow, the *Encyclopedia*'s intro was lost and replaced with the jacket notes from *Beneath the Weave,* a book "for anyone who has ever owned a rug mat, or plans to."

The reference to O'Donoghue's name "being smeared" on the *Encyclopedia*'s front cover pertains to the demand he made of Simmons that he be given sole credit for the book: "Edited by Michael O'Donoghue." Simmons, taken slightly aback, consented. No one at the *Lampoon* had ever requested such billing, but given O'Donoghue's track record of self-promotion, it's hard to see Simmons, or anyone, surprised by his demand. But there was also the need to top Hendra, to mark this extension of his territory. For what it was worth, O'Donoghue wanted all to know, especially Hendra, who the *Encyclopedia* belonged to.

The *Encyclopedia of Humor* was finally released in September 1973. In light of the missed deadlines it is an impressive piece of work. There are lulls, as Kelly noted, and the entries are not in true alphabetical order—"Automobile" comes before "Astrology," and so on. But the editorial mix provides for first-rate material and shows many *Lampoon* regulars at the top of their game. Brian McConnachie's ethereal presence comes through in two fine comic strips, "Swamp Sluts" and "Heading for Trouble." In both, dialogue is tied loosely to action, but the words convey a reality separate from the images—a McConnachie specialty. There are several Bruce McCall drawings augmented by his vivid text, the best being an "All Purpose Atrocity Poster" in which blanks are furnished for the name of America's latest enemy, indifferent, of course, to all human life. (McCall also penned many of the *Encyclopedia*'s smaller, unsigned entries.) Edward Gorey's illustrations accompany each letter in the alphabet, and Ed Bluestone's maxims presage Jack Handey's *Deep Thoughts*:

When I see a speeding ambulance, I wish it would crash so I could get a whiff of that oxygen.

The sooner all the animals are extinct, the sooner we'll find their money.

When I look at the moon, the stars, and the planets, there's not a doubt in my mind that God is a fag.

A free press is vital because slaves would be too stupid to write the news.

Doug Kenney contributed one of his finest pieces, "First Blowjob." The story concerns young, pert Connie Phillips, who attends her senior prom with football star Jeff. It is a by-the-numbers date, complete with small talk and minor flirtation. After the prom, Jeff drives Connie to a secluded spot and gives her a tiny box. Connie believes this to be an engagement ring; she is flattered but reminds Jeff that they must first graduate from State College before matrimony can be seriously considered. Jeff is puzzled, corrects her. "*I'm* not going to the State College," he says.

"My folks are sending me to the State *Mental Hospital*—that box I gave you has a couple of Dramamines in it so you don't gag too much when you give me my blowjob."
"Y-your what?" said Connie tonelessly.
"My blowjob," Jeff explained. "You know, where a guy crams his meat into your gullet and you eat on it until he goes spooey all over your uvula."

Jeff forces Connie to suck, then swallow; he ties her to the steering wheel of his convertible, changes into a Nazi uniform, and produces a car aerial removed from a hood: " 'Gee,' exclaimed Jeff as he began to lash out viciously at her unprotected body. 'I've been wanting to try this ever since I first heard Negro music!' "

"First Blowjob" is written in a *Saturday Evening Post* vernacular, and again it's Kenney who captures the dark side of the 1950s. There is a hint of Terry Southern here, too, primarily in the "Gee whiz!" dialogue uttered amid date rape and abuse. O'Donoghue, who saw similarities between Southern and Kenney, encouraged his *Lampoon* colleague to read the works of the Texas wonder. Thus did masters meet.★

When not "bugging" people for material, P. J. O'Rourke collaborated with O'Donoghue on two pieces: "Krash Course," in which "The Name-On-Request Correspondence School of Home Study" teaches the unemployed to fly 747s in their spare time; and "Battling Buses of World War II," a tribute to the little-known Army Bus and Trolley Corps. It is a silly but well-executed idea, filled with O'Donoghue-inspired puns and jokes: "1939—Shadow of the Bus Fumes Large Over Europe"; "The Buses of Navaronne"; "Highways at War: Death Takes Its Tollroads"; "Destination Tokyo, With Connections for Kyoto, Osaka, and Yokohama." The concept was O'Rourke's. He and O'Donoghue were riding in a bus when, according to O'Donoghue, "he said, 'You know, my dad used to be a rear-door gunner on one of these buses.' And then we started whipping up this whole scenario, with the slogan, 'Very few ever came back because nobody went over.' "

Though influenced by O'Donoghue, O'Rourke continued to seek and strike his signature note. His solo pieces for the *Encyclopedia* pale against the material written with O'Donoghue. For all the energy evident in his work, there is an odd sterility to many of O'Rourke's jokes, a sterility he would eventually smash through. For the moment, however, it was O'Donoghue who did the smashing; and in the *Encyclopedia* he expended all of himself in an effort to finish the project.

With his name on the book's cover, O'Donoghue was responsible for the final product and thus left nothing to chance. Spare notions, old ideas, random thoughts scribbled in notebooks—O'Donoghue used everything he had. He flipped through the cards in his metal box looking for ideas he could expand upon or recycle. Parts of his "happening" work surfaced in "Mona Guerrilla Theater," a series of short, strange monologues written with McConnachie. Material from his *Evergreen* days took up some space, including a bit of verse composed years before: "Life: One thing led/To another and/Before we knew it/We were

---

★Southern also appears in the *Encyclopedia*. In a letter addressed to *Ms.* magazine, he states that feminists will never be taken seriously because of their "animal-like" behavior during sex. This was Southern's second *Lampoon* piece, the first being in the November 1972 issue, where in mock investigative tones he exposes a group of Vietnam veterans that licks the assholes of dead Vietcong—"stiff-gook rimming," as he calls it. O'Donoghue, who longed to see Southern in the *Lampoon,* was pleased when his idol finally contributed.

dead." This small item was enlarged and illustrated so it filled a page. His dirty limericks, first published in *Other Scenes,* were put into service as well. In order to fill up *that* page, Sean Kelly added a few limericks of his own, the subject of each being O'Donoghue.

A writer who'd mastered all media
Tried a humorous Encyclopedia.
When his deadlines had past
He admitted at last
To habitual sins of Acedia.

But not all of O'Donoghue's *Encyclopedia* work reflected hurry and strain. "Cowgirls at War," a lesbian S&M comic drawn by Russ Heath, shows a pair of "Sagebrush Sallys" mouthing romantic clichés while engaging in rough sex. They stop only to kill off the German soldiers who have surrounded their bullet-pocked hacienda. Although much of the dialogue is taken from O'Donoghue's play *Someday What You Really Are Is Going to Catch Up With You . . . ,* it is reworked in a highly entertaining manner, the result superior to the original. Then there's "The Churchill Wit," a collection of anecdotes that highlight Sir Winston's "clever" side. Next to a photo of the old boor—doctored so he gives us the finger—are several examples of his "precious gift of humor."

At an elegant dinner party, Lady Astor once leaned across the table to remark, "If you were my husband, Winston, I'd poison your coffee."

"And if you were my wife, I'd beat the shit out of you," came Churchill's unhesitating retort.

When the noted playwright George Bernard Shaw sent him two tickets to the opening night of his new play with a note that read: "Bring a friend, if you have one," Churchill, not to be outdone, promptly wired back, "You and your play can go fuck yourselves."

Churchill was known to drain a glass or two and, after one particularly convivial evening, he chanced to encounter Miss Bessie Braddock, a Socialist member of the House of Commons, who, upon seeing his condition, said, "Winston, you're drunk." Mustering all his dignity, Churchill drew himself to his full height, cocked an eyebrow and rejoined, "Shove it up your ass, you ugly cunt."

"The Churchill Wit" is perhaps O'Donoghue's best *Encyclopedia* entry. It is a strong, one-joke premise that loses nothing along the way. But for sheer bite one must recognize Anne Beatts. Her *Encyclopedia* pieces are minor when compared to her other *Lampoon* work; yet each, save for one (an interminable *Jungle Book* parody seemingly designed to fill pages), hits the reader quickly, then recedes, a mode of attack no doubt learned from O'Donoghue. Beatts intensifies alphabetically: First, a bumper sticker that reads "WARNING! I Speed Up to Run Down Little Animals!" Next, a plea to businesses to "Hire the Veteran. He needs the money." Plenty, it seems, as he is now a junkie with a "hundred-dollar-a-day habit." Finally, listed under "Liberals, Concerned," is "Beneath the Family of Man"—a "photographic exhibition of our times."

Here Beatts matches famous quotes to grisly photos, and the effect is that of *Faces of Death* as scripted by Bartlett's. A pile of severed human heads illustrates the Kipling line "If you can keep your head when all about you are losing theirs . . ." Under the words of General P. H. Sheridan, "The only good Indian is a dead Indian," lie several dead Indian women and children. The human remains found in a Nazi crematorium inspire Shakespeare's observation "Golden lads and girls all must, as chimney-sweepers, come to dust" (the same inscription found on Phoebe Zeit-Geist's tombstone), while Alexander Pope's adage "The proper study of mankind is man" is set next to two Nazi doctors at work on a dismembered corpse.

"Beneath the Family of Man" is satirical hardball played with the right touch of misanthropy. Thus the piece inspired its share of negative mail. Readers found it "disgusting," "sadistic," and in "extremely poor taste." A teenage girl wrote that the piece "epitomized your complete disregard for some of the world's worst tragedies" and that she was "nauseated and offended" by the *Encyclopedia* overall. An older man stated, "*Encyclopedia of Humor* my ass. I've got news for you guys—concentration camps are not funny." In response to this criticism—specifically concerning the photo of the severed heads, which truly unnerved a number of readers—O'Donoghue told the press that "people [are] writing Crayola-scrawled messages to us, blaming us for cutting off the heads. Hell, we didn't behead anybody. Those pictures came from UPI." Yet no amount of reader reaction could match the quiet anger displayed by Volkswagen, itself run down by Beatts's humor.

Beatts wished to knock Ted Kennedy off the Chappaquiddick bridge by using a Volkswagen ad. She drew on her experience as a copywriter to conceive the perfect image: a VW Bug floats on a body of water, as impervious to sinking as Jesus Himself. The copy reads, "If Ted Kennedy drove a Volkswagen, he'd be president today." Like the best *Lampoon* parodies, the ad has force because it looks real—so real, in fact, that the official VW symbol was used instead of a mock logo. This proved a major editing error, for once Volkswagen's lawyers saw their client's name tied to a slander of the Kennedys, they acted. The company brought a $30 million lawsuit against the *Lampoon* for infringement of its trademark, and this Matty Simmons could not contest. Doubtless the many bloodshot hours spent on the *Encyclopedia*'s completion led to the editorial oversight, but that would not do as a legal argument. In order to avoid a financial calamity, Simmons had to recall unsold copies of the book and destroy the offending ads in each.

At the time of the lawsuit, 450,000 softcovers of the *Encyclopedia* had been distributed, and of these some 315,000 had been sold. Volkswagen's action was widely reported and this, of course helped make the book a best-seller. And as more people read the *Encyclopedia,* more were angered or put off by its humor. Again, it was Beatts's work that riled those who chose to complain; but since O'Donoghue was the book's editor most of the mail was addressed to him, including a nasty letter from four Vietnam vets who took exception to Beatts's "Hire the Veteran" piece. They informed O'Donoghue that they would bind him, throw him in a bag, hang it up, and then beat him with large sticks until every bone in his body was broken. Yet O'Donoghue worried more about the Kennedy reaction to the VW ad: "I just know I'm going to be standing around at a cocktail party and some people I know who know the Kennedys are going to come up to me and punch me in the mouth." This statement was issued for the sake of publicity, but after so much negative mail O'Donoghue no doubt believed that physical retribution was possible, if not probable.

Volkswagen promised to cease legal action once the ads were destroyed and an apology was made in the *Lampoon*. Simmons complied on all fronts, then sent an inner-office memo to his staff: "The Volkswagen lawsuit has been settled and although there were no damages to this company from the point of view of settlement, it once again points to the absolute need to refrain from the use of anybody's trademark or copyright." If the magazine was to attack icons, Simmons reasoned, let it trash America's most cherished commodity: celebrity.

At the close of 1973 the *Lampoon*'s circulation neared 800,000. Ad revenues were up, the company's name established in print, on record, and on stage. Exhausted by but proud of the *Encyclopedia,* O'Donoghue had no desire to return to the magazine's monthly grind. He felt he contributed heavily to the *Lampoon*'s success, and as the company expanded into show business, O'Donoghue rightfully demanded a larger, hotter piece of the action.

six

I've only been attracted to two kinds of women. One is the very smart, complex, intelligent woman, preferably with a sense of humor, with whom I can have a long and very absorbed relationship. And the other kind are frothing sex weasels. The trouble with complex women is that there's always a minotaur in the labyrinth.

Earlier in 1973, before the *Encyclopedia* was tackled, O'Donoghue and Beatts were becoming quite serious as a couple and a creative team. Each generated considerable energy and together they formed an acid-tipped comic alliance. The artistic arrangement had O'Donoghue as mentor to Beatts the student; Beatts possessed the necessary satirical tools; O'Donoghue showed her a new way to ply them. In return Beatts corrected O'Donoghue's often atrocious spelling, but more important, she influenced the way he would look for the rest of his life.

O'Donoghue's metamorphosis was one of personality and artistic temperament. But in terms of wardrobe and weight his image was less calculated—that is, until he began making money at the *Lampoon*. At this point he sought to complete the package, to shed not only pounds but the scruffy, tattered look that supposedly lent him a bohemian air. Here Beatts was crucial: "I got him out of those Hush Puppies and little torn shirts he was wearing," she said. She steered him toward old white suits and Hawaiian shirts, walking sticks and wing tip shoes. He trimmed his beard and cut short his thinning hair. Most of O'Donoghue's new wardrobe was found in thrift stores outside Manhattan. "You could buy a 1930s white suit for twenty dollars," said Beatts. "You could buy Hawaiian shirts for three dollars." She recognized his enchantment with the fashions of the 1930s; to him "it was a sense that things that were older were better."

But there was more to this shift in style than nostalgia. The new look fit O'Donoghue's flair for self-dramatization and gave him a feeling of polish and authority. It was a form of serious camp, a foppish exterior that augmented the dark thoughts within. "Michael was an extraordinarily self-conscious person because he was an extraordinarily *conscious* person," observed Sean Kelly. "Michael was one of those people who could walk into a room, say something about that room, the saying of which destroys the people who live there. They're pegged forever by class, by race, by their limitations. Now if you have this curse or gift, how do you yourself dress? Because anything you put on marks you as the kind of asshole *who* wears the kind of thing you're wearing."

Through his attraction to the 1930s, O'Donoghue was drawn to the geometric grace of art deco. He'd flirted with this style when still in jeans and army jacket. He collaborated with the artist Charles White III on " '30s," a poem that appeared in the August 1970 *Evergreen Review.* " '30s" is a minor ditty about Broadway vampires, "the elegant undead" who feed on chic New Yorkers. White's black-and-white deco images accompany each stanza and are partially obscured by blots of blood. (O'Donoghue and White teamed many times during the *Lampoon* years, most prominently on the album cover of *Radio Dinner.*) In a May 1972 *Lampoon* piece, "The Zircon As Big As the Taft," F. Scott and Zelda Fitzgerald frolic in an art deco environment and commit "madcap" acts such as eating their dog, riding atop bread trucks, killing the writer Carl Van Vechten by striking his head with a salt shaker. Illustrated by David Palladini, "Zircon" is colorful but remote; its cool deco surface flattened O'Donoghue's jokes. It was the type of piece that mystified Michael Gross, who, while laying it out, would wonder, "What's funny about this?"

O'Donoghue's work had always contained a touch of the effete. So, too, had his personality, despite the bohemian trappings. But as the white suits replaced his torn shirts, what once was sheer affectation became matter-of-fact, the final stitch in his overall design. "When Michael found art deco he was one happy guy," said Sean Kelly. "Michael was real happy when he hit on that one because he didn't have to worry about [an identity] anymore." He'd outgrown the downtrodden look but "he couldn't put on a business suit, he couldn't put on a leisure suit, he couldn't put on a safari suit." The 1930s, or at least his romanticized version of that decade, provided the perfect cover. No one could comment on his new style because the style was a comment in itself.

Beatts, too, dressed in antique clothes: backless dresses, wide-brimmed hats, 1930s/1940s-era shoes. She complemented O'Donoghue visually, and this, added to their deepening collaboration and romance, pleased him immensely. "She had everything," he would later say. "It was like one-stop shopping." Like him, Beatts enjoyed the theatrical element of their relationship. They forged a cool deco surface of their own. Comparisons to Nick and Nora Charles of *Thin Man* fame were made by those witness to their transformation. But the image that struck many in the *Lampoon* world was that of Zelda and Scott Fitzgerald, an image no doubt sanitized as Beatts and O'Donoghue would not care to be seen as insane or alcoholic. Their Zelda and Scott were cutting as well as stylish; in this they were closer to themselves than to the literary couple that for most people defined the American Jazz Age.

Transformation aside, Matty Simmons wanted O'Donoghue, old or new, back in the magazine. Though stung by Volkswagen's lawsuit, Simmons was happy with the *Encyclopedia*'s critical and respectable commercial success. Now it was time for his heavy-hitter to return to the fold and produce as brilliantly as before. But *Lemmings*'s triumph—*Hendra's* triumph—gnawed at O'Donoghue, and he insisted that he be given a showbiz project as well. Simmons agreed, and plans were made to bring the *Lampoon* to radio under O'Donoghue's direction. As with *Radio Dinner,* sound production would be a crucial part of the new project, so O'Donoghue again turned to the person he knew would deliver the goods, Bob Tischler. After *Radio Dinner,* Tischler had resumed his duties at Wendell Craig full-time. In order for him to work on the radio show he would have to quit a steady job and join what on paper seemed experimental. After all, the days of radio comedy were past, and old characters and routines were fresh only in the far reaches of space. Yet Tischler was taken with the concept, and he left his job to assist O'Donoghue.

Actually, Tischler would do more than assist: He would become one of the best collaborators with whom O'Donoghue ever worked. On *Radio Dinner,* Tischler had dealt primarily with Hendra because O'Donoghue kept clear of technical matters. But Hendra was not part of the new venture; O'Donoghue, as creative director, would have to deal directly with Tischler and, more often than not, defer to his judgment. This placed O'Donoghue in a less than authoritative position, but he had little choice if the project was to succeed. He knew that Tischler was the right person for the job—indeed, the only person he felt he could trust—and it was this recognition that ultimately strengthened their creative bond.

O'Donoghue had no "master plan" concerning the radio show's format. The basic idea was to have *Lampoon* contributors write sketches and song parodies, hire actors to read the lines or sing the lyrics, then piece the thing together with audio links and segues. Most important to O'Donoghue was that the show reflect radio's golden age in style as well as quality, a point he stressed to all concerned.

Polly Bier, a television producer brought in to assist Tischler, received one of O'Donoghue's pep talks. "His visions of the show sounded really very exciting," she said. "He talked about doing some very innovative stuff, about using radio in a way it hadn't been used for a long time. . . . There were a lot of pieces written that used old radio announc-

ers, perfect recreation of the forties, perfect recreation of the fifties . . ."
To this end O'Donoghue used actors such as Norman Rose, Sid Davis,
George Coe, and Tischler's former employer Wendell Craig. Each had
a distinct, resonant voice that recalled radio's earlier period, the kind of
voice that filled rooms and imaginations.

Many of the magazine's editors were keen on being part of the show,
too; and before long scripts floated in from Doug Kenney, Bruce McCall,
George Trow, and Brian McConnachie (the latter two would double
extensively as performers). And then there was the cast of *Lemmings*,
stage-tested and ready to go. Initially, O'Donoghue wanted no contact
with the actors in Hendra's production, the exception being Christopher
Guest, who had worked with O'Donoghue on *Radio Dinner* and whose
range as a comic actor and musician could not be ignored. But with
Guest came the other *Lemmings*, most prominently Chevy Chase and
John Belushi, both of whom performed from the first show on.*

The son of an eminent publishing executive, Chase knew Guest from
their days at Bard College in upstate New York. After Bard, Chase
became involved with Channel One, a comedy video group directed by
Ken Shapiro. (Channel One's sketches were later captured in the film
The Groove Tube, which featured Chase and a young Richard Belzer.)
Chase's involvement with the group led to his receiving a call from
Guest, who was cast in *Lemmings*. The show needed a comic actor who
could play drums, so Chase auditioned for Hendra and was, in his mind,
"awful. I mean, I really wasn't an actor. I couldn't get onstage and act.
It was kind of scary. But I would fill the drum part pretty well and my
audition consisted of some impersonation of gays or some strange thing
which seemed to be in back then." Nevertheless, Hendra was taken with
Chase and hired him on the spot.

Belushi came to *Lemmings* by way of Chicago's illustrious Second
City. A native of Wheaton, Illinois, Belushi had forged his craft in summer stock and his own improvisational group, the West Compass Players.
When he joined Second City he plowed through the traditions of earlier
members such as Alan Arkin, Mike Nichols, and Barbara Harris, whose
humor tended to be erudite, and established a new era in which the
language of the street and the energy of youth prevailed. In many ways
Belushi's influence on Second City was similar to O'Donoghue's experience with *Evergreen Review:* Each tapped a vibrant form—Belushi rock
'n' roll, O'Donoghue comic books—that creatively jolted their respective
venues. Hendra saw this up close in Chicago when he went to catch

*Hendra and Simmons remember this differently, each saying in his book that Chase
and Belushi were gradually woven into the *Radio Hour* because of O'Donoghue's hatred
for Hendra. But both actors appeared in the first show (as did another *Lemmings* cast
member, Gary Goodrow), and are credited at the end by O'Donoghue himself.

Belushi's act. For his part, Belushi, who wanted badly to be in *Lemmings,*
made certain that Hendra missed nothing, even if it meant upstaging the
other players. "I pitied his fellow actors as this rolling, bearded landmine
crashed through their set," Hendra later wrote, "threatening to destroy them
if his purpose was thwarted, blow their heads off if they got in his way."

Chase's and Belushi's involvement with Hendra didn't mark them as
"traitors" in O'Donoghue's eyes. After all, neither one was part of the
magazine and so both were free of political taint. Not so for Sean Kelly,
whose solid ties to *Lemmings* and Hendra led to increasing tension between himself and O'Donoghue. But O'Donoghue would overlook this
if Kelly chose to take his side in the cold war with Hendra.

"I was summoned into the Presence," Kelly recalled, "and informed
that Hendra was the Beast from the Thousand Fathoms, that he was a
prick and how could I work with him." O'Donoghue wanted Kelly
exclusively for the radio show; Kelly responded by saying that he had
worked hard on *Lemmings* and couldn't leave simply because O'Donoghue asked him to. He *would,* he said, contribute to both shows, since
he desired to work with O'Donoghue and didn't see why there had to
be a conflict. O'Donoghue, reluctant, gave in; he needed Kelly and did
not want to sabotage the radio project before it began. Yet inside he
seethed: His respect for Kelly's comic brilliance was sullied by what he
considered betrayal through indecision. He would work with Kelly but
gradually ceased to view him as a friend.

Hendra also lobbied Kelly and told him that as a team they had a
bright future. Though loath to choose a "master," as he put it, or to
take sides in the ongoing conflict, Kelly fell into Hendra's sphere "by
attrition. . . . Tony and I would get together with our kids, and Michael
and Anne were at Reno Sweeney's [a fashionable Manhattan nightclub].
It wasn't some sort of thing where I felt 'Fuck you, O'Donoghue!' By
no means." But regardless of Kelly's intentions, O'Donoghue refused to
see the situation in any way save his own: Hendra was garbage, as was
anyone associated with him. Nothing more need be said or considered.*

*I have always wanted to do a radio show. They are quite exciting. Sound is
very comforting. You can do enormous things with sound. If you want to do*

---

*Looking back, Kelly believed that Hendra "asked for" O'Donoghue's anger. "Tony's
an interesting theological case," he said. "Tony knows good and evil, and he chooses to
do evil in a Graham Greene, fucked up way to affirm its existence. . . . If you're with
your best friend's former girlfriend, the worst thing you can do under the circumstances
is to fuck her. Tony chooses to do the evil thing regardless of the consequences. . . .
Now this doesn't mean that he isn't capable of great generosity, isn't extraordinarily
intelligent or talented. But in retrospect, I realize that Tony fucked Amy Ephron because
it was the wrongest thing he could do short of killing her." Suffice it to say that Kelly
and Hendra later had a major falling out of their own.

500,000 Etruscans charging Troy or wherever the Etruscans charged, you can do it very easily with a few sound effects and some screams, and you have it.

By fall 1973 *The National Lampoon Radio Hour* was in production. The first shows were taped at Bell Sound, on Fifty-fourth Street, while a permanent studio was being built on the eleventh floor at 635 Madison—seven flights above the *Lampoon* offices. Here O'Donoghue demanded panache: he called the new studio the "Radio Ranch" and saw to it that the decor matched the theme. The reception/office area was to convey a Prairie Moon feel, complete with cactus-shaped furniture and painted desert backdrops. This was in line with his romantic view of bygone radio days, a time when the medium ranked second only to Hollywood; when, as a boy, he lay for hours in front of the family set, listening to and cataloging his favorite shows in scrapbooks. Also, the Radio Ranch conceit matched his new look, for one never saw Jack Benny sport ripped denim flairs.

O'Donoghue's mania for structure led him to devise a schedule that he insisted the contributors heed: "All material (save music) must be in at least one month before a theme's air date. This is an absolute deadline and . . . cannot be changed." But O'Donoghue did not foresee the amount of work needed to produce a weekly show. Soon after the program's debut the deadlines became less absolute as he and Tischler scrambled to fill air time with whatever material they could obtain. After recording a number of bits, the two worked into the night editing raw tape to broadcast length while locating the music and sound effects that best brought out the humor. Oftentimes O'Donoghue slept on the studio couch while Tischler, varied lengths of tape hanging all around him, fashioned the bits into a fluid whole. He then would wake O'Donoghue, play the just-edited stretch, and get the sleepy director's opinion before another round of work began.

The extensive labor made for smooth listening. *The National Lampoon Radio Hour* debuted on November 17, 1973, and was syndicated in some eighty-four markets nationwide. The number would quickly rise past one hundred, and by early 1974 the show would reach somewhere between two hundred and six hundred markets (Tischler's and Simmons's numbers, respectively), bringing the *Lampoon* name to its largest audience yet, a feat unmatched until the release of *Animal House* five years later. What the audience heard in those initial broadcasts was the *Lampoon* sensibility fleshed out in bold audio strokes. There was an immediacy that one would not find on *Radio Dinner* because it, like all albums, was frozen in time. The *Radio Hour* moved, fluctuated; routines, one-liners, long sketches, and song parodies came at the listener in such a way that a strange rhythm was achieved, exactly as O'Donoghue and Tischler intended. "It's very fast and staccato, like a radio 'Laugh-In,' " O'Donoghue told the *Milwaukee Journal* just after the show's debut. "It's quite different in pace from the old style of radio. I've listened to that kind and it's really slow."

Though the *Radio Hour* did reflect the speed of television, the trappings of old radio were present in the show. This was especially so in "Laughs From the Past," in which the sound of a scratched 78 rpm disc (which was smashed to pieces every week) signaled a classic routine by Abbott and Costello, Spike Jones and his City Slickers, or Henry Morgan. In time less "traditional" humorists such as Lenny Bruce and Nichols and May were heard in the segment, and this bridged the space between comedy's old and new guard: Here tradition and innovation subverted each other, which gave the *Radio Hour* its unique flavor. And that a segment such as "Laughs From the Past" was prepackaged helped O'Donoghue and Tischler immensely; it was one less piece they needed to rehearse, record, and edit.

> *"We could say we're smoking reefer on the radio*
> *While we're really eating cookies and you'd never know.*
> *We could tell you we look great*
> *When we're really overweight*
> *You can get away with so much on the radio . . ."*
> —From the *National Lampoon Radio Hour* theme song

O'Donoghue was the *Radio Hour*'s host. Each week he introduced the show in the guise of a contemporary actress such as Jill St. John or Karen Valentine, the joke being that his mellifluous voice was unchanged. The show itself was equal parts absurdity, nostalgia, and satire (as Richard Nixon faced the possibility of impeachment, the *Hour* contained more political humor), and at times the elements mixed beautifully. An early example of this came in the wake of Israel's victory over Egypt in the Yom Kippur War.

O'Donoghue played a news correspondent reporting from the frontlines. His voice is barely heard through the static of a ham radio, then fades and is replaced by jaunty Irish music on an old 78. The song, "The Jews Have Got Their Irish Up," a novelty record from the 1940s, compares the Jewish armies of the pre-Israel period to Irishmen fighting the same enemy, the British. Yet the song seems almost a parody, something that Sean Kelly might have written with Tischler's technical help. It was woven so well into the fabric of the show that doubtless many listeners thought it an original *Lampoon* piece. But as with "Laughs From

With engineer Bob Tischler

the Past," the song and other bits like it fit the format of "classic" radio while relieving O'Donoghue and Tischler of additional work.

Filling time on the *Radio Hour* became paramount. Along with the prerecorded items, original sketches were often given long musical openings and closings. On one level this lent a sketch an "authentic" radio sound, as though an orchestra was in the studio assisting the actors at the mikes. But the tactic also took up extra minutes, as did some of the talk show parodies overseen by O'Donoghue and on occasion by George Trow. The parodies revolved around a central theme—butter in taxis, Pat Nixon giving advice, authors hawking controversial books—and from here the actors improvised until the premise ran dry or O'Donoghue felt there was enough material to edit down. The final length of a talk show parody depended on the amount of quality humor there was as well as on the amount of time it covered. Thus the occasional rambling sketch in which a discussion could go on for seven or eight minutes—an eternity in radio. This became somewhat of an inside joke and formed the basis of a routine written by Chevy Chase. Protesting the "charge" that the producers deliberately padded the *Radio Hour,* Chase defended the show at length, doing what he said the producers didn't do, pad. He later repeated this bit in a cold opening on *Saturday Night Live.*

Recurring characters and bits were another way to fill a show. Although O'Donoghue belittled this concept on artistic grounds, the brutal weekly schedule ensured that whatever material worked would be used again and again. Repeats were essential and formed the backbone of the *Radio Hour.*

- Christopher Guest established two recurring characters: Roger De-Swans, an effete British actor who introduced odd interpretations of such dramatic classics as Samuel Beckett's *Waitng for Godot* and Anton Chekov's *The Seagull;* and Flash Bazbo, a moronic science fiction hero created by Doug Kenney.
- Anne Beatts, whose voice recalled Gracie Allen and Jack Benny's wife, Mary Livingston, hosted "Recipe Corner," which consisted of her correcting erroneous recipes given the previous week. As one of the few women in the cast, Beatts performed in a multitude of sketches.
- George Trow played Mr. Chatterbox, a Walter Winchell–type reporter who gossiped about the sins and styles of high society. Trow's energetic performances made the bit a *Radio Hour* highlight, and he closed each segment by admonishing the audience, "Do try to mix with a better class of people."
- Brian McConnachie, like Beatts, regularly appeared on the show. And he, too, had a recurring role as the *Radio Hour*'s "Public Disservice" announcer who offered ridiculous advice about insignificant matters.
- John Belushi's Marlon Brando wandered in and out of various bits reciting lines from *Last Tango in Paris*. He also played Craig Baker, a nineteen-year-old "perfect master" whose idea of meditation and higher consciousness was to hang out and drink beer with his suburban pals.

Bruce McCall didn't perform but he did create rich, aural imagery. His "Megaphone Newsreel," a takeoff on the movie house newsreels of the 1930s and 1940s, possessed the intricacy of his artwork. Narrated by Wendell Craig, whose deep comic voice captured the period tone, "Megaphone" marched "around the world" and "into your face" with news about a stolen muffin crime spree, a Mississippi flood caused by an overflowing bathtub, tricycle races, and garbage men on motorcycles. Craig's description of events was so precise that one could practically *see* houses half submerged in floodwater or muffins being swiped. This same attention to detail was heard in other McCall pieces; "The Camera Club of the Air," in which contestants call in to a panel of judges and describe their photos over the phone; and a documentary on the menace of wood rot, complete with the sound of a projector showing the film.

MADGE: Oh, Jane. I feel so run-down lately. You know, no pep, irregularity, nagging headache. Some mornings I just don't feel I can face the world. And last night my Ted said I'm no fun anymore. Jane, isn't there something I can take to relieve my symptoms and feel my old self again?

JANE: Afraid not, Madge. What you've got is an advanced, malignant tumor of the brain. ("Wacky" music up and out.)

In the first seven shows, which ran to the end of 1973, there was an energy and enthusiasm that lifted the lesser material and sharpened the stronger pieces. Part of this stemmed from the excitement of the new project: Many *Lampoon* writers preferred the studio to their offices at the magazine (though they did manage to meet their monthly deadlines); and since the radio show was but an elevator ride away, it served as a refuge for those either bored with or stuck on an idea. O'Donoghue welcomed any and all staffers who wanted to contribute (Hendra excepted), and his devotion to the project inspired the writers who came upstairs to give him their best effort—either on page or in performance. As he had at the magazine, O'Donoghue drew an appreciative crowd, and at times this worried Matty Simmons who wanted the *Radio Hour* to succeed but not at the expense of the *Lampoon* itself.

Creatively, the *Radio Hour* was quite successful. Some of the best humorists of a generation collaborated weekly to recapture and redefine the lost art of radio comedy. To be sure the field was uncrowded: O'Donoghue often compared the show to the Pony Express. But in its brief resuscitation of the dead beast, the *Radio Hour* set in motion a number of careers of comedy writers and actors who challenged, then altered, the mainstream of humor in the same way that the directors of "New Hollywood"—Coppola, Lucas, Spielberg, Scorsese—changed the film industry. Not Cheech nor Chong nor the Firesign Theatre could match the show's range of talent and the brilliance found there. The *Radio Hour* was the final word in the statement made in print by the *Lampoon*. The school of "Just kidding, folks!" was burned to the ground while hippie comedians were beaten with pipes. You weren't going to see the *Lampoon* "kids" perform their schtick on the *Tonight Show,* amusing the tourists with their "zany" antics.

The material on the *Radio Hour* could be much harsher than some of the humor in the magazine. The immediacy of sound was one obvious advantage: Hearing a rifle shot makes more of an impression than seeing "BLAM!" in a comic panel. Indeed, many of O'Donoghue's jokes worked better when heard, especially if they suggested or contained violence. In a parody of the Charmin tissue ads of the period—in which Mr. Whipple admonishes women for "squeezing the Charmin" in his store—O'Donoghue beats the living hell out of Whipple while telling him, "I'm gonna squeeze your Charmin and then I'm gonna squeeze your Mop & Glo and then I'm gonna squeeze your Frankenberry . . ."

In print, both the beating and the dialogue would be on equal terms; on radio, the sound of Whipple's face being rearranged nearly drowns out O'Donoghue's words. Imbalance is necessary for the joke to come off.

Such was the case for a variety of pieces, including Anne Beatts's little gem, "The Nazi Dr. Dolittle." This piece *did* appear both in the magazine and on the show, and the difference is clear; after all, when the punch line is "He *made* the animals talk," sounds of torture must be heard or the heat is lost. But for sheer audio aggression nothing on the *Radio Hour* topped O'Donoghue's routine about Ed Sullivan that appeared on show number five.

> You know, Ed Sullivan, we kid him a lot but Ed Sullivan is one of the greats of this business. And in the cab on the way over to the studio tonight I had a funny thought: What if Ed Sullivan were tortured. And when I say tortured what I mean is, What if steel needles, say six inches long, were plunged into Ed's eyes? I think it would go something like this . . .

A beat is taken, then O'Donoghue begins screaming at the top of his lungs. The screams are like a series of explosions, each one setting off the next; as O'Donoghue turns away from the microphone his screams become cries before ending as grunts. The pain caused by the needles is made explicit and is not "joked up" for the sake of a laugh. In this O'Donoghue was a method comic: His migraines were so intense that it was all he could do *but* scream. To him it felt as though needles were indeed being thrust in his sockets. He expressed this by wishing the pain on others—preferably showbiz figures he despised—but in the end it was he who acted out the pain, for he alone knew how profound it could be.

Tischler had seen this bit in its embryonic form at Franconia College, and O'Donoghue did a less-violent version in private for friends such as McConnachie and Nelson Lyon. But when it came time to record O'Donoghue threw everything into the performance. "He was just beating the shit out of the studio," recalled Chevy Chase. "I mean we were up there in the window looking down from the control room and Michael was cutting himself, you know, hitting mikes and knocking chairs over, doing the act, which was so wonderful and we were in hysterics." Lyon viewed the needles in the eyes as "the ultimate use of pain and torture for shattering humorous effect. It's not just a joke. It's a moment in art that reverberates with significance and meaning. It's an unspeakable image. That's the great Michael O'Donoghue creation." As Luis Buñuel was forever tied to the sliced cow's eye in *Un Chien Andalou,* so the needles bit would mark O'Donoghue for most of his career. It became a signature of sorts, a broken and bleeding Jackie Gleason screaming "How sweet it AIN'T!!" before crashing into the orchestra pit.

The commitment shown in his Ed Sullivan "impression" was heard in every piece O'Donoghue recorded for the show. He couldn't manage accents and didn't create characters, but when the part called for it he displayed passion as well as subtlety. After all, he did have a history in theater and his artistic persona was perhaps his most realized conception. Performing in sketches, then, proved scarcely a challenge. In fact, it's interesting how well the other *Lampoon* writers performed as actors. They more than held their own with seasoned pros such as George Coe and Norman Rose, not to mention the *Lemmings* crowd of Christopher Guest, John Belushi, Alice Playten, Gary Goodrow, and Chevy Chase.

Although hired as an actor for *Lemmings,* Chase was primarily a writer who felt he had much to learn when it came to the boards. But on the *Radio Hour,* Chase blossomed; his voice was perfect for the medium and he established an intimacy with the microphone that he would later bring in front of television cameras. Like O'Donoghue, Chase did not engage in "impressions" per se but would on occasion attempt broad accents— his version of Senator Sam Ervin's decrepit southern twang was recognizable but not exact, more a cracker tonality than character study. For the most part Chase used his own voice, whether he played a suicide hot line operator or the English writer Roald Dahl (in a sketch in which Dahl's wife, the actress Patricia Neal, tries to serve him coffee but because of her stroke can't distinguish a cup from a magazine), and this, too, he would repeat when working on television.

John Belushi also blossomed on the show. In *Lemmings* he was the star attraction, his comic velocity the main engine that drove the Woodstock parody. But radio demands a different speed and Belushi adjusted to this reality in the first *Radio Hour.* In a takeoff on *Waiting for Godot,* Belushi delivers Beckett's stark dialogue seriously; when Godot arrives, late due to traffic, Belushi and the other actors deviate from the script ("Hi, good to see you . . .") but maintain the same tone—no need for embellishment or banging about. Indeed, the majority of Belushi's *Radio Hour* work showed him to be a skilled comic actor, someone who could find the fluctuation in a mood and play it right as well as for laughs. This aspect of Belushi's talent was either ignored or dismissed once he achieved stardom as the "slob" in *Animal House.* But Belushi took pride in his craft and stressed this to journalists who expected a drug-crazed buffoon.

This is Michael O'Donoghue speaking for the editors of the National Lampoon. *In the past few weeks we've received quite a few letters, telegrams, even irate phone calls protesting some of the things we've done here on the show, and I think that's wonderful because that's what this country's all about, the right to disagree. I'm going to say that again—the right to disagree. You have an opinion and the other guy has an opinion. If you don't see eye to eye you can always kill him because that's how we settle things here. For almost two hundred years that's been the American way, and if you can't get to him, as is sometimes the case, you can always harm his loved ones or set fire to his pets. It's all part of voicing your beliefs under our system.*

O'Donoghue dubbed the *Radio Hour* as "sixty minutes of mindless hostility" and "sixty minutes chock full of mirth, merriment, and racial slurs." Provocation was part of the mission. Slanders were thrown at the French, and Native Americans were portrayed as so crazy that keeping them in reservations was the only answer. Germans, Italians, and Indians received their lumps, as did the major monotheist religions. As with similar material in the magazine, these and other assaults were primarily ironic and mounted to expose bigotry's core—though at times this distinction was intentionally blurred, usually at the hands of O'Donoghue.

In the *Lampoon* he probed the sanctity of the Holocaust while trying to twist swastikas and barbed wire into jokes. He even proposed a special issue to be titled *National Socialist Lampoon*—what the magazine would be had the Germans won the war.★ Among the issue's theme-related jokes was the observation, "Consider that most of the Jews Hitler killed would be dead by now anyway, or very old and sick . . . what has it been, thirty-five, forty years? So, you know, things are beginning to even out."

This he used in one of his *Radio Hour* closings, the part of the show in which he mused briefly about life and art. But the comment inspired little negative listener reaction, and the critics took no issue with this or any of the "hostile" remarks heard weekly. In fact the *Los Angeles Times* used "mirth, merriment, and racial slurs" as a headline atop its positive review of the show and advised: "To those who would be offended, avoid it at all costs. But those with a sense of the absurd can't afford to miss it." Doubtless the *Times* meant listeners, but one of the show's sponsors, lacking an absurdist sensibility, took the paper's advice and decided to avoid the *Radio Hour* "at all costs."

Like any commercial enterprise, the *Radio Hour* needed corporate money to survive. As Matty Simmons explained, the radio stations "took the programs on a barter basis, which meant [the stations] kept a number of the commercial spots, resold them, and kept the money." Thus national advertisers were needed to pay the *Radio Hour*'s bills. Thanks to

---

★Neither this nor the related "Pro-Semitism" issue was ever published, though it would have been interesting to see if O'Donoghue could pull off "Fiddler in the Oven."

Lampoon co-founder Rob Hoffman's soft drink connections, advertising director Gerry Taylor snagged 7-Up as the show's first major sponsor. This was somewhat of a coup since the magazine itself, despite its healthy circulation figures, never managed to get an advertiser of equal weight. The Uncola was aboard, its happy jingle—"We see the light of 7-Up"— sung amid the sound of long knives being sharpened.

Will the Lord Jesus be able to feed all those people with that single loaf of Wonder Bread and that half a can of tuna? We'll find out just as soon as we take this break to hear all about how you can vulcanize your sneakers at home for just pennies per shoe.

O'Donoghue's desire to subvert traditional radio extended to commercial bumpers, the slick lead-ins to the ads themselves. He penned a number of these, and one of his favorites was "But first this word from Schnell, the death camp of bottled beers." Doug Kenney, who shared O'Donoghue's animus toward corporate greed, jumped into the action as well. Although proficient as a cut-and-slash artist when he wanted to be, much of Kenney's *Radio Hour* material veered more to the strange and absurd, even when the subject was political. But in the fifth installment of the show Kenney shot a bullet through a can of the sponsor's product: "Don't touch that dial! The *National Lampoon Radio Hour* will be right back after this insincere commercial message written by some cynical Nazi solely for the purpose of ripping off your parents' money." This led right into the 7-Up song as Uncola sprayed in all directions.

If 7-Up wasn't put off by Kenney's blast, which did not mention the company *by name,* then show number seven easily took up the slack. By this time O'Donoghue was emotionally and physically drained, and he began to move away from his demanding schedule. He started by taking the seventh show off and was replaced as emcee by Sean Kelly (who kept reminding listeners that he was *not* Michael O'Donoghue). The show's theme was the approaching impeachment of Richard Nixon, and Kelly used material from the first act of *Lemmings,* which included bits such as the "Impeachment Day Parade," hosted by Chevy Chase and Rhonda Coullet; and "Mission Impeachable," in which hired thug E. Howard Hunt is instructed to undermine what remained of the democratic process. The "Impeachment" show was the most overtly political installment of the radio series, and much of the material was recycled in a *Lampoon* record album, *The Missing White House Tapes.*

Someone in 7-Up's chain of command took offense to the program, and the word went out that America's cleanest soft drink would no longer finance such filth. The company's ads appeared in one more show before being pulled, leading Sean Kelly to call 7-Up "the Unsponsor."

The *Radio Hour* never fully recovered from 7-Up's exit; and since no other major company was eager to hawk its products in this treasonous, tasteless environment, the show fell back on reliable but less influential sponsors such as A&M Records and Fender guitars. Before long the *Radio Hour* served to promote the magazine, its "Best Of" editions, and *The Missing White House Tapes.* Also heard were ads for another publication that Simmons owned called *Ingenue.* (The yet-to-be famous novelist Jamaica Kincaid, a contributor to *Ingenue,* appeared in several of these ads.) But the damage was done and the *Radio Hour* continued to lose money.

After his brief hiatus O'Donoghue returned, but the pressure remained and the strain began to show. Janis Hirsch, who sold block bookings for *Lemmings* before working on the *Radio Hour* with Belushi's girlfriend, Judy Jacklin, witnessed several of O'Donoghue's outbursts during this period, including an argument he had with George Trow. As she told Tony Hendra:

> One day, we were just sitting there doing grunt work, and Michael and George began having a fight during George's recording of "Mr. Chatterbox." They were having some kind of battle and it carried over into our office. Judy and I just dropped our pencils and watched for a while. They were fighting with words we had to look up in the dictionary. Prehistoric creatures and so on. And then they started throwing things. When I saw them each trying to pick up the desks, we ran into the little partition area and hid. It was really scary. . . .

O'Donoghue was fond of Hirsch, and he often revealed to her his softer, quieter side. Part of this fondness was shown through his humor; he dubbed Hirsch "Wobbles the Duck" due to the remnants of her childhood bout with polio. (O'Donoghue changed the name slightly for use as the *Radio Hour*'s signature line: "Honk! Honk! Why it's Wobbles the Goose!") But the fact that he would fight with of all people Trow suggested that he was directing the show on borrowed time. At first he made light of the backstage stress and mentioned it on air. When reading Trow's name on the list of credits he joked that his friend "threw a chair at me!" In his closing thoughts at the end of show nine he promised:

> Next week we'll be taking a long hard look at sleazy radio shows hosted by irritable people who've been up all night and are so sick and tired of doing the closings that they just throw in the first dumb, pointless joke that occurred to them, such as defining "honorable discharge" as how the Japanese address their clap symptoms.

"We're working hundred-hour weeks," he told a journalist at the time. "It's astounding. I've threatened to play the entire sound track from *The Thomas Crown Affair* when things really get desperate. And I'll do it, too." Things *were* getting a bit desperate for O'Donoghue: Although the grind produced some outstanding comedy, money was continually lost, the show was doomed, and O'Donoghue knew he would soon return full-time to the magazine—a prospect he found uninspiring. From the moment he began work on the *Encyclopedia* to his entanglement with the *Radio Hour,* O'Donoghue's presence in the *Lampoon* dwindled. Many issues went out minus an O'Donoghue piece; others displayed his secondary work. His absence was truly felt in two issues where one would have expected him most: January 1973 "Death" and September 1973 "Postwar"—an issue that included parodies of Nazism by Bruce McCall and George Trow but nothing from the Master himself.

Though hammered by his schedule, O'Donoghue continued to prosper financially, and in the spring of 1973 he sought better living conditions. O'Donoghue's new style no longer matched the shadows and dirt of the Spring Street loft; he and Anne Beatts moved into the Chelsea Hotel while Beatts shopped around for a cleaner, upscale space. (Oddly enough, Amy Ephron came back into O'Donoghue's life and sublet the loft while the apartment hunt was on—a situation that Beatts found at best curious.) She eventually discovered a prewar floor-through apartment at 23 West Sixteenth Street. It boasted fourteen-foot ceilings, Corinthian columns, and mirrored French doors, leading O'Donoghue to call it "the Winter Palace." It was the stylish frame into which he and Beatts eagerly stepped.

Unlike the loft, which was simply a large, sparsely decorated space, the new apartment was a formal living area. There was a drawing room, a dining room, a bedroom, and polished wood panel floors; a patio/garden area sat in back, a small but elegant French balcony in front. O'Donoghue's persona would flourish in this perfect setting for all of his curios and strange objects. Everything would be carefully, *carefully* arranged according to his design. Each item, no matter how small, was to fit into the larger narrative he created for the Palace. Nelson Lyon compared O'Donoghue's system to a Cornell Box, named after the artist Joseph Cornell, who was known for his meticulous arrangement and sculpting of objects within a box.* Overall it was, in Lyon's words, "the fulfillment of the fantasy."

---

*In his book *American Visions,* Robert Hughes wrote of Cornell's "small voyages of discovery, scavenging for relics of the past in New York junk shops and flea markets. To others these deposits might be refuse, but to Cornell they were the strata of repressed memory, a jumble of elements waiting to be grafted and mated to one another." As Hughes grasped Cornell's art, so too did Lyon understand O'Donoghue's method.

Luigi, a decent man who is down on his luck, approaches "Mr. Mika" for a loan. He receives $1,000 along with O'Donoghue's best wishes. As O'Donoghue leaves for a charity function, Pops the janitor enters.

POPS: There goes the greatest guy in show business.

LIUGI: Ah, he's a saint!

POPS: Luigi, did you know that during the Korean War when he was entertaining the troops up at the front, five minutes before he was to go on they handed him a telegram that his wife was dead, killed in a car wreck. But he went on anyway. He said, "I owe it to the boys."

LUIGI: I heard abouta that.

POPS: Well, here's something nobody knows: Mike has terminal cancer.

LUIGI: Ah! Mama mia!

POPS: That's right. I was sweeping up his dressing room the other day when I found his medical report behind a trunk.

LUIGI: Justa like him not to tella anybody.

POPS: Yep. They only gave him a few months to live. He's living on borrowed time right now. Lesser man would be in the hospital, but not him.

LUIGI: Itsa no wonder theya call him "Mr. Show Business."

The glamour O'Donoghue once saw in the "showbiz" end of the *Lampoon* now acquired a slight tarnish. He preferred the *Radio Hour* to the magazine but wished above all to rest and reevaluate his professional situation. This was not yet to be, and work continued in the studio. His jokes about the strain of directing the show became tougher and thus closer to his true mental state. This was heard in show number twelve, in which recurring bits such as Beatts's "Recipe Corner" and the minimalist serial "The Lost Glider" abruptly end with gunshots. An announcer is then machine-gunned in mid-statement. O'Donoghue, as Debra Paget, steps forward to explain the situation.

Let me just call time-out here to talk seriously about what humor is, and more importantly, what it should be. You know, we *NatLampers* are often accused of confusing humor with pointless violence. To quote a recent letter sent me by a West Virginia psychologist, "You shoot people on your show as casually as *Laugh-In* used to douse them in water." Point well taken. But before dismissing all of this as mere mindless hostility, let me remind our critics of something the American author and essayist William Rose Benét once said when he was—

Debra is riddled with bullets, her anecdote dead on arrival. Appropriately enough, O'Donoghue included in this show a song by Kinky Friedman and the Texas Jewboys called "The Ballad of Charles Whitman." The song tells the story of the deranged ex-Marine who in 1966 climbed a tower in Austin, Texas, and began shooting passersby with a high-powered rifle before he was mowed down by police. "The Ballad" stands alone as a classic; but its appearance on the *Radio Hour* reflected O'Donoghue's growing interest in serial killers and mass murderers as American "folk artists"—insane virtuosos who transcended the common act of murder. Only in America, O'Donoghue felt, could killers achieve celebrity due to their unique and creative methods of bloodletting. If the Holocaust was the grand opera of genocide, then serial killers were troubadors who performed to small audiences in the heartland.

In darker moments O'Donoghue harbored his own murderous fantasies. Nelson Lyon recalled an afternoon cab ride with O'Donoghue during which his friend revealed a desire to be a hit man. Lyon believed it came "from a private reverie of pain or discomfort: 'I'd just like to be a hit man. That's what I'd really like to be. Just a hit man. I could really do it.' It was not a tossed off remark. He was articulating how he felt; this was an expression of the mood he was in. It wasn't a disastrous mood, it was just Michael. That's what he said and that's what he meant." Lyon felt that of all O'Donoghue's dramas the most poignant was his need to connect with people. To adapt George Eliot, O'Donoghue was sensitive to the degree that he heard grass grow. This made him subject to pain and agony (mostly self-inflicted), unlike the average rube, who doesn't see the need for elaborate defense mechanisms (and who may be better off). He was brighter than most people he met and "unorthodox" in creative tastes. How then to proceed? to connect? Though he exposed his soft side to a select few, the majority were kept at a distance. The "others" never vanished.

No matter how genuine the desire, O'Donoghue was not hit man material. Physically he was slight, if strong for his build, and he did begin carrying a small, open blade in his pocket (for protection on the street, he said). But O'Donoghue could never grab a loaded weapon, peer through its scope, and fire at civilians. To him the *thought* alone was potent enough to strengthen a piece or bolster his persona. It was a conceit that required nerve. Like Nazism and the Holocaust, the use of hit men and serial killers as comic fodder carried risk, pushed ever hot buttons.

This is not to say that O'Donoghue was insincere when handling bloody subjects. He kept files on depraved individuals and the crimes they committed (indeed, one file was titled "Psycho"); he studied their motives, if any, and picked through their mental debris. Here he paralleled his hero, Sherlock Holmes: No act was too savage or too bizarre that it couldn't serve a purpose; and for O'Donoghue to nourish the style of humor that now bore his signature, he had to dip into the well where the mangled bodies lay.

An early example of his fascination with serial killers appeared in the December 1973 *Lampoon*. His target was Dean Corll, a particularly twisted man who handcuffed teenage boys to a wooden board in his Houston, Texas, home before sodomizing, torturing, then murdering them. In August 1973 Corll was shot to death by one of his teen "help-ers" whom he paid to bring potential victims to his lair. When police searched Corll's house they found the remains of twenty-seven boys— the serial killing record to that date (later broken by the equally twisted John Wayne Gacy, the killer party clown). O'Donoghue surveyed the crime scene and discovered "Dean Corll's Favorite Jokes," which he took upon himself to "edit." Set next to a photo of a glaring Corll, the "jokes" are punctuated with the screams of tortured boys and explicit descriptions of sex crimes. One "joke" in particular exhibited a run-on style of writ-ing that O'Donoghue used when he wished to gauge the lunatic pulse.

"Jeez, I wish you was tattooed!" said "Specks" to the teenage hitchhiker who, wearing only a black sack over his head, was chained to a makeshift plywood pillory. "I might even let you live if you was tattooed. Since you ain't, however, here's what I'm gonna do. I'm gonna fuck you an' then I'm gonna carve Nazi slogans in your neck and then I'm gonna force-feed you Kitty Litter an' then I'm gonna spot weld your face an' then I'm gonna dress you up in latex an' piss on you an' then I'm gonna slice off your lips an' then I'm gonna take Polaroids of you an' then I'm gonna put your eyes out an' then I'm gonna nail your tongue to the floor an' then I'm gonna fuck you again an' then I'm gonna give you a Drano enema an' then I'm gonna shoot you in the head with a .22 and bury you under the old boathouse in a lot of quicklime. But maybe, just maybe, I'll let you go if you beg for mercy right now. Do you know how to beg for mercy?"

"No, but if you hum a few bars, I can fake it!"

As "Specks" addressed his prey, so it seemed O'Donoghue was ad-dressing the *Radio Hour*. The segments italicized by gunfire suggested growing impatience on his part, and by early 1974 something—any-thing—had to give. The show's terminal condition became more evident with episode fourteen, the tip-off being O'Donoghue's reading of the credits at the beginning. The episode ran for half an hour, broke for local commercials, and never returned. Letters and phone calls came to the *Lampoon* in the week following the broadcast, and most carried the same complaint: Local stations fucked up and didn't play the show's second half; was anyone at the *Radio Hour* aware of this? At the end of the next show, O'Donoghue answered the complaints.

> Hello, this is Michael O'Donoghue, and before we return with part two of tonight's *National Lampoon Radio Hour* I'd just like to warn our listeners that we've had some reports that certain stations aren't playing the second half of the show. And one station has even gone so far as to claim that we've switched over to being only a half an hour long. Now, I don't know who they think *they're* kidding—the show is called the *National Lampoon Radio "Hour."* Of course the unfortunate thing is that we've put all the good stuff, the really funny things and the weird bits and the more hard-hitting stuff and even the so called material of an adult nature in the last half of the show. . . . Let me just say, don't let these radio stations push you around, okay?

A week later, Doug Kenney followed this lead.

> As you probably have heard, however, a number of fascist pig station managers are refusing to play the last half of the show. In fact, when our listeners call up to complain, they are being told that the show is now only a half hour long, which is, of course, an outright lie.

But the conspiracy was too much for the *Radio Hour* to resist, and O'Donoghue and Henry Beard finally announced that as a goodwill gesture they would donate the show's second half hour to the United Council of Churches. They hoped, they said, that the council would build up what the *Radio Hour* routinely tore down.

Of course, the *Radio Hour* was bleeding heavily and thus its second half hour was lopped off. It was Bob Tischler's idea to not announce the change in format and to blame everything on the stations. The ruse worked briefly before listeners saw through it; O'Donoghue received some very nasty letters from fans who felt betrayed (though a few exhibited a mock anger in an attempt to imitate the *Lampoon* sensibility), and a number of station managers were left unsmiling. But at this point such reactions were drowned out by static, white noise that steadily engulfed the *Radio Hour.*

Despite the show's poor health the material remained first-rate, and the episode for Easter contained some of the best and most devastating satire in the *Radio Hour*'s entire run. The target, naturally, was Christianity—mythology, belief system, predatory faith. The *Lampoon* had been there many times before, skewering religion and spirituality from a variety of angles. But in this particular instance the concentration of blows was so great that it lent credence to the charge that the *Lampoon* was indeed staffed by the godless and profane. And that the show was billed as an

Easter "special" . . . well, reportedly the flames in Hell rose a bit higher that day.

Part of the episode slams the pious and hypocritical, a not especially "tasteless" tactic. After all, many in the Lord's flock do the same but for reasons other than satire. We hear Norman Vincent Peale, fatuous Christian author dedicated to profitable uplift, lecturing the starving, disease-ridden masses of Bangladesh on proper spiritual values and blaming their situation on their own "negative thinking." The answer? Buy his books and see the light. Later, Peale pulls the same act on Jesus Christ Himself and pitches the Savior's original ideas back to the source, price tag attached. Also in this vein is a bit in which St. Jude snubs Danny Thomas—the celestial unimpressed with the mortal, another time-honored premise that with minor adjustments would work easily on the mainstream stage. But is the episode's direct lunge at God's throat that singed the ears of many listeners and put it beyond "respectability."

It is one thing for an adult to say "God is dead" or "God doesn't exist." The relative unpopularity of these sentiments in America insure their marginalization. But call the Creator a heartless murderer and insist He be taken to task and righteous heads are turned. Put this criticism in the mouth of a child and the flock can become a wolf pack. "What can you expect from a God who crucified His own Son?" asks an adolescent pondering the state of the world. He later reads from a list of charges written in the language of Scripture:

God so loved the world that He gave it His only begotten Son . . . and His only begotten spinal meningitis . . . and His only begotten bombing of Dresden . . . and His only begotten nerve gas . . . and His only begotten retarded children . . . and His only begotten Attica massacre . . .

The young voice trails off as the evidence mounts. God is alive and remains at large; His henchmen sing His praises in a militant version of "Onward Christian Soldiers" in which the faithful are urged to maim and kill unbelievers as an offering to Him.

"The program you produced for Easter was not humorous and at best very sick satire," wrote the head of religious services at an Oregon penitentiary, one of many letters from the offended. "In my opion [sic] we have no right to downgrade the religious beliefs of any person and especially on a high holy day for the given religion. Parts of the Easter Special verged on blasphemy and several sections including the 'Onward Christian Soldier' take-off were blasphemy." Other letter writers were convinced that the Lampoon was "evil" and "sacrilegious" to allow such material on the air. But for all its nasty kick, the Easter show ended on a gentle, self-satirizing note. After reading the closing credits, O'Donoghue is approached by two priests whose parish is shut down. They ask for help and O'Donoghue, reprising his generous "Mr. Show Business" character, is badgered into giving them the *Lampoon*'s office building as the site for the new parish. The magazine and radio show have forty-eight hours to pack up and leave, a scenario to warm the hearts of *Lampoon* haters everywhere.

But the magazine remained solid and in the black; there would be no surrender, no retreat. The *Radio Hour,* however, lagged financially behind the *Lampoon* and was $400,000 in debt. The show also sapped O'Donoghue's creative energy, and his once-dominant presence on air shrank to his reading the closing credits. O'Donoghue wanted out. Matty Simmons saw this as an opportunity to bring his star contributor back to the magazine full-time. After all, why waste such talent on a dead-end project? He proposed that O'Donoghue continue as creative supervisor of the *Radio Hour* but that he hire other people to perform the day-to-day labor. "The magazine, I reminded him, was still at the core of *Lampoon* operations," Simmons later wrote, "and we needed his input, and even more importantly, his output. He reminded me that he wouldn't work with Hendra. I assured him that he wouldn't have to, that he could deal with Kenney or McConnachie. He agreed."

According to Anne Beatts, O'Donoghue and Simmons were involved in "hardball" negotiations regarding not only O'Donoghue's future employment with the magazine but royalties and perks as well. (Noel Silverman, Beatts's lawyer, advised O'Donoghue throughout.) At some point before Easter Sunday 1974, O'Donoghue and Simmons came to an agreement in which O'Donoghue was to resume his magazine duties the Monday following the holiday weekend. But then a problem arose. Beatts, who was visiting Chicago, flew into New York on Easter Sunday and met O'Donoghue at the *Radio Hour*'s offices. They were about to join friends for brunch when Beatts noticed that "someone else's stuff" was in her desk. "And I freaked out," she recalled, "and I tried to pull a power play because I said, 'This is not acceptable that while I'm gone my desk has been given away!' " Beatts suspected that Simmons's son Michael was to blame (though Michael believed her memory to be "faulty" and thought that Beatts wanted a bigger office with a window). She then demanded that her material be deleted from that week's *Radio Hour,* but this was a near impossibility since the show was edited and ready to be sent to stations nationwide. This led O'Donoghue to phone Simmons at home.

Relaxing after a "particularly hectic week," Simmons picked up the receiver and heard O'Donoghue's animated voice. According to Simmons, O'Donoghue complained about Beatts's desk and said that it had been moved into the show's recording studio. "I didn't even know such a desk existed," wrote Simmons, who quoted O'Donoghue as screaming, "Anne Beatts has to have a desk at the radio show! And she's got to have an office. She must have it or else!" Simmons told him to stay calm and that they would discuss the matter during office hours. "No, we discuss it now or I quit!" O'Donoghue reportedly said, to which Simmons replied, "Okay, if that's how you feel about it, you can quit!" O'Donoghue needed no further encouragement, and he and Beatts severed their *Lampoon* ties.

To this point O'Donoghue and Simmons had what Simmons termed "a very good relationship." O'Donoghue threw tantrums, of course, and he periodically rushed into Simmons's office to complain of slights suffered and work not rendered precisely to his taste. But O'Donoghue knew that Simmons valued him; he was paid better than most of the other editors and could own his material without fear that Simmons would contest it. When O'Donoghue had problems with the IRS, Simmons helped him out of the jam. When he spoke of his brain-shattering migraines, Simmons's wife took him to her acupuncturist in search of relief. (Never found: O'Donoghue turned white as the needles went in; like Ed Sullivan, O'Donoghue viewed the procedure as torture, and he returned to the solace of Percodan.) Despite the theatrics and emotional explosions, O'Donoghue was always on speaking terms with Simmons. But after their discussion on Easter, the two did not speak again for nineteen years. (O'Donoghue wrote in one of his notebooks, "I'd rather buttfuck cancer than shake hands with Matty Simmons.")

Beatts felt that O'Donoghue should have tried to "hold Matty up" and tell him that the show wasn't going out until the problem was resolved. "But that was not something Michael could or would do," Beatts admitted, adding that a break was inevitable given the circumstances. "At that point I think Matty felt he could get someone else to do Michael's job and then he would be well rid of Michael," she said. "Michael had always been such a difficult person, with the feuds, etc." In fact, many people at the magazine were weary of O'Donoghue's tantrums and vendettas, including Henry Beard, who was not the confrontational type, and Brian McConnachie, whom O'Donoghue had once accused of comic theft. The accusation surprised, then enraged, McConnachie; he angrily told O'Donoghue, "I don't have to steal material," then realized that the accusation was a test to see if he was still on O'Donoghue's side. Then there was Tony Hendra, who, frozen out of O'Donoghue's world, was glad to see his former friend go. "I was not a passive party," he later said.

I decided once it became clear to me that Michael was not going to reconcile, I said, "Fuck him. I'm not giving up this great thing that I found here. If he wants to be an asshole, I'll cut him out." And I did my best to cut him out. And I did, I drove him out. I was still at the *Lampoon* in its real glory year, which was 1974, and he was nowhere. So in terms of that, I won and I'd set out to win. I thought he was behaving like a total asshole and I was really resentful that I was being blamed for all of this. So I quite deliberately joined battle with O'Donoghue and said, "Fuck you. If you're going to take this attitude I'm going to beat you." And I did. I got rid of him.*

Despite the staff's battle fatigue with O'Donoghue, there was a general sense of loss when it became clear that he would never return. Janis Hirsch colored the day following his resignation "Black," and Hendra noted that the office mood was somber. And though O'Donoghue had been nearly absent in the magazine for the better part of a year, the sudden permanence of this fact rocked all concerned. It was perhaps fitting that O'Donoghue's final *Lampoon* appearance was in the December 1973 "Self-Indulgence" issue. Here the editors savaged as well as flaunted themselves; the issue is filled with in-jokes and references to running feuds, personality disorders, egomania, and the like. Numerous photos and caricatures of the editors appeared in several parodies, including a *Lampoon* "Sunday Comics" section and a takeoff on teen magazines called "Poon Beat." To the average reader who knew nothing of *Lampoon* office politics, "Self-Indulgence" was indeed just that. To the editors the issue made perfect satirical sense: Having shot everything in sight, why not turn the gun on yourself? If nothing else it lent the impression that not even the *Lampoon* wits were above a decent razing.

O'Donoghue's turbulent side receives plenty of play in the issue. In an editoral cartoon we see O'Donoghue in a diaper throwing a childish fit. In "Poon Beat" we learn of a particularly bloody gag he pulls on Sean Kelly after hours, a bit that would later surface in *Animal House* (next page).

And in the "Sunday Comics" we see O'Donoghue on an average day in the office (page 265).

But violence alone could not explain O'Donoghue. In a "Poon Beat" photo he and Beatts, dressed ever stylishly, are slipping clothes onto their maid before she "begins her day's chores" in the Winter

*In his book, written years before the above statement was made, Hendra sounded less triumphant about O'Donoghue's departure: "It was hard to imagine the *Lampoon* without O'Donoghue somewhere in its entrails, whether he was charming the pants off a newcomer or punching his own thigh in homicidal rage. A council of war had to be held to discuss what the magazine—and the organization—would be like without him. . . . It was a closed-door meeting—the most serious one we'd ever had, and there were the strictest instructions that we not be disturbed. . . ."

MICHAEL'S sPLIT PERSONALITY!

Michael O'Donoghue—easily the most popular POONBEAT personality if fan mail is any indication—has a real problem!

Of course, on the surface he seems "just one of the gang," a little older, a little balder perhaps, but basically a warm, whimsical, twinkly-eyed Irish rogue who devotes all his spare time to his favorite charity—the Michael O'Donoghue Memorial Fun Fur Kitten Farm in Rochester, New York!

But sometimes, Michael shows AN-OTHER SIDE of his "kookiness" that is even wackier! For example, when he overheard Sean making fun of his narrow shoulders and weak, characterless chin, Michael decided to play a practical joke on Sean!

Late Friday afternoon, when everybody was gone, Michael sneaked back up in the service elevator and crept into Sean's office leading, of all things, a large horse! Closing the door so no one might hear, our rascally scamp raised his cane to the prankish pony and CLUBBED IT TO DEATH! He just kept HITTING and HITTING and HITTING it until the head looked like thirty pounds of Alpo!

Well, you can imagine the look on Sean's face early Monday morning when he found the horribly mangled carcass sprawled out on his rug! And Sean's face looked even funnier when he discovered that the rascally animal's extremities had s-t-i-f-f-e-n-e-d over the weekend and now couldn't be dragged through the door until Mr. Csynyswzcky, the super, came up and chopped them off with a power——
[Continued on page 135]

Palace. This scenario is amplified in "Underwear for the Deaf,"* a color photo layout where a woman wearing panties for the hearing-impaired encounters a strange, masked duo in a restaurant. They trick the near-deaf lass into taking an oceanliner cruise with them, and once on board they begin to fondle her crotch and lick her feet. The woman merely responds with, "Eh? What? Come Again?"

The masked couple are played by O'Donoghue and Beatts; and the notion of luring women onto ships for "fun" apparently was attempted in real life. According to Brian McConnachie, with whom the couple often socialized, all three were in a strip club when O'Donoghue sent a note to a dancer inviting her and her sister to accompany him and Beatts on an ocean liner cruise. All expenses would be paid, promised O'Donoghue, but the dancer declined his offer. McConnachie saw this as pure theater, a heightened performance by a pair of writers whose act had transcended the magazine.

Michael O'Donoghue, née Donoghue, wishes to announce that as of Easter Sunday, 1974, he is no longer in any way, shape, form, or reasonable facsimile thereof connected with, adjoined to, or even hanging around a lot any more the *National Lampoon* magazine or the *Radio Hour.*"
—Editorial note, *National Lampoon*, August 1974

*Written by O'Donoghue and photographed by David Kaestle, "Underwear for the Deaf" was conceived as a series of strips in which deaf girls wearing the magic panties encountered those who sought to take advantage of their impairment. "Underwear" was one of the few pieces that O'Donoghue did not own outright, and after he left the *Lampoon* the magazine continued to run the strips well into 1976.

O'Donoghue got the rest he desired; no more *Radio Hour* all-nighters, no more having to tolerate the *Lampoon* "Dead." Of course, this also meant he would receive no more *Lampoon* paychecks. He and Beatts had put little money away as they were living up to their incomes. There were many dinners in expensive restaurants (a habit that became somewhat of a joke: in the dust jacket notes for the *Encyclopedia of Humor,* O'Donoghue wrote of himself, "all he's done is take Anne Beatts out to fancy restaurants he can't afford where the two of them try to order their food in French and get served things like a high chair in a plate of Vichy water"), their wardrobe expanded, new and stranger kitsch items filled their apartment. In addition, Beatts earned less than O'Donoghue: "Michael always said that he brought home the bread and I brought home the rolls," she recalled. Still, here was a couple whose work on the nation's most notorious magazine was highly regarded. Surely there were creative and financial opportunities beyond the *Lampoon?*

Rather than search for immediate employment, O'Donoghue, in Beatts's words, "took to his bed, a lot." The cult reputation he had earned through *Phoebe Zeit-Geist* expanded magnificently at the *Lampoon* and began to touch those in the mainstream. But if professional openings existed, O'Donoghue wasn't interested. He preferred to stay at home in bed with his cats, Toots, Black Cat, and Cow. He would pop a Percodan or smoke a joint, then lie back, place his hands over his throat, and watch hours and hours of television. There was depression here; resignation, too. After four solid years of intensive creative output, O'Donoghue removed himself from the world and viewed its reflection on TV. To him television represented the lowest and coarsest values of a society in decay—and this he found attractive. Television's rhythms and seductive glare kept him amused and transfixed for days on end. The content of programs and commercials was appreciated on its own terms, but the bright, flashing images themselves were mesmerizing, especially when he was stoned. "Really a nice way to spend one's life," he said, "using TV more as a kaleidoscope than anything else, colored beads to fascinate the animal . . ."

But the world demanded its membership dues; bills piled up, rent had to be paid. Beatts graduted from roll-bringer to breadwinner by default. She received work from former *Lampoon* contributor Terry Catchpole, who edited the front section of the skin magazine *Oui*. Beatts wrote short, pithy items for this section and urged O'Donoghue to do the same. The magazine had money and paid its contributors on time. Catchpole certainly was interested, so O'Donoghue pulled himself from bed to compose several small pieces.

Although clearly not his best work, a few *Oui* bits stand out: A mural artist who specializes in strange and exotic paintings-for-hire is erased by the corporate trust division of New York Chemical Bank; an unknown writer of the 1930s has the misfortune of calling his novel *Gadsby*, which not only suffers in comparison to Fitzgerald's masterpiece but is entirely written without the use of the letter *e*; looking back on his days as a long-haired 1960s bohemian, O'Donoghue states for the record, "I always unswervingly maintained that a National Guardsman had a perfect right to blow the head off anyone who stuck a flower in his gun." Each piece is finely tuned and arranged down to the final punctuation mark. When O'Donoghue chose to work he maintained a perfectionist ethic no matter how minor the piece.

After several appearances in *Oui*, which included some caption writing, O'Donoghue again withdrew. He wasn't that interested in penning small items, but something had to be found and soon. By midsummer the money situation was getting serious. Beatts borrowed money from her stepmother, sold secondhand items to a flea market, rolled pennies to pay the electric bill. Then another old *Lampoon* colleague showed up and offered them a project. The cartoonist Picha had been backed by Belgian investors to produce an X-rated, feature-length cartoon parodying Tarzan. Having seen the success of Ralph Bakshi's *Fritz the Cat,* the Belgians wanted to cash in on what they hoped would be a profitable X-rated cartoon market. Picha gave O'Donoghue and Beatts the job of rewriting his original shooting script. Beatts began translating the French script into English while O'Donoghue combed his notebooks and files for jokes and concepts he could weave into the existing narrative.

The treatment's original title, *Tarzoon,* had to be changed because neither Picha nor his investors had ever purchased the rights to the Edgar Rice Burroughs character. Thus the film became known as *Shame of the Jungle*—a nod of sorts to another (and better) parody of Tarzan, Jay Ward's *George of the Jungle*. In script form, *Shame* is an interesting blend of *Lampoon*ish humor and visual gags, and in many areas the O'Donoghue stamp shines clearly. The plot: A bald alien creature named Queen Bazonga (who resembles Cruella DeVil of *101 Dalmations*) wants a hair transplant. She settles on Shame's mate, June, a foulmouthed, sex-starved jungle woman who constantly berates Shame for his inferior cocksmanship: "You're pathetic! I've had more fun with a Waterpik! What did you do, graduate from the Evelyn Wood School of Fucking? You fairy!" No Maureen O'Sullivan, she.

Shame, meanwhile, is a bumbling oaf; with his simian companion, Flicka (who better meets June's sexual needs), he moves clumsily through the jungle, tripping over branches, crashing into trees. An unlikely hero, he nevertheless is pressed into service once June is kidnapped by the evil queen's military guards, known as the Peckerheads. Shame and Flicka pursue June to the queen's lair, a large alien spaceship manned by marching, uncircumcised penises. After a brief run-in with the queen, who is literally fucked to death by her guards, Shame finds June as the ship lifts off. They eject from the craft before it slams into a mountain range that resembles a naked woman lying spread-eagled on the ground. They embrace as a phallic mushroom cloud rises in the distance.

The shooting script for *Shame* reads well, especially the narration. O'Donoghue's description of events recalls the panels in *Phoebe Zeit-Geist* as well as some of his early *Lampoon* work (parts of "Pornocopia," the captions to "What Fangs on the Neck?"). When Shame is captured by the Peckerheads, we are told, "Fate, like the swirling winds that whimsically shape the Bedouin sands, has saved Shame from a firing squad's blindfold . . . only to deliver him into the arms of a demented queen. But it matters little whether Death wears an empty scabbard or a filmy gown. . . ." Much of the narration is written in this manner and does not translate well from page to sound track. Had *Shame* been a silent film the narrator's speeches would have made fine title cards. But with the eye focused on the animation the ear cannot follow such extensive wording, and so the narration is lost in the mix of music and cartoon sound effects. In fact, the majority of the action as written fails to come off on-screen. Part of this is due to the cheap animation, but the lack of true comic pacing is what does *Shame* in. The result is as dispiriting as the comedy is flat.

The fault certainly did not lie with O'Donoghue and Beatts. In better hands their script might have clicked; and given the obvious budget constraints and horrible direction, it's amazing that a few of the film's sequences do work: The Molar Men, squat African stereotypes of the kind often seen in Hollywood cartoons of the 1930s and 1940s devour every animal and human they encounter as they chase Shame through the jungle. Their large teeth cut quickly into hide and tissue, and within seconds each victim is reduced to bone. The Molar Men sequence moves well, is humorously graphic, and represents the only sustained comic action in the film. Other nice bits, the penis army marching in swastika formation, an angelic white missionary smashing an African child's head with a crucifix, are isolated and brief and soon disappear as garish colors and a grating musical sound track flood the screen.

Shame of the Jungle, like other *Fritz the Cat* facsimiles of the period, is preoccupied with sex for its own sake. Almost all the characters in this film, from people to elephants to bugs, fuck for no other reason than to show cartoon characters fucking. No doubt this was in the original French script, and Beatts and O'Donoghue did their best to give the scenes some comic boost. But they were hired guns, not original screen-writers, and thus had to work with what they were handed. O'Donoghue also directed *Shame*'s English-speaking sound track, which featured the voices of such *Radio Hour* actors as Christopher Guest and John Belushi, who played Craig Baker, the beer-swilling "perfect master" he had cre-ated for the radio show. (Bob Tischler worked as the film's sound editor, and Bill Murray, who became a *Radio Hour* regular after O'Donoghue's exit, can be heard reading the news in an unusual "black" dialect.) De-spite the talent on hand, *Shame*'s fate was predestined. It opened in New York in early 1975, ran for two weeks then was pulled. When asked about his participation in the film, O'Donoghue would say it was done by "the *other* Michael O'Donoghue and Anne Beatts."*

Shame was written strictly for the money, though it was Beatts's feeling that O'Donoghue could never take a job for mere financial rea-sons; once he created something it became part of him, and if asked to alter his creation he was often violently unyielding. "Compromise was not in his vocabulary in any way," said Beatts, who had seen O'Dono-ghue rage around the *Lampoon* offices if anyone dared retouch his work. But without the security of a regular job—or, in O'Donoghue's case, the stature of editorship that allowed for such displays—compromise was a necessary evil; the freelancer knows no dignity. With *Shame*, O'Dono-ghue was granted some latitude and wrote what he wanted; with maga-zines and newspapers, however, criteria differed from editor to editor, but none were going to be steamrolled into accepting whatever O'Donoghue submitted no matter his reputation or track record.

---

*The French, predictably, loved *Shame*. It ran on the Champs-Elysée for six months and became a cult hit.

In late fall 1974, Beatts convinced a friend at the *Village Voice* to hire her and O'Donoghue as restaurant reviewers. She thought the job was perfect: They loved to dine out, and since they were getting paid to eat they finally could afford to dine in some of the city's better restaurants. Despite Beatts's enthusiasm the *Voice* gig would prove short-lived. Their first review was of the Artist and Writers Restaurant, located on West Fortieth Street. Written in the first person by Beatts, the review is not a standard survey of food, quality of service, and prices—though this information is included. From the opening sentence—"We sat beneath a large, faded photograph of the cancer-riddled Babe taking a last bow at Yankee Stadium"—one senses these correspondents have attitude. They find the food "adequate," but the Blue Willow–pattern china on which it is served makes up for the lack of excellence. Rice pudding sends Beatts into a reverie about nannies, and she and O'Donoghue look down on a couple engaged in "earnest" conversation.

If the first review had edge it was Beatts's edge: stylish, smart, slightly disdainful—qualities that can confuse the average editor but not over-whelm him. O'Donoghue's edge was something else entirely and seemed out of place in a piece about food. It was his perspective that dominated the second *Voice* review—of, fittingly enough, Luchow's, the famous German restaurant on East Fourteenth Street. Again, the opening sets, as it were, the table:

> Luchow's expresses both halves of the German character: brutality (the brass band) and sentimentality (the string quartet). Dining there is a sado-masochistic experience. You cringe during the oom-pah-pahs and weep during the waltzes. Nevertheless, we declined a quiet table in the anteroom (known as the Polish Corridor).

They are instead seated near the restaurant's Christmas tree. "The 54-foot-high Christmas tree is festooned with hand-painted soccer balls and a million lights," O'Donoghue observes. "It looks like the last thing the folks at Nagasaki saw before they turned into tuna melts." The brightness of the lights is thus perfectly conveyed, but Beatts's and O'Donoghue's editor at the *Voice* was not amused by the line and ordered it cut. Beatts had no problem with this demand, but O'Donoghue stood firm. It was fine the way it was, he told her; no change was necessary. Beatts reminded him that they needed the work. O'Donoghue didn't care; he wasn't going to allow some liberal jerk-off to ruin their piece. But the line was cut without his consent and the review was published. It was the last one Beatts and O'Donoghue were asked to write.

Nelson Lyon did his part to help. For his November 1974 *Esquire* piece, "Formica With Love," a review of waitresses who hoped to be movie starlets, he employed O'Donoghue as a model. Dressed in white suit and wing tips, O'Donoghue is deadpan as a waitress drips ketchup on his pants. Lyon also introduced O'Donoghue to his close friend Paul Morrissey, who was directing a musical intended for Broadway called *Man in the Moon*. Produced by Andy Warhol, the musical had severe script problems and revisions were quickly needed, so Morrissey hired O'Donoghue to write new dialogue. But O'Donoghue's contribution to *Moon* was deemed inappropriate by Morrissey and the dialogue went unused (the show itself soon died). Once again O'Donoghue was out of work, out of money, and seemingly out of options. He shared his frustration with Lyon, who listened as O'Donoghue spoke somewhat emotionally of his professional and financial situation. It was a side of himself that he reluctantly revealed, a vulnerability he often aggressively suppressed.

Beatts, of course, saw the entire spectrum. But as money became scarce and professional opportunities dwindled, O'Donoghue was harder to live with. "He flipped out about every minor crisis of life," she said; and although his outbursts grew from a career that was stalled, Beatts believed that O'Donoghue suffered from a chemical imbalance. One moment he would be sunny, happy and fine, then something would set him off and he would "go crazy." This was followed by a migraine, which forced him to withdraw until the pain receded; then he would

The "Jesus pose," c. 1974–75

be up again with a smile on his face. "Major mood swings," said Beatts. "He needed to feel bad in order to feel good again." Once into a fit nothing or no one could soothe him until the process completed its jagged course.

Beatts had known about O'Donoghue's temperament before they became involved, but he'd convinced her that she alone could magically calm him:

> It's that terrible hook: "But you are the one woman in the world that I need to make me happy and therefore if we are together I will not be this way." It's a pretty tough assignment. I stepped right into it because the payback was very high. He said he adored me, I was "one-stop shopping." He gave me the most amazing gifts, he laughed at my jokes. . . . Michael at his most charming and good-humored and delightful was sublime. Then there was the dark side. In any relationship of that nature you try to figure out if there is any possible way to get the Dr. Jekyll without the Mr. Hyde. Once Mr. Hyde started coming out of course that was my thought: "How do I separate these two people and only get the good stuff?" I had to acknowledge that wasn't ever going to happen.

The ghost of the *Lampoon,* in the form of a giant dollar sign, haunted the Winter Palace and put O'Donoghue further on edge. In October 1974 the grand contractual payoff to Henry Beard, Doug Kenney, and Rob Hoffman began. They were paid $100,000 with the large chunk, $3 million, to be doled out the following March. This arrangement among the *Lampoon*'s founders and Matty Simmons had always eaten at O'Donoghue. Though he'd had nothing to do with the birth of the magazine, O'Donoghue correctly believed that he had been just as vital to its success as were Beard and Kenney. After all, it was O'Donoghue who sharpened the *Lampoon* through violent artistic effort, and it was his style of humor that ultimately defined the enterprise.* That he was no longer connected to the *Lampoon* was irrelevant: If there was going to be a big payday for those who got the ball rolling, then he certainly was entitled to his share of the profits. And besides, both Beard and Kenney, according to O'Donoghue, had promised that he and George Trow would receive a portion of the settlement.

O'Donoghue made it known that he wanted *something* from the

---

*His influence continued after his exit. One of the major successes for the *Lampoon* that year was *The 1964 High School Yearbook Parody.* Put together by Kenney and P. J. O'Rourke, the *Yearbook* was an extension of the *Ezra Taft* version that originally ran in the "Nostalgia" issue. The premise was O'Donoghue's, though he received no real credit for this in the *Yearbook*'s list of acknowledgments. Yet he never complained and did not begrudge Kenney and O'Rourke their exceptional project.

Lampoon, yet he had trouble expressing precisely what he felt was due him. One evening before the large payoff, Henry Beard visited O'Donoghue and Beatts. Nelson Lyon was there, too; both he and Beard consumed several drinks while O'Donoghue repeatedly tossed a toy basketball into a tiny hoop. The issue of the money was raised but in an offhanded way. It was Lyon's assessment that despite the importance of the topic, Beard and O'Donoghue danced around specifics and avoided direct contact. The two were caught in a scenario of O'Donoghue's making, and if he didn't press the issue Beard certainly wasn't going to do it for him. "Michael had tremendous power of personality and great skills in manipulating conversation and dialogue and setting up scenes. This was artistry," said Lyon; and yet . . .

> He was terribly embarrassed by personal issues he simply could not confront, couldn't resolve, that were too emotionally charged to resolve. This is so ironic because his genius was piercing the veil, talking about things no one dared to talk about, using material no one would dare *think* of using, and exposing to the light all the dark mushrooms in the Freudian cellar—blasting them with light. That was the basis of his humor and his art. But there were crucial areas *he* couldn't confront.

The *Lampoon* payoff was one of them.

As 1975 began, Beatts's and O'Donoghue's professional and financial situation was unchanged. Beatts wrote for whom she could (primarily Terry Catchpole at *Oui*) and had in mind a book of women's humor. O'Donoghue spun out article ideas for *Esquire,* none of which were sold, and started to conceive of a humor magazine he hoped would rival the *Lampoon.* While plans were hatched at Sixteenth Street, a bigger project was in development out west, something that would soon engulf both O'Donoghue and Beatts.

The only difference between television and a lava lamp is that television has slightly better audio.

American television comedy has always been more miss than hit, and the list of those who made a real difference in the way humor is perceived is consequently short: Ernie Kovacs, Lucille Ball, Sid Caesar, and Jackie Gleason bent the medium to conform to their talents and so left indelible marks. Of the vaudevillians who came to TV by way of long stints in radio, only one act, George Burns and Gracie Allen, played with and tweaked the visual form. (Burns continually spoke to the home audience, something the other characters couldn't do; and he kept tabs on the show's action by watching along on his own private set.) The brilliant Fred Allen was too verbal and nontelegenic to succeed on a visual scale, but then he had nothing but contempt for TV; Jack Benny, graceful as always, simply performed his radio show in front of the cameras; and Milton Berle, an early industry giant, placed himself prominently in a variety format where he cavorted with the subtlety of Al Jolson. If television contained vaudeville's corpse, the casket lid rattled well into the early 1960s.

By the early 1970s television comedy had gone through its fantasy stage—talking horses, monster families, witches, genies, flying nuns, singing ferrets—and emerged to meet the real world, or as "real" as producers could handle without losing the element of make-believe. On the rougher end stood Norman Lear and his flagship show, *All in the Family*. Though it became diluted over time as it spat out lesser but successful shows such as *Maude, Good Times, The Jeffersons,* and *Archie Bunker's Place,* the early installments of *All in the Family* came as close to capturing the turbulence of its time than did any other program. The language and attitudes expressed in those episodes would have difficulty appearing in a contemporary sitcom, lest tribal emotions be stirred up and unleashed. Lear took advantage of the small opening given him to explore at length "objectionable" speech, and he found the humor within it.

On the softer side was James L. Brooks and *The Mary Tyler Moore Show*. Less aggressive than *All in the Family, Mary* exhibited a whimsical edge where absurdity and dry wit merged with the show's recurring characters. *Mary* was "real" in that its star played a single woman who was devoted to her career and who did not fall victim to the family trap. Because this was relatively new in television at the time, Brooks could easily have steered Mary Richards toward a more righteous path and made her stereotypically feminist—*Maude*ish, as it were. But the character and the show were complex, the show's humor light but not lacking roots. Indeed, *The Mary Tyler Moore Show* did more to change television comedy than did anything at Lear's end of the spectrum. As great as *All in the Family* initially was, it never sustained its early, vibrant pace. *Mary,* on the other hand, built to a steady speed and maintained it without showing effort. This was attempted in spin-offs such as *Rhoda* and *Phyllis* and in many sitcoms thereafter; but as with any copy or duplicate, the colors remain fullest in the original.

One of the younger writers for *The Mary Tyler Moore Show* was a Pennsylvania native, Marilyn Suzanne Miller. She penned her first *Mary* script at age twenty-two and was soon in the thick of the early 1970s TV comedy scene. Miller found unique the way Brooks trusted her comic instincts. "Jim Brooks at the *Mary* show did something that I don't think anybody does even now," she said.

I wrote a number of those episodes and I said [to Brooks] "No, no, no. You have to leave that joke in. You might not get it but it's a girl joke." Jim would go, "Oh, okay." That doesn't happen even now. He understood that there was a difference betwen men and women and if he was going to do a show with a woman in it he'd better honor things women were telling him. And he listened to women, which was what made him a brilliant producer.

During this period, 1973–1974, Miller had watched Lily Tomlin's network specials that ran first on CBS, then on ABC. Though given free reign to explore different comedic areas on *Mary*, Miller was nevertheless astounded by what Tomlin was doing. The former *Laugh-In* star dispensed with the standard network comedy format and experimented with different moods and styles. The specials, Miller felt, were a cross between traditional sketch comedy and drama that went further than she could ever hope to go on *Mary*, no matter how enlightened her producer. Miller wanted to write for Tomlin and soon made the acquaintance of one of Tomlin's producers, Lorne Michaels. Like James Brooks, Michaels keyed into Miller's style and understood what she had in mind. His sensitivity to women's humor was conditioned partly by his wife, Rosie Shuster, who also wrote for the specials, but mostly by Tomlin, who demanded nothing less from her collaborators. (Michaels's early sensitivity would diminish over time and prompt charges that he had no use for women's humor, charges sometimes voiced by Shuster and Miller themselves.)

The sketches Miller wrote for Tomlin were deep slices of life that bordered on the dramatic. "They were unlike anything one had seen in sketch comedy previously," said Miller, "and they were also from a female point of view. They were supported and applauded and loved, and Lorne was very much a part of that." But the Tomlin specials were a brief detour for Miller; neither CBS nor ABC chose to continue airing comedy that network executives considered "bizarre," and Miller returned to the mainstream as a writer for *Rhoda, The Odd Couple,* and *Maude.*

Miller's participation in the Tomlin shows was not her sole exposure to alternative humor. She also was a devoted reader of the *National Lampoon* and a fan of Michael O'Donoghue's work. In 1973 she had arranged to meet O'Donoghue through a friend at the *Village Voice* who knew Anne Beatts, and when Miller went to New York she was invited to the Winter Palace for dinner and discussion. It seemed that O'Donoghue was equally as anxious to meet her.

"Michael had it in his head that everyone was from a movie," she later observed. "And I think he had it in his head that I was this sophisticated person from Hollywood. So he had me down to Sixteenth Street for dinner one night and it was all Danish food, like he must have thought was very suave food to serve. I was petrified of it, and I think it was that night that Michael figured out who I was, which was like a girl going '*Ehhhh!* What the hell is *this*!' " The connection made, O'Donoghue began to watch Miller's TV work. After an epsiode of *Rhoda* in which sister Brenda dates a man Rhoda suspects is married, O'Donoghue phoned Miller on the West Coast to congratulate her. Miller was thrilled by this recognition, and the two grew close as comedy peers and friends. For O'Donoghue it would prove, in myriad ways, a most profitable relationship.

I don't think television will ever be perfected until the viewer can press a button and cause whoever is on the screen's head to explode.

In early 1975, NBC president Herb Schlosser gazed at the network's late-night weekend schedule and saw *Tonight Show* reruns. There was nothing to appeal to the highly coveted "youth" demographic, and Schlosser wanted this corrected. He began to push for a new comedy/variety program that would air at eleven-thirty on Saturday nights and become, over time, another moneymaking franchise for the network. Schlosser's idea did not enjoy widespread support within NBC's corporate bowels, but the project went ahead under the supervision of the network's director of talent, David Tebet, and the director of late-night television, Dick Ebersol. As the *Saturday Night* project built steam, it was Ebersol, age twenty-seven, who championed Lorne Michaels, age twenty-nine, as the new show's producer and guiding light.*

Michaels was a wunderkind waiting to emerge. Born in Toronto, Ontario, Michaels grew up as a student of television, primarily American television, and he went on to produce plays as a teenage counselor in summer camp and a campus variety show while a student in college. When he was in eleventh grade, Michaels met Rosie Shuster, whose father, Frank Shuster, half of the then-famous comedy team Wayne and Shuster, became Michaels's "biggest influence" and comedy tutor. "He knew about the best American and English comedy," Michaels later said. "Frank would talk endlessly to me, teaching me. He would tell me about Jack Benny—how Benny would pick up a cue and *then* pause. . . . Frank would explain why the first six Marx Brothers movies—*Duck Soup, Animal Crackers,* and others—were funnier than the later ones, including *A Night at the Opera.* . . . Frank was also the first person to tell me about

---

*The corporate politics and personality clashes behind the creation of *Saturday Night* are well documented in *Saturday Night: A Backstage History of Saturday Night Live* by Doug Hill and Jeff Weingrad.

the great movies of Preston Sturges. Frank is a gentle and kind man, with a tremendous love of show business. . . ."

Michaels, too, loved show business, and this led him to form a comedy partnership with Hartz Pomerantz, with whom he performed on CBC radio and television. The team worked briefly as gag writers for Woody Allen and Joan Rivers (of Allen, Michaels remarked, "He was a great teacher, but I don't think Hart and I added anything to his career"), and then were hired in 1968 to contribute to *Laugh-In*. The team's jokes and assorted premises went into the show's comedy blender and came out as mulch; neither Michaels nor Pomerantz recognized their material in its final form. It was this experience that most galled Michaels, and he began to envision a comedy show in which the writing was respected and was part of a larger, more experimental format. After *Laugh-In*, the team returned to Canada and eventually broke up. Michaels produced a half hour comedy pilot for the CBC, "which they said was too serious, too clever, and too avant-garde." It was this pilot, however, that helped win him employment with Lily Tomlin; and it was for his work on her CBS special that Michaels received an Emmy award for his writing. Tomlin soon made him a co-producer on subsequent specials, and here Michaels truly honed his craft.

Dick Ebersol's instincts, as least when it came to Lorne Michaels, were on target. He recognized the young producer's involvement with the groundbreaking Tomlin shows as a necessary component to the *Saturday Night* project. Also, Michaels had a philosophy of humor formed over the years; as early as 1972 he tried to get a similar project off the ground but found no network that would take it. When Michaels pitched his plans for the new late-night show it was clear to Ebersol that he had the right man. "Dick knew I was breaking all the rules, putting parody commercials in with the real ones and all that, and he kept telling me I was vulnerable, but he supported me," Michaels said. After Ebersol and Michaels made the rounds with network executives, the deal was finalized: On April 1, 1975, Michaels was officially hired as the producer of *NBC's Saturday Night*.

Michaels finally had the show he'd always desired. When it came to hiring a staff, he naturally leaned toward those he knew or had worked with. This included Marilyn Miller, who at the time had, as she put it, "seven hundred jobs" writing for shows and potential pilots. She turned Michaels down but insisted that he call O'Donoghue, who, Miller felt, would be perfect for *Saturday Night*. Michaels was intrigued. Though not a reader of the *National Lampoon*, Michaels was familiar with the *Radio Hour*, which ran on KRLA-FM in Pasadena. Despite O'Donoghue's presence on the *Hour*, Michaels focused more on the performances than on any one personality. "On Sunday nights when it would play I would drive around and listen to it," he said. "I was more aware of the comedy in it—again it was performance—than I was of him." Still, Miller's suggestion struck a chord, and just after he was hired by NBC Michaels telephoned O'Donoghue and Beatts.

For O'Donoghue the call came at an opportune time. With his manager, Barry Secunda, he had attempted and failed to receive the backing necessary to finance a new humor magazine he wanted to call *Roustabout*. It was to be a cross between *Playboy* and the *Lampoon,* but since the *Lampoon* had a lock on all the available talent, how could *another* magazine hope to survive, even with Michael O'Donoghue and Anne Beatts on the masthead? (Sean Kelly later said that had *Roustabout* been realized, he would have jumped to it immediately.) Despite this setback the couple had been helped financially. As promised, Doug Kenney gave $30,000 of his *Lampoon* settlement to O'Donoghue and wrote on the check that the money was for "school supplies." In addition, Beatts had secured a deal with Macmillan Books to publish a collection of women's humor called *Titters*. She didn't have time to write for TV, she thought, but was interested enough to accompany O'Donoghue to meet Michaels at the Oyster Bar in Grand Central Terminal. After an initial get-acquainted dinner, the couple invited Michaels to the Winter Palace to further discuss the project and to give the young producer a taste of their performance art.

What initially struck Michaels about the two was their antique clothing and affected manners. "They were kind of, for me, Scott and Zelda," he recalled, adding that their art deco style was "somewhere between full of shit and impressive . . . it was very important to them to have this style. I was more used to that in performers than I was in writers. I didn't know any writers who behaved that way." He arrived at the apartment with a young filmmaker he knew in Los Angeles, Tom Schiller, who was himself part of the new show. Like Michaels, Schiller grew up enamored of television. His father, Bob Schiller, had been a writer for *I Love Lucy,* and as a boy Tom had spent hours on the Desilu lot, where the show's cast and crew served as his extended family. As an adult Schiller worked with film, and in 1973 he made a short subject that featured his mentor, Henry Miller. Now with Michaels, Schiller entered the "family business" of writing television comedy.

Although Michaels and Schiller were wise to the ways of showbiz and Hollywood hype, neither had seen such an arrangement of kitsch and nostalgia as that on display at Sixteenth Street. Like their antique clothing, O'Donoghue and Beatts used their apartment as an extension of their identities—a personal narrative that O'Donoghue fiddled with in the Spring Street loft. As "ironic" and "camp" as the Palace interior must have seemed to the visitors, it contained, at least for O'Donoghue, deeper and more serious meanings. He hoped, on some level, to capture the organized clutter of Sherlock Holmes's Baker Street study and so re-create the security of his bedroom in Sauquoit. Indeed, O'Donoghue had a boylike fascination with the items he collected, and in a large glass case he arranged them into various dioramas and scenes for which only he knew the story line. Little Nazi dolls milled with plastic bears and mouse fairies while a herd of plastic rhinos loitered nearby. Ike and Mamie Eisenhower dinner plates sat next to Jack and Jackie Kennedy salt and pepper shakers (appropriately enough, the JFK shaker had two holes in its head). Items were added, scenes shifted, but the format re-mained in place.

After a number of meetings, including one at the show's barren office space at 30 Rockefeller Plaza, Michaels asked O'Donoghue and Beatts to join *Saturday Night*. At first Beatts refused, citing her book deal and the amount of work that was needed to finish it on deadline. Michaels assured her that she could do both the book *and* the show, and his cool persuasion finally won her over. "He made it sound much easier than it turned out to be," she said. O'Donoghue, on the other hand, offered no resistance: He needed the work and he saw television as a step above the drudgery of magazines. After all, he had always been attracted to "hotter" forms and was in no way contemptuous of show business—so long as he could make it his own. While he made his feelings about television known to Michaels and spoke at length about the medium's emptiness and idiocy, O'Donoghue coveted the access television would bring him.

Of course, not all of his old colleagues were happy with his decision. O'Donoghue's step into television altered his dealings with George Trow, who saw the TV job as a wedge between them. "At a certain moment we parted," he said.

> I remember the moment quite clearly. He'd begun to work for *Saturday Night*. I didn't think that any good could come from working in television. We went to a restaurant in SoHo called Food. He looked at me and said, "But they've given me the camera. They don't always give you the camera." I understood exactly what he meant. He'd spent his life not having the tools needed to do what he needed to do. Someone was giving him a television camera to play with. After that our relationship changed. He went into a different life. I did not participate in that life. But we saw each other two or three times a year, always on the best terms.

Newly energized, O'Donoghue told everyone of "the show" and his plans for it. To Nelson Lyon he said, "I'm going to ride this one to shore," and spoke of *Saturday Night* as a step toward making films. And

while O'Donoghue was contemptuous of the *Lampoon* and all it represented, some of the material he and Beatts developed for the show reflected the magazine's style. (Indeed, a few one-liners from the
Encyclopedia appeared as bumpers in the early shows.) After their hiring,
O'Donoghue and Beatts visited Bruce McCall and his wife, Polly Bier,
in the Hamptons. McCall noticed the pair writing material, trying out
routines, cracking each other up. They continually spoke of "this TV
show" and ran their material by McCall. To his ear it sounded very
*Lampoon*ish, and he wondered what kind of show would allow it.

Lorne Michaels recognized the influence of the *Lampoon* but wanted
little to do with it himself. His was a peculiar position. True, he collected
talent from the *Lampoon,* including the *Radio Hour, Lemmings,* and its
follow-up, *The National Lampoon Show,* which featured Belushi and an
actress from Toronto's Second City, Gilda Radner (whom Michaels did
know in her pre-*Lampoon* days). Yet he felt the *Lampoon* aesthetic to
be too mean and male-oriented for his taste, so he tilted more to the
improvisational comedy of Second City and its various offshoots—the
smooth urbanity of Mike Nichols and Elaine May being one of his
favorites. Michaels distanced *Saturday Night* from the *Lampoon* in every
way he could, and he went so far as to claim that the show owed more
to the *New Yorker* than to Matty Simmons's humor rag.

Had the *National Lampoon* not existed, *Saturday Night* would have
been an entirely different show.* Whichever way it went—whether
toward the British models of Monty Python or *Beyond the Fringe,* the
Lily Tomlin brand of sketch comedy or that of Second City—*Saturday
Night* would have lacked the edge it possessed early in its run because
none of the above schools of humor packed the same savage punch as
the *Lampoon*. Thanks to the magazine, blood was on the floor and fear
was in the air; and try as he might, Michaels could not sidestep this as
he assembled his show. The hiring of O'Donoghue and Beatts, as well
as Belushi and Chevy Chase, was a clear sign of that.

Before the first official meeting of the *Saturday Night* writers in July,
O'Donoghue and Beatts developed a multitude of ideas for the show.
Since there was no fixed format, the two struck out in all directions.
O'Donoghue played with concepts reminiscent of Ernie Kovacs: He liked
the image of a bullet hitting and "cracking" the screen from the inside,
a mark that would remain and partially obscure the sketch that followed.
He also wanted to chroma key film close-ups of Humphrey Bogart and
Judy Garland onto a pair of T-shirts and have them talk to one another.

*According to Simmons, NBC first approached *him* with the idea of a late-night comedy/
variety show in late 1974. The network, he said, wanted to cash in on the *Lampoon*
name. Simmons considered the offer, then rejected it on the grounds that a *Lampoon*
television show would be a drain on the magazine.

There were many single-sentence concepts such as "Oven Mitts of the Gods," "Cutting the Zen Master in Half," and "Attack of the Atomic Sea Monkeys." This latter idea, which belonged to Beatts, reflected a mini-obsession the pair seemed to have with the mail-order "pets." In O'Donoghue's notebooks from the period there are numerous sea monkey sketch and film ideas, and the line "Hey, let's boil the sea monkeys!" pops up several times. The same went for wolverines and badgers, beasts that amused O'Donoghue no end.

Despite the change in his professional life, O'Donoghue continued to brood privately, and he and Beatts engaged in countless arguments. "Michael, far from becoming calmer and sweeter, became more erratic and angrier with me," she said. "We had some pretty major fights to the point that I didn't spend July Fourth weekend with him." (Barry Secunda, who lived upstairs from their apartment, could clearly hear the exchanges, so loud was the yelling.) Beatts believed that O'Donoghue was afraid of the new world of television and that he dealt with the stress by having "more moods." This, added to O'Donoghue's ongoing depression, made for a rather potent stew. To this point she had made allowances for her partner's behavior because "poor Michael, he lost his job and no one understands him, etc." But now that both were gainfully employed, "it seemed there was less to excuse."

After their holiday separation, Beatts and O'Donoghue began work in earnest on the show. They reported to the seventeenth floor of the NBC Building at 30 Rockefeller Plaza, and there mixed with the rest of the show's writing staff. Michaels had assembled an eclectic group of writers, from gag man Alan Zweibel to variety show veteran Herb Sargent (whose credits included the original *Tonight Show* with Steve Allen and the American version of *That Was the Week That Was*) to the apprentice team of Al Franken and Tom Davis, whose place on the show was secured through Tom Schiller's lobbying of Michaels on their behalf. Originally from Minneapolis, Minnesota, Franken and Davis toiled in the comedy club hell of Los Angeles. Their act owed much to Bob and Ray, but they were young and raw and not always employed. They appeared briefly in the Neil Israel film *Tunnelvision* (which also featured Laraine Newman) before they received the call to come to New York.

Once he surveyed the talent on display, O'Donoghue made a mental list of those he liked and those he felt to be inferior. Naturally, he warmed to Chevy Chase, who was initially hired as a writer, simply because he knew him from the *Radio Hour*. He also respected Herb Sargent's experience in the medium. But it was Franken and Davis who first felt the brunt of his comic elitism. Davis was fond of uttering "Far out" when in conversation, and this disgusted O'Donoghue, who ridiculed Davis in front of the entire staff. "He jumped all over me and kicked my butt," Davis remembered, and within two days of the attack he ceased using the phrase. Still, O'Donoghue saw something in Davis that he liked, and soon he took Davis under his wing. O'Donoghue suggested reading material, introduced him to people such as Doug Kenney, and spoke of humor in artistic terms that inspired the young writer.

Franken, on the other hand, inspired nothing but hostility. According to Davis, O'Donoghue disliked his partner "from the beginning. He thought Al was an obnoxious, egomaniacal asshole," and he made Franken the target of many put-downs. Whenever Franken submitted an idea or sketch, O'Donoghue would invariably label it "shit" or dismiss it altogether. In one writers' meeting, Franken and Davis pushed for a sketch they felt was funny, but O'Donoghue and Sargent disagreed. When Franken openly disputed O'Donoghue's opinion the senior writer walked over to Franken, grabbed the script from his hand, took it to the window, and let it drop seventeen floors to the pavement. End of discussion. This angered Franken but delighted Davis: "Franken was always trying to bully me, too, and it was great to see him get kicked in the nuts," he said.

To the other writers O'Donoghue cast a tangible shadow. Rosie Shuster first met him in June when O'Donoghue and Michaels went to Los Angeles to interview prospective talent. To Shuster he appeared very pale, "like a mollusk plucked out of its shell." She found him to be witty and "a little bit intimidating," and she noticed how that vein on his upper left eyebrow twitched periodically. In the weeks leading up to the first show Shuster thought "he was the Master. He had the most honed, barbed wit" among the staff, and she marveled at "the poison blow darts that emitted from his lips." O'Donoghue spoke in an epigrammatic manner and he worked his favorite (and prewritten) lines into conversation, a practice he'd lifted from Oscar Wilde. If he was frightened by what television held in store for him, O'Donoghue either rid himself of the fear or effectively suppressed it: He entered the show with full persona raging and rolled over anyone who stood in his way. "He did have a mythology about himself that was infectious," noted Shuster.

Lorne Michaels, too, succumbed. He treated O'Donoghue "with great deference at the beginning," said Shuster. "I think he was kind of in awe of Michael. He was very enamored of him." Michaels himself admitted that O'Donoghue "was really first among equals" and vital to helping Michaels realize his vision for the show. The producer was impressed with O'Donoghue's poise and generosity; he wanted O'Donoghue's approval and he valued his opinion. Given this type of treatment, O'Donoghue strolled easily to the front of the room, expecting deference as his due. He and Chase, along with Michaels and sometimes Sargent, formed a ruling "brain trust," as Alan Zweibel called it, over the staff.

It was they who would shape the content of *Saturday Night* and bring it before the cameras.

Office space on the seventeenth floor was at first limited. A large room where several writers would share desks, the area was conducive to collaboration and the sharing of ideas. Walls were soon built and offices allocated (which staffers called "rooms"); many of the writers spent nearly all their time there as the offices were better than their apartments. O'Donoghue was one of the exceptions. He received an office early on, and he often left at the end of the day. After all, he had the Winter Palace and didn't need—nor did he desire—to stay overnight. But he did decorate his office to taste and made certain that his work space reflected his personal style. Prominently placed was a picture of mass murderer Richard Speck, whom O'Donoghue claimed to admire, and several photos taken from a magazine called *Stump Love,* which featured nude amputee women in erotic poses.

The office itself was tidy and clean. "The lasting vision I have of Mike was sitting behind a desk that was not cluttered," remembered Chase. "The left side had a drawer with files of his writing, writings which would never get on *Saturday Night*—thoughts and concepts. Then to the left of the [Smith-] Corona typewriter would be a legal pad . . . there'd be a little area for his pencils. And they were all Michael's . . . When you went into that office, you really were in *his* office. His was very retentive and perfect." O'Donoghue also had a cork board on which idea cards were neatly tacked. This inspired a prank committed by Rosie Shuster. When O'Donoghue left for the day, Shuster, with the help of Tom Schiller, sneaked into his office and moved the cards slightly to the right each evening until, after a period of days, the cards moved off the board and onto the next wall while remaining in perfect formation. The cards themselves were filled with, in Shuster's words, "disturbing imagery—dark, weird, twisted, strange, vivid, intense imagery." After a while O'Donoghue put his cards back into place but said nothing about the prank.

As he began to write for the show O'Donoghue erred on the side of detail, sometimes excessively so. Unlike Chase, who had some television writing experience with the Smothers Brothers and Alan King, O'Donoghue did not know the standard way to arrange a script. "The first scripts he would turn in would have AUDIO, VIDEO, in caps. That's Mike," said Chase. "First he'd write it in caps on a legal pad, then he'd type it out with his little Corona, in caps—AUDIO, VIDEO. Well, it's very charming and it's a good way to do your notes, first drafts . . . but there's also a script method whereby you can put music, effects, and you put that in your left hand side, in caps, and you put your stage directions and that's got to be in lower case, but single spaced . . . So, Michael was a little wishy-washy at first." Lorne Michaels noted that O'Donoghue's "work at read-through had the most stage directions in it." As with his print work, every detail and bit of action were precisely described. O'Donoghue left nothing to chance and strove to get his concepts rendered perfectly on air. This would lead to inevitable disaster; live television is nothing if not error-filled, and O'Donoghue would find some of his cherished concepts mangled in front of millions of viewers.

> *We used to kick a fat man in the pants. Now we kick him in the nuts, deck him with a shovel, rearrange his cheekbones, leave him slabbed out on the pavement, looking like a Chinese-laundry ticket. That's the way to deal with a fat man.*

By the end of August the *Saturday Night* cast was set. Along with Gilda Radner and John Belushi—whom Michaels considered trouble and had hired only at the behest of O'Donoghue, Beatts, Chase, and others— there was Laraine Newman, a member of the L.A. improv group the Groundlings, who had appeared in a Lily Tomlin special; Garrett Morris, a graduate of Juilliard and an Off-Broadway playwright; Jane Curtin, a comedic stage actress from Boston; and Dan Aykroyd, another product of Toronto's Second City, who had been a regular on Lorne Michaels's CBC radio and television shows. Here Michaels's "recipe" for the show—he knew the ingedients but not the proportions—blended evenly. This in part owed to the fact that some cast members had already worked together, either in Second City or in the *Lampoon* productions, and thus knew well the strengths and weaknesses of the others. Few new shows enjoy such a head start, yet the talent assembled for *Saturday Night* would reach beyond old routines to create interesting, at times dynamic, comedy organic to the program.

O'Donoghue and Beatts were, of course, familiar with Chase and Belushi; but they soon would grow tight with some of the newer talents on display. Beatts and Rosie Shuster would become a strong writing team as counterbalance to the overwhelming male presence on the show. O'Donoghue would cast Laraine Newman in some of his better, darker, bits; though lean in body, Newman was robust comedically and she welcomed the edge presented her by O'Donoghue. Other collaborations would naturally emerge as O'Donoghue found who best serviced his material. But there was one force on the show that could match as well as exceed anything that O'Donoghue produced: Dan Aykroyd. At first O'Donoghue was put off by the Canadian actor; after one glance at Aykroyd's motorcycle garb, black save for a red cotton handkerchief dangling from his back pocket, O'Donoghue remarked that the guy looked like "rough trade." Aykroyd's memory of their encounter is a touch dramatic but no less entertaining:

> So as I walked for the first time down the hallway at my new job, Mike stepped out from a doorway as if he'd been waiting. Like a hybrid of Nevada trapdoor spider and Indian cobra, he darted and injected: "Jesus, are you in the wrong part of town or what, pal? Aykroyd, you look like the biggest, ugliest leather queen I've seen since Rondo Hatton tried to fuck Montgomery Clift. Listen, they're having a great sale at the Anvil bar on anal drawstring, and from the width of your ass, you'll be needing a yard of 100-pound Fiberglas test!"

Aykroyd said that he knew he should laugh, lest O'Donoghue completely write him off. "Then I looked at him while attempting to summon a rejoinder from my reeling brain. Here was a sartorially impeccable, slender, red-haired, pink Irishman. In his hand he held a long black Egyptian cigarette, and although they were writer's hands, I saw a bony clawlike strength. My first thought was, 'This is someone I don't want to fuck with physically. The hands could snap your throat, and he'll bite, too.' " While he overestimated O'Donoghue's violent potential, Aykroyd keyed into the persona; before long, O'Donoghue would likewise key into Aykroyd. He said that the twenty-two-year-old was 78 rpm in a 45 rpm world.

Saturday Night premiered on October 11, 1975. The cast, now called "The Not Ready For Prime Time Players," was expanded by three: Chase, who pushed for and won an acting spot; George Coe, a *Radio Hour* veteran who appeared in many of *Saturday Night*'s early commercial parodies; and O'Donoghue, who had, after all, plenty of experience as a performer. This experience came in handy as O'Donoghue was slated by Michaels to appear in *Saturday Night*'s opening sketch, "Wolverines." He was to play a professor who would give immigrant John Belushi a lesson in the English language. Minutes before the show aired, O'Donoghue ran into Nelson Lyon who, with actor Michael Murphy, attended the broadcast. Lyon wished O'Donoghue luck and was impressed with his friend's nonchalance, given that O'Donoghue was soon to appear live in front of the largest audience of his life. Though he later would tell interviewers that he was scared to death, O'Donoghue affected a surface calm and coolly sipped from a glass of water. He took his place on the set and the countdown to air began.

The set suggests a dingy study, faded and worn with time. O'Donoghue, dressed in a brown suit, sits in an armchair and reads a newspaper. Offstage, a door closes; steps are heard. Belushi, carrying a bag of groceries, walks down a short flight of stairs and heads to the chair opposite

O'Donoghue. He sets the groceries down as O'Donoghue says, "Good evening." Belushi responds in broken English, "Gudt effning." O'Donoghue folds his paper and leans forward:

"*Good* ev-e-ning."

"*Gudt* eff-e-ning . . . *Gudt* eff-e-ning."

O'Donoghue checks his watch, picks up and opens an old book.

"Let us begin. Repeat after me. I would like . . ."

"I wudt like . . ."

"To feed your fingertips . . ."

"To feedt yur fingerteeps . . ."

"To the wolverines."

"To de wolfureens."

The lesson continues. O'Donoghue reads, "I am afraid we are out of badgers. Would you accept a wolverine in its place? . . . 'Hey!' Ned exclaimed. 'Let's boil the wolverines!' " and Belushi struggles to keep pace. O'Donoghue begins another line but suddenly grabs his chest, a look of pain and shock on his face. He falls from his chair and hits the floor, dead. Belushi briefly ponders the situation, then he, too, grabs his chest and dies instantly. After a beat, Chevy Chase walks on wearing a floor director's headset. He surveys the bodies, mumbles into his microphone, looks to the camera, and says, "Live from New York. It's *Saturday Night!*" The opening montage rolls.

O'Donoghue was quite proud of "Wolverines" (as was his father, Michael James, who wept as he watched his son's television debut). He made a point of telling people that the sketch announced to all that *Saturday Night* was not another TV comedy show: This is *our* humor, he would say, not Paul Lynde's or George Gobel's or Carol Channing's. He also observed that "Wolverines" was so strange that the network censors had no complaints. "It's pretty violent," he later said of the sketch, "but it is curious how you can go around any kind of censorship code just by bizarreness. In 1954 and in 1962 you could have said 'I would like to feed your fingertips to the wolverines' on a television show and no one would have hit it. It's so odd it doesn't relate to—yet it really does strike the brain at a strange angle."

"Wolverines" was odd but great. O'Donoghue and Belushi clicked as though they were a seasoned comedy team, and the death falls they took appeared real, not "funny" in the Redd Foxx "I'm comin' to join you, Elizabeth!" fake heart attack mold. The set was properly seedy looking and the mood was that of a theater stage. This was an element that Michaels insisted on, and throughout the show's first season there was a theatrical feel to many of the sketches.

Saturday Night's first host, George Carlin, was written into a parody of Alexander the Great by O'Donoghue, titled "High School Reunion," but Carlin refused to appear in this or any other sketch. So the opening show revolved around Carlin's stand-up act, and amid the unevenness other O'Donoghue bits stood out. One, "The Academy of Better Careers," promotes a school where people are trained to answer phones for late-night ads such as the one we are watching—a circle of Hell where the phone never stops ringing. Another, "Jamitol," is a takeoff on the then-ubiquitous Geritol ads. O'Donoghue plays Chevy Chase's "wife," who can do it all, including making studded leather vests at their boutique, thanks to the vitamins and iron in Jamitol. O'Donoghue and Chase forgo the standard mincing fag stereotypes and deliver their lines in a straight manner, as it were. This subdued approach makes "Jamitol" seem like an actual ad, an effect heightened by the omission of studio audience laughter. All of *Saturday Night*'s filmed and taped commercial parodies were presented this way in the show's first weeks and often were mistaken for the real thing. A nice satirical touch, but one destined to vanish; soon laughter was piped in over the sound tracks, and the parodies were segregated from the genuine consumerist appeals.

After "Wolverines" and "Jamitol," O'Donoghue appeared on-screen once more as an extra in "Bee Hospital," the first of many sketches that featured the cast in bee costumes. In the opening montage, a series of color-tinted New York photos taken by Edie Baskin, there is a shot of O'Donoghue and Beatts having dinner. Each smiles at the other in a warm, happy way, and one senses that this is a couple deep in love. But offscreen there was trouble as the once-stylish pair slowly broke apart.

In *Saturday Night*'s first season, domestic bliss rarely visited Sixteenth Street. Beatts felt that O'Donoghue had a tough time adjusting to television as well as to *her* professional advancement. The two were now creative equals, though Beatts had an edge with her book deal. "He seemed very resentful about *Titters*," she said. "And we had a project where we were writing another animated feature and we were late." The project, *The Day The Earth Threw Up*, was to be a science fiction spoof, but O'Donoghue had no intention of finishing the screenplay. "And part of the way of not finishing it was having fights," said Beatts. The proposed film's backers wanted O'Donoghue's involvement, and once he abandoned the project they immediately followed suit.

"Despite the difficulties of the previous year, I had been able to cling to the illusion that if we had economic and creative success that our troubles would be over," said Beatts. But success intensified matters, and Beatts looked for ways to lessen the tension. In the fall of 1975 she went into therapy and urged O'Donoghue to do the same. He refused on "artistic" grounds: "I don't care for psychiatry too much. I like eccentricities and craziness and I'd hate to see them resolved. . . . I think therapy interferes with the creative process. It takes off the edge." But what was good for his art was poison to his relationship with Beatts, and soon she began to remove herself from the line of fire. "If Michael flew into a rage, I would go to the movies," she later said, leaving her partner to fume in black mist.

While O'Donoghue ensconced himself in the *Saturday Night* brain trust, Beatts tried to establish her voice on the show. But like the testosterone-heavy *Lampoon, Saturday Night* was basically a men's club. When the show premiered, Beatts and Rosie Shuster were the lone women on the writing staff, and for a time each tended to work separately. Beatts's first job was producing the commercial parodies, which basically meant preparing other people's material for the camera. Beatts herself appeared in an ad called "Speed," in which she played Ellen Sherman, "Cleveland housewife and mother." Ellen enters a kitchen fresh from the market and rattles off her responsibilities and accomplishments in rapid succession as she removes groceries from a paper bag, which she then quickly folds. How does Ellen manage all this? "She takes Speed, the tiny blue diet pill you don't have to be overweight to need." "Speed" was the first piece shot in *Saturday Night*'s studio 8H. (It also served as an audition script for prospective female cast members.) Beatts runs through her lines at a frantic but fluid clip, her timing doubtless enhanced by the twenty-seven takes required to isolate her dialogue from the crackling of folded paper bags. In a sense, "Speed" epitomized Beatts's predicament: Her comic energy was contained on tape amid the current of a live show. The trick for her was breaking free and adding this energy to the mix.

O'Donoghue suffered no such isolation. He was in the thick of things from day one, and his strong comic voice ensured that *Saturday Night* would, at least initially, bear his mark. Perhaps one of the reasons Lorne Michaels deferred to O'Donoghue in this early period was that the former *Lampoon* star knew precisely what he wanted. After all, Michaels had yet to commit to a "total" vision of the show and referred to it as a recipe-in-progress. Also, O'Donoghue was older and secure in his moves, and on a show comprised of young talent he served as a creative anchor. Dan Aykroyd said it was O'Donoghue who showed the rest of the staff what was possible comedically, and Rosie Shuster added that on a certain level everyone on the show wanted his approval. It is no wonder, then, that O'Donoghue believed he would indeed "ride this one to shore."

After the second *Saturday Night*, which consisted mainly of Paul Simon singing his greatest hits (an O'Donoghue piece did appear: "Up Against the Wallpaper," wallpaper decorated with slogans from the 1960s hawked by Jerry Rubin just prior to his "hip" capitalist phase), the show quickly settled into formula: cold opening; montage; guest host

With Chevy Chase, 1975

monologue or related bit; commercial parody and/or first sketch, and so on. Although Michaels insisted that *Saturday Night* was "experimental" and would "find itself" on air, the show by necessity adhered to television's iron rule of familiarity. The format was set and the repeats began. In eight of the first ten episodes the Bees appeared either singly or as a group. This continued throughout the first season, much to the consternation of John Belushi, who declared to the press, "I hate the fucking Bees!" (Yet he would wear the costume well into his final season.) Chevy Chase's Land Shark, which preyed on women in urban apartment buildings, surfaced in episodes four and six in two nearly identical *Jaws* parodies and became somewhat of a running gag during Chase's time on *Saturday Night*. But perhaps the oddest of all the early recurring bits were the segments featuring the Muppets.

Before *Saturday Night* had a cast and a full writing staff, Dick Ebersol signed Jim Henson to develop new Muppet characters for the show. Known primarily for Big Bird, Oscar the Grouch, and the Cookie Monster of *Sesame Street* fame, Henson moved away from these familiar characters to create nasty reptilian creatures that inhabited a barren, volcanic terrain. What the point of it all was is anybody's guess since the new Muppets fit so poorly in the *Saturday Night* mix. These characters got drunk, were lascivious, and lived in craters—offbeat by Henson's standards but tame to those on the show, especially the writers, whose task it was to make the Muppets funny (but within Henson's guidelines). Most put off by the Muppets was O'Donoghue, who referred to them as "those little hairy facecloths. I'd deep-six them in a second." His hatred of the creatures led him to draft a piece called "The Day of the Muppets" in which, after being exposed to an atomic blast, the Muppets mutate into flesh-eating beasts that kill Henson and terrorize the studio audience. Instead, Henson's contract with the show expired in the spring of 1976 and he and *Saturday Night* parted ways. But O'Donoghue would later recycle his atomic concept and expand it into one of his more memorable pieces.

Early on, O'Donoghue attempted a recurring bit. In the fifth episode, hosted by Robert Klein, then a month later in the Candice Bergen Christmas show, there appeared a sketch of his called "Minute Mystery." Taken from the files of the Mexico City police department, the "Mystery" premise is Who Done It? A body is discovered and the home and studio audiences are invited to solve the crime. The second "Mystery" is the better of the two. The body of a professor, O'Donoghue, lies dead on a couch—eyes blank, blood trickling down his forehead. A crime photographer, Mike Mendoza, played by Dan Aykroyd, snaps a shot of the scene for his paper when he notices a beautiful woman holding a gun. She is Winona Foxfire, the professor's assistant. When asked by Mendoza and Lopez, a Mexican cop played by Belushi, what she knows about the murder, Winona says nothing save that she is sexually attracted to men who can't solve mysteries. She entices the two into a ménage à trois and the professor is left to rot.

"Minute Mystery" is filled with O'Donoghue's distinctive language and his flair for detail. Aykroyd's character, after confessing he hasn't the slightest idea who snuffed the professor, gives the audience twenty seconds to find the culprit. Interposing cameras pan the set, which consists of "clues" such as a pair of white wing tips on a silver tray, a book titled *Wool Shrinkage,* a manual lawn mower, and the words "Winona did it!" scrawled in blood on the wall. The wordplay among Aykroyd, Belushi, and Bergen, who plays Winona, is taken from O'Donoghue's rejected *Man in the Moon* dialogue. Bergen tells Belushi "Eat my hair net, Jocko!" and observes that Aykroyd must comb his hair "with buttered toast." Euphemisms for sex—"Trap the clam," "Stuff the bunny," and "Swallow the swan"—are tossed about, and soon the crime scene becomes a parlor game with Winona as the prize. The first "Minute Mystery" follows the same pattern, though without Bergen there to give it juice the sketch consists of obscure leads that intentionally go nowhere. Cameras scan the "clues," some of which are O'Donoghue's kitsch items from his apartment, including a plastic hand sporting a knife wound in the palm and multicolor plastic saints at the end of each finger.

Despite favorable audience reaction, O'Donoghue would abandon "Minute Mystery" and concentrate on single pieces. He continued to appear on camera, often as an extra in other writers' sketches. Of course, O'Donoghue had no problem writing himself into his own work but only if the piece called for it. He found a nice little opening in the fourth episode to perform something that, with the possible exception of Aykroyd, fit no one else in the cast.

O'Donoghue walks calmly down a flight of stairs to a pay phone. He drops in a dime, dials a number, and turns to the camera. He flashes a slight, psychotic smile; thin strands of hair hang awkwardly over his left ear. His call is answered by Laraine Newman, who appears in split-screen at an airport ticket counter. "Good evening. Trans American Airlines," she says. O'Donoghue lowers his voice:

You know what I'd like to do to you, lady? I'd like to stick tacks in your neck. Then I'd like to take a chain saw and run it down your spine. Then I'd like to throw garbage at your face. Then I'd like to rent a truck, fill it full of scrap metal and park it on your kneecaps. Then I'd like to hit you in the lungs with a shovel, throw more garbage at your face, and then lop off your thumbs with a grapefruit knife. Good-bye.

Newman, who has remained straight-faced, replies, "Good-bye, and thank you for calling Trans American."

The bit marked the first on-camera appearance of the "sinister" O'Donoghue, not so much a character as an attitude. He was in essence a comic assassin, the hit man he had romanticized to Nelson Lyon in the cab. O'Donoghue had played with this attitude for some time (the Trans American rant is similar to the one in "Dean Corrl's Favorite Jokes") and in many ways the "assassin" flowed from his ongoing anger, depression, and private insecurities—the very emotions that were driving Anne Beatts from their relationship. Unlike other comedians who masked their sadness with a smile and a gag, O'Donoghue placed his sadness at the center of his humor and allowed it to fill the room. His smile was that of the sadist, the gags stuffed in the mouths of his trembling victims.

Michael Anne

Happy New Year
1976

Season's greetings from Zelda and Scott

As for Beatts, her first real breakthrough came when Lily Tomlin hosted the show in late November. Emboldened by Tomlin's presence, Beatts and Rosie Shuster collaborated on a now-celebrated sketch in which Tomlin played a female hard hat instructor. The premise was a basic comic reversal, placing the women in the position of sexist louts taunting vulnerable men who walked by their work site. The sketch has a fine nasty streak, and when Aykroyd, who plays the target of the women's lust, sobs and asks that the taunting cease, he is ignored and abused even more viciously. Apparently, none of the men on the show wanted to play this role, and Aykroyd was cast by default. One wonders, then, who would have played the man in another sketch Beatts had in mind: "It was about a feminist restaurant, where the man got totally humiliated: His food was served on the floor, the waitresses humiliated him and he was supposed to say, 'Oh, fine, fine. I like this.' We didn't run it. Some of us thought the humor was in the intimidation factor, but not enough of us felt it was really funny."

The hard hat sketch was somewhat of a sea change for Beatts. When Lorne Michaels first interviewed her and O'Donoghue for the *Saturday Night* job, she freely opined that to her the Lily Tomlin specials were self-consciously feminist and that she preferred the camp and absurdity of Cher. In manner and dress, Beatts reflected a similar theatrical style, but the edge of her humor cut through the costume and into the target of choice. If Beatts was to emerge from the male dominance of the show and establish a creative foothold for herself, she had to dispense with the wry and go for the gut. The hard hat sketch did just that; it leveled the playing field, at least for one show, and established Beatts and Shuster as a combined force worth heeding.

O'Donoghue contributed little to the Tomlin episode; neither cared for the humor of the other, and the show that week catered more to Tomlin's tastes. But it was the episode following Tomlin that brought O'Donoghue face-to-face with another master of comic aggression, Richard Pryor. According to *A Backstage History of Saturday Night Live,* O'Donoghue visited Pryor's hotel room and ran by the comedian a joke he'd written for Weekend Update, the weekly news segment that featured Chevy Chase. The joke "quoted" former Alabama Governor George Wallace as saying, "I don't judge a man by the color of his skin. I judge him according to the size of his nostrils." Offended, Pryor reportedly picked up a cognac bottle and threatend to bash in O'Donoghue's skull. Whether Pryor was joking or not, O'Donoghue was intimidated enough to stay away from the show for most of the week.

Lorne Michaels, conversely, dismissed this story and claimed that O'Donoghue and Pryor never met. But he did concur that O'Donoghue remained clear of the show that week, primarily because his humor did not mesh with Pryor's. Whatever the truth of the matter (O'Donoghue always maintained that Pryor did try to "crack my head open with a cognac bottle"), the fact remains that O'Donoghue had material on the show that week, regardless of his physical proximity to the studio. In addition to the Update joke, which aired with a different punch line (George Wallace judges a man by whether he can see him smile in the dark), O'Donoghue contributed to "Exorcist II," in which Laraine Newman, possessed by the Devil, insults a pair of priests with lines such as "You French-kiss your dog on the mouth!" and "Your mama eats kitty litter!" One of the priests was Pryor, and he responded to this last line by trying to strangle Newman—symbolic, perhaps, of his relationship with O'Donoghue?

O'Donoghue must have surfaced at least once that week, for he saw in rehearsals a bit he recognized from the *Lampoon*. In a series of black-outs set in a police line-up, Pryor played a criminal suspect who had been beaten while in custody, handcuffed, and displayed with other "suspects" for identification. In one lineup it was him and three white cops; in another he stood next to a nun, a refrigerator, and a duck. The point, obviously, was that no matter what, Pryor would be fingered by the victim. But the latter lineup stirred memories in O'Donoghue; he recalled that Brian McConnachie had published in the November 1972 *Lampoon* a cartoon in which a black suspect was in a lineup with a nun, a duck, and a little boy. He immediately phoned McConnachie to alert him of the theft: "They're stealing your stuff! It's a disgrace!" O'Donoghue then tried to have the bit removed but was told that it was "in the zeitgeist" and that this type of comedy belonged to their generation.*

Since O'Donoghue had lobbied Lorne Michaels to hire McConnachie anyway, he took the opportunity to, if not get his friend a job with the show, then at least use him to make Michaels uncomfortable. A month later, at John Belushi's birthday party, O'Donoghue introduced McConnachie to Michaels. "Brian," said O'Donoghue as he led the tall writer to meet his boss, "this is the man who's been stealing your material." A pause, then Michaels spoke. "The first words to me from Lorne were a lie," said McConnachie. " 'I've been trying to call you,' he said. " 'I've been leaving messages on your machine.' But I didn't have a machine. I'm waiting there and thinking, 'I know that Michael wants me to take Lorne by the hair and threaten to put his head in the toilet. That's what Michael would like me to do.' His face was lit up, looking to see what trouble would transpire." But McConnachie, knowing he could use a job in television, resisted the temptation to assault Michaels. (A savvy move: McConnachie wrote for *Saturday Night* in its fourth season and contributed periodically to the show for many years thereafter.)

*In a letter later sent to McConnachie by one of the show's lawyers, O'Donoghue is said to have denied making the call.

In the Pryor episode, the show's format was shuffled a touch to accommodate Pryor's demands (that they employ for the week one of his writers, allow his ex-wife to deliver a monologue, hire extra actors, etc.). After this Candice Bergen returned, for Christmas, and from there on the profitable formula remained firmly in place, tweaked now and then depending on the host, related concepts, and so on. As 1976 began, *Saturday Night* truly took off, beginning with the Elliott Gould episode of January 10. Michaels, disappointed with Bergen's Christmas show, remained in New York for the holidays and with Chase and O'Donoghue wrote the bulk of material for Gould's appearance.

Chase's talent for slapstick was featured in a sketch about "interior demolitionists" in which he and Gould are hired to destroy the inside of a suburban home. Belushi played Marlon Brando in "Godfather Group Therapy" and then the leader of "The Killer Bees," South American bandit-bees who rob people of their pollen. In this sketch another recurring character was introduced: Lorne Michaels. He is called upon by a frustrated Chase to save the sketch, which suffers a technical breakdown. The director, Davey Wilson, is "drunk" and the cameramen receive the wrong instructions, which throws the sketch into chaos. It is a breaking of the fourth wall made popular by Monty Python, and in this and subsequent shows Michaels will respond to the calls of "Lorne! Lorne!" whenever something is needed.

O'Donoghue appears in the Gould episode, again as an extra, and in a piece called "Birthright" he is silent but prominent as a clown who sprays a newborn baby in the face with seltzer water (part of a controversial birthing technique known as "Pearl Harbor"). But it was in the following episode, hosted by Buck Henry, where O'Donoghue scored two solid hits as writer and performer.

He had spent several weeks polishing a sketch called "Citizen Kane II," which was both a takeoff on the original film and a comment on the idea that *any* film, no matter how singular and unique, could inspire a sequel. In O'Donoghue's sequel to *Kane* the premise is absurdly transparent: The nurse who heard Charles Foster Kane's last word, "Rosebud," suddenly remembers a few more. She tells this to Mr. Thompson, the reporter who tried and failed to discover what "Rosebud" meant. They visit Kane's former friend and partner, Jed Leland, who is still in the same nursing home and still craving "a good cigar," and attempt to jog his memory one more time.

The nurse says that after Kane muttered "Rosebud" he said "Henri." Leland remembers Henri as a "little Frenchman" who worked for Kane as a printer on the *New York Inquirer*. In flashback we see the day Kane took over the newspaper that would make his media empire. He tries to remedy a slow news day by aiming a gun outside his office window and shooting the pedestrians below. "Take a headline, Bernstein!" he says to his assistant. " 'Crazed Sniper Guns Down Six.' Play up the innocent women and children angle and offer a ten-thousand-dollar reward for the madman's capture." Henri has the front page headline ready almost instantly, but Kane fires him for the delay. "We're running a scandal sheet here, not a newspaper," he informs the hapless printer. Kane bites into a roast beef on rye with mustard, reveals his plans to sell billions of papers by any means necessary, and continues to gun down pedestrians while ordering front-page revisions.

We return to present time. Thompson wonders why a dying Kane would mention an employee he fired fifty years before. The nurse then remembers that Kane said something else: "with mustard." Thompson puts it all together: Rosebud, Henri, with mustard. "I wonder what it means," he says. Leland suggests that it might have been a horse Kane bet on; the nurse thinks perhaps it was a woman he knew. "I guess we'll never know," says Thompson finally. We cut to a shot of a furnace. The door opens, and placed on the flames is a restaurant card that reads, "Roast beef on rye with mustard." The music swells to fade.

In rhythm and in detail, "Citizen Kane II" is perhaps the nearest O'Donoghue ever came to duplicating on air the style of parody he mastered in the *Lampoon*. The piece is a TV cousin to "Tarzan of the Cows" and hinges, like "Tarzan," on a single absurd concept. It is presented in black and white (another *Lampoon* touch; the parody must resemble the original for the humor to work) and the music and sound, especially the echo effects used in Jed Leland's reminiscence, recall the effects used by Orson Welles in his masterpiece. This allows the crowning joke, silly though it is, to shine. In fact, O'Donoghue's joke is so silly that it broke up both Buck Henry, who played Thompson, and Chevy Chase, who was Leland. This was rare on the early *Saturday Night*; the cast members prided themselves on their integrity as comic actors, and they scorned the Carol Burnett school of laughing on camera. But as Chase admitted, it was difficult to keep a straight face when dressed in *Citizen Kane* costume and pondering the "meaning" of "Rosebud, Henri, with mustard."

O'Donoghue's second piece in this episode was a reprisal of his needles-in-the-eyes routine from the *Radio Hour*—a routine familiar to those on staff but never seen on camera. In its original radio form, O'Donoghue spent little time establishing the premise before he screamed and crashed about. For television, however, he knew the routine needed a stronger framework; it had to be presented as a legitimate part of the show. For this he enlisted Buck Henry to introduce him as "the king of impressionists." After Henry's introduction, big band music, worthy of the cheesiest variety fare, blares as O'Donoghue runs onstage. Dressed in a Vegas-style tuxedo, he snaps his fingers and smiles to the audience in "sincere" showbiz fashion.

> Thank you, thank you very very much, ladies and gentlemen, I'd like to . . . You know, when you're in show business it seems you always end up at some bar at four o'clock in the morning arguing over who's the best singer, who's the best dancer, who's the funniest comedian. But I think there's one thing everybody agrees on and that's who's the nicest guy in show business and of course I'm talking about Mr. Mike Douglas . . .

Having recently watched Mike's show, the "king" had a funny thought: What if someone took steel needles—say, fifteen, eighteen inches long "with *real* sharp points"—and plunged them into Mike's eyes? What would his reaction be? O'Donoghue removes his glasses, turns his back to get into character, grabs his face, and screams and thrashes across the stage. At first the image seems ridiculous, but O'Donoghue pushes it and acts as though he is in serious physical pain. Audience members who line the stage watch O'Donoghue in amazement. A few laugh; the rest seem horrified and confused by the man who writhes and kicks just inches from their faces. Finally, O'Donoghue spills off the end of the stage, but his screams continue to fill the studio. Buck Henry walks on applauding. "Uncanny, isn't it?" he says.

O'Donoghue thrashed about so violently that he sustained minor injuries. "I did that on a brick stage," he later said.

> I'd forgotten this one element. I realized I was going to get really hurt—and *did.* As you were doing it you just said, "Go with it. Get as hurt as you're going to get. You're not going to end up in the hospital, and if you do, they'll take care of you." So I took terrific blows and for almost three or four weeks was just a mess of welts. I went off the side of the stage through lights and stuff. At the end of it I just went right over the side off onto a concrete floor. It looked like a Jackson Pollock, parts of my leg.

As with "Wolverines" and the Trans American psycho rant, the needles routine stood out from anything on American television at the time. In a culture where Don Rickles was considered "aggressive" this was completely off the map. When O'Donoghue first met and spoke with Lorne Michaels, he didn't believe that he would be allowed put such material on the air. But as the first season progressed, O'Donoghue discovered that Michaels was serious, and so he looked to inject this material into every opening available on the show. Dark streaks appear in a variety of sketches, some of which O'Donoghue did not conceive but "punched up" with a few choice lines taken from his notebooks or

© Edie Baskin. Used by permission.

Measuring steel needles, with *real* sharp points, on *Saturday Night*

Lampoon pieces. Not every actor on *Saturday Night* appeared comfortable with O'Donoghue's more violent output, or fit the particular style of his work. But once the show settled into a groove and the actors showed their range, O'Donoghue determined who best serviced his material. Almost always it came down to two cast members: Laraine Newman and John Belushi.

Like many others on the show, Newman hailed from an improvisational background. She was particularly adept at character work and sank herself into varied personas almost anonymously. It was this talent that caught Lorne Michaels's and Lily Tomlin's attention in 1974, when they saw Newman at the Groundlings Theater in Los Angeles, and it was the reason Michaels brought her to New York for *Saturday Night* the following year. Physically slight, Newman could nevertheless rip through a scene—that is, if the script called for it. She adapted well to whatever she was given but was oftentimes put off by what she called the "prep school" bent of some of the show's writers. Still, Newman preferred "hard" comedy to soft, and it was with O'Donoghue that she achieved some of her madder television moments.

In the mid-1970s the makers of Camay soap chose Luciana Avedon to sell their "beauty" product. Exotic and icy, Avedon spoke of Camay's cleansing powers in a near-hypnotic manner as she gazed longingly at the soft skin of a little girl. O'Donoghue sensed a vampire quality in Avedon's obsession with youth; he put an Avedon-type wig on Newman, set her in an open coffin, and surrounded her with beautifully framed photos of grotesque-looking children. She rises, turns to the camera, and gestures to the photos:

> I was an ugly child, a hideous teenager, with fur on my ears and webbed fingers. But now I am young and beautiful. How do I do it? The answer is in this, my *Beauty Regimen* book. My book tells how I drink the blood of Girl Scouts and Brownies. It tells how I eat the faces of young virgins. It even tells how I have all my bones replaced with those of cheerleaders and pompom girls. Buy my book or I steal your lungs!

Newman brings Avedon's cool personality in line with O'Donoghue's script. There is no exaggeration, no "playing to" the savage dialogue. An invisible yet tangible current runs through the bit, and one almost believes that Avedon is of the fashionable undead. Newman's skill in grasping the essential part of a character showed also in her depiction of a real-world zombie.

In *Saturday Night*'s third show, Newman appeared as Lynette "Squeaky" Fromme in a sketch titled "Dangerous But Inept." Fromme, a Charles Manson groupie, had recently attempted the assassination of Gerald Ford as an offering to her demented idol. In "Dangerous" Fromme is interviewed by Jane Curtin; questions are asked but Squeaky is focused solely on drilling the bourgeois pig sitting next to her. Yet she cannot get her handgun to fire and she spends the interview fiddling with it and trying, and failing, to kill Curtin. Newman touches on Fromme's insanity, but the sketch is brief, the humor centered on the nonworking gun. We get the idea that Squeaky is clumsy, not dangerous. It would take O'Donoghue to find the truly frightening aspects of Manson and his "girls."

"Dangerous" showed early on that *Saturday Night* considered verboten subjects such as Charles Manson fair comic game. There would be many Manson jokes, mostly on Weekend Update, and O'Donoghue sought to play the pyscho himself in a bit in which Charlie carves a Halloween pumpkin but flips out and stabs it repeatedly instead. This piece did not pass the network censor, but a better and more sinister Manson piece did. For the episode hosted by Louise Lasser in July 1976, the second-to-last show of the first season, O'Donoghue created an image that he later said took a second to see and a lifetime to forget.

We open on a prison cell that holds two women, Squeaky Fromme and Sandra Goode—another Manson follower who hoped to assassinate the president. Both stare, unblinking, into the camera. Bright red hoods cover their heads, on which are carved tiny x's. Goode, played by Jane Curtin, speaks:

> Hi. I'm Sandra Goode and we make these lovely potholders from our own hair. It takes weeks and weeks but we don't care, do we, Squeaky? [Squeaky responds by making gun noises.] And if we make a mistake, even a teeny teeny tiny mistake that you'd never notice in a million years, we start all over again and then we punish ourselves, severely . . .

Goode reads a message to Manson that is hidden in one of the potholders: "Don't drink the water. It's posoned . . . posoned." Angered by the spelling error, Goode and Squeaky punish themselves—Goode sticks fingers in her eyes, Squeaky twists her nipples. Both scream, then calm somewhat as Goode completes her pitch. For only $30 one can own a human hair potholder, but supplies are limited. The women remove their hoods to show their bald pates. Squeaky leans forward and says, "You better buy them, you little piggies. I'm not kidding." They stare silently ahead as the image fades.

On paper, "Potholders" was dark and strange enough; anyone with the slightest imagination could see where O'Donoghue was going. But in performance the visual effect exceeded even O'Donoghue's expectations. Curtin's Goode is naturally crazy, her manner subtle but threatening. Newman's Squeaky, however, is a psychopath lost in a hallucinatory swirl. The odds are even that she'd mutilate herself as well as anyone standing near her, and Newman manages to delicately balance Squeaky's destructive impulses. Her eyes glazed with hatred, her mouth fixed in a semigrin, she imitates the sound of pistol shots, which seems to provide some comfort. When the spelling error in the potholder is found and Squeaky pulls on her tits, the audience laughs but hesitantly. This was not a common sight, and O'Donoghue, standing near the set, was also caught off guard.

"It scared *me* when it was on," he said of the sketch. "Sometimes you don't appreciate how a look will change things. Just before the show Laraine came up to me and said, 'Listen, when I do it, will it be okay if I pinch my nipples and scream?' I didn't quite hear the question and said, 'Yeah, sure, Laraine. Anything you want.' And when she *did* pinch her nipples and scream with a bald wig on, it was really quite a look and one I won't soon forget. . . . My God, it was distasteful! You're not going to see that kind of thing on the Dick Van Dyke show."

John Belushi was less anonymous in his characterizations but he made up for this through sheer presence and force. Subdued on the *Radio Hour,* he returned to the intense open space of his Second City and

Lemmings days. One sees this in "Wolverines" in his quick, beautifully executed seizure. And in *Saturday Night*'s third installment he performed his *Lemmings* version of Joe Cocker, coarse blues voice spurred by balletlike spins, crashes to the floor, and beer poured on face and chest. (Early in the second season Belushi did his Cocker next to Cocker himself, which led to a subtler but still rich performance.) Belushi's power as a comic actor was seemingly too strong for television, and certainly Lorne Michaels was concerned with the power source itself; yet Belushi adapted well to the medium and hit his marks while forcefully in character. Even in the Bee straitjacket he so despised there is, early on, an integrity born of the stage. This, of course, would fade with success as Belushi became a *Saturday Night* mascot, Bee antennae still in place. But when he first took the gig he took it as far as the small screen would allow. The chaos of live television was further enhanced by his creative turbulence.

O'Donoghue understood Belushi from the start, hence their appearance together in "Wolverines." That he knew the actor from the *Radio Hour* of course helped, but their relationship there had been different; as one part of a revolving cast of performers Belushi was not the main vehicle of O'Donoghue's humor. On *Saturday Night,* however, the relationship changed, intensified. Here the visual was everything and Belushi, once unleashed, could get more across in a tumble or a seizure than he could from reciting a speech. This was the current he rode when onstage, and O'Donoghue looked to steer this energy right into the cameras. But Belushi's energy was not easy to corral, and he would, on occasion, expend it elsewhere. In the week before she first hosted the show, Belushi saw Candice Bergen in Lorne Michaels's office and approached her with an idea. As O'Donoghue remembered it:

John had written a sketch that parodied a Sam Peckinpah kind of director, a director who, in order to act out a scene, brutalizes his actresses. John wanted to run this down with Candy, and I was fortunate enough to be sitting in Lorne's office when he did. He grabbed her, threw her against the wall, and then threw her to the ground. Ultimately, it got down to them wrestling on the floor. Lorne, who was sitting behind his desk, wouldn't look at them. And I, with an affinity for the Japanese cinematic school, didn't really want to look either. I mean, being on the periphery of this action was the most fun. Candy was a good sport; she took it. John was ultimately sitting on top of her, banging her head against the floor. John knew this was the way people did it in live television, and he was helping her get accustomed to the technical process.

The Peckinpah sketch ran the week following Bergen's appearance, with Gilda Radner as the abused party. Radner, too, was fine in physical comedy, though she owed more to traditional slapstick than did Belushi. Radner's falls seemed calculated, Belushi's an act of nature. O'Donoghue studied Belushi as he would a rare species of animal and soon came to call him the Bear Man.

O'Donoghue felt that Belushi was most effective when building gradually to an aggressive state, and with this in mind he wrote the first of several Weekend Update "rants." Originally a three-minute segment reserved for topical humor, Update quickly became Chevy Chase's showcase. As the segment expanded, guest "commentators" appeared to give "editorial replies." Chase often remained in shot as the commentators spoke, mugging and undermining whatever point they attempted to make. With Belushi he kept a straight face; Chase introduced Belushi as a "meteorologist" who had something to say about March coming in like a lion and going out like a lamb:

> Thank you, Chevy. Well, another winter is almost over and March, true to form, has come in like a lion and hopefully will go out like a lamb. At least that's how March works here in the United States. But did you know March behaves differently in other countries? In Norway, March comes in like a polar bear and goes out like a walrus. Or take the case of Honduras, where March comes in like a lamb and goes out like a salt-marsh harvest mouse. Let us compare this to the Maldive Islands, where March comes in like a wildebeest and goes out like an ant—a *tiny little* ant about *this big* . . .

Belushi cites other examples of March around the world. In South Africa it comes in like a lion and goes out like a different lion; one has a mane and the other doesn't. And then there's a country where March "hops in like a kangaroo, stays a kangaroo for a while, then it becomes a slightly *smaller* kangaroo. Then for a few days it's sort of a cross between a frilled lizard and a common housecat, then it changes *back* into the smaller kangaroo, and then it goes out like a wild dingo." Belushi is fully revved. "And it's *not* Australia! Now you'd think it would be Australia but it's *not!*" Chase tries to calm him, but Belushi erupts. "NOW LOOK, PAL!" he yells, shoves Chase aside, rattles off more examples until he suffers a heart attack and flies off camera.

So successful was the routine that O'Donoghue and Belushi did little to alter it: Belushi spoke slowly and seemingly rationally, then built to a seizure and died. The "weatherman" character appeared again two episodes later, with Belushi ranting about weather in song titles—"April Showers," "Let It Snow," "Stormy Weather," and so on. But this version surprisingly lacked the necessary verve; when Belushi keeled over it was almost an afterthought, more flop than mad convulsion. In future rants Belushi played himself and went off on tangents unrelated to the subject at hand. (Perhaps his best rant in this line dealt with the "bad luck of the Irish," during which Belushi segued from the topic into a diatribe about his friend, Dan Sullivan.) When he reached seizure point he pushed it to the limit and died in a spectacular, violent manner. Belushi never again simply flopped.

By the middle of *Saturday Night*'s first season the show finally boasted the mix of comedy styles that Lorne Michaels had initially sought. Marilyn Miller joined the program when Lily Tomlin hosted, and her sketches stood out from the more satirical fare. One of her early, celebrated pieces, "Slumber Party," focused on a group of girls who discussed sex in adolescent terms. The piece felt "real" because Miller was never one to succumb to mere jokes; her humor was organic to the situation she portrayed, and in "Slumber Party" that meant wide-eyed girls both sickened and drawn to the mechanics of intercourse. Like Miller, Dan Aykroyd was a singular force on *Saturday Night,* and in the first season he not only created the perfect, rapid-fire pitchman (for Bass-o-matic, Vibromatic, and Mel's Char Palace, "where you find your own cow, you cut your own steaks"), but he became the show's true prodigy. Aykroyd, it seemed, could do anything; and his method of comic acting, at once robotic and fluid, made distinctive the characters he inhabited. He joked that the ultimate *Saturday Night* cast would consist of "humanoids or clones" and doubtless he would have been the prototype. But it's hard to imagine any life-form that could match Aykroyd at his best.

Despite the varied styles that emerged in *Saturday Night*'s first year, the reigning theme for many sketches continued to be death, and this could be all attributed to O'Donoghue. As he had on the *Lampoon,* O'Donoghue set a mood in which death and dying were seen by the show's writers as a legitimate source of humor. Chevy Chase wrote a cold opening featuring the "Dead String Quartet" in which dead musicians "performed" by slumping over their instruments. (Chase scripted a similar bit in which he played poker with the dead, but this never survived dress rehearsal.) Alan Zweibel, the Catskill jokemeister known more for his Weekend Update material, tried his hand at death humor with "Cresk," a toothpaste for the dead. ("Johnny's body will rot, but his teeth won't! Not with new Cresk, now with formaldehyde!") But where Chase lacked a sinister edge and Zweibel imitated *Mad* magazine, it was Franken and Davis who consistently (but not always ably) dealt with bleak topics such as death, disease, and violence.

The first real example of this came on the Candice Bergen Christmas show. The team penned a sketch called "Parents' Nightmare" in which they, too, found humor in the Dean Corll serial murders. Although brief and not as graphic as O'Donoghue's *Lampoon* piece, (Chase's character vaguely describes his participation in the killings) "Nightmare" revealed a side of Franken and Davis that their critics both on and off the show used to denigrate their material; many felt the team was self-consciously tasteless and could not effectively handle the same topics that O'Donoghue had made his name satirizing. O'Donoghue, glancing at their work, concurred.

But despite his condescension to the younger, "lesser," writers and his belief that they wrote "shit," O'Donoghue showed that he, too, was capable of producing less-than-stellar material. For the Dyan Cannon episode in May, O'Donoghue wrote "Bathwater of the Stars," in which the water left over from a celebrity's bath is bottled and sold to the public. Ostensibly a parody of celebrity culture, "Bathwater" is a roll call of B-level personalities such as Doug McClure and Shelley Winters and does nothing but reflect O'Donoghue's disgust for the dregs of show business. Another, better-known bit was "Fluckers." Here the premise is even simpler: If an awful name such as Fluckers is used to promote quality jam, then it corresponds that the worse the brand name, the better the jam. O'Donoghue trots them all out—Nose Hair, Death Camp, Dog Vomit, Monkey Pus, Mangled Baby Ducks, 10,000 Nuns and Orphans All Eaten By Rats, and the topper, Painful Rectal Itch. "Fluckers" received plenty of laughter from the studio audience, but even O'Donoghue partisan Chevy Chase, who uttered the Painful Rectal Itch line, felt the piece was cheap, and his discomfort clearly showed on camera.

"Fluckers" appeared on the April 17 Ron Nessen episode. Nessen, then President Ford's press secretary, hosted *Saturday Night* as a publicity stunt to show that the administration had a sense of humor and could take a joke. Minor intrigue developed: Could the administration co-opt this maverick program, or would *Saturday Night* emerge with its integrity intact? Of course, were *Saturday Night* truly beyond the pale Nessen would go nowhere near it, and Lorne Michaels would naturally reject any official overture. But like *Laugh-In,* which achieved notoriety when it featured Richard Nixon saying "Sock it to *me?*", *Saturday Night* was part of the American entertainment combine and thus subject to mainstream influence—the presidency, to cite one example.* In fact, it was arranged that Ford himself say "Live from New York, it's *Saturday Night.*" So there was no real political tension to be played with or skewered, and the show itself was filled not with satirical strikes against the

*Indeed, Ron Nessen's appearance began a *Saturday Night* political tradition of sorts. Mainstream political figures such as Julian Bond, John Anderson, Ed Koch, George McGovern, Jesse Jackson, Bill Bradley, Lamar Alexander, Rudolph Giuliani, George Pataki, and Steve Forbes have either hosted or appeared on the show—additional proof that in America there is little separation of satire and state.

empire but with gratuitous sex and toilet humor. (One excuse given for this was that due to a technician's strike that week, all the pieces had to conform to stationary camera set-ups—no "subtlety" or "complexity" allowed.) When mixed with different forms this style of humor is fine; but to pile it in one spot simply because the President is watching smacks of something other than satire, and in retrospect a few *Saturday Night* staffers, especially Chase, admitted as much.

The Nessen episode led to a righteous outcry in the mainstream media. It was generally felt that the Ford administration had lowered itself to a grimy depth and that its PR effort had backfired. Of those protesting, it was syndicated columnist Harriet Van Horne who provided some of the more amusing observations. Van Horne bought into the idea of *Saturday Night* as an outlaw show—"uncensored," as she wrongly put it—and she ceded the "natural" right of the president to engage in the manufacture of image. After analyzing the "sleazy" show and the amoral environment that had produced it, Van Horne closed her column on a high note: "But let us cry 'Enough!' to the vulgarity that spits in our faces. Are we not, at long last, sated with gang rapes, mass murder and Nazi cabaret humor? Nobody craves a diet of Disney and John–Boy Waltons, but isn't it time for a diminuendo in the smut and savagery? Have all of us, including President Ford and his press secretary, lost our sense of shame?"

Van Horne's column was widely read and commented on in the *Saturday Night* offices. Though an argument could have been made that the Nessen episode was simply one of the weaker shows of *Saturday Night*'s first season, Van Horne reinforced the image of a satirical program out of control. This made it easier for the *Saturday Night* staff to dismiss this and related criticisms (though the notoriety created by such criticism was embraced). "Who is Harriet Van Horne?" asked Chevy Chase. "Her name alone should suggest the problems that woman must have." O'Donoghue added, "Yes, *dear* Harriet. She called us, I believe, a moral mudslide. She said, and please correct me if I err, that the *Saturday Night* show is the seventies equivalent of the Nazi cabaret acts. She linked us to mass murder. Youth gangs. Most of the decline of the West—we're the headwaters of it, I think." O'Donoghue's tone suggested that *Saturday Night* reflected none of these things, and to a degree this was true. The show had a broader base than just violence and death. But still, some of O'Donoghue's best material was rooted in the very "savagery" Van Horne bewailed. This could not be dismissed, nor should it have been. It was one of the elements that distinguished *Saturday Night* from other mainstream fare.

In the second half of the show's first season, O'Donoghue produced some exceptional violent imagery that seemed at home on television but didn't quite fit existing categories. For the Tony Perkins episode he parodied the film *Psycho* without losing the Hitchcock feel. Perkins as Norman Bates appears in a late-night commercial in which he promotes his school of motel management. Norman stands behind a check-in desk in a dimly lit motel lobby. As he explains the advantages of running one's own motel, the camera cuts suddenly to a stuffed duck hanging near the ceiling; after a few more words, a swift cut to a stuffed owl. Both non sequitur shots pay homage to Hitchcock and help to set a strange tone. The birds cast deep shadows and the camera shakes a bit while recording each image. This gives the piece an off-balance look that heightens the *Psycho* effect. Norman tells prospective managers that they can learn the motel trade in the privacy of their own showers, but are they motel material? He offers a quiz:

Question One—A guest loses her key to her room. Would you:
(a) Give her a duplicate key.
(b) Let her in with your passkey.
(c) Hack her to death with a kitchen knife.

Question Two—Which of the following is the *most* important in running a successful motel?
(a) Cordial atmosphere.
(b) Courteous service.
(c) Hack her to death with a kitchen knife.

The quiz is interrupted by Norman's "mother," who informs him of an "important phone call." Before he leaves to take the call, Norman tells those interested to send their names and addresses to him, but: "There's no obligation whatsoever and no salesman will call so . . . uh . . . d-d-don't b-bother to lock your door. Uh . . . just leave it off th-th-th-th-th-the latch. Or lock it, that's fine, I don't care. I don't care if you lock it . . . 'cause I've got the key. I've got the key right here, I've got the key to room one—I've got the key to room two—I've got the key to room three . . ." Mother again interrupts, and Norman, ever the obedient son, exits while flashing a sinister smile.

"The Norman Bates School of Motel Management" was helped of course, by having Perkins reprise his famous character; he knew best the rhythms of Norman's speech, including his murderous stutter, and O'Donoghue catered to this perfectly. But for all its dark and strange qualities the Norman Bates piece was a parody of a fictional killer in a film that was then over fifteen years old. Claudine Longet, on the other hand, was soon to face trial for manslaughter. Longet was the former Mrs. Andy Williams, and her affair with professional skier Spider Sabich ended when she "accidentally" shot him in the stomach with a gun she claimed Sabich was showing her how to use. This led to a media furor about Longet's guilt or innocence. Chevy Chase wrote an Update story in which Longet killed another skier, Jean-Claude Killy, by demonstrating how she mistakenly shot Sabich; then O'Donoghue expanded the premise by concocting a ski tournament called "The Claudine Longet Invitational."

O'Donoghue got hold of stock footage of downhill skiers tripping and tumbling into the snow. Before each fall the sound of gunfire was dubbed in so that it appeared the skiers were hit by precise shots to the body. Chase and Jane Curtin played the commentators covering the event, and when a gun went off and a skier fell, Chase intoned, "Uh oh! He seems to have been accidentally shot by Claudine Longet!" A one-joke premise in which the gunshots sound like those in a cartoon, the piece nevertheless touched a nerve. The studio audience laughed nervously, while at home Andy Williams was appalled by the implications made at the expense of his estranged wife. He threatened NBC with a lawsuit that was averted when *Saturday Night* broadcast an apology two weeks after the piece aired. It was the only apology the show ever issued, and O'Donoghue reveled in the fact that he was responsible for the entire mess.

Longet was a singular target and easily cut down. The "Invitational" 's edge was the potential legal trouble it stirred up for the show. The piece has been celebrated as "outrageous" by TV critics and O'Donoghue himself, but the merits of the "Invitational" are minor when compared to O'Donoghue's scathing attack on the Los Angeles police department in a sketch called "Police State." O'Donoghue is narrator Jeremy Musk; he tells us that all those people who were jailed on *Dragnet* have been released, every one of them. Thus a new breed of cop is required to bring them in. This new breed is personified by Chase and Dan Aykroyd, who play a police duo that literally kills without question. The order "Stop or I'll shoot!" comes after one suspect has been shot several times, and another has his Miranda rights read him once he is dead. In between the executions the cops discuss what they should have for dinner: "How 'bout Indian? You wanna eat Indian?" Chase asks Aykroyd while a suspect bleeds at their feet. Soon the question shifts from food to murder.

> CHASE: "Hey, Champ. How would you feel about Mexican? Would you like to kill Mexican tonight?"
> AYKROYD: "Didn't we kill Mexican last night?"
> CHASE: "That wasn't Mexican. That was Filipino."
> AYKROYD: "Six of one, amigo. Six of one . . ."

Set within the frame of a cop show, "Police State" incorporates not just the clichés of the genre but includes elements of Joseph Wambaugh's police novels and real-life reports of the LAPD's brutality. The sketch was marred slightly by a technical flaw: As a bridge linking the murder sequences, O'Donoghue had a model-size street intersection built on which toy cars and trucks were to smash into each other. But once the sketch began the toy cars just sat there while the sounds of skids and crashes flooded the audio. Stagehands neglected to push the cars along the tiny street, and while seemingly a minor error, this essentially brought the sketch to a stop until live action resumed. (In the final two segments, however, the cars were thrown into a pile, doused with lighter fluid, and set aflame, which rounded out the sketch as O'Donoghue intended.) Despite the mistake, "Police State" remains an O'Donoghue classic. He not only anticipated "reality" police shows such as *COPS*, but he reflected the racist musings of detectives such as Mark Fuhrman and those L.A. patrolmen who referred to the Rodney King beating as "monkey-slapping time."

Throughout the show's first year O'Donoghue was kept on a moderately long leash by the network's censors. A lot of material that he thought would be forbidden was allowed on air with few, if any, alterations. As he later explained, "There were still Standards and Practices problems and I can understand that. I mean, I understand greed being part of the American system and can work around that. You can't step on the toes of certain advertisers [which] makes fair enough sense. If you understood the guidelines and worked within them, NBC's people would meet you halfway." On *Saturday Night,* O'Donoghue at first dealt with Standards editor Jay Ottley, who was pretty tolerant of the show's stronger content. The same was true of Ottley's boss, Standards vice-president Herminio Traviesas, who, despite personal reservations concerning the show's humor, was considered reasonable by many on staff. For a brief period Ottley's role was assumed by Jane Crowley, who was *not* considered reasonable by anyone, especially O'Donoghue. A strict Catholic, Crowley objected to much of *Saturday Night*'s humor and took a hard line on material she believed offensive or immoral. Yet as is often the case with censorship, Crowley's rigidity led to a contradictory enforcement of network standards. A shining example of this was seen when Raquel Welch hosted on April 24.

In an episode dominated by tit jokes—inescapable, it seemed, with Welch as the host—O'Donoghue contributed two pieces: "The Claudine Longet Invitational" and John Belushi's second weatherman rant for Weekend Update. Given the direct and potentially libelous attack on Longet, one might have expected the "Invitational" to be severely edited, if not cut completely from the show. But the Longet piece sailed directly to air while the Belushi rant was held up. In his review of weather-related songs, O'Donoghue dissected "Don't Rain on My Parade" and wrote, "There are a lot worse things that could happen to a parade than a little rain. What about 'Don't Blow Your Nose on My Parade'? Or 'Don't Throw Up on My Parade'? Or 'Don't Take a Dump on My Parade'? After a few things like that a little rain wouldn't seem so bad, would it?" Crowley objected to "Take a Dump" and demanded that O'Donoghue change it to something else. O'Donoghue angrily appealed but Crowley was adamant. According to a writer for *New Times* magazine who visited the show that week, O'Donoghue went crazy looking for an alternate title.

"I can't *believe* it!" O'Donoghue was quoted as saying. "They took out 'dump'! Can you believe it? They won't let us say 'dump'! You could say 'Don't *Bleed* on My Parade.' They wouldn't mind *that.* But you can't say 'take a dump'!" Hours passed and O'Donoghue continued ranting about the rant. "The challenge here is to come up with something ten times more distasteful—but something they gotta pass. . . . You wanna make 'em squirm, make 'em say, Oh Christ, why didn't I just let him have 'take a dump.' " Finally, O'Donoghue arrived at a title he could live with. "I never had an idea that when you got censors it would be all this trouble . . . But *now* I got 'em! How do you like *this?* . . . 'Don't Drain Your Boils on My Parade.' All that, and what do they gain? Is it any better to talk about *draining boils* than to say 'take a dump'?" Crowley approved of the change and Belushi delivered the line, but his rant, as previously noted, elicited few laughs; it's doubtful that "take a dump" would have improved Belushi's chances. Why Crowley balked at this weak one-liner but allowed the Longet piece on is a mystery of the television mind-set. One is tempted to think that O'Donoghue's dramatic fuss was a cover for the "Invitational," given that at times he filled scripts with profanity to divert attention from the joke he preferred. But as had been the case at the *Lampoon,* O'Donoghue furiously resisted changes in his work. His "take a dump" snit was no doubt genuine, and as *Saturday Night* grew and his influence waned, O'Donoghue would become ever more vocal about the "raping and strangling" of his material.

Most of the sketches O'Donoghue submitted in the first year were aired with few, if any, major revisions. But when it came to Weekend Update he often encountered resistance. The Belushi rant was mild compared to some of the items he wrote for Chevy Chase, a fair number of which were deemed unfit by Jane Crowley and Herminio Traviesas. Regarding the FBI's harassment of Martin Luther King, O'Donoghue wrote,

According to recent disclosures of FBI activities, J. Edgar Hoover himself, disguising his voice, used to call Reverend Martin Luther King late at night, sometimes claiming to be a streetlight inspector, sometimes asking Reverend King if he had Prince Albert in a can. On one occasion, Hoover reportedly ordered six large pizzas, with anchovies, delivered to the black leader's residence. In a related item, FBI Director Clarence Kelley denied rumors that the Bureau's entire investigation into King's death consisted of asking a ouija board, "Who shot the monkey?"

After a busload of schoolchildren in Chowchilla, California, were held hostage in the summer of 1976, O'Donoghue wondered,

What will the smart, fashionable woman be wearing this fall? From California comes the answer—a lovely, floor-length Chowchilla coat. Chowchilla coats—made from the skins of twenty-six school children. They're not in stores yet but it's only a matter of time.

O'Donoghue resubmitted this item during the show's second season, once with Jackie Onassis wearing the coat, "now available in two shades—natural and Mexican"; and after a school bus accident in Macon, Georgia, in which many children lost their lives, he altered the Chowchilla coat to include "big Negro patches." Despite the revisions, or perhaps *in* spite of them, the network censors never allowed this item on; but for the Dick Cavett episode, on January 31, they did approve an O'Donoghue item that provoked a strong viewer response:

The popular TV personality known as "Professor Backwards" was slain in Atlanta yesterday by three masked gunmen. According to reports, neighbors ignored the professor's cries of "PLEH! PLEH!"

The studio audience erupted in gasps and laughter. Chase, who read the item, was unaware that Professor Backwards was indeed a real person and thus he was a bit thrown by the reaction. Within days the show was deluged with mail protesting the joke, and Chase composed a letter of apology that was copied and sent to the offended. "I felt very bad that I had used the joke," he wrote, "and worse that I didn't research the whole story better before taking the chance that someone might be hurt by this item. It is done. It is a lesson learned. I'm sorry you were offended, and only hope no one close to the man was within viewing distance." O'Donoghue, on the other hand, saw no reason to apologize for this or any of his material. "Comedy is a baby seal hunt," he liked to say, and who is less contrite than a veteran seal hunter?

Though the show received its share of bad reviews and negative mail, the majority of mainstream critics enjoyed *Saturday Night* immensely. Tom Shales of the *Washington Post* and John J. O'Connor of the *New York Times* made much of *Saturday Night*'s distinctive place on American TV and celebrated its uniqueness. (O'Connor initially panned the show but changed his view soon after.) The venerable Cleveland Amory of *TV Guide* called the show "rare—if uneven—fun." Even the *New Yorker* took notice. In his meditation on the state of American humor, writer Michael Arlen said that *Saturday Night* projected its comedy "in a recognizable, human, non-celebrity voice—and in a voice, too, that tries to deal with the morass of media-induced show-business culture that increasingly pervades American life." *Saturday Night* did indeed assail television convention and the reigning celebrity culture, but did so by establishing its own conventions and playing to its favored celebrities: Lily Tomlin, Richard Pryor, Elliott Gould, Dick Cavett, Paul Simon— these were not strangers to the mainstream. If anything, *Saturday Night* represented a generational shift in entertainment; the "mavericks" now sat in corporate offices and churned out comedy to attract the demographic most desired by their corporate bosses, eighteen-to-thirty-four-year-old viewers. They also created new celebrities, Chevy Chase first among them. If their comedy was offbeat or strange, well, this was what the prime demographic responded to. Far from being an "outsider" show, *Saturday Night* was inevitable. There were simply too many people creating this type of humor and the networks could no longer ignore or dismiss them. Lorne Michaels understood this as well as anyone, which is why he had pushed for such a show since 1972.

The final crack in *Saturday Night*'s outlaw facade came on May 17, 1976, when the show won four Emmy awards, including Best Writing in a Comedy/Variety Series and Best Comedy/Variety Series. Chevy Chase received an acting award and Dave Wilson won for his direction of the show. *Saturday Night*'s only real competition that night was the *Carol Burnett Show*—a remnant of the variety programs of the 1950s and 1960s. That *Saturday Night* steamrolled the pleasant, crowd-pleasing Burnett and her staff proved that the mainstream had moved to its next stage. "Hip" humor was in, the "cutting edge" advertiser-friendly. Hollywood took notice while across the country in countless living rooms, adolescents and teenagers watched *Saturday Night* religiously and hoped that one day they too would earn a living in comedy. The seeds of a comic boom were planted.

seven

You know the best way to measure a comic sketch on TV? In kilowatts used. Like, would my sketch light up Boulder Dam? So I'm not thinking in terms of laughs—I'm thinking in terms of kilowatts used.

Michael O'Donoghue did nothing to resist the show's success. He not only told his friends that *Saturday Night* was his ticket to a film career, he predicted how the show would evolve, or de-evolve. Tom Davis remembered that before the premiere O'Donoghue told him, "This is going to be a huge hit, and it's going to peak in two years, and then I'm getting out. Then everyone is going to consume each other cannibalistically and say, 'It was my idea! It was my idea!' There'll be a big squabble over money and people won't speak to each other." Davis asked O'Donoghue on what did he base his prediction. O'Donoghue smiled and said, "*The Lampoon.*"

While in Los Angeles for the Emmys, O'Donoghue basked in the postawards glow. He and Anne Beatts rented a bungalow at the Beverly Hills Hotel and threw a party celebrating *Saturday Night*'s full acceptance by mainstream television. Indeed, O'Donoghue referred to the Emmys as the moment when he sold out; he enjoyed the rewards of show business without guilt or second thoughts. O'Donoghue had several reasons to feel good at Emmy time: He was a major part of a critically acclaimed, award-winning show; he was doing well financially; and most important, he and Beatts were back together following a brief separation.

At the end of 1975 and well into 1976, O'Donoghue remained angry and depressed. What caused this mental turmoil was a mystery to Beatts as she watched him either fly off the handle or emotionally withdraw. This led inevitably to conflict. Also, Beatts was finishing *Titters,* which O'Donoghue did not fully support. Beatts herself withdrew from the relationship, and in the spring of 1976 she moved into an apartment of her own. While she continued to see O'Donoghue at the office, she refused to go home with him once work was done. Then, in April,

Beatts was involved in a taxi accident. Though she was not seriously hurt, O'Donoghue showed concern and pushed for a reconciliation. To Beatts he seemed earnest and sincere; after all, in his better moments he revered her and made her the center of attention. Beatts accepted, the fighting ceased, and O'Donoghue appeared to brighten somewhat. During this period he wrote a few less-than-dark pieces for the show, one of which many critics consider the best sketch in *Saturday Night*'s history: "The Last Voyage of the Starship *Enterprise*."

O'Donoghue conceived "Last Voyage" in early April and finished the script in mid-May. While putting the piece together, he sometimes sought chemical assistance. "I would smoke dope and read the [*Star Trek*] books and get little lines in and look at the episodes and even string it together to some extent," he said, and it was, in many ways, his most ambitious effort of the season. The piece would run for nearly twelve minutes and end, Ernie Kovacs–style, with the set completely disassembled.

"Last Voyage" is just that: The crew of the *Enterprise* are followed through space by a 1968 Chrysler Imperial that carries Herb Goodman, the (fictional) head of programming for NBC. The Imperial overtakes the ship, which Goodman boards so he may cancel *Star Trek*. Meantime, the show's characters do everything in their power to prevent this ulti-

With Anne Beatts, near the end of their relationship

mate annihilation, but their prop guns stop working, the ship's power is cut off, and technicians begin to put away the prop computers, console, and turbolift. Dr. McCoy, Mr. Sulu, and Lieutenant Uhura break character and call it quits. Mr. Spock tries to remain logical and in control, but suddenly he flips out and wanders amid the turmoil muttering to himself. Only Captain Kirk resists, but it is fruitless; he is left alone on an empty set to ponder his next career move.

During the many hours he spent polishing "Last Voyage," O'Donoghue captured the precise cadences of *Star Trek*'s major characters. He strove to match the original in every way he could, from the techno-banter on the bridge to the "action" sequence, which here consisted of the camera titling right to left. He extensively detailed the type of costumes he wanted from Wardrobe and insisted that the set lighting convey the same look as a *Star Trek* episode. His script was well served by the cast—Chase's Spock and Aykroyd's McCoy are particularly good. But it is John Belushi's Kirk that truly stands out in the sketch. Known for his Brando and Joe Cocker impressions, Belushi was no serious mimic; there was something of himself in every character he portrayed, and when it came to William Shatner this was especially so. Though made up to look the part, Belushi could not shade Kirk in a distinctive accent or physical outburst: "You gotta *act* it," he said, and act it he did.

Belushi was helped by O'Donoghue's dialogue. Kirk's speeches and exchanges with Spock read as though written for Shatner himself, blended with O'Donoghue's imagery:

I have a hunch, Mr. Spock, that we are about to face a menace more terrifying than the flying parasites of Ingraham B; more insidious than the sand bats of Manark 4; more bloodthirsty than the vampire clouds of Argus 10. I have a hunch that "thing" out there is deadlier than the Romulans, the Klingons, and the Gorns, all rolled into one.

Belushi turned, in his words, "this dumpy little body into William Shatner." He also assumed Shatner's speech patterns, all pauses and quick declarations—"I . . . *havahunch,* Mr. Spock . . ." When informed that "life support systems are still operative," Belushi's Kirk replies, "But for how long, Mr. Spock . . . for-*how*-long?" Throughout rehearsals, including dress, O'Donoghue feared that Belushi lacked the agility to effectively play Kirk. Belushi brought little to the character until the live show, and there, when it counted, he delivered—to the relief of O'Donoghue, who nervously watched just off camera. Belushi's Kirk was first in what would become a long line of Shatner impressions; but when compared to, say, Jim Carrey's over-the-top Kirk on *In Living Color,* Belushi was positively mannered. Indeed, he lent the role more dignity than did Shatner himself in the later *Star Trek* films.

Ambitious, colorful, well-acted, and funny, "Last Voyage" neverthe-less does not live up to its reputation as the "best" sketch ever seen on *Saturday Night*. No doubt familiarity contributed to this assessment: *Star Trek* enjoys a near-cult status in American pop culture and thus is easily understood; one need not strive to "get" the jokes in "Last Voyage" or any subsequent treatment.* *Star Trek* creator Gene Roddenberry called it "delicious" and "imaginatively conceived"; and NBC, which receives O'Donoghue's scorn throughout the piece and in Kirk's final speech—"except for one television network, we have found intelligent life every-where in the galaxy"—allowed "Last Voyage" on as O'Donoghue intended. (In fact, he said that NBC was "good-natured" about the whole thing.) "The Last Voyage of the Starship *Enterprise*" was among the better sketches in the show's first year, but as satire "Police State" had more bite, as parody "Citizen Kane II" showed more imagination. One of O'Donoghue's best *Saturday Night* pieces had not yet been conceived, and when written, it, unlike "Last Voyage," would never get on the air.

"Last Voyage" appeared on the May 29 episode, hosted by Elliott Gould (his second stint that year), following which the show's cast and crew went on extended hiatus. With all of June and half of July off, and with *Titters* finished and in production, O'Donoghue and Beatts set sail for Paris on the QE2. Their reconciliation had for the most part gone smoothly and both looked to a romantic vacation in Europe. In addition to Paris, they traveled to England, Italy, and Greece, took in the sights, and unwound from the pressures of live television—or at least tried to. Beatts saw O'Donoghue sink back into depression from time to time during their trip, and as before this led to clashes between the two. When they returned to New York, Beatts noticed that "Michael seemed very unhappy. He talked about the meaning of life and [how] he was going to stay in a Trappist monastery for a week." Darkness and depres-sion hung over Sixteenth Street for the better part of August. Finally, Beatts reached her rope's end.

"At that point it started to sink in on me that this is who he was and I was not going to make him happy," she said. "And that's what tore it for me because I ran out of reasons to say 'Well, he's only being like this because . . .' So that was it." On Labor Day weekend Beatts

*When William Shatner hosted *Saturday Night Live* in 1986, he appeared in two *Star Trek* sketches, one of which is equal to "Last Voyage": Shatner plays himself addressing a *Star Trek* convention. Standing in front of a crowd of pathetic "Trekkers," Shatner erupts: "Get a life, will you, people! I mean, look at you, look at the way you're dressed. You've turned an enjoyable little job that I did as a lark for a few years into a colossal waste of time. . . . It's just a TV show, dammit! It's just a TV show!"

moved out of the Winter Palace and into the Gramercy Park Hotel. Naturally, O'Donoghue was quite upset and saw her move as a betrayal. "I mean, *everything* was a betrayal," said Beatts. "Hanging his sweater on a hook instead of a hanger was a betrayal." (This in reference to the time when Beatts sent O'Donoghue into hysterics because she had stretched the neck of a favorite sweater.) "My part in [O'Donoghue's obsessions] was to tolerate it and treat it seriously. But he was very convincing to people. I think he got people to treat trivial things very seriously, which he always claimed was what made him what he was, that he was obsessed with trivia."

O'Donoghue lobbied for Beatts's return. As before, he promised to change, do anything to get her back. But Beatts never returned to Sixteenth Street; her break from O'Donoghue was final. The only problem was that she had to work with him on *Saturday Night,* which was about to begin its second season. As Beatts readied herself for the premiere on September 18 (hosted, fittingly enough, by Lily Tomlin), O'Donoghue lay covered in black mist. Migraines came and went. The TV stayed on for hours, its volume jacked up. Dope was smoked, Percodan taken. Amid all this he wrote short, extremely violent pieces in which the characters ended up mutilated, dead, or both. It was a time, as he later put it, of *"snakes on everything."*

> *Actually, I've always found that negative life conditions have produced great work conditions. The worse my life has been, the better my work has been.*

After its critically acclaimed first season, *Saturday Night* entered what proved to be an interesting, transitional period. A major change was the departure of Chevy Chase. An Emmy Award–winning celebrity on the rise, Chase was practically required by the laws of American showbiz to advance to a larger, more lucrative stage—specifically, Hollywood. (He also wished to marry his girlfriend, who lived in Los Angeles.) Talk of his leaving had started earlier that year, and by the beginning of the second season it was decided that Chase would move into prime time as the star of his own comedy specials. Chase was to appear in the first six episodes of *Saturday Night*'s new season, then gradually fade from the show through a few cameo spots. Appearing as Gerald Ford in the September 18 premiere, Chase bruised his testicles falling onto a podium. He was off the show until October 16, then formally left after the Buck Henry episode, on October 30.

In the two episodes Chase missed through injury, the cast and writers caught a glimpse of how *Saturday Night* would soon appear. Jane Curtin assumed the anchor desk on Weekend Update and delivered the "news" in a low-key, straitlaced manner. In time Curtin developed her own

Update persona of a smooth, slightly ironic newswoman who tightened at any incompetence she perceived around her. John Belushi, who had chafed a bit under Chase's sudden fame, stepped forward to fill the gap with considerable comic energy. Like Curtin, Belushi developed an on-air persona, though his was more on the manic side; he began to play "himself" in a number of sketches, sometimes breaking the reality of a scene ("It's no good!" he complained in a *Dragnet* spoof in which he wore a dress and demanded that the sketch be abandoned), other times addressing the camera as John Belushi—whether to announce his retirement from show business so he could train for the 1980 Olympics, or simply to offer to sell the clothes off his back.

Belushi also received a co-writing credit with Dan Aykroyd, to whom he grew rather close. Aykroyd's presence in the first season was unique, but with a year of television behind him, he now pushed into some truly strange areas. At its best, Aykroyd's humor featured elements of mysticism, technology, violence, and mechanics. His premises were conceptual but firm; no matter how odd or ethereal the idea it was always grounded in Aykroyd's sense of reason. Early in the second season he wrote a piece with Marilyn Miller called "The Snake-Handling O'Sheas." A parody of Norman Lear sitcoms in which each character boasts a distinctive identity—Dad's a hard hat, Mom's an executive, Daughter's a nun, and Son's a gay state trooper—the piece veers into religious insanity as the family waves living snakes around while they chant and speak in tongues. The image, like that of the bald Manson women in O'Donoghue's human-hair potholder piece, is uncompromising and direct. And it is Aykroyd, as the state trooper, who emits the eeriest of chants, a furious, primal sound that fit no existing category of humor.

Throughout the second season Aykroyd wrote many conceptual pieces that defied the common notion of sketch comedy. One, "Blog Diet," focuses on a woman desperate to lose weight. She is dragged off by fascist guards to an ice hut in a simulated Arctic environment. There she must catch and eat whatever she can find, but only if she can hide it from Blog, a nutritionist disguised as an Eskimo. Since Blog watches everything on a closed-circuit video system, the woman keeps nothing she catches and thus she presumably sheds pounds. Another, "Dr. X: Family Counselor," concerns a psychotherapist who wears an iron mask and has a metal arm—the result of a nuclear waste spill and rocket sled accident, respectively. Dr. X tries to help the "M" family with their problems, but the son wants to know what happened to his face and arm. Dr. X starts to tell but is overcome by trauma; he screams, then shrugs it off by saying, "Oh, nothing." After several of these outbursts the son is sent to work in Dr. X's lab, where he meets death via a flesh-searing laser.

Aykroyd's work of this period fascinated his co-workers—O'Donoghue and Marilyn Miller especially. Together they would analyze what it was about Aykroyd's humor that made it unique, even for *Saturday Night*. Both had a special fondness for an Aykroyd piece titled "Metal Detector." In it, Aykroyd passes through an airport metal detector over and over again; each pass sets off the alarm and Aykroyd must surrender more metal objects in his possession, silverware, bits of armor, and so forth. A large pile accumulates, and Aykroyd is forced to strip to his waist, where he is covered in chains and locks. Beneath his wool hat is a metallic skullcap. "I love metal!" he exclaims to the beleaguered security guard, who finally allows him through. He sweeps up the pile and heads to his gate. He is followed by the Tin Woodsman from Oz, who naturally sets off the alarm but is waved along by the guard. This must serve as a punch line since the piece itself is nothing but Aykroyd removing metal objects from his trench coat and body.

"Metal Detector" is reminiscent of a Harpo Marx routine; but unlike Harpo, who when faced with a problem or challenge produced a variety of items from his magic coat, Aykroyd is simply a metal freak who must catch his flight. Each time they saw the sketch, from rehearsals to air, O'Donoghue and Miller discussed its logic and tried to discern what made it work. Like most of Aykroyd's second season output, no one explanation would cover the scope and depth of his peculiar humor. Once this season ended and *Saturday Night* became a celebrity/comedy machine, Aykroyd never really returned to those strange areas that inspired his best work. Remnants always remained, primarily in the mechanistic chatter of the Coneheads (which he developed with Tom Davis), but over time Aykroyd's humor became soft and user-friendly. The man who had created "Blog Diet" wound up busting ghosts and turned Beldar Conehead from an alien misanthrope into a cuddly Earth Daddy.

Like Aykroyd's work, Marilyn Miller's output during the second season was distinctive; she composed some beautifully realized comic vignettes. Miller's humor was less conceptual than Aykroyd's and seemed better suited to the theater than to television. Indeed, Miller's pieces were perhaps the most theatrical in *Saturday Night*'s history; she wrote *scenes,* not sketches; the humor was found in the characters, not in the premises. In a piece featuring Lily Tomlin's character Tess, there is pathos, too. Tess is in her dingy apartment eating cereal out of the box. She is visited by a salesman who shows her some commemorative coins celebrating the Apollo space missions. As the salesman hawks his coins, Tess interrupts him with questions and observations that have nothing to do with the situation at hand. She is lonely and has called on the salesman simply to have someone to talk to. He becomes irritated and leaves. If Tess is heartbroken we do not see it; she mutters to herself, grabs the cereal box, and plops in a chair to watch the Three Stooges. Tomlin, as usual, is brilliant. Her character evokes both pity and laughter, for we know that more than one Tess exists in the world, and their existence is as tragic as it is anonymous.

Another piece, set in even dingier surroundings, concerns a young, working-class woman who tries to deal with her husband's impotence. Why he cannot summon his "manly powers" is unclear, but the wife deflects her husband's shame and anger by creating a story about how she came to choose him over his rival while in cheerleader camp. It's a preposterous tale—the letter *H* for "Henry" formed on her knee after she knelt in gravel and prayed for a sign—but it soothes her husband as she promises to love him regardless of his condition. They embrace as the camera pulls back. The young marrieds are played by Sissy Spacek and John Belushi, both of whom give dramatic life to even the tiniest detail in Miller's script. Belushi especially shines here—his emotions range from anger to embarrassment to jealously to vulnerability, and he slips from one into the other with true poise. The scene is shot and acted in *Playhouse 90* fashion, and for a few moments one nearly forgets that the piece is connected to a larger show.

A new but seasoned voice was brought in at the beginning of the second season. Bruce McCall had left the *Lampoon* and freelanced for magazines as diverse as *Esquire* and *Oui*. But work was intermittent, and McCall expressed to O'Donoghue his interest in writing for *Saturday Night*. O'Donoghue set his friend and former colleague up with Lorne Michaels, who, after a midsummer meeting, hired McCall as an apprentice writer. Yet upon his arrival McCall knew immediately that the show was not his proper environment. Most of the staff smoked dope, watched TV, and went to bed at three A.M. McCall, on the other hand, used no drugs, watched very little television, and slid between the sheets by ten-thirty every night. Also, the staff had been together for a year; this had allowed them to form relationships, to adapt to each other's strengths and weaknesses, to develop and refine their own comic vision and language. McCall was the first new writer added to the mix since *Saturday Night* debuted, and this made him feel like an orphan. "I was low man on the totem pole, totally bewildered, and I didn't get it at all," he said, adding that O'Donoghue, who had pressed for his hiring, offered little assistance. "Michael was not available. He was storming around, critiquing everybody else's stuff and getting his own work pushed through."

A first-rate humorist and illustrator, McCall had plenty of ideas— one concept about an Eskimo RAF fighter pilot was bandied about but never realized—yet he admitted that he didn't know how to use the system. "Nobody was helpful," he said. "I was really isolated. I didn't have the nature or the balls to barge into somebody's office and say,

'What do you think of this?' They were all nice in a standoffish way. They tolerated my presence, but I was barely noticed. I wasn't any good at it, and I knew it." McCall did get a few items on the air, primarily some Baba Wawa bits for Gilda Radner, but the richness of his work in the *Lampoon* and on the *Radio Hour* would never be duplicated on *Saturday Night*. Once this became clear to him, McCall quit after only six installments of that year's show. As for O'Donoghue, he was, in McCall's words, "after bigger game."

> He was not a mentor. He was not interested in taking me on as a project and teaching me how to do the show. He was feeling his oats. He wanted to be the biggest force on that show to the point of fighting with Lorne. He always dismissed Lorne as a patsy. *He* knew what was best and this was his chance to elevate humor . . . by God from the moment he got there he was the world's greatest expert on what was funny. He had no doubts about that. He was scathing in his criticism of sketches that were "soft" or "not daring enough." He had a lordly disdain for the scribblings of lesser souls.

O'Donoghue's disdain took on emotional as well as creative features. His breakup with Anne Beatts drove him into even darker waters; he ceased trying to woo Beatts back into a relationship and alternately shunned and vilified her. He wrote a line with her in mind: "If the cops dusted your body, they'd find the fingerprints of every man in town." Beatts, unable to simply shut off her emotions, missed O'Donoghue's company. She didn't regret her decision to leave O'Donoghue but felt the process "was very painful." As Beatts pushed ahead with her duties as the show's script coordinator, O'Donoghue lashed out in his office. "Lots of broken phones," said Tom Davis, whose office was next to O'Donoghue's. "They had to bring a new phone in every other day. He would break the telephone. He would pick up the receiver with a person on the other end and smash it on a desk—'BOOM! BOOM!'—like that. The receiver was broken and the phone was smashed. He'd always be bleeding a little bit himself."

O'Donoghue's mood didn't translate immediately into dark, violent sketches—those were about to arrive. One of his first bits performed in the second season was a song called "The Antler Dance," which he wrote with Paul Shaffer. O'Donoghue wanted to start a silly dance craze, and in the song he tells the listener that "it's so easy you can do it, too":

Put your hands on your head like a big old moose,
Keep your elbows high and your legs real loose,
Then you groove around the floor, kind a leap and prance.
Shake your middle just a little and you're doin' the Antler Dance.

He also began an interesting collaboration with Tom Davis. Though never an official "team," they nevertheless wrote some of the stranger and more obscure pieces to ever appear on *Saturday Night*. One such piece was "Green Cross Cupcakes," which materialized one afternoon in O'Donoghue's office. "I don't know what we were thinking," said Davis. "We were smoking very potent pot and came up with this and it delighted us, and everybody else giggled when we read it at the read-through, so it got done." The piece centers on the scientific "fact" that Green Cross Cupcakes do not cause cancer. A housewife serves her husband Green Cross secure in the knowledge that he will not grow a tumor and die. To stress this, she wheels in a cage holding a dozen or so white rats, all of whom are still alive after five years of eating nothing but Green Cross. She then shows her husband "documented footage" from the Gamma Ray Bakery-Laboratories, where the cupcakes are made and tested: A pair of technicians in lab coats walk a cupcake-filled stretcher past glass cages that hold screaming rats as red lights flash and a siren wails. "No cancer, huh?" says the husband, impressed. "I'll have another, delicious Green Cross Cupcake. In fact, I'll have as many as I like!" As he stuffs his face, the housewife beams and confides, "Cancer-freeness never tasted so good."

The pot Davis and O'Donoghue smoked must have been quite potent, indeed. The commercial parody parts of "Green Cross" are standard, if curious—the housewife in the kitchen praising the cupcakes, the words "Truth in advertising" flashing on and off the screen as she speaks, and so on; but the "footage" from Gamma Ray Labs is strictly humor from and for the unconscious mind. Davis remembered it as "the biggest egg we ever laid," but the studio audience responded favorably, and it's likely that more than a few stoned home viewers shared in the joke that had so delighted Davis and O'Donoghue. As images go, the sight of rats screaming and clawing to get at cancer-free cupcakes is on the unusual side. But this was rather tame compared to another image O'Donoghue conceived during this period.

Fascinated that despite the civil rights movement and the expansion of the black middle class there still existed a toothpaste called Darkie, complete with smiling Negro on the tube, O'Donoghue wrote a takeoff called "Tarbrush"— a toothpaste "made for Negroes and their special needs." A black college girl is dressed for a dance. Her date arrives but is rebuffed after one look. "Kiss off, Kong-nose," she tells him. "I'd rather fingerlick the Colonel." He's confused: "My hair's all fuzzy, I just stole a customized van, and look—matchin' cuff links! Why won't you give me a tumble?" The reason lies in his teeth; they are too white. "And that turns me off!" the girl tells him. "You know what you're sufferin' from? You're sufferin' from Honky Tooth! Honky Tooth—four hundred years of slavery and racial oppression *in your mouth!* Why not give Tarbrush a try?"

He does. Tarbrush is literally a black toothpaste that turns white teeth "a rich, dark ebony." After brushing his teeth jet black, he returns to the girl, who yells, "Oooooo-wheeeee! Now your mouth looks like a load of coal!" They skip the dance and "get it on" instead.

Although supposedly a parody of racist products and negative imagery, "Tarbrush" struck many on *Saturday Night* as being too close to the real thing. Several staff members were made uncomfortable by the piece as it went through production, none more than Garrett Morris, who was to blacken his teeth on camera. According to Tom Davis, Morris had severe misgivings about "Tarbrush," and the concept ultimately hurt his feelings—not the first nor last time, given what Morris had to endure from the white writers, O'Donoghue included. But Morris went on with the piece because it was his job and he respected O'Donoghue. "Tarbrush" was rehearsed but never shown to an audience. Worried that most people would see only the racist imagery and not get what was being satirized, Lorne Michaels pulled the piece from production. Had it aired, "Tarbrush" would doubtless have been among *Saturday Night*'s more notorious, if not reviled, pieces. It was one of many O'Donoghue items that were censored or considered unfit for air during the second season, a development that O'Donoghue saw as ominous.

Weekend Update continued to be a battleground for O'Donoghue. The criteria established by network Standards was at best inconsistent. Although O'Donoghue could get on the following item:

> Michael Goldbaum, the media expert who has been producing President Ford's TV commercials, was fired yesterday when it was discovered that he also produces hard-core pornography. The Ford people caught on when a recent campaign ad with the announcement, "There's a change coming over this land," showed Susan Ford wearing spiked heels, manacles, and a bicentennial dog collar while a masked Nazi tatooed "Vote for my Dad" all over her body.

He was forbidden to use:

> In an attempt to modernize its services, the Catholic church has introduced something new into communion. In addition to dispensing the host, priests will now also dispense a "co-host," which symbolizes the body of Mike Douglas.

O'Donoghue wrote the above item during Jane Crowley's tenure as the show's censor. Given her Catholic beliefs, it was fanciful to think she would allow this on. Yet Crowley apparently had no objections to the president's daughter's being tattooed by a Nazi. Perhaps she considered this political satire, fair game in an election year, whereas mocking the sanctity of communion was never in season. But then she also struck down an O'Donoghue Update joke about a "new strain of gonorrhea" that appeared wherever Ford challenger Ronald Reagan campaigned: "Reagan said he was only spreading conservatism." Whatever the logic, it seemed that violence was fine; sex was okay, depending on the angle, of course; and religion, specifically Christianity, was mostly off-limits. This leeway on violence helped O'Donoghue as he created a recurring character of his own.

While in England with Beatts, O'Donoghue bought an old pair of round eyeglass frames that both he and Beatts thought were a stylish improvement on the wire frames he'd worn for years. Back in New York and in mid-breakup, O'Donoghue had perscription lenses fitted to the new frames, lenses that were now as dark as his mood. They served as "the hidy hole," portable two-way mirrors behind which he could watch the diseased human carnival (of which Beatts was now a part). His eyes effectively blacked out, his "death stare" resembled that of an insect—cold, calculated, indifferent to the misery of "others." What began as a defense mechanism soon became the finishing touch on the costume. Mr. Mike was born.

The character of Mr. Mike evolved rapidly; no research was needed, no experimentation in style or tone was necessary. All had been in place for some time, but it took Beatts's departure to give the monster life. Of course, elements of Mr. Mike had already emerged on the show— the Trans American psycho threats and the needles-in-the-eyes impressions were two prominent examples. Now, however, O'Donoghue operated from a single, cutting point; and here, for good *and* ill, he remained through much of his career. For although Mr. Mike was a "character" in the showbiz sense of the word, he and his creator were organically linked in ways that would seem ridiculous in the case of Aykroyd's Conehead or Belushi's Samurai, or even in their popular manifestation as the Blues Brothers.

Mr. Mike not only sprang from O'Donoghue's anger and pain, his manner was based on two of O'Donoghue's closest friends: George Trow and Nelson Lyon. Trow's influence was evident early on: the stylish demeanor, the elegant wit, the dapper way of dressing. These qualities appeared in Mr. Mike from the beginning, especially in his choice of wardrobe—sleek dark blue suit, white dress shirt open at the collar, matching handkerchief in breast pocket. Lyon's influence, a tone of aggression, mixed well with O'Donoghue's already bleak, aggressive outlook. But it was Lyon's pattern of speech that O'Donoghue adapted for his Mr. Mike monologues. Lyon spoke in a clear, flowing voice that carried with it artistic observations, put-downs, ironical asides, dark humor, and bursts of rich enthusiasm. His large physical presence added to the total effect, and once on a roll he could either captivate or clear a room. Lyon was, in a sense, Neal Cassady to O'Donoghue's Jack Kerouac; Dean Moriarty to Mr. Mike's Sal Paradise.*

Lyon understood Mr. Mike from his inception: "We can't honestly expose ourselves and our inner nature to others; we have to adopt a role or form. Michael daringly projected this unique package of pain, cruelty, masochism, sadism, and shaped it into the sinister comic persona of Mr. Mike." It was Lyon's belief that in the history of humor there never had been a character like this. "Mr. Mike was a pervert, he was a killer, he was a hit man. And if you can take the pain and acknowledge the pain of a thousand needles in your eyes, you should be allowed to dish it out. [O'Donoghue] believed that. So he would dish it out in the form of outrageous and cruel comments and try to give everybody a migraine. That was his conceit, that's what he wanted to pull off conceptually. His work was to inflict pain with artistry and be applauded for it."

Appropriately enough, Mr. Mike first appeared on *Saturday Night* when blood was spilled on camera. Buck Henry hosted the October 30 edition of the show. In a Samurai sketch his forehead was slashed by John Belushi's sword, an act of accidental mayhem that inspired both verbal and visual jokes as the episode progressed. Chevy Chase made the slashing the top story of what was his final Weekend Update, and he, along with other cast members, sported a bandage on the forehead in reference to Henry's on-air injury. O'Donoghue had his bandage put in place as he prepared for his segment, "Least-Loved Bedtime Tales." Thanks to the live TV cutting of Henry, there was added electricity in the studio. The atmosphere was ripe for O'Donoghue's character's debut.

"Least-Loved Bedtime Tales" was a concept O'Donoghue had played with for a number of years, notably in his book pitches to Chris Cerf at Random House: the children's story that ends in violence and death where morals are stubbed out like a half-smoked cigarette. The idea itself wasn't especially fresh. Ernie Kovacs's character Auntie Gruesome told wicked children's tales, and *Mad* magazine often subverted the genre, albeit gently. But O'Donoghue had nothing gentle in mind. His character would *enjoy* relating in full detail the brutality and nastiness of a world in which "innocence" is routinely shot in the face and tossed into a ditch. Why lie to the kids and give them hope that somewhere an answer exists? Better to spell out the savagery simply and directly and trust that

---

*O'Donoghue wasn't the only writer taken with Lyon's persona. The main character in D. Keith Mano's novel *Take Five*, Simon Lynxx, is patterned after Lyon, though Lyon himself saw it as an unflattering caricature.

those listening get the point. "Life is cheap," as Mr. Mike liked to say, "but it still has to come down a little."

O'Donoghue presented the first "Bedtime Tale" as himself. There was no mention of Mr. Mike, but the setting was perfectly his: dark blue suit, soft lighting, classical piano chords floating in the background. The story was titled "The Enchanted Thermos." The littlest Eskimo, lost, alone, half dead with hunger in a barren frigid landscape, happens upon an enchanted thermos from which springs a genie in a parka. The genie offers the Eskimo anything he desires so long as it's made of snow. The Eskimo complains of hunger and wishes for a grand meal, and this the genie instantly provides: snow salad, snow cutlets stuffed with snow, snow casserole, snow pudding, and a generous glass of slush. The Eskimo, delighted, takes a few bites, then slips into a coma. He dies minutes later. The genie goes through the dead Eskimo's pockets and returns to the warmth of his thermos. The end. One final thought: Since the fingernails continue to grow after death, we all become Chinese Mandarins beyond the grave.

Far from alienated, the studio audience spontaneously burst into applause at the end of "The Enchanted Thermos"—a reception "Least-Loved Bedtime Tales" would never again receive. It was enough, however, to win O'Donoghue another "Bedtime Tales" spot on the show two weeks later, hosted by Dick Cavett. This time he introduced himself officially as Mr. Mike, and his story, "The Blind Chicken," was shorter, a bit more violent, and reminiscent of certain Zen parables that O'Donoghue found amusing. A blind chicken lives at the edge of an alligator-infested swamp. One crafty alligator, hungry for chicken meat, knocks at the door of the blind bird's coop. "Who is it?" asks the chicken. The alligator fumbles about as he tries to remember his cover; he says he's one of those things that swim and go quack. "A duck?" says the chicken. Yes, the alligator replies, "I'm a duck." The chicken opens the door, invites him in, and is immediately eaten. A few weeks later the alligator is crushed by a hovercraft. The end.

The look of this particular Mr. Mike segment is striking. There is an air of evil gentility in the lighting that softens O'Donoghue's body and the surrounding set but highlights his dark glasses to the degree that the frames appear as horns jutting out of his head. It's an image that intensifies the story, which is so brief and simple that the audience is left hanging; other than O'Donoghue's acting out the alligator's eating of the chicken, thrashing his head from side to side while emitting loud chomping noises, there is little to grab onto. But the closing aphorism justifies the segment as it defines not only Mr. Mike but O'Donoghue's state of mind since Beatts left him: "Love is a death camp in a costume."

O'Donoghue was onto something now. Although he helped to get

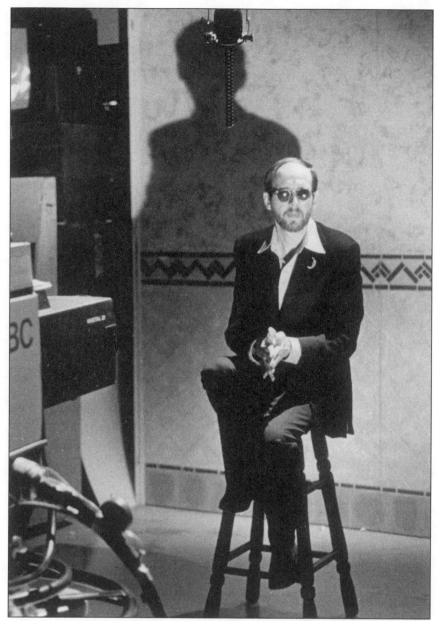

© Edie Baskin. Used by permission.

Mr. Mike on the set

Saturday Night off and running in its first months on the air, he never took part in the creation of recurring characters that came with the show's success. His needles-in-the-eyes routine was performed only twice in the first year (the second time as Tony Orlando and Dawn screaming together in pain) and once in the second year—not enough to rank with the Bees, the Samurai, et al. But with Mr. Mike he could cut and slash away with nothing between him and the audience; his hit man fantasy dramatized and timed to meet the commercial breaks. It was O'Donoghue's effort to remain in the mainstream of a runaway hit show, and he pushed Mr. Mike in front of the cameras as often as Lorne Michaels would allow him.

Like any recurring character, Mr. Mike could never return to his humble roots. The relative simplicity of the first two "Bedtime Tales" gave way to longer, more involved plots. Also, other characters were brought in to listen to and play off the sinister storyteller. In one, host Jodie Foster, fresh from her child hooker role in *Taxi Driver,* dressed in little lace pajamas and sat on Mr. Mike's lap as he told "The Little Train That Died." The familiar tale of the Little Train begins somewhat faithfully: The train pulls a load of scrap metal up a mountain while chanting, "I think I can, I think I can." As he nears the top of the mountain he chugs confidently, "I know I can, I know I can—HEART ATTACK! HEART ATTACK! HEART ATTACK! OH MY GOD THE PAIN! OH MY GOD THE PAIN! I LEFT MY PILLS IN THE ROUND-HOUSE! I LEFT MY PILLS IN THE ROUNDHOUSE!" And he dies. But the story does not end here. Since the Little Train is on an incline, he begins to roll backward, picks up speed, and barrels down the tracks, where sits Freddy the Frog, back turned to the approaching Train. Freddy hops out of the way as the Train smashes into a school bus, killing all the children on board. Later, as the police survey the carnage, one officer looks at Freddy and decides that it's wrong that a frog should survive so many dead humans. So he beats Freddy to death with a softball bat. The end.

In the segment, Jodie Foster serves mainly as a prop. She sits, listens attentively, and smiles during the grisly portions of the story. There is a suggestion of pedophilia here, too, which adds to the overall mood of the piece. After all, aren't bedtime stories for children? And what is Mr. Mike's relation to young Jodie? He sits in an elegant armchair in a subdued but equally elegant room. A piano is softly played nearby. Jodie scampers in, dressed in her nightime lace, and pleads for a "Least-Loved Bedtime Tale." The question of where they are and what happens after storytime is intentionally obscured. But it seems that Mr. Mike is cousin to Nabokov's Humbert, or perhaps one of the more genteel types in Terry Southern's *Candy.*

The dangling of sex before violence is repeated in another Mr. Mike segment in which Gilda Radner plays Fifi, his sexy French maid. As he pets his stuffed flamingo, Mr. Mike notices dust on its dead feathers. He calls for Fifi and reprimands her, but instead of receiving a spanking she is told a "Bedtime Tale" about Willie the Worm. Like Jodie, Fifi sits on Mr. Mike's lap and listens closely. One day while crossing a highway,

Willie is run over by a large truck that mashes the back half of his body. The worm doctor examines poor Willie and tells him that he'll never crawl again. "Not *crawl*! Not *crawl*! But crawling's my whole life!" Willie exclaims, and, determined to prove the worm doctor wrong, he begins extensive physical rehabilitation. Slowly, steadily, Willie's condition improves, and before long he can crawl again. The worm doctor is amazed: "Why, you'd be written up in medical journals, if indeed worms had medical journals," he says. "That's nothing, Doc," replies Willie as he puts on an impressive crawling display that takes him out onto the same highway, where he is run over by a bigger truck. This time his front half is mashed. The end.

Mr. Mike stares off, blankly; pale light reflects in his dark lenses. He seems so taken with Willie's saga that he falls in a near trance, but Fifi rouses him with a kiss, a curtsy, and a *merci beaucoup*. She leaves to attend to her domestic chores, drops her feather duster, and requests that Mr. Mike help her retrieve it. He gets up to "lend" her a hand.

Toward the end of the second season O'Donoghue so established "Least-Loved Bedtime Tales" that he began to play with the format. He took Mr. Mike out of his comfortable salon and placed him in a log cabin with Uncle Remus—the *Song of the South* version as presented by Walt Disney. There the two discuss the adventures of Brer Rabbit. Uncle Remus loves "dat floppy-eared rascal" who's always "a-cookin' up some devilment," and he speaks admiringly of Brer Rabbit's cunning when caught by Brer Fox and Brer Bear: "Dey threaten to skin him alive but dat crafty ole rabbit, he say: 'Skin me alive; do anything you want, but *don't throw me in de briar patch!*' So dey throws him in de briar patch an' he gits away." Mr. Mike shakes his head.

> No, not quite, Uncle Remus. In my story, they respect his wishes and skin him alive. I mean, it's all very amusing to talk about being skinned alive in some children's book, but imagine it actually going down. You know, toward the end when they were cutting the ears away from the sides of the skull, he was screaming: "Throw me in the briar patch; throw me in the molten glass furnace; anything but this!"

Uncle Remus is appalled, then sickened, to discover that Brer Rabbit was eaten by Brer Fox and Brer Bear, who then sold his feet for lucky charms. The old man asks Mr. Mike what the moral is to all this depravity. "There is no moral, Uncle Remus," he answers, "just random acts of meaningless violence." Mr. Mike exits and has his driver take him to Regine's.

Although he had been insulted by "Tarbrush," Garrett Morris turned in a fine performance as Uncle Remus (so enthusiastic was he that he stepped on a few of O'Donoghue's lines). Here the satirical thrust was clear and no one could mistake the piece as racist. If there were any objections to "Mr. Mike Meets Uncle Remus" they centered on the bleakness and violence of O'Donoghue's vision. Indeed, when Mr. Mike described the skinning of Brer Rabbit, audible gasps rose from the studio audience. By this point Lorne Michaels was looking to tone down O'Donoghue's presence on the show. A number of critics and comedy veterans took an even dimmer view of the man and his humor.

Bob Schiller, a former *I Love Lucy* writer who also worked on *All in the Family* and *Maude,* sent a note to his son, Tom, who was starting to make a name for himself on *Saturday Night.* The note read: "Tom, *Half* the sketches Saturday night were about DEATH. Why doesn't O'Donohue [*sic*] shoot himself, get his laugh, and move on to something else?" The elder Schiller was a constant critic of O'Donoghue's work and perspective. When he visited Tom during the week "The Claudine Longet Invitational" was rehearsed, Schiller shook his head and said, "That wasn't funny! My God, that woman has been charged with *murder*! Boy, I wouldn't want to meet the guy who wrote that piece. He must be sick!"

Responded O'Donoghue in an interview:

He's outraged by my death skits, particularly me as "The Mayor of Death." I look at that as a testament, a great one, because it shows that I was able to annoy the man at such a gut level. I respect Bob Schiller, he's a huge figure in comedy. However, he's an old fucking guy and he doesn't affect me, you know what I mean? I understand in terms of craft and skill just how good he is, but the tensions of *our* world are simply not the tensions of *I Love Lucy.* It's not the nuclear family that bothers us. It's, you know, Charles Manson knocking at the door. I have to deal with comedy in a different fashion and he's an old guy and doesn't get that.

But critics closer to O'Donoghue's age and younger rejected what they saw as the "new cruelty" in comedy. A "think piece" on this subject appeared in the *New York Times* on October 2, 1977. Written by Richard Whelan, a Shakespearean actor, "Cruelty Vs. Compassion Among the Comics" compared the old school of Groucho Marx to the young turks represented by Chevy Chase and *Saturday Night.* Whelan portrayed Groucho as a lovable misanthrope who, beneath the crust, possessed the bleeding heart of a true humanitarian.★ As proof, Whelan

★Groucho could certainly be glib about the death of others. Milt Josefsberg, a writer for Jack Benny and a contemporary of Bob Schiller, once wrote about the time when Groucho guest-starred on Benny's radio show during World War II. During a break in rehearsals, Benny's staff and crew gathered around the radio to hear the latest war news. After learning that a number of American ships had been sunk in the Pacific by the Japanese, Groucho asked Josefsberg what type of ships were attacked. "Tankers," said Josefsberg. "You're welcome," replied Groucho, whose joke fell flat among the stunned group in front of him.

© Edie Baskin. Used by permission.

"The Mayor of Death"

cited an episode of *You Bet Your Life* in which an old man believed that Groucho was making fun of him in front of millions of viewers. "Take it easy, old fellow," Whelan quoted the comedian. "It's all a game. Nobody's making fun of you. Now let's try to win some money." Wiping a tear from his eye, Whelan then turned on the "brash" young humorists who, if they had their way, would mock the old man to his grave. "Shut up, Gramps," Whelan imagined them braying. "You're damned right we're making fun of you. That's what we're here for. Don't tell me the way things used to be. Just stick around long enough for a few laughs and then kiss off to terminal dreamland."

Whelan also castigated himself: "Why . . . do I feel slightly unclean after watching 'Saturday Night'? And why, once the stunning effect has dissipated, do I feel let down, guilty, depressed at having enjoyed the shallowness of its humor?" In Whelan's estimation he felt unclean because the *Saturday Night* staff "do not partake of the human comedy." A similar critique was forwarded in the May 23 *Village Voice* by James Wolcott. While Whelan lamented comedy's wicked new turn, Wolcott grabbed the hems of his skirt, jumped on a chair, and shouted "Eeek!" He, too, deplored the "Grand Guignol scumminess" of *Saturday Night* and anticipated Whelan's concerns: "Do breezy one-liners about death or incest really indicate a leap of maturity? It may instead signal that people are becoming increasingly disconnected from the sources of sorrow and pain." It was Wolcott's belief that this "cheap and nasty" disconnection stemmed from the callousness of youth: "[J]okes about death from young comics are always glib and jeering since they're not living with the dread in their bones." Wolcott, then twenty-four, said that because of his youth he understood but did not accept *Saturday Night*'s death humor. Yet the two "young comics" he singled out, Chase and O'Donoghue, were ten and thirteen years his senior, respectively. Not old, but certainly not unfamiliar with the ravages of life and death.

Wolcott directed most of his squeamishness at Chevy Chase, though he did take a pass at O'Donoghue, "a master of hip how-do-you-make-a-dead-baby-float? humor." This made a certain amount of sense, for at the time Chase was *the* prominent example of the *Saturday Night* sensibility; but although Chase could and did make jokes about death, he was never (as his subsequent career has shown) a dark humorist, nor did he mine a sick and dying culture for humor in the manner of O'Donoghue. Indeed, Chase was quite touchy when it came to his public persona, and he dismissed suggestions that he was cruel or callous. Highly sensitive, Chase took Wolcott's criticisms personally, and in the July 7 *SoHo Weekly News,* he went off: "Sure I was hurt, I was really hurt. . . . I'd just like to meet James alone in an alley and ask him, 'Did you ever try it, James? You try it. You get your fucking buns out on the line in front of fifty billion people, try to bridge gaps.. Do it for me.' 'Oh, I can't. I'm a nervous wreck. All I can do is hit fucking typewriter keys.' Well, fuck you. Sit on a knife, baby."

O'Donoghue, although admitting that he'd "like to rearrange Mister What's-his-face's cheekbones with a softball bat," was slightly less defensive. When he read Wolcott's line about the "glib and jeering" youth who live without the fear of death "in their bones," O'Donoghue responded, "Yeah sure. I'll live forever. That's what gives me the right to make jokes about death. I pity those poor bastards whose hair is falling out and in a few years they can't get it up and start pissing blood and get brown spots on their hands. Fortunately, I won't go through that. I don't fear that at all, and of course that's why I make those jibes. Listen, pal—if you make jokes about death, it's not like you're outside the fuckin' *game!*"

The critiques from Schiller, Whelan, and Wolcott were based on the idea that comedy should uplift, not sicken; amuse, not frighten. If death must be dealt with then let it be, in Wolcott's words, "tenderly evocative." Wolcott pointed to a *Bob Newhart* episode in which the Grim Reaper, in standard costume, beckoned our friend Bob. *This,* he suggested, was the tasteful way to handle death. But O'Donoghue wasn't interested in the clichés found on network sitcoms: Death was unpleasant, gruesome, and above all inevitable. Murder, which fascinated O'Donoghue, could not be satirized in cute, uplifting ways. Those who killed were not abstract figures in black robes clutching sickles but aberrant individuals with blood on their hands. One such individual, Gary Gilmore, transcended his crimes, which included shooting a Utah service station attendant twice in the head, by publicly demanding that he be executed by firing squad. The story was made national by an excited press corps that hoped to capture Gilmore's execution on film or tape, while Gilmore himself was negotiating book and movie rights to his saga through an agent.

This was too much for O'Donoghue to pass up. A psychotic redneck had the national press at his feet while public opinion polls showed the majority of Americans favored his execution. The Gilmore spectacle burned brightly in December 1976, just in time for Christmas. With this in mind, O'Donoghue wrote a holiday song he dedicated especially to Gary Gilmore.

Candice Bergen, the host for that year's Christmas show, stands in front of a beautifully decorated tree and introduces O'Donoghue's song. As she reviews Gilmore's story and the media hoopla surrounding it, she seems to have an expression of distaste, as if to anticipate the audience's reaction. The camera fades from her and onto a close-up of Gilda Radner, whose hair and face are pelted by artificial snow. After a Christmas carol music intro, she begins to sing:

> There's a little guy in Utah with a single Christmas wish,
> A single wish that cannot be substituted.
> Doesn't want to get electric trains, get toys or get pet fish
> All he really wants to get is executed.

The shot widens to include the entire cast, all dressed in holiday sweaters amid the steadily falling snow. They join in,

> So, let's kill Gary Gilmore for Christmas
> Let's hang him from atop the Christmas tree.
> Let's give him the only gift that money can't buy
> Put poison in his egg nog, let him drink it, watch him die.

We fade to a close-up of Dan Aykroyd, who talks while the others hum softly behind him.

> Let's throw another yule log on the fire
> And then let's throw Gary Gilmore on there too.
> With a ribbon so gay, and a card that will say,
> "Dear Gary, Merry Christmas to you."

The carolers sing merrily of granting Gilmore's death wish and end with an upbeat "We can thrill Gary Gilmore/If we kill Gary Gilmore/ On this Christmas Day!"

"Let's Kill Gary Gilmore for Christmas" at first shocked, then amused, the studio audience; gasps and moans quickly became laughter as the cast sang of execution in a medley of familiar Christmas carols. It was one of O'Donoghue's finest pieces of the season; yes, the song centered on death, but O'Donoghue had not created the conditions that allowed for such a vulgar display. With fluid satiric timing he reflected the obscenities of murder and media exploitation, but ultimately, he was outdone. After all, how could a little Christmas carol compete with Norman Mailer's *Executioner's Song*?

Despite the perception that *Saturday Night* bore the skull and cross-bones of Mr. Mike, it was becoming clear to O'Donoghue that his once-dominant presence was ebbing fast. Lorne Michaels, who respected O'Donoghue's creative abilities, did not want his show moving into the shadows. He steadily eliminated many of O'Donoghue's darker pieces, sensing that America was not as obsessed with death as was his senior writer. O'Donoghue fought what he saw as disrespect and ingratitude, a battle that would rage the following season. Of the pieces that were eliminated there was one that O'Donoghue especially liked, "Great Moments in Sports," scheduled to air the week Fran Tarkenton hosted the show in 1977.

Bill Murray, then a new cast member (whose early jitters resulted in blown lines and jokes), was to play the Yankee Iron Horse, Lou Gehrig, after he learned he had the rare, fatal nerve disorder that later would bear his name. As Gehrig steps to the microphone to deliver his famous 1939 farewell speech to the fans in Yankee Stadium, he breaks the bad news, each word echoing from dugout to bleacher:

Ladies and gentlemen. A little while ago I found out that I have a fatal disease. (Looks down, then looks up) Perhaps you didn't understand what I just said. *I'm gonna die! And I'm so frightened!* (Now crying) You know, I figured I'd retire in a couple seasons, open a little sporting goods store—*I don't believe it!*—A year from now all you dumb jerk-offs will be sitting here watching some stupid baseball game *and I'll be gone!* (Totally out of control) *It's not fair! It's just not fair. And I'll tell you another thing. Those doctors don't know their head from their . . .*

Gehrig is restrained and is dragged kicking and yelling off the field by two men. We are told that he was placed under heavy sedation until he slipped into a coma and died a few months later. His last words, "Why me?"

"Great Moments" made it to dress rehearsal, but the image of a dying Yankee legend (immortalized by Gary Cooper) behaving in such a manner was deemed insensitive and unfunny and was cut from the program. Of course, O'Donoghue believed otherwise. "Great Moments" cut through myth and jock machismo to show a frightened man faced with extinction. When compared to the sports-related material that *did* get on that night, mostly gentle football spoofs in honor of Tarkenton, O'Donoghue's piece was indeed unsettling and would have run counter to the evening's tongue-in-cheek approach.

As O'Donoghue fought to get his darker material on, other writers dealing with different subjects emerged. In addition to Aykroyd and Marilyn Miller, there was Rosie Shuster, whose absurdist touch was seen in pieces such as "Hollywood Bingo," a game show in which the board is so big that it must be filled out with show business bottom feeders. Once everyone is introduced, there is no time to play the game. Shuster also wrote with Anne Beatts a fine parody of beatnik coffeehouse talent, "Plato's Cave," in which O'Donoghue played an ultracool patron who comments on the acts. Tom Schiller's recurring master strokes that year were the "Bad" sketches—"Bad Playhouse," "Bad Cinema," "Bad Ballet." Hosted by Leonard Pinth-Garnell, played by Aykroyd, "Bad" presented the worst in art, theater, and film; this allowed the cast members to cut loose and be simply awful, which gave "Bad" a diverting, improvisational look. Schiller's deep knowledge of cultural history helped him here as he invented bad schools of acting, cinema, and dance, as well as traditions that no artist of quality would wish to honor. "Bad" was one of the more original premises ever to appear on *Saturday Night*. Unlike the scores of horrible sketches that littered the show over its twenty-plus seasons, Schiller's *intentional* misuse of talent often bordered on brilliance.

O'Donoghue respected Shuster and Schiller and saw value in their work. But he was horrified to see Franken and Davis gain strength and influence as the second season unfolded. While he enjoyed collaborating with Davis, whose work independent of Franken he thought fine, he didn't think much of the team Davis was part of. To O'Donoghue, Franken and Davis's material was nightclub comedy best performed in front of drunks. He saw no philosophy in their humor, no esoteric structure or sensibility. O'Donoghue's judgment was extremely harsh and a bit unfair, for Franken and Davis did write and perform some first-rate material, primarily in the show's third and fourth seasons. (And for a man who hoped to use television as a means to enter Hollywood, one wonders why O'Donoghue would *care* that the team did well.) His assessment was partly colored by his hatred for Franken, but if O'Donoghue genuinely liked something he would say so regardless of personal enmity.

He simply believed that, as a team, Franken and Davis were inferior comics.

O'Donoghue wrote plenty of nondeath humor in the show's second season. But given the emergence of Mr. Mike, it was hard for observers to pick this up. The better pieces ran counter to the perception that O'Donoghue was merely a "dead baby" joke merchant. Among them:

- A farmer's wife prepares her family's breakfast, which includes Quarry—an "all-natural" cereal made from whole rocks and pebbles with no added preservatives; a cereal that's "better tastin' 'cause it's mined."
- Clad in a tuxedo, Garrett Morris sings "The King Kong Dirge," which tells the tragic tale of the giant ape and his forbidden love for Fay Wray, a woman for whom Kong gives his life.
- Gilda Radner plays Lucille Ball in a re-creation of one of the comedienne's most famous gags: Hired to work on an assembly line, Lucy deals with a conveyor belt gone haywire. But instead of boxing candy, she must spray whipped cream and place cherries atop a succession of nuclear warheads. She can't keep pace, and this of course leads to devastation.
- Elliott Gould revives a long-lost song that launched a 1920s dance craze, "The Castration Walk." Gould, John Belushi, and Bill Murray perform the song while grabbing their crotches and falling over each other in pain. Sample lyric: "Well, I went to the rabbi/And he sent me to the *mohel*/But the *mohel* was clumsy/And he made me a goil."

Still, certain habits were hard to break. On the final show of the second season, O'Donoghue was granted another appearance as the needles-in-the-eyes impressionist. This time he widened the routine to include the Mormon Tabernacle Choir. Standing as a conductor before a large group of "singers" in black robes, O'Donoghue leads the choir into the requisite screaming and writhing about. For all the noise and supposed bedlam, this version of O'Donoghue's routine is stale. Gone is the minimalist beauty of the original performance—one man stretching the pain of ruptured eyes to incredible lengths while spectators shuffle nervously in their seats. In the choir version, only O'Donoghue goes full tilt; the "singers" scream but aren't as committed to the piece as its creator. The image speaks volumes. O'Donoghue always held himself above the majority of the show's talent. Though his feelings never changed, *Saturday Night's* direction did, and before long he would thrash and scream with all his might while the show, Emmy laden, went off to meet its commercial destiny.

I think television is almost a substitute for life in this country. It's never been treated seriously. It's America's leading art form and nobody ever talks about it like art. The two greatest art forms of America are comic strips and television. They're treated like jokes or something, and they're incredibly powerful forms.

After two years of television under his cinched belt, O'Donoghue took advantage of the time and pleasures professional success allowed him. The Winter Palace was his base of operations, and with Anne Beatts gone (though he kept her name on the door's buzzer) the kitsch-filled apartment served to define him to the outside world, namely the media. Thanks to his on-camera exposure as Mr. Mike the previous season, journalists high and low visited the Palace, fascinated by and attracted to O'Donoghue's "evil" persona and the colorful props that surrounded him: a life-size stuffed black bear sitting next to a masked little girl mannequin who stared out the front window; a pink flamingo mounted in the bedroom; a panda bear strapped in a toy electric chair; a collection of ultracheap perfumes with names such as Lover's Moon and Atom Bomb. Then there was the collie fur he kept on a hanger in his closet. As he told one interviewer, the fur came "from a dog my friend ran over with his car!" Oftentimes, O'Donoghue said, he'd throw the fur on scraps of food following a dinner party and yell "Fetch!"

Since his days in Rochester with Bread and Circuses, O'Donoghue knew how to court the press. Now on a television-lit stage, his act (to the degree that it *was* an act) captivated those who came to profile him. O'Donoghue played his familiar role of artiste to the fullest. He wore pajama tops with dress slacks; chained-smoked More cigarettes in his preferred European fashion; spoke favorably of his psychotic outbursts and dark inspirations; went on about the need to slaughter sacred cows; and, above all, lamented the creeping censorship of his work on *Saturday Night*. With little prodding, O'Donoghue would go through his files, pull and perform bits and items that he couldn't get on the show. Sometimes he focused on sketches such as "Tarbrush;" but usually he read his censored Weekend Update material, like:

Well, the movie *Earthquake* opened in Rumania this week. Unfortunately, a careless projectionist turned up the Sensurround a bit too much, killing thousands and leaving untold millions homeless.

And in Detroit, a handicapped eight-year-old schoolgirl was attacked by a supposedly tame lion while television cameras rolled. The child, a deaf mute, suffered only minor scratches from the lion but, according to doctors, she did break three fingers screaming for help.

Free from the weekly pressures of the show, O'Donoghue spent many private hours making, as he put it, "significant breakthroughs" in the use of drugs. A regular consumer of Percodan, which was, in essence, a stabilizing chemical to offset his migraines, O'Donoghue also loved to smoke marijuana, and he openly spoke of how the weed opened his brain to different ways of composing a joke or a sketch. "I have a whole theory about marijuana," he said at the time to a reporter from a local New Jersey magazine. "Indeed, the theory was backed up by some book which, if I had any memory left if the marijuana hadn't destroyed it, I could give you the name of the book. Anyhow . . . the theory is that marijuana suppresses the left hemisphere of the brain, which is the linguistic center, leaving the intuitive center in the right half to bubble a bit to the surface. Well, I want the left center in full control when I'm dealing with just where to put this fuckin' semicolon!"

O'Donoghue also stated this theory on *Midday Live,* a local New York show that was hosted by Bill Boggs. Toward the end of *Saturday Night's* second season, John Belushi accepted an invitation to appear on *Midday,* but he would do it only if O'Donoghue accompanied him. Tom Davis recalled that the two had no idea what they were going to do on the show, so they smoked a joint before their appearance. Belushi and O'Donoghue showed up quite stoned, but contained. Perhaps sensing their condition, Boggs asked if drugs played a part in their work. O'Donoghue answered that, yes, drugs were part of his arsenal and that he drew creative inspiration from marijuana. In fact, he added, he was high that very minute. ("Anytime anyone asks me a question like that I always answer him honestly," O'Donoghue later said.) Meanwhile, Belushi began to act a little wild in reaction to Boggs's request that he do Elvis Presley. Boggs's other guest, Steve Allen, was put off by the pair, but the punch line was yet to come.

"Boggs kept asking [Belushi] to do an Elvis Presley imitation," said O'Donoghue, "and I knew John had no ending for it. Finally, he agreed, and to get out of the bit, he picked up a glass of water, threw it at Boggs, hit him in the chest, and knocked over a table full of plants. You should have seen Steve Allen's face. It turned into the Hollywood Wax Museum." The studio audience was equally appalled as they gasped through Belushi's violent routine. O'Donoghue sat back and enjoyed the action, feeding off the embarrassment and horror that filled the set.

O'Donoghue dabbled in powders as well, occasionally snorting cocaine or heroin. Brian McConnachie remembered O'Donoghue's "victory chipmunk dance" when the two expected a coke delivery. O'Donoghue would point his toes and take little leaps in the air—"It was the first time I saw anyone so childishly gleeful about a drug coming his way," said McConnachie. But O'Donoghue never really favored powders, and he ingested them only at "special" moments. Hallucinogens, on the other hand, were always welcome. In the February 1978 issue of *High Times*, O'Donoghue spoke at length about his many acid experiences and the effects the drug had on his imagination and psyche.

> I swear to Christ, one time on acid I could actually make the clouds into any shape I wanted and I would go "*Shazam:* A badger!"—and it would be a badger. And I would say, "Okay, *shazam:* A battleship!" *Whsss!*—and there has been nothing to prove that I actually didn't do this.

> In Mexico they have big insects like birds . . . I have an abnormal fear of insects—bordering on hysteria. I was just slipping into this acid and I realized uh, oh, Jesus Christ, you are here in insect land—ah, you better fucking deal with this. So, what I did is I went over and I found the scariest insects I could find, and I said, "Okay, come here, okay, let's have a look at you. Okay, little sticky feet." Don't like him, but he's not so weird I can't deal with him. Little devil. "Let's pet you. Let's give you a name—" and got on with that. Got over it and it was really good, because if I had let him sneak up on me it would have been like *The Hellstrom Chronicle.*

It was during this same visit to Mexico—where he went during the summer with Edie Baskin, *Saturday Night's* official photographer, whom he was dating—that O'Donoghue nearly killed himself. Attending a party in Yalapa, O'Donoghue went the chemical limit: "I had acid, smoke, mushrooms, and an illegal wine called ricea, which is made out of the roots of some tree. It is illegal to sell it in Mexico. It puts a kind of frosty blue glow around objects, and it's quite exciting. And then nitrous oxide." Tripping heavily and wandering over the rocky terrain, O'Donoghue suddenly fell off a mountain. "I went right over the mountain for about fifty feet, like the kids who dive for the pearls in the waves, and really damaged my head pretty good," he said. "I just stood up and fell backwards. It was really a humiliating thing. Just like Fred MacMurray on drugs—really." Afterward, still stinging from his cuts and scrapes, O'Donoghue jotted a line to himself: "Don't worry about finding the path. The path is what's easiest to follow."

Despite his near-fatal drop and a brush with large glowing insects, O'Donoghue survived his Mexican sojourn. Back in New York by mid-summer 1977, he and Chevy Chase rented a house in the genteel hamlet of East Hampton, Long Island. There the two began work on a screenplay for United Artists, which had signed Chase to star in an unnamed comedy project. Having left *Saturday Night* and starred in a prime time special on NBC, Chase was a hot property in Hollywood and there was a rush to get him into films. But Chase insisted that O'Donoghue be

© Edie Baskin. Used by permission.

After the fall in Mexico

included in anything he did. If he was to cash in on his *Saturday Night* fame then who better to assist him than the guy who helped define the show? O'Donoghue needed no convincing; after years of hard work he felt that the film project was his due, and it was time that Hollywood (America, too) got a taste of the O'Donoghue style splashed across shopping mall screens.

At a time when the "blockbuster" movie concept was picking up speed, *Star Wars* then the latest example, O'Donoghue and Chase decided to go back in time. Both were attracted to the old movie house experience where, for a nickel, patrons saw coming attractions, a newsreel, a cartoon, a bouncing-ball song or "soundie," a chapter of an ongoing serial adventure, and one, perhaps two, feature films. Here was a format rich in satiric possibilities. The TV- and mall-oriented consumer would be shown what moviegoing was like—pre-Spielberg and Lucas. But only the wrapping would evoke warm nostalgia, for O'Donoghue and Chase had a bevy of strange, violent, absurd, and potentially offensive ideas in mind as the project, *Saturday Matinee,* started to come together.

Chase spent a limited amount of time in the East Hampton house. His life and career now centered in Los Angeles; he had an office at MGM, a nice home, and a wife, Jaqueline Carlin, for whom he had left *Saturday Night.* (Carlin appeared in a few of the show's early commercial parodies.) There were demands and responsibilities to be met. But before heading west, Chase relaxed in the large rented house. When not discussing the screenplay, he and O'Donoghue acted as lords of the manor born; and like the couple they played in the "Jamitol" commercial, characters they reprised in a "lovers' spat" on Weekend Update, the pair lent the impression that there was more to their relationship than the writing of a film. "We almost wanted people to believe we were gay," said Chase. "We walked around in white robes in this twelve-bedroom house, and slept together—all that crap." When not in robes, they wrapped themselves in white sheets and strolled casually about. Their gay game ended when Chase returned to L.A., but the dressing in white continued as O'Donoghue, in tandem with Lorne Michaels and Paul Simon, hosted the first of several White Parties.

The White Party concept appealed immensely to O'Donoghue's sense of style and sophistication. Amid the quiet wealth of the Hamptons, where Manhattan's clever upper crust mingle every summer, came the ultimate theatrical amusement—beautiful people dressed elegantly in white, exchanging witticisms and glances on a great, manicured lawn where harp music blended with the scent of sea air. Dandyism and affectation ran rampant. It echoed the kind of party that rich patrons of the arts threw in the 1920s so to be near the creative folk, only now the creative folk patronized themselves. One dissenter to this affair was Anne Beatts, who arrived in a red dress; a drop of blood on ivory. Beatts was no newcomer to retro-fashion and saw the humor in dressing against type. O'Donoghue got the joke, too, for one look at Beatts and his iron door fell off its hinges. He warmed to his former lover and suggested they go away together, a suggestion Beatts seriously considered. But at a later date she saw O'Donoghue pick a fight with Edie Baskin and flashed back, Vietnam-style, to the battles at Sixteenth Street. "That was *exactly* the same as the kind of fights that we had had," she said, "and I went, 'Oh, man. Narrow escape.' "

The best definition I've come up with for comedy was astonishment. Once you see how the form works it no longer astonishes you. The magician's got to come up with a new trick. He can't keep pulling the same small rabbit out of the big hat.

The third season of *Saturday Night,* now called *Saturday Night Live,* would solidify the show as a cultural force. Although some interesting material made it to air during this year, there would be no more Blog Diets, no more bald female psychos or snake-handling nuns and state troopers. *SNL*'s success guaranteed that sooner or later a pop sensibility would dominate the show, that the humor would rely less on the unconscious mind and instead be a conscious part of an overall marketing effort. Inevitable, unavoidable, and clearly desirable. No one on staff seemed to have a problem with this metamorphosis, including O'Donoghue, who, for all his commitment to artistic daring, remained in thrall to showbiz and the glitter that fell around it. From this point on and to the end of his career he would attempt—not always successfully—to balance philosophy and desire; to find that middle space where he could bludgeon and slaughter all that was sacred but do so with the *finest* instruments.

O'Donoghue was now Mr. Mike, no longer host of "Least-Loved Bedtime Tales" but an on-camera presence as ubiquitous as the Bees, Baba Wawa, and the Coneheads. Mr. Mike could pop up at any time, and his appearances throughout the third season effectively blunted the impact of his humor. When Mr. Mike walked on set, everyone knew he would say something "dark" or punctuate a scene with a predictably violent reference. Mr. Mike was so familiar a character that he almost seemed reassuring; he might as well have worn Bee antennae for all the "shock" he now delivered. This is not to say that O'Donoghue ceased to be funny or that his material was Hallmark safe. But the bright commercial light that shone on *SNL* eliminated the shadows where O'Donoghue did his best work. The assassin lost what assassins need most—the element of surprise.

Again, O'Donoghue knew fully well what was happening, yet did little to smash up the arrangement. And had he desired to seriously lash out, to breathe fresh psychotic fire into the show, chances are he would have failed. Unlike what was true during the first season and part of the second, the *SNL* staff no longer feared or felt intimidated by O'Donoghue. It was as much Franken and Davis's show now as it ever was O'Donoghue's—perhaps more so. The team had become, in Davis's words, "Lorne's hired guns." If a writer's piece wasn't working, Michaels would bring in Franken and Davis to confront the writer and tell him or her that it wasn't working. Also, the team appeared on air in "The Franken and Davis Show," essentially a replacement bit for ensemble pieces that fell from the show's rotation. This gave them name recognition that no other writer on the show enjoyed, the exception, of course, being O'Donoghue. Franken and Davis climbed the *SNL* food chain through sheer determination and a willingness to do whatever it took to get their material on.

O'Donoghue, conversely, refrained from such effort. Given his history with the show and his senior status, he thought he shouldn't have to fight to see his material performed. Though he encountered almost no resistance when it came to Mr. Mike (who fit neatly on the *SNL* conveyor belt), he struggled to convince Lorne Michaels that his non–Mr. Mike material should enjoy similar access. Some of the pieces he pushed, such as "Lawn Dentist" and "Disco College," were weak and deserved rejection. But O'Donoghue *did* have some interesting ideas, many of which were edgier than anything he gave Mr. Mike that year. He toyed with pure imagery—no jokes, no premises, no punch lines, just wrinkles in the video pattern. A favorite image was a tarantula dancing on a butter dish and nothing more; he also wanted to see live gunfire in the studio (for example, a marksman shooting plates or large pictures), and he wanted to conduct an actual book burning and toss everything from Tennyson to *Peanuts* onto the flames—"To burn a book is to have read it." Clearly, none of this would do and thus was not done.

Some of O'Donoghue's more "conventional" ideas never passed muster as well. Among them were ad parodies, by now an *SNL* staple. One was a public service announcement in which the elderly are systematically wiped out, the tag being "Old people: Please don't kill them." Another was a commercial for "Spray-On Laetrile." A girl is sad because she cannot attend her senior prom. "I have cancer!" she complains, treating malignancy as though it were acne. But her boyfriend has the answer: Spray-On Laetrile; one *psssst* and "You can kiss cancer good-bye!" O'Donoghue was particularly miffed that this didn't get on, especially since "Green Cross Cupcakes," which also dealt with cancer, had. The one real difference between the two pieces is that in "Green Cross" cancer is prevented, and in "Laetrile" cancer is eliminated. Perhaps the directness of "Laetrile" was its downfall, whereas "Green Cross" was so strange that the cancer references were less threatening. Whatever the reasoning, "Laetrile" never survived read-throughs.

O'Donoghue began to chafe under what he viewed as pure censorship, and he even outlined a cold opening called "Dead Censor": Herminio Traviesas dies, the show's master script is destroyed, and the writers bring out suppressed pieces like the "Dutch Enema Sketch" and "Eating Bowls of Drool." The pieces are so foul, however, that Traviesas comes back to life and orders them cut—Standards reaches from beyond the grave. But O'Donoghue's growing complaints about censorship were directed less at the network and more in the direction of Lorne Michaels. He created a scenario in which he was the abused artist and Michaels was the pig producer. O'Donoghue felt that Michaels had betrayed his early promises of creative freedom, that he worried more about status and money than about the art of humor, and this was why much of O'Donoghue's material never made it on camera. Like the many ongoing themes in his life, O'Donoghue polished this scenario as he would a fine piece of silver. Before long it defined relations between the two.

"I got tired of being lectured to by Lorne 'The Rabbi' Michaels," O'Donoghue later said. "I had learned enough about television to just do what I wanted to do. Like at the *Lampoon,* where we did what we did. Lorne would not relinquish control and it was tiresome. You were always fighting a war on two fronts. One just to get the material itself on the air and make it right and one with Lorne Michaels." But others on *SNL* saw the situation in more complex terms. Tom Davis noted that Lorne Michaels "loved Michael, worshipped Michael, envied Michael, snubbed Michael. I think that Michael was jealous of Lorne's wealth and power, and Lorne owned the show. There was enmity between the two of them, in part due to Michael's envy and jealousy." Rosie Shuster, who knew Michaels as well as anyone, said that her ex-husband began to see O'Donoghue as a "problem child" who was hard to manage. O'Donoghue "would pout, he would sulk, he would get peevish, he would repair to his office, he would leave early. There were displays of testiness." When he presented an idea at read-throughs, it "was like he was presenting treasures." If an idea was rejected, it was because "they don't get it." As the season progressed, O'Donoghue, in Shuster's estimation, became "trapped in this confinement of his own creation."

If he was trapped in the role of Mr. Mike, then O'Donoghue made sure that his creation appeared as often as possible. He played the host of "The Ricky Rat Club," in which Ratkateers sporting names such as Sleazeball, Phlegma, and of course Annette paid homage to a live rat undergoing chemotherapy. He headed a musical group, the Mr. Mike and Tina Turner Revue, whose backup singers, the Mikettes, dressed exactly as O'Donoghue did. The group sang a version of "Proud Mary" in which a factory worker rabbit has his ears caught in a big wheel, leading to the lyric "Big wheel keep on turnin'," after which the rabbit is reduced to tomato bisque. This latter bit was full of flash: Garrett Morris strutted about as Tina Turner, shaking his ass and waving his arms to the house band's lively rendition of "Proud Mary" while Mr. Mike pulled stuffed rabbits from a prop guitar and tossed them across the stage. But there was very little to the piece itself. O'Donoghue seemed content to simply appear and go through the motions as the three female cast members danced around him in Mr. Mike outfits. One feels no thrust, sees no edge, hears no gasps. To whatever degree Lorne Michaels muted O'Donoghue's comic voice, he was helped by the man himself.

There was one Mr. Mike segment that season that was potentially tasteless, and therefore true to the character's essence, but that, in the end, delivered a feathery blow. Near the close of the episode hosted by Ray Charles, the cast gathers around a piano to sing and chat with the musical legend. Mr. Mike shows up and says he has a surprise. He credits Charles for being "a heck of a good sport" regarding all the blind jokes told that evening. But as Mr. Mike solemnly reminds us, "Blindness is nothing to kid about." And so in Charles's name, the network is donating a painting to the Lighthouse of the Blind "in the hope that someday all will be able to see it." Mr. Mike pulls the cover from the painting and within its ornate frame are the words "PLEASE DON'T TELL HIM." He describes the "painting" to Charles as Claude Monet's *The Old Windmill*. He notes the "shimmering iridescence" and the subtle interplay between light and shadow, but Mr. Mike admits that it's "hard to describe, really, you sort of have to see it." Charles appears touched, and Mr. Mike exits, after which Charles confides to the audience that ten big black guys are going to "whup" Mr. Mike "upside his head and break every bone in his body. So please don't tell him." The audience and cast applaud.

The ending to this bit lets both the audience and O'Donoghue off the hook. Only a cruel and insensitive person would pull such a stunt on a blind black man; therefore, he must be punished for his misdeed. The nervous laughter heard during the description of the "painting" turns to relief once Charles admits he's wise to the gag. This is not the Mr. Mike who less than a year earlier said, unsmiling, "It's all very easy to laugh at yourself. The difficult thing is learning to laugh at others." Apparently it is not only difficult but now virtually impossible. The sole Mr. Mike piece where the character's misantrophy burns is the one in which Laraine Newman stumbles into a waterfront bar and must sing the aria from *Madame Butterfly* before receiving a "Least-Loved Bedtime Tale." Mr. Mike breaks his promise, makes no apologies for his cruelty, and demands that Newman hit the road. The only redeeming act he performs is helping a drunk Laraine get drunker.

Perhaps sensing the character's staleness, O'Donoghue planned to kill off Mr. Mike at the end of the third season. He would lay dying in bed, sad Irish music in the background, and tell a story about a dog he had when he was four years old. It would be a sweet, heart-tugging reminiscence that resulted in the violent death of the dog—the final Bedtime Tale. Mr. Mike would then collapse and meet the darkness he always mocked. An interesting idea (he also considered eliminating Mr. Mike in full-tilt, blood-gushing fashion), though how serious O'Donoghue was in realizing it is anyone's guess. Ultimately, he did appear as Mr. Mike in the final show that season. Dressed in a white suit, bathed in soft focus and light, Mr. Mike sings "Baby Ghouls," a ditty about dead little girls in blood stained party dresses who dance in the rain and feed on the living. Laraine Newman plays a cute ghoul who bites deeply into Mr. Mike's neck, her mouth dripping with his blood. But Mr. Mike is okay; he looks to Newman, then to the audience, and smiles brightly. It was all a joke! Mr. Mike lives on.

Apart from the jealousy, the sulking, the cries of censorship and defanging of his creation, O'Donoghue produced two exceptional pieces during *SNL*'s third year. The first aired on the October 8 episode, hosted by Madeline Kahn. Aware of Kahn's fine singing voice, to which he catered in the first season by having Kahn sing "I Feel Pretty" while dressed as the Bride of Frankenstein, O'Donoghue wrote a gospel tune for her titled "Silver Balls and Golden Pins." Bill Murray is a preacher who urges all to find the Lord while bowling. One's faith is sometimes tested, though, and God doesn't always guide your ball; but through diligence and weekend practice your average will rise, and one day you'll wake up in the biggest bowling alley there is. The balls are silver, the pins are golden, and the lane is the Milky Way. "You rent your shoes from angels and they fit real good, but friend, just one word of advice," says Murray. "There ain't no beer frame in Heaven."

Interspersed throughout Murray's sermon are portions of the song. Kahn, clad in a gold dress, stands atop a large bowling trophy. As she sings of redemption and the bowler's final glory, the gold-plated trophy men who surround her come to life and form a chorus. Kahn's voice rises to holy crescendo; possessed by the spirit of the Lord, she reaches to the sky and belts out the song's final stanza:

> In an alabaster alley
> Silver balls and golden pins
> You'll be bowling with the Master
> But the Master always wins.

"Silver Balls and Golden Pins" is less a comedy piece and more an alternative gospel ballad. Once the song picks up steam and Kahn lets it rip, one doesn't laugh so much as be moved by the music. The bowling alley becomes a revival tent, and here O'Donoghue's appreciation for different forms of popular music really shows. A similar appreciation, this time for low-rent science fiction films, burst forth on *SNL* in early 1978.

Late in the second season, O'Donoghue and Tom Davis conceived "Attack of the Atomic Lobsters," an ambitious piece that combined film, animation, and live action in the studio. The idea was that due to massive amounts of atomic waste dumped in the ocean, mutations began to appear, the most serious and deadly being giant lobsters that descend on Manhattan, crawl up the side of the RCA Building, smash into the *SNL* studio, and kill everyone in sight. The piece, as planned, would take up two large chunks of airtime separated only by a commercial break. O'Donoghue and Davis were excited by the prospect of "destroying" *SNL* in front of millions of viewers. But to the show's director, Dave Wilson, "Atomic Lobsters" seemed a technical nightmare, one that he resisted. The piece was put off until the following season.

Wilson never changed his mind about "Atomic Lobsters," but the piece finally appeared on the January 28 episode, hosted by Robert Klein. The concept unfolds over the better part of the show. Jane Curtin reports

on Weekend Update that a Russian satellite has crashed in the northern
Atlantic. Radiation is leaking at an incredible rate, throwing ocean life
off balance and creating bizarre mutations, including a herd of lobsters
now the size of helicopters. The report ends, and so too, supposedly,
does the joke. But later, as Robert Klein is about to introduce that
evening's musical guest, Bonnie Raitt, Curtin runs onstage, bulletin in
hand. The mutant lobsters have moved down the eastern seaboard, and
more have been seen in other cities across the country. President Carter
has declared a state of national emergency, and since no weapon seems
to stop them, all appears lost. Klein jokes that Orthodox Jews have
nothing to fear since lobsters don't eat *them,* either.

After Bonnie Raitt's song, there is a rather long sketch in which
Curtin and Gilda Radner play suburban Jewish housewives smoking a
joint. Radner's character, Rhonda Weiss, gets so stoned that paranoia
sets in; Curtin tries to ease her anxiety but soon she, too, is overwhelmed
by the herb. Suddenly, a loud, weird scream disrupts the sketch. Curtin
and Radner break character and ask the technicians what's wrong. The
screaming continues. John Belushi, dressed as a Bee, enters and says it
sounds like the roar of a giant lobster. The scene then shifts to Rockefeller Center, where the lobsters are killing tourists. (The lobsters' movements recall the work of the great stop-action animator Ray Harryhausen,
best known for his mythical creatures and monsters in films such as *Jason
and the Argonauts*.) Eerie music fills the sound track, music so strange that
it seems to be running backward. In a matter of minutes the lobsters
climb the RCA Building and enter the *SNL* studio.

The studio audience screams in terror. At home base, Robert Klein
describes the final moments as a record for the survivors, if there are
any. The house band plays "Nearer My God to Thee" as soldiers fire
their useless weapons at the offscreen invaders. The lobster roars multiply.
Members of the cast and staff run for their lives, though most are dazed
and bleeding. Belushi is beheaded by a pincer, his body tossed at Klein's
feet. Pools of blood spread across the studio floor, where lie numbers of
disfigured bodies. A blind black man (not Ray Charles) walks into the
scene just as the band is ripped to shreds, their instruments cut off in
mid-note. "Lawdy, lawdy, there's a lobster comin'!" he says but can do
nothing about it, and he joins the growing pile of dead. All is chaos,
but the bills have to be paid, so Klein breaks for a commercial.

We return to a studio in ruins. Smoke drifts over the debris and
wreckage; the audience, technicians, and staff have all been wiped out.
A lone soldier holding a bullhorn walks through and squeezes off a few
rounds from his .45 as Klein speaks to a hand-held camera, his voice
weak, his time short. A giant lobster claw reaches for him, knocks the
camera to the floor, and the screen goes to static. The show's announcer,

Don Pardo, yells out to Klein, but he too is devoured. The credits roll over lobster roars and static. Two voices, O'Donoghue and Davis, assess the situation. O'Donoghue has a plan: The only way to stop the beasts is to eat them. They'll need millions of gallons of boiling water, enough to fill Central Park pond. Also enormous lemons, helpings of butter, nutcrackers, and bibs. The plan becomes a dinner menu, and O'Donoghue and Davis argue about the proper dessert (a swimming pool full of Jell-O? a rum raisin cake the size of a tennis court?) and what constitutes an appetizer. Their voices fade into the static.

"Atomic Lobsters" came off on air nearly without a hitch, but in dress rehearsal there were audio and visual problems, and this sent O'Donoghue into hysterics. Tom Davis watched as his colleague threw scripts into the air, kicked chairs, screamed about incompetence, and generally raised total hell. Audience members exited the studio hushed and intimidated by this mad display; they steered away from O'Donoghue's tantrum, an outburst Davis felt was justified. "Fucking Davey didn't want to do it and he was fighting us all the way," he said of the director, Wilson. O'Donoghue wanted the piece done right for the live show, and for the most part it was.

There were a few mistakes, most notably a camera shot that showed soldiers firing at nothing which ruined the illusion of lobsters in the studio. (There were reports that O'Donoghue went crazy following the live show, too, but Davis maintained that the chief outburst occurred after dress.) Still, "Atomic Lobsters" remains a distinctive moment in SNL's history. In a season in which the writers looked to "feed the machine," as Rosie Shuster described the show's writing process at the time, O'Donoghue attempted to break the thing apart. It was a symbolic effort, a spirited rush against an immovable object. For one night SNL was reduced to rubble; the show had become repetitive and deserved annihilation. Yet like the lobsters themselves, SNL kept coming, the machine squashing everything in its path.

"Atomic Lobsters" proved a fitting epitaph for O'Donoghue's time on the show. At the end of the season he quit so he could pursue a career in film.★ Thanks to Mr. Mike, he was now a certified SNL commodity. He hoped to cash in on this, write the kind of material he wanted without interference, become famous, wear fine clothing, drive

★In Hill's and Weingrad's A Backstage History of Saturday Night Live, they write that O'Donoghue resigned in a huff, telling Lorne Michaels, "Fuck you and fuck your show." O'Donoghue himself told the SoHo Weekly News that he quit because two (unnamed) writers stole one of his ideas and were not "stepped on hard" by Michaels. Whatever the case, O'Donoghue hid his animosity well on the air. In the last show of the third season he not only plays a smiling, singing Mr. Mike, but during the "good night" sequence at the end of the program he waves to the camera, smiles, and shakes several hands.

fast cars, smoke great dope, fuck beautiful women, live the life of a decadent celebrity-artist. It was a role that O'Donoghue tailor-made for himself.

Living well and ripping your enemy's still-beating heart out with your bare hands is the best revenge.

From mid- to late 1977, the *Saturday Matinee* script fattened to an unfilmable length. O'Donoghue wrote the bulk of the screenplay, which covered nearly every aspect of the movie house experience from the 1930s to the 1970s. There was a newsreel, a sports novelty, a documentary, a musical number, a cartoon, a concession stand ad, and a charity ad, as well as several film strips, five coming attractions, and two features. The first draft ran well over two hundred pages, and once Chevy Chase wrote *his* bits, that number would dramatically increase. But Chase held back, preferring instead to play off O'Donoghue and add to the items he was then writing.

"I think probably what happened was, I was stymied," said Chase. "I hadn't written my part of the script, although I helped Michael a lot with his. . . . I came up with a lot of the things in that script—thoughts, moments. We were good at that together." Among the items yet written by Chase were the coming attractions to *Blind Bikers,* a parody of sleazy biker films of the 1960s, and *The Life of God,* a late-1950s, Cinemascope religious epic. If stuck on an idea, the two consulted the Answer Bat—a stuffed brown bat, wings spread, encased in a solid glass bubble, a curio from the collection in Sixteenth Street. But O'Donoghue, inspired, needed few answers as he produced pages and pages of detailed action and dialogue, index fingers stabbing his Smith-Corona, More cigarettes smoked in a continuous chain.

Saturday Matinee was finished during the third season of *SNL,* and there is a sense that O'Donoghue poured his energy into the screenplay once it became clear that many of his ideas were not going to be executed on the show. But there is enthusiasm as well; after all, O'Donoghue was writing with and for Chevy Chase, whose professional heat ensured that the project would make it to the screen. Since *Saturday Matinee* was made up of numerous parts, Chase was cast in various roles—some thirteen by the time the first draft was finished—more of the rising star to go around. An exercise in nostalgia and a parody of fading cinematic forms, *Saturday Matinee* was nevertheless intended to be a blockbuster of its own. So dense and intricate was the screenplay that when filmed it would submerge the audience in a flood of amusing, offensive, horrifying, ridiculous, bizarre images and references. Laughter was but *one* of the responses O'Donoghue and Chase hoped to provoke in what was perhaps the most ambitious project either was ever involved with.

> After the show, why not drop by and say hello to our projectionist? He will be glad to give you a tour of the projection room and show you his cock.
>
> The Management

After a brief travelog, faded and worn stock footage of topless African women dancing and jumping about, breaks apart and leaves the screen blank, a brightly colored title card announces that it is time to follow the bouncing ball and sing "The Animal Song" with the Chase Brothers. Multiple Chevy Chases appear in black tie, and while all speak in the same tone of voice, each boasts specific features: one wears a cowboy hat, another thick round glasses; one weighs six hundred pounds, another sports a banana peel on his shoulder. Then there is Chevy himself, unchanged. Once he announces the song, his brothers exit, clumsily banging into one another as they make their escape. Left alone, Chevy asks the audience to sing with him instead. The ball begins to bounce as the lyrics roll beneath him:

> *A rooster says "Good morning!"*
> *With a cock-a-doodle-do*
> *Good morning!*
> *A horse's neigh is just his way*
> *Of saying "How are you?"*
> *A lion growls "Hello!" and owls*
> *Ask "Why?" and "Where?" and*
> *"Who?"*
> *May I suggest you get undressed*
> *And show them your wazoo.*
>
> *The animals, the animals*
> *Let's talk dirty to the animals*
> *"Fuck you, Mr. Bunny!"*
> *"Eat shit, Mr. Bear!"*
> *If they don't love it,*
> *They can shove it.*
> *Frankly we don't care.*

The "audience" is heard singing on the sound track, starting slowly but quickly building to chorus proportions. More insults are hurled at the animals—" 'Up yours, Mr. Hippo!'/'Piss off, Mr. Fox!'/Go tell a chicken/'Suck my dick!' an'/Give it chicken pox . . ."—before Chevy concludes,

> From birds in the treetops
> To snakes in the grass.
> But never tell an alligator
> "Bite my—"
> No, never tell an alligator
> "Bite my—"
> Don't ever tell an alligator
> "Bite my
> Snatch!"

while the "audience," fooled, sings "Ass." Their collective silhouette is seen on-screen cheering and applauding as Chevy pulls a shade down over the shadows.

Next comes *Captain Windjammer,* a Hollywood sea adventure presented in the MGM style. The opening shot is of an old, leather-bound book, its corners decorated in metal, lying on a table cluttered with sailing maps, charts, and other nautical-oriented items. A hand reaches into frame and opens the book, which shows us the film's title, the names of its stars (Errol Flynn and Olivia de Havilland), and its producer (David O. Selznick). More pages are turned; more names are shown—supporting players, screenwriters, technical crew, director, and so on. The pages that follow the credits set the scene: It is 1581, Philip II of Spain terrorizes his neighbors, his empire extends to the ocean, and only one man can stop him, Captain Jeremy Windjammer. "This is his story . . ." Music swells, a long beat is taken, but instead of live action we see more pages turned. In fact, th ntire film is written down and the audience must read it. In glorio t we see described the sinking of ships, cutlass duels, the overthr Philip, Windjammer standing victorious. Finally, the book is clos "film" ends.

Following *Captain Windjammer* intended coming attractions, three of which Chase did not finish g. Of the remaining two, only *Original Shaft* has punch. (The other, Company, is a fags-in-foxholes spoof that relies heavily on "boys will be girls" jokes, delivered by rugged frontline soliders.) As its title indicates, *Original Shaft* is a precursor to the blaxploitation classic. Made in 1934, it shows Shaft not as the heroic black detective "who goes up against the mob and shoots about five hundred white people in the face" but as a grinnin', shufflin' Negro who all but made the Nation of Islam inevitable. This Shaft works for an unseen white boss to whom he is obedient and loyal. "Ah kin see mah face in dem hubcaps, boss," says Shaft while washing the car; "You mus' be haulin' aroun' gold bars in dese-heah suitcases, boss," he says, carrying bags at the train station. With friends Dishwax, who plays Bones to his Tambo, and Flotilla the maid, Shaft undoes the modest civil rights gains made by Stepin Fetchit; but there is hope:

BOSS: The trouble with you jungle bunnies is—
SHAFT: Ahh, boss, ahh, we doan' wanna be called "jungle bunnies" no moh.
BOSS: What *do* you want to be called, Shaft?
SHAFT: Ahh, we wanna be called "jungle *rabbits!*"

Shaft's self-esteem, while sincere, could never withstand the punishing blows suffered by *Invisible Dog,* a cartoon mutt whose tragic existence follows Shaft's. Patterned on the animated mayhem of Tex Avery and the *Tom and Jerry*–era Hanna-Barbera, *Invisible Dog* is, simply, a dog that can't be seen but can be heard yelping and whimpering after getting brained by a succession of falling safes and pianos, a bathtub, a road-leveler, and a brick house. The *Dog*'s sad life is comparable to the unfortunate animals in Mr. Mike's "Least-Loved Bedtime Tales," and the connection to *SNL* is made explicit in the next segment, *Avalanche of Sports.* Here the Lou Gerhig *"I'm gonna die!"* bit is presented in its original *Saturday Night* form, altered slightly to fit the different medium. After all, what's considered tasteless for television oftentimes needs to be jacked up for the big screen.

To this point, *Saturday Matinee* runs sixty-three pages, roughly half of an average screenplay for a ninety-minute film. But the above is a mere warm-up for the project's main event: *Planet of the Cheap Special Effects,* a science fiction feature that is the sum of nearly every space movie in existence, from *Abbott and Costello Go to Mars* to *Cat Women of the Moon* to *Earth vs. the Flying Saucers* to *World Without End.* O'Donoghue and Chase screened almost fifty films to get the right look, the proper dialogue, the *perfect* sound and visual effects, and so on. Well, perhaps not the perfect sound and visual effects, for if nothing else, *Planet* is an ode to the low-budget, small-studio output of the 1950s and early 1960s in which production values and script quality bordered on Ed Wood territory.★ It was an area of pop culture that truly excited O'Donoghue, and his eagerness to capture this in *Planet* fairly jumps from every page.

The plot of *Planet of the Cheap Special Effects* is familiar and appropri-

---

★Indeed, Wood himself felt he could cash in with a sci-fi quickie of his own, the classic *Plan Nine From Outer Space.* Not screened by O'Donoghue and Chase, *Plan Nine* nevertheless contains much of what the pair were after in their *Planet* film. It was left to Tim Burton and Johnny Depp to pay homage to the cross-dressing *auteur.*

ately thin: An American space team, the Astro Squad, blasts off to find life on Mars, but once "there" they are reminded of home—oxygen, trees, blue skies, English-speaking inhabitants, et al. Soon it turns out that they are not on Mars but on the Earth of the near future. As they make their escape some of the squad are killed, and by the end only the ship's captain remains, whizzing through space in search of the time warp that will take him home . . . or will it? Until then he is the final human adrift in the dark void.

It is in the details where *Planet* springs to life. And there are many, *many* details. Ever the perfectionist and anal to a fault, O'Donoghue loads the script down with paragraph-long, sometimes page-long, camera instructions, film references, costume suggestions, alternate dialogue, and various ways a scene or scenes may be interpreted. He leaves nothing to chance and dotes on each sequence like a mad choreographer who plans a dance down to the smallest twitch or breath. The problem, of course, is that any director who saw this mass of notes would toss them aside and go with *his* vision of how a scene should be set, lit, filmed. But O'Donoghue seemed not to worry about this prospect; he had the film fully mapped in his head, and this he followed until his destination was reached.

References from the 1950s abound in *Planet*. There is a minor commie plot and a talking mule named Mr. Bob; the spaceship's interior is decorated with metal office furniture, a Coke machine, a Norge refrigerator, bunk beds, and a large black dial phone, while the ship's equipment has brand names such as Motorola, Philco, and Sylvania; the captain, Dan Argus (to be played by Chase), smokes Chesterfield cigarettes, even when en route to Mars. But the majority of references emerge once the Astro Squad sets foot on the "alien" planet. Here, in a landscape devastated by atomic war, O'Donoghue's imagination attains ramming speed.

The Astro Squad, a group out of central casting—Doc, the goateed intellectual; Larry, the ladies' man; Righty, the ship's coward; Buzz, the newspaperman brought along to record the journey—move through a strange but familiar terrain. "I have the craziest feeling that I've been here before," says Captain Argus as he walks past an orange tree and into a tropical jungle. They are, of course, on Earth; but as they walk lightning flashes above them and changes the sky's color, and they notice that the lush green background is now black and white. Then Doc makes another discovery:

DOC: Have you noticed it? We're out of sync.
ARGUS: What do you mean, "out of sync"?
DOC: I mean that sometimes our words don't match our lips . . .
ARGUS: It's strange, Doc. Very strange. Everything about this planet
        is phony and unconvincing.

But soon the squad encounters something real, a woman, Flirtatia. Buxom and blond, clad in a revealing ancient Greek costume, high heels, and sunglasses, Flirtatia fights off a Spine-Mangler, a hideous mutant male creature missing a jaw and growing a dwarf hand out of its temple. The squad members kill the Mangler with their Blaster rays and befriend Flirtatia, who then takes them to a cave where dwell the inhabitants of Starlos: a race of gorgeous women between the ages of seventeen and twenty-one, all of whom are endowed with large breasts and good posture. There they meet Queen Voluptua, "Ruler of the Lost City of Lah." Voluptua behaves in much the same fashion as the multititted queen in *Shame of the Jungle*. She is a beautiful tyrant and killer who craves companionship and tenderness—that is, when she isn't terrorizing her subjects. Voluptua invites the squad to stay the night and informs them that all in Starlos are skilled practitioners of oral sex. "Forward my mail!" exclaims Larry.

From here there is hell to pay. It turns out that the women of Starlos are zombie sex kittens controlled by the Brain, a human brain in an electrified plastic dome that operates in the ruins of a once-posh hotel. The Brain thrives on the blood of space explorers the galaxy over; his agent of doom is Bloodmaster 3000, "a steel Dracula to feed my genius!" says the Brain, who receives the blood the giant vampire robot drains from its victims. The Astro Squad is on the menu, but they face other predators as well. In addition to the Spine-Manglers are volcanic lung worms and a thing called the Flying Lunch—half fly, half macaroni-and-cheese casserole. The Lunch was created through a food transmitter accident; it's the size of a cocker spaniel, has insect legs and a mouth that drools cheese and eats flesh. Like its fellow predators, there's nothing cheap about the Lunch. It is intended to frighten the film's characters *and* the audience.

Captain Argus fights his way back to the ship, Flirtatia in tow. Most of the squad is wiped out; only Argus, Flirtatia, and Doc survive. They blast off and head, they believe, home. While Argus tells his new love of the sex life they'll have on Earth, Flirtatia crumbles to dust, her five-hundred-year-old body exposed to nonradioactive air. Doc, too, is different, for he's been turned into a zombie. He and Argus battle while the cheap planet, ripped by volcanic eruptions, explodes in the distance. Deprived of his power source, Doc dies; but before he goes, Argus asks a question that has nagged him since they landed:

ARGUS: Doc, why are the effects so cheap, and the plots so flimsy?
DOC: I'm afraid that's something we'll never know. There are
       doors that Man was never meant to open.

Throughout *Planet of the Cheap Special Effects* we are reminded just how low-budget this post-atomic world is. The film's color stock changes for no reason; the voice track and sound track go out of sync; rear projection alternates with painted backdrops and neither corresponds with the action in the foreground; characters bump into shoddy scenery pieces, behind which are stenciled "Sex Kittens From Beyond the Stars," the "original" title of the film we are watching and of the film within it. When the Great Atomic War of 1956 began, *Sex Kittens* was in production. Its cast of starlets survived and mutated into Starlos, buxom zombie blow job artists who seduce, then kill, space travelers. Radiation has kept them young and pert, and they are controlled by the Brain through a radio telepathy device embedded in the base of the skull. What "civilization" they do have is based entirely on the 1955 Frederick's of Hollywood catalog, the only "book" not destroyed in the war. The Lost City of Lah is, of course, Los Angeles; the Brain's home, the Beverly Hills Hotel, a haunt favored by Hollywood bloodsuckers.

Planet of the Cheap Special Effects contains elements of comedy and horror. Not content to merely parody bad science fiction films, a simple, redundant exercise, O'Donoghue wanted to shift without warning from the corny to the ultraviolent—and, in places, combine the two. This he attempts with the Flying Lunch. Seen buzzing around on black wire, consistent with the planet's cheapness, the Lunch savagely rips open a squad member's throat and gnaws on the flesh within. Blood sprays over cheese and macaroni, an image at once ridiculous and terrifying—at least in O'Donoghue's mind. In those pre–Industrial Light and Magic days, such balance would have been difficult to achieve, though in the hands of either David Lynch or Cronenberg . . . perhaps. This was but one of the many challenges laid down in the *Planet* screenplay. The immediate challenge, however, was cutting the screenplay itself.

The *Planet* portion of *Saturday Matinee* ran 164 pages, far longer than an average screenplay for a feature film, much less one that was part of a larger project. As it stood in first draft, *Saturday Matinee* would probably have clocked in at just under four hours, a comedy marathon that only a Fassbinder could appreciate. The blue pencil was thus desperately needed. But O'Donoghue, understandably proud of his first-rate work, refused to cut anything. Chase, who shared O'Donoghue's high opinion of the screenplay, told his friend that rewrites were a necessity in Hollywood and that the film would not be made unless they did some serious editing. O'Donoghue, according to Chase, remained obstinate: *Saturday Matinee* was a masterpiece, *Planet* the jewel. It was perfect the way it was. Now Chase faced a dilemma: Should he go ahead and cut the script himself or should he respect O'Donoghue's position, which meant the project would die? "That was the problem, and I understood it as Michael's right as an artist and I felt stymied," Chase later said.

"He was irresponsible in that way," said Chase of O'Donoghue's position. "And that's what it is and that's my view. It's a shame, but those are the exigencies of the commercial/professional world that he liked to make fun of, that he didn't want to be a part of, and yet he did want to be a part of." Chase said he told O'Donoghue, " 'You're going to have to learn to compromise to some degree.' And he wouldn't. . . . 'I can't compromise. I'm Michael O'Donoghue.' [In Hollywood] you gotta act, you've got to convince and kiss ass. That's not Michael. It is the most morally repugnant, ethically reprehensible business, and if you have a hair in your ass as an artist you won't cave in. You'll suffer the slings and arrows but you won't get the outrageous fortune." Chase knew that cutting *Saturday Matinee* on his own would invite O'Donoghue's wrath, but his decision *not* to cut the script and thus not make the film ensured that O'Donoghue would be angry with him anyway. So Chase did nothing and turned his attention to two projects then offered him: *Animal House* and *Foul Play,* the latter of which he chose as his feature film debut.

As expected, O'Donoghue viewed Chase's inaction as a betrayal. And since the deal was with United Artists and the film was a vehicle for Chase, O'Donoghue could not shop the script around; *Saturday Matinee* would gather dust while *Planet of the Cheap Special Effects* earned a following among a small number of Hollywood writers, producers, players.★ His hard work come to naught, O'Donoghue complained bitterly to friends about what he saw as Chase's lack of support. Soon people from O'Donoghue's manager, Barry Secunda, to Marilyn Miller regarded Chase as a person who tried to ruin O'Donoghue in Hollywood or who sold him down the river so that he could make lesser, commercially viable films. O'Donoghue himself never personally confronted Chase with his feelings; there was no outburst, no high-pitched screaming of "Scum!" Still, the *Saturday Matinee* experience permanently changed O'Donoghue's relationship with Chase, and from that point on theirs was a classic comedy love/hate affair.

Better a daughter in a cathouse than a son writing screenplays. She'll suck a lot less dick.

★In 1987, *Amazon Women on the Moon* was released. A sketch-oriented film that owed plenty to *The Groove Tube, Tunnelvision,* and *Kentucky Fried Movie,* its centerpiece bit was a 1950s sci-fi movie called *Amazon Women on the Moon,* in which a crew of astronauts encounters a race of beautiful lunar women. *Planet* may or may not have inspired this parody, for the genre was pretty well known. But *Amazon*'s intentional cheap look, replete with scratches and jumps in the film, its "plot" and specific gags (the rocket sounds like a stalled car when started), suggests that its writers were at the very least aware of the *Planet* screenplay.

Saturday Matinee collapsed, but O'Donoghue did not lack offers. In the spring of 1978 he was contacted by Woody Allen, who wanted O'Donoghue in his next film project. Allen had created a minor character that complemented O'Donoghue's *SNL* persona, and his own character, Isaac Davis, was a writer for a "hip" sketch comedy show. The film, later titled *Manhattan,* contains several masked references to *SNL.* Isaac thinks he's wasting his time writing material for an audience conditioned by television, but other characters speak positively of the show and its "chancy," off-the-wall humor—just as a fair number of fashionable Manhattanites spoke of *SNL* at the time. (Gary Weis, *SNL*'s former in-house filmmaker, plays one of Isaac's television colleagues.) Though his character is not connected to the comedy show and he is on-screen for all of a few minutes, O'Donoghue resonates.

Originally, O'Donoghue's character, Dennis, was written into three scenes. He first appears with Diane Keaton at an ERA benefit party. Keaton's character, Mary, is overeducated and pretentious; she is chatting with Dennis when Isaac shows up and complains about a Nazi march in New Jersey. Dennis interrupts to say that he and Mary are discussing orgasms, which is the theme of a project he has in the works:

DENNIS: I'm about to direct a film of my own script, and the premise is this guy screws so great . . .

ISAAC: *Screws* so great?

DENNIS: . . . Screws so great that when he brings a woman to orgasm she's so fulfilled that she dies, right? Now, this one [to Mary] finds this hostile.

MARY: Hostile? God, it's *worse* than hostile. It's aggressive-homicidal!

ISAAC: She *dies*?

MARY: You'll have to forgive Dennis. He's Harvard direct to Beverly Hills. It's Theodor Reik with a touch of Charles Manson.

Dennis, Mary, Isaac, and a few others leave the party and go to a Chinese restaurant. In a cab en route, Dennis reveals his survivalist side.

I jog, I work out at the gym, I lift weights. I study the martial arts, judo. I shoot my pistol at a target range. I keep prepared—because there's no question, a social upheaval is coming eventually—somebody's going to organize the lower classes, the blacks, the workers—and when they come charging up my lawn past my swimming pool in Beverly Hills, they've got no way of knowing I'm a Marxist.

In the restaurant, the discussion turns to culture. Dennis believes that all the old forms such as print and jazz are finished because "Video is where it's at—when the big screens get perfected and the cable is developed—you can sit home and watch sixty channels—once that happens it means movies are dead—like when films came in theater was dead." Isaac, not exactly bemused, replies, "Jazz is dead, the printed word is dead, movies are dead, theater is dead—I think the dead people are having all the fun."

By linking Dennis to sex, violence, and death, and by making him a theorist of social and cultural decay, Woody Allen brings O'Donoghue into his urbane world but strictly on his terms. Fans of Mr. Mike are appeased, the Allen faithful unthreatened. O'Donoghue was, of course, elated to be cast in *Manhattan,* Allen's first effort since his success with the Academy Award–winning *Annie Hall*; and though O'Donoghue saw this as confirmation of his rising celebrity status, he confessed to nervousness when he shot his scenes in early August. "I remember my first scene was a major scene in a Chinese restaurant," he said. "I got there and no one even spoke to me! I said, 'Hello, my name is Michael O'Donoghue. I'm in this film.' I mean, common courtesy has gone right by the board. And then Woody turns to the cameraman and says, 'Okay, you ready to lay one down?' I did this take *very* badly. *Very badly.* I was jittery and missed lines. I was *really* shaken after it and I thought, 'Holy shit, am I in trouble!' "

With Diane Keaton in *Manhattan*

Despite his stage and television experience, O'Donoghue was not relaxed as a performer. "Usually, I'm chickenshit as an actor—don't give enough, back off, and get afraid," he once admitted. Yet during the filming of the restaurant scene, O'Donoghue discovered "a cheap, but very good trick. I started eating Chinese food—rapidly—throughout the fucking thing . . . but I'd blow lines 'cause I had this Moo Goo Gai Pan hanging out of my mouth. This threw my timing and made it very natural because I had to finish a mouthful before talking. It's just using props aggressively, but it works." Due to the excessive heat that hit New York late that summer, O'Donoghue suffered migraines and took Percodan thoughout the filming of his scenes. He was "zone-y" and in a "narco haze," he said, but remained cogent enough to pick up his cues and deliver his lines. Still, his mind was not at its sharpest.

> I remember one time missing a line at the Museum of Modern Art [the site of the party scene]. We had like seven hundred extras there and I blew a take. I said to [Diane] Keaton, "You know, the thing about Percodan is that— two things actually—you can't remember your lines but you don't give a fuck so it kind of balances out." 'Cause I didn't care if I'd blown the take and Gordon Willis, who shot *The Godfather,* had to crank it up again. I was on Percs.

Woody Allen cut the scenes in the cab and the Chinese restaurant and edited O'Donoghue down to the orgasm/death line at the party. It seemed appropriate, somehow, that O'Donoghue be reduced to a brief but impressive appearance. It was the ultimate commercialization of his persona—Woody Allen's Mr. Mike. A sinister quip then he's off, presumably to slash through the crowd at Elaine's.

Back at NBC, the commercialization of O'Donoghue was especially desired by Paul Klein, head of network programming for the East Coast, and by Lorne Michaels. Although O'Donoghue spent his final season on *SNL* complaining about the show's "rot" and how his material was being censored or neutered to fit this new order, he remained a valuable resource to the show and, oddly enough, to the network. *SNL* was a force, and so it made television sense to spin off elements of the show and see what could work and where. Chevy Chase's specials were the first step in this direction, and there were plans to make Gilda Radner the next Carol Burnett by giving her a prime-time show. Then there was O'Donoghue, who, despite his toning down of Mr. Mike the previous year, was certainly *not* ready for the "family hour." But Klein and Michaels saw possibilities in late night, where O'Donoghue could present *his* humor *his* way free from the dictates of the *SNL* format. His specials would air in *SNL*'s time slot when the show was on hiatus. Thus NBC would cash in on O'Donoghue's "weird" humor without his disrupting *SNL*.

O'Donoghue was up for it. He placed himself above *SNL* so often in the press that anything less than his own set of projects would be considered a step back. First he wanted to do something called *Eyes*. The camera would remain in close-up on O'Donoghue's eyes (seen through his dark blue lenses) as he read selections from Alisteir Crowley's mystical texts and Octave Mirbeau's *The Torture Garden*. A compelling idea, but not what the network ordered. He then decided to write a TV movie. Intent on getting fresh creative input, O'Donoghue hired a crew of young writers to assist him in what he called Project X. He didn't want the standard TV scribe or anyone associated with *SNL,* but he still needed people he knew and could trust. So he turned to a trio of friends, Emily Prager, Dirk Wittenborn, and Mitch Glazer, and together they formed an unusual but effective team.

O'Donoghue knew Prager from her time on the *National Lampoon Radio Hour,* where she played a variety of female characters that she drew from a well of voices and accents. Surrounded by the likes of O'Donoghue and Doug Kenney (with whom she had a romantic relationship), Prager eventually moved into comedy writing. Before long her material appeared in the *Lampoon,* and much of her work bore the unmistakable style of O'Donoghue. Like him, Prager could wound with flair; and like him, she was fond of the comic bon mot:

Anyone who could murder an unborn fetus shouldn't be allowed to mother a child.

If God had meant women to give blow jobs, she wouldn't have given them teeth.

Dirk Wittenborn was a young novelist and world traveler. He knew Lorne Michaels, which exposed him to O'Donoghue, and the two struck up an intense friendship; for a time, Wittenborn lived upstairs from O'Donoghue on Sixteenth Street. Wittenborn's style was a bit drier than O'Donoghue's, but he was smart, confident, and when needed swung a mean comic club. Mitch Glazer was a *Rolling Stone* writer who previously worked for the magazine's brash competition, *Crawdaddy,* where he wrote the first in-depth profile of John Belushi seen in the national press (this at a time when practically every *SNL* story focused on Chevy Chase). But the profile's long opening paragraph played not to Belushi but to O'Donoghue, who read with glee and satisfaction Glazer's description of his "sinister" self. "Michael O'Donoghue looks like a chemist in a Marseille heroin lab who sells children on the side," it began. "Michael

would be very effective with piano wire on a dark foggy street . . ."
Though Glazer had no real comedy writing experience, his style and
take on O'Donoghue were enough to win him a job.

The Project X team settled into third-floor offices in Manhattan's
Brill Building in mid-1978. The first project, titled *War of the Insect Gods,*
was to be a sci-fi horror film about mutant cockroaches—a nod not only
to "Atomic Lobsters" but to O'Donoghue's primal fear of insects. A tiny
alien spacecraft lands in New York. Out crawls a silver roach from outer
space. It mixes and breeds with its Earth cousins, spreads its genes, which
mutate at an astounding rate, and this causes the cockroaches to grow
rapidly in size and intelligence. Soon, packs of giant roaches hunt down
and destroy millions of humans. At first they chew people up in the
standard manner (tear into the body, rip the flesh, crunch the bones),
but as their brains develop they set traps and stock the now-looted stores
with poisoned canned food. Roach police squads are formed, and "officers" kill their prey with technologically advanced death rays. Humans
become insects, insects the exterminators.

War of the Insect Gods ends with a stunning, terrifying scene.
Throughout the story a human exterminator named Ed looks for ways
to resist the roaches. He accidentally discovers that ether is their Kryp-
tonite; he fills bottle upon bottle with the clear, deadly liquid and enlists
a few human survivors to help him kill the beasts. As they make their
way up Park Avenue, where roach congregation is high, they are struck
with awe by the sight before them. A ceremony is in progress:

> Giant roaches fill the Avenue and cling to the sides of buildings. Each roach
> carries a bright light. Focus of ceremony is a beautifully garbed roach and
> his attendants, who are performing an elaborate ritual, a grand spectacle,
> full of pageantry but unfathomable to human minds. The roaches no longer
> seem ugly and frightening. Now they glisten in the light. They are beautiful.

A white, transparent nymph roach emerges from an egg case, "diaph-
anous, luminescent, beautiful beyond all belief." It is the Insect God, the
symbol of spirituality in the roach-dominated world. It spreads its wings
and flies into the dark sky above as we hear a reading from the Book
of Joel: "The insects shall enter the windows like a thief. The earth shall
quake before them, the heavens tremble. The sun and the moon shall
be dark and the stars shall withdraw their shining."

War of the Insect Gods, delivered in the fall, went straight into the
dumper. Paul Klein wasn't thrilled with the idea of a film in which
roaches take over New York (which he felt had already occurred, albeit
on a smaller, less brutal scale) and thought it would cost too much to
make, given *War*'s reliance on special effects, apocalyptic scenes of a city

in ruins, and so on.★ He told O'Donoghue he wanted a smaller project, a TV show, something shot on videotape. Klein mentioned the odd documentary film from the early 1960s, *Mondo Cane*. Perhaps O'Donoghue could parody its haphazard style, jump from image to image, and cover the oddities of the contemporary world. O'Donoghue saw plenty of possibilities in the suggestion; he returned to Project X and with Prager, Wittenborn, and Glazer began assembling *Mr. Mike's Mondo Video*. By November the shooting script was completed and approved by the network, and *Mondo* went in front of the cameras with O'Donoghue as director.

As the shooting progessed it became clear that O'Donoghue, in Prager's words, "absolutely knew nothing about direction, and he made lots of mistakes. But he was very good-humored about it and he was very happy to be able to do it. He didn't take it for granted." Wittenborn noticed some nervousness in O'Donoghue as the project went along; to him it seemed that "Michael bit off more than he could chew," that the combination of acting, directing, and basically overseeing every aspect of the production tended to wear him down a bit. Then he would perk up and push the others with comments such as, "It's Emmy time! I can feel it!" But there were endless takes, especially in a sequence called "Cat Swimming School," which consisted of Wittenborn as a swimming instructor tossing cats into a pool. "Michael just loved it, he was like a kid," said Wittenborn. "I mean, he was gleeful—definite interesting streak in him . . . He was getting to see cats thrown in the water! He liked it so much he did it over and over again. I said, 'Michael, I think it should be a little shorter. Michael, let's cut it.' There was this working to death, I thought."

Shooting ended in early 1979, and O'Donoghue began to edit the footage in post-production. Prager was there to help, but O'Donoghue knew he needed an experienced technical hand and so brought in his *Radio Hour* colleague Bob Tischler. When first shown the raw footage, Tischler was taken aback: Continuity was lacking, props would jump from shot to shot, the lighting was substandard. "It was very frustrating because [O'Donoghue] didn't really know what he was doing," said Tischler. "He knew comedically what he wanted but he didn't know how to get it. . . . It was a source of conflict for us."

Tischler waded into *Mondo* and attempted to make the thing look presentable. There was so much to fix that at times he threw up his hands and complained that the project was out of control. O'Donoghue wasn't pleased with Tischler's criticism and felt that it was more personal

★The premise of monster roaches destroying New York was ultimately realized in the 1997 horror film, *Mimic*, which starred Mira Sorvino. Project X was nearly twenty years ahead of the curve.

than professional. Tischler said it was simple: What you do is take good footage and make it better, not take ill-conceived and poorly executed footage and try to save it. Postproduction proceeded as O'Donoghue and Tischler became angrier and angrier with one another. Lorne Michaels, who was *Mondo*'s executive producer, grew anxious over the way the project was developing. It was his money (of which he reportedly lost $250,000), and when Michaels met with a very frustrated Tischler and heard what was going on, his anxiety deepened.

Tischler and his technical crew saved what they could of *Mondo,* but the show's humor, some of which was first-rate, remained hampered by O'Donoghue's poor direction. Tischler found his friend's intolerance for incompetence hypocritical, since in this case O'Donoghue couldn't direct and didn't admit to it. O'Donoghue, on the other hand, justified *Mondo*'s ragged look on the grounds that it was *supposed* to be ragged. This was the "next thing" in video comedy, O'Donoghue said, a rapid-fire, lunatic spree of images and music. Perhaps Tischler didn't get *that*. The project represented the first time the two ever seriously fought. So intense was their conflict that once *Mondo* was completed they didn't speak for several months.

O'Donoghue handed *Mondo* to NBC on April 1. Paul Klein, who, Prager thought, resembled "Walter Matthau as a network executive," remained supportive of O'Donoghue's effort, though he was perplexed by some of its humor and images. But Herminio Traviesas, still in charge of network Standards and Practices, loathed the thing. When *Mondo*'s opening scene of O'Donoghue holding a handgun and sitting cross-legged in a grimy, rabbit-filled room appeared on his monitor, Traviesas wondered just what in hell his network had sponsored.

> Good evening. I'm Mr. Mike, inviting you to come with me into a world where the bizarre is commonplace *and* the commonplace bizarre. It is an odyssey of aggressive weirdness. Whatever raw, savage acts man's hellish brain can conceive, our cameras are there, scouring the globe, seeking out the cheap thrills, the pointless perversities, the shabby secrets, the grotesque, the pathetic—"

He looks sharply over his shoulder—has he heard something? The rabbits scuffle and cluster along the wall, no doubt in fear of getting shot. The mood is set, and from here we enter "the incredible world of *Mr. Mike's Mondo Video.*"

Ragged and coarse images accelerate. Cats are thrown into pools. Lingerie models in multicolor afros jump over a campfire. Girls in net stockings kiss each other. *Hawaii Five-0*'s Jack Lord is worshiped as the living god. Bare-breasted African women dance in a living room. An elephant is electrocuted. People wearing Mao masks invade a suburban home and shoot leisure items. A hand appears silently between folds of flesh, disappears. Pat Nixon watches as a pygmy dances at her feet. Nazi oven mitts. Gig Young's groceries. A peek up Cheryl Tieg's dress. Japanese models bathe in dolphin blood. The song of the harpooned humpback whale. Christmas on other planets. The Mouse Princess hit by two trains. A French waiter verbally and physically abuses American tourists. More bare-breasted African women dancing. Crazed Libyans burn photos of Mr. Mike.

Dan Aykroyd appears, says hello, removes his boots, and shows us why he is a "genetic mutant": The second and third toes of each foot are joined by a webbed mass of flesh. Aykroyd presses the head of a Phillips screwdriver between the webbed toes to prove that the mass is organic and very much a part of him. A secret govenment film displays the latest weapon of the American war machine: Laser Bra 2000. Army test models strip to their underwear and shoot targets with laser rays that emit from the bra's nipple. But perhaps most *Mondo* of all are the number of sexy American gals who drop their handsome boyfriends in favor of creeps:

MARGOT KIDDER: Blackheads drive me wild.

TERRI GARR: If you want to get to first base with me, honey, spit when you talk.

JANE CURTIN: When my date blows his nose in his hankerchief and then looks at it, I can't say no.

GILDA RADNER: I go the limit for a guy with bad breath. And if he has plaque on his teeth? Wigga! Wigga!

DEBORAH HARRY: I think it's cute when guys miss the toilet.

But the crowning touch comes as Jill Duis whispers, "When I reach down and feel a firm colostomy bag, I know I'm with a real man."

Mondo Video ends on a bloodstained beach where Mr. Mike, after insulting the local natives for their addiction to America's discarded fads, stares up to the tropical sky, a spear lodged in his chest, a rabbit hopping from his pocket and away. Traviesas, perhaps inspired by this scene, announced a week after receiving the tape that *Mondo Video* would "appear on this network over my dead body." This led to a number of meetings among Traviesas, Klein, O'Donoghue, and Michaels as they negotiated what material could stay and what had to go. The network ordered a third of the show cut. It made a list; among the demands: no webbed toes, no gals who love creeps, no throwing cats into the pool, and above all, no topless African women shaking their "you-know-whats" at the camera!

After consideration, O'Donoghue agreed to the cuts. Then the network wanted *another* third of the show cut, then a few more items. Trim this part, tone that down, etc. It was Lorne Michaels's view that the network boys simply didn't get it. But to O'Donoghue the increasing demands were an affront. *Fuck* NBC, he said. They approved the shooting script and then balked. Typical corporate pigs. "The censors remind me of those Jap soldiers they keep finding in caves, still fighting a phantom army, unaware that the war was lost years ago," wrote O'Donoghue to himself during the storm. As he searched for answers, O'Donoghue knew one thing: "*Mr. Mike's Mondo Video* is the show NBC isn't proud as a peacock about."

Sensing a marketing angle and convinced that O'Donoghue's humor would sell, Paul Klein bought *Mondo Video* from the network for an estimated $375,000. He struck a deal with New Line Cinema to release *Mondo* nationally to movie theaters as "The TV show that can't be shown on TV!" But there was one problem: Most of *Mondo* had been shot on videotape. This necessitated a video-to-film transfer, which gave *Mondo* a ragged look beyond O'Donoghue's dreams. The "film" appeared murky, and when added to the uneven premises, the below-average production values, and the fact that it was paced for television, *Mondo Video* was a bomb ready to drop.

Mondo's "Gala World Premiere" took place at the Forum Theatre in Manhattan on September 19, 1979. The premiere was, by every account, a prime disaster. Mitch Glazer heard people in the audience ask one another, "Is this funny?" People squirmed in their seats. Very few laughed. That *Mondo* had commercial breaks added to the tension. When the "film" ended, patrons moved on to a dime-a-dance hall called the Tango Palace for a post–premiere party. But among the Project X crowd, spirits were low. Wittenborn was embarrassed by *Mondo*'s reception, and Prager had more than a few cups of blue *Mondo* punch. O'Donoghue kept pretty much to himself during the party; according to onlookers he didn't seem pleased. Once *Mondo* was released nationally and reports filtered in of crowds ripping up seats and beating up ushers, O'Donoghue brightened, at least to the press. "I'm quite thrilled, in fact," he said in a small entertainment publication, *Good Times*.

People just don't dislike this movie, they REALLY DISLIKE this movie. There was a report in Toronto that a third of the audience tried to get their money back. We've had a guy beaten up, a screen slashed. I mean, there's a difference between disliking a movie and this. I'm touched that some primal chord is being struck there.

MR. MIKE'S
MONDO VIDEO

WITH SATURDAY NIGHT LIVE STAR MICHAEL O'DONOGHUE AND FRIENDS

PRODUCED & DIRECTED BY MICHAEL O'DONOGHUE   EXECUTIVE PRODUCER LORNE MICHAELS
WRITTEN BY MITCHELL GLAZER   MICHAEL O'DONOGHUE   EMILY PRAGER   DIRK WITTENBORN
PRODUCTION DESIGN BY FRANNE & EUGENE LEE   A P.K.O. PRESENTATION
COLOR BY ROMAGLO   FROM NEW LINE CINEMA

Plus Special  MR. BILL SHOW

Newspaper ad for "the TV show that can't be shown on TV," 1979

With Mitch Glazer at the *Mondo Video* premiere party

Apparently, the "film" struck a chord in Hollywood as well. Following *Mondo*'s brief but infamous release, O'Donoghue was offered a deal to write, direct, and star in three films for Paramount. He was to receive a substantial fee, reportedly a million dollars (1979 currency, of course). *People, Rolling Stone,* and *Newsweek* all hailed him as the next Woody Allen or Mel Brooks. Though seemingly on top of the world, O'Donoghue's career began a decade-long slide. He reached his peak with *Mondo Video* and set off down the trail to Hollywood and true, mind-shattering frustration.

eight

Making people laugh is the lowest form of comedy.

O'Donoghue's first film for Paramount, to be produced by Bert Schnieder of *Easy Rider* and *Five Easy Pieces* fame, was called *The Dreammaster.* Unlike *Saturday Matinee,* this film was not intended by O'Donoghue to be a comedy or a parody of familiar genres. "It's . . . about a man," he explained at the time.

> Actually, a person of no particular gender. A person who can manipulate your dreams from a mythical city . . . very bleak and geometric like an Alphaville. . . . He has a ray that beams common phobic dreams. It's like a machine, a TV transmitter that goes directly to your head while you sleep. So he can drive people to leap out of windows due to the fear of what they *think* is going on. You immediately fall into his power. . . . As this person becomes more and more powerful and the world falls closer and closer to fascistic order, the one protaganist who can get near him seeks to destroy him.

This was the *simple* explanation. O'Donoghue's idea, inspired by the Vincent Price film *The Last Man on Earth,* was too abstract to be effectively realized, so he turned to Nelson Lyon and asked him to collaborate on the script. Although the two men had been friends for nearly eight years, this was the first time they worked together (O'Donoghue tried to get Lyon to write for the *Lampoon,* but Lyon turned down the offer). Lyon entered the project with confidence, pleased to be part of a major studio film. He also was a serious student of cinema and had an encylcopedic knowledge of both American and European film history. Since there was no story as such, Lyon and O'Donoghue discussed what or who the Dreammaster was and why it would terrorize humanity. They developed its stated purpose: to save the human race and to bring order and morality and control to mankind. O'Donoghue came up with an opening image of a man in a high-rise apartment waking from a deep sleep to find insects crawling all over his room and bed. Horrified, he jumps through a plate glass window and hits the pavement. The insects, of course, were dreamed. From this they began work on the screenplay.

Like the endless, terrifying dreams Lyon and O'Donoghue went on to create, *The Dreammaster* screenplay ran past the standard film length and was weighed down by O'Donoghue's numerous details—shades of *Saturday Matinee*. The two spent several months filling the script with scenes of poetic violence and horror, and delved into the psychology of dreams and theories of astral states. Lyon termed the process "flying blind"; he helped to shape the script and get the action going. O'Donoghue, he felt, had trouble sustaining a story, and this led to some arguing, but nothing like the outbursts that had surrounded *Mondo Video*. One reason for this was that O'Donoghue knew that Lyon was capable of titanic anger of his own—and being the smaller and slighter of the two, O'Donoghue chose not to provoke his friend. But control was maintained simply because both spoke the same creative language. "He was the most rational and reasonable person I've ever worked with because he was the brightest," said Lyon. "You could discuss the pros and cons, the strengths and weaknesses of an idea without ego or having to prove anything. We just examined the value of the ideas."

But *Dreammaster* lacked a real story. With two thirds of the script clocking in at over 160 pages and no ending in sight, O'Donoghue and Barry Secunda worked out a deal with Bert Schneider and *The Dreammaster* was officially designated an "abandoned project." For the third time in two years, O'Donoghue saw another screenplay bite the dust. He was especially bitter about this ongoing cycle of enthusiasm, research, work, rejection; and the only thing he had to show as a "film" in all this time was *Mondo Video* and *that* couldn't even make it to late-night TV. He was depressed, in debt, and had no new film project ready to replace *Dreammaster*. Fortunately for him, another, grander, failure was in progress as his and Lyon's script fell from sight.

In 1980, while O'Donoghue and Lyon attempted to bring *Dreammaster* to term, two momentous events occurred within the bowels of *Saturday Night Live*. First, Lorne Michaels, having lost Dan Aykroyd and John Belushi after the fourth season and suffering an uneven fifth season with a depleted cast, resigned as producer of the show, taking everyone with him—almost. Second, NBC Entertainment president Brandon Tartikoff picked *SNL*'s associate producer, Jean Doumanian, as Michaels' replacement. The network valued the show as a franchise and wanted to keep the ad revenues rolling in. Did Doumanian have any real production or comedy experience? No, but she had worked in the *SNL* atmosphere, knew the original cast, and was responsible for booking the musical acts. Plus, she was outwardly confident that she could keep the show moving at the same steady clip. Good enough, it was felt. But when the first Doumanian *SNL* episode premiered in November of that year, the smell of death started to rise from the show. By March 1981, the stench was overbearing.

Not much more can be said about Jean Doumanian's moment in the *SNL* saddle.* It was one of television's classic dives, a slow-motion descent into the tarpits of comedy and imagination. The cast would have been booed off a Weimar cabaret stage, the writers' scripts deemed unworthy of a bonfire. After twelve mind-boggling episodes, NBC stepped in and cleared away the mess that the network had helped to create. Tartikoff, anxious to maintain a connection to the old show, hired Dick Ebersol as Doumanian's replacement. Ebersol had been there at the show's inception and recently was the producer of *The Midnight Special.* Surely he would have some ideas on how to keep the prized franchise from sinking. Ebersol did. He called Lorne Michaels.

Michaels, who still could not fathom why NBC went with Doumanian, was more than happy to help Ebersol in what was a desperate situation. To succeed, Ebersol knew he needed someone who understood comedy to oversee the writers and cast, to give the show direction. This Doumanian didn't do, and she paid the price. Michaels suggested that Ebersol contact O'Donoghue. After all, he was a mentor to the younger writers on the original show and his sensibility had influenced the show's formation. Also, O'Donoghue was well-known and well-liked by most of the press (an exception being Tom Shales of the *Washington Post,* who found O'Donoghue's humor to be "dour"); his hiring would restore credibility to a discredited show. Since Ebersol was left with the ruins of a once proud enterprise, who better to help rebuild it than O'Donoghue? Ebersol followed Michaels's advice.

Lorne Michaels certainly cared about the sad state of his creation, and what he told Ebersol about O'Donoghue was true. But Michaels had another reason to recommend his former star writer: O'Donoghue was in serious financial debt, and the cancellation of *Dreammaster* left him hanging until a second film project could be sold to Paramount. By recommending him for the job, Michaels made sure that O'Donoghue could return to the high life to which he'd grown accustomed.† As

*Hill's and Weingrad's *Backstage History of Saturday Night Live* provides everything one could possibly want to know about the Doumanian era. A chilling, fascinating read.
†Despite their sometimes rocky relationship, Michaels often made certain that O'Donoghue got work when needed. This included a live, Weekend Update prime-time special that was scheduled to air just before the 1980 presidential election. O'Donoghue was hired as a writer-performer and was set to appear in front of a White House in flames, urging viewers not to vote. However, NBC pre-empted the special and it never aired.

expected, Ebersol offered O'Donoghue the position of supervising producer. O'Donoghue told Ebersol that he hated the show and that it should die a natural death; all he wanted to do was put *SNL* out of its misery. Although Ebersol had been brought in to save and not destroy what was left of the show, he still wanted O'Donoghue regardless of his position. The offer stood, and O'Donoghue accepted.

When he was hired in mid–March 1981, O'Donoghue insisted that Ebersol hire the Project X team of Prager, Wittenborn, and Glazer as writers, as well as John Belushi's wife, Judy Jacklin. He also wanted Prager to be a cast member. He then called Bob Tischler, with whom he had made up after the *Mondo* fiasco, and explained the situation. O'Donoghue was enthusiastic about the opportunity and asked Tischler to join him on the show. O'Donoghue would be Reich Marshall, Tischler Deputy Reich Marshall; together they would inject this dying, rotting enterprise with a jolt of comic energy before its final collapse. To Tischler the opportunity was unique, and although he made good money producing records, he went, with John Belushi's encouragement, to assist O'Donoghue.

With less than a month before the April 11 premiere, Ebersol got busy. He spent the first weeks of his reign firing a good number of Doumanian's staff, hiring new talent, attempting to recapture the feel of the old show. He lured back Matt Neuman, a writer from *SNL*'s fifth season; he sent out feelers to a number of the show's veterans, including Marilyn Miller, who soon joined the new show as well. And, of course, he had O'Donoghue, who wished to introduce himself to the staff in a memorable way. "It was an emergency situation," he later said. "It was like walking into some sad, failing corporation—no pictures on the walls and a lot of sad, angry people sitting around." Aware that morale was low and tension high, O'Donoghue prepared an over-the-top rant in order to break down egos and resistance and lay the groundwork for the reshaping to come. He wanted to burn his mark into the staff's hide and steer them away from the Doumanian carnage.

Ebersol gathered the staff and prepared them. The captive audience watched as the fabled Mr. Mike stepped forward—"a celebrity's entrance, very theatrical," noted Barry Blaustein, a writer who survived Doumanian's show. O'Donoghue paused, then fired away. He said that the material on the new *SNL* was "dog shit" and made him "puke." He railed against everyone in the room. He ticked off the many things that were wrong with the show—so many, in fact, that he sarcastically wondered if the staff was up to the job. His voice seethed with contempt and rose with anger each time he wished to press a point. Matt Neuman, who had nothing to do with Doumanian's show, spoke up to say, "You don't mean me, too?" O'Donoghue looked at Neuman and replied, "Matt, your stuff is particularly vile." Some were appalled by O'Donoghue's behavior, including Catherine O'Hara, who had been wooed from *SCTV* to join the *SNL* cast. The first-rate comic actress, who would have been a boon to the new show, quit soon after the rant.

O'Donoghue produced a spray paint can and began to write DANGER on the wall. "We've got to have more danger on this show," he said, then ordered the staff to mark up the walls with the spray paint he provided. There was a sense of elation among most of the staff as they dutifully grabbed cans and did as they were told. Barry Blaustein, who sat back and enjoyed O'Donoghue's "show biz" performance, noted the absurdity of a bunch of upper-middle-class kids spray-painting walls and saying, "Yes, that's what danger is . . ." Blaustein understood O'Donoghue's intent, to free up the minds of a demoralized staff; but even the most exuberant among them, he said, were slightly embarrassed the next day when they came to work and saw the graffiti-lined walls. Better to be embarrassed by what one writes on a wall than what one writes for a show. Though in retrospect ridiculous, O'Donoghue's performance got results and inspired the writers to create in a leaden environment.

"This is a real raise-the-*Titanic* job, a real Alamo challenge," O'Donoghue said to the *Detroit Free-Press* a week before the premiere. "I don't think we can save it, but I think we can give it a real Viking funeral. We owe it that." It was the line he fed to every media outlet in the days leading up to the new show: Don't expect anything other than a full-scale video interment; *SNL* is dead, the rest is symbolism and ceremony. No one in the press quite bought this, nor did they want to. Most TV writers felt betrayed by Doumanian and demanded "their" old show back, or at least something that resembled the sacred Glory Days. With O'Donoghue on board expectations naturally rose. Of *course* he would talk of funerals and the impossibility of raising the dead. This was Mr. Mike, after all. And where there was Mr. Mike there were great quotes and the promise of interesting comedy. "Lorne talked to me recently," he added in the same *Free-Press* piece, "and said it's kind of a cheap thrill to sit and watch something you worked on go down the dumper and be able to say, 'They couldn't do it without me.' I saw it happen with the *Lampoon,* but it wasn't as bad as this. This was worse. This was really a humiliation."

Due to an impending Writers Guild strike, much of the premiere show was written over a week before air, the final touches added hours before the strike deadline. After this the writers were not allowed near the *SNL* offices or the set. O'Donoghue saw to it that the sketches chosen for production were readied, and he inspired the actors to give their all. It would be the first outing since Doumanian's departure; surely they desired to come out aggressively and serve notice that *this* no longer

Back on *Saturday Night Live*, 1981

was a "dog shit" show? Distancing themselves from the previous regime was certainly a motivating factor, but for most of the actors the premiere was more an audition than a crusade to salvage or even bury *SNL*. Four of Doumanian's cast members remained—Joe Piscopo, Eddie Murphy, Gail Matthius, and Denny Dillon. Murphy, superior to the others in sheer talent, felt little pressure. If *SNL* survived there was no question that he would remain. The same went for Piscopo, though he expressed some doubt about the future of the show. As for Matthius and Dillon, this was it; neither had made a lasting impression while under Doumanian, and if they were to stay on each needed to turn in a strong performance—unlikely given their previous effort. The remaining cast members were rookies and so had to make their presence known immediately.

The combination of the writers' strike, tension within the cast, the pressure of following one of the biggest disasters in American television, and the expectations of the network, the critics, and those who still voluntarily watched *SNL* led to a fascinating installment. Not only was there a sense of "danger"—in this case, whether the show would break apart or not—there was among the actors a nervous energy similar to that of caged animals. This, added to the hurried feel of the sketches, gave the "new" *SNL* the jagged, uneven look that O'Donoghue cherished. As he told the *New York Daily News* after the premiere, "Comedy is best when it's riding on the edge."

Among those who wished Ebersol and O'Donoghue luck in their endeavor was Chevy Chase. The *SNL* vet stopped by the show's offices just days before the premiere, and Ebersol, stuck for a host, asked Chase if he would fill the spot. O'Donoghue apparently felt Ebersol's suggestion was sound. Although convinced that Chase had betrayed him, O'Donoghue saw the promotional advantage of a prominent ex–cast member's helping *SNL* in its hour of need. He also had mixed feelings: He fluctuated between public ridicule of his old friend and the occasional private embrace, but he never really closed the iron door on their relationship. Chase, on the other hand, held O'Donoghue in the highest regard, and this no doubt influenced his decision to accept Ebersol's offer on such short notice. After weeks of hasty repair, the show, tatters and all, finally received its unveiling.

In the cold opening Chase rummages through the props of *SNL* past and finds the clay form of Mr. Bill. Here in a single frame are the first and last big stars of the original show: Chase, who stumbled into instant success; and the ever-suffering Mr. Bill, who by the fourth season was all but an honorary cast member (and who was often confused with Mr. Mike, a confusion fed by the violence in *The Mr. Bill Show*). Both "old-timers" talk sorrowfully of *SNL*'s current state, where laughter is heard only in memory. Then, as if to enhance the very nostalgia that the two have strained to evoke, Chase stumbles once more and flattens Mr. Bill. He looks up and shouts, "Live from New York, it's *Saturday Night!*" reclaiming the tagline from the likes of Charles Rocket and Anne Risley, two of Doumanian's favorites. A remnant of the Lorne Michaels era thus takes back occupied ground.

From here the show swerved all over the place. One of the sharper turns featured Joe Piscopo, whose solid impression of Frank Sinatra distinguished him from the Doumanian crowd. Piscopo's Sinatra has become a spokesman for the "beautiful American guys and chicks out of work" in the automobile industry. Before a large American flag he sings "It's Time for You" (with lyrics such as "Whenever I see those Datzun Z's/I want to punch out a Japanese") as the "victims" of "Jap" encroachment are displayed in an all-out nationalist appeal: a little girl confined to a wheelchair because her father's import crashed into a cow; a proud

World War II veteran who gave his arm in the fight against the Nips only to see "them" as the ultimate victors. The Chairman of the Board is moved, and he remembers when "we were shooting *From Here to Eternity,* I'd have to leave the set *every* day because of the tears in my eyes."

Eddie Murphy delivered a fine impression of Bill Cosby, though the bit, a commercial parody in which Cos served beer instead of Jell-O to children, struck a lesser, lighter chord. A "slice-of-life" sketch in which an Italian father and son—played by Second City alumni Tony Rosato and Tim Kazurinsky, respectively—argue before the son's wedding was filled with over-the-top gestures, accents, and dialogue worthy of Doumanian's show. ("I'm sorry I called you a wop, Pop," mutters the son after a blow-up.) Kazurinsky also appeared in "I Married a Monkey," a soap opera spoof that featured live chimpanzees screeching and jumping around the set, sending the audience into hysterics. As Ed Sullivan and Johnny Carson had discovered years earlier, animals let loose on TV practically guarantee an enthusiastic response, and Kazurinsky tapped into this without shame. The episode was padded out with sketches focusing on the terminally self-righteous, a family at home reading aloud the descriptions of guns printed on bubble gum cards, and a parody of Irene Cara singing the theme to *Fame,* which at the time was heard slightly less than the National Anthem.

Some of the evening's tougher material surfaced on Weekend Update. Chevy Chase resumed command of his old anchor desk, but due to the constraints of the writers' strike the "stories" he read were not as topical as he might have liked. (After one weak joke, Chase ad-libbed, "The writers' strike continues.") Into this breach stepped O'Donoghue, who, under the pen name Edith Wharton, unloaded many of his censored Update jokes from the show's first three years, including the one in which the Catholic church dispenses a communion "co-host" that symbolizes the body of Mike Douglas. O'Donoghue also got on air a favorite joke of his originally written as an exchange between former Update anchors Jane Curtin and Dan Aykroyd, revised to include his screenwriting partner:

> How long does it take to cook a baby in a microwave oven? Exactly fifty-five seconds per pound, claims Mr. Nelson Lyon of Glancing Bow, Michigan, who turned his small fry into a small roast in just eight minutes and fifteen seconds. And to that let me simply add, "Well done!"

The one topical event that did receive treatment was the attempted assassination of Ronald Reagan by John Hinckley. After being shot, Reagan reportedly told jokes to ease the fears of those around him, off-the-cuff one-liners for which he had become renowned. O'Donoghue seized upon this and "discovered" that there were "missing jokes" that the president told between the site of the shooting and the hospital. Wounded and coughing up blood, Reagan quipped:

All in all I'd rather be in Philadelphia than speeding through Washington with a bullet in my lung.

I don't want to say I'm hurt, but I'm hemorrhaging internally.

Why did the assassin cross the road? To shoot me.

The "missing jokes" set the tone for another shooting-related piece inspired by Jimmy Stewart's statement that he would take a bullet for his old Hollywood pal. In a filmed segment, Laurie Metcalf, who was brought to *SNL* from the Steppenwolf Theatre in Chicago, asked New Yorkers on the street if they, like Stewart, would take a bullet for the president, and if so, where. The answers given were straightforward and serious—from a teenaged boy who said he'd do it only for his mother, to a middle-aged businessman who declared, "When this country gets back to law and order, that's when I'd take a bullet for the president." O'Donoghue ordered that the studio microphones be cut so that audience laughter would not undermine the mood of the piece. It was perhaps the most resonant portion of the program.*

Like the episode itself, the reviews were mixed. Tom Shales of the *Washington Post* dismissed it as "Desperation City and largely unconvincing" and proposed that *SNL* was "an idea whose time has gone." Janet Maslin of the *New York Times* took a more moderate view. She contended that although *SNL* was once again "watchable," it appeared to be "headed for an unadventuresome but sometimes witty format." Marvin Kitman of Long Island's *Newsday* went overboard, splashing and raising foam in a crazed and artless manner. A confirmed O'Donoghue fan, Kitman had cranked up the hyperbole on behalf of *Mondo Video* to such a degree that O'Donoghue used one of his quotes in a press release, so it was no surprise that Kitman found *SNL* to be "IMPROVED" and "BETTER-TASTING" (his caps). Kitman was enthusiastic to the point of incoherence, and toward the end of his column he caught a glimpse of himself in the mirror. "Excuse me for sounding so hyper about the

---

*And it proved to be Metcalf's sole appearance on that show, after which she was let go. Metcalf went on to win multiple Emmy Awards for her performance as Jackie on the hit sitcom *Roseanne,* and one wonders how she might have fared had she been kept as an *SNL* cast member.

new show and the new people. I am so emotionally involved and I hate myself. This is only a TV show."

Yes, and as such certain niceties are expected of television performers. This may explain why many critics, Kitman included, came down on Al Franken, who appeared on Weekend Update to deliver a postmortem on the Jean Doumanian era. Disliked by both O'Donoghue and Ebersol, Franken nevertheless was booked to perform a variation of the "Al Franken Decade" routine he had established on the original SNL. Again, Ebersol desired above all else a connection to the old show, and Franken obliged, blasting both Doumanian *and* Ebersol in a particularly nasty and funny monologue. He spoke of NBC's "horrendous mistake" in hiring Doumanian and conceded, "No English-speaking person could do a worse job than Jean." And what of "Dick 'Mr. Humor' Ebersol"? Not only had he attempted to steal credit for the success of the original SNL, credit "which should rightfully go to Lorne Michaels and me, Al Franken," but he was responsible for a number of horrible programs such as *Roller Girls* and *The Waverly Wonders*. "I know Dick," said Franken, "and I can tell you that he doesn't know dick."

Although he and partner Tom Davis were slated to host SNL the following week, Franken echoed O'Donoghue in his plea to viewers that the show be killed off. Of course, this was the last thing that Ebersol and NBC Entertainment president Brandon Tartikoff wanted. But with the writers' strike ongoing it seemed that SNL was indeed finished. "The show was raped and strangled by the Writers Guild," said O'Donoghue to a reporter on the Tuesday following the premiere. The Guild's restrictions were such that even though there was enough prestrike material written for another show, only Ebersol would be allowed to oversee dress rehearsal and make the changes necessary for air. O'Donoghue told the press that this would be "too much" for Ebersol to handle alone. "We realized that there was no way for the show to get around the writers' strike so we canceled," he said.★

O'Donoghue hosted a "The Day the Laughter Ended Party" in his Sixteenth Street apartment days after the premiere, and some fifty guests representing SNL past and present drank and pondered the future of the show. Dan Aykroyd and John Belushi, both of whom were to appear in the next installment, lent encouragement to newer members such as Joe Piscopo, who believed that his big opportunity had passed. But Brandon Tartikoff allayed fears of cancellation when he gave Ebersol the green light for a new season in the fall. Until then SNL was officially on hiatus, and O'Donoghue, paid for the shows missed because of the strike, de-

★In *A Backstage History,* Hill and Weingrad report that in addition to the strike, Ebersol loathed the material that Franken and Davis had written for their appearance and this was another reason why a second show was nixed.

cided to visit Ireland with his live-in girlfriend. He had long desired to see his ancestral land and hoped, as he once said to *Rolling Stone,* to "piss on the Blarney Stone."

I like my women the way I like my eggs—loose and scrambled.

After his breakup with Anne Beatts in 1976, O'Donoghue dated a number of women, including Edie Baskin, Carrie Fisher, and Margot Kidder, but long-term commitment appeared out of the question. By the time *Mondo Video* was released in 1979, O'Donoghue was seeing Carol Caldwell, a Georgia-based writer who had moved to New York to pursue her career. They met four years earlier, when O'Donoghue gave a speech to the Atlanta Society of Communicating Arts, of which Caldwell was president. The two began a correspondence. Once Caldwell came north to live and work, O'Donoghue pulled her into his world of ideas and customs. "I think both of us knew that it was pretty much inevitable that we were going to get together," said Caldwell, who felt O'Donoghue was "bruised and beaten up" following his affair with Kidder. "I think a soft-spoken southern girl was just the kind of comfort he needed."

In the summer of 1980, Caldwell joined O'Donoghue on a trip to southern France, where he and Nelson Lyon wrote much of *The Dreammaster* screenplay. It was there that Caldwell first saw his "horrifying tantrums." A local dry cleaner shrank many of O'Donoghue's clothes, and this drove him to a fine frothing rage. "I was in awe," remembered Caldwell. "He was insane. He was foaming at the mouth like a rabid dog. He was screaming at the top of his lungs and was beating things, hitting the couch. He was totally freaked out that the French had shrunk his clothes. . . . It was pretty terrifying." While she worked on her own projects, Caldwell said that she and Lyon's French lover, Viviane, who recently had given birth to a daughter, "basically served these two *pashas* who worked all day, storming around in one room. We cooked for them, cleaned up after them, sexed them and made their lives livable in this remote place." Caldwell felt that the French trip centered on O'Donoghue and Lyon, but she still found the experience "wonderful" because she was falling in love with O'Donoghue.

Upon their return to New York, Caldwell moved into the Sixteenth Street apartment. Because O'Donoghue was in debt, "our life was not as showy as it could have been." Caldwell began to get freelance work with *Esquire* and *Rolling Stone,* and this brought much-needed money into the house. The fact that she wrote for some of the more prominent national magazines threatened O'Donoghue, she said. "Michael was very jealous of this. Terry [McDonnell, her editor] sent me off to spend a week with William Hurt in Saratoga for a *Rolling Stone* cover story. Michael was very nervous that I was going to run off with Bill Hurt." O'Donoghue tagged along for part of Caldwell's assignment, including a visit to Club 57, an East Village performance space. This lent additional color to her piece: Hurt feels he doesn't fit in such a bohemian atmosphere, so O'Donoghue, "master of disguise and wise to the streets," offers a quick makeover. He "draws out a scarred black switchblade and saws off the sleeves of Bill's workshirt, slashes the pockets, then adds an Ash Wednesday smear to his forehead." Instant assimilation.

Caldwell received similar if less cutting treatment from O'Donoghue. He brought her into a celebrity world to which he was wise, a trip Caldwell described as "heady" and that put her "in hog heaven." He also introduced her to a variety of drugs, though ultimately Caldwell preferred alcohol, O'Donoghue marijuana and Percodan. And despite the occasional flare-up, O'Donoghue was on his best behavior with Caldwell, who, he felt, personified genteel southern womanhood, a gentility that reinforced his own stylish image. Caldwell believed that O'Donoghue's elitist manners were a renunciation of his past.

She noticed, too, that O'Donoghue sometimes dumped on his peers and close friends. "Michael was very small about [the *SNL* crowd's] good fortunes. And I would consistently say to him, 'Michael, when these other people are doing well, it's only good for you. Their success means that you have success coming.' He would get tied in knots about other people's success," knots that were tied by frustration. Although he had yet to realize his Hollywood dream, he watched as Chevy Chase, John Belushi, and Dan Aykroyd starred in commercial films, and Doug Kenney co-wrote hit comedies such as *Animal House* and *Caddyshack*. O'Donoghue was especially harsh toward Belushi regarding Steven Spielberg's *1941,* in which Belushi was a featured star. "Michael's opinion meant a lot to John, who looked up to Michael as a big brother," said Caldwell. "John adored him. Michael would not go see the movie. He was spitting cruel to [Belushi] whenever the subject came up." This did not mean that O'Donoghue disliked Belushi; indeed, the two were the closest of friends. But with O'Donoghue's friendship came the occasional slap across the face, a practice he claimed to take pride in. Sometimes a slap was a test of loyalty, other times an expression of anger or contempt. It all depended on where one stood in relation to the man.

Lorne Michaels received his share of abuse as well. "He was always very, *very* ugly about Lorne," Caldwell recalled. "Meanwhile, Lorne invariably would come in and bail his ass out of huge financial problems"— like suggesting that Ebersol hire him for *SNL*. Michaels's generosity allowed O'Donoghue to finally deliver on the promises he made to Caldwell. *Now* they could live life properly and make up for their meager condition. The first step in this new direction was the trip to Ireland.

Obsessed as always with ritual and theme, O'Donoghue planned no ordinary vacation. He arranged it so that he and Caldwell traveled through southern Ireland by horse-drawn Gypsy wagon. In order to set the right mood, he showed Caldwell the film *Golden Earrings,* in which Marlene Dietrich plays a Gypsy in a caravan. But for Caldwell the experience, although bracing, was less than cinematic. O'Donoghue was skittish around horses, whereas she had grown up around them, so it fell to her to take the wagon's reins. While Caldwell steered their horse along, O'Donoghue sat beside her "in his fashionable James Joyce clothes" and wrote poetry and took notes of their journey. They worked their way north, finished the caravan portion of their trip, and spent the rest of their time in hotels. Before they'd left the States, Caldwell's editor at *Rolling Stone* said that if she and O'Donoghue found themselves in Northern Ireland he wanted a story from there. His request provided the excuse they needed to visit this war-ravaged section of the old country.

The couple went through "extremely dangerous" areas of the North, said Caldwell. "Michael was a coward, he was terrified of everything, but here we were in an extremely titillating, dangerous situation." And despite his fear of physical harm, O'Donoghue was excited to be there; he tapped into a source of danger that no comedy show could ever achieve or duplicate. By day he and Caldwell toured the quiet, depressed, bombed-out parts of Belfast and Derry; at night the cities became war zones. One evening the two hit the sidewalk as a British tank rolled up

In Ireland, summer 1981

beside them and fired just over their heads. This did not deter O'Donoghue, who by now, Caldwell observed, was "becoming a rabid Irish nationalist." Before they left the North they met secretly with IRA members in Belfast. The meeting "thrilled" O'Donoghue to the degree that when he returned home he made a financial contribution to the organization.

Overall, the Irish trip was, in Caldwell's words, "mythological" and helped to tighten their romantic bond. "I had an extremely vivid and important dream while we were in Ireland," remembered Caldwell. "Michael was *the* 'O'Donoghue.' He was mounted on a horse and leading his people back into prominence, and he was carrying this fabulous flag that I saw very clearly: It was the flag of the O'Donoghues." Back in New York, Caldwell had a local flagmaker stitch together the flag of her dream—a yellow crescent moon and stars set against a navy blue background. She presented it to O'Donoghue "in this great ceremony [that] really convinced him of how important it was that he connect with his Irish heritage and his role in it." Later, Caldwell discovered that this was indeed the historical flag of the O'Donoghue clan, a fact that further warmed O'Donoghue's nationalist emotions.

It's not the show I want it to be. I want it to be more than the old SNL*, to make the golden years look like* Hee-Haw*. I want my own work on that old show to look like it was done by some old fart.*

Leading his people to prominence was one thing; but whether O'Donoghue could bring *SNL* back to its place in the corporate comedy sun was something else again. When he returned to the show in the fall of 1981, he was "happy and euphoric and fully functioning," said Caldwell, who saw him bounce out of bed in the morning, ready to work. His earlier desire to give the show a Viking funeral had been replaced with a passion to make *SNL* vital, electric, alive, and, of course, dangerous. Since the single show in April, Dick Ebersol and Bob Tischler, neither of whom took the summer off, had performed major surgery. Removed were the rest of Doumanian's crew, save for cast members Eddie Murphy and Joe Piscopo, and writers Barry Blaustein, David Sheffield, and Pamela Norris. Gone too were O'Donoghue's additions, Mitch Glazer, Dirk Wittenborn, Judy Jacklin, and Emily Prager, who, as an actress, was given little to do. Ebersol and Tischler kept the cast members they'd hired in the spring, then added Mary Gross from Chicago's Second City and Broadway veteran Christine Ebersole.

To O'Donoghue, the arrangement made in his absence was a "fucking comedy nightmare." Although in April he had praised the work of the new hires, including saying some kind words on behalf of Tim

Kazurinsky's "I Married a Monkey," he now took a dark view of the cast, especially Kazurinsky. He considered Eddie Murphy first-rate and was drawn to the acting and musical talents of Christine Ebersole. But as for the others, O'Donoghue felt they were "all losers" and "shit" and he wished he could fire them before the season premiere. In order to help realize *his* vision of *SNL,* O'Donoghue hired as writers Nelson Lyon and Terry Southern, and he made additional demands that he hoped would break the show free from its rigid format.

First, he wanted the announcer, Don Pardo, and the director, Dave Wilson, fired. Both represented *SNL*'s old guard, and if the show were to evolve it needed to lose this dead weight. Ebersol kept Wilson, but he did agree to fire Pardo, who, if O'Donoghue had had his way, would have learned of his dismissal as he announced the opening of the season's first show. Instead of an on-air humiliation, Pardo was let go in private and was replaced with the more reserved Mel Brandt. Next, O'Donoghue wanted to get rid of the show's traditional cold opening, the words "Live from New York, it's *Saturday Night!*" and the decorative photo stills of New York. The new opening was to be a fast-moving, black-and-white film montage of "the most dangerous city in America": a stripped car, the interior of a punk rock club, S&M gays and leather queens, Doberman guard dogs, a tenement fire, a chalk outline of a corpse on a sidewalk, a black drug dealer holding joints. The purpose of this new opening, he wrote in a memo, was to "echo the 'new romance' of New York, the romance of *Taxi Driver* and *Cruising.*"

Ebersol's instincts naturally reflected the corporate line of order and continuity, but he agreed to O'Donoghue's demands; the format was altered slightly and the new opening credit sequence approximated the "dangerous" tone O'Donoghue had outlined. The atmosphere surrounding the show was less chaotic than in the spring, yet Ebersol recognized O'Donoghue's importance and thus approved many of the changes his "Chief of Staff" sought. As Nelson Lyon, sensitive to NBC's position at the time, put it, "Behind this facade of authority there is stupidity and fear. But when they need you they need you, and they let you do anything. The fascist corporation will let *you* be in turn a bully and a fascist. It suits their purposes." And although O'Donoghue's executive office was clean and neat, fresh flowers on his desk every morning, his office door projected a different image: In green spray paint was crudely drawn a skull and crossbones with the title REICH MARSHALL spelled out in caps. All that was needed was some barbed wire spotted with the blood of prisoners who attempted escape.

O'Donoghue wished to impress upon cast and crew his desire for menacing comedy, and to this end he played up the persona of Lyon, who arrived in New York in September. "You think *I'm* bad," O'Dono-

ghue said to the staff, "wait till you see who I'm bringing *in*." Lyon
came to the show dressed completely in black, a fashion statement he
maintained throughout the season. His size, intelligence, verbal intensity,
and proximity to O'Donoghue had the desired effect. Lyon made his
presence known—"the Dark One," as O'Donoghue called him, a label
that would distinguish his work and, in time, contribute to his misfortune. As for O'Donoghue's other new import, Terry Southern, there
was considerably less fanfare. A literary force who wrote some of the
funniest and strangest dialogue uttered in modern cinema—think of the
speeches made by General Jack Ripper in *Dr. Strangelove,* of the president
informing the Soviet premier that Moscow is about to be nuked—Southern was quieter in person and much older than the rest of the show's
staff. He also feared the process of writing for live television. After a
sketch of his called "Sex with Brookie," in which two guys discuss the
finer points of fucking Brooke Shields, was rejected, Southern drew back
and chose instead to add a line or a sight gag to the scripts of other
writers, primarily Lyon and O'Donoghue.

The reasons given for Southern's low output on *SNL* that year depended on who did the talking. Southern himself said little about his
experience, but Lyon remembered encountering the writer in a bar before the show premiered. Southern nervously sipped from a glass of
Scotch and confessed to Lyon his fear of doing the show. Southern asked
if Lyon would add his name to Lyon's scripts and keep him on staff.
Lyon agreed. After all, this was a comic genius at low ebb; slack had to
be given. Rosie Shuster, who returned to *SNL* that season, confirmed

Lyon's account. "He
couldn't pull his oar any
longer," she said of Southern, and Shuster, too, did
what she could to help the
legendary humorist.

If what Lyon and Shus-
ter said was true, then
O'Donoghue's efforts to
prop up his idol were zeal-
ous indeed. Though at the
time O'Donoghue disclosed
few details about Southern's
contribution or lack thereof,
he later used Southern's
presence on the show to
hammer those whose work
he despised. "He came in

With Nelson Lyon, fall 1981

to play the game and he played it very well," O'Donoghue told Lee Hill, a Canadian writer and Southern's biographer.

I can show you some things he wrote from that period which were spectacular. He had not lost his chops. The problem was that these *actors* were from the wacky, wacky school of Second City, belting it out for the cheap seats. They didn't get the nuance of Terry. They didn't know who he was. They just thought he was this old fart and they didn't give him any respect and they couldn't act his stuff, which required *acting,* good actual acting, which they couldn't do and they still can't do.

In the rehearsal period leading up to the season premiere, O'Donoghue grew progressively hostile toward most of the cast and some of the writers. He openly decried their "lack of talent" and said that he did not want to deal with them. "There was this moaning and groaning about the cast," observed Lyon, "this 'lack of inspiration' coming from the cast. That was Michael's complaint." Lyon concurred that the cast was not great, but he felt that O'Donoghue had no one but himself to blame. After all, O'Donoghue chose to visit Ireland instead of staying in New York with Ebersol and Tischler and helping them rebuild the show. Had he remained, he would have been in a stronger position to shape *SNL* more to his tastes, or at least could have resisted some of Ebersol's and Tischler's weaker decisions. But as matters stood, O'Donoghue was stuck with a show not of his making. His dreams of complete creative control began to fade and were replaced with bitterness and anger.

O'Donoghue's interest in *SNL* diminished; he focused more on his own work and left the heavier chores to Tischler. Initially brought in to assist O'Donoghue, Tischler was now his equal, a status that changed by the week. As O'Donoghue withdrew from the daily grind, Tischler stepped into the breach to work with the writers and help Ebersol chart the direction of the show. Tischler thus earned Ebersol's trust and became what O'Donoghue had been hired to be: the senior foreman on *SNL*'s assembly line, there to oversee the manufacturing of marketable comedy. Tischler espoused no grand theories of humor, nor did he see the show as a metaphor for decay. He was there to fix what needed to be fixed and to ensure that *SNL* regained the ground lost during Doumanian's reign. Tischler's philosophy was simple: One worked to make something better; if not, there was no point to the labor. It was the code of the comedy professional, a code personified by Tischler as he strove to achieve that which O'Donoghue rejected.

Although he felt O'Donoghue to be selfish and unprofessional, Tischler defended his friend to Ebersol, who spoke of firing the increasingly disruptive writer. O'Donoghue had all but abdicated his supervisory role, but Tischler maintained that O'Donoghue gave the show edge, that he inspired the writers to push past established boundaries. In this sense Tischler remained loyal to O'Donoghue despite his disdain for his friend's behavior. But many on staff, especially those whom O'Donoghue berated with ball-cutting ferocity, saw him as a hypocrite. Here was a comedy legend, a man who insisted that his comedy approached art, and most of the material *he* offered at read-throughs was from old scripts that hadn't gotten on the original *SNL*. This was true. Always keen to recycle his work, O'Donoghue presented weak sketches such as "Lawn Dentist" and "Disco College" as though they were written on scrolls. Neither sketch made it to air, but one old piece, "Spray-on Laetrile," did—after Standards softened its harsh treatment of cancer. "I lost some rhythms," O'Donoghue said of the change. "I lost some things that seem pretty silly to me. But they weren't silly to [Standards]."

Tussling over the proper way to mock cancer proved minor when compared to the other battles O'Donoghue waged that year. If he was not serious about being supervising producer, he compensated for this by reverting to outraged artiste. Of course, nothing set him off like someone in authority altering his material, and his energies were spent fighting those he thought wished to silence him. He wrote, promoted, defended, then ultimately mourned a pair of sketches that shared a common theme: the fascist abuse of power and the absurdist means used to justify that power. One sketch attained near-mythical status, due in part to the ceaseless hype generated by O'Donoghue. The other was lesser known but much more powerful, and was perhaps one of the best pieces O'Donoghue ever wrote for *SNL*.

The first sketch, "The Last Ten Days in Silverman's Bunker," was intended to be the acme of television satire, "a breakthrough piece," as O'Donoghue put it. Over the summer O'Donoghue read of the troubles that befell Fred Silverman, who as president of NBC tried to conjure some of the ratings "magic" that had made him famous at ABC. But at ABC Silverman was helped by Aaron Spelling, whose pop culture antennae guided the network to the top of the TV heap with shows such as *Charlie's Angels* and *The Love Boat*. At NBC, however, the insects scurried in all directions and Silverman oversaw a programming department that delivered things such as *Supertrain, Hello Larry,* and *Pink Lady and Jeff,* a "comedy-variety" show co-hosted by two Japanese women who barely spoke English. The network's ratings continued to hit the pavement, Silverman flipped out, and by June 1981 NBC purged itself of this destructive force. Here, O'Donoghue thought, were the makings of a fine, nasty piece. He enlisted Nelson Lyon to help him write the script, which finally ran thirty-two pages.

"The Last Ten Days in Silverman's Bunker" opens on Rockefeller

Center, home of the "Nazional Broadcasting Company." The building's exterior is framed in black and white with red tint and shot in the style of Leni Reifensthal, the brilliant if morally corrupt German filmmaker. From this we sense a broadcasting empire, but inside we see the reality: debris-strewn corridors abandoned by executives who fled the inevitable collapse of the network. The place is a television graveyard. Among the remnants hangs a gold peacock that resembles a Nazi eagle; it grips in its talons the network logo "N." Footsteps echo as a hand-held camera surveys the scene. A narrator speaks:

> One is reminded of what the poet Shelley once wrote: "Look upon my works, ye Mighty, and despair! Nothing beside remains. Round the decay of that colossal wreck, boundless and bare, the lone and level sands stretch far away." He might have been describing these very corridors, now deserted, littered with mute evidence of the final convulsions. Here, deep within a stone deco fortress, one man manipulated the destinies of two hundred million people; a twisted genius whose strange experiments lobotomized his helpless victims; a power-mad tyrant who reduced a proud nation to a vast wasteland. This is his story.

The tyrant, of course, is Fred Silverman, the Führer of sleazy broadcasting, Hitler to Pat Weaver's Bismarck. The bulk of the sketch centers on Silverman's mad programming schemes that he believes will turn the ratings war in NBC's favor. Surrounded by his aides Göring, Goebbels, Himmler, and John Chancellor, Silverman reels off ideas for the kind of tits-and-ass shows that made him a success at ABC. Half crazed and manic, Silverman pitches away.

> Even now I am planning a new show that will sweep the country—a game show called *Look Up Her Dress,* host—Marjoe Gortner. So we get these (INDICATES BIG BREASTS WITH HIS HANDS) "intelligent" women contestants to stand on this big piece of Plexiglas, right? (HE LIES ON THE FLOOR TO DEMONSTRATE) Now the cameraman is down like this shooting up through the Plexiglas, right, and Marjoe is asking them questions. Real tricky questions. And if they get any of them wrong, we get to *Look Up Her Dress*! And if they don't beat the buzzer, and if they're thinkin' about it, we still get to *Look Up Her Dress*!

Later, Silverman learns that all of NBC's "pilots" are lost. He lashes out at his aides.

> *Traitors! Cowards!* You have *betrayed* me! Disloyalty has undermined our resistance. But *I promise you* from the ruins of our schedule will arise a new

network, a network of hit shows like . . . *Hollywood Sex Clinic*! Catch this—Jack Klugman, M.D., asks Hollywood's most "talented" actresses—major balloon smugglers, if you *grasp* the *concept*—he asks them a series of strangely intimate questions, questions specifically designed to debase and humiliate them. This sort of question: "Do you *swallow* the whoopee juice, *spit* the whoopee juice out, or smear the whoopee juice on the walls and mirror?" . . . How do you think Miss Susan Anton would field that one? Huh? *Huh?*

Silverman's obsession with big tits inspires another show, *Tom Edison, the Woman,* a "sort of offbeat docufantasy that asks the question: What if . . . Tom Edison was a remarkable woman with an extraordinary pair of twin Zepplins? What sort of 'gadgets' might she invent?" He also proposes a version of *Private Benjamin* called *The Lieutenant Wore Tampax*. But as Silverman slips further into insanity, the network falls into chaos, and nothing can stop his being yanked from power. He briefly considers suicide, cyanide with a bullet chaser, then simply gives up and goes home. "Let the memory of this ruthless madman serve as a ghastly reminder to all Mankind," the narrator instructs us. "It happened once. It must never happen again." We are left with a flashback of Silverman's early NBC period, when his power was absolute and unquestioned. He stands in front of the network affiliates, is clad in full Gestapo garb, affects a Hitleresque pose. The crowd cheers his every word.

> Nothing will stop us. Nothing. We will assault their intelligence. We will destroy their brains but not their buying power. We stand united. One network, unified under the banner of the Nationalist Broadcast Company. One audience. One leader. Two . . .

Silverman makes his "big breast" gesture. The crowd roars approvingly.

"The Last Ten Days in Silverman's Bunker" enjoyed the support of Ebersol and Tischler. Sets were built, and initially the piece was to air on the premiere show. But John Belushi, who was to play Silverman (as he had on the original *SNL*), remained in Los Angeles. "I talked to him quite frequently and asked him *when* he was going to come back to New York to do the show," said Nelson Lyon, in whose L.A. house Belushi was living at the time. "He was kind of mumbly and incoherent on the phone, and *I* didn't know what the hell was going on, and no one was telling me what was going on." Belushi said he was working on a screenplay called *Noble Rot* and that he couldn't make the trip. O'Donoghue, who heard rumors that Belushi was involved in a strange scene, became frustrated with his friend's absence and wanted "Silverman's Bunker" *on.*

After several delays the piece finally was scheduled to air on the December 5 installment, with host Tim Curry slated to replace Belushi.

Then, a week before its appearance, "Silverman's Bunker" was shut down by Silverman's successor, Grant Tinker, who found the piece "tacky" and a potential "discourtesy" to the former NBC president. There was also the fear that Silverman might sue for libel. Ebersol accepted the network's decision and told *TV Guide,* "Ordinarily the legal department says change this or that and the sketch will be fine, but in this case they objected to the entire thing." Ebersol added that the decision was "a major disappointment. It was brilliantly written. This was our major effort of the year, aiming for the hardest and highest level. But there's no court of last resort when NBC says, 'Guys, you can't do this.' They own the show."

O'Donoghue, on the other hand, resisted. It was he who first called attention to the piece in a *New York* magazine article about the show. "It should offend Fred pretty much," he said, and this helped bring the weight of the network down on the sketch. When it was clear that NBC's decision was final, O'Donoghue went on an all-out PR blitz. He mailed copies of "Silverman's Bunker" to TV critics around the country in the hope that a series of supportive columns would force Tinker and his lawyers to rethink their position. He portrayed himself as the victim of "corporate censorship" sponsored by "sleazy and cynical men who determine our lives." He praised the piece to the heavens, spoke of its satirical power and sweeping indictment of network corruption. But O'Donoghue's effort, an impressive, theatrical display, did nothing to resurrect the sketch. It did, however, further alienate Ebersol, whose corporate sensibilities were ruffled by O'Donoghue's public dissent.

Nelson Lyon, who learned of the network's decision two hours before he was to film the Reinfensthal prologue, which he'd conceived, didn't see the point to "Silverman's Bunker." He co-wrote the sketch because "it was a job," but he never shared O'Donoghue's view that "Silverman's Bunker" was a neglected masterpiece. "It's a favorite of a lot of people," he said, "and it has a kind of cult status that Michael manufactured because it was never done." Still, Lyon didn't see the point in attacking someone who in the grand scheme of things was small potatoes. "Who knows about this guy? Who gives a shit about a TV executive? It's not like Orson Welles taking on William Randolph Hearst. Hearst had a life. Silverman had nothing. We tried to read about him to get some hook or angle, but his life was a blank. He was an executive other executives wanted to trash or celebrate depending on their interests or agendas. That's it. Silverman was no Führer. It was a sketch without a reason for being."

There *are* fine moments in "Silverman's Bunker," particularly in the details. "Higher ratings!" accompanies each fascist salute; beneath a portrait of the RCA dog, Victor, reads the line "His Master's Race"; amid the sound of small arms fire and a Bob Hope record, Hermann Göring, his face done up in mascara and lipstick, joins a decadent party where characters from NBC shows cavort with women in 1940s lingerie; a young David Letterman, wounded in the ratings war, vomits blood and dies as Silverman touts him as Johnny Carson's replacement. But ultimately the piece ran too long to sustain the single joke that Fred Silverman was a fascist jerk. O'Donoghue wanted the sketch to run without commercials, which, given its length, would have been roughly twenty minutes. He believed this constituted a groundbreaking event—the longest sketch in the history of *Saturday Night Live*—"the most ambitious sketch we have ever done," he said to *TV Guide*. But the effort he put into seeing "Silverman's Bunker" aired might have been better spent in support of the *other* satire of fascism he wrote that season.

The sketch, titled "The Good Excuse," was to have aired on the Halloween episode of *SNL,* hosted by Donald Pleasence. Set within a dramatic program, *Scripts the Dog Ate the Ending to Playhouse,* "The Good Excuse" is introduced by playwright Neil Simon. The "play" concerns the first American soldier ever to set foot in Auschwitz. "Like most men in Patton's Third Army," says Simon,

> Private Owen Turner had heard dark rumors of Gestapo death factories. But the stories were too bizarre to believe, stories of slave labor, mass graves, gas chambers, lunatic medical experiments, acts of inconceivable barbarism including lampshades sewn from human skin and piles of gold teeth wrenched from the victims' mouths. On January 27th, 1945, Private Turner was part of a force that liberated the Auschwitz Extermination Camp and he discovered that the nightmare was all too real.

The camp commandant, SS Colonel Rudolph Franz Hoess, stuffs documents into a stove in an attempt to destroy as much evidence as he can before he is captured. Private Turner kicks open the door and shoves his rifle barrel into Hoess's throat. "Before I splatter your brains all over this wall," hisses Turner, "I want to know one thing—how could you have done this? What possible reason is there for a civilized being to commit the atrocities you have? What sort of obscene monster systematically murders millions of women and children?" Hoess replies simply, "We had a good excuse." This angers Turner even more.

> TURNER: That's one excuse I'd like to hear, you Kraut filth! I'd like to hear what justifies this living hell!

HOESS: Well, the war is lost. I suppose there's no harm in telling you. Do you mind if I whisper it?

Hoess whispers a few words into Turner's ear. The soldier's attitude changes; his rifle is lowered.

TURNER: Gee, I ah . . . I guess I owe you an apology.

HOESS: Don't be too hard on yourself. You had no way of knowing.

TURNER: When I saw that hundred-foot mound of human skulls outside your office, I just naturally jumped to the conclusion that you were some kind of demented fiend. What can I say—I'm sorry.

Having thwarted Turner, Hoess is confronted by Mordecai Sussman, a gaunt Jewish survivor of the camp. Sussman wears the gold star, his head is shaven, blue numbers are tattooed on his forearm. He is about to smash Hoess in the face with a shovel when Turner steps between them. "Hey, hey, hold on there! I think you should hear the man out first," says the American. " 'Hear him out?' " replies Sussman. "What possible explanation is there for the genocide of a race—to herd doctors and lawyers and university professors naked into cattle cars and slaughter them like animals?" Hoess again whispers his excuse. "Boy," Sussman says, tossing the shovel aside, "I had you guys all wrong. . . . It just looked so bad, you know, what with tossing babies in the air and catching them on the bayonets."

They share a laugh at what now seems silly, when a Russian soldier enters and drills the wall above Hoess's head with bullets. Before he can kill Hoess, however, both Turner and Sussman speak on behalf of the Nazi—"He had a good excuse!" exclaims Sussman. Turner suggests that Hoess explain the reason for mass extermination so that all may hear. Hoess begins to speak, but a big sheepdog runs across the stage with "The Good Excuse" script in its mouth. Neil Simon chases the dog but cannot catch it. "What a shame," he says. "Now we'll never know what that good excuse was." He waves and bids us a fond farewell.

"The Good Excuse" is simple, aggressive, direct; it slashes the face of piety without losing its moral objective, namely, that the Holocaust and anti-Semitism are not and should not be beyond the satirist's reach. "It's a hard thing to attack," O'Donoghue later said, "because everyone attacks it in the same pedestrian way. Holocaust movies don't stir up what that time was like; it's just another old tired image that doesn't affect me." The piece affected Ebersol, though. When he read "The Good Excuse" he immediately vetoed it, and this drove O'Donoghue away from the show for two days. As Ebersol proudly told *New York*, "I'll tell you one thing. I was smart enough . . . not to put on a piece about Nazi concentration camps. As long as I'm with the show, there's not gonna be comedy about the Holocaust." The point to the sketch was clearly missed, or perhaps not understood, by Ebersol. "The point was," explained O'Donoghue, "there was no good excuse, there couldn't be a good excuse, and the very fact of saying there was a good excuse is how ludicrous it could be." No doubt the sight of a tattooed Jewish prisoner laughing it up with a Nazi blinded Ebersol to the absurdity and ultimate focus of the piece. Had it aired, "The Good Excuse," *not* "Silverman's Bunker," would have broken new ground and made for memorable television.

Although "The Good Excuse" did not appear on the Halloween show, the musical act booked for that night did. Fear was one of the better bands that emerged from the Los Angeles punk scene of the early 1980s. Their music conformed somewhat to the punk style of brief, explosive riffs; but unlike the average L.A. thrash band, Fear's songs contained a nice mix of brutality and melody. They fractured jazz and blues and threw the results into fast, harsh arrangements. O'Donoghue was introduced to Fear by John Belushi, who was perhaps the band's most famous admirer (he was often seen wearing a Fear pin). After listening to their music, O'Donoghue shared Belushi's enthusiasm and succeeded at getting Fear on *SNL*. Here was a band that personified danger, especially when playing live. Not only did O'Donoghue want Fear, he wanted to project the chaos of a punk club into American living rooms, and to this end he and Belushi brought in some forty skinheads from Washington, D.C., to slam dance and stage dive while the band performed. (According to an *SNL* publicist at the time, Belushi had planned to slam with the skinheads but refrained at the last minute.)★

O'Donoghue's instincts proved correct. Fear's performance on *SNL* remains one of the true highlights in the show's history. (This, admittedly, is a minority view: Ebersol hated Fear, and it is doubtful that Lorne Michaels would have allowed such unruly elements on any of his programs.) Like Elvis Costello before them—in a 1977 appearance Costello stopped singing "Less Than Zero," a pause that quickened the pulse of Lorne Michaels, then stormed into "Radio, Radio"—Fear *controlled* their moment on live television, although to the untrained eye their moment appeared out of control. During the slow, opening chords of

★Belushi did, however, appear in the opening of the Halloween show. He said nothing, merely looked into a mirror and raised his eyebrows, which inspired a roar from the studio audience. Although in New York and thus, ostensibly, available to do "Silverman's Bunker," Belushi, according to Lyon, was in no shape to rehearse and perform the long, complicated sketch.

"Beef Baloney," the skinheads stirred at the foot of the stage, ready to explode. When the band broke open at high speed, the slamming, diving, stomping, and shoving commenced with a vengeance. Fear played a set of three songs during which band members dodged and at times collided with the dancers. Lead singer Lee Ving dove into the frenzied crowd while bodies spilled across the stage, the action oddly in sync with Fear's driving rhythm. It all seemed to be taking place in an abandoned warehouse on the edge of town rather than in the confines of NBC. *SNL*'s traditional music segment was thus beautifully vandalized in front of millions of onlookers.

With John Belushi and Lee Ving of Fear

O'Donoghue was elated. Now *this,* he felt was good television. Ebersol, however, was sickened by the sight before him. At the peak of the action he crouched near the skinheads and tried to direct their movements, but to no avail. Someone yelled "New York sucks!" into a microphone that had fallen to the stage, and Ebersol raced to the control room and ordered a fade to black. As Fear launched into "Let's Have a War" and a dancer was about to smash the show's Halloween pumpkin, the mikes went dead and a short film, *Prose and Cons,* which mocked Norman Mailer's love of murderous authors such as Jack Henry Abbott, filled the screen. In the studio, Fear ceased playing and the skinheads walked off the set. Ebersol remained angry and reportedly raged in the control room. But for sheer drama nothing could top the *New York Post,* which ran an item the following Tuesday in which "inside" sources spoke of "a riot, mindless, out-of-control destruction of property," and other horrors. "This was a life-threatening situation," said a source. "They went crazy. It's amazing that no one was killed." Ebersol responded swiftly and seriously to the *Post*'s fabrications, but O'Donoghue simply laughed away the negative reaction to Fear. "They're just a band like the Carpenters," he said.

For the next installment, hosted by Lauren Hutton, O'Donoghue had asked William S. Burroughs to read from his novels *Naked Lunch* and *Nova Express*. Lyon and O'Donoghue went to see Burroughs give a public reading and, again, O'Donoghue wanted to transmit the electricity of this event to live TV. As with Fear, Ebersol approved O'Donoghue's suggestion that Burroughs appear (how much damage could an old man inflict?), yet was not particularly taken with the legendary writer. Burroughs's segment was to be four minutes, but in dress rehearsal his reading ran two minutes longer than planned. Between dress and air Ebersol told O'Donoghue to have Burroughs cut the additional time.

"I am about to reply to him about why you can't cut two minutes out of *Naked Lunch*," O'Donoghue recalled, but Ebersol told him,

"Okay this goes . . . cut from Benway . . . lose all this poetry shit here and go right to. . . ." And I know that I can't do it. There's no way I can explain this to this jerk, so I go "Right Dick, be right back." I leave the room and go down and hang with Eddie Murphy, and come back and say, "Okay, it's out. This is out and this is out." Never went to Burroughs and never cut anything, because once you are on live, what are they going to do? Cut in the middle?

Burroughs sat at a gray metal desk and read edited bits from his novels (for all their comic brilliance, there was no chance of hearing unexpurgated sections of *Naked Lunch* and *Nova Express* on network television). Each bit featured Burroughs's notorious character Dr. Benway. In "Twilight's Last Gleaming," from *Nova Express*, an explosion on a ship causes a drunken Benway to widen a patient's small incision. Another explosion, and Benway abandons the operation to board a lifeboat reserved for women. The show's music coordinator, Hal Willner, thought to animate the segment with sounds of an explosion. And since in the original text there run the lyrics to "The Star-Spangled Banner," he felt the segment should end with a resounding version of the anthem. Willner remembered how it played on air.

We wanted the anthem to finish naturally as Burroughs completed the text, so I timed him reading the piece twice—and he was consistent. On the air, he sped up his delivery (live TV often does that to people) and the music "almost" finished. To this day, when I see that clip . . . my stomach turns when I hear that music not quite end. Anyway our National Anthem worked well—the contrast was perfect. It presented a vision of dark Americana.

The studio audience enjoyed the segment. Burroughs drew laughter from them as if he were an old vaudeville sage, which wasn't far from the truth, given his familiarity with the material. Despite the slight rush his timing was excellent, and the image of a lone man reading once-forbidden material at a desk, like the image of Fear and the skinheads, nudged *SNL* that year away from its standard comedy format. "You know, there's enough wacky, wacky humor on that show," said O'Donoghue. "Why can't you have William Burroughs read one of the more important comedy books? It's more than just a sketch. It's a literary event to have that man there. The kids aren't going to lunge for the set and immediately say, 'Jeez, it's some old guy there. I'll never watch this show again.' They'll stay with it." O'Donoghue knew what it would take to move *SNL* to a newer, hopefully deeper level. Unfortunately, his devotion to this task was at best sporadic; and when caught in a tough spot it was far easier for him to play the "brutalized artist" than to throw everything he had into getting what he wanted. If *SNL* was to be dangerous, then O'Donoghue needed to be the show's demolition expert. Yet all too often he blew himself apart instead of blasting away the show's rotting foundation.

O'Donoghue's major gripe that year was, of course, the cast. He never wavered in his admiration of Eddie Murphy and Christine Ebersole, who, when given the chance, showed remarkable comic ability. But the bulk of the cast did nothing to inspire him, except in negative ways. One of his favorite sports was bashing Tim Kazurinsky, to whom O'Donoghue pinned all the worst aspects of Second City, a company he felt was well past its prime. Kazurinsky was a prolific writer and an energetic performer, but his comedy was tame and generic, and this guaranteed a nasty response from O'Donoghue. The same was true, though to a much lesser degree, of Mary Gross. On Second City's stage Gross was an outstanding improvisational actress; however, her theatrical talents did not translate well on camera, and there was a certain stiffness to her performances. O'Donoghue didn't savage Gross, at least not until late in his tenure, but neither did he consider her "A-team." Still, he wrote some strange, poetic characters for her to play, including the Mouse Queen, a mad young woman in Victorian dress who "ruled" the thousands of mice at her feet and scooped them up in her arms, letting them "stream down over her like gentle cascades of refreshing spring water."

O'Donoghue also cast Gross as a tiny fairy in "Nick the Knock," a

sketch he used to humiliate Joe Piscopo. When it came to sheer "wacki-
ness," few could outdo Piscopo. His characters often bounced off the
walls, eyes bulging, expressions broad. (The exceptions to this were his
Frank Sinatra impression and his fine performances in the "Solomon and
Pudge" sketches, in which he and Eddie Murphy played old men in a
bar.) One of his more popular creations in this line was Paulie Herman,
known as the "Jersey Guy"—"I'm from Jersey. Are *you* from Jersey?"
Though a hit on Doumanian's show, Paulie Herman was snuffed by
O'Donoghue, who despised the character. This didn't mean, however,
that an over-the-top Piscopo was necessarily a bad thing, especially if
O'Donoghue could steer him in an embarrassing direction. The inspiration came after O'Donoghue noticed Piscopo doing a voice in the offices
that he did at home for his son. "I'm Nick the Knock, do-dee-o-do,
hum–dee-dee-dum-dum," went the voice, and O'Donoghue told Piscopo that he'd write a sketch that featured Nick. Piscopo complained
that Nick would ruin his image, but O'Donoghue persisted, and with
the help of writer Pamela Norris the sketch was readied for air.★

Many on *SNL* thought "Nick the Knock" was one of the worst
sketches to appear that year. Piscopo certainly believed this, for obvious
reasons (and he blanched when O'Donoghue suggested that Nick be a
recurring character). Although the sketch was motivated by O'Donoghue's desire to blast Piscopo, the result was a bit more interesting than
its detractors claimed.

The curtains of a puppet theater open to reveal a backdrop of ancient
Egyptian ruins on a desert plain. Nick, a distant puppet cousin of Mr.
Punch, hops into view, mumbling and bumbling about. He places a 78
on a gramophone and winds it up; a yodeling song begins, but Nick,
impatient, smashes the record. Light music is then heard as a tiny fairy
flutters to the stage. "Hello, Nick," she says. "I've brought you another
poem. Nick, although you are very strange, I like to think I see beauty
in you that others are too busy to notice. So I have brought you this—
the gift of Truth." As she recites the poem, Nick's aggressive features
soften. He is mesmerized by the cadence and taken with the line "Truth
never dies," which he attempts to mouth himself. Suddenly, there's a
knock at the stage door. Nick opens it and is hit in the face with a bat.
A second knock, another bat to the face. This snaps him back to his
natural violent state; he grabs the fairy and tells her, "I'm going to eat

---

★Norris was one of the few *SNL* writers O'Donoghue liked. She understood O'Donoghue's brand of humor and incorporated it in her own work. Perhaps their best collaboration was "Bizarro Reagans," in which the faults of the real First Family are virtues in
the Bizarro World. Norris wrote most of the sketch, and O'Donoghue appeared as the
narrator, a disembodied head floating through outer space.

your spine," which he does, her green blood running down his chin. Nick tosses aside the fairy's corpse and exits. The curtains close.

"Nick the Knock" was met with near silence from the studio audience. The piece occupied the space opposite *SNL*'s game show parodies and the ever-popular "I Married a Monkey," and perhaps that is why it was deemed a failure. "Nick" represented a style of conceptual humor not seen on *SNL* since the second season, a style that looked more and more out of place under Ebersol. It was a contrast that marked *SNL* for most of that year—the steady, professional comedy of Ebersol and Tischler interrupted by the occasional burst of O'Donoghue's darker passions and conceits. This made for an uneven but not awful show, though it was clear which style would ultimately prevail.

The final spasms came on the Christmas show, hosted by Bill Murray. O'Donoghue had collaborated with Lyon, Rosie Shuster, and Terry Southern on a piece called "At Home With the Psychos." Set in a house near a cracked nuclear reactor, "Psychos" centers on an insane salesman who believes that the survivors of World War III will develop a blowhole "not unlike that of a whale." He plans to get rich by selling a complete line of blowhole accessories—deodorizers, beautifiers, stimulators, the works. His family are equally insane: His wife wears a mohawk hairdo and suffers from stigmata; his daughter is a blind ballerina; his son is a human time bomb, wrapped in dynamite and tickling a detonating switch. Mother fires a shotgun in the house; daughter French-kisses her dad; son calls himself "Mr. Tibbs" and warns the others to not step in his shadow. The action revolves around the blowhole, which, in the original script, was to be shown. But once Standards got a look at the thing—a mutated vagina-like opening with teeth that appeared to come out of a Gahan Wilson drawing—they rejected it. O'Donoghue promised to make the blowhole suitable for broadcast, but when the time came for another look it was evident that O'Donoghue had done little to change what Standards objected to. "Psychos" ran without the blowhole, though it was referred to and "seen" by the characters peering into Dad's briefcase.

O'Donoghue's blowhole deception angered Tischler, who felt that his time had been wasted intentionally. After months of continued loyalty, Tischler ceased to defend O'Donoghue. This left O'Donoghue open to Ebersol, with whom O'Donoghue battled "over a million little issues, and I felt he was wrong on at least half of them," said Tischler. Ebersol, who later told a reporter, "I worked very hard to make Michael part of that show, but after a while, it just became impossible," had tired of the constant, interoffice warfare. The publicity stunt concerning "Silverman's Bunker" had convinced Ebersol that coexistence with O'Donoghue was no longer an option; and the final evidence was provided by O'Donoghue himself when, during a pre–Christmas staff meeting, he vilified everyone on the show as worthless, including Eddie Murphy, whom he considered the best actor in the cast. By this point O'Donoghue's "dark side took over," as Nelson Lyon put it, and it seemed that he was practically begging to be canned. At the end of the year Ebersol and Tischler met with O'Donoghue and his manager, Barry Secunda, to discuss and settle the matter. O'Donoghue wanted Tischler to resign as a show of support, but Tischler refused, which O'Donoghue considered an act of betrayal. When *SNL* resumed production in January 1982, O'Donoghue was gone, though he left behind a tart note to the staff:

January 25, 1982

To the Cast and Crew of SNL . . .

> *Just to set the matter straight, I was fired on Sunday, January 19th, by Dick Ebersol, with the cooperation of Robert Tischler. I did not leave by "mutual consent" and if either claims otherwise, he is, to steal a phrase from Louisa May Alcott, a "lying cunt." I don't know why I was dismissed because Ebersol refused to meet with me and tell me.*
>
> *I'm quite pleased by what we did together. We turned the show around and then some. There was more to be proud of than embarrassed by, and there were a few truly blazing moments. My thanks to you all.*
>
> *As for me, I plan to get out of show business and write my memoirs. Of course, there's always my work with the little deaf girls, so I'll be busy, busy, busy.*
>
> *P.S. Any chance of getting the Allman Bros. back for another eight or nine more sets????*

O'Donoghue's dismissal provided him a platform to denounce *SNL* and speak of his "rape" at the hands of NBC. He called Ebersol "a major wimp" possessed of "an average *Wide World of Sports* sense of humor." He said that their conflict was inevitable because "There's always gonna be creative differences between me and anyone who wears a Gucci belt buckle." In an interview with TV critic Eric Mink, then of the *St. Louis Post-Dispatch*, O'Donoghue reflected a bit more on his time with the show. "I never got the sucker airborne," he complained. "When I left, I realized something I hadn't realized before. Most of my energies had been spent blocking the second-rate efforts of second-rate sensibilities. . . . I think of [comedy] conceptually, where it's going to be three years from now. That's where I wanted to take the show. . . . Conceptually, the nation has moved on. We did some good things, but

I never walked out of the place saying, 'Wow, we really gave America an eyeful this time.' "

For Tischler, O'Donoghue's exit prompted mixed feelings. He felt bad about the way things had turned out, but he thought O'Donoghue had conducted himself terribly. "If he had shown up and been the Michael O'Donoghue of old, really worked and worked on pieces and showed people through his writing how good he was . . . This was a guy who was pathetic in a way, who really was a genius," but who, Tischler believed, failed to use his powers effectively. Tischler also thought that O'Donoghue "made a big mistake" when he spray-painted the walls during his first "danger" rant. In essence, O'Donoghue had painted himself into a corner that he couldn't get out of without compromising his image or position on the show. In fact, O'Donoghue's image was enhanced by his firing: He could now lay claim to the "censored" artist role he performed so well. He could also fire shots at *SNL* from a safe distance. "I suspect it'll be a nice, respectable comedy show," he told Mink after his departure. "Not too exciting, not too embarrassing. It will just float along at about a C-plus, B-minus level."

The show did settle into a safe, commercial groove once O'Donoghue left. NBC received what it had ordered, and the hilarity is ongoing. It is, in retrospect, perhaps fanciful to assume that any *one* person could have derailed *SNL* and sent it crashing into a crowd of bored spectators. O'Donoghue must have believed this himself, for it would explain his self-destructive behavior throughout the rebuilding process. Despite his talk of "danger" and the few instances where he honored his pledge, O'Donoghue knew he would never be allowed to produce the show entirely to his taste, and had he been allowed to do so the result would have been one endless migraine. After all, if *Mondo Video* made him suffer, imagine his running a live, ninety-minute network comedy show almost every week for a season. It would be like Sherlock Holmes's being put in charge of Scotland Yard. The demands of authority would stall his creative drive; administrative tasks would flatten inspiration and ideas.

O'Donoghue was destined to play the outsider, a role he initially chose and to which, in the end, he had to submit. His experience on *SNL* '81 was the beginning of this end. The world of comedy he had helped to discover and define spun away from him, and there was very little he could do to stop it.

I was there the morning John died. He was lying on the floor of his bungalow. When I tried to revive him, the "big guy" opened his eyes and whispered, "Dope is for dopes." And he died. It was the last thing he ever said. I took his wallet and left.

The death of death humor, at least the kind practiced by the original *National Lampoon* and *Saturday Night Live,* was initially caused by a fall off a cliff in Hawaii and then finalized by an overdose in a Hollywood bungalow.

The first blow came in late summer 1980. Having scored big with *Animal House*, promoting the release of *Caddyshack,* and about to co-produce a Chevy Chase vehicle, *Modern Problems,* Doug Kenney went to Hawaii to rest, dry out from drugs and alcohol, and prepare for the next career push. The trip had been suggested by Chase, who, with Kenney's film production partner, Alan Greisman, accompanied the writer. "The three of us were just sort of playboys," said Chase. "We were doing whatever we could to have fun and get away from the world." This included some intake of recreational chemicals, the drying out being more a slowing down. But according to Chase, Hawaii was fine, and soon Kenney was joined by his girlfriend, Kathryn Walker, who flew to the islands to spend time with him before they were to move in together back in L.A. After Chase and Walker returned to the mainland, Kenney remained in Hawaii, alone. He rented a Jeep, drove to the island of Kauai, parked the Jeep, walked through some shrubs near the edge of a cliff, removed his shoes, and, depending on one's view, either slipped or intentionally walked off the cliff's edge, hit the rocks below, and died.

Grief spread through Kenney's circle. Anger, too. One of the prime architects of modern humor, on the verge of Hollywood fame and power, had been wiped out in mid-step. Since no one but Kenney knew why or how he fell, comments on his death will always be speculative. However, most of Kenney's friends and associates ruled out suicide. "If I had to guess, I'd say he was stoned and he slipped," said Alan Greisman. Added Kenney's close friend Lucy Fisher, "I can imagine Doug taking off his shoes on a beautiful sunset evening to walk in the grass, then having the footing go out from under him." Whatever the reality of his death, Kenney's unfulfilled Hollywood destiny was mourned as well. "The sky would have been the limit. He'd have done incisive, hysterical exposés of American culture," said Greisman. Henry Beard thought Kenney would have gone the Woody Allen route, writing and directing "personal and complete" films. Emily Prager opined, "Doug would have been really, really powerful in Hollywood. The course of comedy was changed by his death."

This is true, though to what extent the course was changed remains unexamined and unknown. Amazingly, there has been no extensive look at the life and work of Doug Kenney, who, to put it mildly, was a major comic force. One explanation for this cultural void can be found in the October 1981 issue of *Esquire*. There beneath the headline THE LIFE AND

DEATH OF A COMIC GENIUS, Robert Sam Anson dissected the Harvard sensation under a black light. And although all of Kenney's friends are quoted in the piece, which suggests full cooperation, they were stunned by the result: Anson's Doug Kenney was not the Doug *they* knew. Anson had turned their bright star into a drug-addled, insecure wreck; moreover, he engaged in nickel-and-dime psychology. According to Anson, Kenney was constantly haunted by his dead brother, Daniel, forming the basis for a life of self-loathing and death wishes. In Anson's eyes, Kenney was indeed brilliant, the cream of his generation; but boy, was the guy fucked up! Begging for Mommy's and Daddy's love with an ounce of cocaine up his nose, it was no wonder that Kenney fell off that cliff. But then, aren't all comedians tortured souls seeking approval and affirmation?

If Robert Sam Anson took a twisted view of Kenney, he certainly had help. Throughout the piece Kenney's friends provide observations and anecdotes that highlight the humorist's dark side. No doubt they provided other facts about Kenney; his sensitivity, kindness, and quick wit were touted by everyone who knew him. But it's the dark side that sells, something that *Lampoon* veterans should know better than anyone. Their collective horror at what Anson did betrayed either a naiveté about the glossy world of tell-all, admittedly then in its nascent stage, or an inability to take a punch below the belt, a form of assault the *Lampoon* itself could and did specialize in. Those who savaged the corrupt and filthy aspects of life were savaged in return, and they found the experience anything but humorous.

Just after Kenney's death but before the *Esquire* piece appeared, Sean Kelly was approached by several publishing houses and was asked to write Kenney's biography. There was real interest in Kenney's saga, the midwestern boy who helped remake American print and film comedy before dying mysteriously—the stuff of great nonfiction. Kelly, too, was taken with the idea and began to put out feelers to those who, like himself, knew and had worked with Kenney. But when the results of Anson's back-alley autopsy hit the racks, the circle closed around Kenney's grave and any hope of cooperation was lost. Kelly abandoned the project.

The code of silence remained until fall 1993, when *Harvard Magazine* published the "approved" profile of Kenney, written by Craig Lambert. As in Anson's piece, Kenney's dark side was shown; but Lambert took care to expose the full picture, and his article, "The Life of the Party," serves as the lone testament to Kenney's life and work. Kenney remains a mystical figure in the annals of American humor, and his presence is still felt by his friends. Harold Ramis, who collaborated with Kenney on *Animal House* and *Caddyshack,* and who told Lambert that he speaks to Kenney in his dreams, paid tribute to the man in his film *Multiplicity.*

The lead character, played by Michael Keaton, is named "Doug Kinney." After a series of cloning experiments, Kinney is sliced three ways. By the end of the film the "Dougs" come to terms with their identities, and of course all live happily ever after.

The second, fatal blow to the *Lampoon/SNL* comic sensibility came on March 5, 1982, the day John Belushi was found dead in his room at the Chateau Marmont. Much has been said and written about the events that led to Belushi's demise; but when probing the subject one cannot overlook Bob Woodward's *Wired,* the Albert Goldman-esque study of drugs, drug buying, drug taking, drug abuse, and comedy. While not technically a biography, *Wired* presents to us "The Short Life and Fast Times of John Belushi" via Woodward's stilted prose. He analyzes comedy as he would a Supreme Court decision or the presidential nominating process, and as a result, *Wired* is perhaps the most humorless book ever written about a comedian. It resembles a stiff old bore ruining the jokes he feels obligated to tell.

Woodward's prime focus is not on humor but on Belushi's drug habit. Apparently, drugs were part of the counterculture in the 1960s and early 1970s, and those shaped by this culture, such as John Belushi, continued to ingest drugs as they attained professional success. Even more incredible was the fact that some people actually *died* from drug overdoses; and, strangely enough, Belushi was one of them. Woodward's tour of Belushi's pain and weaknesses ends with an up-close inspection of the Final Days and their highlight, the comedian's bloated dead body. "The right side," Woodward points out, "where blood had apparently settled, was dark and ghastly." Then Bill Wallace, Belushi's friend and one-time karate instructor, who first discovered the body, "reached in John's mouth with trembling fingers and drew out phlegm, which spilled and puddled on the bed sheet in a thick stain. There was a rancid odor." Regrettably, Woodward's publisher, Simon and Schuster, failed to spring for a scratch-and-sniff edition of the book.

As with Robert Sam Anson's piece on Doug Kenney, *Wired* scandalized those who had opened up to Woodward and trusted that he would tell the full story. After all, wasn't this the man who brought down Nixon? (Or was *that* Robert Redford?) Surely he was on their side. In reality, Woodward's brief against Nixon stemmed from his desire to expose the sins of the administration and help rinse "clean" the status quo. Woodward was no radical and did not share the perspective of the American counterculture. Nor did he understand its humor, but, as he said in his introduction, he was "curious" about the world that surrounded Belushi and to what extent it contributed to the comedian's death. His curiosity led him along the used-syringe trail to those phlegm-stained sheets in the Chateau Marmont. Now *there* was an angle: a "cautionary" tale about drug abuse that served to satisfy the crude voyeur in everyone. Predictably, *Wired* sold remarkably well and went through several print-ings.* It also spawned a film version that starred Michael Chiklis as Belushi, a film so bizarre that it may be found in the Adult Horror section of America's finer video stores.

The shock that *Wired* caused among the faithful was in every sense postmortem. When the book was released in 1984, much of the original *Lampoon/SNL* crowd had already abandoned the dark, violent, concep-tual humor that previously defined them. Belushi's death symbolized the abyss, the breaking point between oblivion and showbiz success. The *Lampoon* and *SNL* had influenced the larger culture enough to allow Chevy Chase, Dan Aykroyd, Bill Murray, and many others safe passage in Hollywood, while P. J. O'Rourke, who rejected screenwriting for magazine work and novelty books, cashed in his *Lampoon* chips to be-come the right-wing "bad boy" of publishing. *Wired* merely confirmed that their career choices were the correct ones. And given their retreat to softer ground, their reaction to *Wired* was fitting and appropriate. They would rail against Woodward's character assassination with heads held high and hit the occasional self-righteous note. It was as if this generation of humorists was somehow special and thus above the filthy depths of popular culture. But as Hal Willner so accurately put it, had *Wired* been about someone else—Sinatra, Elvis, Liza Minnelli—many of these people would get a kick out of the sheer nastiness of the thing: *Wired* would be seen for what it is. Instead, *they* were the target and this simply was unacceptable.

When backing away from an abyss, it helps to push off something tangible. In Belushi's case that tangible figure was Nelson Lyon, who had the singular misfortune of being with the comedian just hours before his death. Lyon was in Los Angeles while on hiatus from *SNL*. After O'Donoghue's departure, Lyon came into his own as a writer for the show. One of his best pieces, "The Mild One," in which Bruce Dern played a philosophical biker who broke down the egos of his enemies, secured for Lyon a creative identity independent of O'Donoghue. Flush with success, he sought to relax at his L.A. home and gear up for *SNL*'s final installments of the season. Then, on March 2, 1982: "There's a knock at the door," Lyon recalled.

---

*Judy Jacklin, who remarried and added Pisano to her name, attempted to answer Wood-ward with a book of her own, *Samurai Widow*. It is a heartfelt effort that does some justice to Belushi's memory. But Jacklin lacked the grit necessary to write an effective rebuttal. *Samurai Widow* seems more a balm for herself and her close friends than a parallel history of her husband and his craft. Thus, *Wired* stands in the public mind as the only true "biography" of John Belushi.

> John Belushi knew I was in town, and he comes over with this creature I'd
> never met in my life by the name of Cathy Smith. He said, "Roll up your
> sleeve, I've got a surprise for you," and for forty-eight hours I did. For forty-
> eight hours I indulged in drug taking with John Belushi. And I thought it was
> a lark even though it involved Cathy Smith shooting us both up. I'd never
> been shot up with any drug in my life, I'd never taken heroin in my life.

Still, Lyon sensed no menace. "It was fun," he said. "It was in the
middle of the day. This was not some dimly lit, dark Viper Room toilet.
It was my house. [Belushi] comes over, he's one of my real best friends.
We were really close." The drug taking stretched into the early hours
of March 5. Lyon was in Belushi's bungalow at the Chateau, as were,
at different times, Robin Williams and Robert De Niro. Finally, Lyon
called it quits and hailed a cab to take him home. It wasn't until later
that afternoon that he learned the news from Carol Caldwell, who, like
O'Donoghue, was in town to work on a screenplay. Lyon didn't believe
what he was told and phoned the Chateau for confirmation. After a
"breath–catching silence," the hotel switchboard operator told him, "We
cannot discuss that." Lyon then knew that Belushi was indeed gone.
"And then the reports started and the horror began."

Lyon spent that afternoon grappling with shock and fear. "I was
there," he said,

> wrong place, wrong time, wrong everything, and I felt an immediate hit of
> tremendous guilt. This outlaw lark was indeed lethal, and I should have
> stopped it. I should not have participated in it in the first place. I felt terrible.
> I should have said, "John, no, I'm not going to get shot with drugs. What
> are *in* these drugs?" That was one of the eerie mysteries. As God as my
> witness, heroin was never discussed. "This is something special. A cocktail."
> That's how it was referred to.

That evening, Caldwell and O'Donoghue visited Lyon and his live-in
lover, Viviane, for dinner. Lyon took O'Donoghue into an adjacent room
and gave him the details. "Mike O'Donoghue was the only person who
knew exactly what happened. I told him. He was my partner, he was my
friend, at that time my best friend. And I told him everything. I trusted
him and he was very sympathetic." O'Donoghue advised Lyon to keep
quiet. At the time it was thought that Belushi had died of a heart attack;
drugs were not immediately mentioned. Lyon, and now O'Donoghue, were
the only ones who knew that Belushi had to have overdosed.

Eventually, the truth behind Belushi's death emerged, and when it
did Lyon was caught in the crosshairs of anger, resentment, and fear.
"John died and it was the change of my life," he said. "Friends I had

drifted away from me. They were scared of me. . . . I was inwardly shattered and tortured and about to be considered a 'sinister figure' as the person who was with him last. An unknown writer for *Saturday Night Live* who dressed in black; a mysterious character [who wrote] witty, dark humor; Michael O'Donoghue's partner: 'What's he all about, this Nelson Lyon?' " O'Donoghue found a lawyer for Lyon who immediately instructed him to remain silent and not tell anyone, not even Judy Jacklin, the events of that fatal night. Lyon admitted that his silence, then denial that drugs were taken was "really a foolish thing to do. . . . My instincts were to talk, to tell the world what happened and get the damn thing behind me and over with."

But this, as he discovered to his dismay, proved impossible. Lyon was tagged by many in Belushi's circle as being partly responsible for the comedian's death. Bob Tischler observed, "It was really, really hypocritical. I mean, all these people took drugs with John. None of them did anything to stop him from taking drugs. Nelson just happened to be in the wrong place at the wrong time." Others were in the same wrong place at the same wrong time but managed to escape criticism. "Why weren't people angry at Robin Williams?" asked Tischler. "Why weren't people angry at Robert De Niro?" The fact was that Lyon was a convenient scapegoat. He lacked the celebrity muscle of Williams and De Niro, and thanks to his "sinister" persona he could be dismissed as just another "dark" influence that hovered near Belushi at the end. (Woodward did his part, portraying Lyon as a marginal figure who assumed center stage in the final hours.) This stigma lasted for years and to a degree still does. But the ultimate question is this: Had Lyon overdosed instead, would the same people then blame Belushi for Lyon's death? The answer is obvious.

The funniest death to me is a movie producer doing Quaaludes, falling asleep in his hot tub and parboiling. I don't know if it has ever actually happened, but the idea is sure humorous to me.

O'Donoghue's reaction to the deaths of Kenney and Belushi was mixed. He was of course saddened by the passing of his friends (he spoke of the hole in his life created by Belushi's absence), and he attended both funerals and paid his private respects. But he also was handy with a quip, which showed that when faced with the death of a peer, O'Donoghue did not succumb to mushy tributes and sermonizing. In the wake of Kenney's fall from the cliff, O'Donoghue said simply, "Too bad he wasn't shaking hands with Chevy when it happened." After Belushi's body was discovered and taken from his bungalow, O'Donoghue said the corpse looked like a beached whale. "You know, it shocked me the first two or three hundred times I saw the footage on TV of poor old bloated John being carried out of the Chateau Marmont in a body bag. But now I know it just means it's time for the news."

Unlike most of the *Lampoon/SNL* crowd, O'Donoghue was not terribly hurt by either the *Esquire* article on Kenney or by Woodward's book. Instead, he parodied *Wired* in a missive sent to friends during the 1984 Christmas season. Titled, "Parts Left Out of *Wired*: The Short, Fat Life of John Belushi," the letter depicts Mitch Glazer as a drug-addled sex hound who's trying to get "into" Candice Bergen. Written in Woodward's flat style, the "missing" page shows Glazer whacked out on angel dust while an icy, prissy Bergen spurns his crazed advances. It was a two-for-one: O'Donoghue slammed Woodward's penchant for salacious copy and tweaked a friend in a most unflattering way. It was the kind of thing that those close to O'Donoghue expected of him and appreciated. It also was symbolic of his creative output during the final decade of his life.

From 1984 to his death in 1994, O'Donoghue played pretty much to a private audience. Gone was the talk of his being the "Woody Allen of the Eighties"; instead, O'Donoghue wrote screenplay after unproduced screenplay, worked on various collections of poetry that were never published (though in 1979 he privately released a thin volume titled *Bears*), tinkered with but did not finish a book, *Letters from France,* an uneven though at times ripe put-down of all things French. Another book, *Stunt Dog,* and a project titled *Bad Barbie,* on which he was to work with his friend, Trey Speegle, also remained unfinished. In 1992 he put together a gallery showing in SoHo of paint-by-numbers art that received some favorable press notices. These were among the many projects that kept O'Donoghue busy during this period, but save for one major film, neither he nor his work was seen by anything resembling a mass audience.

O'Donoghue certainly hadn't anticipated such a decline in popularity. When he left *SNL* at the end of 1981, he was profiled by a number of columnists nationwide. His tales of corporate censorship were played up, his notoriety celebrated, his work described as the definitive cutting edge. But O'Donoghue was savvy enough to realize that his "dangerous" persona could take him so far before becoming a liability. Thus he began to play down what had taken him years to polish. "I have a terrible image," he told one reporter. "[T]his idea of me as a nutcake lunatic is not true." He decried the notion that he was into violence for violence's sake. "I'd like to not be known just as Mr. Mike of *Saturday Night Live,*" he said in 1983. "I'm in show business, if only in a strange way."

He branched out: A song written for *SNL*, "Single Bars and Single Women" (which Christine Ebersole performed beautifully), was recorded by Dolly Parton and became a Top Ten hit on the country music charts in 1982. "Single Bars" was so popular that ABC turned it into a TV movie the following year, and O'Donoghue was featured in the country music press. This led to contacts with Nashville-based composers and musicians, and he continued to write country-western songs on the side. Three years later he tried to enter the world of musical comedy with *Jump,* based on the tales of Uncle Remus, written with Timothy Mayer (a first-rate playwright from Harvard and friend to the old *Lampoon* crowd), set to the music of Van Dyke Parks. After some six months of work, however, Parks's demands for extensive script changes drove O'Donoghue into a fury and *Jump,* much to his regret and anger, failed to be produced.

In 1985, *SNL* beckoned once more. After a five-year hiatus, Lorne Michaels returned to the show and brought along his trusted lieutenants, Franken and Davis, who were made co-producers, and Jim Downey, who became head writer. O'Donoghue was ostensibly hired to write and produce short films and videos. He had several scripts in hand, including one, *The Psycho,* in which Cupid employs automatic weapons instead of bow and arrow; and an "emotionally moving" piece about Jean Seberg's being harassed by the FBI. O'Donoghue claimed that Michaels and his "regime" would allow none of his ideas on air. "They wanted hard laughs, more of the same," he said. But according to Marilyn Miller, it became an arrangement that O'Donoghue manipulated to his advantage: "He didn't have to write anything, he didn't have to come into the office or even leave the house or actually make a video, and Lorne paid him." When he saw that his old friend Chevy Chase was to host the November 16 installment of that season, O'Donoghue wrote an inspired opening monologue and distributed it among the show's staff:

CHEVY: Right after I stopped doing cocaine, I turned into a giant garden slug and, for the life of me, I don't know why. Hi, I'm Chevy Chase. Have you noticed that, in the years since I left *Saturday Night Live,* my eyes have actually gotten smaller and closer together so they now look like little pig eyes? Why? Again, I don't have a clue. As I was saying to Alan King the other day at the Alan King Celebrity Tennis Tournament, "Alan, I need more money. What I can't fit in my wallet, I'll eat or I'll shove up my ass, but I *must have more!*" And when I looked in the mirror, my eyes were the size of Roosevelt dimes and had moved another inch closer to my nose. "What is going on here?!?" I exclaimed to my new wife, who looks like my old wife except she's new. Still, the fans showed up for my last movie—*The Giant Garden Slug's European Vacation*—a movie any man would be proud of, particularly if that man was Cantinflas. There's much more I can say but I have a twenty lodged in my lower colon and it's just driving me crazy. My next film is called *The Giant Garden Slug Blows Eddie Murphy While John Candy Watches* and it opens tomorrow at Red Carpet Theaters everywhere. Don't miss it.

Chase found the monologue hilarious and asked Michaels to let him deliver it on the show. Michaels refused, and this helped fuel O'Donoghue's negative assessment of *SNL*. A month later the *New York Times* did a story on the "Struggles at the New 'Saturday Night.' " In the story, Michaels speaks of the challenge to "redefine [*SNL*] as an 80's show," while in the next paragraph O'Donoghue passes judgment. "I think the show is an embarrassment. It's like watching old men die. It's sad, sluggish, old, witless and very disturbing. It lacks intelligence and it lacks heart, and if I were grading it I'd have to give it an F." O'Donoghue's comments came while the show received a flurry of negative reviews. It was felt, either by Michaels or NBC president Brandon Tartikoff, that O'Donoghue's comments were uncalled for and he was fired. "I didn't know that my job required lying about my opinion of the show," he later said. This proved to be O'Donoghue's final stint with *SNL*, though he remained "nailed" to the show's "cross" for the rest of his life.

O'Donoghue was given one more shot at television exposure in 1991. The Fox network ordered a pilot for a weekly series that would bear O'Donoghue's stamp. The result, *TV*, was arguably like *Mondo Video* in that it moved quickly from bit to bit. But the pilot owed more to *SCTV* than anything else, the premise being a fictional network's broadcasting day—twenty-four hours of television in thirty minutes. It was a narrow target, one festooned with familiar forms: commercials, cop shows, news updates, soap operas, public service announcements. And while there are a few humorous items—alien brain gobblers discuss their favorite dish, a gunslinger wears a dress so he is assured of a duel—*TV* is by and large flat and uninspired.

O'Donoghue wrote the majority of the pilot, a hodgepodge of unproduced jokes and sketches taken from his files (including a small piece of "Silverman's Bunker"). Fox refused to pick up the show, and this, of course, set O'Donoghue off: "Fox is the scaredest, most frightened group of men I have ever seen in my life and probably the dumbest, too." Given that at the time Fox aired shows such as *Herman's Head* and *Charlie Hoover* (starring a miniature Sam Kinison, a classic bit of casting), their rejection of *TV* must have seemed ridiculous to O'Donoghue. But *his* cheap, fictional network could never compete with the real thing. In this case, reality was decidedly stranger than fiction.★

But it was Hollywood success that O'Donoghue truly craved—"I want to direct movies. . . . I want to produce movies"—and in 1982 he made an all-out effort to finally realize what for him was an ever-elusive dream. "I've never been one of those snotty New York writers who sneer at L.A.," he said to Paul Slansky, who profiled him for *Playboy*. "I think the concept of a sybaritic culture is terrifying to a lot of people from the Northeast, but not to me." And to prove that he was no snob, O'Donoghue openly embraced the corrupt and foul lifestyles of those in Hollywood's fast lane.

> Everybody lies all the time in L.A. People just lie as a matter of course. They go to those screenings and they have to walk past the producer and his wife after the movie's over—"Jeez, I just loved it, Sol; most exciting film in years. Yes, I think *Night of the Lepus* is a classic"—and something in them snaps. Something deep within them snaps and it never returns. Then they just lie about everything. "Great dinner, honey. Great salad. Great sex." *Great* has become a meaningless word; it's just a rhythm word now. I am always happy in L.A.

This was said at the beginning of his sojourn. Over the years he would work on and see projects stalled, canceled, or otherwise abandoned. Dust settled on the pile of scripts; *Biker Heaven, Factory of Fear, Arrive Alive, Kittens in a Can, The House Guest, Drop Dead, The Badger*. His enthusiasm soured, and back into the victimized mode he fell. He compared his plight to that of William Faulkner, another literary talent brutalized and castrated by the Hollywood system. He advised those who desired to join the game that they should "lube up" and go for the big bucks because in L.A. writers ranked lower than call girls. "Hollywood is the world's biggest whorehouse," he wrote after years of ass-numbing abuse; and while none of these complaints is particularly original (the screenwriter's lament has existed since the silent era), O'Donoghue's experience in lotusland convinced him that his creative voice was no longer fashionable.

Screenwriting took a lot out of O'Donoghue; it was a tedious, compromise-laden process that oftentimes left him shaking, bewildered, or simply beat. This was why he detested rewrites and revisions, the

---

★In 1993, when Fox hired Chevy Chase to host a late-night talk show, Chase offered O'Donoghue the job as head writer. "I don't think so, Chevy," said O'Donoghue, "maybe triple the money before I come to L.A. and save your ass." Seven months later, *The Chevy Chase Show* premiered and was canceled within weeks, a fate that O'Donoghue had predicted when he turned down the job.

marrow of the Hollywood system. And it was why, to a point, he never saw his better material produced.

His final collaboration with Nelson Lyon came in 1982, when the pair wrote the sequel to *Easy Rider,* called *Biker Heaven* (Terry Southern, who contributed a few lines, was given co-writing credit). The project was to reunite the original cast of Peter Fonda, Dennis Hopper, and Jack Nicholson, and was much wilder, more violent, and funnier than the first film. Set in 2068, in the aftermath of a nuclear war, Billy and Captain America are resurrected from the dead and sent on a mission by the Leader, the Biker God. They are to recover the original Gasden flag—"Don't Tread on Me"—and use it as a unifying emblem for the nation's rebirth. They snort the powdered skull of Crazy Horse and set off, encountering numerous factions and tribes: Black Panzers, Cannibal Cops, Aryan Krusaders, Cycle Sluts, Desert Demons. The two bikers finally make it to Washington, D.C., and hold aloft the new flag, the symbol of an American "Fuck you!" to those who destroyed the dream. The power of the moment inspires the statue of Lincoln to rise from his marble seat and thrust forward his middle finger. A heavy metal version of the "Battle Hymn of the Republic" erupts as Billy and Captain America burst into flames and return to Biker Heaven.

America was reborn, but *Biker Heaven* died. Lyon said that there was no real force behind the project to get it filmed. At various times either the stars of *Biker Heaven* or its producer, Bert Schneider, wavered as Lyon cut the script down to a commercial length. But the emotional states suffered by both writers exacted a heavy toll as well. Lyon was still dealing with Belushi's death and the unpleasantness that followed; and O'Donoghue received his walking papers from Carol Caldwell. The breakup caught him off guard, and he reacted as only he knew how. "We were writing *Biker Heaven,*" said Lyon, "and during a particularly anxious moment he threw a phone through the window of our writers' bungalow" on the Zoetrope lot. Purple-faced and screaming in anger, O'Donoghue "was in full rant. A crowd of people gathered around the bungalow. These people are really not alarmed by anything, but Mike succeeded in getting these people to knock on the door and ask what was the matter." Lyon told them that he and O'Donoghue were running lines from their script. The crowd dispersed.

"He was particularly weird-looking," Lyon recalled. "He was in a kind of phantomasque—he was wearing black tights, like a black super-villain's outfit, so he was fashion coordinated for the rage. He was obsessed with Carol, the betrayal, his anger at being rejected." Once it was clear that *Biker Heaven* would not be made, O'Donoghue and Lyon ended their partnership but remained close friends. From there O'Dono-ghue turned to Mitch Glazer, with whom he felt he had a better chance at commercial success. In 1983 they worked in earnest on *Arrive Alive,* a comedy about a sleazy hotel detective named Mickey Crews who runs afoul of powerful, murderous forces. But the project seemed cursed,* and when *Arrive Alive* finally went in front of the cameras in 1989, the rushes were so bad that filming was stopped two weeks after it began. The problem was that Willem Dafoe, not known for his comic acting, was cast as Mickey. Glazer said that Dafoe tried to bring the material to life but the footage was "painful" to watch, the performance "terrifying."

During the 1980s O'Donoghue and Glazer had secured a reputation in Hollywood as notorious pitchmasters. Glazer played good cop, was accessible and easy to get along with; O'Donoghue played bad cop and did his best to menace the pig producers. "Michael was at his best as a partner," said Glazer. "He was such an enforcer. He had Hollywood so frightened. Not that it ever helped him, but he was intimidating." In his mirrored shades, linen suits, Panama hat, the ever-present More cigarette in hand, O'Donoghue cut an unusual screenwriting figure. "Just *that* alone in Hollywood makes no sense," Glazer observed, but their agent, John Burnam of William Morris, succeeded in getting them meeting after meeting.

Sometimes O'Donoghue would deliberately sabotage a meeting. Once he and Glazer met with a producer who wanted them to write a movie about "a guy who passes the bar, becomes a lawyer, and sets up his office *in* a bar. So he's passed the bar and his office is in a bar." The producer asked for their thoughts. Glazer replied, "Yeah, that's possible. I can see that." O'Donoghue stared at the producer through his dark shades, sighed heavily, and said, "It's not something I would ever, *ever* want to write. Talk to Glazer." He then got up and left the office, while Glazer had to deal with the now irate producer who yelled, "Who is this guy? I've never been treated like this!" and made the standard "You'll never work in this town again!" threats.

Other times, O'Donoghue improvised to win a pitch, seemingly for the sake of winning it. After being given a poster for a prospective movie called *New Year's 2000,* he and Glazer walked around the Universal lot before they were to meet the director, Walter Hill. They had nothing to bring to the meeting until O'Donoghue said, "You know what would be a great idea, Glazer? If we made it a musical and basically had all these different bands write their own videos and then we don't have to write any dialogue at all." The two went into the meeting and O'Donoghue made the pitch: The film would open on a James Taylor concert in 1999 with Taylor singing "Sweet Baby James" to a crowd of old

---

*The saga of *Arrive Alive* is fully described in an entertaining book, *A Pound of Flesh* by Art Linson, who was the film's producer.

hippies. Then, suddenly, three black helicopters arrive carrying the Rock Police, who machine-gun everyone in sight, followed by the film's opening credits. "And they gave us the deal," said Glazer, but neither wanted to do the project.

O'Donoghue and Glazer finally did see a script of theirs filmed and released: *Scrooged*, an updated comic handling of *A Christmas Carol*, which came out in 1988. The plot to *Scrooged* runs more or less in line with Dickens' original story; but in the newer version Scrooge is Frank Cross, the ruthless president of a sinking television network, IBC. In a last-ditch effort to turn the network around and grab the all-important holiday ratings, Cross schedules a programming blitzkrieg of specials such as *The Night the Reindeer Died,* in which Santa and Lee Majors save Christmas with the help of advanced weaponry, and *Bob Goulet's Old Fashioned Cajun Christmas*, in which the singer roasts chestnuts on the bayou. All this leads to Christmas Eve, when IBC will present a live staging of *A Christmas Carol*, complete with the Solid Gold dancers and gymnast Mary Lou Retton, who, as Tiny Tim, tosses aside her crutches and vaults down a London street.

The only element of Christmas that warms Frank Cross is the rise in ad revenues for the network. Other than that he is a prime corporate prick who abuses everyone and trusts no one. As he plans for the big gala show, his job and reputation on the block, he is visited by the trio of ghosts who show him the error of his ways. After looking in on his colorless childhood, his change in character as he rises to power, and his future of isolation and death, Cross is redeemed. He hijacks the very show on which his career rests and uses the live transmission to share his redemption with an audience of millions. He is human again, and television serves to project his humanity.

It was the final confessional scene that O'Donoghue and Glazer sought an approach they could stomach. They settled on the example of New York on Christmas Eve, where for one night people are nice to one another. "That was a miracle we could live with," said Glazer. They wrote the redemption speech with this in mind, but Bill Murray, who played Cross, worried about how to "act" it. He phoned Glazer and confessed his nervousness; Murray felt he had to emote, but Glazer told him to just say the lines and to play the scene as written. When the scene was shot, Murray, who wanted a big acting moment, went emotionally wild; Glazer, standing with O'Donoghue off-camera, thought the actor was having a breakdown. The camera followed Murray as he ignored his marks and improvised his speech. When he finished, the crew applauded his performance. After the applause died down, O'Donoghue said aloud, "What was *that*? The Jim Jones Hour?" The film's director, Richard Donner, who thought that a grip had said this, turned and punched O'Donoghue solidly in the arm. Donner apologized, but O'Donoghue's arm remained bruised for a week.

As a director, Richard Donner had the commercial touch.★ He did well with films such as *Superman* and *Lethal Weapon,* but *Scrooged* made him nervous. He wanted laughs instantly and during filming tended to extract broad takes from the actors. O'Donoghue felt that Donner didn't understand humor, that to him loud and fast equaled funny. Thus the subtler material never made it on film (though Bill Murray's closing improv did), and the scenes that were meant to be played straight received the Donner comedy treatment: mugging, yelling, elbows in the ribs. "Only about 40 percent of what Mitch Glazer and I wrote made it onto the screen," an angry O'Donoghue later told *Premiere,* "and even that got twisted. We wrote a fucking masterpiece. We wrote *It Happened One Night.* We wrote a story that could make you laugh and cry. You would have wanted to share it with your grandchildren every fucking Christmas for the next 100 years. The finished film was a piece of unadulterated, unmitigated shit. I've seen that picture once, and I'll never see it again. The only good thing is that big checks came out of *Scrooged,* which allowed me to get a house in Ireland."

You only live once, and usually not even then.

It was in his Irish home that O'Donoghue could escape from the various pressures of Hollywood and New York. And it was with his second wife, Cheryl Hardwick, that O'Donoghue found some semblance of peace in his final years.

Hardwick hailed from Pittsburgh and had arrived in 1967 in New York, where she studied music at Julliard, then later composed scores for Off-Broadway shows. By the mid-1970s she was friends with another pianist, Paul Shaffer, who introduced her to Howard Shore—hired by Lorne Michaels to head the first *Saturday Night* in-house band. When Hardwick discovered that O'Donoghue was part of this new show, she pushed for and won a spot in the band. She and O'Donoghue grew friendly with one another during *SNL*'s first three seasons; but it wasn't until 1985 that the two began to have a serious relationship. They performed as a team that year at New York's Bottom Line: O'Donoghue

★Sydney Pollack was slated to be the film's original director, and O'Donoghue blew him nothing but shit during read-throughs. Once he sat in front of Pollack, with studio executives looking on, and said, "Sydney with a Y? What are you, a Vegas stripper? What Jew does Sydney with a Y?" Another time, after Pollack found a credibility problem with the script's depiction of ghosts, O'Donoghue went crazy. "It's a *ghost,* Sydney! How the fuck do you know what it would do? You're a logic Nazi!" Not surprisingly, Pollack eventually gave way to Donner.

Wedding day, with (from left) Paul Shaffer, Bill Murray, Jane Curtin, and Herb Sargent

read poetry and sang; Hardwick accompanied him on the piano. Here both saw the possibility of lifelong collaboration. Each had had countless relationships, affairs, and one-night stands; but now that they were getting older they wanted the stability of a central relationship.

Hardwick proposed marriage to O'Donoghue on Valentine's Day 1985. He didn't answer her until June, when over dinner at the Algon-quin Hotel, he got on his knee and gave Hardwick a Cracker Jack ring. The deal was finalized that August when the two met in Paris on Hard-wick's birthday; O'Donoghue, dressed in a white linen suit, greeted her with a stuffed toy duck. They married in New York on October 26, 1986. At the reception the couple reprised their act, as they would do for the next several years: O'Donoghue sang while Hardwick, in an elegant white wedding gown, played piano.

Hardwick moved into the Sixteenth Street apartment; but it was in Ireland that her relationship with O'Donoghue seemed best defined. The couple visited the west coast of Ireland in the summer of 1988, and they stayed in an old cottage. The following year, *Scrooged* money in the bank, they bought a large house called Garraunbaun in County Galway in the town Clifden; and here O'Donoghue's fantasies of country living were realized. He and Hardwick would spend the better part of five months of each year in the house where O'Donoghue played Country Squire. He learned to ride horses, played croquet, went for walks around the estate.

Hardwick and O'Donoghue

He also took time to write. In 1990 he contributed a short play to *Spin* magazine called *The Paris of the Prairie,* one of his better pieces of work in his later years. Two old geezers sit in a rest home, their heads wrapped in gauze. They wax nostalgic about life in Dagotown, where the bank had a screen door on its vault and people draped furs over their mailboxes because theft and dishonesty were unknown. Then, of course, the town changed for the worse. The geezers look to lay blame on the "niggers" and the "spics"; but since the niggers owned the bank and the spics ran the *son et lumiére* shows, it had to be someone else. "Moon men," says the first geezer. "They landed in big silver saucers and nothing was ever the same." The second geezer unwraps his gauze to reveal a third eye in his forehead. "I'm a moon man," he answers, so it wasn't them. The list of possible culprits grows, everything from the "toad clones" to "the beast that eats your face and was stabbed a million times but is still moving," but they finally admit that blame is useless because they both "like it a lot more now." They go back to reading newspapers. "The Missouri Waltz" is heard on a nearby piano. The second geezer's third eye blinks.

The Paris of the Prairie (which was performed in New York in April 1990 with O'Donoghue and George Trow as the geezers) was printed untouched by *Spin*'s then editor-in-chief, Bob Guccione Jr. This impressed O'Donoghue, who by this time saw very little of his work published. And it helped convince him to accept Guccione's offer of

In Ireland, with Nelson Lyon

writing a monthly column for *Spin*. Titled "Not My Fault!" the column served as O'Donoghue's final public stage; and of the pieces published from December 1993 to January 1995, only a handful show him at full stride. In one he connects fast food to random shootings and skewers meat industry propaganda. In another he hammers the dying remnants of the Rat Pack before veering into the pathology of daytime talk shows: "The person in the most pain wins." But it was in his last column, published after his death, where O'Donoghue displayed real passion. He focuses on the plight of the Tutsis in Rwanda and is mystified that there is a relief effort on behalf of their oppressors, the Hutus.

"Have we all become so United Colors of Benetton that genocide is now nothing more than a harmless foible, hardly worth mentioning?" he asks. "I must say, this is a refreshing new approach to charity work which, traditionally, has always focused on the victim. Now comes this novel idea of rewarding the aggressor, and it opens the door to some exciting possibilities." After offering a few suggestions of his own, including a Serb-Aid concert, he admits, "It just breaks my heart that Rudolf Hess didn't live to see this day . . . killers need love, too."

O'Donoghue wrote several *Spin* columns in Ireland; and although he enjoyed the monthly outlet he felt that his effort was ultimately wasted. "Frankly, trying to talk to the 'X Generation' is like poking a dead body with a stick," he said. "I don't get much reaction from these things, I don't get much money, no pussy—I get nothing, frankly. . . . I don't think anything you put in words means that much anymore." There was always the option of film, though by mid-1994 O'Donoghue didn't seem terribly optimistic on that front. But his spirits were lifted when he and Hardwick were visited in Garraunbaun that summer by Quentin Tarantino and his girlfriend at the time, former *SNL* cast member Julia Sweeney. Tarantino, who awaited the fall release of *Pulp Fiction,* discussed movies with O'Donoghue during his two week stay, and the

In Ireland, with Quentin Tarantino and Julia Sweeney

two spoke of a possible film collaboration.* Tarantino told O'Donoghue of his love of *Lampoon* humor, and O'Donoghue returned the compliment by praising *Reservoir Dogs*. Hardwick and Sweeney looked on as two generations connected, with Tarantino aware that the man to whom he was speaking had made possible his commercial mix of savagery and humor.

As pleasant as Garraunbaun was, O'Donoghue could still ignite when the moment seized him. It was in the Ireland house, Hardwick remembered, that she finally named the "demon" that provoked O'Donoghue to such screaming fits of rage.

One summer afternoon, Hardwick and some houseguests planned to take a boat out to a nearby island and then go swimming. O'Donoghue was to join them, but his swimming trunks had been misplaced. As he searched his bedroom he became increasingly irate and finally he blew up. Hardwick, who was downstairs, could hear him throwing a major

---

*Hired to punch up the script to the Tony Scott film *Crimson Tide,* Tarantino based some of the dialogue on his discussions with O'Donoghue. Check the scene in which submarine movies are assessed.

tantrum. When quiet returned she went to their room, and there she noticed a scrawl on a yellow pad next to the bed. Taking a closer look, she saw that O'Donoghue had written "Swimtrun"; but in his anger O'Donoghue wrote off the side of the pad and carved "ks" into the wood of the nightstand. This Hardwick took as an omen, and she looked to "tame the beast by naming the beast." His temper gradually cooled after that; his fuse grew a bit longer. But whenever O'Donoghue seemed ready to explode, Hardwick would say, "I think Swimtrun is coming. . . ."

Back in New York, the shadow of the beast fell hard. In his *Village Voice* obituary, Darius James best captured the early-morning scene of November 8, 1994. O'Donoghue, wrote James,

> . . . awoke with what he believed was another of the migraines that had tormented him throughout his life. He got out of bed, went to his bathroom and took some medication to relieve the pain. Later, he awoke a second time and exclaimed "OH MY GOD!!" His wife, Cheryl Hardwick, reported that his eyes were the color of blood and that she could see bolts of "lightning flash behind his eyeballs." She immediately telephoned EMS.
>
> Three hours later at St. Vincent's, a doctor informed Ms. Hardwick that Michael had suffered a massive cerebral hemorrhage and was now officially "brain dead." His body was put on life support, his organs donated to children.

When we die, I suspect that our last thoughts are not about the Great Truths which we seldom hear nor do we spend our final moments recalling some Wondrous Beauty so infrequently glimpsed—the light streaming through a Sequoia tree, a Polynesian sunset—that sort of thing. No, I suspect our last thoughts are those dopey advertising slogans which have been clubbed and beaten and pounded into our minds thousands and thousands of times so that even as our brains begin to melt and the worms commence to gnaw at the softer parts and the light flickers and fades, even as we are swept toward the Eternal Void, we'll still be mumbling over and over, "Looks like a pump, feels like a sneaker . . . Looks like a pump, feels like a sneaker . . . Looks like a pump, feels . . ."

Is there today a comedy demon comparable to O'Donoghue's "Swimtrun"? If so, he would be difficult to find in the clean and minty-fresh world of American humor. Like accounting and corporate law, comedy is another legitimate profession with room for the aggressive "go-getter." The career summit for most comedians is film stardom by way of a sitcom, preferably one named after themselves. Thus comics cannot risk offending or alienating their target audience; after all, who wants to *pay* to have some grim bastard shove reality back in your face? Comedy should lift the soul and warm the heart. This is the function of laugh tracks, a mechanism through which we share the joy.

Just before his death, O'Donoghue attended a book party in Manhattan with Marilyn Miller. As luminaries and celebrities drifted by, O'Donoghue asked his friend, "Why didn't I get this? Why did it turn out this way for me?" Miller responded, "Because, Michael, you didn't want it. You kicked it in the teeth." As she later put it, "Michael was absolutely unedited, and you can't be unedited and [be] a success." Well, it's certainly a trick few can pull off, and for a time O'Donoghue was one of the few who did. But a change in climate coupled with a pattern of self-destructive acts caused success to wilt, then die. O'Donoghue was a comedy trailblazer; and when someone clears away the rot and makes possible new avenues of expression, they usually are run down by the subsequent traffic. And in most cases, O'Donoghue met the traffic head-on.

Where does one look for the "unedited" expression that was O'Donoghue's specialty? Two writers, Bruce Wagner and Darius James, tap into

In repose, near the end of his life

this vein. Wagner's *Wild Palms,* as both comic strip and TV movie, effectively rendered a brutal, kaleidoscopic dreamscape as "reality"—a shadow world that kills. In his novel *Negrophobia,* James rips the entrails from racist guts and uses them as props in his private minstrel show. But the semi-underworld of 'zines is perhaps the best contemporary example of raw sensation captured in print. "Taste" is extremely relative as editors and writers fire images and words as if from the barrel of a rusted shot-gun. Most are self-reverential, some ironic, a few so utterly vile as to cause sickness.

One 'zine in this line was *Boiled Angel,* in which Mike Diana exposed the nastiest parts of his imagination: sodomized babies ground into dog food, wife abuse, cannibalism, blasphemy. Diana was so unedited that he was jailed briefly by the state of Florida for breaking obscenity laws. Another 'zine, *Answer Me!* took for granted horrors such as rape and mass murder; and in one edition there are rankings for history's best serial killers, many of whom are proud Americans. *Answer Me!*'s creator, Jim Goad, received a book contract from a savvy Simon and Schuster in 1996, but the house failed to market the result, *The Redneck Manifesto,* perhaps fearing an unwholesome (and thus uncommercial) tie-in to the Oklahoma City bombing. To the book's critics, Goad's humorous, angry tome appeared little more than a cry from Ruby Ridge, and his effort was ignored.

Without doubt, the most successful, unedited personality is Howard Stern, who owes his professional existence to the *National Lampoon.* Stern is a middlebrow wit who plays the lowbrow game brilliantly; his humor is a variation of stalk-and-slash but there is nothing affected about it. He goes for the throat as casually as he would go to the bathroom—and at times it seems he does both at once. He is backed by an equally brilliant sound collagist named Fred Norris, in whose sound effects for the Stern show one can hear O'Donoghue: Several times each morning, Norris plays a tape of a man screaming violently, a piteous scream filled with unspeakable pain. It is O'Donoghue's voice taken from the *Radio Hour*'s "Let's Torture Ed Sullivan." The needles continue to maim; the ghost kicks and wails through the morning rush.

epilogue

few months after he died, O'Donoghue's ashes were spread across the lawn in Garraunbaun, where he often destroyed opponents in croquet. His dream of returning to his ancestral land was finalized. "I've always been very influenced by dreams," he once said, and this he took quite seriously. Much of his conceptual humor and verse came from the notes he made in the middle of the night as he strained to recapture a shadow cadence or image.

> *I'm flying too close to the moon.*
> *What is the light that dreams are lit with?*
> *Will it be over soon?*

While researching and writing this book, I encountered Michael O'Donoghue in my dreams at least a half dozen times. In one he showed me how he threw a tantrum (something I had never seen in life); in another he padded about a book-lined study and explained his feelings about dying. But the dream that haunted and enthralled me most took place in a field at night.

He holds a basket of fireflies in a tender, loving fashion. The fireflies' light glows on and off; they seem to have human faces, but their features remain nonspecific. There is a melodic hum, and at first I think it's the fireflies; but as I move away I realize that it is O'Donoghue who is humming. He's serenading the fireflies and they pulsate in time to the humming. As I drift back, O'Donoghue is enveloped by the dark; the fireflies continue to pulsate and glow until they look like a distant lamp swinging in his arms.

The following day, when I went through his files, I discovered a notebook I hadn't noticed before. I opened it, and there on the page before me was a drawing of a firefly, beneath which were notes on the species. A few pages later I again saw the word *fireflies*, this time as a title that O'Donoghue considered for a collection of his poetry. I began to feel some strange psychic pull; but then on the next page I was confronted by two words written in thick black marker:

"BLOW ME."

But since it fell into my lot
That I should rise
And you should not
I gently rise and softly call
Goodnight
And joy be to you all
Irish traditional

MICHAEL O'DONOGHUE

1940-1994

The prayer card from his wake

index

All material by Michael O'Donoghue is copyright © 1998 by the Estate of Michael O'Donoghue and is used by permission. All rights reserved.

Visual material presented in *Mr. Mike* appears courtesy of Cheryl Hardwick. The following exceptions are noted:

Page(s)	Credit
15, 28	Photos courtesy of Jane Donohue.
90	Genosite excerpt copyright © 1965 by Michael O'Donoghue. Originally appeared in *Evergreen Review*, March 1965.
116	"Buddy Can You Spare A Fin?" copyright © 1965 by Michael O'Donoghue and Frank Springer. Originally appeared in *Evergreen Review*, June 1965.
121, 122	"Paris in the Twenties" excerpt and "2 Poems" copyright © 1965 by Michael O'Donoghue. Originally appeared in *Evergreen Review*, September 1965.
123, 124	*Phoebe Zeit-Geist* excerpt copyright © 1965 by Michael O'Donoghue and Frank Springer. Originally appeared in *Evergreen Review*, November 1965.
128 (top)	*Phoebe Zeit-Geist* excerpt copyright © 1966 by Michael O'Donoghue and Frank Springer. Originally appeared in *Evergreen Review*, April 1966.
128 (bottom)	*Phoebe Zeit-Geist* excerpt copyright © 1966 by Michael O'Donoghue and Frank Springer. Originally appeared in *Evergreen Review*, June 1966.
129	*Phoebe Zeit-Geist* excerpt copyright © 1966 by Michael O'Donoghue and Frank Springer. Originally appeared in *Evergreen Review*, August 1966.
130	*Phoebe Zeit-Geist* excerpt copyright © 1966 by Michael O'Donoghue and Frank Springer. Originally appeared in *Evergreen Review*, October 1966.
131	*Phoebe Zeit-Geist* excerpt copyright © 1966 by Michael O'Donoghue and Frank Springer. Originally appeared in *Evergreen Review*, December 1966.
132	*Phoebe Zeit-Geist* excerpt copyright © 1967 by Michael O'Donoghue and Frank Springer. Originally appeared in *Evergreen Review*, February 1967.
133	*Phoebe Zeit-Geist* excerpt copyright © 1967 by Michael O'Donoghue and Frank Springer. Originally appeared in *Evergreen Review*, April 1967.
134, 135	*Phoebe Zeit-Geist* excerpts copyright © 1967 by Michael O'Donoghue and Frank Springer. Originally appeared in *Evergreen Review*, June 1967.
136, 137	*Phoebe Zeit-Geist* excerpts copyright © 1966 by Michael O'Donoghue and Frank Springer. Originally appeared in *Evergreen Review*, October 1967.
138, 139	*Phoebe Zeit-Geist* excerpts copyright © 1966 by Michael O'Donoghue and Frank Springer. Originally appeared in *Evergreen Review*, October 1966.
158	"Marigold Flagg" excerpt copyright © 1966 by Michael O'Donoghue. Originally appeared in *Evergreen Review*, August 1966.
159, 160	*Phoebe Zeit-Geist* excerpts copyright © 1968 by Michael O'Donoghue and Frank Springer. Originally appeared in *The Adventures of Phoebe Zeit-Geist*.
164, 165	*Rock* excerpts copyright © 1968 by Michael O'Donoghue and Philip Wende. Originally appeared in *The Incredible, Thrilling Adventures of the Rock*.
167	Photo courtesy of George W.S. Trow.
187–190	"Tarzan of the Cows" excerpts copyright © 1971 by Twenty-First Century Communications, Inc., rights assigned to Michael O'Donoghue. Originally appeared in *National Lampoon*, April 1971.
193	"Kill the Children Federation" copyright © 1971 by Twenty-First Century Communications, Inc., rights assigned to Michael O'Donoghue. Originally appeared in *National Lampoon*, August 1971.
194, 195	"Children's Letters to the Gestapo" copyright © 1971 by Twenty-First Century Communications, Inc., rights assigned to Michael O'Donoghue. Originally appeared in *National Lampoon*, September 1971.
198	Photo by Dirck Halstead. (Courtesy of Cheryl Hardwick)
203	"The Vietnamese Baby Book" excerpt copyright © 1971 by Twenty-First Century Communications, Inc., rights assigned to Michael O'Donoghue. Originally appeared in *National Lampoon*, January 1972.
264, 265	"Michael's Split Personality!" and the "Poonwise!" excerpt copyright © 1973 by Twenty-First Century Communications, Inc., rights assigned to Michael O'Donoghue. Originally appeared in *National Lampoon*, December 1973.

296   Photo copyright © Edie Baskin. Used by permission.

324   Photo copyright © Edie Baskin. Used by permission.

328   Photo copyright © Edie Baskin. Used by permission.

337   Photo copyright © Edie Baskin. Used by permission.

355   Photo from *Manhattan* copyright © 1979 Metro-Goldwyn-Mayer, Inc. All rights reserved. Courtesy of MGM CLIP + STILL.